WORD VIRUS
the WILLIAM S. BURROUGHS reader

WORD VIRUS

the WILLIAM S. BURROUGHS reader

edited by james grauerholz
and ira silverberg

with an introduction by ann douglas

Grove Press   New York

Published simultaneously in Canada
Printed in the United States of America

FIRST EDITION

All selections from *The Cat Inside* (© 1992 William S. Burroughs), *Exterminator!* (© 1966, 1967, 1969, 1973 William S. Burroughs), *Interzone* (© 1989 William S. Burroughs), *My Education* (© 1995 William S. Burroughs), *Queer* (© 1985 William S. Burroughs) and *The Western Lands* (© 1987 William S. Burroughs) are used by permission of Viking Penguin, a division of Penguin Putnam Inc.

All selections from *Cities of the Red Night* (© 1981 William S. Burroughs) and *The Place of Dead Roads* (© 1983 William S. Burroughs) are reprinted by permission of Henry Holt and Company, Inc.

All selections from *The Burroughs File* (© 1987 William S. Burroughs) and *The Yage Letters* (© 1963, 1975 William S. Burroughs and Allen Ginsberg) are reprinted by permission of City Lights Books.

All selections from *The Adding Machine* (© 1985, 1986 William S. Burroughs) are published by arrangement with Seaver Books.

All selections from *Junky* (© 1953, 1977, renewed 1981 William S. Burroughs) *The Job* (© 1968, 1970, renewed 1997, 1998 William S. Burroughs) and *The Third Mind* (© 1974, 1978 William S. Burroughs and Brion Gysin) are used by permission of The William S. Burroughs Trust.

The excerpt from *And the Hippos Were Boiled in Their Tanks* (an unpublished manuscript by William S. Burroughs and Jack Kerouac) is used by permission of The William S. Burroughs Trust and with the gracious consent of the Estate of Jack Kerouac, John Sampas, Executor.

The essay "Personal Magnetism" by William S. Burroughs was first published in *Literary Outlaw: The Life and Times of William S. Burroughs*, by Ted Morgan (New York: Henry Holt and Company, 1988) and is used by permission of The William S. Burroughs Trust.

All selections from *Naked Lunch* (© 1959, 1962, renewed 1987, 1990 William S. Burroughs), *The Soft Machine* (© 1961, 1966, renewed 1989, 1994 William S. Burroughs), *The Ticket that Exploded* (© 1962, 1967, renewed 1990, 1995 William S. Burroughs), *Nova Express* (© 1964, renewed 1992 William S. Burroughs) and *The Wild Boys* (© 1971 William S. Burroughs) are reprinted from editions published by Grove Press.

Library of Congress Cataloging-in-Publication Data
Burroughs, William S., 1914–97
    Word virus : the William S. Burroughs reader / edited by James
Grauerholz and Ira Silverberg.
        p.   cm.
    "Collected in one volume the essential writings of America's
foremost literary innovator."
    ISBN 0-8021-1629-9
    1. Beat generation—Literary collections.   2. Burroughs, William
S., 1914–97 —Biography.   3. Authors, American—20th century—
Biography.   I. Grauerholz, James.   II. Silverberg, Ira.
III. Title.
PS3552.U75A6   1998
813'.54—dc21   97-48269
                                                      CIP

DESIGN BY LAURA HAMMOND HOUGH

Grove Press
841 Broadway
New York, NY 10003

98 99 00 01   10 9 8 7 6 5 4 3 2 1

contents

INTERZONE (1954–59)

THE CUT-UPS (1960–67)

LATE WORK (1984–97)

editor's preface
by ira silverberg

Word Virus: The William S. Burroughs Reader collects passages, routines, chapters, and condensations of the entire literary output of William S. Burroughs. While this is a rather formidable anthology, it only represents about 10 percent of Burroughs' published work.

We have attempted, through our selections, to follow recurring themes and characters in Burroughs' work as well as to chronicle the shifts in style and content which took place throughout the years he wrote. The anthology is meant as much for the general reader as it is for the scholar, and provides links between Burroughs' life and his writing through the chapter introductions written by James Grauerholz. Writer and scholar Ann Douglas' introductory essay provides both an overview of the work and a history of the writer and his contemporaries.

In choosing from almost fifty years of Burroughs' work, we have focused our attention on his most memorable passages and the trademark "routines," along with those which demonstrate a continuity of Burroughs' vision. While stylistic changes took place over time, Burroughs had several literary, artistic, and political concerns which permeated his work. His lack of comfort with the human body, his mistrust of authority and control, his utopian visions, and his early themes of gay liberation are all to be found here. Throughout, one sees these concerns repeat, multiply, take new shape, and adjust to the surroundings in which Burroughs places them. One also sees the formal and physical experimentation with the work—the cut-ups, the fold-ins, the collaborations.

While Burroughs has been frequently relegated to one iconic label or other— "High Priest of Junk," "Godfather of Punk," or "Gay Rights Pioneer"—we have tried to show another side of his character by chronicling the maturation of his emotional concerns. "El Hombre Invisible" emerges through these texts as a man looking for an answer, searching for reconciliation. By including his introduction to *Queer* (in which he writes of the killing of his wife, Joan), as well as the soul-searching texts of his later years, a more complex Burroughs emerges, one which the labels preclude. William Burroughs just wanted to live, and ultimately die, peacefully. He tried hard in his final years to exorcise the demons which both haunted him and infused his work with a characteristic sense of discomfort and otherness.

The dichotomy of the gun-toting, substance-abusing queer seeking spiritual refuge might strike some as anticlimactic. But William Burroughs was not what he appeared to be to many of his fans. The work which so many revere as biblical texts in the church of addiction were always seen by the writer himself as cautionary rather than visionary. In constructing this book, we found the visionary texts in routines like "Electronic Revolution" and in the landscapes which presage Ridley Scott's *Blade Runner* and William Gibson's *Neuromancer*.

Organized, for the most part, chronologically, *Word Virus* isolates specific periods in Burroughs' writing life. We have intentionally left out collages and letters (with the exception of *The Yagé Letters,* which provides an introduction to *Interzone* and *Naked Lunch*), as they both fall outside the parameters of this collection and are ultimately better presented in their original publications. We have, however, included collaborations with Kells Elvins, Jack Kerouac, and Brion Gysin.

We begin this anthology with very early work in the chapter titled "The Name Is Burroughs," where his literary characteristics can be seen in his teen years. Here, too, we present a chapter from *And the Hippos Were Boiled in Their Tanks,* an early, unpublished collaboration with Jack Kerouac. Burroughs and Kerouac alternated chapters in constructing this novel and this chapter represents Burroughs' first attempt at conjuring the scene around him at Columbia in the 1940s. The mythology of *And the Hippos . . .* is elaborated upon by James Grauerholz.

As the anthology progresses, there is the occasional lapse in chronology. The routine called "The Name Is Burroughs," the *Queer* introduction, and the pieces in the chapter titled "Inspector Lee: Nova Heat" all fall out of sequence for reasons pertaining to the overriding themes of their respective chapters. These instances are also explained in further detail in Grauerholz's introductions. The chapters are broken down as follows: "The Name Is Burroughs," "A Hard-Boiled Reporter," "Interzone," "The Cut-Ups," "Inspector Lee: Nova Heat," "Queer Utopia," "The Red Night Trilogy," and "Late Work."

Word Virus ends with sections from the last major work published during Burroughs' life, *My Education: A Book of Dreams*. His last two years of journal writing, which will be published at a later date, have been excluded, as it was our wish to honor the *Word Virus* manuscript that Burroughs approved before his death.

The editing of *Word Virus: The William S. Burroughs Reader* was completed at the end of July 1997, one week before William Burroughs succumbed to a fatal heart attack.

I recall the afternoon I delivered the manuscript to his home. The box it was in was eight inches tall and weighed ten pounds. It landed on William's dining table with a thud and I said, "Here, William, is our attempt at boiling down your life's work." He immediately opened the box, carefully inspected the table of contents, thumbed through some pages, and said, "My dear, you boys have been working very hard and appear to have done a complete job." He thumbed through a bit more and added, "Well, it all seems to be in order." He then closed the box. An anticlimax for sure, but I was well aware of his reticence in such matters, and also sure that he'd have a thorough going-over of the manuscript when I left.

I visited William the next day, and at some point he nodded at the box and said, "I think we shall call it *Just for Jolly*. You realize, of course, these are words of Jack the Ripper, uttered in response to a query as to the motivation for his crimes. 'Just for jolly,' he said. And indeed what else shall we call a life's work?" He'd been reading about Jack the Ripper in those final days; he'd also been reading a great deal of Tennyson, and was fond in particular of the poem "Ulysses," from which we tried to find a line or two for an alternate title. I reminded him of our working title, the title which ultimately stuck, and it took some time to convince him that the book should have a moniker more true to his oeuvre. And so, *Word Virus* it was.

It should be said here, both as a disclaimer and as a testament to the collaborative spirit which William engendered, that this anthology has been put together by two members of the Burroughs "family"—family in the queer sense of the word, the family one chooses. James Grauerholz had been in William Burroughs' life as friend, companion, manager, and editor from 1974 until William's death in 1997. He was the most important partner Burroughs ever had and continues as Burroughs' literary executor. His diligence, hard work, and love of William, the man and the writer, allowed William to enjoy his final years in comfort, and provided him with the luxury of time to pursue his art and writing.

I came onto the Burroughs scene in 1981 and lived in Lawrence, Kansas, from 1982 until the beginning of 1984. Through William and James I became immersed in the world of letters and chose a career in publishing, where, among other things, I have worked as William's personal publicist and as his publisher (both at High Risk Books and at Grove Press).

While we have both been close to the man, so too have we been close to the work. It is with the inspiration from William's writing and friendship that we have endeavored to present a fair portrait of his life's work through our selections.

New York City, 1998

"punching a hole in the big lie": the achievement of william s. burroughs

by ann douglas

"When did I stop wanting to be President?" Burroughs once asked himself, and promptly answered, "At birth certainly, and perhaps before." A public position on the up-and-up, a career of shaking hands, making speeches, and taking the rap held no appeal for one who aspired to be a "sultan of sewers," an antihero eye-deep in corruption, drugs, and stoic insolence, watching "Old Glory float lazily in the tainted breeze."

Burroughs started out in the 1940s as a founding member of the "Beat Generation," the electric revolution in art and manners that kicked off the counterculture and introduced the hipster to mainstream America, a movement for which Jack Kerouac became the mythologizer, Allen Ginsberg the prophet, and Burroughs the theorist. Taken together, their best-known works—Ginsberg's exuberant take-the-doors-off-their-hinges jeremiad *Howl* (1956); Kerouac's sad, funny, and inexpressibly tender "true story" novel *On the Road* (1957); and Burroughs' avant-garde narrative *Naked Lunch* (1959), a Hellzapoppin saturnalia of greed and lust—managed to challenge every taboo that respectable America had to offer.

Over the course of his long career, Burroughs steadfastly refused to honor, much less court, the literary establishment. Invited in 1983 to join the august Academy and Institute of Arts and Letters, he remarked, "Twenty years ago they were saying I belonged in jail. Now they're saying I belong in their club. I didn't listen to them then, and I don't listen to them now." Adept in carny routines and vaudevillian sleights of hand, Burroughs was a stand-up comic, a deadpan ringmaster of Swiftian satire and macabre dystopias, who claimed an outsider role so extreme as to constitute extraterrestrial status. "I'm apparently some kind of agent from another planet," he told Kerouac, "but I haven't got my orders decoded yet."

Unlike Ginsberg and Kerouac, however, Burroughs, born in 1914 to a well-to-do Wasp family in St. Louis, was part of the American elite. Indeed, as he often noted, his personal history seemed inextricably intertwined with some of the most important and ominous events of the modern era. In the 1880s, his paternal grandfather had invented the adding machine, a harbinger of the alliance of technology and corporate wealth that made possible the monstrously beefed-up defense industry of the Cold War years. Burroughs' maternal uncle, Ivy Lee, a pioneer of public relations, had helped John D. Rockefeller Jr. improve his image after the Ludlow Massacre of 1914, in which Colorado state militia shot two women and eleven children in a dispute between miners and management. In the 1930s, Lee served as Hitler's admiring publicist in the United States, an achievement that Congressman Robert LaFollette branded "a monument of shame."

Thin, physically awkward, with a narrow, impassive, even hangdog face as an adolescent, Burroughs qualified easily as the most unpopular boy in town. One concerned parent compared him to "a walking corpse." (Burroughs agreed, only wondering whose corpse it was.) Already interested in drugs, homosexuality, and con artistry, devoid of team spirit and "incurably intelligent," he was at best a problematic student, a troubling presence at several select schools, among them the Los Alamos Ranch School in New Mexico, the site J. Robert Oppenheimer commandeered in 1943 for the scientists engaged in the Manhattan Project. Los Alamos birthed the bombs that destroyed Hiroshima and Nagasaki and brought into being what Burroughs sardonically referred to as "the sick soul, sick unto death, of the atomic age," the central theme of his work.

In 1936, Burroughs graduated from Harvard, a place whose pretensions he loathed; a blank space appeared in the yearbook where his photograph should have been. He then traveled to Vienna and saw for himself what the Nazi regime his uncle had promoted was up to. For Burroughs, as for Jean Genet, one of his literary heroes, Hitler became a seminal figure; he never forgot that everything Hitler had done was legal. During the 1940s, Burroughs worked as a drug pusher and a thief, but he was guilt-free; a life of petty crime was less "compromising" than the "constant state of pretense and dissimulation" required by any job that contributed to the status quo. When gangsters write the laws, as Burroughs was sure they did, not only in the Third Reich but in most of the post-WWII West, ethics become fugitives, sanity is branded madness, and the artist's only option is total resistance. "This planet is a penal colony and nobody is allowed to leave," Burroughs wrote in *The Place of Dead Roads* (1984). "Kill the guards and walk."

In September 1951, in a drunken attempt at William Tell–style marksmanship, Burroughs inadvertently shot and killed his wife, Joan, while the couple was living in Mexico with their four-year-old son, Billy. Burroughs never considered himself anything but homosexual. He saw his intermittent sexual relations with Joan as a stopgap measure when the "uncut boy stuff" he preferred was unavailable. Joan worshipped him, but he admitted to a friend that the marriage was in some sense "an impasse, not amenable to any solution." Regarding the feminine sex in general as a grotesque mistake of nature, a biological plot against male independence and self-expression, he never made a woman central to his fiction. Starring roles went instead to wickedly updated, flagrantly queer versions of the classic male hero, to tricksters, gunmen, pirates, and wild boys. Like Genet, Burroughs saw homosexuality (as opposed to effeminacy and faggotry, for which he had no tolerance) as inherently sub-versive of the status quo. Women were born apologists; (queer) men were rebels and outlaws. Nonetheless, Burroughs knew that rules are defined by their exceptions. He adored Joan's brilliantly unconventional mind and elusive delicacy. He never fully recovered from her death.

Cool, even icy in manner, acerbic in tone, Burroughs once remarked that all his intimate relationships had been failures—he had denied "affection . . . when needed or supplied [it] when unwanted." He had not responded to his father's sometimes abject pleas for love nor visited his mother in her last years in a nursing home. In 1981, after an impressive debut as a novelist, Billy Burroughs, who had been raised by his grandparents, died of cirrhosis, be-lieving that his father had "signed my death warrant."

Although the cause of Joan's death was ruled "criminal imprudence" and Burroughs spent only thirteen days in jail, he held himself responsible. He had been "possessed," and, in the magical universe Burroughs believed we inhabit, to be the subject of a successful possession was the mark of carelessness, not victimhood. If you knew, as he did, that life is a contest between the invading virus of the "Ugly Spirit" and the vigilant, if existence is predicated on preter-natural watchfulness, what excuse could there possibly be for falling asleep on the job? In a sea swarming with sharks, he remarked, it is strongly advisable not to look like a "disabled fish."

In the introduction to *Queer* (1985), he tells his readers that Joan's death "maneuvered me into a lifelong struggle in which I had no choice but to write my way out"; his art was grounded in his culpability. It mattered greatly to him that Calico, one of the beloved cats of his later years, who reminded him of Joan, had never been mistreated, had never required or suffered discipline at his hands. A matchless revisionist of received wisdom, Burroughs thought there was a very real point in closing the barn door after the horse had gone. Mistakes, he explained in *Exterminator!* (1973), are made to be corrected. Filled with the ironies of belatedness as it is, life is education to the last breath, and beyond.

In the same spirit, Burroughs rejected the notion that his familial and geo-graphic proximity to the forces of darkness represented by corporate wealth, Hitler, and the Manhattan Project were "coincidence," a word he disdained. For his first novel, *Junky* (1953), he took his nom de plume, "William Lee," from his mother and his uncle; always uncannily alert to the subterranean implications of his friend's personae, Kerouac described *Junky* as the work of a "Goering-like sophisticate." Nor did Burroughs leave unexamined the class and race privileges to which he had been born. As a lifelong student of the ways in which power passes itself off as nature, he believed that nothing hap-pens without our consent; we are always complicit in what we take to be our God-given circumstances. "To speak is to lie—to live is to collaborate."

"I don't mind people disliking me," Burroughs wrote in *Queer*. "The ques-tion is, what are they in a position to do about it?" In his case, the answer was "apparently nothing, at present," but he knew how and where his relative immunity was manufactured. He escaped the full rigor of the law not only in the case of Joan's death, but on various occasions when he was caught red-handed with illegal drugs, not because the wind is ever tempered to the shorn lamb, but because those who have usually get more. He always had some family funds at his disposal, and he was quite aware that he possessed, in Kerouac's word, "finish"—it was visible at all times that he did not belong to the "torturable classes."

Almost alone among the major white male writers of his generation, Burroughs viewed whiteness and wealth as in some sense criminal and certainly man-made, a con job passed off as a credential. Whites, he liked to complain, were the only ethnic group who marshaled an army before they had enemies. This hardly meant that Burroughs wanted, as both Genet and Kerouac on occasion said they did, to cease being white; he conducted no romance with negritude, an infatuation he took to be simply another form of the sentimentalism he disdained. He remained imperturbably himself in all climates, speaking no language but English despite the years he spent living in various parts of North Africa and Latin America. Strangers sometimes mistook him for a banking official, even a CIA or FBI agent, and he was never averse to trading on his patrician aura in a tight spot. "Keep your snout in the public trough" was a Burroughs maxim.

Burroughs remarked in *Junky* that one reason he drifted into a life of "solo adventure" and addiction was that a drug habit supplied the close-to-the-margin knowledge of emergency his comfortable background had forestalled. Yet, finally, his aim was not to undertake slumming expeditions among his social inferiors but to use his wit and his mind to write his way out of his condition. It was a task for which he was superbly equipped.

Among his contemporaries, only Thomas Pynchon and Kurt Vonnegut begin to match the wild brilliance of Burroughs' laconic extravaganzas of black humor. In one inspired moment in *The Place of Dead Roads* (1983), Burroughs' stand-in, William Hall, is driving on a dimly lit road at night, wondering if he'll be able to summon the "correct emotions" for the parents of the child he imagines himself running over. Suddenly a man swings into view, carrying a dead child under one arm; he slaps it down on a porch, and asks, "This yours, lady?" None of Burroughs' peers were his equal in brainpower megawattage, in sheer, remorseless intelligence. In his own phrase, he was a "guardian of the knowledge," a Wittgenstein of the narrative form. A critique of the family is implicit in Burroughs' fantasy about the dead child; even the most hallucinatory inventions of his imagination are grounded in hard, clear, powerfully analytic and authoritative thought. Dickens and Tolstoy remind us that great authors need not be intellectual geniuses, but part of the special excitement and pleasure in reading Burroughs at his best lies in the shock of encountering someone so much smarter than oneself. Burroughs' work is an intellect booster, Miracle-Gro for the mind—the reader has been handed the strongest binoculars ever made and for the first time sees the far horizon click into focus.

Burroughs claimed that after one look at this planet, any visitor from outer space would say, "I WANT TO SEE THE MANAGER!" It's a Burroughs axiom that the manager is harder to locate than the Wizard of Oz, but Burroughs holds what clues there are to his whereabouts; his work draws the "Wanted, Dead or Alive" poster, and his delineations are executions, fearless and summary. "The history of the planet," he wrote, "is a history of idiocy highlighted by a few morons who stand out as comparative geniuses." In an essay titled "The Hundred-Year Plan," he compared Cold War politicians, bravely proffering patriotic stupidity, crass ignorance, and a gung-ho weapons program as qualifications for office, to prehistoric dinosaurs, whom he imagined gathering for a convention many millennia past. Faced with downscaling or extinction, a dinosaur leader announces, "Size is the answer . . . increased size. . . . It was good enough for me. . . . (Applause) . . . We will increase . . . and we will continue to dominate the planet as we have done for three hundred million years! . . . (Wild Applause)." In this arena, Burroughs believed his elite status worked for him. Revolutionaries are always disaffected members of the ruling class; only the enemy within can lay hands on top-secret information. The insider is the best spy.

Like Hemingway, like Ginsberg and Kerouac, Burroughs aspired to "write his own life and death," to leave something like a complete record of his experiment on the planet; by his own admission, there is finally only one character in his fiction—himself. In a guarded but uncannily astute review of *The Wild Boys* (1971), Alfred Kazin analyzed what he took to be the solipsism of Burroughs' narrative form; Burroughs wanted "to make the fullest possible inventory and rearrangement of all the stuff natural to him . . . to put his own mind on the internal screen that is his idea of a book." Yet Burroughs was not in any usual sense a confessional or autobiographical writer.

A leader of postmodern literary fashion in the 1960s, Burroughs early discarded the Western humanistic notions of the self traditionally associated with autobiography. In a 1950 letter, he commented severely on Ginsberg's recent discovery that he was "just a human like other humans." "Human, Allen, is an adjective, and its use as a noun is in itself regrettable." Burroughs took his starting point to be the place where "the human road ends." In his fiction, identity is an affair of ventriloquism and property rights—everything is potentially up for reassignment or sale. In a compulsive gambling session described in *Naked Lunch,* a young man loses his youth to an old one; lawyers sell not their skills, but their luck to the hapless clients they defend. Most things in Burroughsland function as addictive substances, and the "self" can be simply the last drug the person in question has ingested. Or it may be a random object, someone else's discard, an "article abandoned in a hotel drawer."

Yet if postmodernism is, as a number of its critics have said, a disavowal of responsibility, Burroughs was no postmodernist. In his view, the elite's last shot at virtue lay in taking responsibility for the consequences of its power, and Burroughs for one—and almost the only one in the ranks of recent, major, white male American authors—was willing not only to shoulder responsibility, but to extend it. In Burroughs' magical universe, if we are everywhere complicit, we are also everywhere active. "Your surroundings are *your* surroundings," he wrote in *The Soft Machine*. "Every object you touch is alive with your life and your will."

When Burroughs wrote, in a famous line from *Naked Lunch,* that he was merely a "recording instrument," he wasn't implying, as a number of his critics and fans have thought, that he made no choices, exerted no control over what he wrote, but rather that he wanted to learn how to register not the pre-packaged information he was programmed by corporate interests or artistic canons to receive, but what was actually there. In a 1965 interview with *The Paris Review,* he explained that while the direction of Samuel Beckett, a novelist he admired greatly, was inward, he was intent on going "outward." For Burroughs, the "control machine" is almost synonymous with the Western psyche. The point, as he saw it, was to get outside it, to beat it at its own game by watching and decoding the extremely partial selections it makes from the outside world and then imposes on us as "reality."

Like Marshall McLuhan, himself a fan and brilliant expositor of Burroughs' work, Burroughs saw that Western man had "externalized himself in the form of gadgets." The media extend to fabulous lengths man's nervous system, his powers to record and receive, but without content themselves, cannibalizing the world they purportedly represent and ingesting those to whom they in theory report, like drugs inserted into a bodily system, they eventually replace the organism they feed—a hostile takeover in the style of *The Invasion of the Body Snatchers*. Instead of reality, we have the "reality studio"; instead of people, "person-impersonators" and image-junkies looking for a fix, with no aim save not to be shut out of the "reality film." But Burroughs believed that a counteroffensive might still be possible, that the enemy's tactics can be pried out of their corporate context and used against him by information bandits like himself. Computers might rule the world, but the brain is the first computer; all the information people have forgotten is stored there. The problem is one of access.

In the 1960s, as he developed the "cut-up" method of his first trilogy, *The Soft Machine* (1961), *The Ticket That Exploded* (1962), and *Nova Express* (1964), Burroughs became fascinated by tape recorders and cameras. A how-to writer for the space age for whom science fiction was a blueprint for action, dedicated to "wising up the marks," he instructed readers in the art of deprogramming. Walk down the street, any street, recording and photographing what you hear and see. Go home, write down your observations, feelings, associations, and thoughts, then check the results against the evidence supplied by your tapes and photos. You will discover that your mind has registered only a tiny fraction of your experience; what you left unnoticed may be what you most need to find. "Truth may appear only once," Burroughs wrote in his journal in 1997; "it may not be repeatable." To walk down the street as most people perform the act is to reject the only free handout life has to offer, to trample on the prince in a rush for the toad, storming the pawnshop to exchange gold for dross. What we call "reality," according to Burroughs, is just the result of a faulty scanning pattern, a descrambling device run amok. We're all hard-wired for destruction, in desperate need of rerouting, even mutation.

How did this happen? How did Western civilization become a conspiracy against its members? In his second trilogy, *Cities of the Red Night* (1981), *The Place of Dead Roads* (1984), and *The Western Lands* (1987), which taken as a whole forms his greatest work, Burroughs fantasized the past which produced the present and excavated its aborted alternatives, the last, lost sites of human possibility. The first is the United States that disappeared in his boyhood, the pre- and just post-WWI years when individual identity had not yet been fixed and regulated by passports and income taxes; when there was no CIA or FBI; before bureaucracies and bombs suffocated creative consciousness and super-highways crisscrossed and codified the American landscape—"sometimes paths last longer than roads," Burroughs wrote in *Cities of the Red Night.* In the heyday of the gunman, of single combat, and of the fraternal alliances of fron-tier culture, the promises of the American Revolution were not yet synony-mous with exclusionary elite self-interest. Now, however, Burroughs wrote, there are "so many actors and so little action"; little room is left for the inde-pendent cooperative social units he favored, for the dreams that he saw as the magical source of renewal for whole peoples as well as individuals.

Globally, Burroughs located a brief utopian moment a century or two earlier, a time when one's native "country" had not yet hardened into the "nation-state" and the family did not police its members in the interests of "national security"; before the discovery by Western buccaneers and entre-preneurs of what was later known as the Third World had solidified into colonial and neocolonial empire, effecting a permanent and inequitable re-distribution of the world's wealth; before the industrial revolution had pro-duced an epidemic of overdevelopment and overpopulation and capitalism had become an instrument of global standardization.

Burroughs had no sympathy for the regimented, Marxist-based Commu-nist regimes of Eastern Europe. He saw the Cold War administrations of the U.S. and the U.S.S.R. not as enemies but as peers and rivals vying to see who could reach the goal of total control first. Yet both Burroughs and Karl Marx had an acute understanding of just how revolutionary the impact of plain com-mon sense could be in a world contorted by crime and self-justification, and in a number of areas their interests ran along parallel lines. Unlike Ginsberg or Kerouac, Burroughs unfailingly provides an economic assessment of any culture, real or imaginary, he describes; how people make a (legal or illegal) living is always of interest to him. Like Marx, he was certain that "laissez-faire capitalism" could not be reformed from within: "A problem cannot be solved in terms of itself." He, too, saw the colonizing impulse that rewrote the world map between the sixteenth and nineteenth centuries as a tactic to "keep the underdog under," an indispensable part of capitalism's quest for new markets and fresh supplies of labor.

Burroughs never accepted the geopolitics that divided the American continent into separate southern and northern entities. Both were part of the same feeding system, though the South was the trough, the North the hog. Traveling in Colombia in search of the drug *yagé* in April 1953, Burroughs reported to Ginsberg that he was mistaken for a representative of the Texaco Oil Company and given free lodging and transportation everywhere he went. In fact, as Burroughs knew, Texaco had surveyed the area, discovered no oil, and pulled out several years before. The Colombian rubber and cocoa industries, totally dependent on American investment, were drying up as well. Colombians, however, refused to believe it; they were still expecting the infrastructure of roads, railroads, and airports that U.S. industry could be counted on to build to expedite the development, and removal, of a Third World country's material wealth. Burroughs had no more sympathy for the losers in the neocolonial con game than he did for any other "mark." "Like I should think some day soon boys will start climbing in through the transom and tunneling under the door" was his derisive comment on Colombian delusions about U.S. investment.

The literary critic Tobin Siebers, writing about post-WWII literary culture, has speculated that the postmodern disavowal of agency, almost entirely the work of First World, white, male writers and theorists, is both an expression and an evasion of racial and economic guilt. Looking at the defining phenomena of the twentieth century, its holocausts, genocides, gulags, and unimaginably lethal weapons of destruction, who would want to advertise himself as part of the group that engineered and invented them? Postmodernism allows whites to answer the question "Who's responsible?" by saying, "It looks like me, but actually there is no real 'me'"—no one, in postmodernspeak, has a firmly defined or authentic self. In the universe of total, irreversible complicity postmodernism posits, the cause-and-effect sequence of individual action and consequence, motive and deed, is severed. Where Burroughs breaks with the postmodern position is that in his fiction, though everyone is complicit, everyone is also responsible, for everyone is capable of resistance. There are no victims, just accomplices; the mark collaborates with his exploiter in his own demise.

"We make truth," Burroughs wrote in his journal shortly before his death on August 2, 1997. "Nobody else makes it. There is no truth we don't make." What governments and corporations assert as truth is nothing but "lies"; such bodies are inevitably "self-righteous. They have to be because in human terms they are wrong." For Burroughs as for the postmodernists, identity was artifice, but for him it was made that way, betrayed that way, and can be remade differently. To deny the latter possibility is the last and worst collusion because it's the only one that can be avoided. Burroughs' final trilogy is a complex, funny, impassioned attempt, with one always aware of the death sentence under which it apparently operates, to "punch a hole in the big lie," to parachute his characters behind the time lines of the enemy and make a different truth.

As he explained it in *Cities of the Red Night,* what Burroughs had in mind was a globalization of the Third World guerrilla tactics that defeated the U.S. in Vietnam. He prefaces the novel with an account of an actual historical personage, Captain Mission, a seventeenth-century pirate who founded an all-male, homosexual community on Madagascar, a libertarian society that outlawed slavery, the death penalty, and any interference in the beliefs and practices of its members. Although Captain Mission's relatively unarmed settlement didn't survive, Burroughs elaborates what its "New Freedoms" could have meant if it had: fortified positions throughout the Third World to mobilize resistance to "slavery and oppression" everywhere.

Despite his scorn for those lining up to welcome their destroyers, Burroughs did not traffic with the racialized thinking that—in historical fact—buttressed and excused the empire-building process, the definition of Third World people of color as inherently lazy, dishonest, incorrigibly irrational, and unable to look after their own welfare. The Western virtues of rationality and instrumentalism were largely suspect to Burroughs in any case; he shared the so-called primitive belief in an animistic universe which the skeptical West categorically rejected. In *Cities of the Red Night,* Burroughs is explicit that whites would be welcome in his utopia only as "workers, settlers, teachers, and technicians"— no more "white-man boss, no Pukka Sahib, no Patróns, no colonists." As he recounts the history of seven imaginary cities in the Gobi desert thousands of years ago, Burroughs explains that before the destruction of the cities by a meteor (itself a forerunner of late-twentieth-century nuclear weaponry), an explosion which produced the "Red Night" of the title, all the people of the world were black. White and even brown and red-skinned people are "mutations" caused by the meteor, as was the albino woman-warrior whose all-female army conquered one of the original cities, reducing its male inhabitants to "slaves, consorts, and courtiers."

Burroughs' cosmological myth resembles the Black Muslim fable, embraced notably by Elijah Muhammad and Malcolm X, about the creation of a white race of "devils" by an evil black scientist named Yacub intent on destroying the all-black world that has rejected him. Yet Burroughs never signed up for the fan clubs of the Third World revolutionaries so compelling to young, left-wing Americans in the 1960s; to his mind, heroes like Che Guevara were simply devices for those running the "reality film," a gambit designed to leave the "shines cooled back . . . in a nineteenth century set." Burroughs claimed to belong to only one group, the "Shakespeare squadron"; in the historical impasse in which he lived, language was his only weapon.

Language as he found it, however, was rigged to serve the enemy, an ambush disguised as an oasis—in the West, language had become the "word virus," the dead heart of the control machine. Burroughs' avant-garde experiments in montage, the cut-up, and disjunctive narrative were attempts to liberate Western consciousness from its own form of self-expression, from the language that we think we use but which, in truth, uses us. "Writers are very powerful," Burroughs tells us; they can write, and "unwrite," the script for the reality film.

Defending *Naked Lunch* during the obscenity trial of 1966 as an example of automatic writing, Norman Mailer noted that "one's best writing seems to bear no relation to what one is thinking about." Many post-WWII writers showed a quickened interest in the random thought that reroutes or classifies the plan of a novel or essay, but Burroughs came closest to reversing the traditional roles of design and chance. For him, conscious intent was a form of prediction, and prediction is only possible when the status quo has reason to assume it will meet no significant opposition. In his fiction, the continuity girl, the person who keeps the details of one sequence of film consistent with the next, has gone AWOL; there are no shock absorbers. Jump cuts replace narrative transitions; straight chronological, quasi-documentary sequences are spliced with out-of-time-and-space scenes of doom-struck sodomy and drug overdoses. Lush symbolist imagery and hard-boiled, tough-guy slang, the lyric and the obscene, collide and interbreed. Burroughs' early style was founded on drug lingo and jive talk; he was fascinated by their mutability, their fugitive quality, the result of the pressure their speakers were under to dodge authority and leave no records behind. His later work elaborates and complicates this principle. No one form of language can hold center stage for long. Fast-change artistry is all; sustained domination is impossible.

The novelist Paul Bowles, a friend of Burroughs', thought the cut-up method reflected an "unsatisfied desire on the part of the mind to be anonymous," but it also came out of Burroughs' need to work undercover, at the intersections where identities and meanings multiply faster than language can calculate or record. The cut-up method was not a refusal of authorship. The writer still selects the passages, whether from his own work, a newspaper, a novel by someone else, or a sign glimpsed out a train window, which he then cuts up and juxtaposes. You always know what you're doing, according to Burroughs. Everyone sees in the dark; the trick is to maneuver yourself into the position where you can recognize what you see.

The first step is to realize that the language, even the voice that you use, are not your own, but alien implants, the result of the most effective kind of colonization, the kind that turns external design into what passes for internal motivation and makes what you are allowed to get feel like what you want. In *The Ticket That Exploded,* Burroughs challenged his readers to try and halt their "subvocal speech," that committee meeting inside the head that seldom makes sense and never shuts up, the static of the self, the lowest idle of the meaning-fabricating machine. Who are you talking to? Burroughs wants to know. Is it really yourself? Why has Western man "lost the option of silence"? The nonstop monologue running in our heads is proof of possession, and the only way to end it is to cut the association lines by which it lives, the logic by which we believe that "b" follows "a" not because it in fact does, but because we have been aggressively, invasively conditioned to think so. Like the Jehovah who is its front man, Western language has become prerecorded sequence, admitting of no alternatives.

"In the beginning was the word," the Bible says, but the only beginning the line really refers to, Burroughs reminds us, is the beginning of the word itself, the recorded word, literacy as the West understands it, a period that makes up only a tiny fraction of human history. Burroughs suggests that people try communicating by pictures, as the Chinese and Mayans did, even by colors and smells; words are "an around-the-world oxcart way of doing things." English as spoken shuts out the infinite variations in which meaning presents itself; the body thinks too, though the Western mind can only imperfectly translate its language. Burroughs wanted to abolish "either/or" dichotomies from our speech, change every "the" to an "a," and root out the verb "to be," which is not, as it claims, a description of existence, but a "categorical imperative of permanent condition," a way of programming people to disavow change, no matter how imperative.

Burroughs' ambitions amounted to nothing less than an attempt to uproot and transform Western concepts of personhood and language, if not personhood and language themselves, to produce a new emancipation proclamation for the twenty-first century. Inevitably, in his last novel, *The Western Lands*, he judged his attempt a failure, but he also noted that even to imagine success on so radical a scale was victory. By the time of his death, Burroughs was recognized as one of the major American writers of the postwar era and he had become a formative influence, even a cult figure, for several generations of the young, leaving his mark on punk rock, performance art, and independent film.

When Norman Mailer shared a podium with Burroughs at the Jack Kerouac School of Disembodied Poetics of the Naropa Institute in Boulder in 1984, he found him an impossible act to follow. The kids loved him, Mailer noted with some envy; they laughed uproariously at his every line. They knew he was "authentic." The critic Lionel Abel thought that Burroughs and his Beat colleagues had established the "metaphysical prestige" of the drug addict and the criminal; though modern skepticism destroyed the belief in transcendence, the human "need for utterness," not to be denied, had found its satisfaction in "trans-descendence." In a cameo role in Gus Van Sant's *Drugstore Cowboy* (1989), a movie about young addicts in Seattle, with his dead-white poker face, dark, quasi-clinical garb, and low-pitched, deliberate, nasal intonation, Burroughs is clearly an iconic apparition from the underground, the hipster as Tiresias, the master of "the crime," as he described it in *Naked Lunch*, "of separate action."

Burroughs was never comfortable with the "Beat" label. In a 1969 interview with Daniel Odier, while acknowledging his close personal friendships with several of the Beat writers, he remarked that he shared neither their outlook nor their methods. Kerouac believed that the first draft was always the best one and emphasized spontaneity above all else; Burroughs counted on revision. He used the word "beat" sparingly and literally, to mean "no fire, no intensity, no life," while Kerouac and Ginsberg said it meant "high, ec-static, saved." Unlike Ginsberg, Kerouac, or Gregory Corso, whose entire careers can be seen as part of the Beat movement, Burroughs belongs to an-other literary tradition as well, that of the avant-garde novelists headed by Vladimir Nabokov, Thomas Pynchon, John Hawkes, William Gaddis, John Barth, and Don DeLillo. His affinities with their direct forebears, T. S. Eliot and Ernest Hemingway in particular, are defining ones; for all his innovations, he is visibly carrying on the work of high modernist irony, as Kerouac and Ginsberg most decidedly are not, and this fact may account for the willing-ness of the American critical establishment to grant Burroughs a more respectful hearing than it has yet accorded his Beat peers.

Nonetheless, the affinities between Burroughs and the Beats are stronger than those he had with any other group. When he first met the much younger Ginsberg and Kerouac in 1944, he instantly took on a mentor role, handing Kerouac a copy of Oswald Spengler's *Decline of the West,* with an instruction to "EEE di fy your mind, my boy, with the grand actuality of fact." Ginsberg said that while Columbia University (where both Ginsberg and Kerouac had been students) taught them about "the American empire," Burroughs in-structed them about the "end of empire." As John Tytell has pointed out, their pathway to "beatitude" sprang directly out of his "nightmare of devastation." In Tangiers in 1955, as Burroughs began the work that would become *Naked Lunch*—a book that Kerouac named and that he and Ginsberg helped to type and revise—he wrote Kerouac that he was trying to do something similar to Kerouac's "spontaneous prose" project, whose guidelines Kerouac had writ-ten out in 1953 at Ginsberg's and Burroughs' request; Burroughs was writ-ing "what I see and feel right now to arrive at some absolute, direct transmission of fact on all levels."

Kerouac's extended, astute, funny, and loving portraits of Burroughs as "Will Dennison" in *The Town and the Country* (1950) and "Old Will Lee" in *On the Road* not only served as advance publicity for *Naked Lunch,* but by Burroughs' own admission helped to elaborate the persona he adopted. In his essay "Remembering Kerouac," Burroughs said that Kerouac had known Burroughs was a writer long before he himself did. Over the course of his long life, Burroughs had other seminal, creative friendships and partnerships, most notably with the avant-garde artist Brion Gysin. Yet in some not altogether fanciful sense, Burroughs became what Kerouac and Ginsberg had first imag-ined and recognized him to be.

The novelist Joyce Johnson, a friend of Kerouac's, claims that the Beat Generation "has refused to die." Unlike the "Lost Generation" of the 1920s headed by F. Scott Fitzgerald and Hemingway which, within a decade, as the "Jazz Age" gave way to the Depression, was decisively repudiated by its own members, the Beat movement continues even today, a half century after its inception, sustaining its veterans and attracting new members—those for whom the respectable is synonymous with boredom and terror, if not crime, who regard the ongoing social order as suffocating, unjust, and unreal, who be-

lieve that honesty can still be reinvented in a world of lies and that the answers, if there are any, lie not in the political realm but in the quest for new
forms of self-expression and creative collaboration across all traditional class,
race, and ethnic boundaries, in fresh recuperative imaginings of ourselves and
our country, in physical, spiritual, and metaphysical explorations of roads still
left to try. "What's in store for me in the direction I don't take?" Kerouac
asked.

Burroughs deconstructed the word, but he never abandoned it; it was, after
all, his "fragile lifeboat," the "mainsail to reach the Western lands." Though
he turned to painting as his main artistic outlet and published no novels after
1987, he continued to write, as Kerouac and Ginsberg had, up to the very day
he died. If he had never been known as a Beat writer, if there had been no
Beat movement, his avant-garde experiments in form, his wit, his mastery of
language would ensure his inclusion in college courses on the post-WWII
narrative. But it is his talismanic power to beckon and admonish his readers,
to reroute their thoughts and dreams, that has made him widely read outside
the academy as well as within it, and this is what he shares with his Beat companions and no one else, certainly not with the reclusive Thomas Pynchon or
the at times grotesquely overexposed Norman Mailer. Like Ginsberg and
Kerouac, Burroughs is there yet elsewhere. He, too, practiced literature as
magic.

The uncannily perceptive Herbert Huncke, a hustler, homosexual, addict,
and writer, was the fourth seminal figure of the first Beat circle. Initially, he
had been troubled by Burroughs' coldness. On one occasion, however, when
Burroughs passed out drunk in his apartment, Huncke saw a different man.
Awake, Burroughs was "the complete master of himself," Huncke wrote in
The Evening Sun Turns Crimson (1980), but asleep, he seemed a "strange,
otherworld" creature, "relaxed and graceful," touched with a mysterious
beauty, "defenseless and vulnerable . . . lonely and as bewildered as anyone
else." At that instant, Huncke said, "a certain feeling of love I bear for him to
this day sprang into being." At moments, Kerouac glimpsed in Burroughs "that
soft and tender curiosity, verging on maternal care, about what others think
and say" that Kerouac believed indispensable to great writing. Burroughs was
a Beat writer because he, too, wanted to decipher what he called the "hieroglyphic of love and suffering," and he learned about it largely from his relations with other men.

In the age that coined the word "togetherness" as a synonym for family
values, the Beats, each in his own style, mounted the first open, sustained assault in American history on the masculine role as heterosexual spouse, father,
and grown-up provider. In the midst of the Cold War crusade against all de-
viations from the masculine norm, in the era that could almost be said to have
invented the idea of classified information, they openly addressed homosexuality, bisexuality, and masturbation in their work, declassifying the secrets of
the male body, making sexuality as complex as individual identity, and pushing their chosen forms to new limits in the process.

Though Kerouac did not consider himself homosexual, he had intermit-tent sex with Ginsberg throughout the 1940s and early 1950s. Ginsberg and Burroughs had also been lovers, and their deep and steady friendship outlasted their physical affair. Shortly before his death from cancer on April 5, 1997, Ginsberg telephoned Burroughs to tell him that he knew he was dying. "I thought I would be terrified," Allen said, "but I am exhilarated!" These were his "last words to me," Burroughs noted in his journal; it was an invitation a "cosmonaut of inner space," in his favored phrase of self-description, could not fail to accept. He died four months later.

Some of Burroughs' last journal entries were about Allen and "the courage of his total sincerity." Though Kerouac's self-evasions had strained Burroughs' patience long before Kerouac's death in 1969, he always loved the passage in *On the Road* in which Kerouac spoke of feeling like "somebody else, some stranger . . . my whole life was a haunted life, the life of a ghost." Burroughs, too, knew what it was to be "a spy in somebody else's body where nobody knows who is spying on whom." In *The Western Lands,* Burroughs imagined a new kind of currency, underwritten not by gold or silver but by moral virtues and psychological achievements. Rarest of all are the "Coin of Last Resort," awarded those who have come back from certain defeat, and the "Contact Coin," which "attests that the bearer has contacted other beings." Finally, love between men was simply love, and love, Burroughs wrote in his journal the day before he died, is "What there is. Love."

Selected Bibliography

Abel, Lionel. "Beyond the Fringe." *Partisan Review*. 30 (1963): 109–112.

Burroughs, William S. "Final Words." *The New Yorker*. (August 18, 1997): 36–37.

Fiedler, Leslie A. "The New Mutants." *Partisan Review*. 32(1965): 505–525.

Huncke, Herbert. *The Herbert Huncke Reader*. Ed. Benjamin G. Schafer. New York: William and Morrow Company, 1997.

Johnson, Joyce. "Reality Sandwiches." *American Book Review*. 18 August-September (1997): 13.

Kazin, Alfred. "He's Just Wild about Writing." *The New York Times Book Review*. (December 12, 1971): 4, 22.

Kerouac, Jack. *Vanity of Duluoz: An Adventurous Education, 1935–1946*. 1968; rpt., New York: Penguin Books, 1994.

Knickerbocker, Conrad. "William Burroughs: An Interview." *The Paris Review*. 35 (1965): 13–49.

McCarthy, Mary. "Burroughs' Naked Lunch." *William S. Burroughs at the Front: Critical Reception, 1959–1989*. Ed. Jennie Skerl and Robin Lydenberg. Carbondale: Southern Illinois University Press, 1991: 33–39.

McLuhan, Marshall. "Notes on Burroughs." *The Nation* (December 28, 1964): 517–519.

Morgan, Ted. *Literary Outlaw: The Life and Times of William S. Burroughs*. 1988; rpt., New York: Avon Books, 1990.

Siebers, Tobin. *Cold War Criticism and the Politics of Skepticism*. New York: Oxford, 1993.

Tanner, Tony. *City of Words: American Fiction 1950–1970*. London: Jonathan Cape, 1971.

Tytell, John. *Naked Angels: Kerouac, Ginsberg, Burroughs*. New York: Grove Weidenfeld, 1976.

Watson, Steven. *The Birth of the Beat Generation: Visionaries, Rebels, and Hipsters, 1944–1960*. New York: Pantheon, 1995.

editors' note

The editor's selections from William Burroughs' writings are arranged chronologically, for the most part. Source citations are by book title and chapter title (if any) and include some embedded subheadings, following the author's text. All selections from novels begin with the first pages of the full book, and end with the last pages of the book; the author's sequence is followed. Collections of shorter pieces are grouped according to the title of the published collection, and the title of each piece is given. When a titled chapter or passage from a novel is not presented in its entirety, this is indicated in the table of contents and in the heading of the passage. Where the chapters of a book are neither numbered nor titled, cuts are indicated by a double line-space. In *The Place of Dead Roads* and *The Western Lands,* chapter numbers and section titles are omitted in favor of a listing of first lines from the selected passages, to offer a reader a map of the works.

THE NAME IS
BURROUGHS

the name is burroughs
by james grauerholz

William Seward Burroughs (II) was born a few years after the beginning of "the American Century," descended from two respectable upper-middle-class families, one of which would give its name to a great American company. His hometown of St. Louis was a city old and large enough to incorporate the traditions of the Eastern seaboard while serving as the jumping-off point for the American West. He was a child of privilege and destiny—but it was not a destiny that his ancestors or his peers could have foreseen, or even imagined.

Burroughs' paternal grandfather, William Seward Burroughs, was an indefatigable inventor best known for perfecting the adding machine. As a young man in Ohio after the Civil War, Burroughs worked as a bookkeeper—a job that in those times was done by hand—and after seven tedious years as a copyist, he became obsessed with the idea of a mechanical device that would make handwritten accounts obsolete. In 1882, aged twenty-five years, Burroughs moved to St. Louis for its warmer climate. With Joseph Boyer, he formed the American Arithmometer Company four years later, but it took five years more to perfect his invention. Thereafter the company prospered, but the inventor's health was failing; tubercular at thirty-nine, he moved to Citronelle, Alabama, and died there two years later, in 1898. The loyal Boyer renamed the firm the Burroughs Adding Machine Company and moved it to Detroit. He placed an imposing obelisk in St. Louis' Bellefontaine Cemetery, over Burroughs' grave in the family plot, with the inscription: "Erected by his associates as a tribute to his genius."

William Burroughs' father, Mortimer, was the eldest of the inventor's four children, and the only one to hold on to a few shares when the company offered to buy all the family's inherited stock. Mortimer, then only fourteen, displayed an acumen that was confirmed when he finally sold the stock three decades later, in 1929, just three months before the Crash. His brother, Harold, became addicted to morphine, and committed suicide in 1915; his sister Jenny wandered drunk on the streets of St. Louis and vanished in Seattle; and his youngest sister, Helen, married and moved to Colorado. The Burroughs family disintegrated; the "Burroughs millions," with which William Burroughs would often complain that Jack Kerouac, in his novels, had unhelpfully invested him,

3

never existed. And yet the Burroughs company loomed large in American cyberbusiness during the 1950s and 1960s, with its own skyscraper in New York, and the legend had an inevitable credibility for many years.

Mortimer graduated at M.I.T. and returned to St. Louis. In 1910, he married an elegant, ethereal St. Louis woman of twenty-two named Laura Lee—a debutante who was tall and thin, much given to seeing ghostly apparitions and reading meaning into all seeming happenstance. The daughter of a circuit-riding Methodist minister, the Rev. James Wideman Lee, Laura used crystal ball and Ouija board to contact the spirits of the departed. She had a gift for flower arranging, and authored three illustrated promotional booklets of floral arrangements for the Coca-Cola company in the 1930s. Laura Lee's brother, Ivy Ledbetter Lee, had graduated Princeton at the turn of the century, and he (and his contemporary Edward L. Bernays) invented what is now called "public relations." Ivy Lee was an interesting and roguish character, who worked to polish the public images of such disparate figures as John D. Rockefeller Sr. and Adolf Hitler. He lived in New York in high style, and was a public figure of his time, mentioned in the newspapers and even in a popular song of the twenties. By the early thirties his work for Germany's ruling National Socialist Party had brought him to the attention of the House Un-American Activities Committee, and a few months after testifying before HUAC in 1934, he died of complications from a brain tumor—before he could see what his Nazi friends would unleash on the world.

Mortimer and Laura's first child, Mortimer Jr., was born in 1911, after which Burroughs *père* was known as "Mote," to distinguish him from his son, "Mort." Three years after Mort came along, William Seward Burroughs II was born at home, on February 5, 1914, at 4664 Pershing Avenue in the Central West End of St. Louis, near the city's vast Forest Park, in a redbrick house which Mote had built for his family on a tree-lined street secluded behind wrought-iron gates. After six years at the private Community School, Willy and his brother Mort were sent to the John Burroughs School (named after the American naturalist and wildlife conservationist, no relation to Burroughs' family), in the St. Louis suburb of Ladue. In 1926, when Willy was twelve, the Burroughs family moved to a new house at 700 South Price Road, nearer to the school. His classmates were other members of the white upper class—most of them from families wealthier, in fact, than Burroughs' own. Their teachers were well paid, and their curricula were based on the classical education by which these scions-in-waiting were to be prepared for social and business leadership. Most of the male graduates of the Burroughs School went on to Ivy League colleges, as did Burroughs himself.

The public environment of William Burroughs' childhood was shaped by traditions of class and quality, with roots in the British origins of the first American settlers. It was calculated to produce worthy heirs to great fortunes, new captains of industry for the nation. But Willy Burroughs and his brother Mort were at the lower end of the social scale, based on their family's middling fortune, and Willy in particular was keenly aware of never quite fitting in. The private environment of Burroughs' childhood may have contributed to this. His father was reserved in demeanor, and closer to his elder son, Mort; father and younger son were never able to connect on an emotional level, a fate that would play out again in the relationship between Burroughs and his own son years later. Burroughs' mother was distant and vague, but she doted on Willy, and may have contributed an element of narcissism to his personality.

But young Willy was also raised by the household help, for his parents had sufficient means to retain a small group of servants. Otto Belue, the African-American gardener, was only about a dozen years older than Willy, and he often played with the boy as he worked in the garden. And there were Irish nannies for the children, two of whom left lifelong impressions upon Burroughs. One nanny taught him old Irish curses and witchcraft, which much intrigued him; another, Mary Wells, took him along on a picnic with her veterinarian boyfriend, who apparently sexually abused the four-year-old boy. This incident of childhood molestation left Burroughs with what he felt was a repressed psychic wound—which he was not able to recall to consciousness until forty years later, in the late 1950s, during what would be the last of a long series of psychiatric and psychoanalytic relationships for Burroughs, beginning when he was twenty-six.

Young Burroughs, a thin, bookish boy, who already at age eight entertained dreams of a glamorous life as a writer, immersed himself in the pulp fiction of the day—an exposure to popular-entertainment forms of writing that would be apparent in his later writing. His earliest known composition that survives is a short essay published in his school magazine, the *John Burroughs Review*, in February 1929 when Burroughs was just fifteen. "Personal Magnetism" shows a deftness and balance that prefigures Burroughs' adult talent, and reveals his fascination with magic, sensational powers, and control. There is no way to know how much his school editor changed the text, but it reads like Burroughs.

A serious accident happened in 1927, when Burroughs was thirteen years old: he caused an explosion while playing with his chemistry set, and badly burned his right hand. He was taken to a doctor's office just a few blocks from his home and given an "adult dose" of morphine, by injection. Burroughs later recalled that this made a deep impression on him: "As a boy, I was much plagued by nightmares. I remember a nurse telling me that opium gives you sweet dreams, and I resolved that I would smoke opium when I grew up." Also in 1927 a book was published which Burroughs read, with profound consequences: Jack Black's *You Can't Win*. This autobiography of a turn-of-the-century opium-smoking safecracker and itinerant stickup man in the American West captured the imagination of the teenaged boy. Jack Black moved in a world where "the Johnson Family" (of fair, compassionate strangers of the road, with the natural democracy of the equally suffering) offered an attractive alternative to what Burroughs saw as the enforced, institutionalized hypocrisy of middle-class America—as exemplified by his uncle, Ivy Lee, whom he visited in New York, with his parents, at holidays.

Mote and Laura took the family on a vacation cruise to France in 1929—the first of many extracontinental journeys in Burroughs' life. Young Willy had persistent sinus troubles, so in 1930 his parents sent him and his brother to the Los Alamos Ranch School for Boys in northern New Mexico. The school was founded and run by A. J. Connell, a sort of Lord Baden-Powell for the American Southwest: he stressed an idealized Boy Scout–like existence, emphasizing physical hardening and manly bonding, for both of which Burroughs was rather ill-suited. The roster of fellow L.A.R.S. alumni included many future American industrialists, as well as the author Gore Vidal—who, late in Burroughs' life, reminisced with him about the sexual importunities of Connell. Vidal was in the same class as Burroughs' brother, Mort. Later, during WWII, the Ranch School was commandeered as the ultrasecret home for the Manhattan Project. Burroughs always hated Robert Oppenheimer and the other scientists who developed the atomic bomb, and the president from Missouri who ordered its use on Japan. Among L.A.R.S. alumni, however, this was probably a minority view.

The New Mexico experience was trying for Burroughs, in several ways; for one thing, it was a separation from his mother that proved unexpectedly stressful for him. He was soon in trouble for going down to Santa Fe with a classmate and passing out on chloral hydrate, or "knockout drops"—no doubt inspired by reading tales in boys'-adventure magazines about shanghaied sailors. Also at Los Alamos, he was first indulging his dream of being a writer, and he kept a torrid diary of his romantic feelings toward one of the other boys. As Burroughs later wrote, when he finally retrieved this diary—among his possessions shipped home after the episode with the "Mickey"—he quickly destroyed the dangerous pages.

Burroughs finished his high school credits at the Taylor School in St. Louis after his ignominious retreat from the Ranch School, and in 1932, at eighteen, he left home for Harvard University in Cambridge, Massachusetts. One of his friends there, Richard Stern, was from a wealthy Kansas City family, and he was instrumental in exposing Burroughs to the gay subculture of New York City in the early 1930s. They would drive down to Greenwich Village, where they found lesbian dives, piano bars, and a homosexual underground—exposing Burroughs to some social stereotypes that he found repulsive, but also giving him his first inkling of a way of life that was an alternative to the straight world. Burroughs went home to St. Louis in the summers, and by one account he lost his heterosexual virginity at age twenty-one with an African-American prostitute in an East St. Louis brothel, which he then frequented for a time.

As Burroughs' older brother grew up, Mort proved to be a sensible, stoic member of his family and of society—in marked contrast to his brother William. He studied architecture at Princeton and Harvard, then spent the rest of his life in St. Louis. During WWII, Mort had steady employment as a drafts-man for the Emerson Electric engineering company, where he worked until retirement. He married a St. Louis woman and raised two daughters there, and attended to his parents for as long as they lived, even after they retired to Palm Beach, Florida. Throughout his life, William Burroughs owed much of his freedom to his brother's dutiful help to the family—which began in ear-nest just as the younger Burroughs was moving as far away from all of them as possible.

Burroughs had already embraced, at least in his mind, a wide social under-ground of the imagination; since boyhood, he was fascinated with gangsters and hoboes, an underworld with roots in nineteenth-century America. He affected various eccentricities, such as keeping a pet ferret in his rooms in Claverly Hall at Harvard, in emulation of Saki's "Sredni Vashtar" character. And he kept pistols, with one of which he almost killed Stern one day, firing it at him without realizing the gun was loaded—an ominous foreshadowing. Burroughs' love of guns began in the 1920s, when the pacification of the Western frontier was still a living memory in eastern Missouri; but he had a special fascination for all weapons and techniques of self-defense and mastery over others, even as a young boy.

Burroughs completed his baccalaureate in American Literature at Harvard in 1936, and—after a "grand tour" through Eastern Europe, which brought him fact-to-face with the open homosexuality of the Weimar era in Germany and Austria—he stayed on in Vienna, took classes in medicine there, and briefly attended a school for fledgling diplomats. He followed the rise of the Nazis in Germany, and the impending *Anschluss* of Austria; he picked up boys in Vienna's ancient steam baths, the Romanische Baden, and moved in a rarefied world of exiles, runaways, queers, and spies. In 1937, he agreed to marry a woman he knew from his trips to Dubrovnik: Ilse Klapper, a German Jew in her thirties, the doyenne of a circle of gay intellectuals Burroughs had met there. The marriage was Ilse's idea, to escape the Nazi invasion. Burroughs did not share the anti-Semitism prevalent in the society from which he sprang; he did not seek his parents' permission, nor would they have given it. He married Ilse in Athens, and gave her the status she needed to flee to New York. Burroughs met up with her there, and although they remained friendly for years, they separated at once, and he formally divorced her nine years later.

Burroughs took psychology courses at Columbia University in New York City, but returned to Cambridge in the summer of 1938 to study anthropol-ogy. He was twenty-four years old, and his roommate was his best friend from St. Louis, Kells Elvins. Kells was an intelligent, handsome man who was irre-sistible to women; he married three of them in his short life. Undoubtedly, Burroughs' attraction to Elvins was partly sexual, but there is no evidence the relationship was ever physically consummated. Elvins was studying criminal psychology, and Burroughs also wanted to understand the criminal mind. During their time as graduate students, they wrote the farcical vignette

"Twilight's Last Gleamings," drunkenly acting out the scenes on a screened porch, with lightning in the night sky.

Kells Elvins is an important figure in Burroughs' life; his innate mordant humor helped to shape Burroughs' writing. With the savage, take-no-prisoners satire of college men, informed by a shared appreciation of the psychopathic mind, they tapped a vein of cruel funniness that goes back through Nashe, Sterne, Swift, Voltaire, and Petronius to Aristophanes. The figure of "pure glittering shamelessness," exemplified by the boat captain's rushing into the first lifeboat in women's clothing, would be a touchstone of all Burroughs' work. This volume also includes an essay from a mid-1970s *Crawdaddy* column, in which Burroughs offers a more explicit retrospective introduction to "Twilight's Last Gleamings"—it is invaluable for understanding the auto-biographical Burroughs *Ur*-hero, "Audrey"/"Kim." This character also represents a visceral rejection—on grounds of hypocrisy, if not melodrama—of the "hero principle" as it was inculcated in young men of his social class. Burroughs gained mastery over the Wasp hero he was expected to be, and could never become, by seizing upon and elaborating a post-Nietzschean "antihero" concept.

The manuscript used for this version of "Twilight's Last Gleamings" was evidently typed on a Spanish typewriter, and therefore was typed—either from memory or (less likely) a copy of the original manuscript—after Burroughs moved to Mexico in 1949. But as the 1938 pages are lost, this is the fullest extant version of this seminal work, whose characters, ideas, and scenes would recur throughout all of Burroughs' writing, sometimes verbatim. (The reader will also find at least two further echoes of this story, in *Nova Express* and *The Wild Boys*.) It marks the birth of "Doctor Benway," one of Burroughs' archetypes—less than a year after his medical-school experiences in Vienna. In the heyday of Burroughs' later performing career, 1974–87, "Twilight's Last Gleamings" was a staple of his public readings, never failing to get a rise from the audience.

Kells Elvins went to Huntsville, Texas, to work as a psychologist at the state prison, and in late 1938 Burroughs visited him for a few weeks, then returned to New York City for the winter. Except for his friendship with Ilse Klapper, who was working as secretary for a fellow émigré, the Broadway playwright Ernst Toller, Burroughs' activities during this year remain unclear. After Toller's suicide, when Klapper worked for the actor Kurt Kasznar and the writer Jean Latouche, Burroughs may have unknowingly met Brion Gysin, who worked on the costumes for Latouche's Broadway hit *Cabin in the Sky*.

In late summer 1939, perhaps on Ilse's recommendation, Burroughs went from New York to Chicago to attend five lectures given by a Polish count named Alfred Korzybski, who spoke about his newly minted Theory of General Semantics. Burroughs retained from Korzybski's talks the conviction that words were false signposts that had a life of their own, and the insight that what Korzybski called "either/or thinking" could only lead to intellectual stalemate and self-deceit. In their postulation of the universal answer—"both/ and"—Korzybski and Burroughs alike tread close to the path of the Hindu philosopher Nagarjuna and his Seven-Fold Negation, so that the groundwork of Buddhist principles is not far from Burroughs' own revelations about language and reality in his early adulthood.

In the fall of 1939, Burroughs enrolled again at Columbia, to study anthropology. Staying at the University Club, he ran into a Harvard man named Bill Gilmore, who knew the homosexual scene in Greenwich Village. Gilmore introduced Burroughs to a young man named Jack Anderson, with whom Burroughs was infatuated from their first meeting. He moved into a room in the boardinghouse in the Village where Anderson lived, and it was at this point, in early 1940, that he contacted his first analyst, Dr. Herbert Wiggers, to begin a course of treatment which centered on his obsession with Anderson.

Jack was bisexual, and when he persisted in bringing men (and women!) back to his room for sex, Burroughs was so distraught that he cut off the end of his left little finger, with a new pair of poultry shears, alone in a hotel room. Carrying the severed digit in a handkerchief, Burroughs triumphantly presented himself to Dr. Wiggers—who immediately committed him to Bellevue. Accompanied in a taxicab by his father, his "wife" Ilse, and his friend Gilmore, Burroughs was transferred to the Payne Whitney clinic. Burroughs' account of this traumatic incident, a sketch called "The Finger," dates from the early 1950s and is included in the 1988 *Interzone* collection. His case file, recently discovered by the psychohistorian Peter Swales, contains examples of Burroughs' early attempts at "automatic writing," and shows his interest in the anthropology of the Kwakiutl and Crow Indians. Burroughs was reportedly a quiet, cooperative patient, and after four weeks he was sent home to St. Louis.

Mote and Laura owned a small landscaping business, and Burroughs became their deliveryman, a job he found intolerably boring. His parents sent him to a new analyst, whom he did not like. He kept in touch with Jack Anderson, who visited him in St. Louis, and the two of them promptly got into a drunken car wreck in Mote's automobile. Again, we have Burroughs' own account of the incident: "Driving Lesson," in *Interzone*. The image of two boys in a car speeding out of control toward a catastrophic wreck recurs in his later work—*The Wild Boys* and *Port of Saints*, in particular—as an erotic scenario, and as a breakthrough to a parallel dimension. One of Burroughs' lifelong regrets was his inability to show gratitude or love at this time to his father, who rescued him from the legal and financial consequences of the accident.

In late 1940, Burroughs got a pilot's license at a flying school in Lockport, Illinois. He lived in nearby Chicago for several months after that, seeing a new analyst, and applying for officers' training programs in various branches of the military—war was in the air, and that promised adventure. But Burroughs was flatfooted and nearsighted. He was turned down by all the armed services, as well as by the Office of Strategic Services, the precursor of today's Central Intelligence Agency. His interviewer was a fellow Harvard man who noted that Burroughs "had no clubs." After his failed OSS interview in Washington, Burroughs went up to New York again. He lived there for a year, working for an advertising agency—a job he got through family connections. As an adman, Burroughs was indifferent; he laughed at marketing slogans that his company did not consider funny at all. For sheer ludicrousness, his favorite campaign was for a high-colonic enema called "The Cascade"—for which he penned the motto: "Well done! thou true and faithful servant!"

Burroughs found another psychiatrist, who referred him after a few months to yet another analyst; meanwhile, he was reunited with Anderson, and they lived together on West Twelfth Street in the Village, but no longer as lovers. Burroughs' attraction to Anderson had waned, and Anderson's dependence on him had become a financial burden; it also gave a backdrop to his ongoing psychoanalytic sessions and his efforts to deal with his homosexuality. Even if he had wanted to return to an academic career, his college record was spotty, and he was no longer interested in his studies. Although none of Burroughs' 1940s correspondence with his family survives, his parents probably insisted on his continuing in analysis as a condition of the allowance they were paying him: two hundred dollars a month, at a time when a dollar-fifty bought a steak dinner with all the trimmings.

Talk of the war in Europe was everywhere; in December 1941 the Japanese attacked Pearl Harbor, and the U.S. joined World War II. The spring of 1942 found Burroughs back in St. Louis, recuperating from a bout with mononucleosis. That summer, he was unexpectedly called up in the draft and conscripted as an infantryman. Burroughs' long-fantasized military career, when it finally began, was over rather quickly. Feeling he belonged in the officer corps, he did not take well to his basic training at Jefferson Barracks, near St. Louis, and he asked his mother for help to escape from the army. Laura made an appointment with Dr. David Riock, who referred him to Chestnut Lodge in Maryland, near Washington, D.C. After a visit to that facility in June, Burroughs decided not to enroll in a psychotherapeutic program, which they told him could last a year.

In September, Burroughs was honorably discharged and returned home to St. Louis, but not for long—he soon moved back to Chicago. He was following up on some "underworld connections" he had made during his short stint as an inductee at Jefferson Barracks, and he had become involved in the relationship between two of his friends from St. Louis: David Kammerer and Lucien Carr. Like Kells Elvins, David Kammerer is one of the overlooked sources of Burroughs' personal philosophy. Kammerer was a brilliant conversationalist, his monologues ranging from the classics to the "Sunday funnies." At thirty-one, he was the same age as Mort, through whom he met Burroughs. Kammerer had been Lucien Carr's youth-group leader when Lucien was in junior high, and he introduced the teenager to Burroughs. Kammerer was romantically fascinated with Carr, who seems to have enjoyed the attention. When Carr went away to Andover, and then Bowdoin, Kammerer followed; in fall 1942, Kammerer followed Carr to the University of Chicago, where they were joined by Burroughs and his shadowy "army friends." Lucien Carr was then seventeen.

In Chicago, Burroughs associated with thieves and young veterans. He plotted to stick up a Turkish bath and ambush an armored truck, but both schemes failed. He was an employee-dishonesty investigator for a short time, but for the most part he worked as an exterminator—a job he later employed as a metaphor in his work. Burroughs also found a new analyst, whom he consulted for eight months. The Chicago period is a stage in Burroughs' romanticized life amidst "the criminal element" which began with his reading of *You Can't Win*.

At first, Kammerer's fixation on an idealized image of Lucien appeared to Burroughs as a psychological affectation, comparable to wearing a monocle. Burroughs amused himself by endlessly analyzing "the affair" privately with Kammerer, like characters in an André Gide novel. They were an unholy trinity of high-spirited adventurers; their pranks and escapades got Burroughs thrown out of his rooming house, and culminated in an ambiguous suicide attempt by Carr, whereupon Carr was brought home to St. Louis by his parents.

When Carr enrolled at Columbia University, Kammerer followed him to New York. In the spring of 1943, so did Burroughs, taking an apartment at 69 Bedford Street in Greenwich Village, half a block from Kammerer's place. He found work briefly as a bartender and a process server, but with his parents' allowance, he had no real need to work. Kammerer did maintenance work at Columbia University, where Carr lived in the dorms. A salon grew up around the Kammerer-Carr friendship, in Dave's Morton Street flat, with other Columbia students coming to sit at Dave's feet as he held forth. Lucien was the star pupil; his intellectual and physical fearlessness, and his beauty, drove David Kammerer mad.

In late 1943, in his Columbia dormitory, Lucien Carr met a fellow student named Allen Ginsberg, who introduced himself. Carr took Ginsberg down to Kammerer's apartment, where Ginsberg met Burroughs for the first time. In early spring 1944, Carr took Burroughs to meet a former Columbia student of his acquaintance, a high school football prodigy from Lowell, Massachusetts, named Jack Kerouac. Now the "Beat troika" was complete: a bourgeois, Communist-raised Jew from Paterson, New Jersey; a proletarian Catholic from a Massachusetts mill town; and a patrician Wasp manqué from St. Louis, gateway to the West—but the other two Missourians, Carr and Kammerer, were the center of the action. While Carr's bold ideas inspired Ginsberg and Kerouac (both wrote copiously of the ongoing melodrama in their journals), Burroughs remonstrated with Kammerer to get over his growing obsession.

In March 1944, Burroughs commenced another psychiatric analysis, this time with Dr. Paul Federn. In his case notes, Federn dubbed Burroughs a "Gangsterling"—a "wanna-be" gangster. His patient's other life, however, revolved around the apartments of two young Barnard women, Joan Vollmer and Frankie Eddie Parker, who were as unconventional as the young soldiers, sailors, and students who circulated around them in their salons at a succession of addresses near Columbia, on Manhattan's Upper West Side. Again, Lucien Carr had provided the introductions, and Burroughs, Ginsberg, and Kerouac began to spend time with Vollmer and Parker and their friends. David Kammerer, whom Carr was now avoiding, became ever more desperate.

Ginsberg and Kerouac drank eagerly from the fountain of wisdom they found in this strange, erudite older man: William Burroughs, at the ripe old age of thirty. He gave them "reading lists" of classic work, such as Rimbaud, Swift, Spengler; but he himself was still under the influence of Jack Black and, latterly, Dashiell Hammett and Raymond Chandler, whose "hard-boiled detective" style would manifest in his early writing. Burroughs was inclined to feel that he understood psychology as well as, or better than, the psychiatrists for whom his parents were paying, and he commenced a "lay analysis" of Ginsberg and Kerouac; these sessions went on intermittently for more than a year. Burroughs quickly "diagnosed" Kerouac's abnormal attachment to his mother, and intuited Ginsberg's sexual ambivalence. In fact, Ginsberg's early infatuation with Burroughs can be seen as a transference toward the older man, who listened so acceptingly and made such penetrating comments. But Burroughs was not attracted to Ginsberg physically, and in any case there was no seduction.

Inevitably, Dave Kammerer's obsession with Lucien Carr led to a final confrontation, late one night in mid-August 1944 in Morningside Park, near the Hudson River. Kammerer had taken his pursuit of Carr to unprecedented lengths, and on this night he reached the climax of his desperation. Carr, in profound confusion and provocation, and perhaps in simple self-defense, stabbed Kammerer repeatedly with a Boy Scout knife. He weighted the body and sank it in the Hudson. Carr ran for guidance to Kerouac, who helped him dispose of Kammerer's eyeglasses, and then to Burroughs, who advised him to get a good lawyer and turn himself in. Not long after, Carr did just that, and—after pleading guilty to first-degree manslaughter "in defense of his honor"—he was sentenced to two years in Elmira Reformatory, which he served with good behavior.

The Kammerer manslaughter was a shock to the circle of friends. Kerouac and Burroughs were both charged as accessories in the crime, which brought unwelcome attention to Burroughs from his parents; he returned to St. Louis with his father, who had come to New York to post bond. Kerouac's father refused to bail out his son, so Kerouac married his Columbia girlfriend, Edie Parker, and went to live with her and her parents in their hometown of Grosse Pointe, Michigan; within a few months, Kerouac returned alone to New York.

In the fall of 1944, Burroughs convinced his parents that he needed to go back to New York to continue his psychoanalysis. On his return, he was referred by Dr. Federn to Dr. Lewis Wolberg, who practiced hypnotherapy and narcotherapy, and who shared Burroughs' interest in the criminal mind. Under hypnosis on Wolberg's couch, Burroughs produced seven or eight submerged personalities, including a prissy English governess, a redneck tobacco farmer, a stoic old Negro, a mystical Chinese peasant savant, and a raving idiot, restrained in chains. Meanwhile Burroughs continued his amateur analysis of Ginsberg and Kerouac, who were still reeling from the death of Kammerer and the imprisonment of Carr.

Joan Vollmer was an attractive, cynical, and daring young woman in her early twenties, from upstate New York. With a little matchmaking from Ginsberg and perhaps Kerouac, Vollmer and Burroughs had become intellectually and emotionally linked, and their relationship graduated to sex by the spring of 1945. Eyewitnesses speak of the uncanny contact of their two "keen intelligences"; when Burroughs and Vollmer experimented with telepathic games, the results were eerie. The affair with Joan may also have been the first time Burroughs could feel self-assured with a woman.

By the summer of 1945, Burroughs was living with Vollmer and her one-year-old daughter, Julie, in their apartment on West 115th Street. Kerouac had begun writing a quasi-fictional account of the affair between Carr and Kammerer, a work he called "I Wish I Were You." After completing an unsatisfactory short draft, he showed it to Burroughs, and soon they were working together on a new version, which they called "And the Hippos Were Boiled in Their Tanks"—after a line from radio personality Jerry Newman's deliberately scrambled newscasts. The war in Europe had ended in May, and by the time Kerouac submitted the "Hippos" manuscript to the Ingersoll & Brennan literary agency that fall, the war in Asia was over, too—thanks to the Manhattan Project and a place called Los Alamos. Burroughs was still in touch with Ilse Klapper, whose comment on Hiroshima and Nagasaki was: "It is unbelievable what a shit we are in."

The "Hippos" manuscript—dated "August 1945"—was retyped by Kerouac, a fast and accurate typist, and his is the only handwriting on the typescript. The chapters are marked to show their alternating authorship, and the pages attributed to "Will Dennison" clearly are in Burroughs' voice. The passage here, attributed to "Dennison," is the first chapter of the novella. "Mike Ryko" is Kerouac, "Phillip Tourian" is Carr, and "Ramsay Allen" is Kammerer. Dennison's mention of "my old lady" presumably refers to Joan Vollmer, and "Agnes O'Rourke" appears to be one of the lesbians from Kammerer's Greenwich Village circle. The "Pied Piper Bar" was the West End, a hangout for Columbia students and a frequent watering hole for the group. From Kerouac's later correspondence, we know that no publishers took an interest in the "Hippos" manuscript in the mid-forties—and indeed, it is not very well written, overall. Moreover, Carr objected to the exploitation of his troubled story by his two friends, and the manuscript was stashed away by Kerouac and forgotten. It turned up at the offices of Kerouac's agent, Sterling Lord, in the early 1970s. The jejune text cannot be published as a serious novel, but "Hippos"—and the earlier draft—will undoubtedly be published, with biographical commentary, someday.

The first section of this book begins with an excerpt from Burroughs' own "literary autobiography," written in 1972 after he had reviewed thousands of his own pages for an archive-sale project. "The Name Is Burroughs" is taken from a short piece written in the mid-1960s, which Burroughs grafted onto the beginning of the longer 1972 text to create a chapter for *The Adding Machine*. In this selection, Burroughs recaptures some of his earliest themes; for example, Lord Cheshire, stranded on an ice floe near the Pole with the others starving around him, lies bravely to Reggie as he gives the boy the last of his lime juice—"Yes . . . I've had mine. . . ."—an act of self-sacrifice that will recur in Burroughs' 1954 short story "The Junky's Christmas" and again in 1971, in " 'The Priest,' They Called Him."

Burroughs also refers to the sentimental effect of his childhood reading of *The Biography of a Grizzly,* written and illustrated by Ernest Seton Thompson in 1900, which ends with the noble, aged bear "Wahb" feebly slinking into "Death Gulch, that fearful little valley where everything was dead, where the very air was deadly"—there to await his death. In these notes, Burroughs is openly chagrined at his earliest writing attempts. Indeed, there is something—as he tells us—painful about them, or strained, as if a young man were trying on masks, looking for one that would fit.

from
the adding machine

THE NAME IS BURROUGHS

The name is Bill Burroughs. I am a writer. Let me tell you a few things about my job, what an assignment is like.

You hit Interzone with that grey anonymously ill-intentioned look all writers have.

"You crazy or something walk around alone? Me good guide. What you want Meester?"

"Well uh, I would like to write a bestseller that would be a good book, a book about real people and places . . ."

The Guide stopped me. "That's enough Mister. I don't want to read your stinking book. That's a job for the White Reader." The guide's face was a grey screen, hustler faces moved across it. "Your case is difficult frankly. If we put it through channels they will want a big piece in advance. Now I happen to know the best continuity man in the industry, only handles boys he likes. He'll want a piece of you too but he's willing to take it on spec."

People ask what would lead me to write a book like *Naked Lunch*. One is slowly led along to write a book and this looked good, no trouble with the cast at all and that's half the battle when you can find your characters. The more far-out sex pieces I was just writing for my own amusement. I would put them away in an old attic trunk and leave them for a distant boy to find . . . "Why Ma this stuff is terrific—and I thought he was just an old book-of-the-month-club corn ball."

Yes I was writing my bestseller . . . I finished it with a flourish, fading streets a distant sky, handed it to the publisher and stood there expectantly.

He averted his face . . . "I'll let you know later, come around, in fact. Always like to see a writer's digs." He coughed, as if he found my presence suffocating.

A few nights later he visited me in my attic room, leaded glass windows under the slate roof. He did not remove his long black coat or his bowler hat. He dropped my manuscript on a table.

"What are you, a wise guy? We don't have a license on this. The license alone costs more than we could clear." His eyes darted around the room. "What's that over there?" he demanded, pointing to a sea chest.

"It's a sea chest."

"I can see that. What's in it?"

"Oh, nothing much, just some old things I wrote, not to show anybody, quite bad really . . ."

"Let's see some of it."

Now, to say that I never intended publication of these pieces would not be altogether honest. They were there, just in case my bestseller fell on the average reader like a bag of sour dough—I've seen it happen, we all have: a book's got everything, topical my God, the scene is present-day Vietnam (Falkland Islands!) seen through a rich variety of characters . . . How can it miss? But it does. People just don't buy it. Some say you can put a curse on a book so the reader hates to touch it, or your book simply vanishes in a little swirl of disinterest. So I had to cover myself in case somebody had the curse in; after all, I am a professional. I like cool remote Sunday gardens set against a slate-blue mist, and for that set you need the Yankee dollar.

As a young child I wanted to be a writer because writers were rich and famous. They lounged around Singapore and Rangoon smoking opium in a yellow pongee silk suit. They sniffed cocaine in Mayfair and they penetrated forbidden swamps with a faithful native boy and lived in the native quarter of Tangier smoking hashish and languidly caressing a pet gazelle.

I can divide my literary production into sets: where, when and under what circumstances produced. The first set is a street of red brick three-story houses with slate roofs, lawns in front and large back yards. In our back yard my father and the gardener, Otto Belue, tended a garden with roses, peonies, iris and a fish pond. The address is 4664 Pershing Avenue and the house is still there.

My first literary endeavor was called "The Autobiography of a Wolf," written after reading *The Biography of a Grizzly*. In the end this poor old bear, his health failing, deserted by his mate, goes to a valley he knows is full of poison gas. I can see a picture from the book quite clearly, a sepia valley, animal skeletons, the old bear slouching in, all the old broken voices from the family album find that valley where they come at last to die. "They called me the Grey Ghost. . . . Spent most of my time shaking off the ranchers." The Grey Ghost met death at the hands of a grizzly bear after seven pages, no doubt in revenge for plagiarism.

There was something called *Carl Cranbury in Egypt* that never got off the ground. . . . Carl Cranbury frozen back there on yellow lined paper, his hand an inch from his blue steel automatic. In this set I also wrote westerns, gangster stories, and haunted houses. I was quite sure that I wanted to be a writer.

When I was twelve we moved to a five-acre place on Price Road and I attended the John Burroughs School which is just down the road. This period was mostly crime and gangster stories. I was fascinated by gangsters and like most boys at that time I wanted to be one because I would feel so much safer with my loyal guns around me. I never quite found the sensitive old lady English teacher who molded my future career. I wrote at that time Edgar Allan Poe things, like old men in forgotten places, very flowery and sentimental too, that flavor of high school prose. I can taste it still, like chicken croquettes and canned peas in the school dining room. I wrote bloody westerns too, and would leave enigmatic skeletons lying around in barns for me to muse over . . .

"Tom was quick but Joe was quicker. He turned the gun on his unfaithful wife and then upon himself, fell dead in a pool of blood and lay there drawing flies. The vultures came later . . . especially the eyes were alike, a dead blue opaqueness." I wrote a lot of hangings: "Hardened old sinner that he was, he still experienced a shudder as he looked back at the three bodies twisting on ropes, etched against the beautiful red sunset." These stories were read aloud in class. I remember one story written by another boy who later lost his mind, *dementia praecox* they called it: "The captain tried to swim but the water was too deep and he went down screaming, 'Help, help, I am drowning.'"

And one story, oh very mysterious . . . an old man in his curtained nineteen-twenties Spanish library chances on a forgotten volume and there written in letters of gold the single word "ATHENA." . . . "That question will haunt him until the house shall crumble to ruins and his books shall moulder away."

At the age of fourteen I read a book called *You Can't Win*, being the life story of a second-story man. And I met the Johnson Family. A world of hobo jungles, usually by the river, where the bums and hobos and rod-riding pete men gathered to cook meals, drink canned heat, and shoot the snow . . . black smoke on the hip behind a Chink laundry in Montana. The Sanctimonious Kid: "This is a crooked game, kid, but you have to think straight. Be as positive yourself as you like, but no positive clothes. You dress like every John Citizen or we part company, kid." He was hanged in Australia for the murder of a constable.

And Salt Chunk Mary: "Mary had all the no's and none of them ever meant yes. She received and did business in the kitchen. Mary kept an iron pot of salt chunk and a blue coffee pot always on the woodstove. You eat first and then you talk business, your gear slopped out on the kitchen table, her eyes old, unbluffed, unreadable. She named a price, heavy and cold as a cop's blackjack on a winter night. She didn't name another. She kept her money in a sugar bowl but nobody thought about that. Her cold grey eyes would have seen the thought and maybe something goes wrong on the next day, Johnny Law just happens by or Johnny Citizen comes up with a load of double-ought buckshot into your soft and tenders. It wouldn't pay to get gay with Mary. She was a saint to the Johnson Family, always good for a plate of salt chunk. One time Gimpy Gates, an old rod-riding pete man, killed a bum in a jungle for calling Salt Chunk Mary an old fat cow. The old yegg looked at him across the fire, his eyes cold as gunmetal . . . 'You were a good bum, but you're dogmeat now.'

He fired three times. The bum fell forward, his hands clutching coals, and his hair catching fire. Well, the bulls pick up Gates and show him the body: 'There's the poor devil you killed, and you'll swing for it.' The old yegg looked at them coldly. He held out his hand, gnarled from years of safe-cracking, two fingers blown off by the 'soup'. 'If I killed him, there's the finger pulled the trigger and there's the tendon pulled the finger.' The old yegg had beaten them at their own game."

This inspired me to write some crime stories . . . "'Here's to crime!' he shouted and raised a glass of champagne, but he crumpled like a pricked balloon as the heavy hand of Detective Sergeant Murphy fell on his shoulder." . . . "Joe Maguire regarded the flushed face of the dealer with disfavor. 'A coke bird,' he decided. 'Better cut him off the payroll; get coked up and shoot a good client.'"

I did a short story too, with a trick ending about this gangster who goes to a fortune-teller . . . "'This man is a criminal,' she thought shrewdly, 'a gangster, perhaps . . . he must have made enemies.' 'I see danger,' she said. The man's face twitched—he needed to snow. 'I see a man approaching . . . he has a gun . . . he lifts the gun . . . he—' With an inarticulate cry the man leapt to his feet and whipped out an automatic, spitting death at the fortune-teller . . . blood on the crystal ball, and on the table, a severed human hand."

After reading Eugene Aram's *Dream*—which I committed to memory and recited to the class in sepulchral tones—I wrote a series about murderers who all died of brain fever in a screaming delirium of remorse, and one character in the desert who murdered all his companions—sitting there looking at the dead bodies and wondering why he did it. When the vultures came and ate them he got so much relief he called them "the vultures of gold" and that was the title of my story, *The Vultures of Gold*, which closed this rather nauseous period.

At fifteen I was sent to the Los Alamos Ranch School for my health, where they later made the first atom bomb. It seemed so right somehow, like the school song . . .

> *Far away and high on the mesa's crest*
> *Here's the life that all of us love best*
> *Los Allll-amos.*

Far away and high on the mesa's crest I was forced to become a Boy Scout, eat everything on my plate, exercise before breakfast, sleep on a porch in zero weather, stay outside all afternoon, ride a sullen, spiteful, recalcitrant horse twice a week and all day on Saturday. We all had to become Boy Scouts and do three hours a week of something called C.W.—Community Work—which was always something vaguely unpleasant and quite useless too, but A.J. said it was each boy's cooperative contribution to the welfare and maintenance of the community. We had to stay outdoors, no matter what, all afternoon—they even timed you in the john. I was always cold, and hated my horse, a sulky strawberry roan. And the C.W. was always hanging over you. There were crew-leaders, you understand, many of them drunk with power—who made life hell for the crew.

This man had conjured up a whole city there. The school was entirely self-sufficient, raised all the food, etcetera. There was a store, a post office, and one of the teachers was even a magistrate. I remember once he got a case which involved shooting a deer out of season and he made the most of it, went on for days. He had founded the school after he quit the Forest Service because some inspirational woman told him "Young man, there is a great constructive job waiting for you and if you don't do it now you will only have to do it later under much more difficult circumstances." So he rubbed a magic lamp of contributions . . . "I know what's best for boys," he said, and those Texas oilmen kicked in.

What I liked to do was get in my room against the radiator and play records and read the Little Blue Books put out by Haldeman-Julius, free-thinker and benevolent agnostic . . . Remy de Gourmont . . . Baudelaire . . . Guy de Maupassant . . . Anatole France . . . and I started writing allegories put in a vaguely Oriental setting, with dapper jewel thieves over the wine, engaged in philosophical discussions I prefer not to remember.

"To observe one's actions with detachment while making them as amusing as possible seems to me . . ."

"Very interesting," said the imperturbable detective popping up from behind a potted rubber plant. "You are all under arrest."

I had a bad rep with the other boys . . . "burns incense in his room . . . reading French books . . ." Later at Harvard during summer trips to Europe I started satirical novels about the people I met; one of them begins " 'But you see I don't know much about love,' she said coyly, twisting an old-fashioned."

Then I had an English period, gentlemen adventurers and all that . . .

"My god, that poor old chief!" He broke down sobbing.

The other looked at him coldly and raised an eyebrow: "Well after all, Reggie, you didn't expect him to *give* us the emeralds, did you?"

"I don't know what I expected, but not that *piranha* fish!"

"It was much the easiest and most convenient method."

"I can't stick it, Humphreys. Give me my share. I'm clearing off."

"Why certainly." He took seven magnificent emeralds from the side pocket of his yellow silk suit and placed them on the table. With a quiet smile he pushed four stones to Reggie.

Reggie was touched. "I mean, hang it all, it was your idea, Humphreys, and you did most of the work."

"Yes Reggie, you funked it."

"Then why?"

"I am thinking of Jane."

Reggie made a hasty exit, "I can't thank you enough" over his shoulder. Humphreys leaned forward, looking at the three emeralds quizzically.

"You'll be missing your mates, won't you now? . . . Ali!"

"Yes master."

"A white man has just left. He is carrying four green stones. I want those stones, do you understand Ali?"

"Yes master I understand."

Exit Ali, fingering his kris.

And *then* I read Oscar Wilde. Dorian Gray and Lord Henry gave birth to Lord Cheshire, one of the most unsavory characters in fiction, a mawkishly sentimental Lord Henry . . . Seven English gentlemen there in the club, planning an expedition to the Pole:

"But *which* pole, Bradford?"

"Oh hang it all, who cares?"

"Why Reggie, you're as excited as a child!"

"I am, and I glory in it—let's forget we were ever gentlemen!"

"You seem to have done that already," said Lord Cheshire acidly.

But it seems the cynical Lord Cheshire had more kindness in him than all the others put together when the supplies gave out . . . "Poor Reggie there, rotten with scurvy, I can't bear to look at him, and Stanford is cracking, and there have been rumors about Cuthbert . . . Morgan drinks all day, and James is hitting the pipe . . ." So I leave him there on an ice floe, rotten with scurvy, giving his last lime juice to Reggie and lying bravely about it.

"Have you had yours?" the boy said softly.

"Yes," said Lord Cheshire, "I've had mine."

And I wrote a story for *True Confessions,* about a decent young man who gets on the dope. He was grieving the loss of a favorite dog, sitting on a park bench looking at the lake, smell of burning leaves . . .

" 'Hello kid, mind if I sit down?' The man was thin and grey with pinpoint eyes, the prison shadow in them like something dead. 'If you don't mind my saying so, you look down in the dumps about something.' "

In a burst of confidence the young man told him about the dog. ". . . he went back inside the burning house. You see, he thought I was in there."

"Kid, I got a pinch of something here make you forget about that old dead dog . . ."

That's how it started. Then he fell into the hands of a sinister hypnotist who plied him with injections of marijuana.

"Kill, kill, kill." The words turned relentlessly in his brain, and he walked up to a young cop and said "If you don't lock me up I shall kill you." The cop sapped him without a word. But a wise old detective in the precinct takes a like to the boy, sets him straight and gets him off the snow. It was a hard fight but he made it. He now works in a hardware store in Ottawa, Illinois . . . the porch noise, home from work . . . "And if any kind stranger ever offers me some pills that will drive all my blues away, I will simply call a policeman."

A story about four jolly murderers was conceived in the Hotel La Fonda on a rare trip to Santa Fe when I was feeling guilty about masturbating twice in one day. A middle-aged couple, very brash and jolly; the man says "Sure and I'd kill my own grandmother for just a little kale . . ."

"We have regular rates of course," the woman observed tartly.

I formed a romantic attachment for one of the boys at Los Alamos and kept a diary of this affair that was to put me off writing for many years. Even now I blush to remember its contents. During the Easter vacation of my second year I persuaded my family to let me stay in St. Louis, so my things were packed and sent to me from the school and I used to turn cold thinking maybe the boys are reading it aloud to each other.

When the box finally arrived I pried it open and threw everything out until I found the diary and destroyed it forthwith, without a glance at the appalling pages. This still happens from time to time. I will write something I think is good at the time and looking at it later I say, my God, tear it into very small pieces and put it into somebody else's garbage can. I wonder how many writers have had similar experiences. An anthology of such writing would be interesting.

Fact is, I had gotten a real sickener—as Paul Lund, an English gangster I knew in Tangier, would put it . . . "A young thief thinks he has a license to steal and then he gets a real sickener like five years maybe."

This lasted longer. The act of writing had become embarrassing, disgusting, and above all *false*. It was not the sex in the diary that embarrassed me, it was the terrible falsity of the emotions expressed. I guess Lord Cheshire and Reggie were too much for me—for years after that, the sight of my words written on a page hit me like the sharp smell of carrion when you turn over a dead dog with a stick, and this continued until 1938. I had written myself an eight-year sentence.

Cambridge, Massachusetts, 1938 . . . I was doing graduate work in anthropology at Harvard and at the same time Kells Elvins, an old school friend from John Burroughs, was doing graduate work in psychology. We shared a small frame house on a quiet tree-lined street beyond the Commodore Hotel. We had many talks about writing and started a detective story in the Dashiell Hammett/Raymond Chandler line. This picture of a ship captain putting on women's clothes and rushing into the first lifeboat was suddenly *there* for both of us. We read all the material we could find in Widener's Library on the *Titanic,* and a book based on the *Morro Castle* disaster called *The Left-handed Passenger*.

On a screened porch we started work on a story called *Twilight's Last Gleamings* which was later used almost verbatim in *Nova Express*. I was trying to contact Kells to see if he had the original manuscript and to tell him that I was using the story under both our names when his mother wrote me that he had died in 1961.

I see now that the curse of the diary was broken temporarily by the act of collaboration. We acted out every scene and often got on laughing jags. I hadn't laughed like that since my first tea-high at eighteen when I rolled around the

floor and pissed all over myself. I remember the rejection note from *Esquire:*
"Too screwy and not effectively so for us."

I liked to feel that manuscript in my hands and read it over with slow shameless chuckles. The words seemed to come through us, not out of us. I have a
recurrent writer's dream of picking up a book and starting to read. I can never
bring back more than a few sentences; still, I know that one day the book itself will hover over the typewriter as I copy the words already written there.

After that I lost interest again and the years from 1938 to 1943 were almost
entirely unproductive. In 1943 I met Kerouac and Ginsberg. Kerouac and I
collaborated on a novel based on the Carr-Kammerer case, which we decided
not to publish, and again I lost interest in writing.

I can remember only one attempt between 1943 and 1949. I was living in
Algiers, Louisiana, across the river from New Orleans. I was on heroin at the
time and went over to New Orleans every day to score. One day I woke up
sick and went across the river, and when I got back I tried to recapture the
painful over-sensitivity of junk sickness, the oil slick on the river, the hastily-
parked car.

personal magnetism

"Are you bashful? Shy? Nervous? Embarrassed? If so, send me two dollars and I will show you how to control others at a glance; how to make your face appear twenty years younger; how to use certain Oriental secrets and dozens of other vital topics."

I am none of these things, but I would like to know how to control others at a glance (especially my Latin teacher). So I clipped the coupon, beginning to feel more magnetic every minute.

In a week, I received an impressive red volume with magnetic rays all over the cover. I opened the book and hopefully began to read. Alas! The book was a mass of scientific drivel cunningly designed to befuddle the reader, and keep him from realizing what a fake it was.

I learned that every time one yawns, a quart of magnetism escapes, that it takes four months to recuperate from a cigarette. And as for a cocktail! Words fail me. Another common exit of magnetism is light literature of any kind, movies, and such unmagnetic foods as cucumbers and eggs. I never realized that a cucumber was so potent. They always impressed me as watery and tasteless.

And how is magnetism acquired? So far as I can make out, one must sit perfectly still for hours reading the dictionary or something equally uninteresting, then, laden with magnetism, one should arise with tensed eye (whatever that is) and with slow, steady steps, bear down on one's quarry like a steam roller.

Did I find out how to control others at a glance? I certainly did, but never had the nerve to try it. Here is how it is done: I must look my victim squarely in the eye, say in a low, severe voice, "I am talking and you must listen," then, intensify my gaze and say, "You cannot escape me." My victim completely subdued, I was to say, "I am stronger than my enemies." Get thee behind me Satan. Imagine me trying that on Mr. Baker!

I think the book was right in saying that by following its instructions I could make myself the center of interest at every party. Interest is putting it mildly!

twilight's last gleamings

(with Kells Elvins)

PLEASE IMAGINE AN EXPLOSION ON A SHIP

A paretic named Perkins sat askew on his broken wheelchair. He arranged his lips.

"You pithyathed thon of a bidth!" he shouted.

Barbara Cannon, a second-class passenger, lay naked in a first-class bridal suite with Stewart Lindy Adams. Lindy got out of bed and walked over to a window and looked out.

"Put on your clothes, honey," he said. "There's been an accident."

A first-class passenger named Mrs. Norris was thrown out of bed by the explosion. She lay there shrieking until her maid came and helped her up.

"Bring me my wig and my kimono," she told the maid. "I'm going to see the captain."

Dr. Benway, ship's doctor, drunkenly added two inches to a four-inch incision with one stroke of his scalpel.

"There was a little scar, Doctor," said the nurse, who was peering over his shoulder. "Perhaps the appendix is already out."

"The appendix *out!*" the doctor shouted. "*I'm* taking the appendix out! What do you think I'm doing here?"

"Perhaps the appendix is on the left side," said the nurse. "That happens sometimes, you know."

"Can't you be quiet?" said the doctor. "I'm coming to that!" He threw back his elbows in a movement of exasperation. "Stop breathing down my neck!" he yelled. He thrust a red fist at her. "And get me another scalpel. This one has no edge to it."

He lifted the abdominal wall and searched along the incision. "I know where an appendix is. I studied appendectomy in 1904 at Harvard."

The floor tilted from the force of the explosion. The doctor reeled back and hit the wall.

"Sew her up!" he said, peeling off his gloves. "I can't be expected to work under such conditions!"

* * *

At a table in the bar sat Christopher Hitch, a rich liberal; Colonel Merrick, retired; Billy Hines of Newport; and Joe Bane, writer.

"In all my experience as a traveler," the Colonel was saying, "I have never encountered such service."

Billy Hines twisted his glass, watching ice cubes. "Frightful service," he said, his face contorted by a suppressed yawn.

"Do you think the captain controls this ship?" said the Colonel, fixing Christopher Hitch with a bloodshot blue eye. "Unions!" shouted the Colonel. "Unions control this ship!"

Hitch gave out with a laugh that was supposed to be placating but ended up oily. "Things aren't so bad, really," he said, patting at the Colonel's arm. He didn't land the pat, because the Colonel drew his arm out of reach. "Things will adjust themselves."

Joe Bane looked up from his drink of straight rye. "It's like I say, Colonel," he said. "A man—"

The table left the floor and the glasses crashed. Billy Hines remained seated, looking blankly at the spot where his glass had been. Christopher Hitch rose uncertainly. Joe Bane jumped up and ran away.

"By God!" said the Colonel. "I'm not surprised!"

Also at a table in the bar sat Philip Bradshinkel, investment banker; his wife, Joan Bradshinkel; Branch Morton, a St. Louis politician; and Morton's wife, Mary Morton. The explosion knocked their table over.

Joan raised her eyebrows in an expression of sour annoyance. She looked at her husband and sighed.

"I'm sorry this happened, dear," said her husband. "Whatever it is, I mean."

Mary Morton said, "Well, I declare!"

Branch Morton stood up, pushing back his chair with a large red hand. "Wait here," he said. "I'll find out."

Mrs. Norris pushed through a crowd on C Deck. She rang the elevator bell and waited. She rang again and waited. After five minutes she walked up to A Deck.

The Negro orchestra, high on marijuana, remained seated after the explosion. Branch Morton walked over to the orchestra leader.

"Play 'The Star-Spangled Banner,'" he ordered.

The orchestra leader looked at him.

"What you say?" he asked.

"You black baboon, play 'The Star-Spangled Banner' on your horn!"

"Contract don't say nothing 'bout no Star-Spangled Banner," said a thin Negro in spectacles.

"This old boat am swinging on down!" someone in the orchestra yelled, and the musicians jumped down off the platform and scattered among the passengers.

Branch Morton walked over to a jukebox in a corner of the saloon. He saw "The Star-Spangled Banner" by Fats Waller. He put in a handful of quarters. The machine clicked and buzzed and began to play:
"OH SAY CAN YOU? YES YES"

Joe Bane fell against the door of his stateroom and plunged in. He threw himself on the bed and drew his knees up to his chin. He began to sob.

His wife sat on the bed and talked to him in a gentle hypnotic voice. "You can't stay here, Joey. This bed is going underwater. You can't stay here."

Gradually the sobbing stopped and Bane sat up. She helped him put on a life belt. "Come along," she said.

"Yes, honey face," he said, and followed her out the door.
"AND THE HOME OF THE BRAVE"

Mrs. Norris found the door to the captain's cabin ajar. She pushed it open and stepped in, knocking on the open door. A tall, thin, red-haired man with horn-rimmed glasses was sitting at a desk littered with maps. He glanced up without speaking.

"Oh Captain, is the ship sinking? Someone set off a bomb, they said. I'm Mrs. Norris—you know, Mr. Norris, shipping business. Oh the ship *is* sinking! I know, or you'd say something. Captain, you will take care of us? My maid and me?" She put out a hand to touch the captain's arm. The ship listed suddenly, throwing her heavily against the desk. Her wig slipped.

The captain stood up. He snatched the wig off her head and put it on.

"Give me that kimono!" he ordered.

Mrs. Norris screamed. She started for the door. The captain took three long, springy strides and blocked her way. Mrs. Norris rushed for a window, screaming. The captain took a revolver from his side pocket. He aimed at her bald pate outlined in the window, and fired.

"You Goddamned old fool," he said. "Give me that kimono!"

Philip Bradshinkel walked up to a sailor with his affable smile.

"Room for the ladies on this one?" he asked, indicating a lifeboat.

The sailor looked at him sourly.

"No!" said the sailor. He turned away and went on working on the launching davit.

"Now wait a minute," said Bradshinkel. "You can't mean that. Women and children first, you know."

"Nobody goes on this lifeboat but the crew," said the sailor.

"Oh, I understand," said Bradshinkel, pulling out a wad of bills.

The sailor snatched the money.

"I thought so," said Bradshinkel. He took his wife by the arm and started to help her into the lifeboat.

"Get that old meat outa here!" screamed the sailor.

"But you made a bargain! You took my money!"

"Oh, for Chrissakes," said the sailor. "I just took your dough so it wouldn't get wet!"

"But my wife is a woman!"

Suddenly the sailor became very gentle.

"All my life," he said, "all my life I been a sucker for a classy dame. I seen 'em in the Sunday papers laying on the beach. Soft messy tits. They just lay there and smile dirty. Jesus they heat my pants!"

Bradshinkel nudged his wife. "Smile at him." He winked at the sailor. "What do you say?"

"Naw," said the sailor, "I ain't got time to lay her now."

"Later," said Bradshinkel.

"Later's no good. Besides she's special built for you. She can't give me no kids and she drinks alla time. Like I say, I just seen her in the Sunday papers and wanted her like a dog wants rotten meat."

"Let me talk to this man," said Branch Morton. He worked his fingers over the fleshy shoulder of his wife and pulled her under his armpit.

"This little woman is a mother," he said. The sailor blew his nose on the deck. Morton grabbed the sailor by the biceps.

"In Clayton, Missouri, seven kids whisper her name through their thumbs before they go to sleep."

The sailor pulled his arm free. Morton dropped both hands to his sides, palms facing forward.

"As man to man," he was pleading. "As man to man."

Two Negro musicians, their eyes gleaming, came up behind the two wives. One took Mrs. Morton by the arm, the other took Mrs. Bradshinkel.

"Can we have dis dance witchu?"

"THAT OUR FLAG WAS STILL THERE"

Captain Kramer, wearing Mrs. Norris's kimono and wig, his face heavily smeared with cold cream, and carrying a small suitcase, walked down to C Deck, the kimono billowing out behind him. He opened the side door to the purser's office with a pass key. A thin-shouldered man in a purser's uniform was stuffing currency and jewels into a suitcase in front of an open safe.

The captain's revolver swung free of his brassiere and he fired twice.

"SO GALLANTLY STREAMING"

Finch, the radio operator, washed down bicarbonate of soda and belched into his hand. He put the glass down and went on tapping out S.O.S.

"S.O.S. . . . S.S. *America* . . . S.O.S. . . . off Jersey coast . . . S.O.S. . . . son-of-a-bitching set . . . S.O.S. . . . might smell us . . . S.O.S. . . . son-of-a-bitching crew . . . S.O.S. . . . *Comrade* Finch . . . comrade in a pig's ass . . . S.O.S. . . . Goddamned captain's a brown artist . . . S.O.S. . . . S.S. *America* . . . S.O.S. . . . S.S. Crapbox . . ."

Lifting his kimono with his left hand, the captain stepped in behind the radio operator. He fired one shot into the back of Finch's head. He shoved the small body aside and smashed the radio with a chair.

"O'ER THE RAMPARTS WE WATCH"

Dr. Benway, carrying his satchel, pushed through the passengers crowded around Lifeboat No. 1.

"Are you all right?" he shouted, seating himself among the women. "I'm the doctor."

"BY THE ROCKETS' RED GLARE"

When the captain reached Lifeboat No. 1 there were two seats left. Some of the passengers were blocking each other as they tried to force their way in, others were pushing forward a wife, a mother, or a child. The captain shoved them all out of his way, leapt into the boat and sat down. A boy pushed through the crowd in the captain's wake.

"Please," he said. "I'm only thirteen."

"Yes yes," said the captain, "you can sit by me."

The boat started jerkily toward the water, lowered by four male passengers. A woman handed her baby to the captain.

"Take care of my baby, for God's sake!"

Joe Bane landed in the boat and slithered noisily under a thwart. Dr. Benway cast off the ropes. The doctor and the boy started to row. The captain looked back at the ship.

"OH SAY CAN YOU SEE"

A third-year divinity student named Titman heard Perkins in his stateroom, yelling for his attendant. He opened the door and looked in.

"What do you want, thicken thit?" said Perkins.

"I want to help you," said Titman.

"Thtick it up and thwitht it!" said Perkins.

"Easy does it," said Titman, walking over toward the broken wheelchair. "Everything is going to be okey-dokey."

"Thneaked off!" Perkins put a hand on one hip and jerked the elbow forward in a grotesque indication of dancing. "Danthing with floothies!"

"We'll find him," said Titman, lifting Perkins out of the wheelchair. He carried the withered body in his arms like a child. As Titman walked out of the stateroom, Perkins snatched up a butcher knife used by his attendant to make sandwiches.

"Danthing with floothies!"

"BY THE DAWN'S EARLY LIGHT!"

A crowd of passengers was fighting around Lifeboat No. 7. It was the last boat that could be launched. They were using bottles, broken deck chairs and fire axes. Titman, carrying Perkins in his arms, made his way through the fighting unnoticed. He placed Perkins in a seat at the stern.

"There you are," said Titman. "All set."

Perkins said nothing. He sat there, chin drawn back, eyes shining, the butcher knife clutched rigidly in one hand.

A hysterical crowd from second class began pushing from behind. A big-faced shoe clerk with long yellow teeth grabbed Mrs. Bane and shoved her forward. "Ladies first!" he yelled.

A wedge of men formed behind him and pushed. A shot sounded and Mrs. Bane fell forward, hitting the lifeboat. The wedge broke, rolling and scrambling. A man in an ROTC uniform with a .45 automatic in his hand stood by the lifeboat. He covered the sailor at the launching davit.

"Let this thing down!" he ordered.

As the lifeboat slid down toward the water, a cry went up from the passengers on deck. Some of them jumped into the water, others were pushed by the people behind.

"Let 'er go, God damn it, let 'er go!" yelled Perkins.

"Throw him out!"

A hand rose out of the water and closed on the side of the boat. Springlike, Perkins brought the knife down. The fingers fell into the boat and the bloody stump of hand slipped back into the water.

The man with the gun was standing in the stern. "Get going!" he ordered. The sailors pulled hard on the oars.

Perkins worked feverishly, chopping on all sides. "Bathtardth, thonthabitheth!" The swimmers screamed and fell away from the boat.

"That a boy."

"Don't let 'em swamp us."

"Atta boy, Comrade."

"Bathtardth, thonthabitheth! Bathtardth, thonthabitheth!"

"OH SAY DO DAT STAR-SPANGLED BANNER YET WAVE"

The Evening News

Barbara Cannon showed your reporter her souvenirs of the disaster: a life belt autographed by the crew, and a severed human finger.

"I don't know," said Miss Cannon. "I feel sorta bad about this old finger."

"O'ER THE LAND OF THE FREE"

and the hippos were boiled in their tanks

unpublished manuscript written in 1945 by "William Lee and John Kerouac;" Will Dennison chapters written by William Burroughs, Mike Ryko chapters by Jack Kerouac

CHAPTER ONE

WILL DENNISON:

The bars close at three A.M. on Saturday nights so I got home about 3:45 after eating breakfast at Riker's on the corner of Christopher Street and Seventh Avenue. I dropped the *News* and *Mirror* on the couch and peeled off my seersucker coat and dropped it on top of them. I was going straight to bed. At this point, the buzzer rang. It's a loud buzzer that goes through you so I ran over quick to push the button and release the outside door. Then I took my coat off the couch and hung it over a chair so no one would sit on it, and I put the papers in a drawer. I wanted to be sure they would be there when I woke up in the morning. Then I went over and opened the door. I timed it just right so that they didn't get a chance to knock.

Four people came into the room. Now I'll tell you in a general way who these people were and what they looked like, since the story is mostly about two of them. Phillip Tourian is seventeen years old, half-Turkish and half-American. He has a choice of several names but prefers Tourian. His father goes under the name of Rogers. Curly black hair falls over his forehead, his skin is very pale, and he has green eyes. He was sitting down in the most comfortable chair with his leg over the arm before the others were all in the room. This Phillip is the kind of boy literary fags write sonnets to, which start out, "Oh raven-haired Grecian lad . . ." He was wearing a pair of very dirty slacks and a khaki shirt with the sleeves rolled up showing hard muscular forearms.

Ramsay Allen is an impressive-looking grey-haired man of forty or so, tall and a little flabby. He looks like a down-at-heels actor, or someone who used to be somebody. Also he is a Southerner and claims to be of a good family, like all Southerners. He is a very intelligent guy but you wouldn't know it to see him now. He is so stuck on Phillip he is hovering over him like a shy vulture, with a foolish sloppy grin on his face. Al is one of the best guys I know and you couldn't find better company. And Phillip is all right too. But when they get together, something happens, and they form a combination which gets on everybody's nerves.

Agnes O'Rourke has an ugly Irish face, close-cropped black hair, and she always wears pants. She is straightforward, manly, and reliable. Mike Ryko is a nineteen-year-old red-haired Finn, a sort of merchant seaman, dressed in dirty khaki.

Well, that's all there were, the four of them, and Agnes held up a bottle. "Ah, Canadian Club," I said. "Come right in and sit down," which they all had anyway by this time, and I got out some cocktail glasses and everyone poured himself a straight shot. Agnes asked me for some water which I got for her.

Phillip had some philosophical idea he had evidently been developing in the course of the evening and now I was going to hear about it.

He said, "I've figured out a whole philosophy on the idea of waste as evil and creation as good. So long as you are creating something it is good. The only sin is waste of your potentialities."

That sounded pretty silly to me so I said, "Well of course I'm just a befuddled bartender, but what about Lifebuoy Soap ads, they're creations all right."

And he said, "Yeah, but you see that's what you call wasteful creation. It's all dichotomized. Then there's creative waste, such as talking to you now."

So I said, "Yeah, well but where are your criteria to tell waste from creation? Anybody can say that what he's doing is creation whereas what everybody else is doing is waste. The thing is so general it don't mean a thing."

Well, that seemed to hit him right between the eyes. I guess he hadn't been getting much opposition. At any rate he dropped the philosophy and I was glad to see it go because such ideas belong in the "I don't want to hear about it" department as far as I'm concerned.

Phillip then asked me if I had any marijuana and I told him not much, but he insisted he wanted to smoke some, so I got it out of the desk drawer and we lit a cigarette and passed it around. It was very poor stuff and the one stick had no effect on anyone.

Ryko, who had been sitting on the couch all this time without saying anything, said, "I smoked six sticks in Port Arthur Texas and I don't remember a thing about Port Arthur Texas."

I said, "Marijuana is very hard to get now, and I don't know where I'll get any more after this is gone," but Phillip grabbed up another cigarette and started smoking it. So I filled my glass with Canadian Club.

Right then it struck me as strange, since these guys never have any money, where this Canadian Club came from, so I asked them.

Al said, "Agnes lifted it out of a bar." It seems Al and Agnes were standing at the end of the bar in the Pied Piper having a beer, when Agnes suddenly said to Al, "Pick up your change and follow me, I've got a bottle of Canadian Club under my coat." Al followed her out more scared than she was. He hadn't even seen her take it. This took place earlier in the evening and the fifth was now about half gone.

I congratulated Agnes and she smiled complacently. "It was easy," she said. "I'm going to do it again."

Not when you're with me, I said to myself.

Then there was a lull in the conversation and I was too sleepy to say anything. There was some talk I didn't hear and then I looked up just in time to see Phillip bite a large piece of glass out of his cocktail glass and begin chewing it up, which made a noise you could hear across the room. Agnes and Ryko made faces like someone was scratching fingernails on a blackboard.

Phillip chewed up the glass fine and washed it down with Agnes' water. So then Al ate a piece too and I got him a glass of water to wash it down with.

Agnes asked if I thought they would die, and I said no, there was no danger if you chewed it up fine, it was like eating a little sand. All this talk about people dying from ground glass was hooey. Right then I got an idea for a gag, and I said, "I am neglecting my duties as a host. Is anyone hungry? I have something very special I just got today."

At this point Phillip and Al were picking stray pieces of glass out from between their teeth. Al had gone into the bathroom to look at his gums in the mirror, and they were bleeding. "Yes," said Al from the bathroom. Phillip said he'd worked up an appetite on the glass. Al asked me if it was another package of food from my old lady and I said, "As a matter of fact, yes, something real good."

So I went into the closet and fooled around for a while and came out with a lot of old razor blades on a plate with a jar of mustard.

Phillip said, "You bastard I'm really hungry," and I felt pretty good about it and said, "Some gag, hey?"

Ryko said, "I saw a guy eat razor blades in Chicago. Razor blades, glass, and light globes. He finally ate a porcelain plate."

By this time everyone was drunk except Agnes and me. Al was sitting at Phillip's feet looking up at him with a goofy expression on his face. I began to wish that everybody would go home.

Then Phillip got up swaying a little bit and said, "Let's go up on the roof." And Al said, "All right," jumping up like he never heard such a wonderful suggestion. I said, "No don't. You'll wake up the landlady. There's nothing up there anyway."

Al said, "To hell with you Dennison," sore that I should try to block an idea coming from Phillip. So they lurched out the door and started up the stairs. The landlady and her family occupy the floor above me, and above them is the roof.

I sat down and poured myself some more Canadian Club. Agnes didn't want any more and said she was going home. Ryko was now dozing on the couch, so I poured the rest in my own glass, and Agnes got up to go.

I could hear some sort of commotion on the roof and then I heard some glass break in the street. We walked over to the window and Agnes said, "They must have thrown a glass down on the street." This seemed logical to me so

I stuck my head out cautiously and there was a woman looking up and swearing. It was getting grey in the street.

"You crazy bastards," she was saying, "what you wanta do, kill somebody?"

Now I am a firm believer in the counter-attack, so I said, "Shut up. You're waking everybody up. Beat it or I'll call a cop," and I shut off the lights as though I had gotten up out of bed and gone back again. After a few minutes she walked away still swearing, and I was swearing myself, only silently, as I remembered all the trouble those two had caused me in the past. I remembered how they had piled up my car in Newark and got me thrown out of a hotel in Washington, D.C. when Phillip pissed out the window. And there was plenty more of the same. I mean Joe College stuff about 1910 style. This happened whenever they were together. Alone they were all right.

I turned on the lights and Agnes left. Everything was quiet on the roof. "I hope they don't get the idea to jump off," I said to myself because Ryko was asleep. "Well they can roost up there all night if they want to. I'm going to bed," and I undressed and got into bed leaving Ryko sleeping on the couch.

A HARD-BOILED
REPORTER

a hard-boiled reporter
by james grauerholz

By the fall of 1945, William Burroughs and Joan Vollmer were involved with a frenetic Benzedrine-fueled scene around Times Square and the Village, in the course of which Vollmer began to exhibit disturbing symptoms of dissociation and hallucination. Her husband, Paul Adams, came home on leave from the service and, disgusted by her condition, divorced her. Kerouac was hospitalized with phlebitis in his legs, aggravated by the "speed" and his long hours at the typewriter. But the drug that would change Burroughs' life first appeared in the hands of Jack Anderson, in January 1946: Anderson asked him to fence a hot Thompson submachine gun and sixteen boxes of morphine tartrate syrettes, stolen from the Brooklyn Navy Yard. From his very first experience with junk, Burroughs knew he had found his *Rheingold*.

An acquaintance of Burroughs', Bob Brandenburg, took him to meet a potential buyer for the drugs: a petty thief named Phil White. With White, Burroughs met Herbert Huncke, a Times Square hustler and thief from Chicago, with a rap sheet as long as the needle tracks on his arm. Huncke's ancestry and childhood were reminiscent of Jack Black territory: a Midwestern underworld of broken lives and hustlers on the edge. Huncke had a quasiliterary charm to his conversation, and he appeared to Burroughs and his friends as the supreme examplar of underground cool and "beatness."

Burroughs was now living with Joan Vollmer and scoring for morphine on the Upper West Side. His new tutors—Huncke and White—introduced him to the fine art of "hitting a croaker": persuading a physician to prescribe narcotics, usually by faking symptoms. Burroughs was also in training to become a "lush roller"; he apprenticed himself to Phil White, robbing sleeping drunks on the subway. But things eventually went wrong: one of their victims woke up and became violent, and Burroughs had to kick the man, breaking his ribs. This episode awakened Burroughs to the real danger and horror of this way of life, which he then abandoned. In April 1946, Burroughs was arrested for obtaining narcotics with a forged prescription. Joan Vollmer asked his erstwhile psychiatrist, Dr. Wolberg, to sign a surety bond for his release. While awaiting trial, Burroughs took up dealing heroin in the Village with a friend

of Huncke's named Bill Garver, a junky and overcoat thief with a Philadel-
phia Main Line background, about Burroughs' age.

Burroughs' sentencing came up in June, and a condition of his suspended
sentence was that he return to St. Louis—again. This time, he was reunited
with Kells Elvins, who was home from Texas. They hatched a plan to raise
ruby-red grapefruit and vegetables near the Rio Grande River town of Pharr,
Texas. Burroughs' separation from the "bad influence" of his New York friends
was favored by his parents, who had endured several years of their son's catas-
trophes. Elvins made a good impression on them, though, and with their help,
Burroughs bought land in Texas and lived with Elvins in a house near Pharr.
Around this time, they made a car trip to Mexico, where Burroughs finally
got a Mexican divorce from Ilse Klapper, and they found a *practicante* to inject them with the "Bogomolets serum": a supposedly rejuvenating and life-
prolonging substance developed by a Russian doctor.

Within a few months, Vollmer suffered a breakdown and was picked up
by the police as she sat on the sidewalk, incoherent, her little daughter, Julie,
next to her. She was hospitalized in Bellevue, and Burroughs responded at
once, going to New York to gain her release. Now he asked her to marry
him, and although the marriage was never formalized, Burroughs always
believed that their only child was conceived in a New York hotel room that
October. Burroughs brought Vollmer and her daughter back with him to
Pharr, and after a Christmas visit to his parents in St. Louis, the young couple
began to look for a remote area in eastern Texas where Burroughs could grow
a cash crop of marijuana. They finally settled in New Waverly, near Houston and not far from Huntsville, where Elvins had worked in the state prison.
Vollmer promptly sent word to New York for Huncke to come down and
be their "farmhand."

While Vollmer carried her child and Burroughs shot dope in his orgone
accumulator and read Wilhelm Reich and Mayan anthropology, Huncke visited Houston for drugs and cultivated their pot patch. He brought back cases
of Benzedrine inhalers for Vollmer, and despite her pregnancy, she used them
eagerly. In New York she had hallucinated violent scenes in an adjacent apartment; Huncke later wrote a vignette of Vollmer at the farm, late at night under
a full moon, distractedly scraping the little skinks and lizards off the trees by
the house. On July 21, 1947, William Seward Burroughs Jr. (III) was born in
a hospital in nearby Conroe, Texas. The new grandparents paid a visit: Mote
and Laura came down from St. Louis to see little Billy and the family, but
their visit was brief. This was for the best, for if they had stayed, they might
have realized that the "neighbor" was a New York street hustler, their daughter-
in-law was strung out on speed, and their son was a heroin-addicted marijuana
farmer.

In late August, Neal Cassady and Allen Ginsberg arrived for a visit. Cassady
was the new paragon on the scene, and his intensity had already captivated
Ginsberg and Kerouac. Cassady was bisexual, and Ginsberg was in love with
him. Burroughs was less impressed, and in any case, the Ginsberg-Cassady

romance quickly fizzled, and Ginsberg shipped out on a merchant liner in early September. Cassady drove Burroughs to New York in a rickety old Jeep, carrying the pot harvest, which proved unsalable. Back in New York, Burroughs acquired a new habit, and in January 1948 he went to Lexington, Kentucky, for a cure at the federal hospital there. Living in New Waverly again for only a few months, Burroughs was arrested in Beeville, Texas, while having sex with his wife in their car on the side of the road. This incident, and his marijuana crop failure, contributed to his sudden decision to sell his land and move the family to New Orleans. Huncke returned to New York and resumed stealing.

The Burroughs family lived in Louisiana for a little more than a year, most of that time in a "shotgun shack" at 509 Wagner Street in Algiers, just across the Mississippi River from the French Quarter. Burroughs was soon readdicted, and he fell into a circle of junkies around Lee Circle and Dupont Street. Having learned from Bill Garver how to deal heroin in New York, he now began to deal in New Orleans, with a new partner, Joe Ricks. In January 1949, Burroughs was visited by Kerouac and Cassady (who again failed to impress him) on a cross-country run that Kerouac describes in *On the Road*. Then in April, Herbert Huncke's larceny, out of Ginsberg's apartment in New York, came to a head with a car chase and arrest that landed Huncke back in jail and Ginsberg in Columbia Presbyterian Psychiatric Institute, where he met Carl Solomon—to whom he would dedicate his 1955 breakthrough poem, *Howl*.

Burroughs was also arrested, the same month, after a car chase through New Orleans, and charged with possession of illegal guns and drugs. He was jailed—a disaster, because he was heavily addicted and went into withdrawal in his cell. With Joan's and his lawyer's help, Burroughs was moved from jail to a hospital, where he spent a few weeks and came out clean. But as his case progressed through the courts, Burroughs began to realize that eventual prison time was a very possible outcome. He remembered Mexico, from his trip three years earlier with Elvins, and his lawyer winked encouragingly at Burroughs' "vacation" plans.

Burroughs went to Mexico City in September 1949. He found an apartment on Cerrada de Medellín in the Colonia Roma neighborhood, registered for classes at the English-language Mexico City College (using his G.I. Bill educational benefits), and returned to Algiers to relocate his family. A lot of the other American students in Mexico were recent G.I.s in their late teens and early twenties, many of them more intrigued by the climate, the booze, and the women than by any particular studies; their "headquarters" was the Bounty Bar, co-owned by two Americans and a Mexican. Burroughs found a lawyer, Bernabé Jurado, to help him apply for Mexican citizenship, and in Jurado's office, toward the end of 1949, he first encountered David Tesorero—"Old Dave" (or "Old Ike," as he is called in *Junky*).

Dave was a junky of many years' standing, and he tutored Burroughs in the ways of the Mexican dope underworld. One woman had gained monopoly over the heroin trade in Mexico City, by graft and blackmail, and she maintained her franchise with an iron hand. "Lola la Chata," they called her. There was little opportunity for Burroughs and Tesorero to go into business dealing, and they were dissatisfied with the quality and cost of Lola's product. But miraculously, Old Dave was able to register as an addict and obtain a legitimate government medical prescription for fifteen grams of morphine sulfate per month, at wholesale prices: cheap, legal, and pure.

This precipitated Burroughs' worst drug habit to date, and led to strains in his relationship with Vollmer. In September 1950—after a visit to Mexico City the previous month by Lucien Carr and his girlfriend—she went to see her friend John Herrmann in Cuernavaca, and there filed for divorce from her common-law husband. The next month, Kells Elvins and his new wife arrived in Mexico City. Burroughs and Vollmer were soon reconciled, and they began to spend time with the Elvinses.

Burroughs and Ginsberg stayed in contact through letters. Ginsberg was in his literary-agent phase, seeking publishers in New York for his friends. He urged Burroughs to write a first-person account of his life as a drug addict, for the potboiler market. By late 1950, Burroughs was working on a manuscript. He wrote in longhand on lined paper tablets, and his work was typed up by Alice Jeffreys, the wife of an American friend from the Bounty scene. Elvins was now seeing Burroughs fairly often, and, as before, encouraging him to go on with his writing. But Burroughs was disappointed with Jeffreys' work on the manuscripts he called *Junk*, which he felt she had overcorrected, so he bought a typewriter and learned to type, with four fingers: the index and middle finger of each hand.

Burroughs' citizenship papers were still not straightened out, and he was subjected to various police shakedowns, in the course of which his formerly rosy view of Mexico as a "haven of non-interference" soured considerably. In midwinter he resolved to quit junk, and after an agonizing, slow-withdrawal "cure," he managed to do so. But with the departure of junk came the return of libido, and after six years with Vollmer—who was visibly disintegrating under the accumulated damage of the Benzedrine and now the all-day tequila, and suffering a recurrence of her childhood poliomyelitis—Burroughs was hungering to connect with a young American boy. There were plenty of those, at Mexico City College and at the Bounty Bar. In the spring of 1951, Burroughs began to pursue several of them.

Off junk, and after a bad period of drinking heavily, Burroughs settled into a routine of writing at home with Vollmer, while the neighbor women looked after Billy and Julie, and going out to the Bounty to drink and troll for young Americans. In June, around the time he moved his family to a now-demolished building at 210 Orizaba, he turned his attentions to a nineteen-year-old named Lewis Marker, from Jacksonville, Florida. Marker had served in the Air Force, and was a student at Mexico City College. He was by no means homosexual, nor was he immediately drawn to Burroughs—who now laid siege on Marker, following his movements, setting up meetings with him, and focusing his powers of imagination and performance upon the boy.

He was competing with an American woman, Betty Jones ("Mary" in *Queer*), for Marker's attention.

Vollmer's condition, meanwhile, was worsening. She felt abandoned, and her tequila intake climbed. For a long time she had tolerated Burroughs' pursuit of boys, and he had never made any secret of his essential homosexuality. But she was visibly declining, her hair falling out, her slight limp becoming more pronounced, her wistful features swelling with alcohol; she could scarcely care for the children. Out of her own despair, or her mounting disappointment with Burroughs, she had begun to mock him in front of their friends, deliberately humiliating and verbally emasculating him when he would launch into one of his grandiose tales.

Before long Burroughs and his "routines" had captivated Marker, who must have had some affection for this man of thirty-seven, because in June 1951 he agreed to accompany him on a trip to Ecuador, in search of *yagé*, a hallucinogenic vine that was said to convey telepathic powers. Their sexual relationship was unequal, with Burroughs very much the pursuer, and the strains of traveling together in the Third World—combined with the failure of Burroughs' quest for the spirit-vine—resulted in the breakdown of their connection, even before the end of the trip.

Exhausted by hard travel and disappointed by their failure to find any *yagé*, Burroughs and Marker split up and returned separately to Mexico City in early September, after six weeks in each other's constant company. Forsaken by Marker and traveling home alone, Burroughs must have dreamed of a further escape from the wreckage of his and Vollmer's lives in Mexico—to South America, where they and their children would dwell in deep jungle, living by basic human skills. Eleven years earlier, Burroughs had been desperate enough to cut off part of a finger over his unrequited love; now his desolation was even greater.

Joan Vollmer was in her own extremity: while Burroughs was in Ecuador in mid-August, Lucien Carr and Allen Ginsberg visited her in Mexico City. They were surprised to find Burroughs gone, and no one knew when he might return. But the three old Columbia friends spent a week on a wild, drunk-driving carouse, which enamored Carr with Vollmer and terrified Ginsberg and the two children. They survived their trip to the volcano of Paricutín, and just before Burroughs returned, Ginsberg and Carr left Mexico.

On September 6, 1951, Burroughs had made arrangements to meet someone about selling a gun at the apartment of John Healy, an American who was a part owner of the Bounty. Vollmer was with Burroughs, and Healy was at work downstairs, in the bar. Burroughs may have been surprised to find Marker staying in Healy's apartment—or he may have staged the visit precisely because he knew he might find Marker there. But Marker was not alone: his childhood friend and fellow ex-serviceman, Eddie Woods, had just arrived from Florida, and they were drinking heavily in the early evening. It was probably the first time Burroughs and Marker had seen each other since they'd parted, in Ecuador, a few days before.

The gun was on the table, and Burroughs was boasting for the benefit of the two boys, perhaps to show Marker that he didn't care—or, perhaps, to show how much he did. He told them about his plan to move his family to South America to live off the land, killing and eating the plentiful wild boars. Joan said that if Bill was their hunter, they'd starve to death. Burroughs took the bait, and dared her to "show the boys what kind of a shot old Bill is"—to put her gin glass on her head, for him to shoot it off, à la William Tell. She put the glass on her head, turned a little sideways, giggled and smiled, and said: "I can't look; you know I can't stand the sight of blood. . . ."

Time stood still for the two drunken boys as they watched the skinny older man raise his pistol, too proud or too ashamed to back down, and aim at the glass on his wife's head. He fired before they could raise any protest—but he missed, and Vollmer's head jerked back, then slowly tilted forward onto her chest, bright red cranial blood oozing from the wound. In the ensuing silence, Marker said, "I think your bullet has hit her, Bill," and Burroughs moved to his wife's chair and took her in his arms, calling her name disconsolately. Her drinking glass lay unbroken on the floor.

Joan Vollmer breathed her last at the nearby Red Cross station in Colonia Roma, while Burroughs waited outside. He was taken into custody and jailed, then transferred the next day to another jail. Allen Ginsberg, passing through Galveston, Texas, read of the shooting in a local newspaper. In Mexico City the event was front-page news for three days, but it was soon superseded by other killings and scandals. And now Burroughs' many legal fees and attendances upon Bernabé Jurado came to his rescue: Jurado took the case, made a great fuss, greased some palms, and got his client out of Lecumberri Prison in record time, just thirteen days. The Mexican press at first sensationalized the "gringo killer," but when his story kept changing, the articles took on a scoffing, scandalized tone, and by the time of his release on bail, his case was little noted.

Burroughs' brother, Mort, arrived from St. Louis, sent by their parents; Vollmer's parents also showed up, and they departed with Julie, to raise her in New York State. They left Mort to arrange for their daughter's burial, in the Panteón Americano. After a tearful reconciliation with his brother William, Mort took his little nephew to live with Mote and Laura, who had retired to Palm Beach, Florida. Marker, Healy, and Woods were all in hiding from the Mexican cops, and they did not re-emerge until Jurado had coached them on what had happened. After some preliminary hearings, for which Jurado suborned the testimony of two ballistics witnesses, Burroughs' case slipped into judicial limbo . . . but it could not remain there forever.

Marker was at first solicitous of Burroughs, who fell ill after his release from prison, but he soon tired of their domestic situation, and left Mexico in January 1952 to return to his stateside haunts. Burroughs wrote long letters to Marker, but in his letters to Ginsberg, he complained of the boy's silence. The Ecuador trip and his wife's death had come when most of Burroughs' writing on the first drafts of *Junk* was already finished; while he awaited judgment and sentencing, he turned his efforts to chronicling the affair with Marker (whom he called "Eugene Allerton"), as if somehow a book could explain the devastating thing that had happened. This new writing he thought of as *Queer*—which, in 1952, was a book title that no American publisher would touch.

Around Christmas 1951, Burroughs learned of Phil White's death in the Tombs, New York City's municipal prison. Ginsberg conveyed Huncke's account: White had informed on a friend and then, disgraced, hanged himself in his cell. Ginsberg also reported that he had failed to interest New Directions Press in publishing Burroughs' junk memoirs. But Carl Solomon, long since discharged from Columbia Psychiatric and still in touch with Ginsberg, had been hired as an editor by his uncle, A. A. Wyn, a New York publisher whose imprint, Ace Books, was among the first to market pocket-sized, cheaply bound editions, or "paperbacks." Solomon persuaded his uncle to give a contract to Ginsberg for Burroughs' memoirs as a drug addict, to be bound together in a double book with an antinarcotics tract by a former drug agent, for "balance." In April 1952, Wyn accepted *Junk* for publication. The title was changed to *Junkie,* and Ginsberg passed along Solomon's request for an autobiographical Preface for the book.

"Prologue," the document Burroughs reluctantly produced, is an extraordinary confession. Using his mother's maiden name for a pseudonym—"William Lee"—and changing certain names and places in his account to further obscure his identity, he tells his own story and gives us the keys to his intellectual development. He describes his early fascination with criminals, and his misadventures in that vein as a boy; he hints at his crush on Kells Elvins, and at the sexual torments of his Los Alamos days; and he gives a clear idea of his jaundiced attitude toward the twelve years of psychoanalysis he had undergone.

Meanwhile, the final drafts of *Junkie* were now in the hands of Ginsberg and Solomon, and over Ginsberg's objections, Wyn's editors insisted on adding numerous "medical disclaimers" in the text, repudiating various comments by Burroughs as being contrary to "accepted medical authority." These disclaimers were all removed when, in 1976, from a photocopy of the original typescript, Burroughs revised and de-expurgated the book, restoring a chapter about the Rio Grande Valley days and various passages late in the book and reverting to his own spelling of the title: *Junky.*

Burroughs consciously allowed the influence of detective fiction, already evident in the "Hippos" manuscript, to guide his writing style in *Junky.* He tried to tell the facts of what had happened to him, what he had done, and most of all, what he had seen and heard. With unusual frankness, he told a plain, unvarnished tale of his addiction, and described his homosexual encounters, too. Many of the characters are familiar: "Herman" is Herbert Huncke (who never felt particularly flattered by this passage); "Roy" is Phil White, aka "The Sailor"; "Bill Gains" is William Garver; "Old Ike" is David Tesorero;

"Lupita" is Lola la Chata; and "my old lady" is Joan Vollmer Burroughs. She
appears only a handful of times, but always in a supportive light: helping
Burroughs out of jail in New Orleans; trying to stop his runaway drug use in
Mexico. At the end of the book, wrapping up his story, Burroughs writes: "My
wife and I are separated." This euphemism reflects his unwillingness to address the tragedy of her death.

Burroughs was writing *Queer* when, in May 1952, Jack Kerouac arrived for a
two-month visit and became his roommate at 210 Orizaba. Kerouac's *Mexico
City Blues* was composed at this time. In *Queer*, Burroughs chose to cast his
story in the third person—as befitted the shift in his own consciousness of himself from autobiographer to author—creating himself as the protagonist, "Lee."
Also during this year Burroughs began sleeping with a young Mexican boy
named Angelo Porcayo, whom he always remembered as affectionate and
uncomplicated. Perhaps this simpler arrangement aided Burroughs in showing
himself, not as the cool, implacable narrator of *Junky*, but as the self-hating,
desperate, inexplicably love-addled character "Lee."

That summer, Bill Garver arrived from the States and took a room in the
Orizaba building. Kerouac and Burroughs were not domestically compatible,
and Burroughs was relieved when Kerouac left in August. During the final
editing stages of *Junky*, Ginsberg told Burroughs that Ace Books refused to
include the homosexual material, and Burroughs abandoned the *Queer* manuscript just at the point where Marker had abandoned him: in Puyo, Ecuador.
But he continued writing to Marker, in Florida, despite the absence of reply.
Finally Marker came down to Mexico, in the fall of 1952. It was a short visit;
Burroughs accompanied Marker to Jacksonville and Hollywood, Florida, where
he met Eddie Woods and Betty Jones again. It was the end of Burroughs'
eighteen-month involvement with Lewis Marker.

Burroughs went on to Palm Beach, to spend Christmas with his parents
and his now four-year-old son, Billy. At about the same time, Bernabé Jurado
fled Mexico to escape prosecution for shooting a teenaged boy who accidentally scratched his car. In his letters to Ginsberg, Burroughs talked of his plans
to go back to Panama and South America very soon, and of his hopes, which
would prove vain, that Marker would join him there. Although Burroughs
couldn't mention it to his parents, his first book, *Junky*, was scheduled for
publication by Ace Books in New York the following summer. But he did tell
them about his "research trip" to Puyo, and about his plans for the next trip.
Mote and Laura agreed to underwrite their wayward son's new expedition: to
Colombia, South America. They did not know that the object of his quest was
yagé.

Burroughs set out in January 1953, and he wrote a continuous stream of
letters back to Ginsberg during the seven-month trip. Marker's disappearance
created a void for Burroughs' "routines," and he was now writing primarily
for Ginsberg's edification and enjoyment. Through Harvard connections,
Burroughs met the American ethnobotanist Richard Evans Schultes ("Dr.

Schindler"), who assisted him in his quest. After many further misadventures—including official detainment over an error in his travel papers and a few sexual encounters with light-fingered native boys—in the early summer, Burroughs finally located and partook of the *yagé* elixir, several times, in the Putumayo river town of Pucalpa. If he was searching for a drug that could heighten the telepathy between two kindred souls—such as himself and Marker, or Ginsberg—and bring them into psychic union, Burroughs found instead an intensely hallucinatory and solitary voyage inward.

Transcribing his trip notes on a typewriter rented by the hour, Burroughs spent a few months in Lima, Peru. He was thirty-nine years old, an exile for the past five years, and about to be a published writer. He was finally reconciled to his homosexuality, but still seeking the perfectly telepathic partner, and his feelings for Ginsberg—whom he had treated condescendingly during the Columbia years, when Burroughs was thirty and Allen only eighteen— were now his primary emotional longing. In August he headed north from Lima, through Panama City and back to Mexico, and he sent Allen his last installment, a short piece he called "Mexico City Return." In this text, Burroughs recounts asking people from the old Bounty gang for any news of Marker—while at the same time professing his new indifference, as shown by the "Skip Tracer" sequence that ends the piece.

In 1984, the long-lost *Queer* manuscript became available again, and Burroughs agreed to revise the book for publication. The original text ended abruptly with the failure of his first *yagé* quest, and he needed something to give the book a better ending: "Mexico City Return" provided a dénouement. Burroughs also agreed to write a new introduction for *Queer,* but he found it difficult to face rereading the manuscript. He put it off, and eventually wrote a handful of notes—which did not seem sufficient for introducing this long-rumored and much-anticipated book. At his suggestion, I dipped into his letters to Kerouac and Ginsberg from the same period, and using them we cobbled together a broader Introduction.

The portion of the *Queer* "Introduction" included here, however, is taken entirely from Burroughs' new writings from early 1985. It is the part most commonly quoted, because in it Burroughs makes his first formal statement on Joan's death and what it meant to him. Before then, in interviews, he would either tell the truth and change the subject, or—more often—pass off the old accidental-discharge lie fabricated for him by Jurado many years before.

In September 1953 Burroughs finally quit Mexico and went to Palm Beach, where his parents were operating a small gift shop called Cobblestone Gardens and raising Billy, now five years old. Burroughs was with them only briefly; he soon left for Ginsberg's New York apartment on East Seventh Street for their all-important reunion after six years apart. But Ginsberg had come into his own: no longer an impressionable teenager, he was now twenty-seven, and confident in his queer identity. Although he loved Burroughs, he did not want him for a lover. Somehow their friendship realigned itself, and they finished editing *The Yagé Letters* by the end of the year. The book was published ten years later, by City Lights, just after the U.S. publication of *Naked Lunch* in 1962 by Barney Rosset's Grove Press.

The Yagé Letters is not, strictly speaking, a collection of letters, but rather an epistolary novella, again substituting variations on Burroughs' own biography, obscuring his past: Ohio for Missouri, Cincinnati for St. Louis. As Burroughs is now performing for Ginsberg, he is portraying himself in a tougher, more worldly light than his actual circumstances may have warranted. One can also see how pioneering was his interest in psychedelics (for example, he learns about "ololiuqui," which in the 1960s would become known as "morning glory seeds," containing lysergic compounds). But the most important development is the further entrance of Burroughs' dreams into his writing, and his elaboration of the "routine" beyond the early form created for "Allerton's" sake. In a letter from May 1953, Burroughs describes a dream of sailors wiping their asses with a treaty, and encloses the routine "Roosevelt After Inauguration." City Lights' printers in 1963 refused to include "Roosevelt" in the first edition of *The Yagé Letters;* the routine was first published by Ed Sanders' Fuck You Press on the Lower East Side of New York in 1964; twenty years later, City Lights restored it to its edition.

As for the publication of *Junkie* in the spring of 1953, it was not reviewed in print, nor was it expected to be; it did, however, confer a certain notoriety upon its author in the hipster circles of Greenwich Village, in places like the venerable San Remo Bar, which Burroughs and Ginsberg frequented at this time. And because the Ace Books double edition was among the very first wave of cheap, soft-cover pocket-sized paperbacks, the first six months of sales exceeded 113,000 copies. But with a royalty of only three cents per copy (regardless of the cover price), this did not earn much money for Burroughs.

The *yagé* manuscript was finished, and Burroughs was ready to move on. He could not stay in New York with Ginsberg, now that he knew his desire was not reciprocated. A friend of Ginsberg's named Alan Ansen (a Harvard man, younger than Burroughs) was heading to the Mediterranean in early 1954. Burroughs decided to accompany him; it would be his first return to the Continent in seventeen years. His past was littered with the failures of his loves and other efforts: his wife was dead, the Columbia circle was shattered, and almost all his former friends had left him. But he still had his parents' allowance, and the knowledge that he had become a writer.

PROLOGUE

I was born in 1914 in a solid, three-story, brick house in a large Midwest city. My parents were comfortable. My father owned and ran a lumber business. The house had a lawn in front, a back yard with a garden, a fish pond and a high wooden fence all around it. I remember the lamp-lighter lighting the gas streetlights and the huge, black, shiny Lincoln and drives in the park on Sunday. All the props of a safe, comfortable way of life that is now gone forever. I could put down one of those nostalgic routines about the old German doctor who lived next door and the rats running around in the back yard and my aunt's electric car and my pet toad that lived by the fish pond.

Actually my earliest memories are colored by a fear of nightmares. I was afraid to be alone, and afraid of the dark, and afraid to go to sleep because of dreams where a supernatural horror seemed always on the point of taking shape. I was afraid some day the dream would still be there when I woke up. I recall hearing a maid talk about opium and how smoking opium brings sweet dreams, and I said: "I will smoke opium when I grow up."

I was subject to hallucinations as a child. Once I woke up in the early morning light and saw little men playing in a block house I had made. I felt no fear, only a feeling of stillness and wonder. Another recurrent hallucination or nightmare concerned "animals in the wall," and started with the delirium of a strange, undiagnosed fever that I had at the age of four or five.

I went to a progressive school with the future solid citizens, the lawyers, doctors and businessmen of a large Midwest town. I was timid with the other children and afraid of physical violence. One aggressive little lesbian would pull my hair whenever she saw me. I would like to shove her face in right now, but she fell off a horse and broke her neck years ago.

When I was about seven my parents decided to move to the suburbs "to get away from people." They bought a large house with grounds and woods and a fish pond where there were squirrels instead of rats. They lived there in a comfortable capsule, with a beautiful garden and cut off from contact with the life of the city.

I went to a private suburban high school. I was not conspicuously good or bad at sports, neither brilliant nor backward in studies. I had a definite blind spot for mathematics or anything mechanical. I never liked competitive team games and avoided these whenever possible. I became, in fact, a chronic malingerer. I did like fishing, hunting and hiking. I read more than was usual for an American boy of that time and place: Oscar Wilde, Anatole France, Baudelaire, even Gide. I formed a romantic attachment for another boy and we spent our Saturdays exploring old quarries, riding around on bicycles and fishing in ponds and rivers.

At this time, I was greatly impressed by an autobiography of a burglar, called *You Can't Win*. The author claimed to have spent a good part of his life in jail. It sounded good to me compared with the dullness of a Midwest suburb where all contact with life was shut out. I saw my friend as an ally, a partner in crime. We found an abandoned factory and broke all the windows and stole a chisel. We were caught, and our fathers had to pay the damages. After this my friend "packed me in" because the relationship was endangering his standing with the group. I saw there was no compromise possible with the group, the others, and I found myself a good deal alone.

The environment was empty, the antagonist hidden, and I drifted into solo adventures. My criminal acts were gestures, unprofitable and for the most part unpunished. I would break into houses and walk around without taking anything. As a matter of fact, I had no need for money. Sometimes I would drive around in the country with a .22 rifle, shooting chickens. I made the roads unsafe with reckless driving until an accident, from which I emerged miraculously and portentously unscratched, scared me into normal caution.

I went to one of the Big Three universities, where I majored in English literature for lack of interest in any other subject. I hated the University and I hated the town it was in. Everything about the place was dead. The University was a fake English setup taken over by the graduates of fake English public schools. I was lonely. I knew no one, and strangers were regarded with distaste by the closed corporation of the desirables.

By accident I met some rich homosexuals, of the international queer set who cruise around the world, bumping into each other in queer joints from New York to Cairo. I saw a way of life, a vocabulary, references, a whole symbol system, as the sociologists say. But these people were jerks for the most part and, after an initial period of fascination, I cooled off on the setup.

When I graduated without honors, I had one hundred fifty dollars per month in trust. That was in the depression and there were no jobs and I couldn't think of any job I wanted, in any case. I drifted around Europe for a year or so. Remnants of the postwar decay lingered in Europe. U.S. dollars could buy a good percentage of the inhabitants of Austria, male or female. That was in 1936, and the Nazis were closing in fast.

I went back to the States. With my trust fund I could live without working or hustling. I was still cut off from life as I had been in the Midwest suburb. I fooled around taking graduate courses in psychology and jiu-jitsu lessons. I decided to undergo psychoanalysis, and continued with it for three years. Analysis removed inhibitions and anxiety so that I could live the way I wanted to live. Much of my progress in analysis was accomplished in spite of my analyst who did not like my "orientation," as he called it. He finally abandoned analytic objectivity and put me down as an "out-and-out con." I was more pleased with the results than he was.

After being rejected on physical grounds from five officer-training programs, I was drafted into the Army and certified fit for unlimited service. I decided I was not going to like the Army and copped out on my nut-house record—I'd once got on a Van Gogh kick and cut off a finger joint to impress someone who interested me at the time. The nut-house doctors had never heard of Van Gogh. They put me down for schizophrenia, adding paranoid type to explain the upsetting fact that I knew where I was and who was President of the U.S. When the Army saw that diagnosis they discharged me with the notation, "This man is never to be recalled or reclassified."

After parting company with the Army, I took a variety of jobs. You could have about any job you wanted at that time. I worked as a private detective, an exterminator, a bartender. I worked in factories and offices. I played around the edges of crime. But my hundred and fifty dollars per month was always there. I did not have to have money. It seemed a romantic extravagance to jeopardize my freedom by some token act of crime. It was at this time and under these circumstances that I came in contact with junk, became an addict, and thereby gained the motivation, the real need for money I had never had before.

The question is frequently asked: Why does a man become a drug addict?

The answer is that he usually does not intend to become an addict. You don't wake up one morning and decide to be a drug addict. It takes at least three months' shooting twice a day to get any habit at all. And you don't really know what junk sickness is until you have had several habits. It took me almost six months to get my first habit, and then the withdrawal symptoms were mild. I think it no exaggeration to say it takes about a year and several hundred injections to make an addict.

The questions, of course, could be asked: Why did you ever try narcotics? Why did you continue using it long enough to become an addict? You become a narcotics addict because you do not have strong motivations in any other direction. Junk wins by default. I tried it as a matter of curiosity. I drifted along taking shots when I could score. I ended up hooked. Most addicts I have talked to report a similar experience. They did not start using drugs for any reason they can remember. They just drifted along until they got hooked. If you have never been addicted, you can have no clear idea what it means to need junk with the addict's special need. You can't decide to be an addict. One morning you wake up sick and you're an addict.

I have never regretted my experience with drugs. I think I am in better health now as a result of using junk at intervals than I would be if I had never been an addict. When you stop growing you start dying. An addict never

stops growing. Most users periodically kick the habit, which involves shrinking of the organism and replacement of the junk-dependent cells. A user is
in a continual state of shrinking and growing in his daily cycle of shot-need
for shot completed.

Most addicts look younger than they are. Scientists recently experimented
with a worm that they were able to shrink by withholding food. By periodically shrinking the worm so that it was in continual growth, the worm's life
was prolonged indefinitely. Perhaps if a junky could keep himself in a constant state of kicking, he would live to a phenomenal age.

Junk is a cellular equation that teaches the user facts of general validity. I
have learned a great deal from using junk: I have seen life measured out in
eyedroppers of morphine solution. I experienced the agonizing deprivation
of junk sickness, and the pleasure of relief when junk-thirsty cells drank from
the needle. Perhaps all pleasure is relief. I have learned the cellular stoicism
that junk teaches the user. I have seen a cell full of sick junkies silent and immobile in separate misery. They knew the pointlessness of complaining or
moving. They knew that basically no one can help anyone else. There is no
key, no secret someone else has that he can give you.

I have learned the junk equation. Junk is not, like alcohol or weed, a means
to increased enjoyment of life. Junk is not a kick. It is a way of life.

SELECTIONS

My first experience with junk was during the War, about 1944 or 1945. I had
made the acquaintance of a man named Norton who was working in a shipyard at the time. Norton, whose real name was Morelli or something like that,
had been discharged from the peacetime Army for forging a pay check, and
was classified 4-F for reasons of bad character. He looked like George Raft,
but was taller. Norton was trying to improve his English and achieve a smooth,
affable manner. Affability, however, did not come natural to him. In repose,
his expression was sullen and mean, and you knew he always had that mean
look when you turned your back.

Norton was a hard-working thief, and he did not feel right unless he stole
something every day from the shipyard where he worked. A tool, some canned
goods, a pair of overalls, anything at all. One day he called me up and said he
had stolen a tommy gun. Could I find someone to buy it? I said, "Maybe.
Bring it over."

The housing shortage was getting under way. I paid fifteen dollars a week
for a dirty apartment that opened onto a companionway and never got any
sunlight. The wallpaper was flaking off because the radiator leaked steam when
there was any steam in it to leak. I had the windows sealed shut against the
cold with a caulking of newspapers. The place was full of roaches and occasionally I killed a bedbug.

I was sitting by the radiator, a little damp from the steam, when I heard Norton's knock. I opened the door, and there he was standing in the dark hall with a big parcel wrapped in brown paper under his arm. He smiled and said, "Hello."

I said, "Come in, Norton, and take off your coat."

He unwrapped the tommy gun and we assembled it and snapped the firing pin.

I said I would find someone to buy it.

Norton said, "Oh, here's something else I picked up."

It was a flat yellow box with five one-half grain syrettes of morphine tartrate.

"This is just a sample," he said, indicating the morphine. "I've got fifteen of these boxes at home and I can get more if you get rid of these."

I said, "I'll see what I can do."

At that time I had never used any junk and it did not occur to me to try it. I began looking for someone to buy the two items and that is how I ran into Roy and Herman.

I knew a young hoodlum from upstate New York who was working as a short-order cook in Riker's, "cooling off," as he explained. I called him and said I had something to get rid of, and made an appointment to meet him in the Angle Bar on Eighth Avenue near 42nd Street.

This bar was a meeting place for 42nd Street hustlers, a peculiar breed of four-flushing, would-be criminals. They are always looking for a "setup man," someone to plan jobs and tell them exactly what to do. Since no "setup man" would have anything to do with people so obviously inept, unlucky, and unsuccessful, they go on looking, fabricating preposterous lies about their big scores, cooling off as dishwashers, soda jerks, waiters, occasionally rolling a drunk or a timid queer, looking, always looking, for the "setup man" with a big job who will say, "I've been watching you. You're the man I need for this setup. Now listen . . ."

Jack—through whom I met Roy and Herman—was not one of these lost sheep looking for the shepherd with a diamond ring and a gun in the shoulder holster and the hard, confident voice with overtones of connections, fixes, setups that would make a stickup sound easy and sure of success. Jack was very successful from time to time and would turn up in new clothes and even new cars. He was also an inveterate liar who seemed to lie more for himself than for any visible audience. He had a clean-cut, healthy country face, but there was something curiously diseased about him. He was subject to sudden fluctuations in weight, like a diabetic or a sufferer from liver trouble. These changes in weight were often accompanied by an uncontrollable fit of restlessness, so that he would disappear for some days.

The effect was uncanny. You would see him one time a fresh-faced kid. A week or so later he would turn up so thin, sallow and odd-looking, you would have to look twice to recognize him. His face was lined with suffering in which his eyes did not participate. It was a suffering of his cells alone. He himself—the conscious ego that looked out of the glazed, alert-calm hoodlum eyes—would have nothing to do with this suffering of his rejected other self, a suffering of the nervous system, of flesh and viscera and cells.

He slid into the booth where I was sitting and ordered a shot of whiskey. He tossed it off, put the glass down and looked at me with his head tilted a little to one side and back.

"What's this guy got?" he said.

"A tommy gun and about thirty-five grains of morphine."

"The morphine I can get rid of right away, but the tommy gun may take a little time."

Two detectives walked in and leaned on the bar, talking to the bartender. Jack jerked his head in their direction. "The law. Let's take a walk."

I followed him out of the bar. He walked through the door sliding sideways. "I'm taking you to someone who will want the morphine," he said. "You want to forget this address."

We went down to the bottom level of the Independent Subway. Jack's voice, talking to his invisible audience, went on and on. He had a knack of throwing his voice directly into your consciousness. No external noise drowned him out. "Give me a thirty-eight every time. Just flick back the hammer and let her go. I'll drop anyone at five hundred feet. Don't care what you say. My brother has two .30-caliber machine guns stashed in Iowa."

We got off the subway and began to walk on snow-covered sidewalks between tenements.

"The guy owed me for a long time, see? I knew he had it but he wouldn't pay, so I waited for him when he finished work. I had a roll of nickels. No one can hang anything on you for carrying U.S. currency. Told me he was broke. I cracked his jaw and took my money off him. Two of his friends standing there, but they kept out of it. I'd've switched a blade on them."

We were walking up tenement stairs. The stairs were made of worn black metal. We stopped in front of a narrow, metal-covered door, and Jack gave an elaborate knock inclining his head to the floor like a safecracker. The door was opened by a large, flabby, middle-aged queer, with tattooing on his forearms and even on the backs of his hands.

"This is Joey," Jack said, and Joey said, "Hello there."

Jack pulled a five-dollar bill from his pocket and gave it to Joey. "Get us a quart of Schenley's, will you, Joey?"

Joey put on an overcoat and went out.

In many tenement apartments the front door opens directly into the kitchen. This was such an apartment and we were in the kitchen.

After Joey went out I noticed another man who was standing there looking at me. Waves of hostility and suspicion flowed out from his large brown eyes like some sort of television broadcast. The effect was almost like a physi-

cal impact. The man was small and very thin, his neck loose in the collar of
his shirt. His complexion faded from brown to a mottled yellow, and pancake makeup had been heavily applied in an attempt to conceal a skin erup-
tion. His mouth was drawn down at the corners in a grimace of petulant
annoyance.

"Who's this?" he said. His name, I learned later, was Herman.

"Friend of mine. He's got some morphine he wants to get rid of."

Herman shrugged and turned out his hands. "I don't think I want to bother,
really."

"Okay," Jack said, "we'll sell it to someone else. Come on, Bill."

We went into the front room. There was a small radio, a china Buddha with
a votive candle in front of it, pieces of bric-a-brac. A man was lying on a studio couch. He sat up as we entered the room and said hello and smiled pleasantly, showing discolored, brownish teeth. It was a Southern voice with the
accent of East Texas.

Jack said, "Roy, this is a friend of mine. He has some morphine he wants
to sell."

The man sat up straighter and swung his legs off the couch. His jaw fell
slackly, giving his face a vacant look. The skin of his face was smooth and
brown. The cheekbones were high and he looked Oriental. His ears stuck
out at right angles from his asymmetrical skull. The eyes were brown and
they had a peculiar brilliance, as though points of light were shining behind
them. The light in the room glinted on the points of light in his eyes like an
opal.

"How much do you have?" he asked me.

"Seventy-five half-grain syrettes."

"The regular price is two dollars a grain," he said, "but syrettes go for a
little less. People want tablets. Those syrettes have too much water and you
have to squeeze the stuff out and cook it down." He paused and his face went
blank: "I could go about one-fifty a grain," he said finally.

"I guess that will be okay," I said.

He asked how we could make contact and I gave him my phone number.

Joey came back with the whiskey and we all had a drink. Herman stuck his
head in from the kitchen and said to Jack, "Could I talk to you for a minute?"

I could hear them arguing about something. Then Jack came back and
Herman stayed in the kitchen. We all had a few drinks and Jack began telling
a story.

"My partner was going through the joint. The guy was sleeping, and I was
standing over him with a three-foot length of pipe I found in the bathroom.
The pipe had a faucet on the end of it, see? All of a sudden he comes up and
jumps straight off the bed, running. I let him have it with the faucet end, and
he goes on running right out into the other room, the blood spurting out of
his head ten feet every time his heart beat." He made a pumping motion with
his hand. "You could see the brain there and the blood coming out of it."

Jack began to laugh uncontrollably. "My girl was waiting out in the car. She called me—ha-ha-ha!—she called me—ha-ha-ha!—a cold-blooded killer."

He laughed until his face was purple.

A few nights after meeting Roy and Herman, I used one of the syrettes, which was my first experience with junk. A syrette is like a toothpaste tube with a needle on the end. You push a pin down through the needle; the pin punctures the seal; and the syrette is ready to shoot.

Morphine hits the backs of the legs first, then the back of the neck, a spreading wave of relaxation slackening the muscles away from the bones so that you seem to float without outlines, like lying in warm salt water. As this relaxing wave spread through my tissues, I experienced a strong feeling of fear. I had the feeling that some horrible image was just beyond the field of vision, moving, as I turned my head, so that I never quite saw it. I felt nauseous; I lay down and closed my eyes. A series of pictures passed, like watching a movie: A huge, neon-lighted cocktail bar that got larger and larger until streets, traffic, and street repairs were included in it; a waitress carrying a skull on a tray; stars in the clear sky. The physical impact of the fear of death; the shutting off of breath; the stopping of blood.

I dozed off and woke up with a start of fear. Next morning I vomited and felt sick until noon.

Roy called that night.

"About what we were discussing the other night," he said. "I could go about four dollars per box and take five boxes now. Are you busy? I'll come over to your place. We'll come to some kind of agreement."

A few minutes later he knocked at the door. He had on a glen plaid suit and a dark, coffee-colored shirt. We said hello. He looked around blankly and said, "If you don't mind, I'll take one of those now."

I opened the box. He took out a syrette and injected it into his leg. He pulled up his pants briskly and took out twenty dollars. I put five boxes on the kitchen table.

"I think I'll take them out of the boxes," he said. "Too bulky."

He began putting the syrettes in his coat pockets. "I don't think they'll perforate this way," he said. "Listen, I'll call you again in a day or so after I get rid of these and have some more money." He was adjusting his hat over his asymmetrical skull. "I'll see you."

Next day he was back. He shot another syrette and pulled out forty dollars. I laid out ten boxes and kept two.

"These are for me," I said.

He looked at me, surprised. "You use it?"

"Now and then."

"It's bad stuff," he said, shaking his head. "The worst thing that can happen to a man. We all think we can control it at first. Sometimes we don't want to control it." He laughed. "I'll take all you can get at this price."

Next day he was back. He asked if I didn't want to change my mind about selling the two boxes. I said no. He bought two syrettes for a dollar each, shot them both, and left. He said he had signed on for a two-month trip.

One night, Roy and I got on the subway at Times Square. A flashily dressed man weaving slightly was walking ahead of us. Roy looked him over and said, "That's a good fucking mooch. Let's see where he goes."

The mooch got on the IRT headed for Brooklyn. We waited standing up in the space between cars until the mooch appeared to be sleeping. Then we walked into the car, and I sat down beside the mooch, opening *The New York Times*. The *Times* was Roy's idea. He said it made me look like a businessman. The car was almost empty, and there we were, wedged up against the mooch with twenty feet of empty seats available. Roy began working over my back. The mooch kept stirring and once he woke up and looked at me with bleary annoyance. A Negro sitting opposite us smiled.

"The shine is wise," said Roy in my ear. "He's O.K."

Roy was having trouble finding the poke. The situation was getting dangerous. I could feel sweat running down my arms.

"Let's get off," I said.

"No. This is a good mooch. He's sitting on his overcoat and I can't get into his pocket. When I tell you, fall up against him, and I'll move the coat at the same time. . . . *Now!* . . . For Chris' sake! That wasn't near hard enough."

"Let's get off," I said again. I could feel fear stirring in my stomach. "He's going to wake up."

"No. Let's go again. . . . *Now!* . . . What in hell is wrong with you? Just let yourself flop against him hard."

"Roy," I said, "for Chris' sake let's get off! He's going to wake up."

I started to get up, but Roy held me down. Suddenly he gave me a sharp push, and I fell heavily against the mooch.

"Got it that time," Roy said.

"The poke?"

"No, I got the coat out of the way."

We were out of the underground now and on the elevated. I was nauseated with fear, every muscle rigid with the effort of control. The mooch was only half asleep. I expected him to jump up and yell at any minute.

Finally I heard Roy say, "I got it."

"Let's go then."

"No, what I got is a loose roll. He's got a poke somewhere and I'm going to find it. He's got to have a poke."

"I'm getting off."

"No. Wait." I could feel him fumbling across my back so openly that it seemed incredible that the man could go on sleeping.

It was the end of the line. Roy stood up. "Cover me," he said. I stood in front of him with the paper shielding him as much as possible from the other passengers. There were only three left, but they were in different ends of the car. Roy went through the man's pockets openly and crudely. "Let's go outside," he said. We went out on the platform.

The mooch woke up and put his hand in his pocket. Then he came out on the platform and walked up to Roy.

"All right, Jack," he said. "Give me my money."

Roy shrugged and turned his hands out, palm up. "What money? What are you talking about?"

"You know Goddamned well what I'm talking about! You had your hand in my pocket."

Roy held his hands out again in a gesture of puzzlement and deprecation. "Aw, what are you talking about? I don't know anything about your money."

"I've seen you on this line every night. This is your regular route." He turned and pointed to me. "And there's your partner right there. Now, are you going to give me my dough?"

"What dough?"

"Okay. Just stay put. We're taking a ride back to town and this had better be good." Suddenly, the man put both hands in Roy's coat pockets. "You sonofabitch!" he yelled. "Give me my dough!"

Roy hit him in the face and knocked him down. "Why you—" said Roy, dropping abruptly his conciliatory and puzzled manner. "Keep your hands off me!"

The conductor, seeing a fight in progress, was holding up the train so that no one would fall on the tracks.

"Let's cut," I said. We started down the platform. The man got up and ran after us. He threw his arms around Roy, holding on stubbornly. Roy couldn't break loose. He was pretty well winded.

"Get this mooch off me!" Roy yelled.

I hit the man twice in the face. His grip loosened and he fell to his knees.

"Kick his head off," said Roy.

I kicked the man in the side and felt a rib snap. The man put his hand to his side. "Help!" he shouted. He did not try to get up.

"Let's cut," I said. At the far end of the platform, I heard a police whistle. The man was still lying there on the platform holding his side and yelling "Help!" at regular intervals.

There was a slight drizzle of rain falling. When I hit the street, I slipped and skidded on the wet sidewalk. We were standing by a closed filling station, looking back at the elevated.

"Let's go," I said.

"They'll see us."

"We can't stay here."

We started to walk. I noticed that my mouth was bone dry. Roy took two goofballs from his shirt pocket.

"Mouth's too dry," he said. "I can't swallow them."

We went on walking.

"There's sure to be an alarm out for us," Roy said. "Keep a lookout for cars. We'll duck in the bushes if any come along. They'll be figuring us to get back on the subway, so the best thing we can do is keep walking."

The drizzle continued. Dogs barked at us as we walked.

"Remember our story if we get nailed," Roy said. "We fell asleep and woke up at the end of the line. This guy accused us of taking his money. We were scared, so we knocked him down and ran. They'll beat the shit out of us. You have to expect that."

"Here comes a car," I said. "Yellow lights, too."

We crawled into the bushes at the side of the road and crouched down behind a signboard. The car drove slowly by. We started walking again. I was getting sick and wondered if I would get home to the morphine sulphate I had stashed in my apartment.

"When we get closer in we better split up," Roy said. "Out here we might be able to do each other some good. If we run into a cop on the beat we'll tell him we've been with some girls and we're looking for the subway. This rain is a break. The cops will all be in some all-night joint drinking coffee. For chris' sake!" he said irritably. "Don't round like that!"

I had turned around and looked over my shoulder. "It's natural to turn around," I said.

"Natural for thieves!"

We finally ran into the BMT line and rode back to Manhattan.

Roy said, "I don't think I'm just speaking for myself when I say I was scared. Oh. Here's your cut."

He handed me three dollars.

Next day I told him I was through as a lush-worker.

"I don't blame you," he said. "But you got a wrong impression. You're bound to get some good breaks if you stick around long enough."

Eventually, I got to Texas and stayed off junk for about four months. Then I went to New Orleans. New Orleans presents a stratified series of ruins. Along Bourbon Street are ruins of the 1920s. Down where the French Quarter blends into Skid Row are ruins of an earlier stratum: chili joints, decaying hotels, oldtime saloons with mahogany bars, spittoons, and crystal chandeliers. The ruins of 1900.

There are people in New Orleans who have never been outside the city limits. The New Orleans accent is exactly similar to the accent of Brooklyn. The French Quarter is always crowded. Tourists, servicemen, merchant seamen, gamblers, perverts, drifters, and lamsters from every State in the Union. People wander around, unrelated, purposeless, most of them looking vaguely sullen and hostile. This is a place where you enjoy yourself. Even the criminals have come here to cool off and relax.

But a complex pattern of tensions, like the electrical mazes devised by psychologists to unhinge the nervous systems of white rats and guinea pigs, keeps the unhappy pleasure-seekers in a condition of unconsummated alertness. For one thing, New Orleans is inordinately noisy. The drivers orient themselves largely by the use of their horns, like bats. The residents are surly. The transient population is completely miscellaneous and unrelated, so that you never know what sort of behavior to expect from anybody.

New Orleans was a strange town to me and I had no way of making a junk connection. Walking around the city, I spotted several junk neighborhoods: St. Charles and Poydras, the area around and above Lee Circle, Canal and Exchange Place. I don't spot junk neighborhoods by the way they look, but by the feel, somewhat the same process by which a dowser locates hidden water. I am walking along and suddenly the junk in my cells moves and twitches like the dowser's wand: "Junk here!"

I didn't see anybody around, and besides I wanted to stay off, or at least I thought I wanted to stay off.

In the French Quarter there are several queer bars so full every night the fags spill out on to the sidewalk. A room full of fags gives me the horrors. They jerk around like puppets on invisible strings, galvanized into hideous activity that is the negation of everything living and spontaneous. The live human being has moved out of these bodies long ago. But something moved in when the original tenant moved out. Fags are ventriloquists' dummies who have moved in and taken over the ventriloquist. The dummy sits in a queer bar nursing his beer, and uncontrollably yapping out of a rigid doll face.

Occasionally, you find intact personalities in a queer bar, but fags set the tone of these joints, and it always brings me down to go into a queer bar. The bring-down piles up. After my first week in a new town I have had about all I can take of these joints, so my bar business goes somewhere else, generally to a bar in or near Skid Row.

But I backslide now and then. One night, I got lobotomized drunk in Frank's and went to a queer bar. I must have had more drinks in the queer joint, because there was a lapse of time. It was getting light outside when the bar hit one of those sudden pockets of quiet. Quiet is something that does not often happen in a queer joint. I guess most of the fags had left. I was leaning against the bar with a beer I didn't want in front of me. The noise cleared like smoke and I saw a red-haired kid was looking straight at me and standing about three feet away.

He didn't come on faggish, so I said, "How you making it?" or something like that.

He said: "Do you want to go to bed with me?"

I said, "O.K. Let's go."

As we walked out, he grabbed my bottle of beer off the bar and stuck it under his coat. Outside, it was daylight with the sun just coming up. We staggered through the French Quarter passing the beer bottle back and forth. He was leading the way in the direction of his hotel, so he said. I could feel my stomach knot up like I was about to take a shot after being off the junk a long time. I should have been more alert, of course, but I never could mix vigilance and sex. All this time he was talking on in a sexy Southern voice which was not a New Orleans voice, and in the daylight he still looked good.

We got to a hotel and he put me down some routine why he should go in first alone. I pulled some bills out of my pocket. He looked at them and said, "Better give me the ten."

I gave it to him. He went in the hotel and came right out.

"No rooms there," he said. "We'll try the Savoy."

The Savoy was right across the street.

"Wait here," he said.

I waited about an hour and by then it occurred to me what was wrong with the first hotel. It'd had no back or side door he could walk out of. I went back to my apartment and got my gun. I waited around the Savoy and looked for the kid through the French Quarter. About noon, I got hungry and ate a plate of oysters with a glass of beer, and suddenly felt so tired that when I walked out of the restaurant my legs were folding under me as if someone was clipping me behind the knees.

I took a cab home and fell across the bed without taking off my shoes. I woke up around six in the evening and went to Frank's. After three quick beers I felt better.

There was a man standing by the jukebox and I caught his eye several times. He looked at me with a special recognition, like one queer looks at another. He looked like one of those terra-cotta heads that you plant grass in. A peasant face, with peasant intuition, stupidity, shrewdness and malice.

The jukebox wasn't working. I walked over and asked him what was wrong with it. He said he didn't know. I asked him to have a drink and he ordered Coke. He told me his name was Pat. I told him I had come up recently from the Mexican border.

He said, "I'd like to get down that way, me. Bring some stuff in from Mexico."

"The border is pretty hot," I said.

"I hope you won't take offense at what I say," he began, "but you look like you use stuff yourself."

"Sure I use."

"Do you want to score?" he asked. "I'm due to score in a few minutes. I've been trying to hustle the dough. If you buy me a cap, I can score for you."

I said, "O.K."

We walked around the corner past the NMU hall.

"Wait here a minute," he said, disappearing into a bar. I half-expected to get beat for my four dollars, but he was back in a few minutes. "O.K.," he said, "I got it."

I asked him to come back to my apartment to take a shot. We went back to my room, and I got out my outfit that hadn't been used in five months.

"If you don't have a habit, you'd better go slow with this stuff," he cautioned me. "It's pretty strong."

I measured out about two-thirds of a cap.

"Half is plenty," he said. "I tell you it's strong."

"This will be all right," I said. But as soon as I took the needle out of the vein, I knew it wasn't all right. I felt a soft blow in the heart. Pat's face began to get black around the edges, the blackness spreading to cover his face. I could feel my eyes roll back in their sockets.

I came to several hours later. Pat was gone. I was lying on the bed with my collar loosened. I stood up and fell to my knees. I was dizzy and my head ached. Ten dollars were missing from my watch-pocket. I guess he figured I wasn't going to need it any more.

Several days later I met Pat in the same bar.

"Holy Jesus," he said, "I thought you was dying! I loosened your collar and rubbed ice on your neck. You turned all blue. So I says, 'Holy Jesus, this man is dying! I'm going to get out of here, me!'"

A week later, I was hooked. I asked Pat about the possibilities of pushing in New Orleans.

"The town is et up with pigeons," he said. "It's really tough."

One day I was broke and I wrapped up a pistol to take it in town and pawn it. When I got to Pat's room there were two people there. One was Red McKinney, a shriveled-up, crippled junkie; the other was a young merchant seaman named Cole. Cole did not have a habit at this time and he wanted to connect for some weed. He was a real tea head. He told me he could not enjoy himself without weed. I have seen people like that. For them, tea occupies the place usually filled by liquor. They don't have to have it in any physical sense, but they cannot have a really good time without it.

As it happened I had several ounces of weed in my house. Cole agreed to buy four caps in exchange for two ounces of weed. We went out to my place, Cole tried the weed and said it was good. So we started out to score.

Red said he knew a connection on Julia Street. "We should be able to find him there now."

Pat was sitting at the wheel of my car on the nod. We were on the ferry, crossing from Algiers, where I lived, to New Orleans. Suddenly Pat looked up and opened his bloodshot eyes.

"That neighborhood is too hot," he said loudly.

"Where else can we score?" said McKinney. "Old Sam is up that way, too."

"I tell you that neighborhood is too hot," Pat repeated. He looked around resentfully, as though what he saw was unfamiliar and distasteful.

There was, in fact, no place else to score. Without a word, Pat started driving in the direction of Lee Circle. When we came to Julia Street, McKinney said to Cole, "Give me the money because we are subject to see him any time. He walks around this block. A walking connection."

Cole gave McKinney fifteen dollars. We circled the block three times slowly, but McKinney did not see "the Man."

"Well, I guess we'll have to try Old Sam," McKinney said.

We began looking for Old Sam above Lee Circle. Old Sam was not in the old frame rooming house where he lived. We drove around slowly. Every now and then Pat would see someone he knew and stop the car. No one had seen Old Sam. Some of the characters Pat called to just shrugged in a disagreeable way and kept walking.

"Those guys wouldn't tell you nothing," Pat said. "It hurts 'em to do anybody a favor."

We parked the car near Old Sam's rooming house, and McKinney walked down to the corner to buy a package of cigarettes. He came back limping fast and got in the car.

"The law," he said. "Let's get out of here."

We started away from the curb and a prowl car passed us. I saw the cop at the wheel turn around and do a doubletake when he saw Pat.

"They've made us, Pat," I said. "Get going!"

It was five in the afternoon when we left the hospital and took a cab to Canal Street. I went into a bar and drank four whiskey sodas and got a good lush kick. I was cured.

As I walked across the porch of my house and opened the door, I had the feel of returning after a long absence. I was coming back to the point in time I left a year ago when I took that first "joy bang" with Pat.

After a junk cure is complete, you generally feel fine for a few days. You can drink, you can feel real hunger and pleasure in food, and your sex desire comes back to you. Everything looks different, sharper. Then you hit a sag. It is an effort to dress, get out of a car, pick up a fork. You don't want to do anything or go anywhere. You don't even want junk. The junk craving is gone, but there isn't anything else. You have to sit this period out. Or work it out. Farm work is the best cure.

Pat came around as soon as he heard I was out. Did I want to "pick up"? Just one wouldn't hurt any. He could get a good price on ten or more. I said no. You don't need will power to say no to junk when you are off. You don't want it.

Besides, I was charged in State, and State junk raps pile up like any other felony. Two junk raps can draw you seven years, or you can be charged in State on one and Federal on the other so that when you walk out of the State joint the Federals meet you at the door. If you do your Federal time first, then the State is waiting for you at the door of the Federal joint.

I knew the law was out to hang another on me because they had messed up the deal by coming on like Federals and by searching the house without a warrant. I had a free hand to arrange my account of what happened since there was no statement with my signature on it to tie me down. The State could not introduce the statement I had signed for the Federals without bringing up the deal I had made with that fair-play artist, the fat captain. But if they could hang another charge on me, they would have a sure thing.

Usually, a junky makes straight for a connection as soon as he leaves any place of confinement. The law would expect me to do this and they would be watching Pat. So I told Pat I was staying off until the case was settled. He borrowed two dollars and went away.

A few days later I was drinking in the bars around Canal Street. When a junky off junk gets drunk to a certain point, his thoughts turn to junk. I went into the toilet in one bar, and there was a wallet on the toilet-paper box. There is a dream feeling when you find money. I opened the wallet and took out a twenty, a ten and a five. I decided to use some other toilet in some other bar and walked out leaving a full martini.

I went up to Pat's room.

Pat opened the door and said, "Hello, old buddy, I'm glad to see you."

Sitting on the bed was another man, who turned his face to the door as I came in. "Hello, Bill," he said.

I looked at him a long three seconds before I recognized Dupré. He looked older and younger. The deadness had gone from his eyes and he was twenty pounds thinner. His face twitched at intervals like dead matter coming alive, still jerky and mechanical. When he was getting plenty of junk, Dupré looked anonymous and dead, so you could not pick him out of a crowd or recognize him at a distance. Now, his image was clear and sharp. If you walked fast down a crowded street and passed Dupré, his face would be forced on your memory— like in the card trick where the operator fans the cards rapidly, saying, "Take a card, any card," as he forces a certain card into your hand.

When he was getting plenty of junk, Dupré was silent. Now he was garrulous. He told me how he finally got so deep in the till, he lost his job. Now he had no money for junk. He couldn't even raise the price of PG and goofballs to taper off. He talked on and on.

"It used to be, all the cops knew me before the War. Many's the seventy-two hours I put in right over in the Third Precinct. It was the First Precinct then. You know how it is when you start to come off the stuff." He indicated his genitals, pointing with all his fingers, then turning the hand palm up. A concrete gesture as though he had picked up what he wanted to talk about and was holding it in his palm to show you. "You get a hard-on and shoot off right in your pants. It doesn't even have to get hard. I remember one time I was in with Larry. You know that kid Larry. He was pushing a while back. I said, 'Larry, you got to do it for me.' So he took down his pants. You know he had to do that for me."

Pat was looking for a vein. He pursed his lips in disapproval. "You guys talk like degenerates."

"What the matter, Pat?" I said. "Can't you hit it?"

"No," he said. He moved the tie-up down to his wrist to hit a vein in his hand.

Later, I stopped by my lawyer's office to talk about the case and to ask whether I could leave the State and go to the Rio Grande Valley in Texas, where I owned farm property.

"You're hot as a firecracker in this town," Tige told me. "I have permission from the judge for you to leave the State. So you can go on to Texas any time you like."

"I might want to take a trip to Mexico," I said. "Would that be okay?"

"So long as you are back here when your case comes up. There are no restrictions on you. One client of mine went to Venezuela. So far as I know, he's still there. He didn't come back."

As soon as I hit Mexico City, I started looking for junk. At least, I always had one eye open for it. As I said before, I can spot junk neighborhoods. My first night in town I walked down Dolores Street and saw a group of Chinese junkies standing in front of an Exquisito Chop Suey joint. Chinamen are hard to make. They will only do business with another Chinaman. So I knew it would be a waste of time trying to score with these characters.

One day I was walking down San Juan Létran and passed a cafeteria that had colored tile set in the stucco around the entrance, and the floor was covered with the same tile. The cafeteria was unmistakably Near Eastern. As I walked by, someone came out of the cafeteria. He was a type character you see only on the fringes of a junk neighborhood.

As the geologist looking for oil is guided by certain outcroppings of rock, so certain signs indicate the near presence of junk. Junk is often found adjacent to ambiguous or transitional districts: East Fourteenth near Third in New York; Poydras and St. Charles in New Orleans; San Juan Létran in Mexico City. Stores selling artificial limbs, wig-makers, dental mechanics, loft manufacturers of perfumes, pomades, novelties, essential oils. A point where dubious enterprise touches Skid Row.

There is a type person occasionally seen in these neighborhoods who has connections with junk, though he is neither a user nor a seller. But when you see him the dowser wand twitches. Junk is close. His place of origin is the Near East, probably Egypt. He has a large straight nose. His lips are thin and purple-blue like the lips of a penis. The skin is tight and smooth over his face. He is basically obscene beyond any possible vile act or practice. He has the mark of a certain trade or occupation that no longer exists. If junk were gone from the earth, there might still be junkies standing around in junk neighborhoods feeling the lack, vague and persistent, a pale ghost of junk sickness.

So this man walks around in the places where he once exercised his obsolete and unthinkable trade. But he is unperturbed. His eyes are black with an insect's unseeing calm. He looks as if he nourished himself on honey and Levantine syrups that he sucks up through a sort of proboscis.

What is his lost trade? Definitely of a servant class and something to do with the dead, though he is not an embalmer. Perhaps he stores something in his body—a substance to prolong life—of which he is periodically milked by his masters. He is as specialized as an insect, for the performance of some inconceivably vile function.

* * *

The Chimu Bar looks like any cantina from the outside, but as soon as you walk in you know you are in a queer bar.

I ordered a drink at the bar and looked around. Three Mexican fags were posturing in front of the jukebox. One of them slithered over to where I was standing, with the stylized gestures of a temple dancer, and asked for a cigarette. There was something archaic in the stylized movements, a depraved animal grace at once beautiful and repulsive. I could see him moving in the light of campfires, the ambiguous gestures fading out into the dark. Sodomy is as old as the human species. One of the fags was sitting in a booth by the jukebox, perfectly immobile with a stupid animal serenity.

I turned to get a closer look at the boy who had moved over. Not bad. *"¿Por qué triste?"* ("Why sad?") Not much of a gambit, but I wasn't there to converse.

The boy smiled, revealing very red gums and sharp teeth far apart. He shrugged and said something to the effect that he wasn't sad or not especially so. I looked around the room.

"Vámonos a otro lugar," I said. ("Let's go someplace else.")

The boy nodded. We walked down the street into an all-night restaurant, and sat down in a booth. The boy dropped his hand onto my leg under the table. I felt my stomach knot with excitement. I gulped my coffee and waited impatiently while the boy finished a beer and smoked a cigarette.

The boy knew a hotel. I pushed five pesos through a grill. An old man unlocked the door of a room and dropped a ragged towel on the chair. *"¿Llevas pistola?"*—("You carry a pistol?")—asked the boy. He had caught sight of my gun. I said yes.

I folded my pants and dropped them over a chair, placing the pistol on my pants. I dropped my shirt and shorts on the pistol. I sat down naked on the edge of the bed and watched the boy undress. He folded his worn blue suit carefully. He took off his shirt and placed it around his coat on the back of a chair. His skin was smooth and copper-colored. The boy stepped out of his shorts and turned around and smiled at me. Then he came and sat beside me on the bed. I ran one hand slowly over the boy's back, following with the other hand the curve of the chest down over the flat brown stomach. The boy smiled and lay down on the bed.

Later we smoked a cigarette, our shoulders touching under the cover. The boy said he had to go. We both dressed. I wondered if he expected money. I decided not. Outside, we separated at a corner, shaking hands.

Some time later I ran into a boy named Angelo in the same bar. I saw Angelo off and on for two years. When I was on junk I wouldn't meet Angelo for months, but when I got off I always ran into him on the street somewhere. In Mexico your wishes have a dream power. When you want to see someone, he turns up.

Once I had been looking for a boy and I was tired and sat down on a stone bench in the Alameda. I could feel the smooth stone through my pants, and the ache in my loins like a toothache when the pain is light and different from any other pain. Sitting there looking across the park, I suddenly felt calm and happy, seeing myself in a dream relationship with The City, and knew I was going to score for a boy that night. I did.

Angelo's face was Oriental, Japanese-looking, except for his copper skin. He was not queer, and I gave him money; always the same amount, twenty pesos. Sometimes I didn't have that much and he would say: *"No importa."* ("It does not matter.") He insisted on sweeping the apartment out whenever he spent the night there.

Once I connected with Angelo, I did not go back to the Chimu. Mexico or Stateside, queer bars brought me down.

The meaning of *"mañana"* is "Wait until the signs are right." If you are in a hurry to score for junk and go around cracking to strangers, you will get beat for your money and likely have trouble with the law. But if you wait, junk will come to you if you want it.

I had been in Mexico City several months. One day I went to see the law-yer I had hired to get working and residence papers for me. A shabby middle-aged man was standing in front of the office.

"He ain't come yet," the man said. I looked at the man. He was an old-time junky, no doubt about it. And I knew he didn't have any doubts about me either.

We stood around talking until the lawyer came. The junky was there to sell some religious medals. The lawyer had told him to bring a dozen up to his office.

After I had seen the lawyer, I asked the junky if he would join me for sup-per and we went to a restaurant on San Juan Létran.

The junky asked me what my story was and I told him. He flipped back his coat lapel and showed me a spike stuck in the underside of his lapel.

"I've been on junk for twenty-eight years," he said. "Do you want to score?"

There is only one pusher in Mexico City, and that is Lupita. She has been in the business twenty years. Lupita got her start with one gram of junk and built up from there to a monopoly of the junk business in Mexico City. She weighed three hundred pounds, so she started using junk to reduce, but only her face got thin and the result is no improvement. Every month or so she hires a new lover, gives him shirts and suits and wrist watches, and then packs him in when she has enough.

Lupita pays off to operate wide open, as if she was running a grocery store. She doesn't have to worry about stool pigeons because every law in the Fed-eral District knows that Lupita sells junk. She keeps outfits in glasses of alco-hol so the junkies can fix in the joint and walk out clean. Whenever a law needs money for a quick beer, he goes over by Lupita and waits for someone to walk out on the chance he may be holding a paper. For ten pesos ($1.25) the cop lets him go. For twenty pesos, he gets his junk back. Now and then, some ill-advised citizen starts pushing better papers for less money, but he doesn't push long. Lupita has a standing offer: ten free papers to anybody who tells her about another pusher in the Federal District. Then Lupita calls one of her friends on the narcotics squad and the pusher is busted.

Lupita fences on the side. If anyone makes a good score, she puts out a grapevine to find out who was in on the job. Thieves sell to her at her price or she tips the law. Lupita knows everything that happens in the lower-bracket underworld of Mexico City. She sits there doling out papers like an Aztec goddess.

Lupita sells her stuff in papers. It is supposed to be heroin. Actually, it is pantopon cut with milk sugar and some other crap that looks like sand and remains undissolved in the spoon after you cook up.

I started scoring for Lupita's papers through Ike, the old-time junky I met in the lawyer's office. I had been off junk three months at this time. It took me just three days to get back on.

An addict may be ten years off the junk, but he can get a new habit in less than a week; whereas someone who has never been addicted would have to take two shots a day for two months to get any habit at all. I took a shot daily for four months before I could notice withdrawal symptoms. You can list the symptoms of junk sickness, but the feel of it is like no other feeling and you can not put it into words. I did not experience this junk sick feeling until my second habit.

Why does an addict get a new habit so much quicker than a junk virgin, even after the addict has been clean for years? I do not accept the theory that junk is lurking in the body all that time—the spine is where it supposedly holes up—and I disagree with all psychological answers. I think the use of junk causes permanent cellular alteration. Once a junky, always a junky. You can stop using junk, but you are never off after the first habit.

When my wife saw I was getting the habit again, she did something she had never done before. I was cooking up a shot two days after I'd connected with Old Ike. My wife grabbed the spoon and threw the junk on the floor. I slapped her twice across the face and she threw herself on the bed, sobbing, then turned around and said to me: "Don't you want to do anything at all? You know how bored you get when you have a habit. It's like all the lights went out. Oh well, do what you want. I guess you have some stashed, anyway."

I did have some stashed.

Junk short-circuits sex. The drive to non-sexual sociability comes from the same place sex comes from, so when I have an H or M shooting habit I am non-sociable. If someone wants to talk, O.K. But there is no drive to get acquainted. When I come off the junk, I often run through a period of uncontrolled sociability and talk to anyone who will listen.

Junk takes everything and gives nothing but insurance against junk sickness. Every now and then I took a good look at the deal I was giving myself and decided to take the cure. When you are getting plenty of junk, kicking looks easy. You say, "I'm not getting any kick from the shots any more. I might as well quit." But when you cut down into junk sickness, the picture looks different.

During the year or so I was on the junk in Mexico, I started the cure five times. I tried reducing the shots, I tried the Chinese cure, but nothing worked.

After my Chinese fiasco, I made up some papers and gave them to my wife to hide and dole out according to a schedule. I had Ike help me make up the papers, but he had an inaccurate mind, and his schedule was all top-heavy on the beginning and suddenly ended with no reduction. So I made up my own schedule. For a while I stayed with the schedule, but I didn't have any real push. I got stuff from Ike on the side and made excuses for the extra shots.

I knew that I did not want to go on taking junk. If I could have made a single decision, I would have decided no more junk ever. But when it came to the process of quitting, I did not have the drive. It gave me a terrible feeling of helplessness to watch myself break every schedule I set up as though I did not have control over my actions.

One morning in April, I woke up a little sick. I lay there looking at shadows on the white plaster ceiling. I remembered a long time ago when I lay in bed beside my mother, watching lights from the street move across the ceiling and down the walls. I felt the sharp nostalgia of train whistles, piano music down a city street, burning leaves.

A mild degree of junk sickness always brought me the magic of childhood. "It never fails," I thought. "Just like a shot. I wonder if all junkies score for this wonderful stuff."

I went into the bathroom to take a shot. I was a long time hitting a vein. The needle clogged twice. Blood ran down my arm. The junk spread through my body, an injection of death. The dream was gone. I looked down at the blood that ran from elbow to wrist. I felt a sudden pity for the violated veins and tissue. Tenderly I wiped the blood off my arm.

"I'm going to quit," I said aloud.

I made up a solution of hop and told Ike to stay away for a few days. He said, "I hope you make it, kid. I hope you get off. May I fall down and be paralyzed if I don't mean it."

In forty-eight hours the backlog of morphine in my body ran out. The solution barely cut the sickness. I drank it all with two nembutals and slept several hours. When I woke up, my clothes were soaked through with sweat. My eyes were watering and smarting. My whole body felt itchy and irritable. I twisted about on the bed, arching my back and stretching my arms and legs. I drew my knees up, my hands clasped between the thighs. The pressure of my hands set off the hair-trigger orgasm of junk sickness. I got up and changed my underwear.

There was a little hop left in the bottle. I drank that, went out and bought four tubes of codeine tablets. I took the codeine with hot tea and felt better.

Ike told me, "You're taking it too fast. Let me mix up a solution for you."
I could hear him out in the kitchen crooning over the mixture: "A little cinnamon in case he starts to puke . . . a little sage for the shits . . . some cloves to
clean the blood . . ."

I never tasted anything so awful, but the mixture leveled off my sickness at
a bearable point, so I felt a little high all the time. I wasn't high on the hop; I
was high on withdrawal tone-up. Junk is an inoculation of death that keeps
the body in a condition of emergency. When the junky is cut off, emergency
reactions continue. Sensations sharpen, the addict is aware of his visceral processes to an uncomfortable degree, peristalsis and secretion go unchecked. No
matter what his actual age, the kicking addict is liable to the emotional excesses of a child or an adolescent.

About the third day of using Ike's mixture, I started drinking. I had never
been able to drink before when I was on the junk, or junk sick. But eating hop
is different from shooting the white stuff. You can mix hop and lush.

At first I started drinking at five in the afternoon. After a week, I started
drinking at eight in the morning, stayed drunk all day and all night, and woke
up drunk the next morning.

Every morning when I woke up, I washed down benzedrine, sanicin, and a
piece of hop with black coffee and a shot of tequila. Then I lay back and closed
my eyes and tried to piece together the night before and yesterday. Often, I
drew a blank from noon on. You sometimes wake up from a dream and think,
"Thank God, I didn't really do that!" Reconstructing a period of blackout
you think, "My God, did I really do it?" The line between saying and thinking
is blurred. Did you say it or just think it?

After ten days of the cure I had deteriorated shockingly. My clothes were
spotted and stiff from the drinks I had spilled all over myself. I never bathed.
I had lost weight, my hands shook, I was always spilling things, knocking
over chairs, and falling down. But I seemed to have unlimited energy and a
capacity for liquor I never had before. My emotions spilled out everywhere.
I was uncontrollably sociable and would talk to anybody I could pin down. I
forced distastefully intimate confidences on perfect strangers. Several times
I made the crudest sexual propositions to people who had given no hint of
reciprocity.

Ike was around every few days. "I'm glad to see you getting off, Bill. May
I fall down and be paralyzed if I don't mean it. But if you get too sick and
start to puke—here's five centogramos of M."

Ike took a severe view of my drinking. "You're drinking, Bill. You're drinking and getting crazy. You look terrible. You look terrible in your face. Better
you should go back to stuff than drink like this."

When I jumped bail and left the States, the heat on junk already looked like
something new and special. Initial symptoms of nationwide hysteria were clear.
Louisiana passed a law making it a crime to be a drug addict. Since no place

or time is specified and the term "addict" is not clearly defined, no proof is necessary or even relevant under a law so formulated. No proof, and consequently, no trial. This is police-state legislation penalizing a state of being. Other states were emulating Louisiana. I saw my chance of escaping conviction dwindle daily as the anti-junk feeling mounted to a paranoid obsession, like anti-Semitism under the Nazis. So I decided to jump bail and live permanently outside the United States.

Safe in Mexico, I watched the anti-junk campaign. I read about child addicts and Senators demanding the death penalty for dope peddlers. It didn't sound right to me. Who wants kids for customers? They never have enough money and they always spill under questioning. Parents find out the kid is on junk and go to the law. I figured that either Stateside peddlers have gone simpleminded or the whole child-addict setup is a routine to stir up anti-junk sentiment and pass some new laws.

Refugee hipsters trickled down into Mexico. "Six months for needle marks under the vag-addict law in California." "Eight years for a dropper in Washington." "Two to ten for selling in New York." A group of young hipsters dropped by my place every day to smoke weed.

There was Cash, a musician who played trumpet. There was Pete, a heavy-set blond, who could have modeled for a clean-cut American Boy poster. There was Johnny White, who had a wife and three children and looked like any average young American. There was Martin, a dark, good-looking kid of Italian stock. No zoot-suiters. The hipster has gone underground.

Bill Gains threw in the towel and moved to Mexico. I met him at the airport. He was loaded on H and goofballs. His pants were spotted with blood where he had been fixing on the plane with a safety pin. You make a hole with the pin, and put the dropper over (not in) the hole, and the solution goes right in. With this method, you don't need a needle, but it takes an old-time junky to make it work. You have to use exactly the right degree of pressure feeding in the solution. I tried it once and the junk squirted out to the side and I lost it all. But when Gains made a hole in his flesh, the hole stayed open waiting for junk.

Bill was an old-timer. He knew everybody in the business. He had an excellent reputation and he could score as long as anyone sold junk. I figured the situation must be desperate when Bill packed in and left the States.

"Sure, I can score," he told me. "But if I stay in the States I'll wind up doing about ten years."

I took a shot with him, and the what-happened-to-so-and-so routine set in.

"Old Bart died on the Island. Louie the Bell Hop went wrong. Tony and Nick went wrong. Herman didn't make parole. The Gimp got five to ten. Marvin the waiter died from an overdose."

I remembered the way Marvin used to pass out every time he took a shot. I could see him lying on the bed in some cheap hotel, the dropper full of blood hanging to his vein like a glass leech, his face turning blue around the lips.

"What about Roy?" I asked.

"Didn't you hear about him? He went wrong and hanged himself in the Tombs." It seems the law had Roy on three counts, two larceny, one narcotics. They promised to drop all charges if Roy would set up Eddie Crump, an old-time pusher. Eddie only served people he knew well, and he knew Roy. The law double-crossed Roy after they got Eddie. They dropped the narcotics charge, but not the two larceny charges. So Roy was slated to follow Eddie up to Riker's Island, where Eddie was doing pen indefinite, which is maximum in City Prison. Three years, five months, and six days. Roy hanged himself in the Tombs, where he was awaiting transfer to Riker's.

Roy had always taken an intolerant and puritanical view of pigeons. "I don't see how a pigeon can live with himself," he said to me once.

I asked Bill about child addicts. He nodded and smiled, a sly, gloating smile. "Yes, Lexington is full of young kids now."

At this time, I was not on junk, but I was a long way from being clean in the event of an unforeseen shake. There was always some weed around, and people were using my place as a shooting gallery. I was taking chances and not making one centavo. I decided it was about time to move out from under and head south.

When you give up junk, you give up a way of life. I have seen junkies kick and hit the lush and wind up dead in a few years. Suicide is frequent among ex-junkies. Why does a junky quit junk of his own will? You never know the answer to that question. No conscious tabulation of the disadvantages and horrors of junk gives you the emotional drive to kick. The decision to quit junk is a cellular decision, and once you have decided to quit you cannot go back to junk permanently any more than you could stay away from it before. Like a man who has been away a long time, you see things different when you return from junk.

I read about a drug called *yagé*, used by Indians in the headwaters of the Amazon. *Yagé* is supposed to increase telepathic sensitivity. A Colombian scientist isolated from *yagé* a drug he called *telepathine*.

I know from my own experience that telepathy is a fact. I have no interest in proving telepathy or anything to anybody. I do want usable knowledge of telepathy. What I look for in any relationship is contact on the nonverbal level of intuition and feeling, that is, telepathic contact.

Apparently, I am not the only one interested in *yagé*. The Russians are using this drug in experiments on slave labor. They want to induce states of automatic obedience and literal thought control. The basic con. No build-up, no routine, just move in on someone's psyche and give orders. The deal is certain to backfire because telepathy is not in itself a one-way setup, or a setup of sender and receiver at all.

I decided to go down to Colombia and score for *yagé*. Bill Gains is squared away with Old Ike. My wife and I are separated. I am ready to move on south and look for the uncut kick that opens out instead of narrowing down like junk.

Kick is seeing things from a special angle. Kick is momentary freedom from the claims of the aging, cautious, nagging, frightened flesh. Maybe I will find in *yagé* what I was looking for in junk and weed and coke. *Yagé* may be the final fix.

from
queer
(SELECTIONS)

Lee turned down Coahuila, walking with one foot falling directly in front of the other, always fast and purposeful, as if he were leaving the scene of a holdup. He passed a group in expatriate uniform: red-checked shirt outside the belt, blue jeans and beard, and another group of young men in conventional, if shabby, clothes. Among these Lee recognized a boy named Eugene Allerton. Allerton was tall and very thin, with high cheekbones, a small, bright-red mouth, and amber-colored eyes that took on a faint violet flush when he was drunk. His gold-brown hair was differentially bleached by the sun like a sloppy dyeing job. He had straight, black eyebrows and black eyelashes. An equivocal face, very young, clean-cut and boyish, at the same time conveying an impression of makeup, delicate and exotic and Oriental. Allerton was never completely neat or clean, but you did not think of him as being dirty. He was simply careless and lazy to the point of appearing, at times, only half awake. Often he did not hear what someone said a foot from his ear. "Pellagra, I expect," thought Lee sourly. He nodded to Allerton and smiled. Allerton nodded, as if surprised, and did not smile.

Lee walked on, a little depressed. "Perhaps I can accomplish something in that direction. Well, *a ver*. . . ."

The Ship Ahoy had a few phony hurricane lamps by way of a nautical atmosphere. Two small rooms with tables, the bar in one room, and four high, precarious stools. The place was always dimly lit and sinister-looking. The patrons were tolerant, but in no way bohemian. The bearded set never frequented the Ship Ahoy. The place existed on borrowed time, without a liquor license, under many changes of management. At this time it was run by an American named Tom Weston and an American-born Mexican.

Lee walked directly to the bar and ordered a drink. He drank it and ordered a second one before looking around the room to see if Allerton was there. Allerton was alone at a table, tipped back in a chair with one leg crossed over the other, holding a bottle of beer on his knee. He nodded to Lee. Lee tried to achieve a greeting at once friendly and casual, designed to show interest without pushing their short acquaintance. The result was ghastly.

As Lee stood aside to bow in his dignified old-world greeting, there emerged instead a leer of naked lust, wrenched in the pain and hate of his deprived body and, in simultaneous double exposure, a sweet child's smile of liking and trust, shockingly out of time and out of place, mutilated and hopeless.

Allerton was appalled. "Perhaps he has some sort of tic," he thought. He decided to remove himself from contact with Lee before the man did something even more distasteful. The effect was like a broken connection. Allerton was not cold or hostile; Lee simply wasn't there as far as he was concerned. Lee looked at him helplessly for a moment, then turned back to the bar, defeated and shaken.

Lee finished his second drink. When he looked around again, Allerton was playing chess with Mary, an American girl with dyed red hair and carefully applied makeup, who had come into the bar in the meantime. "Why waste time here?" Lee thought. He paid for the two drinks and walked out.

He took a cab to the Chimu Bar, which was a fag bar frequented by Mexicans, and spent the night with a young boy he met there.

Lee left his apartment for the Ship Ahoy just before five. Allerton was sitting at the bar. Lee sat down and ordered a drink, then turned to Allerton with a casual greeting, as though they were on familiar and friendly terms. Allerton returned the greeting automatically before he realized that Lee had somehow established himself on a familiar basis, whereas he had previously decided to have as little to do with Lee as possible. Allerton had a talent for ignoring people, but he was not competent at dislodging someone from a position already occupied.

Lee began talking—casual, unpretentiously intelligent, dryly humorous. Slowly he dispelled Allerton's impression that he was a peculiar and undesirable character. When Mary arrived, Lee greeted her with a tipsy old-world gallantry and, excusing himself, left them to a game of chess.

"Who is he?" asked Mary when Lee had gone outside.

"I have no idea," said Allerton. Had he ever met Lee? He could not be sure. Formal introductions were not expected among the G.I. students. Was Lee a student? Allerton had never seen him at the school. There was nothing unusual in talking to someone you didn't know, but Lee put Allerton on guard. The man was somehow familiar to him. When Lee talked, he seemed to mean more than what he said. A special emphasis to a word or a greeting hinted at a period of familiarity in some other time and place. As though Lee were saying, "*You* know what I mean. *You* remember."

Allerton shrugged irritably and began arranging the chess pieces on the board. He looked like a sullen child unable to locate the source of his ill temper. After a few minutes of play his customary serenity returned, and he began humming.

After that, Lee met Allerton every day at five in the Ship Ahoy. Allerton was accustomed to choose his friends from people older than himself, and he looked forward to meeting Lee. Lee had conversational routines that Allerton had never heard. But he felt at times oppressed by Lee, as though Lee's presence shut off everything else. He thought he was seeing too much of Lee.

Allerton disliked commitments, and had never been in love or had a close friend. He was now forced to ask himself: "What does he want from me?" It did not occur to him that Lee was queer, as he associated queerness with at least some degree of overt effeminacy. He decided finally that Lee valued him as an audience.

It was a beautiful, clear afternoon in April. Punctually at five, Lee walked into the Ship Ahoy. Allerton was at the bar with Al Hyman, a periodic alcoholic and one of the nastiest, stupidest, dullest drunks Lee had ever known. He was, on the other hand, intelligent and simple in manner, and nice enough when sober. He was sober now.

Lee had a yellow scarf around his neck, and a pair of two-peso sunglasses. He took off the scarf and dark glasses and dropped them on the bar. "A hard day at the studio," he said, in affected theatrical accents. He ordered a rum Coke. "You know, it looks like we might bring in an oil well. They're drilling now over in quadrangle four, and from that rig you could almost spit over into Tex-Mex where I got my hundred-acre cotton farm."

"I always wanted to be an oilman," Hyman said.

Lee looked him over and shook his head. "I'm afraid not. You see, it isn't everybody can qualify. You must have the calling. First thing, you must look like an oilman. There are no young oilmen. An oilman should be about fifty. His skin is cracked and wrinkled like mud that has dried in the sun, and especially the back of his neck is wrinkled, and the wrinkles are generally full of dust from looking over blocks and quadrangles. He wears gabardine slacks and a white short-sleeved sport shirt. His shoes are covered with fine dust, and a faint haze of dust follows him everywhere like a personal dust storm.

"So you got the calling and the proper appearance. You go around taking up leases. You get five or six people lined up to lease you their land for drilling. You go to the bank and talk to the president: 'Now Clem Farris, as fine a man as there is in this Valley and smart too, he's in this thing up to his balls, and Old Man Scranton and Fred Crockly and Roy Spigot and Ted Bane, all of them good old boys. Now let me show you a few facts. I could set here and gas all morning, taking up your time, but I know you're a man accustomed to deal in facts and figures and that's exactly what I'm here to show you.'

"He goes out to his car, always a coupe or a roadster—never saw an oilman with a sedan—and reaches in back of the seat and gets out his maps, a huge bundle of maps as big as carpets. He spreads them out on the bank president's desk, and great clouds of dust spring up from the maps and fill the bank.

"'You see this quadrangle here? That's Tex-Mex. Now there's a fault runs right along here through Jed Marvin's place. I saw Old Jed too, the other day when I was out there, a good old boy. There isn't a finer man in this Valley than Jed Marvin. Well now, Socony drilled right over here.'

"He spreads out more maps. He pulls over another desk and anchors the maps down with cuspidors. 'Well, they brought in a dry hole, and this map. . . .' He unrolls another one. 'Now if you'll kindly sit on the other end so it don't roll up on us, I'll show you exactly why it was a dry hole and why they should never have drilled there in the first place, 'cause you can see just where this here fault runs smack between Jed's artesian well and the Tex-Mex line over into quadrangle four. Now that block was surveyed last time in 1922. I guess you know the old boy done the job. Earl Hoot was his name, a good old boy too. He had his home up in Nacogdoches, but his son-in-law owned a place down here, the old Brooks place up north of Tex-Mex, just across the line from. . . .'

"By this time the president is punchy with boredom, and the dust is getting down in his lungs—oilmen are constitutionally immune to the effects of dust—so he says, 'Well, if it's good enough for those boys I guess it's good enough for me. I'll go along.'

"So the oilman goes back and pulls the same routine on his prospects. Then he gets a geologist down from Dallas or somewhere, who talks some gibberish about faults and seepage and intrusions and shale and sand, and selects some place, more or less at random, to start drilling.

"Now the driller. He has to be a real rip-snorting character. They look for him in Boy's Town—the whore district in border towns—and they find him in a room full of empty bottles with three whores. So they bust a bottle over his head and drag him out and sober him up, and he looks at the drilling site and spits and says, 'Well, it's your hole.'

"Now if the well turns out dry the oilman says, 'Well, that's the way it goes. Some holes got lubrication, and some is dry as a whore's cunt on Sunday morning.' There was one oilman, Dry Hole Dutton they called him—all right, Allerton, no cracks about Vaseline—brought in twenty dry holes before he got cured. That means 'get rich,' in the salty lingo of the oil fraternity."

Joe Guidry came in, and Lee slid off his stool to shake hands. He was hoping Joe would bring up the subject of queerness so he could gauge Allerton's reaction. He figured it was time to let Allerton know what the score was—such a thing as playing it too cool.

They sat down at a table. Somebody had stolen Guidry's radio, his riding boots and wrist watch. "The trouble with me is," said Guidry, "I like the type that robs me."

"Where you make your mistake is bringing them to your apartment," Lee said. "That's what hotels are for."

"You're right there. But half the time I don't have money for a hotel. Besides, I like someone around to cook breakfast and sweep the place out."

"*Clean* the place out."

"I don't mind the watch and the radio, but it really hurt, losing those boots. They were a thing of beauty and a joy forever." Guidry leaned forward, and glanced at Allerton. "I don't know whether I ought to say things like this in front of Junior here. No offense, kid."

"Go ahead," said Allerton.

"Did I tell you how I made the cop on the beat? He's the *vigilante*, the watchman out where I live. Every time he sees the light on in my room, he comes in for a shot of rum. Well, about five nights ago he caught me when I was drunk and horny, and one thing led to another and I ended up showing him how the cow ate the cabbage . . .

"So the night after I make him I was walking by the beer joint on the corner and he comes out *borracho* and says, 'Have a drink.' I said, 'I don't want a drink.' So he takes out his *pistola* and says, 'Have a drink.' I proceeded to take his *pistola* away from him, and he goes into the beer joint to phone for reinforcements. So I had to go in and rip the phone off the wall. Now they're billing me for the phone. When I got back to my room, which is on the ground floor, he had written '*El Puto Gringo*' on the window with soap. So, instead of wiping it off, I left it there. It pays to advertise."

The drinks kept coming. Allerton went to the W.C. and got in a conversation at the bar when he returned. Guidry was accusing Hyman of being queer and pretending not to be. Lee was trying to explain to Guidry that Hyman wasn't really queer, and Guidry said to him, "He's queer and you aren't, Lee. You just go around pretending you're queer to get in on the act."

"Who wants to get in on your tired old act?" Lee said. He saw Allerton at the bar talking to John Dumé. Dumé belonged to a small clique of queers who made their headquarters in a beer joint on Campeche called The Green Lantern. Dumé himself was not an obvious queer, but the other Green Lantern boys were screaming fags who would not have been welcome at the Ship Ahoy.

Lee walked over to the bar and started talking to the bartender. He thought, "I hope Dumé tells him about me." Lee felt uncomfortable in dramatic "something-I-have-to-tell-you" routines and he knew, from unnerving experience, the difficulties of a casual come-on: "I'm queer, you know, by the way." Sometimes they don't hear right and yell, "What?" Or you toss in: "If you were as queer as I am." The other yawns and changes the subject, and you don't know whether he understood or not.

The bartender was saying, "She asks me why I drink. What can I tell her? I don't know why. Why did you have the monkey on your back? Do you know why? There isn't any why, but try to explain that to someone like Jerri. Try to explain that to any woman." Lee nodded sympathetically. "She says to me, why don't you get more sleep and eat better? She don't understand and I can't explain it. Nobody can explain it."

The bartender moved away to wait on some customers. Dumé came over to Lee. "How do you like this character?" he said, indicating Allerton with a wave of his beer bottle. Allerton was across the room talking to Mary and a chess player from Peru. "He comes to me and says, 'I thought you were one of the Green Lantern boys.' So I said, 'Well, I am.' He wants me to take him around to some of the gay places here."

* * *

Lee and Allerton went to a Russian restaurant for dinner. Lee looked through the menu. "By the way," he said, "the law was in putting the bite on the Ship Ahoy again. Vice squad. Two hundred pesos. I can see them in the station house after a hard day shaking down citizens of the Federal District. One cop says, 'Ah, Gonzalez, you should see what I got today. Oh la la, such a bite!'

"'Aah, you shook down a *puto* queer for two *pesetas* in a bus station crapper. We know you, Hernandez, and your cheap tricks. You're the cheapest cop inna Federal District.'"

Lee waved to the waiter. "Hey, Jack. *Dos* martinis, much dry. *Seco*. And *dos* plates Sheeshka Babe. *Sabe?*"

The waiter nodded. "That's two dry martinis and two orders of shish kebab. Right, gentlemen?"

"Solid, Pops. . . . So how was your evening with Dumé?"

"We went to several bars full of queers. One place a character asked me to dance and propositioned me."

"Take him up?"

"No."

"Dumé is a nice fellow."

Allerton smiled. "Yes, but he is not a person I would confide too much in. That is, anything I wanted to keep private."

"You refer to a specific indiscretion?"

"Frankly, yes."

"I see." Lee thought, *Dumé never misses.*

The waiter put two martinis on the table. Lee held his martini up to the candle, looking at it with distaste. "The inevitable watery martini with a decomposing olive," he said.

Lee bought a lottery ticket from a boy of ten or so, who had rushed in when the waiter went to the kitchen. The boy was working the last-ticket routine. Lee paid him expansively, like a drunk American. "Go buy yourself some marijuana, son," he said. The boy smiled and turned to leave. "Come back in five years and make an easy ten pesos," Lee called after him.

Allerton smiled. *Thank god*, Lee thought. *I won't have to contend with middle-class morality.*

"Here you are, sir," said the waiter, placing the shish kebab on the table.

Lee ordered two glasses of red wine. "So Dumé told you about my, uh, proclivities?" he said abruptly.

"Yes," said Allerton, his mouth full.

"A curse. Been in our family for generations. The Lees have always been perverts. I shall never forget the unspeakable horror that froze the lymph in my glands—the lymph glands that is, of course—when the baneful word seared my reeling brain: **I was a homosexual.** I thought of the painted, simpering female impersonators I had seen in a Baltimore night club. Could it be possible that I was one of those subhuman beings? I walked the streets in a daze, like a man with a slight concussion—just a minute, Doctor Kildare, this isn't your script. I might well have destroyed myself, ending an existence which seemed to offer nothing but grotesque misery and humiliation. Nobler, I thought, to die a man than live on, a sex monster. It was a wise old queen—Bobo, we called her—who taught me that I had a duty to live and to bear my burden proudly for all to see, to conquer prejudice and ignorance and hate with knowledge and sincerity and love. Whenever you are threatened by a hostile presence, you emit a thick cloud of love like an octopus squirts out ink . . .

"Poor Bobo came to a sticky end. He was riding in the Duc de Ventre's Hispano-Suiza when his falling piles blew out of the car and wrapped around the rear wheel. He was completely gutted, leaving an empty shell sitting there on the giraffe-skin upholstery. Even the eyes and the brain went, with a horrible shlupping sound. The Duc says he will carry that ghastly shlup with him to his mausoleum . . .

"Then I knew the meaning of loneliness. But Bobo's words came back to me from the tomb, the sibilants cracking gently. 'No one is ever really alone. You are part of everything alive.' The difficulty is to convince someone else he is really part of you, so what the hell? Us parts ought to work together. Reet?"

Lee paused, looking at Allerton speculatively. *Just where do I stand with the kid?* he wondered. He had listened politely, smiling at intervals. "What I mean is, Allerton, we are all parts of a tremendous whole. No use fighting it." Lee was getting tired of the routine. He looked around restlessly for some place to put it down. "Don't these gay bars depress you? Of course, the queer bars here aren't to compare with Stateside queer joints."

"I wouldn't know," said Allerton. "I've never been in any queer joints except those Dumé took me to. I guess there's kicks and kicks."

"You haven't, really?"

"No, never."

Lee paid the bill and they walked out into the cool night. A crescent moon was clear and green in the sky. They walked aimlessly.

"Shall we go to my place for a drink? I have some Napoleon brandy."

"All right," said Allerton.

"This is a completely unpretentious little brandy, you understand, none of this tourist treacle with obvious effects of flavoring, appealing to the mass tongue. My brandy has no need of shoddy devices to shock and coerce the palate. Come along." Lee hailed a cab.

"Three pesos to Insurgentes and Monterrey," Lee said to the driver in his atrocious Spanish. The driver said four. Lee waved him on. The driver muttered something, and opened the door.

Inside, Lee turned to Allerton. "The man plainly harbors subversive thoughts. You know, when I was at Princeton, Communism was the thing. To come out flat for private property and a class society, you marked yourself a stupid lout or suspect to be a High Episcopalian pederast. But I held out against the infection—of Communism I mean, of course."

"*Aquí.*" Lee handed three pesos to the driver, who muttered some more and started the car with a vicious clash of gears.

"Sometimes I think they don't like us," said Allerton.

"I don't mind people disliking me," Lee said. "The question is, what are they in a position to do about it? Apparently nothing, at present. They don't have the green light. This driver, for example, hates gringos. But if he kills someone—and very possibly he will—it will not be an American. It will be another Mexican. Maybe his good friend. Friends are less frightening than strangers."

Lee opened the door of his apartment and turned on the light. The apartment was pervaded by seemingly hopeless disorder. Here and there, ineffectual attempts had been made to arrange things in piles. There were no lived-in touches. No pictures, no decorations. Clearly, none of the furniture was his. But Lee's presence permeated the apartment. A coat over the back of a chair and a hat on the table were immediately recognizable as belonging to Lee.

"I'll fix you a drink." Lee got two water glasses from the kitchen and poured two inches of Mexican brandy in each glass.

Allerton tasted the brandy. "Good Lord," he said. "Napoleon must have pissed in this one."

"I was afraid of that. An untutored palate. Your generation has never learned the pleasures that a trained palate confers on the disciplined few."

Lee took a long drink of the brandy. He attempted an ecstatic "aah," inhaled some of the brandy, and began to cough. "It *is* god-awful," he said when he could talk. "Still, better than California brandy. It has a suggestion of cognac taste."

There was a long silence. Allerton was sitting with his head leaning back against the couch. His eyes were half closed.

"Can I show you over the house?" said Lee, standing up. "In here we have the bedroom."

Allerton got to his feet slowly. They went into the bedroom, and Allerton lay down on the bed and lit a cigarette. Lee sat in the only chair.

"More brandy?" Lee asked. Allerton nodded. Lee sat down on the edge of the bed, and filled his glass and handed it to him. Lee touched his sweater. "Sweet stuff, dearie," he said. "That wasn't made in Mexico."

"I bought it in Scotland," he said. He began to hiccough violently, and got up and rushed for the bathroom.

Lee stood in the doorway. "Too bad," he said. "What could be the matter? You didn't drink much." He filled a glass with water and handed it to Allerton. "You all right now?" he asked.

"Yes, I think so." Allerton lay down on the bed again.

Lee reached out a hand and touched Allerton's ear, and caressed the side of his face. Allerton reached up and covered one of Lee's hands and squeezed it.

"Let's get this sweater off."

"O.K.," said Allerton. He took off the sweater and then lay down again. Lee took off his own shoes and shirt. He opened Allerton's shirt and ran his hand down Allerton's ribs and stomach, which contracted beneath his fingers. "God, you're skinny," he said.

"I'm pretty small."

Lee took off Allerton's shoes and socks. He loosened Allerton's belt and unbuttoned his trousers. Allerton arched his body, and Lee pulled the trousers and drawers off. He dropped his own trousers and shorts and lay down beside him. Allerton responded without hostility or disgust, but in his eyes Lee saw a curious detachment, the impersonal calm of an animal or a child.

Later, when they lay side by side smoking, Lee said, "Oh, by the way, you said you had a camera in pawn you were about to lose?" It occurred to Lee that to bring the matter up at this time was not tactful, but he decided the other was not the type to take offense.

"Yes. In for four hundred pesos. The ticket runs out next Wednesday."

"Well, let's go down tomorrow and get it out."

Allerton raised one bare shoulder off the sheet. "O.K.," he said.

Thursday Lee went to the races, on the recommendation of Tom Weston. Weston was an amateur astrologer, and he assured Lee the signs were right. Lee lost five races, and took a taxi back to the Ship Ahoy.

Mary and Allerton were sitting at a table with the Peruvian chess player. Allerton asked Lee to come over and sit down at the table.

"Where's that phony whore caster?" Lee said, looking around.

"Tom give you a bum steer?" asked Allerton.

"He did that."

Mary left with the Peruvian. Lee finished his third drink and turned to Allerton. "I figure to go down to South America soon," he said. "Why don't you come along? Won't cost you a cent."

"Perhaps not in money."

"I'm not a difficult man to get along with. We could reach a satisfactory arrangement. What you got to lose?"

"Independence."

"So who's going to cut in on your independence? You can lay all the women in South America if you want to. All I ask is be nice to Papa, say twice a week. That isn't excessive, is it? Besides, I will buy you a round-trip ticket so you can leave at your discretion."

Allerton shrugged. "I'll think it over," he said. "This job runs ten days more. I'll give you a definite answer when the job folds."

"Your job. . . ." Lee was about to say, "I'll give you ten days' salary." He said, "All right."

Allerton's newspaper job was temporary, and he was too lazy to hold a job in any case. Consequently his answer meant "No." Lee figured to talk him over in ten days. "Better not force the issue now," he thought.

* * *

They left by bus a few days later, and by the time they reached Panama City, Allerton was already complaining that Lee was too demanding in his desires. Otherwise, they got on very well. Now that Lee could spend days and nights with the object of his attentions, he felt relieved of the gnawing emptiness and fear. And Allerton was a good traveling companion, sensible and calm.

From Manta they flew on to Guayaquil. The road was flooded, so the only way to get there was by plane or boat.

Guayaquil is built along a river, a city with many parks and squares and statues. The parks are full of tropical trees and shrubs and vines. A tree that fans out like an umbrella, as wide as it is tall, shades the stone benches. The people do a great deal of sitting.

The city, like all Ecuador, produced a curiously baffling impression. Lee felt there was something going on here, some undercurrent of life that was hidden from him. This was the area of the ancient Chimu pottery, where salt shakers and water pitchers were nameless obscenities: two men on all fours engaged in sodomy formed the handle for the top of a kitchen pot.

What happens when there is no limit? What is the fate of The Land Where Anything Goes? Men changing into huge centipedes . . . centipedes besieging the houses . . . a man tied to a couch and a centipede ten feet long rearing up over him. Is this literal? Did some hideous metamorphosis occur? What is the meaning of the centipede symbol?

Lee got on a bus and rode to the end of the line. He took another bus. He rode out to the river and drank a soda, and watched some boys swimming in the dirty river. The river looked as if nameless monsters might rise from the green-brown water. Lee saw a lizard two feet long run up the opposite bank.

He walked back towards town. He passed a group of boys on a corner. One of the boys was so beautiful that the image cut Lee's senses like a wire whip. A slight involuntary sound of pain escaped from Lee's lips. He turned around, as though looking at the street name. The boy was laughing at some joke, a high-pitched laugh, happy and gay. Lee walked on.

Six or seven boys, aged twelve to fourteen, were playing in a heap of rubbish on the waterfront. One of the boys was urinating against a post and smiling at the other boys. The boys noticed Lee. Now their play was overtly sexual, with an undercurrent of mockery. They looked at Lee and whispered and laughed. Lee looked at them openly, a cold, hard stare of naked lust. He felt the tearing ache of limitless desire.

He focused on one boy, the image sharp and clear, as if seen through a telescope with the other boys and the waterfront blacked out. The boy vibrated with life like a young animal. A wide grin showed sharp, white teeth. Under the torn shirt Lee glimpsed the thin body.

He could feel himself in the body of the boy. Fragmentary memories . . . the smell of cocoa beans drying in the sun, bamboo tenements, the warm dirty river, the swamps and rubbish heaps on the outskirts of the town. He was with the other boys, sitting on the stone floor of a deserted house. The roof was gone. The stone walls were falling down. Weeds and vines grew over the walls and stretched across the floor.

The boys were taking down their torn pants. Lee lifted his thin buttocks to slip down his pants. He could feel the stone floor. He had his pants down to his ankles. His knees were clasped together, and the other boys were trying to pull them apart. He gave in, and they held his knees open. He looked at them and smiled, and slipped his hand down over his stomach. Another boy who was standing up dropped his pants and stood there with his hands on his hips, looking down at his erect organ.

A boy sat down by Lee and reached over between his legs. Lee felt the orgasm blackout in the hot sun. He stretched out and threw his arm over his eyes. Another boy rested his head on his stomach. Lee could feel the warmth of the other's head, itching a little where the hair touched Lee's stomach.

Now he was in a bamboo tenement. An oil lamp lit a woman's body. Lee could feel desire for the woman through the other's body. "I'm not queer," he thought. "I'm disembodied."

Lee walked on, thinking, "What can I do? Take them back to my hotel? They are willing enough. For a few Sucres. . . ." He felt a killing hate for the stupid, ordinary, disapproving people who kept him from doing what he wanted to do. "Someday I am going to have things just like I want," he said to himself. "And if any moralizing son of a bitch gives me any static, they will fish him out of the river."

Lee's plan involved a river. He lived on the river and ran things to please himself. He grew his own weed and poppies and cocaine, and he had a young native boy for an all-purpose servant. Boats were moored in the dirty river. Great masses of water hyacinths floated by. The river was a good half-mile across.

Lee walked up to a little park. There was a statue of Bolívar, "The Liberating Fool" as Lee called him, shaking hands with someone else. Both of them looked tired and disgusted and rocking queer, so queer it rocked you. Lee stood looking at the statue. Then he sat down on a stone bench facing the river. Everyone looked at Lee when he sat down. Lee looked back. He did not have the American reluctance to meet the gaze of a stranger. The others looked away, and lit cigarettes and resumed their conversations.

Lee sat there looking at the dirty yellow river. He couldn't see half an inch under the surface. From time to time, small fish jumped ahead of a boat. There were trim, expensive sailing boats from the yacht club, with hollow masts and beautiful lines. There were dugout canoes with outboard motors and cabins of split bamboo. Two old rusty battleships were moored in the middle of the river—the Ecuadoran Navy. Lee sat there a full hour, then got up and walked back to the hotel. It was three o'clock. Allerton was still in bed. Lee sat down on the edge of the bed.

"It's three o'clock, Gene. Time to get up."

"What for?"

"You want to spend your life in bed? Come on out and dig the town with me. I saw some beautiful boys on the waterfront. The real uncut boy stuff. Such teeth, such smiles. Young boys vibrating with life."

"All right. Stop drooling."

"What have they got that I want, Gene? Do you know?"

"No."

"They have maleness, of course. So have I. I want myself the same way I want others. I'm disembodied. I can't use my own body for some reason." He put out his hand. Allerton dodged away.

"What's the matter?"

"I thought you were going to run your hand down my ribs."

"I wouldn't do that. Think I'm queer or something?"

"Frankly, yes."

"You do have nice ribs. Show me the broken one. Is that it there?" Lee ran his hand halfway down Allerton's ribs. "Or is it further down?"

"Oh, go away."

"But, Gene . . . I am due, you know."

"Yes, I suppose you are."

"Of course, if you'd rather wait until tonight. These tropical nights are so romantic. That way we could take twelve hours or so and do the thing right." Lee ran his hands down over Allerton's stomach. He could see that Allerton was a little excited.

Allerton said, "Maybe it would be better now. You know I like to sleep alone."

"Yes, I know. Too bad. If I had my way we'd sleep every night all wrapped around each other like hibernating rattlesnakes."

Lee was taking off his clothes. He lay down beside Allerton. "Wouldn't it be booful if we should juth run together into one gweat big blob," he said in baby talk. "Am I giving you the horrors?"

"Indeed you are."

Allerton surprised Lee by an unusual intensity of response. At the climax he squeezed Lee hard around the ribs. He sighed deeply and closed his eyes.

Lee smoothed his eyebrows with his thumbs. "Do you mind that?" he asked.

"Not terribly."

"But you do enjoy it sometimes? The whole deal, I mean."

"Oh, yes."

Lee lay on his back with one cheek against Allerton's shoulder, and went to sleep.

Lee went to Quito to get information on the *yagé*. Allerton stayed in Salinas. Lee was back five days later.

"*Yagé* is also known to the Indians as *ayahuasca*. Scientific name is *Bannisteria caapi*." Lee spread a map out on the bed. "It grows in high jungle on the Amazon side of the Andes. We will go on to Puyo. That is the end of the road. We should be able to locate someone there who can deal with the Indians, and get the *yagé*."

They took a river boat to Babahoya. Swinging in hammocks, sipping brandy, and watching the jungle slide by. Springs, moss, beautiful clear streams and trees up to two hundred feet high. Lee and Allerton were silent as the boat powered upriver, penetrating the jungle stillness with its lawnmower whine.

From Babahoya they took a bus over the Andes to Ambato, a cold, jolting fourteen-hour ride. They stopped for a snack of chick-peas at a hut at the top of the mountain pass, far above the tree line. A few young native men in gray felt hats ate their chick-peas in sullen resignation. Several guinea pigs were squeaking and scurrying around on the dirt floor of the hut. Their cries reminded Lee of the guinea pig he owned as a child in the Fairmont Hotel in St. Louis, when the family was waiting to move into their new house on Price Road. He remembered the way the pig shrieked, and the stink of its cage.

They passed the snow-covered peak of Chimborazo, cold in the moonlight and the constant wind of the high Andes. The view from the high mountain pass seemed from another, larger planet than Earth. Lee and Allerton huddled together under a blanket, drinking brandy, the smell of wood smoke in their nostrils. They were both wearing Army-surplus jackets, zipped up over sweatshirts to keep out the cold and wind. Allerton seemed insubstantial as a phantom; Lee could almost see through him, to the empty phantom bus outside.

From Ambato to Puyo, along the edge of a gorge a thousand feet deep. There were waterfalls and forests and streams running down over the roadway, as they descended into the lush green valley. Several times the bus stopped to remove large stones that had slid down onto the road.

Lee was talking on the bus to an old prospector named Morgan, who had been thirty years in the jungle. Lee asked him about *ayahuasca*.

"Acts on them like opium," Morgan said. "All my Indians use it. Can't get any work out of them for three days when they get on *ayahuasca*."

Old man Morgan went back to Shell Mara on the afternoon bus to collect some money owed him. Lee talked to a Dutchman named Sawyer who was farming near Puyo. Sawyer told him there was an American botanist living in the jungle, a few hours out of Puyo.

"He is trying to develop some medicine. I forget the name. If he succeeds in concentrating this medicine, he says he will make a fortune. Now he is having a hard time. He has nothing to eat out there."

Lee said, "I am interested in medicinal plants. I may pay him a visit."

"He will be glad to see you. But take along some flour or tea or something. They have nothing out there."

Later Lee said to Allerton, "A botanist! What a break. He is our man. We will go tomorrow."

"We can hardly pretend we just happened by," said Allerton. "How are you going to explain your visit?"

"I will think of something. Best tell him right out I want to score for *yagé*. I figure maybe there is a buck in it for both of us. According to what I hear, he is flat on his ass. We are lucky to hit him in that condition. If he was in the chips and drinking champagne out of galoshes in the whorehouses of Puyo, he would hardly be interested to sell me a few hundred Sucres' worth of *yagé*. And, Gene, for the love of Christ, when we do overhaul this character, please don't say, 'Doctor Cotter, I presume.'"

It was dark when they reached Cotter's place, a small thatched hut in a clearing. Cotter was a wiry little man in his middle fifties. Lee observed that the reception was a bit cool. Lee brought out the liquor, and they all had a drink. Cotter's wife, a large, strong-looking, red-haired woman, made some tea with cinnamon to cut the kerosene taste of the Puro. Lee got drunk on three drinks.

Cotter was asking Lee a lot of questions. "How did you happen to come here? Where are you from? How long have you been in Ecuador? Who told you about me? Are you a tourist or travelling on business?"

Lee was drunk. He began talking in junky lingo, explaining that he was looking for *yagé*, or *ayahuasca*. He understood the Russians and the Americans were experimenting with this drug. Lee said he figured there might be a buck in the deal for both of them. The more Lee talked, the cooler Cotter's manner became. The man was clearly suspicious, but why or of what, Lee could not decide.

Dinner was pretty good, considering the chief ingredient was a sort of fibrous root and bananas. After dinner, Cotter's wife said, "These boys must be tired, Jim."

Cotter led the way with a flashlight that developed power by pressing a lever. A cot about thirty inches wide made of bamboo slats. "I guess you can both make out here," he said. Mrs. Cotter was spreading a blanket on the cot as a mattress, with another blanket as cover. Lee lay down on the cot next to the wall. Allerton lay on the outside, and Cotter adjusted a mosquito net.

"Mosquitos?" Lee asked.

"No, vampire bats," Cotter said shortly. "Good night."

"Good night."

Lee's muscles ached from the long walk. He was very tired. He put one arm across Allerton's chest, and snuggled close to the boy's body. A feeling of deep tenderness flowed from Lee's body at the warm contact. He snuggled closer and stroked Allerton's shoulder gently. Allerton moved irritably, pushing Lee's arm away.

"Slack off, will you, and go to sleep," said Allerton. He turned on his side, his back to Lee. Lee drew his arm back. His whole body contracted with shock. Slowly he put his hand under his cheek. He felt a deep hurt, as though he were bleeding inside. Tears ran down his face.

* * *

He was standing in front of the Ship Ahoy. The place looked deserted. He could hear someone crying. He saw his little son, and knelt down and took the child in his arms. The sound of crying came closer, a wave of sadness, and now he was crying, his body shaking with sobs.

He held little Willy close against his chest. A group of people were standing there in convict suits. Lee wondered what they were doing there and why he was crying.

When Lee woke up, he still felt the deep sadness of his dream. He stretched out a hand towards Allerton, then pulled it back. He turned around to face the wall.

Cotter was evasive when Lee asked about *ayahuasca*. He said he was not sure *yagé* and *ayahuasca* were the same plant. *Ayahuasca* was connected with *brujería*—witchcraft. He himself was a white *brujo*. He had access to *brujo* secrets. Lee had no such access.

"It would take you years to gain their confidence."

Lee said he did not have years to spend on the deal. "Can't you get me some?" he asked.

Cotter looked at him sourly. "I have been out here three years," he said.

Lee tried to come on like a scientist. "I want to investigate the properties of this drug," he said. "I am willing to take some as an experiment."

Cotter said, "Well, I could take you down to Canela and talk to the *brujo*. He will give you some if I say so."

"That would be very kind," said Lee.

Cotter did not say any more about going to Canela. He did say a lot about how short they were on supplies, and how he had no time to spare from his experiments with a curare substitute. After three days Lee saw he was wasting time, and told Cotter they were leaving. Cotter made no attempt to conceal his relief.

from EPILOGUE: MEXICO CITY RETURN

Every time I hit Panama, the place is exactly one month, two months, six months more nowhere, like the course of a degenerative illness. A shift from arithmetical to geometrical progression seems to have occurred. Something ugly and ignoble and subhuman is cooking in this mongrel town of pimps and whores and recessive genes, this degraded leech on the Canal.

A smog of bum kicks hangs over Panama in the wet heat. Everyone here is telepathic on the paranoid level. I walked around with my camera and saw a wood and corrugated iron shack on a limestone cliff in Old Panama, like a penthouse. I wanted a picture of this excrescence, with the albatrosses and vultures wheeling over it against the hot grey sky. My hands holding the camera were slippery with sweat, and my shirt stuck to my body like a wet condom.

An old hag in the shack saw me taking the picture. They always know when you are taking their picture, especially in Panama. She went into an angry consultation with some other ratty-looking people I could not see clearly. Then she walked to the edge of a perilous balcony and made an ambiguous gesture of hostility. Many so-called primitives are afraid of cameras. There is in fact something obscene and sinister about photography, a desire to imprison, to incorporate, a sexual intensity of pursuit. I walked on and shot some boys—young, alive, unconscious—playing baseball. They never glanced in my direction.

Down by the waterfront I saw a dark young Indian on a fishing boat. He knew I wanted to take his picture, and every time I swung the camera into position he would look up with young male sulkiness. I finally caught him leaning against the bow of the boat with languid animal grace, idly scratching one shoulder. A long white scar across right shoulder and collarbone. I put away my camera and leaned over the hot concrete wall, looking at him. In my mind I was running a finger along the scar, down across his naked copper chest and stomach, every cell aching with deprivation. I pushed away from the wall muttering "Oh Jesus" and walked away, looking around for something to photograph.

A Negro with a felt hat was leaning on the porch rail of a wooden house built on a dirty limestone foundation. I was across the street under a movie marquee. Every time I prepared my camera he would lift his hat and look at me, muttering insane imprecations. I finally snapped him from behind a pillar. On a balcony over this character a shirtless young man was washing. I could see the Negro and Near Eastern blood in him, the rounded face and *café-au-lait* mulatto skin, the smooth body of undifferentiated flesh with not a muscle showing. He looked up from his washing like an animal scenting danger. I caught him when the five o'clock whistle blew. An old photographer's trick: wait for a distraction.

That night I had a recurrent dream: I was back in Mexico City, talking to Art Gonzalez, a former roommate of Allerton's. I asked him where Allerton was, and he said, "In Agua Diente." This was somewhere south of Mexico City, and I was inquiring about a bus connection. I have dreamed many times I was back in Mexico City, talking to Art or Allerton's best friend, Johnny White, and asking where he was.

I flew up to Mexico City.

I checked into an eight-peso hotel near Sears, and walked over to Lola's, my stomach cold with excitement. The bar was in a different place, redecorated, with new furniture. But there was the same old bartender behind the bar, with his gold tooth and his moustache.

"*¿Cómo está?*" he said. We shook hands. He asked where I had been, and I told him South America. I sat down with a Delaware Punch. The place was empty, but someone I knew was bound to come in sooner or later.

The Major walked in. A retired Army man, grey-haired, vigorous, stocky. I ran through the list crisply with the Major:

"Johnny White, Russ Morton, Pete Crowly, Ike Scranton?"

"Los Angeles, Alaska, Idaho, don't know, still around. He's always around."

"And oh, uh, whatever happened to Allerton?"

"Allerton? Don't believe I know him."

"See you."

"'Night, Lee. Take it easy."

I walked over to Sears and looked through the magazines. In one called *Balls: For Real Men,* I was looking at a photo of a Negro hanging from a tree: "I Saw Them Swing Sonny Goons." A hand fell on my shoulder. I turned, and there was Gale, another retired Army man. He had the subdued air of the reformed drunk. I ran through the list.

"Most everybody is gone," Gale said. "I never see those guys anyway, never hang around Lola's anymore."

I asked about Allerton.

"Allerton?"

"Tall skinny kid. Friend of Johnny White and Art Gonzalez."

"He's gone too."

"How long ago?" No need to play it cool and casual with Gale. He wouldn't notice anything.

"I saw him about a month ago on the other side of the street."

"See you."

"See you."

I put the magazine away slowly and walked outside and leaned against a post. Then I walked back to Lola's. Burns was sitting at a table, drinking a beer with his maimed hand.

"Hardly anybody around. Johnny White and Tex and Crosswheel are in Los Angeles."

I was looking at his hand.

"Did you hear about Allerton?" he asked.

I said, "No."

"He went down to South America or some place. With an Army colonel. Allerton went along as guide."

"So? How long has he been gone?"

"About six months."

"Must have been right after I left."

"Yeah. Just about then."

I got Art Gonzalez's address from Burns and went over to see him. He was drinking a beer in a shop across from his hotel, and called me over. Yes, Allerton left about five months ago and went along as guide to a colonel and his wife.

"They were going to sell the car in Guatemala. A '48 Cadillac. I felt there was something not quite right about the deal. But Allerton never told me anything definite. You know how he is." Art seemed surprised I had not heard from Allerton. "Nobody has heard anything from him since he left. It worries me."

I wondered what he could be doing, and where. Guatemala is expensive, San Salvador expensive and jerkwater. Costa Rica? I regretted not having stopped off in San José on the way up.

Gonzalez and I went through the where-is-so-and-so routine. Mexico City is a terminal of space-time travel, a waiting room where you grab a quick drink while you wait for your train. That is why I can stand to be in Mexico City or New York. You are not stuck there; by the fact of being there at all, you are travelling. But in Panama, crossroads of the world, you are exactly so much aging tissue. You have to make arrangements with Pan Am or the Dutch Line for removal of your body. Otherwise, it would stay there and rot in the muggy heat, under a galvanized iron roof.

That night I dreamed I finally found Allerton, hiding out in some Central American backwater. He seemed surprised to see me after all this time. In the dream I was a finder of missing persons.

"Mr. Allerton, I represent the Friendly Finance Company. Haven't you forgotten something, Gene? You're supposed to come and see us every third Tuesday. We've been lonely for you in the office. We don't like to say 'Pay up or else.' It's not a friendly thing to say. I wonder if you have ever read the contract *all the way through*? I have particular reference to Clause 6(x) which can only be deciphered with an electron microscope and a virus filter. I wonder if you know just what *'or else'* means, Gene?

"Aw, I know how it is with you young kids. You get chasing after some floozie and forget all about Friendly Finance, don't you? But Friendly Finance doesn't forget you. Like the song say, 'No hiding place down there.' Not when the old Skip Tracer goes out on a job."

The Skip Tracer's face went blank and dreamy. His mouth fell open, showing teeth hard and yellow as old ivory. Slowly his body slid down in the leather armchair until the back of the chair pushed his hat down over his eyes, which gleamed in the hat's shade, catching points of light like an opal. He began humming "Johnny's So Long at the Fair" over and over. The humming stopped abruptly, in the middle of a phrase.

The Skip Tracer was talking in a voice languid and intermittent, like music down a windy street. "You meet all kinds on this job, Kid. Every now and then some popcorn citizen walks in the office and tries to pay Friendly Finance with *this* shit."

He let one arm swing out, palm up, over the side of the chair. Slowly he opened a thin brown hand, with purple-blue fingertips, to reveal a roll of yellow thousand-dollar bills. The hand turned over, palm down, and fell back against the chair. His eyes closed.

Suddenly his head dropped to one side and his tongue fell out. The bills dropped from his hand, one after the other, and lay there crumpled on the red tile floor. A gust of warm spring wind blew dirty pink curtains into the room. The bills rustled across the room and settled at Allerton's feet.

Imperceptibly the Skip Tracer straightened up, and a slit of light went on behind the eyelids.

"Keep that in case you're caught short, Kid," he said. "You know how it is in these spic hotels. You gotta carry your own paper."

The Skip Tracer leaned forward, his elbows on his knees. Suddenly he was standing up, as if tilted out of the chair, and in the same upward movement he pushed the hat back from his eyes with one finger. He walked to the door and turned, with his right hand on the knob. He polished the nails of his left hand on the lapel of his worn glen plaid suit. The suit gave out an odor of mold when he moved. There was mildew under the lapels and in the trouser cuffs. He looked at his nails.

"Oh, uh . . . about your, uh . . . account. I'll be around soon. That is, within the next few . . ." The Skip Tracer's voice was muffled.

"We'll come to *some* kind of an agreement." Now the voice was loud and clear. The door opened and wind blew through the room. The door closed and the curtains settled back, one curtain trailing over a sofa as though someone had taken it and tossed it there.

from INTRODUCTION

An addict has little regard for his image. He wears the dirtiest, shabbiest clothes, and feels no need to call attention to himself. During my period of addiction in Tangiers, I was known as "El Hombre Invisible," The Invisible Man. This disintegration of self-image often results in an indiscriminate image hunger. Billie Holliday said she knew she was off junk when she stopped watching TV. In my first novel, *Junky,* the protagonist "Lee" comes across as integrated and self-contained, sure of himself and where he is going. In *Queer* he is disintegrated, desperately in need of contact, completely unsure of himself and of his purpose.

The difference of course is simple: Lee on junk is covered, protected and also severely limited. Not only does junk short-circuit the sex drive, it also blunts emotional reactions to the vanishing point, depending on the dosage. Looking back over the action of *Queer,* that hallucinated month of acute withdrawal takes on a hellish glow of menace and evil drifting out of neon-lit cocktail bars, the ugly violence, the .45 always just under the surface. On junk I was insulated, didn't drink, didn't go out much, just shot up and waited for the next shot.

When the cover is removed, everything that has been held in check by junk spills out. The withdrawing addict is subject to the emotional excesses of a child or an adolescent, regardless of his actual age. And the sex drive returns in full force. Men of sixty experience wet dreams and spontaneous orgasms (an extremely unpleasant experience, *agaçant* as the French say, putting the teeth on edge). Unless the reader keeps this in mind, the metamorphosis of Lee's character will appear as inexplicable or psychotic. Also bear in mind that the withdrawal syndrome is self-limiting, lasting no more than a month. And Lee has a phase of excessive drinking, which exacerbates all the worst and most dangerous aspects of the withdrawal sickness: reckless, unseemly, outrageous, maudlin—in a word, appalling—behavior.

After withdrawal, the organism readjusts and stabilizes at a pre-junk level. In the narrative, this stabilization is finally reached during the South American trip. No junk is available, nor any other drug, after the paregoric of Panama. Lee's drinking has dwindled to several good stiff ones at sundown. Not so different from the Lee of the later *Yagé Letters*, except for the phantom presence of Allerton.

So I had written *Junky*, and the motivation for that was comparatively simple: to put down in the most accurate and simple terms my experiences as an addict. I was hoping for publication, money, recognition. Kerouac had published *The Town and the City* at the time I started writing *Junky*. I remember writing in a letter to him, when his book was published, that money and fame were now assured. As you can see, I knew nothing about the writing business at the time.

My motivations to write *Queer* were more complex, and are not clear to me at the present time. Why should I wish to chronicle so carefully these extremely painful and unpleasant and lacerating memories? While it was I who wrote *Junky*, I feel that I was being written in *Queer*. I was also taking pains to ensure further writing, so as to set the record straight: writing as inoculation. As soon as something is written, it loses the power of surprise, just as a virus loses its advantage when a weakened virus has created alerted antibodies. So I achieved some immunity from further perilous ventures along these lines by writing my experience down.

At the beginning of the *Queer* manuscript fragment, having returned from the insulation of junk to the land of the living like a frantic inept Lazarus, Lee seems determined to score, in the sexual sense of the word. There is something curiously systematic and unsexual about his quest for a suitable sex object, crossing one prospect after another off a list which seems compiled with ultimate failure in mind. On some very deep level he does not want to succeed, but will go to any length to avoid the realization that he is not really looking for sex contact.

But Allerton was definitely *some* sort of contact. And what was the contact that Lee was looking for? Seen from here, a very confused concept that had nothing to do with Allerton as a character. While the addict is indifferent to the impression he creates in others, during withdrawal he may feel the compulsive need for an audience, and this is clearly what Lee seeks in Allerton: an audience, the acknowledgment of his performance, which of course is a mask, to cover a shocking disintegration. So he invents a frantic attention-getting format which he calls the Routine: shocking, funny, riveting. "It is an Ancient Mariner, and he stoppeth one of three. . . ."

The performance takes the form of routines: fantasies about Chess Players, the Texas Oilman, Corn Hole Gus' Used-Slave Lot. In *Queer,* Lee addresses these routines to an actual audience. Later, as he develops as a writer, the audience becomes internalized. But the same mechanism that produced A.J. and Doctor Benway, the same creative impulse, is dedicated to Allerton, who is forced into the role of approving Muse, in which he feels understandably uncomfortable.

What Lee is looking for is contact or recognition, like a photon emerging from the haze of insubstantiality to leave an indelible recording in Allerton's consciousness. Failing to find an adequate observer, he is threatened by painful dispersal, like an unobserved photon. Lee does not know that he is already committed to writing, since this is the only way he has of making an indelible record, whether Allerton is inclined to observe or not. Lee is being inexorably pressed into the world of fiction. He has already made the choice between his life and his work.

The manuscript trails off in Puyo, End of the Road town. . . . The search for *yagé* has failed. The mysterious Doctor Cotter wants only to be rid of his unwelcome guests. He suspects them to be agents of his treacherous partner Gill, intent on stealing his genius work of isolating curare from the composite arrow poison. I heard later that the chemical companies decided simply to buy up the arrow poison in quantity and extract the curare in their American laboratories. The drug was soon synthesized, and is now a standard substance found in many muscle-relaxing preparations. So it would seem that Cotter really had nothing to lose: his efforts were already superseded.

Dead end. And Puyo can serve as a model for the Place of Dead Roads: a dead, meaningless conglomerate of tin-roofed houses under a continual downpour of rain. Shell has pulled out, leaving prefabricated bungalows and rusting machinery behind. And Lee has reached the end of his line, an end implicit in the beginning. He is left with the impact of unbridgeable distances, the defeat and weariness of a long, painful journey made for nothing, wrong turnings, the track lost, a bus waiting in the rain . . . back to Ambato, Quito, Panama, Mexico City.

When I started to write this companion text to *Queer,* I was paralyzed with a heavy reluctance, a writer's block like a straitjacket: "I glance at the manuscript of *Queer* and feel I simply can't read it. My past was a poisoned river from which one was fortunate to escape, and by which one feels immediately threatened, years after the events recorded. —Painful to an extent I find it difficult to read, let alone to write about. Every word and gesture sets the teeth on edge." The reason for this reluctance becomes clearer as I force myself to look: the book is motivated and formed by an event which is never mentioned, in fact is carefully avoided: the accidental shooting death of my wife, Joan, in September 1951.

While I was writing *The Place of Dead Roads,* I felt in spiritual contact with the late English writer Denton Welch, and modelled the novel's hero, Kim Carson, directly on him. Whole sections came to me as if dictated, like table-tapping. I have written about the fateful morning of Denton's accident, which left him an invalid for the remainder of his short life. If he had stayed a little longer here, not so long there, he would have missed his appointment with the female motorist who hit his bicycle from behind for no apparent reason. At one point Denton had stopped to have coffee, and looking at the brass hinges on the café's window shutters, some of them broken, he was hit by a feeling of universal desolation and loss. So every event of that morning is charged with special significance, as if it were underlined. This portentous second sight permeates Welch's writing: a scone, a cup of tea, an inkwell purchased for a few shillings, become charged with a special and often sinister significance.

I get exactly the same feeling to an almost unbearable degree as I read the manuscript of *Queer.* The event towards which Lee feels himself inexorably driven is the death of his wife by his own hand, the knowledge of possession, a dead hand waiting to slip over his like a glove. So a smog of menace and evil rises from the pages, an evil that Lee, knowing and yet not knowing, tries to escape with frantic flights of fantasy: his routines, which set one's teeth on edge because of the ugly menace just behind or to one side of them, a presence palpable as a haze.

Brion Gysin said to me in Paris: "For ugly spirit shot Joan because. . . ." A bit of mediumistic message that was not completed—or was it? It doesn't need to be completed, if you read it: "ugly spirit shot Joan *to be cause,*" that is, to maintain a hateful parasitic occupation. My concept of possession is closer to the medieval model than to modern psychological explanations, with their dogmatic insistence that such manifestations must come from within and never, never, never from without. (As if there were some clear-cut difference between inner and outer.) I mean a definite possessing entity. And indeed, the psychological concept might well have been devised by the possessing entities, since nothing is more dangerous to a possessor than being seen as a separate invading creature by the host it has invaded. And for this reason the possessor shows itself only when absolutely necessary.

In 1939, I became interested in Egyptian hieroglyphics and went out to see someone in the Department of Egyptology at the University of Chicago. And something was screaming in my ear: "YOU DON'T BELONG HERE!" Yes, the hieroglyphics provided one key to the mechanism of possession. Like a virus, the possessing entity must find a port of entry.

This occasion was my first clear indication of something in my being that was not me, and not under my control. I remember a dream from this period: I worked as an exterminator in Chicago, in the late 1930s, and lived in a room-

ing house in the near North Side. In the dream I am floating up near the ceiling with a feeling of utter death and despair, and looking down I see my body
walking out the door with deadly purpose.

One wonders if *yagé* could have saved the day by a blinding revelation. I
remember a cut-up I made in Paris years later: "Raw pealed winds of hate and
mischance blew the shot." And for years I thought this referred to blowing a
shot of junk, when the junk squirts out the side of the syringe or dropper owing
to an obstruction. Brion Gysin pointed out the actual meaning: the shot that
killed Joan.

I had bought a Scout knife in Quito. It had a metal handle and a curiously
tarnished old look, like something from a turn-of-the-century junk shop. I can
see it in a tray of old knives and rings, with the silver plate flaking off. It was
about three o'clock in the afternoon, a few days after I came back to Mexico
City, and I decided to have the knife sharpened. The knife-sharpener had a
little whistle and a fixed route, and as I walked down the street towards his
cart a feeling of loss and sadness that had weighed on me all day so I could
hardly breathe intensified to such an extent that I found tears streaming down
my face.

"What on earth is wrong?" I wondered.

This heavy depression and a feeling of doom occurs again and again in the
text. Lee usually attributes it to his failures with Allerton: "A heavy drag slowed
movement and thought. Lee's face was rigid, his voice toneless." Allerton has
just refused a dinner invitation and left abruptly: "Lee stared at the table, his
thoughts slow, as if he were very cold." (Reading this *I am* cold and depressed.)

I have constrained myself to remember the day of Joan's death, the overwhelming feeling of doom and loss . . . walking down the street I suddenly found
tears streaming down my face. "What is wrong with me?" The small Scout
knife with a metal handle, the plating peeling off, a smell of old coins, the
knife-sharpener's whistle. Whatever happened to this knife I never reclaimed?

I am forced to the appalling conclusion that I would never have become a
writer but for Joan's death, and to a realization of the extent to which this
event has motivated and formulated my writing. I live with the constant threat
of possession, and a constant need to escape from possession, from Control.
So the death of Joan brought me in contact with the invader, the Ugly Spirit,
and maneuvered me into a lifelong struggle, in which I have had no choice
except to write my way out.

*I have constrained myself to escape death. Denton Welch is almost my face. Smell
of old coins. Whatever happened to this knife called Allerton, back to the appalling Margaras Inc. The realization is basic formulated **doing**? The day of Joan's
doom and loss. Found tears streaming down from Allerton pealing off the same
person as a Western shootist. **What are you rewriting?** A lifelong preoccupation
with Control and Virus. Having gained access the virus uses the host's energy,*

blood, flesh and bones to make copies of itself. Model of dogmatic insistence never never from without was screaming in my ear, "YOU DON'T BELONG HERE!"

A straitjacket notation carefully paralyzed with heavy reluctance. To escape their prewritten lines years after the events recorded. A writer's block avoided Joan's death. Denton Welch is Kim Carson's voice through a cloud underlined broken table tapping.

William S. Burroughs
February 1985

from
the yagé letters
(SELECTIONS)

January 15, 1953
Hotel Colón, Panama

Dear Allen,

I stopped off here to have my piles out. Wouldn't do to go back among the Indians with piles I figured.

Bill Gains was in town and he has burned down the Republic of Panama from Las Palmas to David on paregoric. Before Gains, Panama was a p.g. town. You could buy four ounces in any drug store. Now the druggists are balky and the Chamber of Deputies was about to pass a special Gains Law when he threw in the towel and went back to Mexico. I was getting off junk and he kept nagging me why was I kidding myself, once a junky always a junky. If I quit junk I would become a sloppy lush or go crazy taking cocaine.

One night I got lushed and bought some paregoric and he kept saying over and over, "I *knew* you'd come home with paregoric. I *knew* it. You'll be a junkie all the rest of your life" and looking at me with his little cat smile. Junk is a cause with him.

I checked into the hospital junk sick and spent four days there. They would only give me three shots of morphine and I couldn't sleep from pain and heat and deprivation besides which there was a Panamanian hernia case in the same room with me and his friends came and stayed all day and half the night—one of them did in fact stay until midnight.

Recall walking by some American women in the corridor who looked like officers' wives. One of them was saying, "I don't know why but I just can't eat sweets."

"You got diabetes lady," I said. They all whirled around and gave me an outraged stare.

After checking out of the hospital, I stopped off at the U.S. Embassy. In front of the Embassy is a vacant lot with weeds and trees where boys undress to swim in the polluted waters of the bay—home of a small venomous sea snake. Smell of excrement and sea water and young male lust. No letters. I stopped again to buy two ounces of paregoric. Same old Panama. Whores and pimps and hustlers.

"Want nice girl?"

"Naked lady dance?"

"See me fuck my sister?"

No wonder food prices are high. They can't keep them down on the farm. They all want to come in the big city and be pimps.

I had a magazine article with me describing a joint outside Panama City called the Blue Goose. "This is anything-goes joint. Dope peddlers lurk in the men's room with a hypo loaded and ready to go. Sometimes they dart out of a toilet and stick it in your arm without waiting for consent. Homosexuals run riot."

The Blue Goose looks like a Prohibition-era road house. A long one-story building run down and covered with vines. I could hear frogs croaking from the woods and swamps around it. Outside a few parked cars, inside a dim bluish light. I remembered a prohibition-era road house of my adolescence and the taste of gin rickeys in a midwest summer. (Oh my God! And the August moon in a violet sky and Billy Bradshinkel's cock. How sloppy can you get?)

Immediately two old whores sat down at my table without being asked and ordered drinks. The bill for one round was $6.90. The only thing lurking in the men's room was an insolent demanding lavatory attendant. I may add that far from running riot in Panama I never scored for one boy there. I wonder what a Panamanian boy would be like. Probably cut. When they say anything goes they are referring to the joint not the customers.

I ran into my old friend Jones the cab driver, and bought some C off him that was cut to hell and back. I nearly suffocated myself trying to sniff enough of this crap to get a lift. That's Panama. Wouldn't surprise me if they cut the whores with sponge rubber.

The Panamanians are about the crummiest people in the Hemisphere—I understand the Venezuelans offer competition—but I have never encountered any group of citizens that brings me down like the Canal Zone Civil Service. You can not contact a civil servant on the level of intuition and empathy. He just does not have a receiving set, and he gives out like a dead battery. There must be a special low frequency civil service brain wave.

The Service men don't seem young. They have no enthusiasm and no conversation. In fact they shun the company of civilians. The only element in Panama I contact are the hip spades and they are all on the hustle.

Love,

Bill

P.S. Billy Bradshinkel got to be such a nuisance I finally had to kill him:

The first time was in my model A after the spring prom. Billy with his pants down to his ankles and his tuxedo shirt still on, and jissom all over the car seat. Later I was holding his arm while he vomited in the car headlights, looking young and petulant with his blond hair mussed standing there in the warm spring wind. Then we got back in the car and turned the lights off and I said, "Let's again."

And he said, "No we shouldn't."

And I said, "Why not?" and by then he was excited too so we did it again, and I ran my hands over his back under his tuxedo shirt and held him against me and felt the long baby hairs of his smooth cheek against mine and he went to sleep there and it was getting light when we drove home.

After that in the car several times and one time his family was away and we took off all our clothes and afterwards I watched him sleeping like a baby with his mouth a little open.

That summer Billy caught typhoid and I went to see him every day and his mother gave me lemonade and once his father gave me a bottle of beer and a cigarette. When Billy was better we used to drive out to Creve Coeur Lake and rent a boat and go fishing and lie on the bottom of the boat with our arms around each other's shoulders not doing anything. One Saturday we explored an old quarry and found a cave and took our pants off in the musty darkness.

I remember the last time I saw Billy was in October of that year. One of those sparkling blue days you get in the Ozarks in autumn. We had driven out into the country to hunt squirrels with my .22 single shot, and walked through the autumn woods without seeing anything to shoot at and Billy was silent and sullen and we sat on a log and Billy looked at his shoes and finally told me he couldn't see me again (notice I am sparing you the falling leaves).

"But why Billy? Why?"

"Well if you don't know I can't explain it to you. Let's go back to the car."

We drove back in silence and when we came to his house he opened the door and got out. He looked at me for a second as if he was going to say something then turned abruptly and walked up the flagstone path to his house. I sat there for a minute looking at the closed door. Then I drove home feeling numb. When the car was stopped in the garage I put my head down on the wheel sobbing and rubbing my cheek against the steel spokes. Finally Mother called to me from an upstairs window was anything wrong and why didn't I come in the house. So I wiped the tears off my face and went in and said I was sick and went upstairs to bed. Mother brought me a bowl of milk toast on a tray but I couldn't eat any and cried all night.

After that I called Billy several times on the phone but he always hung up when he heard my voice. And I wrote him a long letter which he never answered.

Three months later when I read in the paper he had been killed in a car wreck and Mother said, "Oh that's the Bradshinkel boy. You used to be such good friends didn't you?"

I said, "Yes Mother" not feeling anything at all.

And I got a silo full of queer corn where that come from. Another routine: A man who manufactures memories to order. Any kind you want and he guarantees you'll believe they happened just that way—(As a matter of fact I have just about sold myself Billy Bradshinkel). A line from the Japanese Sandman provides theme song of story, "Just an old second hand man trading new dreams for old." Ah what the Hell! Give it to Truman Capote.

Another bit of reminiscence but genuine. Every Sunday at lunch my grand-mother would disinter her dead brother killed 50 years ago when he dragged his shotgun through a fence and blew his lungs out.

"I always remember my brother such a lovely boy. I hate to see boys with guns."

So every Sunday at lunch there was the boy lying by the wood fence and blood on the frozen red Georgia clay seeping into the winter stubble.

And poor old Mrs. Collins waiting for the cataracts to ripen so they can operate on her eye. Oh God! Sunday lunch in Cincinnati!

February 28, 1953
Hotel Niza, Pasto

Dear Allen:

On my way back to Bogotá with nothing accomplished. I have been conned by medicine men (the most inveterate drunk, liar and loafer in the village is invariably the medicine man), incarcerated by the law, rolled by a local hustler (I thought I was getting that innocent backwoods ass, but the kid had been to bed with six American oilmen, a Swedish botanist, a Dutch ethnographer, a Capuchin father known locally as the Mother Superior, a Bolivian Trotskyite on the lam, and jointly fucked by the Cocoa Commission and Point Four). Finally I was prostrated by malaria. I will relate events more or less chronologically.

I took a bus to Mocoa which is the capital of the Putumayo and end of the road. From there on you go by mule or canoe. For some reason these end of road towns are always God awful. Anyone expecting to outfit himself there will find they have nothing he needs in the stores. Not even citronella—and no one in these end of the road towns knows anything about the jungle.

I arrived in Mocoa late at night and consumed a ghastly Colombian soft drink under the dubious eyes of a national cop who could not make up his mind whether to question me or not. Finally he got up and left and I went to bed. The night was cool, about like Puyo, another awful end of the road town.

When I woke up next morning I began to get bum kicks still in bed. I looked out the window. Cobblestone, muddy streets, one-story buildings mostly shops. Nothing out of the ordinary but in all my experience as a traveler—and I have seen more God awful places—no place ever brought me down like Mocoa. And I don't know exactly why.

Mocoa has about two thousand inhabitants and sixty national cops. One of them rides around all day through the four streets of the town on a motor bicycle. You can hear him from any place in town. Radios with extra loud speakers in every cantina make a horrible discordant noise (there are no juke-boxes in Mocoa where you can play what you want to hear). The police have a brass band they bang around three or four times a day starting in the early morning. I never saw any signs of disorder in this town which is well out of the war zone. But there is an air of unresolved and unsoluble tension about Mocoa, the agencies of control out in force to put down uprising which does not occur. Mocoa is The End Of The Road. A final stalemate with the cop riding around and around on his motor bicycle for all eternity.

I went on to Puerto Limón which is about thirty miles from Mocoa. This town can be reached by truck. Here I located an intelligent Indian and ten minutes later I had a *yagé* vine. But the Indian would not prepare it since this is the monopoly of the *brujo* (medicine man).

This old drunken fraud was crooning over a man evidently down with malaria. (Maybe he was chasing the evil spirit out of his patient and into the gringo. Anyway I came down with malaria two weeks to the day later.) The *brujo* told me he had to be half lushed up to work his witchcraft and cure people. The high cost of liquor was working a hardship on the sick, he was only hitting two cylinders on a short count of lush. I bought him a pint of *aguardiente* and he agreed to prepare the *yagé* for another quart. He did in fact prepare a pint of cold water infusion after misappropriating half the vine so that I did not notice any effect.

That night I had a vivid dream in color of the green jungle and a red sunset I had seen during the afternoon. A composite city familiar to me but I could not quite place it. Part New York, part Mexico City and part Lima which I had not seen at this time. I was standing on a corner by a wide street with cars going by and a vast open park down the street in the distance. I cannot say whether these dreams had any connection with *yagé*. Incidentally you are supposed to see a city when you take *yagé*.

I spent a day in the jungle with an Indian guide to dig the jungle and collect some *yoka*, a vine the Indians use to prevent hunger and fatigue during long trips in the jungle. In fact, some of them use it because they are too lazy to eat.

The Upper Amazon jungle has fewer disagreeable features than the midwest stateside woods in the summer. Sand flies and jungle mosquitoes are the only outstanding pests and you can keep them off with insect repellent. I didn't have any at this time. I never got any ticks or chiggers in the Putumayo. The trees are tremendous, some of them two hundred feet tall. Walking under these trees I felt a special silence, a vibrating soundless hum. We waded through clear streams of water (who started this story you can't drink jungle water? Why not?).

Yoka grows on high ground and it took us four hours to get there. The Indian cut a *yoka* vine and shaved off a handful of the inner bark with a machete. He soaked the bark in a little cold water, squeezed the water out of the bark and handed me the infusion in a palm leaf cup. It was faintly bitter but not unpleasant. In 10 minutes I felt a tingling in my hands and a nice lift somewhat like benzedrine but not so tight. I walked the four hours back over jungle trail without stopping and could have walked twice that far.

After a week in Puerto Limón I went to Puerto Umbria by truck and down to Puerto Assis by canoe. These canoes are about thirty feet long with an outboard motor. This is standard method of travel on the Putumayo. The motors are out of commission about half the time. This is because people take them apart and leave out the pieces they consider nonessential. Also they economize on grease so the motors burn out.

I arrived in Puerto Assis at ten P.M. and as soon as I stepped out of the canoe a federal cop wanted to see my papers. There is more check on papers in the quiet zones like Putumayo than in Villavicencio which is edge of the war zone. In the Putumayo you won't be five minutes whistle stop before they check your papers. They expect trouble to come from outside in the form of a foreigner—god knows why.

Next day the governor, who looked like a degenerate strain of monkey, found an error in my tourist card. The consul in Panama had put down 52 instead of 53 in the date. I tried to explain this was an error, clear enough in view of the dates on my plane tickets, passport, receipts, but the man was bone stupid. I don't think he understands yet. So the cop gave my luggage a shake missing the gun but decided to impound the medicine gun and all. The sanitary inspector put in his two cents suggesting they go through the medicines.

For God's sake, I thought, *go inspect an outhouse.*

They informed me I was under town arrest pending a decision from Mocoa. So I was stuck in Puerto Assis with nothing to do but sit around all day and get drunk every night. I had planned to take a canoe trip up the Rio Quaymes to contact the Kofan Indians who are known *yagé* artists, but the governor would not let me leave Puerto Assis.

Puerto Assis is a typical Putumayo River town. A mud street along the river, a few shops, one cantina, a mission where Capuchin fathers lead the life of Riley, a hotel called the Putumayo where I was housed.

The hotel was run by a whorish-looking landlady. Her husband was a man of about forty, powerful and vigorous, but there was a beat look in his eyes. They had seven daughters and you could tell by looking at him that he would never have a son. At least not by that woman. This giggling brood of daughters kept coming into my room (there was no door, only a thin curtain) to watch me dress and shave and brush my teeth. It was a bum kick. And I was the victim of idiotic pilfering—a catheter tube from my medical kit, a jock strap, vitamin B tablets.

There was a boy in town who had once acted as a guide to an American naturalist. This boy was the local Mister Specialist. You find one of these pests all over South America. They can say, "Hello Joe" or "O.K." or "Fucky fucky." Many of them refuse to speak Spanish thus limiting conversation to sign language.

I was sitting on a worn-out inverted canoe that serves as a bench in the main drag of Puerto Assis. The boy came and sat with me and began talking about the Mister who collected animals. "He collected spiders, and scorpions and snakes." I was half asleep lulled by this litany when I heard, "And he was going to take me back to the States with him," and woke up. *Oh God,* I thought, *that old line.*

The boy smiled at me showing gaps in his front teeth. He moved a little closer on the bench. I could feel my stomach tighten.

"I have a good canoe," he said. "Why don't you let me take you up the Quaymes? I know all the Indians up there."

He looked like the most inefficient guide in the Upper Amazon but I said, "Yes."

That night I saw the boy in front of the cantina. He put his arms around my shoulders and said, "Come in and have a drink, Mister," letting his hand slip down my back and off my ass.

We went in and got drunk under the weary wise eyes of the bartender and took a walk out along the jungle trail. We sat down in the moonlight by the side of the trail and he let his elbow fall into my crotch and said, "Mister," next thing I heard was, "How much you gonna give me?"

He wanted $30 evidently figuring he was a rare commodity in the Upper Amazon. I beat him down to $10 bargaining under increasingly disadvantageous conditions. Somehow he managed to roll me for $20 and my underwear shorts (when he told me to take my underwear all the way off I thought, a passionate type, my dear, but it was only a maneuver to steal my skivvies).

After five days in Puerto Assis I was well on the way to establish myself as a citizen in the capacity of village wastrel. Meanwhile sepulchral telegrams issued periodically from Mocoa. "The case of the foreigner from Ohio will be resolved." And finally, "Let the foreigner from Ohio be returned to Mocoa."

So I went back up the river with the cop (I was technically under arrest). In Puerto Umbria I came down with chills and fever. Arriving in Mocoa on a Sunday, the Commandante was not there so the second-in-command had me locked up in a wood cubicle without even a bucket to piss in. They put all my gear unsearched in with me. A typical South American touch. I could have had a machine gun concealed in my luggage. I took some aralen and lay down shivering under the blanket. The man in the next cell was confined for lack of some document. I never did understand the details of his case. Next morning the Commandante showed up and I was summoned to his office. He shook hands pleasantly, looked at my papers, and listened to my explanation.

"Clearly an error," he said. "This man is free." What a pleasure it is to encounter an intelligent man in such circumstances.

I went back to the hotel and went to bed and called a doctor. He took my temperature and said, *"Caramba!"* and gave me an injection of quinine and liver extract to offset secondary anemia. I continued the aralen. I had some codeine tablets to control malaria headache so I lay there sleeping most of the time for three days.

I will go to Bogotá, have my tourist card reassembled and return here. Travel in Colombia is difficult even with the soundest credentials. I have never seen such ubiquitous and annoying police. You are supposed to register with the police wherever you go. This is unpardonable stupidity. If I was an active Liberal what could I do in Puerto Assis aside from taking the place over at gun point?

As Ever,
William

April 15
Hotel Nuevo Regis, Bogotá

Dear Al:

Back in Bogotá. I have a crate of *yagé*. I have taken it and know more or less how it is prepared. By the way you may see my picture in *Exposure*. I met a reporter going in as I was going out. Queer to be sure but about as appetizing as a hamper of dirty laundry. Not even after two months in the brush, my dear. This character is shaking down the South American continent for free food and transport, and discounts on everything he buys with a "We-got-like-two-kinds-of-publicity-favorable-and-unfavorable-which-do-you-want,-Jack?" routine. What a shameless mooch. But who am I to talk?

Flashback: Retraced my journey through Cali, Popayan and Pasto to Macoa. I was interested to note that Mocoa dragged Schindler and the two Englishmen as much as it did me.

This trip I was treated like visiting royalty under the misapprehension I was a representative of the Texas Oil Company travelling incognito. (Free boat rides, free plane rides, free chow; eating in officers' mess, sleeping in the governor's house.)

The Texas Oil company surveyed the area a few years ago, found no oil and pulled out. But everyone in the Putumayo believes the Texas Company will return. Like the second coming of Christ. The governor told me the Texas Company had taken two samples of oil eighty miles apart and it was the same oil, so there was a pool of the stuff eighty miles across under Mocoa. I heard this same story in a backwater area of East Texas where the oil company made a survey and found no oil and pulled out. Only in Texas the pool was one thousand miles across. The beat town psyche is joined the world over like the oil pool. You take a sample anywhere and it's the same shit. And the governor thinks they are about to build a railroad from Pasto to Mocoa, and an airport. As a matter of fact the whole of Putumayo region is on the down grade. The rubber business is shot, the cocoa is eaten up with broom rot, no price on rotenone since the war, land is poor and there is no way to get produce out. The dawdling schizophrenia of small town boosters. Like I should think someday soon boys will start climbing in through the transom and tunneling under the door.

Several times when I was drunk I told someone, "Look. There is no oil here. That's why Texas pulled out. They won't ever come back. Understand?" But they couldn't believe it.

We went out to visit a German who owned a *finca* near Mocoa. The British went looking for wild coca with an Indian guide. I asked the German about *yagé*.

"Sure," he said, "my Indians all use it." A half hour later I had twenty pounds of *yagé* vine. No trek through virgin jungle and some old white haired character saying, "I have been expecting you my son." A nice German ten minutes from Mocoa.

The German also made a date for me to take *yagé* with the local *brujo* (at that time I had no idea how to prepare it).

The medicine man was around seventy with a baby smooth face. There was a sly gentleness about him like an old time junkie. It was getting dark when I arrived at this dirt floor thatch shack for my *yagé* appointment. First thing he asked did I have a bottle. I brought a quart of *aguardiente* out of my knapsack and handed it to him. He took a long drink and passed the bottle to his assistant. I didn't take any as I wanted straight *yagé* kicks. The *brujo* put the bottle beside him and squatted down by a bowl set on a tripod. Behind the bowl was a wood shrine with a picture of the Virgin, a crucifix, a wood idol, feathers and little packages tied with ribbons. The *brujo* sat there a long time without moving. He took another long swig on the bottle. The women retired behind a bamboo partition and were not seen again. The *brujo* began crooning over the bowl. I caught *"Yagé pintar"* repeated over and over. He shook a little broom over a bowl and made a swishing noise. This is to whisk away evil spirits who might slip in the *yagé*. He took a drink and wiped his mouth and went on crooning. You can't hurry a *brujo*. Finally he uncovered the bowl and dipped about an ounce more or less of black liquid which he handed me in a dirty red plastic cup. The liquid was oily and phosphorescent. I drank it straight down. Bitter foretaste of nausea. I handed the cup back and the medicine man and the assistant took a drink.

I sat there waiting for results and almost immediately had the impulse to say, "That wasn't enough. I need more." I have noticed this inexplicable impulse on the two occasions when I got an overdose of junk. Both times before the shot took effect. I said, "This wasn't enough. I need more."

Roy told me about a man who came out of jail clean and nearly died in Roy's room. "He took the shot and right away said, 'That wasn't enough' and fell on his face out cold. I dragged him out in the hall and called an ambulance. He lived."

In two minutes a wave of dizziness swept over me and the hut began spinning. It was like going under ether, or when you are very drunk and lie down and the bed spins. Blue flashes passed in front of my eyes. The hut took on an archaic far Pacific look with Easter Island heads carved in the support posts. The assistant was outside lurking there with the obvious intent to kill me. I was hit by violent, sudden nausea and rushed for the door hitting my shoulder against the door post. I felt the shock but no pain. I could hardly walk. No coordination. My feet were like blocks of wood. I vomited violently leaning against a tree and fell down on the ground in helpless misery. I felt numb as if I was covered with layers of cotton. I kept trying to break out of this numb dizziness. I was saying over and over, "All I want is out of here." An uncontrollable mechanical silliness took possession of me. Hebephrenic meaningless repetitions. Larval beings passed before my eyes in a blue haze, each one giving an obscene, mocking squawk (I later identified this squawking as the croaking of frogs)—I must have vomited six times. I was on all fours convulsed with spasms of nausea. I could hear retching and groaning as if I was someone else. I was lying by a rock. Hours must have passed. The medicine man was standing over me. I looked at him for a long time before I believed he was really there saying, "Do you want to come into the house?" I said, "No," and he shrugged and went back inside.

My arms and legs began to twitch uncontrollably. I reached for my nembutals with numb wooden fingers. It must have taken me ten minutes to open the bottle and pour out five capsules. Mouth was dry and I chewed the nembutals down somehow. The twitching spasms subsided slowly and I felt a little better and went into the hut. The blue flashes still in front of my eyes. Lay down and covered myself with a blanket. I had a chill like malaria. Suddenly very drowsy. Next morning I was all right except for a feeling of lassitude and a slight backlog nausea. I paid off the *brujo* and walked back to town.

We all went down to Puerto Assis that day. Schindler kept complaining the Putumayo had deteriorated since he was there ten years ago. "I never made a botanical expedition like this before," he said. "All these farms and *people*. You have to walk miles to get to the jungle."

Schindler had two assistants to carry his luggage, cut down trees, and press specimens. One of them was an Indian from the Vaupes region where the method of preparing *yagé* is different from the Putumayo Kofan method. In Putumayo the Indians cut the vines into eight-inch pieces using about five sections to a person. The pieces of vine are crushed with a rock and boiled with a double handful of leaves from another plant—tentatively identified as ololiuqui—the mixture is boiled all day with a small amount of water and reduced to about two ounces of liquid.

In the Vaupes the bark is scraped off about three feet of vine to form a large double handful of shavings. The bark is soaked in a liter of cold water for several hours, and the liquid strained off and taken over a period of an hour. No other plant is added.

I decided to try some *yagé* prepared Vaupes method. The Indian and I started scraping off bark with machetes (the inner bark is the most active). This is white and sappy at first but almost immediately turns red on exposure to air. The landlady's daughters watched us pointing and giggling. This is strictly against Putumayo protocol for the preparation of *yagé*. The *brujo* of Macoa told me if a woman witnesses the preparation the *yagé* spoils on the spot and will poison anyone who drinks it or at least drive him insane. The old

women-are-dirty-and-under-certain-circumstances-poisonous routine. I figured this was a chance to test the woman pollution myth once and for all with
seven female creatures breathing down my neck, poking sticks in the mixture
fingering the *yagé* and giggling.

The cold water infusion is a light red color. That night I drank a quart of
infusion over a period of one hour. Except for blue flashes and slight nausea—
though not to the point of vomiting—the effect was similar to weed. Vividness of mental imagery, aphrodisiac results, silliness and giggling. In this dosage
there was no fear, no hallucinations or loss of control. I figure this dose as
about one third the dose that *brujo* gave me.

Next day we went on down to Puerto Espina where the governor put us up
in his house. That is we slung our hammocks in empty rooms on the top floor.
A coolness arose between the Colombians and the British because the Colombians refused to get up for an early start, and the British complained the
Cocoa Commission was being sabotaged by a couple of "lazy spics."

Every day we plan to get an early start for the jungle. About eleven o'clock
the Colombians finish breakfast (the rest of us waiting around since eight) and
begin looking for an incompetent guide, preferably someone with a *finca* near
town. About one we arrive at the finca and spend another hour eating lunch.
Then the Colombians say, "They tell us the jungle is far. About three hours.
We don't have time to make it today." So we start back to town, the Colombians collecting a mess of plants along the way. "So long as they can collect
any old weed they don't give a ruddy fuck," one of the Englishmen said to me
after an expedition to the nearest *finca*.

There was supposed to be plane service out of Puerto Espina. Schindler and
I were ready to go back to Bogotá at this point, so there we sit in Puerto Espina
waiting on this plane and the agent doesn't have a radio or any way of finding
out when the plane gets there if it gets there and he says, "Sure as shit boys
one of these days you'll look up and see the Catalina coming in over the river
flashing in the sun like a silver fish."

So I says to Doc Schindler, "We could grow old and simple-minded sitting
around playing dominoes before any sonofabitching plane sets down here and
the river getting higher every day and how to get back up it with every motor
in Puerto Espina broke?"

(The citizens who own these motors spend all the time fiddling with their
motors and taking the motors apart and leaving out pieces they consider nonessential so the motors never run. The boat owners do have a certain Rube
Goldberg ingenuity in patching up the stricken motor for one more last spurt—
but this was a question of going up the river. Going down river you will get
there eventually motor or no, but coming up river you gotta have some means
of propulsion.)

Sure you think it's romantic at first but wait til you sit there five days onna
sore ass sleeping in Indian shacks and eating hoka and some hunka nameless
meat like the smoked pancreas of a two-toed sloth and all night you hear them
fiddle-fucking with the motor—they got it bolted to the porch—"buuuuurt

spluuu . . . . ut . . . . spluuuu . . . . ut," and you can't sleep hearing the motor start and die all night and then it starts to rain. Tomorrow the river will be higher.

So I says to Schindler, "Doc, I'll float down to the Atlantic before I start back up that fuckin river."

And he says, "Bill, I haven't been fifteen years in this sonofabitch country and lost all my teeth in the service without picking up a few angles. Now down yonder in Puerto Leguisomo—they got like military planes and I happen to· know the Commandante is Latah." (Latah is a condition occurring in South East Asia. Otherwise normal, the Latah cannot help doing whatever anyone tells him to do once his attention has been attracted by touching him or calling his name.)

So Schindler went on down to Puerto Leguisomo while I stayed in Puerto Espina waiting to hitch a ride with the Cocoa Commission. Every day I saw that plane agent and he came on with the same bullshit. He showed me a horrible-looking scar on the back of his neck. "Machete," he said. No doubt some exasperated citizen who went berserk waiting on one of his planes.

The Colombians and the Cocoa Commission went up the San Miguel and I was alone in Puerto Espina eating in the Commandante's house. God awful greasy food. Rice and fried platano cakes three times a day. I began slipping the platanos in my pocket and throwing them away later. The Commandante kept telling me how much Schindler liked his food—(Schindler is an old South American hand. He can really put down the bullshit)—did I like it? I would say, "Magnificent," my voice cracking. Not enough I have to eat his greasy food. I have to say I like it.

The Commandante knew from Schindler I had written a book on "marijuana." From time to time I saw suspicion seep into his dull liverish eyes.

"Marijuana degenerates the nervous system," he said looking up from a plate of platanos.

I told him he should take vitamin B1 and he looked at me as if I had advocated the use of a narcotic.

The governor regarded me with cold disfavor because one of the gasoline drums belonging to the Cocoa Commission had leaked on his porch. I was expecting momentarily to be evicted from the governmental mansion.

The Cocoa Commission and the Colombians came back from the San Miguel in a condition of final estrangement. It seems the Colombians had found a *finca* and spent three days there lolling about in their pajamas. In the absence of Schindler I was the only buffer between the two factions and suspect by both parties of secretly belonging to the other (I had borrowed a shotgun from one of the Colombians and was riding in the Cocoa Commission boat).

We went on down the river to Puerto Leguisomo where the Commandante put us up in a gun boat anchored in the Putumayo. There were no guns on it actually. I think it was the hospital ship.

The ship was dirty and rusty. The water system did not function and the W.C. was in unspeakable condition. The Colombians run a mighty loose ship.

It wouldn't surprise me to see someone shit on the deck and wipe his ass with the flag. (This derives from a dream that came to me in seventeenth-century English. "The English and French delegates did shit on the floor, and tearing the Treaty of Seville into strips with such merriment did wipe their backsides with it, seeing which the Spanish delegate withdrew from the conference.")

Puerto Leguisomo is named for a soldier who distinguished himself in the Peruvian War in 1940. I asked one of the Colombians about it and he nodded, "Yes, Leguisomo was a soldier who did something in the war."

"What did he do?"

"Well, he did *something*."

The place looks like it was left over from a receding flood. Rusty abandoned machinery scattered here and there. Swamps in the middle of town. Unlighted streets you sink up to your knees in.

There are five whores in town sitting out in front of blue walled cantinas. The young kids of Puerto Leguisomo cluster around the whores with the immobile concentration of tom cats. The whores sit there in the muggy night under one naked electric bulb in the blare of jukebox music, waiting.

Inquiring in the environs of Puerto Leguisomo I found the use of *yagé* common among both Indians and whites. Most everybody grows it in his backyard.

After a week in Leguisomo I got a plane to Villavencenio, and from there back to Bogotá by bus.

So here I am back in Bogotá. No money waiting for me (check apparently stolen), I am reduced to the shoddy expedient of stealing my drinking alcohol from the university laboratory placed at disposal of the visiting scientist.

Extracting *yagé* alkaloids from the vine, a relatively simple process according to directions provided by the Institute. My experiments with extracted *yagé* have not been conclusive. I do not get blue flashes or any pronounced sharpening of mental imagery. Have noticed aphrodisiac effects. The extract makes me sleepy whereas the fresh vine is a stimulant and in overdose convulsive poison.

Every night I go into a café and order a bottle of Pepsi Cola and pour in my lab alcohol. The population of Bogotá lives in cafés. There are any number of these and always full. Standard dress for Bogotá café society is a gabardine trench coat and of course suit and tie. A South American's ass may be sticking out his pants but he will still have a tie.

Bogotá is essentially a small town, everybody worrying about his clothes and looking as if he would describe his job as "responsible." I was sitting in one of these white-collar cafés when a boy in a filthy light grey suit, but still clinging to a frayed tie, asked me if I spoke English.

I said, "Fluently," and he sat down at the table. A former employee of the Texas Company. Obviously queer, blond, German-looking, European manner. We went to several cafés. He pointed people out to me saying, "He doesn't want to know me anymore now that I am without work."

These people, correctly dressed and careful in manner, did in fact look away and in some cases call for the bill and leave. I don't know how the boy could have looked any less queer in a $200 suit.

One night I was sitting in a Liberal café when three civilian Conservative gun men came in yelling *"Viva los Conservadores!,"* hoping to provoke somebody so they could shoot him. There was a middle-aged man of the type who features a loud mouth. The others sat back and let him do the yelling. The other two were youngish, ward heelers, corner boys, borderline hoodlums. Narrow shoulders, ferret faces and smooth, tight, red skin, bad teeth. It was almost too pat. The two hoodlums looked a little hangdog and ashamed of themselves, like the young man in the limerick who said, "I'll admit I'm a bit of a shit."

Everybody paid and walked out leaving the loud-mouthed character yelling *"Viva el Partido Conservador!"* to an empty house.

As Ever,
Bill

May 23
Lima

Dear Al,

Enclose a routine I dreamed up. The idea did come to me in a dream from which I woke up laughing—

Rolled for $200 in traveller's checks. No loss really as American Express refunds. Recovering from a bout of Pisco neuritis, and Doc has taken a lung X-ray. First Caqueta malaria, then Esmeraldas grippe, now Pisco neuritis— (Pisco is local liquor. Seems to be poison)—can't leave Lima until neuritis clears up.

May 24

Ho hum dept. Rolled again. My glasses and a pocket knife. Losing all my fucking valuables in the service.

This is nation of kleptomaniacs. In all my experience as a homosexual I have never been the victim of such idiotic pilferings of articles of no conceivable use to anyone else. Glasses and traveller's checks yet.

Trouble is I share with the late Father Flanagan—he of Boy's Town—the deep conviction that there is no such thing as a bad boy.

Got to lay off the juice. Hand shaking so I can hardly write. Must cut short.

Love,
Bill

ROOSEVELT AFTER INAUGURATION

Immediately after the Inauguration Roosevelt appeared on the White House balcony dressed in the purple robes of a Roman Emperor and, leading a blind toothless lion on a gold chain, hog-called his constituents to come and get their appointments. The constituents rushed up grunting and squealing like the hogs they were.

An old queen known to the Brooklyn Police as "Jerk Off Annie," was named to the Joint Chiefs of Staff, so that the younger staff officers were subject to unspeakable indignities in the lavatories of the Pentagon, to avoid which many set up field latrines in their offices.

To a transvestite lizzie went the post of Congressional Librarian. She immediately barred the male sex from the premises—a world-famous professor of philology suffered a broken jaw at the hands of a bull dyke when he attempted to enter the Library. The Library was given over to Lesbian orgies, which she termed the Rites of the Vested Virgins.

A veteran panhandler was appointed Secretary of State, and disregarding the dignity of his office, solicited nickels and dimes in the corridors of the State Department.

"Subway Slim" the lush worker assumed the office of Under Secretary of State and Chief of Protocol, and occasioned diplomatic rupture with England when the English Ambassador "came up on him"—lush worker term for a lush waking up when you are going through his pockets—at a banquet in the Swedish Embassy.

Lonny the Pimp became Ambassador-at-Large, and went on tour with fifty "secretaries," exercising his despicable trade.

A female impersonator, known as "Eddie the Lady," headed the Atomic Energy Commission, and enrolled the physicists into a male chorus which was booked as "The Atomic Kids."

In short, men who had gone grey and toothless in the faithful service of their country were summarily dismissed in the grossest terms—like "You're fired you old fuck. Get your piles outa here."—and in many cases thrown bodily out of their offices. Hoodlums and riffraff of the vilest caliber filled the highest offices of the land. To mention only a few of his scandalous appointments:

Secretary of the Treasury: "Pantopon Mike," an old-time schmecker.

Head of the FBI: A Turkish Bath attendant and specialist in unethical massage.

Attorney General: A character known as "The Mink," a peddler of used condoms and a short-con artist.

Secretary of Agriculture: "Catfish Luke," the wastrel of Cuntville, Alabama, who had been drunk twenty years on paregoric and lemon extract.

Ambassador to the Court of St. James's: "Blubber Wilson," who hustled his goofball money shaking down fetishists in shoe stores.

Postmaster General: "The Yen Pox Kid," an old-time junky and con man on the skids. Currently working a routine known as "Taking It Off the Eye"—you plant a fake cataract in the savage's eye (savage is con man for sucker)—cheapest trick in the industry.

When the Supreme Court overruled some of the legislation perpetrated by this vile rout, Roosevelt forced that august body, one after the other, on threat of immediate reduction to the rank of Congressional Lavatory Attendants, to submit to intercourse with a purple-assed baboon; so that venerable, honored men surrendered themselves to the embraces of a lecherous snarling simian, while Roosevelt and his strumpet wife and the veteran brown-nose Harry Hopkins, smoking a communal hookah of hashish, watched the lamentable sight with cackles of obscene laughter. Justice Blackstrap succumbed to a rectal hemorrhage on the spot, but Roosevelt only laughed and said coarsely, "Plenty more where that came from."

Hopkins, unable to control himself, rolled on the floor in sycophantic convulsions, saying over and over "You're killin' me, Chief. You're killin' me."

Justice Hockactonsvol had both ears bitten off by the simian, and when Chief Justice Howard P. Herringbone asked to be excused, pleading his piles, Roosevelt told him brutally, "Best thing for piles is a baboon's prick up the ass. Right Harry?"

"Right Chief. I use no other. You heard what the man said. Drop your moth-eaten ass over that chair and show the visiting simian some Southern hospitality."

Roosevelt then appointed the baboon to replace Justice Blackstrap, "diseased."

"I'll have to remember that one boss," said Hopkins, breaking into loud guffaws.

So henceforth the proceedings of the Court were carried on with a screeching simian shitting and pissing and masturbating on the table and not infrequently leaping on one of the Justices and tearing him to shreds.

"He is entering a vote of dissent," Roosevelt would say with an evil chuckle. The vacancies so created were invariably filled by simians, so that, in the course of time, the Supreme Court came to consist of nine purple-assed baboons; and Roosevelt, claiming to be the only one able to interpret their decisions, thus gained control of the highest tribunal in the land.

He then set himself to throw off the restraints imposed by Congress and the Senate. He loosed innumerable crabs and other vermin in both houses. He had a corps of trained idiots who would rush in at a given signal and shit on the floor, and hecklers equipped with a brass band and fire hoses. He instituted continuous repairs. An army of workmen trooped through the Houses, slapping the solons in the face with boards, spilling hot tar down their necks, dropping tools on their feet, undermining them with air hammers; and finally he caused a steam shovel to be set up on the floors, so that the recalcitrant solons were either buried alive or drowned when the Houses flooded from broken water mains. The survivors attempted to carry on in the street, but were arrested for loitering and were sent to the workhouse like common bums. After release they were barred from office on the grounds of their police records.

Then Roosevelt gave himself over to such vile and unrestrained conduct as is shameful to speak of. He instituted a series of contests designed to promulgate the lowest acts and instincts of which the human species is capable. There was a Most Unsavory Act Contest, a Cheapest Trick Contest, Molest a Child Week, Turn In Your Best Friend Week—professional stool pigeons disqualified—and the coveted title of All-Around Vilest Man of the Year. Sample entries: The junky who stole an opium suppository out of his grandmother's ass; the ship captain who put on women's clothes and rushed into the first lifeboat; the vice-squad cop who framed people, planting an artificial prick in their fly.

Roosevelt was convulsed with such hate for the species as it is, that he wished to degrade it beyond recognition. He could endure only the extremes of human behavior. The average, the middle-aged (he viewed middle age as a condition with no relation to chronological age), the middle-class, the bureaucrat filled him with loathing. One of his first acts was to burn every record in Washington; thousands of bureaucrats threw themselves into the flames.

"I'll make the cocksuckers glad to mutate," he would say, looking off into space as if seeking new frontiers of depravity.

INTERZONE

interzone
by james grauerholz

William Burroughs took a steamer to Rome in late December 1953, but after only a few weeks in Rome and Venice he moved on to Tangier, Morocco, where he knew Paul Bowles lived. Burroughs had read *The Sheltering Sky,* and from the people around Alan Ansen he had heard about the permissive environment for Western hashish smokers and boy-lovers in this partitioned city. Tangier was jointly ruled by military forces of the postwar governments of France, England, Spain, and the United States; this "International Zone" would mutate in Burroughs' work into "Interzone," the setting for some of his most prophetic writing.

Soon after his arrival in Tangier, Burroughs turned forty. He continued writing: long letters to Ginsberg, some sent, others not; journals and notes; story sketches; pieces intended for sale to magazines (none were sold). He was introduced to Bowles, but the two writers did not hit it off at first. He met Kiki, a Spanish boy who offered him uncomplicated friendship and sex, for a small price. Burroughs was relieved, after his disastrous pursuits of Anderson and Marker, to have a new *amigo* in his life. He was also readdicted to junk; Kiki helped him to kick in the spring, just in time for a visit from his old friend Kells Elvins.

Burroughs longed for a new romantic beginning with Ginsberg. They corresponded often; in the fall, Burroughs conceived a plan to visit Ginsberg, who was living in San Francisco. He traveled in September to New York, then spent two months in Palm Beach with his parents and Billy, now seven. While he was in Florida, Burroughs was devastated to receive a letter from Ginsberg, who had decided not to receive him in California. The San Francisco trip was canceled, and Burroughs retreated to Tangier.

Still writing, and hooked again, Burroughs began sending Ginsberg the early pages of what he called *Interzone,* expanding upon the short sketches that were published years later in "Lee's Journals": an ongoing first-person account of his habits and cures, routines and table talk, amidst the chaos of that summer's Arab nationalist riots in Tangier. Also at this time he met his great collaborator, Brion Gysin—although at first Burroughs was not especially taken with him. Gysin was a painter and restaurateur whom Burroughs associated with Tangier's uppity queens; Gysin's restaurant, The 1001 Nights, featured dancing boys and the "Master Musicians" from the Moroccan highlands of Joujouka. Burroughs was also initially unimpressed by Gysin's paintings, which he saw at an exhibition soon after arriving in Tangier.

Ginsberg was still in San Francisco, where he had met the teenaged poet Peter Orlovsky, and they were in love. Their partnership would continue, mutatis mutandis, for the rest of their lives. In the early years they were almost always seen together, often naked in public or in photographs, like revolutionary queer newlyweds. With renewed energy, Ginsberg composed *Howl,* and performed it for the first time in October 1955 at the now-legendary Six Gallery reading. A big part of the poem's initial impact was the poet's open homosexuality. Ginsberg was soon offered publication by Lawrence Ferlinghetti, a poet and publisher in San Francisco whose City Lights Books was already a flagship of new poetry and fiction. The "Pocket Poets" edition of *Howl* was published in summer 1956.

Meanwhile, in May, Burroughs went to London for treatment by Dr. John Yerbury Dent, an innovative physician who offered an "apomorphine cure" for addiction. This treatment left a lasting impression on Burroughs as the best drug cure yet, and he later developed it into a metaphor for liberation from other forms of addiction. Burroughs joined Alan Ansen in Venice; as before, with his drug habit removed, Burroughs' drinking got out of control. Ansen's own situation in Venice became delicate, too—he was accused of something involving underage boys. Both men left Italy in September.

Back in Tangier in late 1956, Burroughs made his literary breakthrough. He was off junk, physically fit, often rowing a boat in the harbor, and writing madly. This is the notorious period of the chaotic typed pages that Paul Bowles described as being scattered on every surface, scuffed with heel marks, all over the floor—as Burroughs rushed from ashtray to ashtray, puffing on multiple kif cigarettes and reading hilariously from his new routines. He called this wild, incantatory work of compulsive obscenity his "Word Hoard"—or alternatively, "WORD"—and he was unleashing it as fast as he could.

Jack Kerouac had been living in Mexico, using narcotics with Old Dave Tesorero and Dave's junky girlfriend, Esperanza; Kerouac later called her "Tristessa" in his novella of the same name. Kerouac arrived in Tangier in February 1957 with the news that Old Dave had suddenly keeled over and died on the sidewalk in Mexico City. Kerouac read and discussed Burroughs' "Interzone" manuscript with him, and retyped large portions of it, sharing his keyboard prowess as a favor to his old friend; Kerouac later reported he had many nightmares during this period. He also offered Burroughs a new title for the book: *Naked Lunch.* But Kerouac's neuroses eventually began to annoy Burroughs again, and Jack left Tangier in late April.

Just as Kerouac departed, Ginsberg arrived, with his new boyfriend, Peter Orlovsky. Burroughs was jealous and annoyed, but he took pains to show indifference. Alan Ansen was also in Tangier, and he and Ginsberg took a keen interest in Burroughs' manuscripts. Together they did much collating and typing, creating the next draft of *Naked Lunch*. Before summer, Paul Bowles was back in town, and all of them were spending time with him and his wife, Jane Bowles, and the painter Francis Bacon. The season of "the Beats in Tangier" was soon over, and Ginsberg, Orlovsky, and Ansen left in late June to travel through Spain. Kells Elvins was now living in Copenhagen, and Burroughs spent the month of August with Elvins and his third wife, working on the "Freelandia" section of his book, satirizing what he felt was the oppressive sterility of Scandinavian socialism.

Kerouac's novel *On the Road,* written six years earlier, was finally published in the U.S. by Viking Press at this time, and the book caused an immediate literary sensation. In this context, with Ginsberg's *Howl* already a succés d'estime, Burroughs set his literary sights higher than before. Ginsberg, living in Paris, offered Burroughs' book to Maurice Girodias, whose censorship-defying, English-language Olympia Press seemed a likely publisher; but Girodias refused to deal with the tattered manuscript. When Burroughs returned to Tangier in September 1957, he learned that Kiki had been stabbed to death in Madrid by a jealous lover, and that Bill Garver had died in Mexico of malnutrition and drug abuse. In January, Burroughs went to Paris to meet Ginsberg, and he took a room in the hotel where Ginsberg and Orlovsky, and the young New York poet Gregory Corso, were staying, at no. 9, rue Git-le-Coeur: the "Beat Hotel," as it later came to be known.

Paris in 1958 was the beginning of Burroughs' annus mirabilis. He was writing steadily on *Naked Lunch*. With Ginsberg and Corso as his companions, he met Marcel Duchamp and Louis-Ferdinand Céline, among other notable figures. After Ginsberg left Paris that summer, Burroughs continued to spend time with Corso, who introduced him to a brilliant, eccentric distant cousin of the Rothschild banking family, a wheelchair-bound neurasthenic named Jacques Stern. Together they built up a new drug habit, and in October, Burroughs and Stern went to Dr. Dent's clinic in London for the apomorphine cure. In the course of this trip, they had a falling-out, a rift which was not repaired for two decades.

Lawrence Ferlinghetti had declined Burroughs' chaotic manuscript, but the poet Robert Creeley, an editor at *Black Mountain Review,* published a portion of it in March 1958—a month before Irving Rosenthal and the University of Chicago students who edited the *Chicago Review* planned to publish more excerpts. The Chicago group reaped the whirlwind when a local conservative journalist raised such an outcry that the next issue of the *Review,* which included chapters from *Naked Lunch,* was impounded by university trustees. Widespread resignations from the magazine followed, and Irving Rosenthal and his associates independently published the material in the first issue of *Big Table* a year later.

Brion Gysin moved into the Beat Hotel in November 1958. He had lost his Tangier restaurant the year before, in a tangle with some early members of the Scientology cult. Now Gysin was painting and exhibiting in Paris. Ginsberg later commented that he found Gysin "too paranoid" when they met in 1961, but Burroughs was becoming progressively more paranoid in his worldview, and Burroughs and Gysin soon became inseparable. Gysin had attended the Sorbonne, and his work had first been exhibited with the Surrealists in 1931 in Paris. He knew his way around Paris, he knew *"tout le monde,"* and with his unequaled gift as a raconteur, Gysin propelled Burroughs to a new plateau of independence and competence. Together they formed a "third mind."

In April 1959 Burroughs ventured back to Tangier, but he was quickly in trouble with the authorities, due to information given up by a small-time English thief of Burroughs' acquaintance named Paul Lund. Moroccan independence was also in the air, with outbursts of nationalistic frenzy and xenophobia in the streets. Burroughs made his way back to Paris within the month. In Chicago, *Big Table 1* was finally published, but again Burroughs' work and the magazine that printed it were impounded, this time by U.S. postal authorities. Judge Julius Hoffman ruled that *Naked Lunch* was not obscene, and the magazine was released in the United States in June 1959 with an aura of literary scandal. Maurice Girodias now changed his mind about that "ratty junky," and he sent his emissary, the South African poet Sinclair Beiles, over to the Beat Hotel to ask if Mr. Burroughs could deliver a finished manuscript of *Naked Lunch* within ten days for publication by The Olympia Press.

Burroughs and Gysin took up the challenge; with Beiles' help, they were sending marked-up pages to the typesetters daily and receiving typeset galleys as they went along. The book's final sequence was determined, at Beiles' suggestion, by the "random" order in which chapters had been finished and sent for typesetting; but Burroughs would later pose the paradox: "How random is random?" In any case, the book was at press that same month, and in stores in Paris by August 1959. By now, the Beat Hotel was a thriving international young-hipster meeting-place. Burroughs and Gysin were pushing the limits of cannabis inspiration and paranoid genius, and Burroughs had begun to make drawings and collages with cursive and typewritten texts, photos, drawings, and magazine pictures.

The American poet Harold Norse was also at the hotel, and hung out with Burroughs and Gysin. Around the time *Naked Lunch* was published, Norse introduced Burroughs to someone who would remain with him for six years: a nineteen-year-old, redheaded Briton named Ian Sommerville, who was studying at Cambridge in England and working at the Mistral Bookshop in Paris for the summer. Sommerville had a natural gift for mathematics, audio engineering, photography, and computers, all talents that he later shared with Burroughs in their collaborations. For the moment, though, Sommerville was just helping Burroughs kick a codeine habit. It was the first love affair that Burroughs had dared to undertake since his romantic failures with Marker and Ginsberg.

After Burroughs survived a court appearance in Paris on a trumped-up drug conspiracy charge, he was visited in October 1959 by photographer Loomis Dean and writer David Snell. They were working on a story about the Beat "revolution" for *Life* magazine, and they made a lasting impression on Burroughs: he saw them as mouthpieces and insiders from the world of the Insect-manipulated Control media of the Western world: "LIFE TIME FORTUNE INC." The Burroughs-Gysin "third mind" needed a manifesto for action within this shared worldview, and that same week, Gysin discovered a principle of random text manipulation: he was cutting a matte for one of his drawings when his Stanley knife sliced through some pages of the *New York Herald Tribune* underneath the matte, revealing new, seemingly meaningless phrase combinations that, as a former Surrealist, Gysin recognized as art. Gysin demonstrated the technique to Burroughs, and they quickly adopted the "cut-up method" as a revolutionary approach to writing.

When *Naked Lunch* was edited in 1959, the previous draft, called *Interzone,* was ripped apart and reassembled by Burroughs with Gysin and Beiles. The published version contained most of the routines and "journals," but very little remained of the "WORD" section. That manuscript survived, however, and was discovered by Barry Miles in 1984, in the Ginsberg collection at Columbia University. When Burroughs and I edited the *Interzone* collection four years later, we combined the material published in *Early Routines* (Cadmus Editions, 1981) with a revised version of the "WORD" chapter from the 1958 *Interzone* manuscript. The new *Interzone* was published by Viking in 1989.

"International Zone" is a travel piece that Burroughs wrote for magazine submission; the character he calls "Brinton" is clearly himself, and gives an idea of his assessment of his own persona at this point in his life. Also here are excerpts from "Lee's Journals," including an early statement of Burroughs' radical artistic prolegomenon. Written partly in Tangier's Benchimal Hospital, where Burroughs was undergoing a cure for his Eukodol habit, the "Journals" portray his state of ultimate dejection and lostness, his bravado and his still-wicked humor.

In one bravissimo passage, Burroughs writes, from Benchimal: "God grant I never die in a fucking hospital! Let me die in some *louche* bistro, a knife in my liver, my skull split with a beer bottle, a pistol bullet through the spine, my head in spit and blood and beer, or half in the urinal so the last thing I know is the sharp ammonia odor of piss . . . Anyplace, but not in a hospital, not in bed. . . ." He recites a list of his friends who have died violently already, including David Kammerer, Joan Vollmer, William Cannastra, and a junky named "Marvie" whom Burroughs used to service in Greenwich Village, who overdosed in front of him. Much later in his life, Burroughs wrote: "When you face Death, for that moment, you are immortal."

"WORD," written in 1956 and 1957, marks the turning point in Burroughs' writing: the moment when he dared to gamble everything for immortality. If the voice he was struggling to find seems a bit forced today, we must remember he was trying to do the not-yet-done, and that he chose to omit "WORD" from *Naked Lunch,* perhaps for that reason. But "WORD" is also crammed with lurid snippets and phrases, as from a fevered brain, which show Burroughs straining to achieve a rapid-fire free association, or automatic writing—and this, in turn, would lead him to "the cut-ups."

The publication of *Naked Lunch* in Olympia's "Traveller's Companion" series was a literary event. Too extreme in its content to be printed in the U.S., the book was smuggled into America and England by intellectuals and young travelers. Maurice Girodias also licensed editions to publishers in France, Germany, Italy, and England: Editions Gallimard, Limes Verlag, Sugar Editore, and John Calder Ltd. A few years later, when Barney Rosset was ready to publish *Naked Lunch* in the U.S., Rosset and his editor, Richard Seaver, dealt directly with Burroughs and his New York attorney, Eugene Winick. Girodias was a groundbreaking publisher, but he was unscrupulous with money; in 1967, he lost all his rights in the novel.

Laura Lee Burroughs heard about her son's scandalous book, and she wrote him an angry letter from Palm Beach in late 1959, excommunicating Burroughs from the family. His joshing, reassuring answer to her shows his reliance on her forgiveness and the closeness between mother and son. All that was changing, though, because his mother was beginning to exhibit confusion and incipient dementia. Burroughs' reliance on his parents' money was nearing an end. He had terminated his last psychiatric relationship, after nine months of sessions with a Dr. Schlumberger in Paris that year. Burroughs concluded that the promise of Freudian analysis—to cure neurosis once the original trauma is recovered—was a false promise. He ended by questioning the very concepts of "neurosis" and the psychiatric "cure." At the age of forty-five, Burroughs came into his own.

Burroughs and Gysin were busy with their cut-up experiments, collaborating on small editions of the earliest cut-up texts, like *The Exterminator* (Auerhahn Press) and *Minutes to Go* (Two Cities), both published in early 1960. Sinclair Beiles and Gregory Corso were also invited into the *Minutes to Go* manifesto, but Corso had a problem with the coldness of the method—or, perhaps, of its practitioners. In true Surrealist fashion, Burroughs and Gysin envisioned their discovery as the foundation of a new worldwide movement in all the arts, but specifically in writing—and a literary "Cut-Up Movement" took root during the middle to late 1960s in Germany, England, and the United States. The lasting effect of the cut-ups, however, would be felt in other mediums many years later.

In April 1960, Burroughs was deported from France for drug-related reasons. The Beat Hotel's season in the sun had come to an end; the old Paris crowd was moving on, and a younger group of proto-Beatniks was coming in. Burroughs had a collaborator, a boyfriend, and a literary mission; he had no need of a fixed address. He relocated to a hotel room in London, with a large sea-trunk full of papers from his manic production in 1956–58—which he would now proceed to cut up.

from
interzone

INTERNATIONAL ZONE

A miasma of suspicion and snobbery hangs over the European Quarter of Tangier. Everyone looks you over for the price tag, appraising you like merchandise in terms of immediate practical or prestige advantage. The Boulevard Pasteur is the Fifth Avenue of Tangier. The store clerks tend to be discourteous unless you buy something immediately. Inquiries without purchase are coldly and grudgingly answered.

My first night in town I went to a fashionable bar, one of the few places that continues prosperous in the present slump: dim light, well-dressed androgynous clientele, reminiscent of many bars on New York's Upper East Side.

I started conversation with a man on my right. He was wearing one of those brown sackcloth jackets, the inexpensive creation of an ultra-chic Worth Avenue shop. Evidently it is the final touch of smartness to appear in a twelve-dollar jacket, the costume jewelry pattern—I happened to know just where the jacket came from and how much it cost because I had one like it in my suitcase. (A few days later I gave it to a shoeshine boy.)

The man's face was grey, puffy, set in a mold of sour discontent, *rich* discontent. It's an expression you see more often on women, and if a woman sits there long enough with that expression of rich discontent and sourness, a Cadillac simply builds itself around her. A man would probably accrete a Jaguar. Come to think, I had seen a Jaguar parked outside the bar.

The man answered my questions in cautious, short sentences, carefully deleting any tinge of warmth or friendliness.

"Did you come here direct from the States?" I persisted.

"No. From Brazil."

He's warming up, I thought. I expected it would take two sentences to elicit that much information.

"So? And how did you come?"

"By yacht, *of course.*"

I felt that anything would be an anticlimax after that, and allowed my shaky option on his notice to lapse.

The European Quarter of Tangier contains a surprising number of first-class French and international restaurants, where excellent food is served at very reasonable prices. Sample menu at The Alhambra, one of the best French restaurants: Snails *à la bourgogne,* one half partridge with peas and potatoes, a frozen chocolate mousse, a selection of French cheeses, and fruit. Price: one dollar. This price and menu can be duplicated in ten or twelve other restaurants.

Walking downhill from the European Quarter, we come, by inexorable process of suction, to the Socco Chico—Little Market—which is no longer a market at all but simply a paved rectangle about a block long, lined on both sides with shops and cafés. The Café Central, by reason of a location that allows the best view of the most people passing through the Socco, is the official meeting place of the Socco Chico set. Cars are barred from the Socco between eight A.M. and twelve midnight. Often groups without money to order coffee will stand for hours in the Socco, talking. During the day they can sit in front of the cafés without ordering, but from five to eight P.M. they must relinquish their seats to paying clients, unless they can strike up a conversation with a group of payers.

The Socco Chico is the meeting place, the nerve center, the switchboard of Tangier. Practically everyone in town shows there once a day at least. Many residents of Tangier spend most of their waking hours in the Socco. On all sides you see men washed up here in hopeless, dead-end situations, waiting for job offers, acceptance checks, visas, permits that will never come. All their lives they have drifted with an unlucky current, always taking the wrong turn. Here they are. This is it. Last stop: the Socco Chico of Tangier.

The market of psychic exchange is as glutted as the shops. A nightmare feeling of stasis permeates the Socco, like nothing can happen, nothing can change. Conversations disintegrate in cosmic inanity. People sit at café tables, silent and separate as stones. No other relation than physical closeness is possible. Economic laws, untouched by any human factor, evolve equations of ultimate stasis. Someday the young Spaniards in gabardine trench coats talking about soccer, the Arab guides and hustlers pitching pennies and smoking their *kief* pipes, the perverts sitting in front of the cafés looking over the boys, the boys parading past, the mooches and pimps and smugglers and money changers, will be frozen forever in a final, meaningless posture.

Futility seems to have gained a new dimension in the Socco. Sitting at a café table, listening to some "proposition," I would suddenly realize that the other was telling a fairy story to a child, the child inside himself: pathetic fantasies of smuggling, of trafficking in diamonds, drugs, guns, of starting nightclubs, bowling alleys, travel agencies. Or sometimes there was nothing wrong with the idea, except it would never be put into practice—the crisp, confident voice, the decisive gestures, in shocking contrast to the dead, hopeless eyes, drooping shoulders, clothes beyond mending, now allowed to disintegrate undisturbed.

Some of these men have ability and intelligence, like Brinton, who writes unpublishably obscene novels and exists on a small income. He undoubtedly has talent, but his work is hopelessly unsalable. He has intelligence, the rare ability to see relations between disparate factors, to coordinate data, but he moves through life like a phantom, never able to find the time, place and person to put anything into effect, to realize any project in terms of three-dimensional reality. He could have been a successful business executive, anthropologist, explorer, criminal, but the conjuncture of circumstances was never there. He is always too late or too early. His abilities remain larval, discarnate. He is the last of an archaic line, or the first here from another space-time way—in any case a man without context, of no place and no time.

Chris, the English Public School man, is the type who gets involved in fur farming, projects to raise ramie, frogs, cultured pearls. He had, in fact, lost all his savings in a bee-raising venture in the West Indies. He had observed that all the honey was imported and expensive. It looked like a sure thing, and he invested all he had. He did not know about a certain moth preying on the bees in that area, so that bee-raising is impossible.

"The sort of thing that could only happen to Chris," his friends say, for this is one chapter in a fantastic saga of misfortune. Who but Chris would be caught short at the beginning of the war, in a total shortage of drugs, and have a molar extracted without anesthetic? On another occasion he had collapsed with peritonitis and been shanghaied into a Syrian hospital, where they never heard of penicillin. He was rescued, on the verge of death, by the English consul. During the Spanish occupation of Tangier, he had been mistaken for a Spanish Communist and held for three weeks incommunicado in a detention camp.

Now he is broke and jobless in the Socco Chico, an intelligent man, willing to work, speaking several languages fluently, yet bearing the indelible brand of bad luck and failure. He is carefully shunned by the Jaguar-driving set, who fear contagion from the mysterious frequency that makes, of men like Chris, lifelong failures. He manages to stay alive teaching English and selling whiskey on commission.

Robbins is about fifty, with the face of a Cockney informer, the archetypal "Copper's Nark." He has a knack of pitching his whiny voice directly into your consciousness. No external noise drowns him out. Robbins looks like some unsuccessful species of *Homo non sapiens*, blackmailing the human race with his existence.

"Remember me? I'm the boy you left back there with the lemurs and the baboons. I'm not equipped for survival like *some* people." He holds out his deformed hands, hideously infantile, unfinished, his greedy blue eyes searching for a spot of guilt or uncertainty, on which he will fasten like a lamprey.

Robbins had all his money in his wife's name to evade income tax, and his wife ran away with a perfidious Australian. ("And I thought he was my friend.") This is one story. Robbins has a series, all involving his fall from wealth, betrayed and cheated by dishonest associates. He fixes his eyes on you probingly, accusingly: are you another betrayer who would refuse a man a few pesetas when he is down?

Robbins also comes on with the "I can't go home" routine, hinting at dark crimes committed in his native land. Many of the Socco Chico regulars say they can't go home, trying to mitigate the dead grey of prosaic failure with a touch of borrowed color.

As a matter of fact, if anyone was wanted for a serious crime, the authorities could get him out of Tangier in ten minutes. As for these stories of disappearing into the Native Quarter, living there only makes a foreigner that much more conspicuous. Any guide or shoeshine boy would lead the cops to your door for five pesetas or a few cigarettes. So when someone gets confidential over the third drink you have bought him and tells you he can't go home, you are hearing the classic prelude to a touch.

A Danish boy is stranded here waiting for a friend to come with money and "the rest of his luggage." Every day he meets the ferry from Gibraltar and the ferry from Algeciras. A Spanish boy is waiting for a permit to enter the French Zone (for some reason persistently denied), where his uncle will give him a job. An English boy was robbed of all his money and valuables by a girlfriend.

I have never seen so many people in one place without money, or any prospects of money. This is partly due to the fact that anyone can enter Tangier. You don't have to prove solvency. So people come here hoping to get a job, or become smugglers. But there are no jobs in Tangier, and smuggling is as overcrowded as any other line. So they end up on the bum in the Socco Chico.

All of them curse Tangier, and hope for some miracle that will deliver them from the Socco Chico. They will get a job on a yacht, they will write a bestseller, they will smuggle a thousand cases of Scotch into Spain, they will find someone to finance their roulette system. It is typical of these people that they all believe in some gambling system, usually a variation on the old routine of doubling up when you lose, which is the pattern of their lives. They always back up their mistakes with more of themselves.

Some of the Socco Chico regulars, like Chris, make a real effort to support themselves. Others are full-time professional spongers. Antonio the Portuguese is mooch to the bone. He won't work. In a sense, he can't work. He is a mutilated fragment of the human potential, specialized to the point where he cannot exist without a host. His mere presence is an irritation. Phantom tendrils reach out from him, feeling for a point of weakness on which to fasten.

Jimmy the Dane is another full-time mooch. He has a gift for showing precisely when you don't want to see him, and saying exactly what you don't want to hear. His technique is to make you dislike him more than his actual behavior, a bit obnoxious to be sure, warrants. This makes you feel guilty toward him, so you buy him off with a drink or a few pesetas.

Some mooches specialize in tourists and transients, making no attempt to establish themselves on terms of social equality with the long-term residents. They use some variation of the short con, strictly one-time touches.

There is a Jewish mooch who looks vaguely like a detective or some form of authority. He approaches a tourist in a somewhat peremptory manner. The tourist anticipates an inspection of his passport or some other annoyance. When he finds out it is merely a question of a small "loan," he often gives the money in relief.

A young Norwegian has a routine of approaching visitors without his glass eye, a really unnerving sight. He needs money to buy a glass eye, or he will lose a job he is going to apply for in the morning. "How can I work as a waiter looking so as this?" he says, turning his empty socket on the victim. "I would frighten the customers, is it not?"

Many of the Socco Chico regulars are left over from the Boom. A few years ago the town was full of operators and spenders. There was a boom of money changing and transfer, smuggling and borderline enterprise. Restaurants and hotels turned customers away. Bars served a full house around the clock.

What happened? What gave out? What corresponds to the gold, the oil, the construction projects? Largely, inequalities in prices and exchange rates. Tangier is a clearinghouse, from which currency and merchandise move in any direction toward higher prices. Under this constant flow of goods, shortages created by the war are supplied, prices and currency approach standard rates, and Tangier is running down like the dying universe, where no movement is possible because all energy is equally distributed.

Tangier is a vast overstocked market, everything for sale and no buyers. A glut of obscure brands of Scotch, inferior German cameras and Swiss watches, second-run factory-reject nylons, typewriters unknown anywhere else, is displayed in shop after shop. There is quite simply too much of everything, too much merchandise, housing, labor, too many guides, pimps, prostitutes and smugglers. A classic, archetypical depression.

The guides of Tangier are in a class by themselves, and I have never seen their equal for insolence, persistence and all-around obnoxiousness. It is not surprising that the very word "guide" carries, in Tangier, the strongest opprobrium.

The Navy issues a bulletin on what to do if you find yourself in shark-infested waters: "Above all, avoid making uncoordinated, flailing movements that might be interpreted by a shark as the struggles of a disabled fish." The same advice might apply to keeping off guides. They are infallibly attracted by the uncoordinated movements of the tourist in a strange medium. The least show of uncertainty, of not knowing exactly where you are going, and they rush on you from their lurking places in side streets and Arab cafés.

"Want nice girl, mister?"

"See Kasbah? Sultan's Palace?"

"Want *kief*? Watch me fuck my sister?"

"Caves of Hercules? Nice boy?"

Their persistence is amazing, their impertinence unlimited. They will follow one for blocks, finally demanding a tip for the time they have wasted.

Female prostitution is largely confined to licensed houses. On the other hand, male prostitutes are everywhere. They assume that all visitors are homosexual, and solicit openly in the streets. I have been approached by boys who could not have been over twelve.

A casino would certainly bring in more tourists, and do much to alleviate the economic condition of Tangier. But despite the concerted efforts of merchants and hotel owners, all attempts to build a casino have been blocked by the Spanish on religious grounds.

Tangier has a dubious climate. The winters are cold and wet. In summer the temperature is pleasant, neither too hot nor too cool, but a constant wind creates a sandstorm on the beach, and people who sit there all day get sand in their ears and hair and eyes. Owing to a current, the water is shock-cold in mid-August, so even the hardiest swimmers can only stay in a few minutes. The beach is not much of an attraction.

All in all, Tangier does not have much to offer the visitor except low prices and a buyer's market. I have mentioned the unusually large number of good restaurants (a restaurant guide put out by the American and Foreign Bank lists eighteen first-class eating places where the price for a complete meal ranges from eighty cents to two dollars and a half). You have your choice of apartments and houses. Sample price for one large room with bath and balcony overlooking the harbor, comfortably furnished, utilities and maid service included: $25 per month. And there are comfortable rooms for $10. A tailor-made suit of imported English material that would cost $150 in the U.S. is $50 in Tangier. Name brands of Scotch run $2 to $2.50 a fifth.

Americans are exempt from the usual annoyances of registering with the police, renewing visas and so forth, that one encounters in Europe and South America. No visa is required for Tangier. You can stay as long as you want, work, if you can find a job, or go into business, without any formalities or permits. And Americans have extraterritorial rights in Tangier. Cases civil or criminal involving an American citizen are tried in consular court, under District of Columbia law.

The legal system of Tangier is rather complex. Criminal cases are tried by a mixed tribunal of three judges. Sentences are comparatively mild. Two years is usual for burglary, even if the criminal has a long record. A sentence of more than five years is extremely rare. Tangier does have capital punishment. The method is a firing squad of ten gendarmes. I know of only one case in recent years in which a death sentence was carried out.

In the Native Quarter one feels definite currents of hostility, which, however, are generally confined to muttering in Arabic as you pass. Occasionally I have been openly insulted by drunken Arabs, but this is rare. You can walk in the Native Quarter of Tangier with less danger than on Third Avenue of New York City on a Saturday night.

Violent crime is rare. I have walked the streets at all hours, and never was any attempt made to rob me. The infrequency of armed robbery is due less, I think, to the pacific nature of the Arabs than to the certainty of detection in a town where everybody knows everybody else, and where the penalties for violent crime, especially if committed by a Moslem, are relatively severe.

The Native Quarter of Tangier is all you expect it to be: a maze of narrow, sunless streets, twisting and meandering like footpaths, many of them blind alleys. After four months, I still find my way in the Medina by a system of moving from one landmark to another. The smell is almost incredible, and it is difficult to identify all the ingredients. Hashish, seared meat and sewage are well represented. You see filth, poverty, disease, all endured with a curiously apathetic indifference.

People carry huge loads of charcoal down from the mountains on their backs—that is, the women carry loads of charcoal. The men ride on donkeys. No mistaking the position of women in this society. I noticed a large percentage of these charcoal carriers had their noses eaten away by disease, but was not able to determine whether there is any occupational correlation. It seems more likely that they all come from the same heavily infected district.

Hashish is the drug of Islam, as alcohol is ours, opium the drug of the Far East, and cocaine that of South America. No effort is made to control its sale or use in Tangier, and every native café reeks of the smoke. They chop up the leaves on a wooden block, mix it with tobacco, and smoke it in little clay pipes with a long wooden stem.

Europeans occasion no surprise or overt resentment in Arab cafés. The usual drink is mint tea served very hot in a tall glass. If you hold the glass by top and bottom, avoiding the sides, it doesn't burn the hand. You can buy hashish, or *kief*, as they call it here, in any native café. It can also be purchased in sweet, resinous cakes to eat with hot tea. This resinous substance, a gum extracted from the cannabis plant, is the real hashish, and much more powerful than the leaves and flowers of the plant. The gum is called *majoun*, and the leaves *kief*. Good *majoun* is hard to find in Tangier.

Kief is identical with our marijuana, and we have here an opportunity to observe the effects of constant use on a whole population. I asked a European physician if he had noted any definite ill effects. He said: "In general, no. Occasionally there is drug psychosis, but it rarely reaches an acute stage where hospitalization is necessary." I asked if Arabs suffering from this psychosis are dangerous. He said: "I have never heard of any violence directly and definitely traceable to *kief*. To answer your question, they are usually not dangerous."

The typical Arab café is one room, a few tables and chairs, a huge copper or brass samovar for making tea and coffee. A raised platform covered with mats extends across one end of the room. Here the patrons loll about with their shoes off, smoking *kief* and playing cards. The game is Redondo, played with a pack of forty-two cards—rather an elementary card game. Fights start, stop, people walk around, play cards, smoke *kief*, all in a vast, timeless dream.

There is usually a radio turned on full volume. Arab music has neither beginning nor end. It is timeless. Heard for the first time, it may appear meaningless to a Westerner, because he is listening for a time structure that isn't there.

I talked with an American psychoanalyst who is practicing in Casablanca. He says you can never complete analysis with an Arab. Their superego structure is basically different. Perhaps you can't complete analysis with an Arab because he has no sense of time. He never completes anything. It is interesting that the drug of Islam is hashish, which affects the sense of time so that events, instead of appearing in an orderly structure of past, present and future, take on a simultaneous quality, the past and future contained in the present moment.

Tangier seems to exist on several dimensions. You are always finding streets, squares, parks you never saw before. Here fact merges into dream, and dreams erupt into the real world. Unfinished buildings fall into ruin and decay, Arabs move in silently like weeds and vines. A catatonic youth moves through the marketplace, bumping into people and stalls like a sleepwalker. A man, barefooted, in rags, his face eaten and tumescent with a horrible skin disease, begs with his eyes alone. He does not have the will left to hold out his hand. An old Arab passionately kisses the sidewalk. People stop to watch for a few moments with bestial curiosity, then move on.

Nobody in Tangier is exactly what he seems to be. Along with the bogus fugitives of the Socco Chico are genuine political exiles from Europe: Jewish refugees from Nazi Germany, Republican Spaniards, a selection of Vichy French and other collaborators, fugitive Nazis. The town is full of vaguely disreputable Europeans who do not have adequate documents to go anywhere else. So many people are here who cannot leave, lacking funds or papers or both. Tangier is a vast penal colony.

The special attraction of Tangier can be put in one word: exemption. Exemption from interference, legal or otherwise. Your private life is your own, to act exactly as you please. You will be talked about, of course. Tangier is a gossipy town, and everyone in the foreign colony knows everyone else. But that is all. No legal pressure or pressure of public opinion will curtail your behavior. The cop stands here with his hands behind his back, reduced to his basic function of keeping order. That is all he does. He is the other extreme from the thought police of police states, or our own vice squad.

Tangier is one of the few places left in the world where, so long as you don't proceed to robbery, violence, or some form of crude, antisocial behavior, you can do exactly what you want. It is a sanctuary of noninterference.

from LEE'S JOURNALS

Lee's face, his whole person, seemed at first glance completely anonymous. He looked like an FBI man, like anybody. But the absence of trappings, of anything remotely picturesque or baroque, distinguished and delineated Lee, so that seen twice you would not forget him. Sometimes his face looked blurred, then it would come suddenly into focus, etched sharp and naked by the flashbulb of urgency. An electric distinction poured out of him, impregnated his shabby clothes, his steel-rimmed glasses, his dirty grey felt hat. These objects could be recognized anywhere as belonging to Lee.

His face had the look of a superimposed photo, reflecting a fractured spirit that could never love man or woman with complete wholeness. Yet he was driven by an intense need to make his love real, to change fact. Usually he selected someone who could not reciprocate, so that he was able—cautiously, like one who tests uncertain ice, though in this case the danger was not that the ice give way but that it might hold his weight—to shift the burden of not loving, of being unable to love, onto the partner.

The objects of his high-tension love felt compelled to declare neutrality, feeling themselves surrounded by a struggle of dark purposes, not in direct danger, only liable to be caught in the line of fire. Lee never came on with a kill-lover-and-self routine. Basically the loved one was always and forever an Outsider, a Bystander, an Audience.

Failure is mystery. A man does not mesh somehow with time-place. He has savvy, the ability to interpret the data collected by technicians, but he moves through the world like a ghost, never able to find the time-place and person to put anything into effect, to give it flesh in a three-dimensional world.

I could have been a successful bank robber, gangster, business executive, psychoanalyst, drug trafficker, explorer, bullfighter, but the conjuncture of circumstances was never there. Over the years I begin to doubt if my time will ever come. It will come, or it will not come. There is no use trying to force it. Attempts to break through have led to curbs, near disasters, warnings. I cultivate an alert passivity, as though watching an opponent for the slightest sign of weakness.

Of course there is always the possibility of reckless breakthrough, carrying a pistol around and shooting anybody who annoys me, taking narcotic supplies at gunpoint, *amok* a form of active suicide. Even that would require some signal from outside, or from so deep inside that it comes to the same thing. I have always seen inside versus outside as a false dichotomy. There is no sharp line of separation. Perhaps:

"Give it to me straight, Doc."

"Very well. . . . A year perhaps, following a regime. . . ." He is reaching for a pad.

"Never mind the regime. That's all I wanted to know."

Or simply the explosion of knowing, finally: "This is your last chance to step free of the cautious, aging, frightened flesh. What are you waiting for? To die in an old men's home, draping your fragile buttocks on a bench in the dayroom?"

Such a sharp depression. I haven't felt like this since the day Joan died.

Spent the morning sick, waiting for Eukodol. Kept seeing familiar faces, people I had seen as store clerks, waiters, et cetera. In a small town these familiar faces accumulate and back up on you, so you are choked with familiarity on every side.

Sitting in front of the Interzone Café, sick, waiting for Eukodol. A boy walked by and I turned my head, following his loins the way a lizard turns its head, following the course of a fly.

Running short of money. Must kick habit.

What am I trying to do in writing? This novel is about transitions, larval forms, emergent telepathic faculty, attempts to control and stifle new forms.

I feel there is some hideous new force loose in the world like a creeping sickness, spreading, blighting. Remoter parts of the world seem better now, because they are less touched by it. Control, bureaucracy, regimentation, these are merely symptoms of a deeper sickness that no political or economic program can touch. What is the sickness itself?

Until the age of thirty-five, when I wrote *Junky,* I had a special abhorrence for writing, for my thoughts and feelings put down on a piece of paper. Occasionally I would write a few sentences and then stop, overwhelmed with disgust and a sort of horror. At the present time, writing appears to me as an absolute necessity, and at the same time I have a feeling that my talent is lost, and I can accomplish nothing, a feeling like the body's knowledge of disease, which the mind tries to evade and deny.

This feeling of horror is always with me now. I had the same feeling the day Joan died; and once when I was a child, I looked out into the hall, and such a feeling of fear and despair came over me, for no outward reason, that I burst into tears. I was looking into the future then. I recognize the feeling, and what I saw has not yet been realized. I can only wait for it to happen. Is it some ghastly occurrence like Joan's death, or simply deterioration and failure and final loneliness, a dead-end setup where there is no one I can contact? I am just a crazy old bore in a bar somewhere with my routines? I don't know, but I feel trapped and doomed.

Someone just died in the hospital downstairs. I can hear them chanting something, and women crying. It's the old Jew who was annoying me with his groans. . . . Well, get this stiff outa here. It's a bringdown for the other patients. This isn't a funeral parlor.

What levels and time shifts involved in transcribing these notes: reconstruction of the past, the immediate present—which conditions selection of the material—the emergent future, all hitting me at once, sitting here junk-sick because I got some cut ampules of methadone last night and this morning.

I just went down to the head and passed the dead man's room. Sheet pulled up over his face, two women sniffling. I saw him several times, in fact this morning an hour before he died. An ugly little man with a potbelly and scraggly, dirty beard, always groaning. How bleak and sordid and meaningless his death!

God grant I never die in a fucking hospital! Let me die in some *louche* bistro, a knife in my liver, my skull split with a beer bottle, a pistol bullet through the spine, my head in spit and blood and beer, or half in the urinal so the last thing I know is the sharp ammonia odor of piss— I recall in Peru a drunk passed out in the urinal. He lay there on the floor, his hair soaked with piss. The urinal leaked, like all South American pissoirs, and there was half an inch of piss on the floor— Or let me die in an Indian hut, on a sandbank, in jail, or alone in a furnished room, on the ground someplace or in an alley, on a street or subway platform, in a wrecked car or plane, my steaming guts splattered over torn pieces of metal. . . . Anyplace, but not in a hospital, not in bed . . .

This is really a prayer. "If you have prayed, the thing may chance." Certainly I would be atypical of my generation if I didn't die with my boots on. Dave Kammerer stabbed by his boy with a scout knife, Tiger Terry killed by an African lion in a border-town nightclub, Joan Burroughs shot in the forehead by a drunken idiot—myself—doing a William Tell, trying to shoot a highball glass off her head, Cannastra killed climbing out of a moving subway for one more drink— His last words were "Pull me back!" His friends tried to pull him back inside, but his coat ripped in their hands and then he hit a post— Marvie dead from an overdose of horse—

I see Marvie in a cheap furnished room on Jane Street, where I used to serve him—sounds kinda dirty, don't it?—I mean sell him caps of H, figuring it was better to deliver to his room than meet him someplace, he is such a ratty-looking citizen, with his black shoes and no socks in December. Once I delivered him his cap, and he tied up. I was looking out the window—it is nerve-racking to watch someone look for a vein. When I turned around he had passed out, and the blood had run back into the dropper, it was hanging onto his arm full of blood, like a glass leech— So I see him there on the bed in a furnished room, slowly turning blue around the lips, the dropper full of blood clinging to his arm. Outside it is getting dark. A neon sign flashes off and on, off and on, each flash picking out his face in a hideous red-purple glow—"Use Gimpie's H. It's the greatest!" Marvie won't have to hustle tomorrow. He has scored for the Big Fix.

—Leif the Dane drowned with all hands in the North Sea—he was a drag anyhoo. Roy went wrong and hanged himself in the Tombs—he always used to say: "I don't see how a pigeon can live with himself." And P. Holt, the closest friend of my childhood, cut his jugular vein on a broken windshield . . . dead before they got him out of the car. A few of them died in hospitals or first-aid stations, but they had already had it someplace else. Foster, one of my anthropology friends in Mexico, died of bulbar polio. "He was dead when he walked in the door," the doctor at the hospital said later. "I felt like telling him, 'Why don't you check straight into a funeral parlor, pick your coffin and climb into it? You've got just about time.'"

SPARE ASS ANNIE

When I became captain of the town, I decided to extend asylum to certain citizens who were persona non grata elsewhere in the area because of their disgusting and disquieting deformities.

One was known as Spare Ass Annie. She had an auxiliary asshole in the middle of her forehead, like a baneful bronze eye. Another was a scorpion from the neck down. He had retained the human attribute of voice and was given to revolting paroxysms of self-pity and self-disgust during which he would threaten to kill himself by a sting in the back of the neck. He never threatened anyone else, though his sting would have caused instant death.

Another, and by far the most detrimental, was like a giant centipede, but terminated in human legs and lower abdomen. Sometimes he walked half-erect, his centipede body swaying ahead of him. At other times he crawled, dragging his human portion as an awkward burden. At first sight he looked like a giant, crippled centipede. He was known as the Centipeter, because he was continually making sexual advances to anyone he could corner, and anyone who passed out was subject to wake up with Centipete in his bed. One degenerate hermaphrodite known as Fish Cunt Sara claimed he was the best lay in town: "Besides, he's a perfect gentleman in every sense of the word. He's kind and good, which means nothing to the likes of you. . . ."

These creatures had developed in a region where the priests carried out strange rites. They built boxes from the moist, fresh bones of healthy youths, captives from neighboring tribes. The boys were killed by looping a vine noose around their necks and pushing them off the branch of a giant cypress tree. The branch had been cut off and carved in the form of an enormous phallus, being some fifteen feet long and three feet in circumference. The vine (always a *yagé* plant) was attached to the end of the branch, and the youth was led out and pushed off so that he fell about eight feet, breaking his neck. Then the priests pounced on him, while he was still twitching in orgasmic convulsions, and cut through the flesh with copper knives, tearing out the bones. From these bones they made boxes with great skill and speed, lining the boxes with copper. Runners were dispatched to carry the boxes to a certain high peak where peculiar lights were given off by the rocks. Pregnant women were placed in the boxes and left on the peak for a period of three hours. Often the women died, but those who survived usually produced monsters. The priests considered these monstrosities a way of humiliating the human race before the gods, in the hope of diverting their anger.

These horrible freaks were highly prized, and they lived in the temple. The women who gave birth to the most monsters received gold stars, which they were authorized to wear on ceremonial occasions.

Once a month they held a great festival at which everyone gathered in a round stone temple, open at the top, and prostrated themselves on the floor, assuming the most disgusting and degraded positions possible, so that the gods would see they were not attempting to elevate themselves above their station.

The habit of living in filth and humiliation finally occasioned a plague, a form of acute leprosy, that depopulated the area. The surviving freaks (who seemed immune to the plague) I decided to receive as an object lesson in how far human kicks can go.

from GINSBERG NOTES

When a depressed psychotic begins to recover, that is, when recovery becomes possible, the illness makes a final all-out attack, and this is the point of maximum suicide danger. You might say the human race is now at this point, in a position for the first time, by virtue of knowledge which may destroy us, to step free of self-imposed restrictions and see all life as a fact. When you see the world direct, everything is a delight, and boredom or unhappiness is impossible.

The forces of negation and death are now making their all-out suicidal effort. The citizens of the world are helpless in a paranoid panic. First one thing and then another is seen as the enemy, while the real enemy hesitates—perhaps because it looks too easy, like an ambush. Among the Arabs and the East in general, the West (especially America), or domination by foreigners, is seen as the enemy. In the West: communism, queers, drug addicts.

Queers have been worked over by female Senders. They are a reminder of what the Senders can and will do unless they are stopped. Also many of them have sold out their bodies to Death, Inc. Their souls wouldn't buy a paper of milk sugar shit. But the enemy needs bodies to get around.

Also there is no doubt some drugs condition one to receive, that is, soften one up for the Senders. Junk is not such a drug, but it is a prototype of invasion. That is, junk replaces the user cell by cell until he *is* junk, so the Sender will invade and replace until separate life is destroyed. Nothing but fact can save us, and Einstein is the first prophet of fact. Anyone is free, of course, to deliberately choose insanity and say that the universe is square or heart-shaped, but it is, as a matter of fact, curved.

Similar facts: morality (at this point an unqualified evil), ethics, philosophy, religion, can no longer maintain an existence separate from facts of physiology, bodily chemistry, LSD, electronics, physics. Psychology no longer exists, since a science of mind has no meaning. Sociology and all the so-called social sciences are suspect to be purveyors of pretentious gibberish.

The next set of facts of similar import will most likely come from present research on schizophrenia, the electronics of hallucination and the metabolism of insanity, cancer, the behavior and nature of viruses—and possibly drug addiction as a microcosm of life, pleasure and human purpose. It is also from such research that the greatest danger to the human race will come—probably has already come—a danger greater than the atom bomb, because more likely to be misunderstood.

I am selecting, editing and transcribing letters and notes from the past year, some typed, some indecipherable longhand, for Chapter II of my novel on Interzone, tentatively entitled *Ignorant Armies*.

Find I cannot write without endless parentheses (a parenthesis indicates the simultaneity of past, present and emergent future). I exist in the present moment. I can't and won't pretend I am dead. This novel is not posthumous. A "novel" is something finished, that is, dead—

I am trying, like Klee, *to create something that will have a life of its own, that can put me in real danger, a danger which I willingly take on myself.*

My thoughts turn to crime, incredible journeys of exploration, expression in terms of an *extreme act,* some excess of feeling or behavior that will shatter the human pattern.

Klee expresses a similar idea: "The painter who is called will come near to the secret abyss where elemental law nourishes evolution." And Genet, in his *Journal of a Thief:* "The creator has committed himself to the fearful adventure of taking upon himself, to the very end, the perils risked by his creatures."

Genet says he chose the life of a French thief for the sake of *depth.* By the fact of this depth, which is his greatness, he is more humanly involved than I am. He carries more excess baggage. I only have one "creature" to be concerned with: myself.

Four months ago I took a two-week sleep cure—a ghastly routine. I had it almost made. Another five days sans junk would have seen me in the clear. Then I relapsed. Just before relapse, I dreamed the following:

I was in high mountains covered with snow. It was in a suicide clinic: "You just wait till you feel like it." I was on a ledge with a boy, about sixteen years old—I could feel myself slipping further and further out, out of my *body,* you dig. I don't mean a physical slipping on the ledge. The Plane was coming for me. (Suicide is performed by getting in this Plane with a boy. The Plane crashes in the Pass. No Plane ever gets through.)

Marv reaches out and catches my arm and says: "Stay here with us a while longer."

The suicide clinic is in Turkey. Nothing compulsory. You can leave anytime, even take your boy with you. (Boat whistle in the distance. A bearded dope fiend rushing to catch the boat for the mainland.) My boy says he won't leave with me unless I kick my habit.

Earlier dream-fantasy: I am in a plane trying to make the Pass. There is a boy with me, and I turn to him and say: "Throw everything out."

"What! All the gold? All the guns? All the junk?"

"Everything."

I mean throw out all excess baggage: anxiety, desire for approval, fear of authority, etc. Strip your psyche to the bare bones of spontaneous process, and you give yourself one chance in a thousand to make the Pass.

I am subject to continual routines, which tear me apart like a homeless curse. I feel myself drifting further and further out, over a bleak dream landscape of snow-covered mountains.

This novel is a scenario for future action in the real world. *Junk, Queer, Yagé,* reconstructed my past. The present novel is an attempt to create my future. In a sense it is a guidebook, a map. The first step in realizing this work is to leave junk forever.

I'll maintain this International Sophistico-criminal Mahatma con no longer. It was more or less shoved on me anyway. So I say: "Throw down all your arms and armor, walk straight to the Frontier."

A guard in a uniform of human skin, black buck jacket with carious yellow tooth buttons, an elastic pullover shirt in burnished Indian copper, adolescent Nordic suntan-brown slacks, sandals from the calloused foot sole of a young Malay farmer, an ash-brown scarf knotted and tucked in the shirt. He is a sharp dresser since he has nothing to do, and saves all his pay, and buys fine clothes and changes three times a day in front of an enormous magnifying mirror. He has a handsome, smooth Latin face with a pencil-line mustache, small brown eyes blank and greedy, eyes that never dream, insect eyes.

When you get to the Frontier, this guard rushes out of his *casita,* where he was plucking at his mustache, a mirror slung round his neck in a wooden frame. He is trying to get the mirror off his neck. This has never happened before, that anyone ever actually got to the Frontier. The guard has injured his larynx taking off the mirror frame. He has lost his voice. He opens his mouth and you can see his tongue jumping around inside. The smooth, blank, young face and the open mouth with the tongue moving inside are incredibly hideous. The guard holds up his hand, his whole body jerking in convulsive negation. I pay no attention to him. I go over and unhook the chain across the road. It falls with a clank of metal on stone. I walk through. The guard stands there in the mist, looking after me. Then he hooks the chain up again and goes back inside the *casita* and starts plucking at his mustache.

At times I feel myself on the point of learning something basic. I have achieved moments of inner silence.

from WORD

The Word is divided into units which be all in one piece and should be so taken, but the pieces can be had in any order being tied up back and forth in and out fore and aft like an innaresting sex arrangement. This book spill off the page in all directions, kaleidoscope of vistas, medley of tunes and street noises, farts and riot yipes and the slamming steel shutters of commerce, screams of pain and pathos and screams plain pathic, copulating cats and outraged squawk of the displaced Bull-head, prophetic mutterings of *brujo* in nutmeg trance, snapping necks and screaming mandrakes, sigh of orgasm, heroin silent as the dawn in thirsty cells, Radio Cairo screaming like a berserk tobacco auction, and flutes of Ramadan fanning the sick junky like a gentle lush worker in the grey subway dawn, feeling with delicate fingers for the green folding crackle.

This is Revelation and Prophecy of what I can pick up without FM on my 1920 crystal set with antennae of jissom. Gentle reader, we see God through our assholes in the flashbulb of orgasm. Through these orifices transmute your body, the way out is the way in. There is no blacker blasphemy than spit with shame on the body God gave you. And woe unto those castrates who equate their horrible old condition with sanctity.

Cardinal ———— (who shall be a nameless asshole) read *Baby Doll* in the Vatican crapper and shit out his prostate in pathic dismay. "Revolting," he trills. His cock and balls long since dissolve inna thervith of shit death and taxes.

Armed with a meat cleaver, the Author chase a gentle reader down the Midway and into the Hall of Mirrors, trap him impaled on crystal cocks.

With a cry squeezed out by the hanged man's spasm, I raise my cleaver. . . . Will the Governor intervene? Will the whimpering chair be cheated of young ass? Will the rope sing to empty air? Go unused to mold with old jockstraps in the deserted locker room?

The Word, gentle reader, will flay you down to the laughing bones and the author will do a striptease with his own intestines. Let it be. No holes barred. The Word is recommended for children, and convent-trained cunts need it special to learn what every street boy knows: "He who rims the Mother Superior is a success-minded brown nose and God will reward him on TV with a bang at Question 666."

Mr. America, sugar-cured in rotten protoplasm, smiles idiot self bone love, flexes his cancerous muscles, waves his erect cock, bends over to show his asshole to the audience, who reel back blinded by beauty bare as Euclid. He is hanged by reverent Negroes, his neck snaps with a squashed bug sound, cock rises to ejaculate and turn to viscid jelly, spread through the Body in shuddering waves, a monster centipede squirms in his spine. Jelly drops on the Hangman, who runs screaming in black bones. The centipede writhes around the rope and drops free with a broken neck, white juice oozing out.

Ma looks up from knitting a steel-wool jockstrap and says, "That's my boy."

And Pa looks up from the toilet seat where he is reading *The Plastic Age* he keeps stashed in a rubber box down the toilet on invisible string of Cowper gland lubricant—hardest fabric known, beat ramie hands down and cocks up. Some people get it, some don't. A sleeping acquaintance point to my pearl and say, "*¿Eso, qué es?*" ("What's that?" to you nameless assholes don't know Spanish), and I have secrete this orient pearl before a rampant swine not above passing a counterfeit orgasm in my defenseless asshole. It will not laugh a well-greased siege to scorn—heh heh heh—say, "Mother knows best."

A Marine sneering over his flamethrower quells the centipede with jellied gasoline, ignoring the Defense Attorney scream: "Double Jeopardy: My Client . . ."

The Author will spare his gentle readers nothing, but strip himself brother naked. Description? I bugger it. My cock is four and one-half inches and large cocks bring on my xenophobia. . . . "Western influence!" I shriek, confounded by disgusting alterations. "Landsake like I look in the mirror and my cock undergo some awful sorta sea change. . . ." Like all normal citizens, I ejaculate when screwed without helping hand, produce a good crop of jissom, spurt it up to my chin and beyond. I have observed that small hard cocks come quicker slicker and spurtier.

These things were revealed to me in Interzone, where East meets West coming round the other way. In a great apartment house done in Tibetan Colonial, lamsters from the crime of Iowa look out on snowy peaks and groan with Lotus Posture hip-aches. You hooked on Nirvana, brothers, old purple-assed mandrill gibber and piss down your back and eat your ears off. Carry your great meaningless load in hunger and filth and disease, flop against the mud wall like a cut of wrong meat—the Inspector stamp Reject on you with his seal of shit. And the Nationalist white slaver, "Sidi the Lymph," covers his face with scented Kotex and pass by on the other side; and the bearded old Moslem convert from Ottawa, Illinois, seals a coin in the slack hand intoning Koranic platitudes through his Midwest nose. Chinese boys turn in Dad as a rampant junky, and the Japanese boy has rape his honey-face after subdue her with a jack handle, throw the meat into that volcano and roar home in his hot rod to catch the Milton Berle show. And the Javanese fuck himself with a greased banana in a suburb toilet, and Malays catch halitosis from the copy-writers and run for the 6:12 with *Amok* trot—the reference, you ignorant asshole, is to the typical trotting gait of the *Amok*. He does not walk, he does not run, he *trots*—and read "How-to" books: *Thank God for My Bang-Utot Attack*, and *On Being a Latah*. See footnote whyncha? So East screams past West on the scenic railway over the midways of Interzone.

So glad to have you aboard, reader, but remember there is only one captain of this shit, and back-street drivers will be summarily covered with jissom and exposed to faggots in San Marco. Do not thrust your cock out the train or beckon lewdly with thy piles, nor flush thy beat Benny down the toilet. (Benny is overcoat in antiquated Times Square argot.) It is forbidden to use the signal rope for frivolous hangings, or to burn Nigras in the washroom before the other passengers have made their toilet. Show Your Culture. Rusty loads subject to carrying charges, plenty of room in the rear, folks, move back into the saloon.

Bloody Mary's First-Aid Manual for Boys: . . . Erections: Apply tight tourniquet at once, open the urethra with a rusty razor blade a whore shave her cunt with it and trim her rag. Inject hot carbolic acid into the scrotum and administer antivenin shot of saltpeter directly into the hypothalamus. If you are caught short without your erection kit, feed a *candiru* up it to suck out the poison. In stubborn and relapsing cases pelvectomy is indicated.

The *candiru* woman with steel-wool pubic hairs receives clients in her little black hut across the river. . . .

The Child Molester has lured a little changling into a vacant lot. "Now open your mouth and close your eyes and I'll give you a big old hairy surprise."

"And I've news for thee, uncle," she say, soul kissing a *candiru* up his joint.

A cunt undulates out of a snake charmer's basket. Tourist: "He's pulled the teeth of course."

Do I hear a paretic heckler mutter, "Cathtrathon Complekth God damn it?" Well I'd rather be safe than sorry. Almost anything can lurk up a woman's snatch. Why, a Da is subject to be castrated by his unborn daughter, piranha fingerlings with transparent teeth sharp as glass slivers leave you without a cunt to piss in. Safest way to avoid these horrid perils is come over her and shack up with Scylla, treat you right, kid, candy and cigarettes.

The vibrating chair receives the yellow cop killer, burns his piles white as a dead leech.

Death dressed as an admiral hang Billy Budd with his own hands and Judge Lynch sneer, "Dead suns can't witness." But the witness will rise from the concrete of Hudson with a fossil prick to point out the innocent wise guy.

And when the graves start yielding up the dead—Goddammit I pay rent in perpetuity for the old gash, now she rise like Christ in drag.

It's the final gadget, the last of the big-time gimmicks—wires straight into the hypothalamus orgasm center! White nerves spilling out at ear and winking lewdly from corner of the eye, the queen twitch his switch and pant, "Gawd you heat my synapses! Turn me on DaddyOOOOOOOOOOH!!"

"You cheap bitch! You nausea artist! I wouldn't demean myself to connect your horrible old synapses." So the queen has slink a slug in the pay toilet and blew her top off with an overcharge.

Now the thoughtful reader may have observed certain tendencies in the author might be termed unwholesome. In fact some of you may be taken aback by the practices of this character. The analyst say: "Mr. Lee have you not consider, to thread thy cock on a lifelong oyster string of pearly cunts and get with normal suburban kicks is chic as Cecil Beaton's ass this season in Hell?"

I call in my friends and we spend whole evenings listen to the Bendix sing "Sweet and Low," "The Wash Machine Boogie"; and the sinister cream separator, a living fossil, bitter as rancid yak butter, seeks the bellowing Hoover with a leopard's grunt. Suburbia hath horrors to sate a thousand castrates and stem the topless cocks of Israel.

Going my way, brother? The hitchhiker walks home through gathering mushroom clouds, and we meet in the Dead Ass Café, to break glass ashtrays over our foreheads pulsing in code . . . slip with a broken neck to the ground-floor mezzanine and put sickness up the cunt of Mary, yearly wounded with a frightened girl.

Brothers, the limit is not yet. I will blow my fuse and blast my brains with a black short-circuit of arteries, but I will not be silent nor hold longer back the enema of my word hoard, been dissolving all the shit up there man and boy forty-three years and who ever held an enema longer? I claim the record, folks, and any Johnny-Come-Late think he can out-nausea the Maestro, let him shove his ass forward and do a temple dance with his piles.

"Not bad, young man, not bad. But you must learn the meaning of discipline. Now you will observe in my production every word got some kinda awful function fit into mosaic on the shithouse wall of the world. That's discipline, son. Always at all times know thy wants and demand same like a thousand junkies storm the crystal spine clinics cook down the Grey Ladies."

The bartender has kick the Sellubi, his foot sink in the ass and the Sellubi comes across the dusty floor. The bartender braces himself against the brass rail, put other foot in the Sellubi's back and pops him off into the street.

"Step right up ladies and gents to see this character at the risk of all his appendages and extremities and appurtenances will positively shoot himself out of a monster asshole. . . " An outhouse is carried in on the shoulders of Southern Negroes in dungarees, singing spirituals.

"And the walls come tumbling down."

The outhouse falls in a cloud of powdered wood and termites, and the Human Projectile stands there in his black shit suit. A giant rubber asshole in a limestone cliff clicks open and sucks the Human Projectile in like spaghetti. Noise of distant thunder and the Projectile pops out with a great fart, flies a hundred feet through the air into a net supported by four gliders. His shit suit splits and a round worm emerges and does a belly dance. The worm suit peels off like a condom and the Aztec Youth stands naked with a hard-on in the rising sun, ejaculates bloody crystals with a scream of agony. The crowd moans and whimpers and writhes. They snatch up the stones dissolve in red and crystal light. . . . The boy has gone away through an invisible door.

Nimun with sullen cat eyes look for a scrap of advantage, he snap it up and carry it away to the secret place where he lives and no one can find the way to his place. Old queens claw wildly at his bronze body, scream, "Show me your secret place, Nimun. I'll give you all my hoard of rotten ectoplasm."

"What place? You dreaming, mister? I live in the Mills Hotel."

"But WHERE YOU BEEN?????????"

The Skip Tracer has come to disconnect your hypothalamus for the nonpayment of orgones:

"I got a fact process here, Jack. You haven't paid your orgone bill since you was born already and used to squeak out of the womb, 'Don't pay it Ma. Think of your unborn child. You wanta get the best for me,' like a concealed rat. Know this, Operators, Black and Grey Marketeers, Pimps and White Slavers, Paper Hangers of the world: no man can con the Skip Tracer when he knocks on your door with a fact process. He who gives out no orgones will be disconnected from life for the nonpayment."

"But give me time. I'm caught short. . . ."

"Time ran out in the 5th at Tropical. . . . Disconnect him boys."

"Lost my shoe up him," grumbles the bartender. "My feet are killing me, I got this condition of bunions you wouldn't believe it. Turn on the ventilator, Mike. When a man live on other people's shit he can fart out a stink won't quit. I knew this one Sellubi could fart out smoke rings, and they is bad to shoplift with their prehensile piles. . . ."

"Order in the court! You are accused of soliciting with prehensile piles. What have you got to say in your defense?"

"Just cooling them off, Judge. Raw and bleeding . . . wouldn't you?"

Judge: "That's beside the point. . . . What do you recommend, Doctor?"

Dr. Burger: "I recommend hypothalamectomy."

The Sellubi turns white as a dead leech and shits his blood out in one solid clot. Warm spring rain washes shit off a limestone statue of a life-size boy hitchhiking with his cock. "GOING MY WAY?" in dead neon on a red-brick dais overlook a deserted park in East St. Louis.

The Hoover bellows retreat and the Business Man says to his honey-face, "I'm tired, sweet thing, and got the rag on."

The team hangs Brad in the locker room. Ceremonial dress of shoulder pads and jockstrap. His friend will pull the jockstrap down, let the cock spurt free and break his neck with a stiff arm. He is buried under the school outhouse where black widows lurk is bad to bite young boy ass.

Fearless boy angels fly through the locker room jacking off, "Whooooo-ooooooooooo"— they jet away in white wake of jissom, leave a crystal laugh hang in the air.

Greg sits in the school toilet. Clean sharp turds fall out his tight young ass (turds like yellow clay washed clean in summer rain covered with crystal snail tracks in the morning sun lights the green flame of grass).

The man with black Japanese mustache, each hair frozen in white grease. (Black branches with the white ice cover catch the morning sun over a frozen lake when we get back from the hunting trip.)

Ambivalent alcoholic hangs himself with a great Bronx cheer, blasting out all his teeth, and tears at the noose. (Shivering dog breaks his teeth on the steel trap under a cold white moon.)

"Candy, I Call My Sugar Candy." Hanged boy descends on a rope of toffee, comes in the mouth of a fourteen-year-old girl eats toffee and taps out "Candy" on the neon-lighted table—outside, the blight of Oklahoma beaten by the calm young eyes.

The boy has found the vibrator in his mother's closet. They won't be back before five . . . plenty of time. Drops pants to ankles, cock springs up hard and free with that lovely flip make old queen bones stir with root nerves and ligaments. He grease the tip, and it turns into a vulgar cock given to Bronx cheers at moment of orgasm and other shocking departures from good taste. (Emily Post is writing a million-word P.S. to *Etiquette,* entitled *The Cock in Our House.*) He stands front mirror, stick it slow up his ass to the glad gland give a little fart of pleasure. Bubble filled with fart gas hang in the air heavy as ectoplasm dispersed by the winds of morning sweep the dust out with slow old man hands coughing and spitting in the white blast of dawn. Sperm splash the mirror, turn black and go out in a short circuit with ozone smell of burning iron.

Greg has come up behind Brad in the park, goose him and his hand sink in.

"Hello, Brad." He pulls his hand out with a resounding fart and rubs ambergris over his body, poses for *Health and Strength* in faggot-skin jockstrap.

So there he stand on top of the filing cabinet naked as a prick hang out in the muted blue incense of the lesbian temple. (Cold-eyed nuns rustle by, metallic purity leaves a whiff of ozone.) Funny how a man comes back to something he left behind in a Peoria hotel drawer 1932.

You are nearing the frontier where all the pitchmen and street peddlers, three-card-monte quick-con artists of the world spread out their goods. Old pushers, embittered by years of failure, mutter through the endless grey lanes of junk *amok* with a joint (i.e., a syringe), shooting the passersby. The tourist is torn in pieces by Soul Short-Change hypes fight over pieces. (Piranha fish tear each other to great ribbons of black-market beef. White bone glistens through, covered with iridescent ligaments.)

Neon tubes glow in the blood of the world. Everyone see his neighbor clear as an old message on the shithouse wall stand out in white flames of a burning city.

Greg turns away with a cry of defeat. Bone ache for the Marble God smiling into park covered with weeds.

Fish thrown to the seal by naked boy grin for ooze in verdigris: KEEP THE CHANGE.

Smile sweet as a blast of ozone from a June subway, teeth tinkle like little porcelain balls.

Hold your tight nuts frozen in limestone convolutions.

"I'll be right over stick a greased peccary up her Hairy Ear." Albanian argot for cunt.

Sea of frozen shit in the morning sun and maggots twelve feet long stir underneath, the crust breaks here and there. Asshole farts up sulfur gases and black boiling mud.

Crisp green lettuce heads glitter with frost under a tinkling crystal moon.

"We'll make a heap of money, Clem, if the price is right." He plucks a boy's balls, look over careful for lettuce blight, probing veins and ligaments with gentle old-woman fingers, feel soft for the vein in the pink dawn light; and the young boy wake naked out of wet dream, watch his cock spurt into the morning.

The boy flies screaming in a jet of black blood, turns a red tube in the air, ineffable throbbing pink, rains soft pink cushions on your ass in a soft slow come.

The boy has cut off his limestone balls and tossed them to you with a grin—light on water. Now the body sinks with a slow Bronx cheer to a torn pink balloon hang on rusty nail in the barn. Pink and purple lights play over it from a great black crane swing over rubbish heap go back to stone and trees.

His neck has grown around the rope like a tree. (Vine root in old stone wall. Voice fade to decay, loose a soundless puff of dust, fall slow through the sunlight.)

The boy has eaten a pat of butter, turns into middle-aged cardiac. "That's the way I like to see them," says Doctor Dodo Rindfest—known as Doodles to his many friends. "Them old cardiac rams alla time die up a reluctant ewe."

The old queen wallows in bathtub of boy balls. Others jack off over him jitterbugging, walking through the Piney Woods with a .22 in the summer dawn (chiggers pinpoint the boy's groin in red dots), hanging on the back of freight trains careen down the three-mile grade into a cowboy ballad bellowed out by idiot cows through the honky-tonks of Panhandle.

Screaming round the roller coaster in a stolen car, play chicken with a bronze scorpion big as a trailer truck on route 666 between Lynchburg and Danville.

The boy rise in sea-green marble to jack off on the stones of Venice invisible to the ravening castrates of the world, fill the canals with miasmic mist of whimpering halitosis can't get close enough to offend.

The boy has hit you with soft snowballs burst in light burn you soft and pink and cold as cocaine.

Don't walk out on a poor old queen leave her paralyzed come to an empty house. Spurt into the cold spring wind whip the white wash in Chicago, into the sizzling white desert, into the limestone quarry, into the old swimming hole, bait a boy's hook for a throbbing sunfish burn the black water with light.

The wind sighs through the silk stocking hang in clear blue of Mexico clear against the mountain a wind sock of sweet life. (Sweet smell of boy balls and rusty iron cool in the mouth.)

Attic under the round window eye. Summer dawn the two young bodies glow incandescent pink copulations, cock sink into the brown pink asshole up the pearly prostate, sing out along the white nerves. First soft licks of rimming tighten balls off like a winch up the ass. Rim on, MacDuff, till the pool be drained and fill with dead brown leaves, dirty snow drift across my body frozen in the kiss wakes the soft purple flower of shit.

The boy burglar fucked in the long jail with the Porter Tuck—a bullfighter of my acquaintance recently gored in the right lung—in the lungs risk the Great Divide, ousted from the cemetery for the nonpayment come gibbering into the queer bar with a mouldy pawn ticket to pick up the back balls of Tent City, where castrate salesmen sing the IBM song in quavering falsetto.

Balls on the window ledge fall like a broken flowerpot onto the pavement of arson yearly wounded to the sea.

Slow cunt tease refuse until the conversion of the Jew to Diesel go around raping decent cars with a nasty old Diesel Conversion Unit cancerous, so red the rosette, on earth as in heaven this day our breadfruit of cunt.

Crabs frolic through his forest, wrestling with the angle hard-on all night thrown in the home full of valor by adolescent rustler, hide in the capacious skirts of home on the range and the hunter come home from the Venus Hill take the back road to the rusty limestone cave.

Rock and roll around the floor scream for junk fix the Black Yen ejaculate over the salt marshes where nothing grow, not even a mandrake. (Year of the rindpest. Everything died, even the hyenas had to bite a man's balls and run like smash and grab.)

Talk long enough say *something*. It's the law of averages . . . a few chickens . . . only way to live.

Don't neglect the fire extinguisher and stand by with the Kotex in case one of these Southern belles get hot and burst into flame. (Bronx cheer of a fire-eater.)

Cleave fast to mayhem and let not arson be far from thee and clamp murder to thy breast with WHOOOOOOOOOPS of seal leap at your throat in Ralph's. Not a bit alarmed about that. Think of something else.

We are prepared to divulge all and to state that on a Thursday in the month of September 1917, we did, in the garage of the latter, at his solicitations and connivance, endeavor to suck the cock of one George Brune Brubeck, the Bear's Ass, which act disgust me like I try to bite it off and he slap me and curse and blaspheme like Christopher Marlowe with the shiv through his eye the way it wasn't fitting a larval fag should hear any old nameless asshole unlock his rusty word hoard.

The blame for this atrociously incomplete act rest solidly on the basement of Brubeck, my own innocence of any but the most pure reflex move of self-defense and -respect to eliminate this strange serpent thrust so into my face at risk of my Man Life, so I, not being armed (unfortunately) with a blunderbuss, had recourse to nature's little white soldiers—our brave defenders by land—and bite his ugly old cock in a laudable attempt to circumcise him thereby reduce to a sanitary condition. He, not understanding the purity of my motives, did inopportunely resist my well-meaning would-be surgical intervention, which occasioned to him light contusions of a frivolous nature. Whereupon he did loose upon my innocent head a blast of blasphemies like burning lions or unsuccessful horse abortionists cooked in slow Lux to prevent the shrinkage of their worm.

We are not unaware of the needs of our constituents. Never out of our mind, and you may rest assured that we will leave no turd interred to elucidate these rancid oil scandals. We will not be intimidated by lesbians armed with hog castrators and fly the Jolly Roger of bloody Kotex, nor succumb to the blandishments of a veteran queen in drag of Liz in riding pants. Even the Terrible Mother will be touched by the grace of process.

So leave us throw aside the drained crankcase of Brubeck and proceed to unleaven the yeast bread of cunt and unfurl the jolly condom. . . . I walk up to this chick, flash a condom on her like a piecea tin, you dig, and I say, "Come with me."

"Fresh," she say and slap me hard, the way I know it is this impersonator is a insult. I insinuate a clap up her ass without so much as by-your-leave.

So I says, "I thought you was McCoy. You look so nice and female to an old cowhand."

"Oh go impersonate a purple-assed baboon, you stupid old character. I'd resist you to the last bitch in any sex."

I stand on the Fifth Amendment, will not answer question of the senator from Wisconsin. "Are you or have you ever been a member of the male sex?" They can't make Dicky whimper on the boys. Know how I take care of crooners, don't you? Just listen to them. A word to the wise guy. I mean you gotta be careful of politics these days, some old department get physical kick him right in his Coordinator. Well, that's the hole story, and I guess I oughta know after all these years. Wellcome and Burroughs to the family party, a member in *hrumph* good standing we hope.

Castrates, Don't Let The Son Set On You Here—precocious little prick could get it by ass mosses. (Seaweed in a dark green grotto.)

The Philosophic Doctor sits on his rattan-ass Maugham veranda drinking pink gin fades to a Manhattan analyst looking over a stack of notes.

"So our murderer was, it seems, the bitten Brubeck, who has since recovered and spread his hideous progeny from the wards of Seattle in the parishes of New Orleans, nameless blubby things crawl out of ash pits all covered with shitty sheets, walk around gibber like dead geese."

This refers to a nightmare of the subject's childhood in which he found himself threatened by two figures covered with soiled sheets—poison juices, Goddammit! Dream occur after the subject's collaborating father read him "The Murders in the Rue Morgue," where, as you will doubtless recall, one woman got her head cut clean off and rammed up the chimney. So, Brubeck, you know what you can do with your Liz bitch; and if you don't, my orangutan friend will show you.

"I have frequently observed in the course of my practices, *hrumph*, I mean practice, that homosexuals often express a willingness to, *humph*, copulate with *headless* women—a consummation devoutly to be wished. As one subject expressed it, 'Now I read where this chicken live a week without a head. They feed it through this tube stick out so the neck don't heal over and close up the way a cunt would heal over she didn't open it up every month with an apple corer, to let the old blood out. I mean a broad don't need that head anyhoo.' And recall that it was Medusa's head turned the boys to stone. I suggest that the perilous part of a woman is her hypothalamus, sending solid female static fuck up a man's synapses and leave him paralyzed from the waist down."

So I am prepared to state that the above is true and accurate to the best of my knowledge, so help me God or any other outfit when my dignity and sovereignty be threatened by brutal short-arm aggression. Sworn before me, Harry Q. T. Burford on this day.

"We must have a long talk, son. You see there are men and there are, well, women; and women are different from men."

"In precisely what way, Father?" said young Cesspoll incisively.

"Well, they're, well, they're different, that's all. You'll understand when you're older; and, *hurumph,* that's what I want to talk to you about. When you *do* get older."

"Come see me tonight in my apartment under the school privy. Show you something interesting," said the janitor, drooling green coca juice.

Women seethe with hot poison juices eat it off in a twink. Laws of hospitality be fucked. Take your recalcitrant ass to your own trap. No drones in my dormitories.

"I'm no one's live one," sneered the corpse to the necrophile. "Go back to your own people, you frantic old character."

"Oh be careful. There they go again," says the old queen as his string break, spilling his balls across the floor. "Stop them, will you, James, you worthless old shit! Don't just stand there and let the master's balls roll into the coal bin."

"Is them my peeled balls those kids play marbles with? Why shit sure. Boy, who give you the right to play with my balls?"

"They revert to the public domain after not being claimed forty year, mister."

Well, the wind-up is the fag marries the transvestite Liz disguised as a boy in drag, former heartthrob of Greg hang him for kicks and retire to a locker in Grand Central, subsisting on suitcase and shoe leather. So many tasty ways to prepare it, girls—simmered in saddle soap, singe-broiled in brilliantine, smoked over smoldering ashtrays.

We are in a long white corridor of leaves lit by sunlight.

The Old West dies slow on Hungarian gallows, so while he is fixing (can't hit the hypothalamus anymore) we will shake down the trap for hidden miles and tragic flaws hang a golden lad with his own windblown hair.

When is a boy not a boy? When he is buoyed up by the wind, and the sailplane falls silent as erection.

The blind vet is on the way over to fuck me in the Grand Canal bent over the Academy Bridge. Someone take a picture and cops the film fest for a big brass bidet.

The lamprey seeks a silver fish in the green lagoon.

It would be better off dead. Broken leg. Told by an idiot broken down there you must hear. It is out of the woodpile and into the fire that monkey, and Denmark is rotten with a funeral pyre of bullshit.

"Look into my eyes, baby, mirror of the mad come."

"I can see inside the blue flames running on these long white nerves burn the spine in a slow squeeeeeeeeze."

Mouths leap forward on flesh tubes, clamp and twist.

Johnny on all fours and Marv sucking him and running his fingers down the thigh backs and light over the ass and outfields of the ball park. Johnny's body begins to hump in the middle, each hump a little longer and squeezier like oily fingers inside squeeze your balls soft as pink down, squeeze those sweet marshmallows slow slow slow.

He throws his head back with a great wolf howl.

Call the coroner; my skill naught avail.

Mine it out of your limestone bones, those fossil messages of arthritis; read the metastasis with blind fingers.

Where else you gonna look? Into the atrophied nuts of the priest, coyote of death? (A coyote is character hangs around the halls of the immigration department in Mexico, D.F., engage to help you for a fee with his inside connections.)

"I can get you straight in to the District Supervisor. Got an in. Of course, it cost. I don't want much—all go pay off my *tremendous* connections." His voice breaks in a pathic scream.

"Didja get a stand-on?" said the vulgar old queen to the virginal boy, trembling in white flame of contempt. "Land sakes," said the queen, "so young so cold so fair—I love it." (Silver statue in the moonlight.)

The swindler enters Heaven in a blast of bullshit. Here's a man hang self opening night of the Met. Cut throat of entire staff, take over the stage, single-handed scene-stealer. Prance out in Isolde drag, sing the "Liebestod" in a hideous falsetto, ending in burlesque striptease. "Take it off! Take it off!" chant his stooges, as pink step-ins, stiff with ass blood, fly out over the audience, she spring the trap. Blood burn in neon pink light through his spine spasms and grinding bone grins. Flesh turn to black shit and flake off—wind and rain and bones on moldy beach. The queen is a hard-faced boy, patch over one eye, parrot on shoulder, say, "Dead men tell no tales—or do they?" He prods the skull with a cutlass, and a crab scuttles out. The boy reaches down and pick up a scroll.

"The Map! The Map!"

The map turns to shitty toilet paper in his hands, blow across a vacant lot in East St. Louis, catch on clean barbed wire and burn with a blue flame.

The boy pulls off the patch, parrot flies into the jungle, cutlass turns to machete. He is studying the Map and swatting sand flies.

American queens shriek and howl in revolting paroxysms of self-pity. They declare a nausea contest. The most abject queen of them all gathers his rotting protoplasms for an all-out effort. . . .

"My power's coming! . . . My power's coming!" he screeches.

Orchestra strikes up, and female impersonator prances out in hillbilly drag with hairy knobby knees showing.

"She'll be swishing round the mountain when she comes. . . ."

The queen's familiar spirits are gathering, larval whimpering entities. The queen writhes in a dozen embraces, accommodating the passionate exigencies of invisible partners, now sucking noisily, now throwing his legs over his head with a loud "Whoopeee!" He sidles across the floor with his legs spread, reaches up and caresses one of the judges with a claw . . . he has turned himself into a monster crab with a human body from the waist down. Beneath the skin liquid protoplasm quivers like jellied consommé as he offers up his ass.

The judges start back, appalled.

"He liquefy himself already!"

"Deplorable!"

Other contestants jealously throw off their clothes to reveal an impressive variety of unattractive physiques.

"Look at me!"

"Feast your eyes on *my* ugliness!"

One queen pulls the falsie top off his pinhead and begins cackling like a chicken: "I don't need that old head anyhoo!"

We are not at all innarested to find a prick crawl up the back stairs, make time in the broom closet, remember? and spurt all over the white sheet in the hung-over Sunday dawn. . . . We goin' to home it over the silver plate into the golden toilet and jack out our balls on the mosaic floor into the carp pool, keeps them healthy, fat and sluggish.

Assassin of geraniums! Murderer of the lilies!

Over the bridge to Brighton Rock, place of terrible pleasures and danger, where predatory brainwashers stalk the passersby in black Daimlers. Clients check Molotov cocktails and flamethrowers with the beautiful diseases hatcheck person of indeterminate sex. . . . And the government falls at least once a day.

Set wades in blood up to her cunt, cuts down the blasphemers of Ra with her sick hell of junk.

The snake's venom is paid for with coins of the realm of night. No hiding place . . .

Wooden steps wind up a vast slope, scattered stone huts. Greg licks the black rim of the world in a cave of rusty limestone. Across the hills to Idaho, under the pine trees, boys hang a horse with a broken leg. One plays "I'm Leavin' Cheyenne" on his harmonica, they pass around an onion and cry. They stand up and swing off through the branches with Tarzan cries.

We is all out on a long silver bail.

It was a day like any other when I walk down the Main Line to the Sargasso, pass faces set a thousand years in matrix of evil, faces with eerie innocence of old people, faces vacant of intent. Sit down in the green chair provided for me by other men occupy all the others. Convey my order with usual repetitions— at one time I was threatened by rum and Cinzano, whereas I order mint tea. I sit back and make this scene, mosaic of juxtapositions, strange golden chains of Negro substance seeped up from the Unborn South. So I do not at once dig the deformed child—I call it that for want of a better name: actually it look between unsuccessful baboon and bloated lemur, with a sort of moldy sour bestial look in the eyes—that was sitting to all intents and purposes on the back of my chair.

Shellac red-brick houses, black doors shine like ice in the winter sun. Lawn down to the lake, old people sit in green chairs, huddle in lap robes.

We are on the way over with a bolt of hot steel wool to limn your toilet with spangled orgones. Conspicuous consumption is rampant in the porticoes slippery with Koch spit, bloody smears on the cryptic mosaic—frozen cream cone and a broken dropper. As when a junky long dead woke with a junk-sick hard-on, hears the radiator thump and bellow like an anxious dinosaur of herbivorous tendencies—treeless plain stretch to the sky, vultures have miss the Big Meat. . . .

Will he fight? is the question at issue.

"Yes," snarls President Ra look up from a crab hunt, charge the Jockey Club with his terrible member. "Fuck my sewage canal, will you? Don't like you and don't know you. Some Coptic cocksucker vitiate the pure morning joy of hieroglyph."

"At least we have saved the bread knife," he said.

"The message is not clear," said García, when they brought him the *brujo* rapt in nutmeg.

Priest whips a yipping Sellubi down the limestone stairs with a gold chain.

"Unlawful flight to prevent consummation," lisps the toothless bailiff. The trembling defendant—survivor of the Coconut Grove fire—stands with a naked hard-on.

"Death by Fire in Truck," farts the Judge in code.

"Appeal is meaningless in the present state of our knowledge," says the defense, looking up from electron microscope.

"You have your warning," says the President.

"The monkey is not dead but sleepeth," brays Harry the Horse, with inflexible authority.

The centipede nuzzles the iron door rusted to thin black paper with urine of a million fairies. Red centipede in the green weeds and broken stelae. Inside the cell crouch prisoners of the Colónia. Mugwump sits naked on a rusty bidet, turns a crystal cylinder etched with cuneiforms. Iron panel falls in dust, red specks in the sunlight.

A vast Moslem muttering rises from the stone square where brass statues suffocate.

from
naked lunch

I CAN FEEL THE HEAT CLOSING IN

I can feel the heat closing in, feel them out there making their moves, setting up their devil doll stool pigeons, crooning over my spoon and dropper I throw away at Washington Square Station, vault a turnstile and two flights down the iron stairs, catch an uptown A train. . . . Young, good looking, crew cut, Ivy League, advertising exec type fruit holds the door back for me. I am evidently his idea of a character. You know the type comes on with bartenders and cab drivers, talking about right hooks and the Dodgers, call the counterman in Nedick's by his first name. A real asshole. And right on time this narcotics dick in a white trench coat (imagine tailing somebody in a white trench coat—trying to pass as a fag I guess) hit the platform. I can hear the way he would say it holding my outfit in his left hand, right hand on his piece: "I think you dropped something, fella."

But the subway is moving.

"So long flatfoot!" I yell, giving the fruit his B production. I look into the fruit's eyes, take in the white teeth, the Florida tan, the two hundred dollar sharkskin suit, the button-down Brooks Brothers shirt and carrying *The News* as a prop. "Only thing I read is Little Abner."

A square wants to come on hip. . . . Talks about "pod," and smoke it now and then, and keeps some around to offer the fast Hollywood types.

"Thanks, kid," I say, "I can see you're one of our own." His face lights up like a pinball machine, with stupid, pink effect.

"Grassed on me he did," I said morosely. (Note: Grass is English thief slang for inform.) I drew closer and laid my dirty junky fingers on his sharkskin sleeve. "And us blood brothers in the same dirty needle. I can tell you in confidence he is due for a hot shot." (Note: This is a cap of poison junk sold to addict for liquidation purposes. Often given to informers. Usually the hot shot is strychnine since it tastes and looks like junk.)

"Ever see a hot shot hit, kid? I saw the Gimp catch one in Philly. We rigged his room with a one-way whorehouse mirror and charged a sawski to watch it. He never got the needle out of his arm. They don't if the shot is right. That's the way they find them, dropper full of clotted blood hanging out of a blue arm. The look in his eyes when it hit—Kid, it was tasty. . . .

"Recollect when I am travelling with the Vigilante, best Shake Man in the industry. Out in Chi. . . . We is working the fags in Lincoln Park. So one night the Vigilante turns up for work in cowboy boots and a black vest with a hunka tin on it and a lariat slung over his shoulder.

"So I says: 'What's with you? You wig already?'

"He just looks at me and says: 'Fill your hand stranger' and hauls out an old rusty six shooter and I take off across Lincoln Park, bullets cutting all around me. And he hangs three fags before the fuzz nail him. I mean the Vigilante earned his moniker. . . .

"Ever notice how many expressions carry over from queers to con men? Like 'raise,' letting someone know you are in the same line?

"'Get her!'

"'Get the Paregoric Kid giving that mark the build up!'

"'Eager Beaver wooing him much too fast.'

"The Shoe Store Kid (he got that moniker shaking down fetishists in shoe stores) say: 'Give it to a mark with K.Y. and he will come back moaning for more.' And when the Kid spots a mark he begin to breathe heavy. His face swells and his lips turn purple like an Eskimo in heat. Then slow, slow he comes on the mark, feeling for him, palpating him with fingers of rotten ectoplasm.

"The Rube has a sincere little boy look, burns through him like blue neon. That one stepped right off a *Saturday Evening Post* cover with a string of bullheads, and preserved himself in junk. His marks never beef and the Bunko people are really carrying a needle for the Rube. One day Little Boy Blue starts to slip, and what crawls out would make an ambulance attendant puke. The Rube flips in the end, running through empty automats and subway stations, screaming: 'Come back, kid!! Come back!!' and follows his boy right into the East River, down through condoms and orange peels, mosaic of floating newspapers, down into the silent black ooze with gangsters in concrete, and pistols pounded flat to avoid the probing finger of prurient ballistic experts."

And the fruit is thinking: "What a character!! Wait till I tell the boys in Clark's about this one." He's a character collector, would stand still for Joe Gould's seagull act. So I put it on him for a sawski and make a meet to sell him some "pod" as he calls it, thinking, "I'll catnip the jerk." (Note: Catnip smells like marijuana when it burns. Frequently passed on the incautious or uninstructed.)

"Well," I said, tapping my arm, "duty calls. As one judge said to another: 'Be just and if you can't be just, be arbitrary.'"

I cut into the automat and there is Bill Gains huddled in someone else's overcoat looking like a 1910 banker with paresis, and Old Bart, shabby and inconspicuous, dunking pound cake with his dirty fingers, shiny over the dirt.

I had some uptown customers Bill took care of, and Bart knew a few old relics from hop smoking times, spectral janitors, grey as ashes, phantom porters sweeping out dusty halls with a slow old man's hand, coughing and spitting in the junk-sick dawn, retired asthmatic fences in theatrical hotels, Pantopon Rose the old madam from Peoria, stoical Chinese waiters never show sickness. Bart sought them out with his old junky walk, patient and cautious and slow, dropped into their bloodless hands a few hours of warmth.

I made the round with him once for kicks. You know how old people lose all shame about eating, and it makes you puke to watch them? Old junkies are the same about junk. They gibber and squeal at sight of it. The spit hangs off their chin, and their stomach rumbles and all their guts grind in peristalsis while they cook up, dissolving the body's decent skin, you expect any moment a great blob of protoplasm will flop right out and surround the junk. Really disgust you to see it.

"Well, my boys will be like that one day," I thought philosophically. "Isn't life peculiar?"

So back downtown by the Sheridan Square Station in case the dick is lurking in a broom closet.

Like I say it couldn't last. I knew they were out there powwowing and making their evil fuzz magic, putting dolls of me in Leavenworth. "No use sticking needles in that one, Mike."

I hear they got Chapin with a doll. This old eunuch dick just sat in the precinct basement hanging a doll of him day and night, year in year out. And when Chapin hanged in Connecticut, they find this old creep with his neck broken.

"He fell downstairs," they say. You know the old cop bullshit.

Junk is surrounded by magic and taboos, curses and amulets. I could find my Mexico City connection by radar. "Not this street, the next, right . . . now left. Now right again," and there he is, toothless old woman face and cancelled eyes.

I know this one pusher walks around humming a tune and everybody he passes takes it up. He is so grey and spectral and anonymous they don't see him and think it is their own mind humming the tune. So the customers come in on *Smiles*, or *I'm in the Mood for Love*, or *They Say We're Too Young to Go Steady*, or whatever the song is for that day. Sometime you can see maybe fifty ratty-looking junkies squealing sick, running along behind a boy with a harmonica, and there is The Man on a cane seat throwing bread to the swans, a fat queen drag walking his Afghan hound through the East Fifties, an old wino pissing against an El post, a radical Jewish student giving out leaflets in Washington Square, a tree surgeon, an exterminator, an advertising fruit in Nedick's where he calls the counterman by his first name. The world network of junkies, tuned on a cord of rancid jissom, tying up in furnished rooms, shivering in the junk-sick morning. (Old Pete men suck the black smoke in the Chink laundry back room and Melancholy Baby dies from an overdose of time or cold turkey withdrawal of breath.) In Yemen, Paris, New Orleans, Mexico City and Istanbul—shivering under the air hammers and the steam shovels, shrieked junky curses at one another neither of us heard, and The Man leaned out of a passing steam roller and I copped in a bucket of tar. (Note: Istanbul is being torn down and rebuilt, especially shabby junk quarters. Istanbul has more heroin junkies than NYC.) The living and the dead, in sickness or on the nod, hooked or kicked or hooked again, come in on the junk beam and the Connection is eating Chop Suey on Dolores Street, Mexico D.F., dunking pound cake in the automat, chased up Exchange Place by a baying pack of People. (Note: People is New Orleans slang for narcotic fuzz.)

The old Chinaman dips river water into a rusty tin can, washes down a yen pox hard and black as a cinder. (Note: Yen pox is the ash of smoked opium.)

Well, the fuzz has my spoon and dropper, and I know they are coming in on my frequency led by this blind pigeon known as Willy the Disk. Willy has a round, disk mouth lined with sensitive, erectile black hairs. He is blind from shooting in the eyeball, his nose and palate eaten away sniffing H, his body a mass of scar tissue hard and dry as wood. He can only eat the shit now with that mouth, sometimes sways out on a long tube of ectoplasm, feeling for the silent frequency of junk. He follows my trail all over the city into rooms I move out already, and the fuzz walks in on some newlyweds from Sioux Falls.

"All right, Lee!! Come out from behind that strap-on! We know you" and pull the man's prick off straightaway.

Now Willy is getting hot and you can hear him always out there in darkness (he only functions at night) whimpering, and feel the terrible urgency of that blind, seeking mouth. When they move in for the bust, Willy goes all out of control, and his mouth eats a hole right through the door. If the cops weren't there to restrain him with a stock probe, he would suck the juice right out of every junky he ran down.

I knew, and everybody else knew they had the Disk on me. And if my kid customers ever hit the stand: "He force me to commit all kinda awful sex acts in return for junk"—I could kiss the street good-bye.

So we stock up on H, buy a second-hand Studebaker, and start West.

The Rube is a social liability with his attacks as he calls them. The Mark Inside was coming up on him and that's a rumble nobody can cool; outside Philly he jumps out to con a prowl car and the fuzz takes one look at his face and bust all of us.

Seventy-two hours and five sick junkies in the cell with us. Now not wishing to break out my stash in front of these hungry coolies, it takes maneuvering and laying of gold on the turnkey before we are in a separate cell.

Provident junkies, known as squirrels, keep stashes against a bust. Every time I take a shot I let a few drops fall into my vest pocket, the lining is stiff with stuff. I had a plastic dropper in my shoe and a safety-pin stuck in my belt. You know how this pin and dropper routine is put down: "She seized a safety pin caked with blood and rust, gouged a great hole in her leg which seemed to hang open like an obscene, festering mouth waiting for unspeakable congress with the dropper which she now plunged out of sight into the gaping wound. But her hideous galvanized need (hunger of insects in dry places) has broken the dropper off deep in the flesh of her ravaged thigh (looking rather like a poster on soil erosion). But what does she care? She does not even bother to remove the splintered glass, looking down at her bloody haunch with the cold blank eyes of a meat trader. What does she care for the atom bomb, the bed bugs, the cancer rent, Friendly Finance waiting to repossess her delinquent flesh. . . . Sweet dreams, Pantopon Rose."

The real scene you pinch up some leg flesh and make a quick stab hole with a pin. Then fit the dropper *over, not in* the hole and feed the solution slow and careful so it doesn't squirt out the sides. . . . When I grabbed the Rube's thigh the flesh came up like wax and stayed there, and a slow drop of pus oozed out the hole. And I never touched a living body cold as the Rube there in Philly. . . .

I decided to lop him off if it meant a smother party. (This is a rural English custom designed to eliminate aged and bedfast dependents. A family so afflicted throws a "smother party" where the guests pile mattresses on the old liability, climb up on top of the mattresses and lush themselves out.) The Rube is a drag on the industry and should be led out into the skid rows of the world. (This is an African practice. Official known as the "Leader Out" has the function of taking old characters out into the jungle and leaving them there.)

The Rube's attacks become an habitual condition. Cops, doormen, dogs, secretaries snarl at his approach. The blond God has fallen to untouchable vileness. Con men don't change, they break, shatter—explosions of matter in cold interstellar space, drift away in cosmic dust, leave the empty body behind. Hustlers of the world, there is one Mark you cannot beat: The Mark Inside. . . .

I left the Rube standing on a corner, red brick slums to the sky, under a steady rain of soot. "Going to hit this croaker I know. Right back with that good pure drugstore M. . . . No, you wait here—don't want him to rumble you." No matter how long, Rube, wait for me right on that corner. Goodbye, Rube, good-bye kid. . . . Where do they go when they walk out and leave the body behind?

Chicago: invisible hierarchy of decorticated wops, smell of atrophied gangsters, earthbound ghost hits you at North and Halstead, Cicero, Lincoln Park, panhandler of dreams, past invading the present, rancid magic of slot machines and roadhouses.

Into the Interior: a vast subdivision, antennae of television to the meaningless sky. In lifeproof houses they hover over the young, sop up a little of what they shut out. Only the young bring anything in, and they are not young very long. (Through the bars of East St. Louis lies the dead frontier, riverboat days.) Illinois and Missouri, miasma of mound-building peoples, groveling worship of the Food Source, cruel and ugly festivals, dead-end horror of the Centipede God reaches from Moundville to the lunar deserts of coastal Peru.

America is not a young land: it is old and dirty and evil before the settlers, before the Indians. The evil is there waiting.

And always cops: smooth college-trained state cops, practiced, apologetic patter, electronic eyes weigh your car and luggage, clothes and face; snarling big city dicks, soft-spoken country sheriffs with something black and menacing in old eyes color of a faded grey flannel shirt. . . .

And always car trouble: in St. Louis traded the 1942 Studebaker in (it has a built-in engineering flaw like the Rube) on an old Packard limousine heated up and barely made Kansas City, and bought a Ford turned out to be an oil burner, packed it in on a jeep we push too hard (they are no good for highway driving)—and burn something out inside, rattling around, went back to the old Ford V-8. Can't beat that engine for getting there, oil burner or no.

And the U.S. drag closes around us like no other drag in the world, worse than the Andes, high mountain towns, cold wind down from postcard mountains, thin air like death in the throat, river towns of Ecuador, malaria grey as junk under black Stetson, muzzle loading shotguns, vultures pecking through the mud streets—and what hits you when you get off the Malmo Ferry in (no juice tax on the ferry) Sweden knocks all that cheap, tax free juice right out of you and brings you all the way down: averted eyes and the cemetery in the middle of town (every town in Sweden seems to be built around a cemetery), and nothing to do in the afternoon, not a bar not a movie and I blasted my last stick of Tangier tea and I said, "K.E. let's get right back on that ferry."

But there is no drag like U.S. drag. You can't see it, you don't know where it comes from. Take one of those cocktail lounges at the end of a subdivision street—every block of houses has its own bar and drugstore and market and liquor store. You walk in and it hits you. But where does it come from?

Not the bartender, not the customers, nor the cream-colored plastic rounding the bar stools, nor the dim neon. Not even the TV.

And our habits build up with the drag, like cocaine will build you up staying ahead of the C bring-down. And the junk was running low. So there we are in this no-horse town strictly from cough syrup. And vomited up the syrup and drove on and on, cold spring wind whistling through that old heap around our shivering sick sweating bodies and the cold you always come down with when the junk runs out of you. . . . On through the peeled landscape, dead armadillos in the road and vultures over the swamp and cypress stumps. Motels with beaverboard walls, gas heater, thin pink blankets.

Itinerant short con and carny hype men have burned down the croakers of Texas. . . .

And no one in his right mind would hit a Louisiana croaker. State Junk Law.

Came at last to Houston where I know a druggist. I haven't been there in five years but he looks up and makes me with one quick look and just nods and says: "Wait over at the counter. . . ."

So I sit down and drink a cup of coffee and after a while he comes and sits beside me and says, "What do you want?"

"A quart of PG and a hundred nembies."

He nods. "Come back in half an hour."

So when I come back he hands me a package and says, "That's fifteen dollars. . . . Be careful."

Shooting PG is a terrible hassle, you have to burn out the alcohol first, then freeze out the camphor and draw this brown liquid off with a dropper—have to shoot it in the vein or you get an abscess, and usually end up with an abscess no matter where you shoot it. Best deal is to drink it with goofballs. . . . So we pour it in a Pernod bottle and start for New Orleans past iridescent lakes and orange gas flares, and swamps and garbage heaps, alligators crawling around in broken bottles and tin cans, neon arabesques of motels, marooned pimps scream obscenities at passing cars from islands of rubbish. . . .

New Orleans is a dead museum. We walk around Exchange Place breathing PG and find The Man right away. It's a small place and the fuzz always knows who is pushing so he figures what the hell does it matter and sells to anybody. We stock up on H and backtrack for Mexico.

Back through Lake Charles and the dead slot-machine country, south end of Texas, nigger-killing sheriffs look us over and check the car papers. Something falls off you when you cross the border into Mexico, and suddenly the landscape hits you straight with nothing between you and it, desert and mountains and vultures; little wheeling specks and others so close you can hear wings cut the air (a dry husking sound), and when they spot something they pour out of the blue sky, that shattering bloody blue sky of Mexico, down in a black funnel. . . . Drove all night, came at dawn to a warm misty place, barking dogs and the sound of running water.

"Thomas and Charlie," I said.

"What?"

"That's the name of this town. Sea level. We climb straight up from here ten thousand feet." I took a fix and went to sleep in the back seat. She was a good driver. You can tell as soon as someone touches the wheel.

Mexico City where Lupita sits like an Aztec Earth Goddess doling out her little papers of lousy shit.

"Selling is more of a habit than using," Lupita says.

In Cuernavaca or was it Taxco? Jane meets a pimp trombone player and disappears in a cloud of tea smoke. The pimp is one of these vibration and dietary artists—which is a means he degrades the female sex by forcing his chicks to swallow all this shit. He was continually enlarging his theories . . . he would quiz a chick and threaten to walk out if she hadn't memorized every nuance of his latest assault on logic and the human image.

"Now, baby. I got it here to give. But if you won't receive it there's just nothing I can do."

He was a ritual tea smoker and very puritanical about junk the way some teaheads are. He claimed tea put him in touch with supra blue gravitational fields. He had ideas on every subject: what kind of underwear was healthy, when to drink water, and how to wipe your ass. He had a shiny red face and great spreading smooth nose, little red eyes that lit up when he looked at a chick and went out when he looked at anything else. His shoulders were very broad and suggested deformity. He acted as if other men did not exist, conveying his restaurant and store orders to male personnel through a female intermediary. And no Man ever invaded his blighted, secret place.

So he is putting down junk and coming on with tea. I take three drags, Jane looked at him and her flesh crystallized. I leaped up screaming "I got the fear!" and ran out of the house. Drank a beer in a little restaurant—a mosaic bar and soccer scores and bullfight posters—and waited for the bus to town.

A year later in Tangier I heard she was dead.

THE BLACK MEAT

"We friends, yes?"

The shoe shine boy put on his hustling smile and looked up into the Sailor's dead, cold, undersea eyes, eyes without a trace of warmth or lust or hate or any feeling the boy had ever experienced in himself or even in another, at once cold and intense, impersonal and predatory.

The Sailor leaned forward and put a finger on the boy's inner arm at the elbow. He spoke in his dead, junky whisper.

"With veins like that, Kid, I'd have myself a time!"

He laughed, black insect laughter that seemed to serve some obscure function of orientation like a bat's squeak. The Sailor laughed three times. He stopped laughing and hung there motionless listening down into himself. He had picked up the silent frequency of junk. His face smoothed out like yellow wax over the high cheekbones. He waited half a cigarette. The Sailor knew how to wait. But his eyes burned in a hideous dry hunger. He turned his face of controlled emergency in a slow half pivot to case the man who had just come in. "Fats" Terminal sat there sweeping the café with blank, periscope eyes. When his eyes passed the Sailor he nodded minutely. Only the peeled nerves of junk sickness would have registered a movement.

The Sailor handed the boy a coin. He drifted over to Fats' table with his floating walk and sat down. They sat a long time in silence. The café was built into one side of a stone ramp at the bottom of a high white canyon of masonry. Faces of The City poured through silent as fish, stained with vile addictions and insect lusts. The lighted café was a diving bell, cable broken, settling into black depths.

The Sailor was polishing his nails on the lapels of his glen plaid suit. He whistled a little tune through his shiny, yellow teeth.

When he moved an effluvia of mold drifted out of his clothes, a musty smell of deserted locker rooms. He studied his nails with phosphorescent intensity.

"Good thing here, Fats. I can deliver twenty. Need an advance of course."

"On spec?"

"So I don't have the twenty eggs in my pocket. I tell you it's jellied consommé. One little whoops and a push." The Sailor looked at his nails as if he were studying a chart. "You know I always deliver."

"Make it thirty. And a ten tube advance. This time tomorrow."

"Need a tube now, Fats."

"Take a walk, you'll get one."

The Sailor drifted down into the Plaza. A street boy was shoving a newspaper in the Sailor's face to cover his hand on the Sailor's pen. The Sailor walked on. He pulled the pen out and broke it like a nut in his thick, fibrous, pink fingers. He pulled out a lead tube. He cut one end of the tube with a little curved knife. A black mist poured out and hung in the air like boiling fur. The Sailor's face dissolved. His mouth undulated forward on a long tube and sucked in the black fuzz, vibrating in supersonic peristalsis disappeared in a silent, pink explosion. His face came back into focus unbearably sharp and clear, burning yellow brand of junk searing the grey haunch of a million screaming junkies.

"This will last a month," he decided, consulting an invisible mirror.

All streets of the City slope down between deepening canyons to a vast, kidney-shaped plaza full of darkness. Walls of street and plaza are perforated by dwelling cubicles and cafés, some a few feet deep, others extending out of sight in a network of rooms and corridors.

At all levels criss-cross of bridges, cat walks, cable cars. Catatonic youths dressed as women in gowns of burlap and rotten rags, faces heavily and crudely painted in bright colors over a stratum of beatings, arabesques of broken, suppurating scars to the pearly bone, push against the passerby in silent clinging insistence.

Traffickers in the Black Meat, flesh of the giant aquatic black centipede—sometimes attaining a length of six feet—found in a lane of black rocks and iridescent, brown lagoons, exhibit paralyzed crustaceans in camouflage pockets of the Plaza visible only to the Meat Eaters.

Followers of obsolete unthinkable trades, doodling in Etruscan, addicts of drugs not yet synthesized, black marketeers of World War III, excisors of telepathic sensitivity, osteopaths of the spirit, investigators of infractions denounced by bland paranoid chess players, servers of fragmentary warrants taken down in hebephrenic shorthand charging unspeakable mutilations of the spirit, officials of unconstituted police states, brokers of exquisite dreams and nostalgias tested on the sensitized cells of junk sickness and bartered for raw materials of the will, drinkers of the Heavy Fluid sealed in translucent amber of dreams.

The Meet Café occupies one side of the Plaza, a maze of kitchens, restaurants, sleeping cubicles, perilous iron balconies and basements opening into the underground baths.

On stools covered in white satin sit naked Mugwumps sucking translucent, colored syrups through alabaster straws. Mugwumps have no liver and nourish themselves exclusively on sweets. Thin, purple-blue lips cover a razor-sharp beak of black bone with which they frequently tear each other to shreds in fights over clients. These creatures secrete an addicting fluid from their erect penises which prolongs life by slowing metabolism. (In fact all longevity agents have proved addicting in exact ratio to their effectiveness in prolonging life.) Addicts of Mugwump fluid are known as Reptiles. A number of these flow over chairs with their flexible bones and black-pink flesh. A fan of green cartilage covered with hollow, erectile hairs through which the Reptiles absorb the fluid sprouts from behind each ear. The fans, which move from time to time touched by invisible currents, serve also some form of communication known only to Reptiles.

During the biennial Panics when the raw, peeled Dream Police storm the City, the Mugwumps take refuge in the deepest crevices of the wall sealing themselves in clay cubicles and remain for weeks in biostasis. In those days of grey terror the Reptiles dart about faster and faster, scream past each other at supersonic speed, their flexible skulls flapping in black winds of insect agony.

The Dream Police disintegrate in globs of rotten ectoplasm swept away by an old junky, coughing and spitting in the sick morning. The Mugwump Man comes with alabaster jars of fluid and the Reptiles get smoothed out.

The air is once again still and clear as glycerine.

The Sailor spotted his Reptile. He drifted over and ordered a green syrup. The Reptile had a little, round disk mouth of brown gristle, expressionless green eyes almost covered by a thin membrane of eyelid. The Sailor waited an hour before the creature picked up his presence.

"Any eggs for Fats?" he asked, his words stirring through the Reptile's fan hairs.

It took two hours for the Reptile to raise three pink transparent fingers covered with black fuzz.

Several Meat Eaters lay in vomit, too weak to move. (The Black Meat is like a tainted cheese, overpoweringly delicious and nauseating so that the eaters eat and vomit and eat again until they fall exhausted.)

A painted youth slithered in and seized one of the great black claws sending the sweet, sick smell curling through the café.

from HOSPITAL

The lavatory has been locked for three hours solid. . . . I think they are using it for an operating room. . . .

NURSE: "I can't find her pulse, doctor."
DR. BENWAY: "Maybe she got it up her snatch in a finger stall."
NURSE: "Adrenalin, doctor?"
DR. BENWAY: "The night porter shot it all up for kicks."
    He looks around and picks up one of those rubber vacuum cups at the end of a stick they use to unstop toilets. . . . He advances on the patient. . . . "Make an incision, Doctor Limpf," he says to his appalled assistant. . . . "I'm going to massage the heart."

Dr. Limpf shrugs and begins the incision. Dr. Benway washes the suction cup by swishing it around in the toilet bowl. . . .

NURSE: "Shouldn't it be sterilized, doctor?"

DR. BENWAY: "Very likely but there's no time."

He sits on the suction cup like a cane seat watching his assistant make the incision. . . .

"You young squirts couldn't lance a pimple without an electric vibrating scalpel with automatic drain and suture. . . . Soon we'll be operating by remote control on patients we never see. . . . We'll be nothing but button pushers. All the skill is going out of surgery. . . . All the know-how and make-do . . . Did I ever tell you about the time I performed an appendectomy with a rusty sardine can? And once I was caught short without instrument one and removed a uterine tumor with my teeth. That was in the Upper Effendi, and besides . . ."

DR. LIMPF: "The incision is ready, doctor."

Dr. Benway forces the cup into the incision and works it up and down. Blood spurts all over the doctors, the nurse and the wall. . . . The cup makes a horrible sucking sound.

NURSE: "I think she's gone, doctor."

DR. BENWAY: "Well, it's all in the day's work."

He walks across the room to a medicine cabinet. . . . "Some fucking drug addict has cut my cocaine with Saniflush! Nurse! Send the boy out to fill this RX on the double!"

Dr. Benway is operating in an auditorium filled with students: "Now, boys, you won't see this operation performed very often and there's a reason for that. . . . You see it has absolutely no medical value. No one knows what the purpose of it originally was or if it had a purpose at all. Personally I think it was a pure artistic creation from the beginning.

"Just as a bullfighter with his skill and knowledge extricates himself from danger he has himself invoked, so in this operation the surgeon deliberately endangers his patient, and then, with incredible speed and celerity, rescues him from death at the last possible split second. . . . Did any of you ever see Dr. Tetrazzini perform? I say perform advisedly because his operations were performances. He would start by throwing a scalpel across the room into the patient and then make his entrance like a ballet dancer. His speed was incredible: 'I don't give them time to die,' he would say. Tumors put him in a frenzy of rage. 'Fucking undisciplined cells!' he would snarl, advancing on the tumor like a knife-fighter."

A young man leaps down into the operating theater and, whipping out a scalpel, advances on the patient.

DR. BENWAY: "An *espontaneo*! Stop him before he guts my patient!"

(*Espontaneo* is a bullfighting term for a member of the audience who leaps down into the ring, pulls out a concealed cape and attempts a few passes with the bull before he is dragged out of the ring.)

The orderlies scuffle with the *espontaneo,* who is finally ejected from the hall. The anesthetist takes advantage of the confusion to pry a large gold filling from the patient's mouth. . . .

I am passing room 10 they moved me out of yesterday. . . . Maternity case I assume. . . . Bedpans full of blood and Kotex and nameless female substances, enough to pollute a continent. . . . If someone comes to visit me in my old room he will think I gave birth to a monster and the State Department is trying to hush it up. . . .

Music from *I Am an American.* . . . An elderly man in the striped pants and cutaway of a diplomat stands on a platform draped with the American flag. A decayed, corseted tenor—bursting out of a Daniel Boone costume—is singing *The Star Spangled Banner,* accompanied by a full orchestra. He sings with a slight lisp. . . .

THE DIPLOMAT (reading from a great scroll of ticker tape that keeps growing and tangling around his feet): "And we categorically deny that *any* male citizen of the United States of America . . ."

TENOR: "Oh thay can you thee. . . ." His voice breaks and shoots up to a high falsetto.

In the control room the Technician mixes a bicarbonate of soda and belches into his hand: "Goddamned tenor's a brown artist!" he mutters sourly. "Mike! *rumph,*" the shout ends in a belch. "Cut that swish fart off the air and give him his purple slip. He's through as of right now. . . . Put in that sex-changed Liz athlete. . . . She's a fulltime tenor at least. . . . *Costume?* How in the fuck should I know? I'm no dress designer swish from the costume department! *What's that?* The entire costume department occluded as a security risk? What am I, an octopus? Let's see. . . . How about an Indian routine? Pocahontas or Hiawatha? . . . No, that's not right. Some citizen cracks wise about giving it back to the Indians. . . . A Civil War uniform, the coat North and the pants South like it show they got together again? She can come on like Buffalo Bill or Paul Revere or that citizen wouldn't give up the shit, I mean the ship, or a G.I. or a Doughboy or the Unknown Soldier. . . . That's the best deal. . . . Cover her with a monument, that way nobody has to look at her. . . ."

The Lesbian, concealed in a *papier mâché* Arc de Triomphe fills her great lungs and looses a tremendous bellow.

"Oh say do that Star Spangled Banner yet wave . . ."

A great rent rips the Arc de Triomphe from top to bottom. The Diplomat puts a hand to his forehead. . . .

THE DIPLOMAT: "That any male citizen of the United States has given birth in Interzone or at any other place. . . ."

"O'er the land of the FREEEEEEEEEEE . . ."

The Diplomat's mouth is moving but no one can hear him. The Technician clasps his hands over his ears: "Mother of God!" he screams. His plate begins to vibrate like a Jew's harp, suddenly flies out of his mouth. . . . He snaps at it irritably, misses and covers his mouth with one hand.

The Arc de Triomphe falls with a ripping, splintering crash, reveals the Lesbian standing on a pedestal clad only in a leopard-skin jockstrap with enormous falsie basket. . . . She stands there smiling stupidly and flexing her huge muscles. . . . The Technician is crawling around on the control room floor looking for his plate and shouting unintelligible orders: "Thess thupper thonic!! Thut ur oth thu thair!"

THE DIPLOMAT (wiping sweat from his brow): "To any creature of any type or description . . ."

"And the home of the brave."

The diplomat's face is grey. He staggers, trips in the scroll, sags against the rail, blood pouring from eyes, nose and mouth, dying of cerebral hemorrhage.

THE DIPLOMAT (barely audible): "The Department denies . . . un-American. . . . It's been destroyed. . . . I mean it never was. . . . Categor . . ." *Dies.*

In the control room instrument panels are blowing out . . . great streamers of electricity crackle through the room. . . . The Technician, naked, his body burned black, staggers about like a figure in Götterdämmerung, screaming: "Thubber thonic!! Oth thu thair!!!" A final blast reduces the Technician to a cinder.

Gave proof through the night
That our flag was still there. . . .

from THE MARKET

Panorama of the City of Interzone. Opening bars of *East St. Louis Toodle-oo* . . . at times loud and clear then faint and intermittent like music down a windy street. . . .

The room seems to shake and vibrate with motion. The blood and substance of many races, Negro, Polynesian, Mountain Mongol, Desert Nomad, Polyglot Near East, Indian—races as yet unconceived and unborn, combinations not yet realized pass through your body. Migrations, incredible journeys through deserts and jungles and mountains (stasis and death in closed mountain valleys where plants grow out of genitals, vast crustaceans hatch inside and break the shell of body) across the Pacific in an outrigger canoe to Easter Island. The Composite City where all human potentials are spread out in a vast silent market.

Minarets, palms, mountains, jungle. . . . A sluggish river jumping with vicious fish, vast weed-grown parks where boys lie in the grass, play cryptic games. Not a locked door in the City. Anyone comes into your room at any time. The Chief of Police is a Chinese who picks his teeth and listens to denunciations presented by a lunatic. Every now and then the Chinese takes the toothpick out of his mouth and looks at the end of it. Hipsters with smooth copper-colored faces lounge in doorways twisting shrunk heads on gold chains, their faces blank with an insect's unseeing calm.

Behind them, through open doors, tables and booths and bars, and kitchens and baths, copulating couples on rows of brass beds, criss-cross of a thousand hammocks, junkies tying up for a shot, opium smokers, hashish smokers, people eating talking bathing back into a haze of smoke and steam.

Gaming tables where the games are played for incredible stakes. From time to time a player leaps up with a despairing cry, having lost his youth to an old man or become Latah to his opponent. But there are higher stakes than youth or Latah, games where only two players in the world know what the stakes are.

All houses in the City are joined. Houses of sod—high mountain Mongols blink in smoky doorways—houses of bamboo and teak, houses of adobe, stone and red brick, South Pacific and Maori houses, houses in trees and river boats, wood houses one hundred feet long sheltering entire tribes, houses of boxes and corrugated iron where old men sit in rotten rags cooking down canned heat, great rusty iron racks rising two hundred feet in the air from swamps and rubbish with perilous partitions built on multi-levelled platforms, and hammocks swinging over the void.

Expeditions leave for unknown places with unknown purposes. Strangers arrive on rafts of old packing crates tied together with rotten rope, they stagger in out of the jungle their eyes swollen shut from insect bites, they come down the mountain trails on cracked bleeding feet through the dusty, windy outskirts of the city, where people defecate in rows along adobe walls and vultures fight over fish heads. They drop down into parks in patched parachutes. . . . They are escorted by a drunken cop to register in a vast public lavatory. The data taken down is put on pegs to be used as toilet paper.

Cooking smells of all countries hang over the City, a haze of opium, hashish, the resinous red smoke of *yagé,* smell of the jungle and salt water and the rotting river and dried excrement and sweat and genitals.

High mountain flutes, jazz and bebop, one-stringed Mongol instruments, gypsy xylophones, African drums, Arab bagpipes . . .

The City is visited by epidemics of violence, and the untended dead are eaten by vultures in the streets. Albinos blink in the sun. Boys sit in trees, languidly masturbate. People eaten by unknown diseases watch the passerby with evil, knowing eyes.

In the City Market is the Meet Café. Followers of obsolete, unthinkable trades, doodling in Etruscan, addicts of drugs not yet synthesized, pushers of souped-up Harmaline, junk reduced to pure habit offering precarious vegetable serenity, liquids to induce Latah, Tithonian longevity serums, black marketeers of World War III, excisors of telepathic sensitivity, osteopaths of the spirit, investigators of infractions denounced by bland paranoid chess players, servers of fragmentary warrants taken down in hebephrenic shorthand charging unspeakable mutilations of the spirit, bureaucrats of spectral departments, officials of unconstituted police states, a Lesbian dwarf who has perfected Operation Bangutot, the lung erection that strangles a sleeping enemy, sellers of orgone tanks and relaxing machines, brokers of exquisite dreams and memories tested on the sensitized cells of junk sickness and bartered for raw materials of the will, doctors skilled in the treatment of diseases dormant in the black dust of ruined cities, gathering virulence in the white blood of eyeless worms feeling slowly to the surface and the human host, maladies of the ocean floor and the stratosphere, maladies of the laboratory and atomic war. . . . A place where the unknown past and the emergent future meet in a vibrating soundless hum. . . . Larval entities waiting for a Live One . . .

(Section describing The City and the Meet Café written in state of *yagé* intoxication . . . *Yagé, ayuahuasca, pilde, nateema* are Indian names for *Bannisteria caapi,* a fast-growing vine indigenous to the Amazon region.)

from ISLAM, INC.

And now The Prophet's Hour:

"Millions died in the mud flats. Only one blasted free to lungs.

" 'Eye Eye, Captain,' he said, squirting his eyes out on the deck. . . . And who would put on the chains tonight? It is indicate to observe some caution in the up-wind approach, the down-wind having failed to turn up anything worth a rusty load. . . . Señoritas are the wear this season in Hell, and I am tired with the long climb to a pulsing Vesuvius of alien pricks."

Need Orient Express out of here to no hide place(r) mines are frequent in the area. . . . Every day dig a little it takes up the time. . . .

Jack off phantoms whisper hot into the bone ear. . . .

Shoot your way to freedom.

"Christ?" sneers the vicious, fruity old Saint applying pancake from an alabaster bowl. . . . "That cheap ham! You think I'd demean myself to commit a miracle? . . . That one should have stood in carny. . . .

" 'Step right up, Marquesses and Marks, and bring the little Marks too. Good for young and old, man and beast. . . . The one and only legit *Son of Man* will cure a young boy's clap with one hand—by contact alone, folks—create marijuana with the other, whilst walking on water and squirting wine out his ass. . . . Now keep your distance, folks, you is subject to be irradiated by the sheer charge of this character.'

"And I knew him when, dearie. . . . I recall we was doing an Impersonation Act—very high class too—in Sodom, and that is one cheap town. . . . Strictly from hunger. . . . Well, this citizen, this fucking Philistine wandered in from Podunk Baal or some place, called me a fuckin fruit right on the floor. And I said to him: 'Three thousand years in show business and I always keep my nose clean. Besides I don't hafta take any shit off any uncircumcised cocksucker.' . . . Later he come to my dressing room and made an apology. . . . Turns out he is a big physician. And he was a lovely fellah, too. . . .

"*Buddha*? A notorious metabolic junky. . . . Makes his own you dig. In India, where they got no sense of time, The Man is often a month late. . . . 'Now let me see, is that the second or the third monsoon? I got like a meet in Ketchupore about more or less.'

"And all them junkies sitting around in the lotus posture spitting on the ground and waiting on The Man.

"So Buddha says: 'I don't hafta take this sound. I'll by God metabolize my own junk.'

"'Man, you can't do that. The Revenooers will swarm all over you.'

"'Over me they won't swarm. I gotta gimmick, see? I'm a fuckin Holy Man as of right now.'

"'Jeez boss, what an angle.'

"'Now some citizens really wig when they make with the New Religion. These frantic individuals do not know how to come on. No class to them. . . . Besides, they is subject to be lynched like who wants somebody hanging around being better'n other folks? "What you trying to do, Jack, give people a bad time? . . ." So we gotta play it cool, you dig, cool. . . . We don't shove anything up your soul, unlike certain cheap characters who shall be nameless and are nowhere. Clear the cave for action. I'm gonna metabolize a speed ball and make with the Fire Sermon.'

"*Mohammed*? Are you kidding? He was dreamed up by the Mecca Chamber of Commerce. An Egyptian ad man on the skids from the sauce write the continuity.

"'I'll have one more, Gus. Then, by Allah, I will go home and receive a Surah. . . . Wait'll the morning edition hits the souks. I am blasting Amalgamated Images wide open.'

"The bartender looks up from his racing form. 'Yeah. And theirs will be a painful doom.'

"'Oh . . . uh . . . quite. Now, Gus, I'll write you a check.'

"'You are only being the most notorious paper hanger in Greater Mecca. I am not a wall, Mr. Mohammed.'

"'Well, Gus, I got like two types of publicity, favorable and otherwise. You want some otherwise already? I am subject to receive a Surah concerning bartenders who extendeth not credit to those in a needy way.'

"'And theirs will be a painful doom. Sold Arabia.' He vaults over the bar. 'I'm not taking any more, Ahmed. Pick up thy Surahs and walk. In fact, I'll help you. And *stay out*.'

"'I'll fix your wagon good, you unbelieving cocksucker. I'll close you up tight and dry as a junky's asshole. I'll by Allah dry up the Peninsula.'

"'It's a continent already. . . .'

"Leave what Confucius say stand with Little Audrey and the shaggy dogs. Lao-Tze? They scratch him already. . . . And enough of these gooey saints with a look of pathic dismay as if they getting fucked up the ass and try not to pay it any mind. And why should we let some old brokendown ham tell us what wisdom is? 'Three thousand years in show business and I always keep my nose clean. . . .'

"First, every Fact is incarcerate along with the male hustlers and those who desecrate the gods of commerce by playing ball in the streets, and some old white-haired fuck staggers out to give us the benefits of his ripe idiocy. Are we never to be free of this grey-beard loon lurking on every mountain top in Tibet, subject to drag himself out of a hut in the Amazon, waylay one in the Bowery? 'I've been expecting you, my son,' and he make with a silo full of corn. 'Life is a school where every pupil must learn a different lesson. And now I will unlock my Word Hoard. . . .'

"'I do fear it much.'

"'Nay, nothing shall stem the rising tide.'

"'I can't stem him, boys. *Sauve qui peut.*'

"'I tell you when I leave the Wise Man I don't even feel like a human. He converting my live orgones into dead bullshit.'

"So I got an exclusive, why don't I make with the live word? The word cannot be expressed direct. . . . It can perhaps be indicated by mosaic of juxtaposition like articles abandoned in a hotel drawer, defined by negatives and absence. . . .

"Think I'll have my stomach tucked. . . . I may be old, but I'm still desirable."

(The Stomach Tuck is surgical intervention to remove stomach fat at the same time making a tuck in the abdominal wall, thus creating a Flesh Corset, which is, however, subject to break and spurt your horrible old guts across the floor. . . . The slim and shapely F.C. models are, of course, the most dangerous. In fact, some extreme models are known as O.N.S.—One Night Stands—in the industry.

Doctor "Doodles" Rindfest states bluntly: "Bed is the most dangerous place for an F.C. man."

The F.C. theme song is "Believe Me If All These Endearing Young Charms." An F.C. partner is indeed subject to "fleet from your arms like fairy gifts fading away.")

from ORDINARY MEN AND WOMEN: THE TALKING ASSHOLE

BENWAY: "Did I ever tell you about the man who taught his asshole to talk? His whole abdomen would move up and down you dig farting out the words. It was unlike anything I ever heard.

"This ass talk had a sort of gut frequency. It hit you right down there like you gotta go. You know when the old colon gives you the elbow and

it feels sorta cold inside, and you know all you have to do is turn loose?
Well this talking hit you right down there, a bubbly, thick stagnant sound,
a sound you could *smell.*

"This man worked for a carnival you dig, and to start with it was like a
novelty ventriloquist act. Real funny, too, at first. He had a number he called
'The Better 'Ole' that was a scream, I tell you. I forget most of it but it was
clever. Like, 'Oh I say, are you still down there, old thing?'

" 'Nah! I had to go relieve myself.'

"After a while the ass started talking on its own. He would go in without anything prepared and his ass would ad-lib and toss the gags back at
him every time.

"Then it developed sort of teeth-like little raspy in-curving hooks and
started eating. He thought this was cute at first and built an act around it,
but the asshole would eat its way through his pants and start talking on the
street, shouting out it wanted equal rights. It would get drunk, too, and
have crying jags nobody loved it and it wanted to be kissed same as any
other mouth. Finally it talked all the time day and night, you could hear
him for blocks screaming at it to shut up, and beating it with his fist, and
sticking candles up it, but nothing did any good and the asshole said to
him: 'It's you who will shut up in the end. Not me. Because we don't need
you around here any more. I can talk and eat *and* shit.'

"After that he began waking up in the morning with a transparent jelly
like a tadpole's tail all over his mouth. This jelly was what the scientists call
un-D.T., Undifferentiated Tissue, which can grow into any kind of flesh
on the human body. He would tear it off his mouth and the pieces would
stick to his hands like burning gasoline jelly and grow there, grow anywhere
on him a glob of it fell. So finally his mouth sealed over, and the whole
head would have amputated spontaneous—(did you know there is a condition occurs in parts of Africa and only among Negroes where the little
toe amputates spontaneously?)—except for the *eyes* you dig. That's one thing
the asshole *couldn't* do was see. It needed the eyes. But nerve connections
were blocked and infiltrated and atrophied so the brain couldn't give orders
any more. It was trapped in the skull, sealed off. For a while you could see
the silent, helpless suffering of the brain behind the eyes, then finally the
brain must have died, because the eyes *went out,* and there was no more
feeling in them than a crab's eye on the end of a stalk.

"That's the sex that passes the censor, squeezes through between bureaus, because there's always a space *between,* in popular songs and Grade
B movies, giving away the basic American rottenness, spurting out like
breaking boils, throwing out globs of that un-D.T. to fall anywhere and
grow into some degenerate cancerous life-form, reproducing a hideous
random image. Some would be entirely made of penis-like erectile tissue,
others viscera barely covered over with skin, clusters of three and four eyes
together, criss-cross of mouth and assholes, human parts shaken around
and poured out any way they fell.

"The end results of complete cellular representation is cancer. Democracy is cancerous, and bureaus are its cancer. A bureau takes root anywhere in the state, turns malignant like the Narcotic Bureau, and grows and grows, always reproducing more of its own kind, until it chokes the host if not controlled or excised. Bureaus cannot live without a host, being true parasitic organisms. (A cooperative on the other hand *can* live without the state. That is the road to follow. The building up of independent units to meet needs of the people who participate in the functioning of the unit. A bureau operates on opposite principle of *inventing needs* to justify its existence.) Bureaucracy is wrong as a cancer, a turning away from the human evolutionary direction of infinite potentials and differentiation and independent spontaneous action, to the complete parasitism of a virus.

"(It is thought that the virus is a degeneration from more complex lifeform. It may at one time have been capable of independent life. Now has fallen to the borderline between living and dead matter. It can exhibit living qualities only in a host, by using the life of another—the renunciation of life itself, a *falling* towards inorganic, inflexible machine, towards dead matter.)

"Bureaus die when the structure of the state collapses. They are as helpless and unfit for independent existences as a displaced tapeworm, or a virus that has killed the host.

"In Timbuctu I once saw an Arab boy who could play a flute with his ass, and the fairies told me he was really an individual in bed. He could play a tune up and down the organ hitting the most erogenously sensitive spots, which are different on everyone, of course. Every lover had his special theme song which was perfect for him and rose to his climax. The boy was a great artist when it came to improving new combines and special climaxes, some of them notes in the unknown, tie-ups of seeming discords that would suddenly break through each other and crash together with a stunning, hot sweet impact."

ATROPHIED PREFACE

Wouldn't You?

Why all this waste paper getting The People from one place to another? Perhaps to spare The Reader stress of sudden space shifts and keep him Gentle? And so a ticket is bought, a taxi called, a plane boarded. We are allowed a glimpse into the warm peach-lined cave as She (the airline hostess, of course) leans over us to murmur of chewing gum, dramamine, even nembutal.

"Talk paregoric, Sweet Thing, and I will hear."

I am not American Express. . . . If one of my people is seen in New York walking around in citizen clothes and next sentence Timbuctu putting down lad talk on a gazelle-eyed youth, we may assume that he (the party nonresident of Timbuctu) transported himself there by the usual methods of communication. . . .

Lee The Agent (a double-four-eight-sixteen) is taking the junk cure . . . space time trip portentously familiar as junk meet corners to the addict . . . cures past and future shuttle pictures through his spectral substance vibrating in silent winds of accelerated Time. . . . Pick a shot. . . . Any Shot. . . .

Formal knuckle biting, floor rolling shots in a precinct cell. . . . "Feel like a shot of *Heroin*, Bill? Haw Haw Haw."

Tentative half impressions that dissolve in light . . . pockets of rotten ectoplasm swept out by an old junky coughing and spitting in the sick morning.

Old violet brown photos that curl and crack like mud in the sun: Panama City . . . Bill Gains putting down the paregoric con on a Chinese druggist.

"I've got these racing dogs . . . pedigree greyhounds. . . . All sick with the dysentery . . . tropical climate . . . the shits . . . you *sabe* shit? . . . *My Whippets Are Dying*. . . ." He screamed. . . . His eyes lit up with blue fire. . . . The flame went out . . . smell of burning metal. . . . "Administer with an eye dropper. . . . Wouldn't you? . . . Menstrual cramps . . . my wife . . . Kotex . . . Aged mother . . . Piles . . . raw . . . bleeding. . . ." He nodded out against the counter. . . . The druggist took a toothpick out of his mouth and looked at the end of it and shook his head. . . .

Gains and Lee burned down the Republic of Panama from David to Darien on paregoric. . . . They flew apart with a shlupping sound. . . . Junkies tend to run together into one body. . . . You have to be careful especially in hot places. . . . Gains back to Mexico City. . . . Desperate skeleton grin of chronic junk lack glazed over with codeine and goofballs . . . cigarette holes in his bathrobe . . . coffee stains on the floor . . . smoky kerosene stove . . . rusty orange flame . . .

The Embassy would give no details other than place of burial in the American Cemetery. . . .

And Lee back to sex and pain and time and *yagé*, bitter Soul Vine of the Amazon. . . .

I recall once after an overdose of *majoun* (this is cannabis dried and finely powdered to consistency of green powdered sugar and mixed with some confection or other usually tasting like gritty plum pudding, but the choice of confection is arbitrary, I am returning from The Lulu or Johnny or Little Boy's Room (stink of atrophied infancy and toilet training) look across the living room of that villa outside Tangier and suddenly don't know where I am. Perhaps I have opened the wrong door and at any moment The Man In Possession, The Owner Who Got There First will rush in and scream:

"What Are You Doing Here? Who Are You?"

And I don't know what I am doing there nor who I am. I decide to play it cool and maybe I will get the orientation before the Owner shows. . . . So instead of yelling "Where Am I?" cool it and look around you will find out approximately. . . . You were not there for *The Beginning*. You will not be there for *The End*. . . . Your knowledge of what is going on can only be superficial and relative. . . . What do I know of this yellow blighted young junky face subsisting on raw opium? I tried to tell him: "Some morning you will wake up with your liver in your lap" and how to process raw opium so it is not plain poison. But his eyes glaze over and he didn't want to know. Junkies are like that most of them they don't want to know . . . and you can't tell them anything. . . . A smoker doesn't want to know anything but smoke. . . . And a heroin junky same way. . . . Strictly the spike and any other route is Farina. . . .

So I guess he is still sitting there in his 1920 Spanish villa outside Tangier eating that raw opium full of shit and stones and straw . . . the whole lot for fear he might lose something. . . .

There is only one thing a writer can write about: *what is in front of his senses at the moment of writing*. . . . I am a recording instrument. . . . I do not presume to impose "story" "plot" "continuity." . . . Insofar as I succeed in *Direct* recording of certain areas of psychic process I may have limited function. . . . I am not an entertainer. . . .

"Possession" they call it. . . . Sometimes an entity jumps in the body—outlines waver in yellow orange jelly—and hands move to disembowel the passing whore or strangle the nabor child in hope of alleviating a chronic housing shortage. As if I was usually there but subject to goof now and again. . . . *Wrong! I am never here*. . . . Never that is *fully* in possession, but somehow in a position to forestall ill-advised moves. . . . Patrolling is, in fact, my principal occupation. . . . No matter how tight Security, I am always somewhere *Outside* giving orders and *Inside* this strait-jacket of jelly that gives and stretches but always reforms ahead of every movement, thought, impulse, stamped with the seal of alien inspection. . . .

Writers talk about the sweet-sick smell of death whereas any junky can tell you that death has no smell . . . at the same time a smell that shuts off breath and stops blood . . . colorless no-smell of death . . . no one can breathe and smell it through pink convolutions and black blood filters of flesh . . . the death smell is unmistakably a smell and complete absence of smell . . . smell absence hits the nose first because all organic life has smell . . . stopping of smell is felt like darkness to the eyes, silence to the ears, stress and weightlessness to the balance and location sense. . . .

You always smell it and give it out for others to smell during junk withdrawal. . . . A kicking junky can make a whole apartment unlivable with his death smell . . . but a good airing will stink the place up again so a body can breathe. . . . You also smell it during one of those oil burner habits that suddenly starts jumping geometric like a topping forest fire. . . .

Cure is always: *Let go! Jump!*

A friend of mine found himself naked in a Marrakech hotel room second floor. . . . (He is after processing by a Texas mother who dressed him in girls' clothes as a child. . . . Crude but effective against infant protoplasm. . . .) The other occupants are Arabs, three Arabs . . . knives in hand . . . watching him

. . . glint of metal and points of light in dark eyes . . . pieces of murder falling slow as opal chips through glycerine. . . . Slower animal reactions allow him a full second to decide: Straight through the window and down into the crowded street like a falling star his wake of glass glittering in the sun . . . sustained a broken ankle and a chipped shoulder . . . clad in a diaphanous pink curtain, with a curtain-rod staff, hobbled away to the Commissariat de Police. . . .

Sooner or later The Vigilante, The Rube, Lee The Agent, A.J., Clem and Jody The Ergot Twins, Hassan O'Leary the After Birth Tycoon, The Sailor, The Exterminator, Andrew Keif, "Fats" Terminal, Doc Benway, "Fingers" Schafer are subject to say the same thing in the same words to occupy, at that intersection point, the same position in space-time. Using a common vocal apparatus complete with all metabolic appliances—that is, to be the same person—a most inaccurate way of expressing *Recognition:* The junky naked in sunlight . . .

The writer sees himself reading to the mirror as always. . . . He must check now and again to reassure himself that The Crime Of Separate Action has not, is not, cannot occur. . . .

Anyone who has ever looked into a mirror knows what this crime is and what it means in terms of lost control when the reflection no longer obeys. . . . Too late to dial *Police.* . . .

I personally wish to terminate my services as of now in that I cannot continue to sell the raw materials of death. . . . Yours, sir, is a hopeless case and a noisome one. . . .

"Defense is meaningless in the present state of our knowledge," said The Defense looking up from an electron microscope. . . .

Take your business to Walgreen's

We are not responsible

Steal anything in sight

I don't know how to return it to the white reader

You can write or yell or croon about it . . . paint about it . . . act about it . . . shit it out in mobiles. . . . *So long as you don't go and do it.* . . .

Senators leap up and bray for the Death Penalty with inflexible authority of virus yen. . . . Death for dope fiends, death for sex queens (I mean fiends) death for the psychopath who offends the cowed and graceless flesh with broken animal innocence of lithe movement. . . .

The black wind sock of death undulates over the land, feeling, smelling for the crime of separate life, movers of the fear-frozen flesh shivering under a vast probability curve. . . .

Population blocks disappear in a checker game of genocide. . . . Any number can play. . . .

The Liberal Press and The Press Not So Liberal and The Press Reactionary scream approval: "Above all the myth of other-level experience must be eradicated. . . ." And speak darkly of certain harsh realities . . . cows with the aftosa . . . prophylaxis. . . .

Power groups of the world frantically cut lines of connection. . . .

The Planet drifts to random insect doom. . . .

Thermodynamics has won at a crawl. . . . Orgone balked at the post. . . . Christ bled. . . . Time ran out. . . .

You can cut into *Naked Lunch* at any intersection point. . . . I have written many prefaces. They atrophy and amputate spontaneous like the little toe amputates in a West African disease confined to the Negro race and the passing blonde shows her brass ankle as a manicured toe bounces across the club terrace, retrieved and laid at her feet by her Afghan Hound. . . .

Naked Lunch is a blueprint, a How-To Book. . . . Black insect lusts open into vast, other-planet landscapes. . . . Abstract concepts, bare as algebra, narrow down to a black turd or a pair of aging *cojones*. . . .

How-To extend levels of experience by opening the door at the end of a long hall. . . . Doors that only open in *Silence*. . . . *Naked Lunch* demands Silence from The Reader. Otherwise he is taking his own pulse. . . .

Robert Christie knew The Answering Service. . . . Kill the old cunts . . . keep pubic hairs in his locket . . . wouldn't You?

Robert Christie, mass strangler of women—sounds like a daisy chain—hanged in 1953.

Jack The Ripper, Literal Swordsman of the 1890s and never caught with his pants down . . . wrote a letter to The Press.

"Next time I'll send along an ear just for jolly. . . . Wouldn't you?"

"Oh be careful! There they go again!" said the old queen as his string broke, spilling his balls over the floor. . . . "Stop them will you, James, you worthless old shit! Don't just stand there and let the master's balls roll into the coal-bin!"

Window dressers scream through the station, beat the cashiers with the Fairy Hyp.

Dilaudid deliver poor me (Dilaudid is souped-up, dehydrate morphine).

The sheriff in black vest types out a death warrant: "Gotta make it legal and exempt narcotic. . . ."

Violation Public Health Law 334 . . . Procuring an orgasm by the use of fraud. . . .

Johnny on all fours and Mary sucking him and running her fingers down the thigh backs and light over the outfields of the ball park. . . .

Over the broken chair and out through the tool-house window whitewash whipping in a cold Spring wind on a limestone cliff over the river . . . piece of moon smoke hangs in China blue sky . . . out on a long line of jissom across the dusty floor. . . .

Motel . . . Motel . . . Motel . . . broken neon arabesque . . . loneliness moans across the continent like fog horns over still, oily water of tidal rivers. . . .

Ball squeezed dry lemon rindpest rims the ass with a knife cut off a piece of hash for the water pipe—bubble bubble—indicate what used to be me. . . .

"The river is served, sir."

Dead leaves fill the fountain and geraniums run wild with mint, spill a vending machine route across the lawn. . . .

The aging playboy dons his 1920 autograph slicker, feeds his screaming wife down the garbage-disposal unit. . . . Hair, shit and blood spurt out 1963 on the wall. . . . "Yes sir, boys, the shit really hit the fan in '63," said the tiresome old prophet can bore the piss out of you in any space-time direction. . . .

"Now I happen to remember because it was just two years before that a strain of human aftosa developed in a Bolivian lavatory got loose through the medium of a Chinchilla coat fixed an income tax case in Kansas City. . . . And a Liz claimed Immaculate Conception and give birth to a six-ounce spider monkey through the navel. . . . They say the croaker was party to that caper had the monkey on his back all the time. . . ."

I, William Seward, captain of this lushed up hash-head subway, will quell the Loch Ness monster with rotenone and cowboy the white whale. I will reduce Satan to Automatic Obedience, and sublimate subsidiary fiends. I will banish the candiru from your swimming pools—I will issue a bull on Immaculate Birth Control. . . .

"The oftener a thing happens the more uniquely wonderful it is," said the pretentious young Nordic on the trapeze studying his Masonic homework.

"The Jews don't believe in Christ, Clem. . . . All they want to do is doodle a Christian girl. . . ."

Adolescent angels sing on shithouse walls of the world.

"Come and jack off . . ." 1929.

"Gimpy push milk sugar shit . . ." Johnny Hung Lately 1952

(Decayed corseted tenor sings *Danny Deever* in drag. . . .)

Mules don't foal in this decent county and no hooded dead gibber in the ash pits. . . . Violation Public Health Law 334.

So where is the statuary and the percentage? Who can say? I don't have The Word. . . . Home in my douche bag. . . . The King is loose with a flame thrower and the king killer, tortured in effigy of a thousand bums, slides down skid row to shit in the limestone ball court.

Young Dillinger walked straight out of the house and never looked back. . . .

"Don't ever look back, kid. . . . You turn into some old cow's salt lick."

Police bullet in the alley . . . Broken wings of Icarus, screams of a burning boy inhaled by the old junky . . . eyes empty as a vast plain . . . (vulture wings husk in the dry air).

The Crab, aged Dean Of Lush Workers, puts on his crustacean suit to prowl the graveyard shift . . . with steel claws pulls the gold teeth and crowns of any flop sleep with his mouth open. . . . If the flop comes up on him The Crab rears back claws snapping to offer dubious battle on the plains of Queens.

The Boy Burglar, fucked in the long jail term, ousted from the cemetery for the non-payment, comes gibbering into the queer bar with a moldy pawn ticket to pick up the back balls of Tent City where castrate salesmen sing the IBM song.

Crabs frolicked through his forest . . . wresting with the angel hard-on all night, thrown in the homo fall of valor, take a back road to the rusty limestone cave.

Black Yen ejaculates over the salt marshes where nothing grows not even a mandrake. . . .

Law of averages . . . A few chickens . . . Only way to live. . . .

"Hello, Cash."

"You sure it's here?"

"Of course I'm sure. . . . Go in with you."

Night train to Chi . . . Meet a girl in the hall and I see she is on and ask where is a score?

"Come in sonny."

I mean not a young chick but built. . . . "How about a fix first?"

"Ixnay, you wouldn't be inna condition."

Three times around . . . wake up shivering sick in warm Spring wind through the window, water burns the eyes like acid. . . .

She gets out of bed naked. . . . Stash in the Cobra lamp. . . . Cooks up. . . .

"Turn over. . . . I'll give it to you in the ass."

She slides the needle in deep, pulls it out and massages the cheek. . . .

She licks a drop of blood off her finger.

He rolls over with a hard-on dissolving in the grey ooze of junk.

In a vale of cocaine and innocence sad-eyed youths yodel for a lost Danny Boy. . . .

We sniffed all night and made it four times . . . fingers down the black board . . . scrape the white bone. Home is the heroin home from the sea and the hustler home from The Bill. . . .

The Pitchman stirs uneasily: "Take over here will you, kid? Gotta see a man about a monkey."

The Word is divided into units which be all in one piece and should be so taken, but the pieces can be had in any order being tied up back and forth, in and out fore and aft like an innaresting sex arrangement. This book spill off the page in all directions, kaleidoscope of vistas, medley of tunes and street noises, farts and riot yipes and the slamming steel shutters of commerce, screams of pain and pathos and screams plain pathic, copulating cats and outraged squawk of the displaced bull head, prophetic mutterings of *brujo* in nutmeg trances, snapping necks and screaming mandrakes, sigh of orgasm, heroin silent as dawn in the thirsty cells, Radio Cairo screaming like a berserk tobacco auction, and flutes of Ramadan fanning the sick junky like a gentle lush worker in the grey subway dawn feeling with delicate fingers for the green folding crackle. . . .

This is Revelation and Prophecy of what I can pick up without FM on my 1920 crystal set with antennae of jissom. . . . Gentle reader, we see God through our assholes in the flash bulb of orgasm. . . . Through these orifices transmute your body. . . . The Way OUT is the way IN. . . .

Now I, William Seward, will unlock my word horde. . . . My Viking heart fares over the great brown river where motors put put put in jungle twilight and whole trees float with huge snakes in the branches and sad-eyed lemurs watch the shore, across the Missouri field (The Boy finds a pink arrowhead)

out along distant train whistles, comes back to me hungry as a street boy don't
know to peddle the ass God gave him. . . .

Gentle Reader, The Word will leap on you with leopard man iron claws, it
will cut off fingers and toes like an opportunist land crab, it will hang you and
catch your jissom like a scrutable dog, it will coil round your thighs like a bush-
master and inject a shot glass of rancid ectoplasm. . . . And why a *scrutable* dog?

The other day I am returning from the long lunch thread from mouth to
ass all the days of our years, when I see an Arab boy have this little black and
white dog know how to walk on his hind legs. . . . And a big yaller dog come
on the boy for affection and the boy shove it away, and the yaller dog growl
and snap at the little toddler, snarling if he had but human gift of tongues: "A
crime against nature right there."

So I dub the yaller dog Scrutable. . . . And let me say in passing, and I am
always passing like a sincere Spade, that the Inscrutable East need a heap of
salt to get it down. . . . Your Reporter bang thirty grains of M a day and sit
eight hours inscrutable as a turd.

"What are you *thinking*?" says the squirming American Tourist. . . .

To which I reply: "Morphine have depressed my hypothalamus, seat of libido and emotion, and since the front brain acts only at second hand with
back-brain titillation, being a vicarious type citizen can only get his kicks from
behind, I must report virtual absence of cerebral event. I am aware of your
presence, but since it has for me no affective connotation, my affect having
been disconnect by the junk man for the non-payment, I am not innarested in
your doings. . . . Go or come, shit or fuck yourself with a rasp or an asp—
'tis well done and fitting for a queen—but The Dead and The Junky don't
care. . . ." They are *Inscrutable*.

"Which is the way down the aisle to the water closet?" I asked the blonde
usherette.

"Right through here, sir. . . . Room for one more inside."

"Have you seen Pantopon Rose?" said the old junky in the black overcoat.

The Texas sheriff has killed his complicit Vet, Browbeck The Unsteady,
involved in horse heroin racket. . . . A horse down with the aftosa need a sight
of heroin to ease his pain and maybe some of that heroin take off across the
lonesome prairie and whinny in Washington Square. . . . Junkies rush up yelling: "Heigh oOO Silver."

"But where is the *statuary*?" This arch type bit of pathos screeched out in
tea-room cocktail lounge with bamboo decorations, Calle Juarez, Mexico, D.F.
. . . Lost back there with a meatball rape rap . . . a cunt claw your pants down
and you up for rape that's statutory, brother. . . .

Chicago calling . . . come in please . . . Chicago calling . . . come in please.
. . . What you think I got the rubber on for, galoshes in Puyo? A mighty wet
place, reader. . . .

"Take it off! Take it off!"

The old queen meets himself coming round the other way in burlesque of
adolescence, gets the knee from his phantom of the Old Old Howard . . . down

skid row to Market Street Museum shows all kinds masturbation and self-abuse
. . . young boys need it special. . . .

They was ripe for the plucking forgot way back yonder in the corn hole . . .
lost in little scraps of delight and burning scrolls. . . .

Read the metastasis with blind fingers.

Fossil message of arthritis . . .

"Selling is more of a habit than using."—Lola La Chata, Mexico, D.F.

Sucking terror from needle scars, underwater scream mouthing numb nerve
warnings of the yen to come, throbbing bite site of rabies . . .

"If God made anything better He kept it for himself," the Sailor used to
say, his transmission slowed down with twenty goofballs.

(Pieces of murder fall slow as opal chips through glycerine.)

Watching you and humming over and over "Johnny's So Long at the Fair."

Pushing in a small way to keep up our habit. . . .

"And *use* that alcohol," I say slamming a spirit lamp down on the table.

"You fucking can't-wait hungry junkies all the time black up my spoons
with matches. . . . That's all I need for Pen Indef the heat rumbles a black spoon
in the trap. . . ."

"I thought you was quitting. . . . Wouldn't feel right fucking up your cure."

"Takes a lot of guts to kick a habit, kid."

Looking for veins in the thawing flesh. Hour-Glass of junk spills its last
black grains into the kidneys. . . .

"Heavily infected area," he muttered, shifting the tie-up.

"Death was their Culture Hero," said my Old Lady, looking up from the
Mayan Codices. . . . "They got fire and speech and the corn seed from death.
. . . Death turns into a maize seed."

The Ouab Days are upon us
     raw peeled winds of hate and mischance
          blew the shot.

"Get those fucking dirty pictures out of here," I told her.

The Old Time Schmecker supported himself on a chair back, juiced and
goof-balled . . . a disgrace to his blood.

"What are you one of these goofball artists?"

Yellow smells of skid row sherry and occluding liver drifted out of his clothes
when he made the junky gesture throwing the hand out palm up to cop . . .
     smell of chili houses and dank overcoats and atrophied testicles. . . .

He looked at me through the tentative, ectoplasmic flesh of cure . . . thirty
pounds materialized in a month when you kick . . . soft pink putty that fades
at the first silent touch of junk. . . . I saw it happen . . . ten pounds lost in ten
minutes . . . standing there with the syringe in one hand . . . holding his pants
up with the other
     sharp reek of diseased metal.

Walking in a rubbish heap to the sky . . . scattered gasoline fires . . . smoke
hangs black and solid as excrement in the motionless air . . . smudging the

white film of noon heat . . . D.L. walks beside me . . . a reflection of my toothless gums and hairless skull . . . flesh smeared over the rotting phosphorescent bones consumed by slow cold fires. . . . He carries an open can of gasoline and the smell of gasoline envelopes him. . . . Coming over a hill of rusty iron we meet a group of Natives . . . flat two-dimension faces of scavenger fish. . . .

"Throw the gasoline on them and light it. . . ."

QUICK . . .

white flash . . . mangled insect screams . . .
I woke up with the taste of metal in my mouth back from the dead
trailing the colorless death smell
afterbirth of a withered grey monkey
phantom twinges of amputation . . .
"Taxi boys waiting for a pickup," Eduardo said and died of an overdose in Madrid. . . .
Powder trains burn back through pink convolutions of tumescent flesh
. . . set off flash bulbs of orgasm . . . pin-point photos of arrested motion
. . . smooth brown side twisted to light a cigarette. . . .
He stood there in a 1920 straw hat somebody gave him . . . soft mendicant words falling like dead birds in the dark street. . . .
"No . . . No more . . . *No más* . . ."
A heaving sea of air hammers in the purple brown dusk tainted with rotten metal smell of sewer gas . . . young worker faces vibrating out of focus in yellow halos of carbide lanterns . . . broken pipes exposed. . . .
"They are rebuilding the City."
Lee nodded absently. . . . "Yes . . . Always . . ."
Either way is a bad move to The East Wing. . . .
If I knew I'd be glad to tell you. . . .
"No good . . . *no bueno* . . . hustling myself. . . ."
"No glot . . . C'lom Fliday"
Tangier, 1959

THE CUT-UPS

the cut-ups
by james grauerholz

Living alone at the Empress Hotel in London, visiting Ian Sommerville (who was back in school at Cambridge), and renewing his literary work, William Burroughs began in 1960 to create his "cut-up trilogy": *The Soft Machine, The Ticket That Exploded,* and *Nova Express.* He was mixing new pages with older writing, cutting up everything from his past to write an as-yet-unimagined future. His publishers waged legal and literary battles on his behalf, even as they began to recognize that this new work Burroughs was turning in was hardly as accessible to his growing public as *Naked Lunch* had been—that novel did, after all, contain plenty of satirical humor and titillating sexual and drug-related material.

Now that Burroughs had achieved a measure of fame, he began to attract young admirers; Michael Portman, aged seventeen, was the first of these, stalk-ing Burroughs in the fall of 1960 and making himself irresistible. But "Mikey" was a trouble-child from the English upper classes, and he tried to outdo Burroughs in narcotics and alcohol consumption. This pattern continued, worsening throughout his short life. Portman was around Burroughs and Gysin, in London and Tangier, for only about three years; he died in his late thirties, from what Brion Gysin termed "wretched excess."

A relationship that, in contrast, would last all Burroughs' life, but that—like so many of his important friendships—started off on the wrong foot, began in early 1961 when Burroughs received a letter from Timothy Leary, Ph.D., Harvard. Leary was a psychological researcher, but soon would leave that far behind. His specialty was the relatively new field of hallucinogenic drugs, which he termed "psychedelic"—mind-expanding. The history of these substances encompasses some interesting anthropology and pharmaco-botany—as well as a political intersection with the "Control machine," in the person of the CIA, whose secret experiments with LSD in the fifties and sixties were later revealed to have been widespread. Of course, Burroughs' early interest in *yagé,* had put him in contact with these discoveries, and Leary recognized this. He sent some psilocybin mushrooms to Burroughs in London in early 1961, at a time when Burroughs was planning to spend the summer in Tangier with Ian Sommerville.

Allen Ginsberg and Gregory Corso arrived in Tangier in June 1961, just as
The Olympia Press published *The Soft Machine* in Paris. Alan Ansen was not
far behind, and everyone was now taking a potpourri of psychedelic drugs in
the name of spiritual discovery. Leary arrived in Tangier at the climax of the
summer, and persuaded Burroughs to join him in Newton, Massachusetts, for
a month. As Corso, Ansen, and Ginsberg all departed Tangier in September,
Burroughs flew to Boston to participate in Leary's experiments. But Leary was
entering a messianic phase, and after a few weeks he and Burroughs did not
see eye to eye.

Barney Rosset offered Burroughs a basement apartment in Brooklyn, where
he worked on *Nova Express.* In New York at this time, Le Roi Jones and Diane
Di Prima published their ninth issue of *Floating Bear,* which included the suppressed "Roosevelt After Inauguration" routine—for which they were arrested.
Burroughs spent only two months in Brooklyn, returning to London for his
forty-eighth birthday in February 1962. He came home to the sad news that
Kells Elvins, passing through New York just after Burroughs' departure, had
died of a heart attack. Back at the Empress Hotel, living with Sommerville
(and Portman), Burroughs returned to work on *The Ticket That Exploded,*
finishing the manuscript at this time—just as *Naked Lunch* was finally published in the U.S. by Grove Press in March.

With his publishers in France, England, and the U.S. fighting various court
battles for the right to print his books (and the works of Henry Miller, James
Joyce, Frank Harris, Vladimir Nabokov, and J. P. Donleavy), Burroughs seized
the opportunity to rewrite some of his books between editions. After *The Soft
Machine* was published in Paris in 1961, Burroughs significantly expanded the
text for its 1966 publication by Grove in New York, and again for John Calder's
1968 London edition, giving rise to three separate states of the novel. *The Ticket
That Exploded* appeared in Paris in 1962; for Grove's 1967 edition, Burroughs
expanded the text, but he left it alone for Calder's 1968 edition, so there are
just two states of *Ticket.* Grove was the first publisher of *Nova Express,* in
1964, and the (unchanged) U.K. edition, two years later, was given to Jonathan Cape Ltd., due to the reluctance of Burroughs' U.K. agent to grant
Calder a monopoly.

As Barry Miles pointed out in his 1993 biography of Burroughs, the new
material in the second and third states of *Soft Machine,* and in the second state
of *Ticket,* contain passages that provide a bridge to Burroughs' next phase of
writing: a polemical period that parallels his erotic revival in his early fifties.
For this collection, however, the American editions have been used.

The Edinburgh Conference was an annual literary event in Scotland, and by
the early 1960s it was exerting a notable attraction for American and European literary figures. John Calder arranged for Burroughs to be invited to
Edinburgh, Calder's hometown, in August 1962. Attended by such luminar-
ies as Norman Mailer, Mary McCarthy, and Henry Miller, the conference
became focused on *Naked Lunch,* pro and con. McCarthy's controversial ap-

preciation of the novel—a defection from her social class—gave new momentum to Burroughs' career. His remarks at the conference were entitled "The Future of the Novel," and he ended with this statement: "I am primarily concerned with the question of survival—with Nova conspiracies, Nova criminals, and Nova police—A new mythology is possible in the Space Age, where we will again have heroes and villains with respect to intentions towards this planet—the future of the novel is not in Time, but in Space."

Around Christmas 1962, *The Ticket that Exploded* was published in Paris, and there was bad news from Palm Beach: Burroughs' fifteen-year-old son had accidentally shot a neighbor boy in the neck—an accident with disturbing overtones. But Burroughs was not about to go back to Florida now. In London he had recently met Antony Balch, a filmmaker and distributor who suggested a collaboration, and Burroughs—living with Sommerville, with Balch and Gysin nearby—was in a new period of inspiration. He worked on a film called *Towers Open Fire,* with Balch filming Burroughs, Gysin, and Portman on leftover 35mm B/W negative stock; Sommerville, meanwhile, was busy with Burroughs' tape-recorder experiments. In mid-1963, they went to the Beat Hotel in Paris, where Balch did more filming, and Burroughs gave a few avant-garde son-et-lumière musical performances with Daevid Allen and Terry Riley. In June, Burroughs moved to Tangier with Sommerville and Portman; they lived at 4 calle Larachi, in the Arab quarter.

After a guilt-ridden correspondence with his overburdened older brother Mort, Burroughs agreed to take his son into his Tangier home while the boy attended the local American School. Billy arrived in July 1963, just before his sixteenth birthday. He was thrilled to be near his glamorous father and living in the romantic seediness of Tangier. But his father's homosexuality, and his two younger roommates, were confusing to the adolescent boy. Burroughs offered Billy the freedom to smoke hashish and play guitar, but he realized by December that the situation was too overwhelming for his son, and perhaps for himself. The emotional distance between them was at least as great as that between himself and his own father.

When Billy returned to his grandparents' home in Florida in January 1964, Burroughs made a trip to Paris in a foredoomed attempt to collect several thousand dollars in royalties that Girodias owed him. Just two months earlier, John Calder had published a relatively "safe" selection of Burroughs' writings from *Naked Lunch, Soft Machine,* and *Ticket,* which Burroughs named *Dead Fingers Talk*—again adding new emendations to the excerpts, creating slightly new substates of the latter two novels. And in December 1963, City Lights published *The Yagé Letters,* which by now included a final exchange of letters between Ginsberg, who had reached the *yagé* highlands seven years after his mentor, and Burroughs, who was already becoming the literary seer of his cut-up period.

Back in Tangier in February, Burroughs turned his attention to Jeff Nuttall's *My Own Mag,* a mimeographed publication from England, which featured Burroughs' collaged communiqués in twenty-one issues between 1964 and

1966. All was not quiet on the domestic front, however; Sommerville was picking up Arab men for sex, and as they were living in the Casbah, this flagrant activity brought on the opprobrium of their Arab neighbors—especially the women, who openly harassed them in the street. In May 1964, Burroughs finally began to earn a bit of money from his books, and he and Sommerville moved to a more gracious penthouse apartment in the Lotería Building, in downtown Tangier.

With an assignment from *Playboy* to return to his hometown of St. Louis, Burroughs went to the Chelsea Hotel in New York in December 1964. Sommerville wanted to accompany him, but he had visa problems; these could have been overcome, but Barry Miles, an eyewitness, suggests that Burroughs was willing to walk away from his growing ambivalence toward Sommerville. It was a subtle abandonment, one that would haunt Burroughs for a decade. He had little time to ponder it, though, because in January he received word that his seventy-nine-year-old father had died suddenly in Palm Beach. Burroughs went to Florida for the funeral. Laura seemed to be bearing up fairly well; the faithful Mort and his wife Miggy would keep an eye on her, from their home in St. Louis. Burroughs returned to New York, and rented a loft at 210 Centre Street.

In early 1965, *Naked Lunch* was tried in Boston for obscenity. Burroughs' supporting witnesses included Allen Ginsberg, Norman Mailer, and John Ciardi. At this time Gysin developed a device that he called the "Dream Machine": a slotted, spinning cylinder that was brightly illuminated from within, so that, gazing into it, one experienced alpha-wave "flicker" and mild hallucinations. Gysin came to New York to join Burroughs and to market his invention; the literary agent Peter Matson met both of them at this time, and he represented Burroughs for the next nineteen years. The Dream Machine was a sensation, but no one wanted to manufacture a device that could provoke seizures.

Burroughs' reputation was already such that he was the toast of downtown New York in 1965. He made friends with a circle of young painters around the emerging pop artist Robert Rauschenberg, including David Prentice. A cosmetics-fortune heir named Conrad Rooks invited Burroughs to play a deathly, top-hatted character in his avant-garde film project, *Chappaqua*. Burroughs was royally feted at parties and readings thrown by such hostesses as Panna Grady, in her apartment at the Dakota Hotel, and Wyn Chamberlain, in his penthouse at 222 Bowery, an address which Burroughs would make his own ten years later. Brion Gysin was with Burroughs in New York, using his diplomacy and charm to brighten all social situations, and working daily with him on their collaborative chef d'oeuvre, a text-and-collage work that they called *The Third Mind*. Through Panna Grady, Gysin met the poet John Giorno, a Columbia graduate in his twenties who would play a major role in Gysin's and Burroughs' lives; Giorno and Gysin became lovers.

Burroughs spent time with David Budd, a painter from Sarasota, Florida, with a lively circus-people background, whom Burroughs had first met at the

Beat Hotel in the late 1950s. Budd brought to Burroughs' attention the last words of Dutch Schultz, a New York gangster who was shot down in Newark in 1935 and whose disconnected ramblings, recorded by a stenographer as he lay dying in a hospital, were reminiscent of Burroughs' cut-up texts. This relationship led to a film project in 1968, and Burroughs tried his hand at a screenplay based on the gangster's life story, called *The Last Words of Dutch Schultz*. This text was published in four different states: in England in 1965 by Jeff Nuttall in *My Own Mag;* in Boston, by the *Atlantic Monthly,* in 1969; in London by Cape Goliard Press in 1970; and in New York in 1975, by Viking. But the movie project never took off.

Burroughs' six months in the loft on Centre Street were busy times. He collaborated with Joe Brainard and Ron Padgett on *TIME* ("C" Press, 1965), and again with Ed Sanders, who published *APO-33: A Metabolic Regulator.* Burroughs' collage book with Gysin, *The Third Mind,* was unpublishable in its full-graphics form at the time. (The original boards were finally exhibited by the Los Angeles County Museum of Art in their "Ports of Entry" exhibition in July 1996—more than thirty years after *The Third Mind*'s creation.) Burroughs was also making "scrapbooks," with input from Gysin: usually not very large, these hardbound journal-books were filled with collaged images culled from the press, typed and handwritten texts, drawings in colored inks, and so forth. From 1960 to 1976 he made about two dozen such scrapbooks. Burroughs also began to explore live performance in the mid-1960s; he made several public appearances in New York, sometimes with Gysin. On a trip to Paris around this time, Burroughs recorded his first long-playing record, *Call Me Burroughs,* with Sommerville; Gaît Frogé, the owner of the English Bookshop, published a thousand copies of the vinyl album, and the following year it was released in the United States on Bernard Stollman's ESP-Disk label.

The end of Burroughs' year in New York was at hand. In September 1965, as Gysin made ready to take John Giorno with him to Morocco, Burroughs decided to return to London to see what remained of his domestic situation with Ian Sommerville. Immediately he faced a new visa hassle upon landing at Heathrow, due to his growing media notoriety. Mikey Portman's godfather, the chairman of the Arts Council, intervened with the immigration authorities, but Burroughs was obliged to quit England three months later. He went to Tangier for a brief vacation with Gysin and Giorno.

It was the swan song of the Tangier scene: Paul and Jane Bowles were still there, and many others of the mid-fifties Tangerine set, but most of them for only a little while longer. On Christmas Day 1965, Jay Hazelwood (the longtime *genius loci* of the Parade Bar, the HQ of the expat group) died in his bar, of a heart attack. It marked the end of an era: the "anything-goes" international crowd was fleeing newly independent Muslim Morocco. Burroughs returned in January 1966—the midst of the "Swinging Sixties"—to London, the city that would be his home for the next eight years.

from
the soft machine

DEAD ON ARRIVAL

I was working the hole with the Sailor and we did not do bad. Fifteen cents on an average night boosting the afternoons and short-timing the dawn we made out from the land of the free. But I was running out of veins. I went over to the counter for another cup of coffee . . . in Joe's Lunch Room drinking coffee with a napkin under the cup which is said to be the mark of someone who does a lot of sitting in cafeterias and lunchrooms. . . . Waiting on the Man. . . . "What can we do?" Nick said to me once in his dead junky whisper. "They know we'll wait. . . ." Yes, they know we'll wait . . .

There is a boy sitting at the counter thin-faced kid his eyes all pupil. I see he is hooked and sick. Familiar face maybe from the pool hall where I scored for tea sometime. Somewhere in grey strata of subways all-night cafeterias rooming house flesh. His eyes flickered the question. I nodded toward my booth. He carried his coffee over and sat down opposite me.

The croaker lives out Long Island . . . light yen sleep waking up for stops. Change. Start. Everything sharp and clear. Antennae of TV suck the sky. The clock jumped the way time will after four P.M.

"The Man is three hours late. You got the bread?"

"I got three cents."

"Nothing less than a nickel. These double papers he claims." I looked at his face. Good looking. "Say kid I known an Old Auntie Croaker write for you like a Major. . . . Take the phone. I don't want him to rumble my voice."

About this time I meet this Italian tailor *cum* pusher I know from Lexington and he gives me a good buy on H. . . . At least it was good at first but all the time shorter and shorter . . . "Short Count Tony" we call him . . .

Out of junk in East St. Louis sick dawn he threw himself across the washbasin pressing his stomach against the cool porcelain. I draped myself over his body laughing. His shorts dissolved in rectal mucus and carbolic soap. summer dawn smells from a vacant lot.

"I'll wait here. . . . Don't want him to rumble me. . . ."

Made it five times under the shower that day soapy bubbles of egg flesh seismic tremors split by fissure spurts of jissom . . .

I made the street, everything sharp and clear like after rain. See Sid in a booth reading a paper his face like yellow ivory in the sunlight. I handed him two nickels under the table. Pushing in a small way to keep up The Habit: INVADE. DAMAGE. OCCUPY. Young faces in blue alcohol flame.

"And use that alcohol. You fucking can't-wait hungry junkies all the time black up my spoons. That's all I need for Pen Indef the fuzz rumbles a black spoon in my trap." The old junky spiel. Junk hooks falling.

"Shoot your way to freedom kid."

Trace a line of goose pimples up the thin young arm. Slide the needle in and push the bulb watching the junk hit him all over. Move right in with the shit and suck junk through all the hungry young cells.

There is a boy sitting like your body. I see he is a hook. I drape myself over him from the pool hall. Draped myself over his cafeteria and his shorts dissolved in strata of subways . . . and all house flesh . . . toward the booth . . . down opposite me. . . . The Man I Italian tailor . . . I know bread. "Me a good buy on H."

"You're quitting? Well I hope you make it, kid. May I fall down and be paralyzed if I don't mean it. . . . You gotta friend in me. A real friend and if."

Well the traffic builds up and boosters falling in with jackets shirts and ties, kids with a radio turn from the living car trailing tubes and wires, lush-workers flash rings and wrist watches falling in sick all hours. I had the janitor cooled, an old rummy, but it couldn't last with that crowd.

"Say you're looking great kid. Now do yourself a favor and stay off. I been getting some really great shit lately. Remember that brown shit sorta yellow like snuff cooks up brown and clear . . ."

Junky in east bath room . . . invisible and persistent dream body . . . familiar face maybe . . . scored for some time or body . . . in that grey smell of rectal mucus . . . night cafeterias and junky room dawn smells. Three hours from Lexington made it five times . . . soapy egg flesh . . .

"These double papers he claims of withdrawal."

"Well I thought you was quitting . . ."

"I can't make it."

"Imposible quitar eso."

Got up and fixed in the sick dawn flutes of Ramadan.

"¿William tu tomas más medicina? . . . No me hagas caso, William."

Casbah house in the smell of dust and we made it . . . empty Eukodol boxes stacked four feet along the walls . . . dead on the surplus blankets . . . girl screaming . . . *vecinos* rush in . . .

"What did she die of?"

"I don't know she just died."

Bill Gains in Mexico City room with his douche bag and his stash of codeine pills powdered in a bicarbonate can. "I'll just say I suffer from indigestion." Coffee and blood spilled all over the place. Cigarette holes in the pink blanket. . . . The Consul would give me no information other than place of burial in The American Cemetery.

"Broke? Have you no pride? Go to your Consul." He gave me an alarm clock ran for a year after his death.

Leif repatriated by the Danish. freight boat out of Casa for Copenhagen sank off England with all hands. Remember my medium of distant fingers?—

"What did she die of?"

"End."

"Some things I find myself."

The Sailor went wrong in the end. Hanged to a cell door by his principles: "Some things I find myself doing I'll pack in is all."

Bread knife in the heart . . . rub and die . . . repatriated by morphine script . . . those out of Casa for Copenhagen on special yellow note . . .

"All hands broke? Have you no pride?" Alarm clock ran for a year. "He just sit down on the curb and die." Esperanza told me on Niño Perdido and we cashed a morphine script, those Mexican Nar. scripts on special yellow bank-note paper . . . like a thousand dollar bill . . . or a Dishonorable Discharge from the US Army. . . . And fixed in the cubicle room you reach by climbing this ladder.

Yesterday call flutes of Ramadan: *"No me hagas caso."*

Blood spill over shirts and light. The American trailing in form. . . . He went to Madrid. This frantic Cuban fruit finds Kiki with a *novia* and stabs him with a kitchen knife in the heart. (Girl screaming. Enter the nabors.)

"Quédase con su medicina, William."

Half bottle of Fundador after half cure in the Jew Hospital. Shots of demerol by candlelight. They turned off the lights and water. Paper-like dust we made it. Empty walls. Look anywhere. No good. *No bueno.*

He went to Madrid. . . . Alarm clock ran for yesterday. . . . *"No me hagas caso."* Dead on arrival . . . you might say at the Jew Hospital . . . blood spilled over the American . . . trailing lights and water. . . . The Sailor went so wrong somewhere in that grey flesh. . . . He just sit down on zero. . . . I nodded on Niño Perdido his coffee over three hours late. . . . They all went away and sent papers. . . . The Dead Man write for you like a major. . . . Enter *vecinos*. . . . Freight boat smell of rectal mucus went down off England with all dawn smell of distant fingers. . . . About this time I went to your Consul. He gave me a Mexican after his death. . . . Five times of dust we made it . . . with soap bubbles of withdrawal crossed by a thousand junky nights. . . . Soon after the half maps came in by candlelight . . . OCCUPY. . . . Junk lines falling . . . Stay off . . . Bill Gains in the Yellow Sickness . . . Looking at dirty pictures casual as a ceiling fan short-timing the dawn we made it in the corn smell of rectal mucus and carbolic soap . . . familiar face maybe from the vacant lot . . . trailing tubes and wires. . . . "You fucking can't-wait hungry junkies! . . ." Burial in the American Cemetery. *"Quédase con su medicina. . . ."* On Niño Perdido the girl screaming. . . . They all went way through Casbah House. . . . "Couldn't you write me any better than that? Gone away. . . . You can look any place."

No good. *No Bueno.*

You wouldn't believe how hot things were when I left the States—I knew this one pusher wouldn't carry any shit on his person just shoot it in the line— Ten twenty grains over and above his own absorption according to the route he was servicing and piss it out in bottles for his customers so if the heat came up on them they cop out as degenerates—So Doc Benway assessed the situation and came up with this brain child—

"Once in the Upper Baboonasshole I was stung by a scorpion—the sensation is not dissimilar to a fix—Hummm."

So he imports this special breed of scorpions and feeds them on metal meal and the scorpions turned a phosphorescent blue color and sort of hummed. "Now we must find a worthy vessel," he said—So we flush out this old goofball artist and put the scorpion to him and he turned sort of blue and you could see he was fixed right to metal—These scorpions could travel on a radar beam and service the clients after Doc copped for the bread—It was a good thing while it lasted and the heat couldn't touch us—However all these scorpion junkies began to glow in the dark and if they didn't score on the hour metamorphosed into scorpions straight away—So there was a spot of bother and we had to move on disguised as young junkies on the way to Lexington—Bill and Johnny we sorted out the names but they keep changing like one day I would wake up as Bill the next day as Johnny—So there we are in the train compartment shivering junk sick our eyes watering and burning.

CASE OF THE CELLULOID KALI

The name is Clem Snide—I am a Private Ass Hole—I will take on any job any identity any body—I will do anything difficult dangerous or downright dirty for a price.

The man opposite me didn't look like much—A thin grey man in a long coat that flickered like old film—He just happens to be the biggest operator in any time universe—

"I don't care myself you understand"—He watched the ash spiraling down from the end of his Havana—It hit the floor in a puff of grey dust—

"Just like that—Just time—Just time—Don't care myself if the whole fucking shithouse goes up in chunks—I've sat out novas before—I was born in a nova."

"Well Mr. Martin, I guess that's what birth is you might say."

"I wouldn't say—Have to be moving along any case—The ticket that exploded posed little time—Point is they are trying to cross me up—small timers—still on the old evacuation plan—Know what the old evacuation plan is, Mr. Snide?"

"Not in detail."

"The hanging gimmick—death in orgasm—gills—No bones and elementary nervous system—evacuation to the Drenched Lands—a bad deal on the level and it's not on the level with Sammy sitting in—small timers trying to cross me up—Me, Bradly-Martin, who invented the double-cross—Step right up—Now you see me now you don't—A few scores to settle before I travel— a few things to tidy up and that's where you come in—I want you to contact the Venus Mob, the Vegetable People and spill the whole fucking compost heap through Times Square and Piccadilly—I'm not taking any rap for that green bitch—I'm going to rat on everybody and split this dead whistle stop planet wide open—I'm clean for once with the nova heat—like clean fall out—"

He faded in spiraling patterns of cigar smoke—There was a knock at the door—Registered letter from Antwerp—Ten thousand dollar check for film rights to a novel I hadn't written called *The Soft Ticket*—Letter from somebody I never heard of who is acting as my agent suggests I contact the Copenhagen office to discuss the Danish rights on my novel *Expense Account*— bar backed by pink shell—New Orleans jazz thin in the Northern night.

A boy slid off a white silk bar stool and held out the hand: "Hello, I'm Johnny Yen, a friend of—well, just about everybody. I was more physical before my accident you can see from this interesting picture. Only the head was reduced to this jelly but like I say it the impression on my face was taken by the other man's eyes drive the car head-on it was and the Big Physician (he's very technical) rushed him off to a surgery and took out his eyes and made a quick impression and slapped it on me like a pancake before I started to dry out and curl around the edges. So now I'm back in harness you might say: and I have all of 'you' that what I want from my audience is the last drop then bring me another. The place is hermetic. We think so blockade we thought nobody could get thru our flak thing. They thought. Switch Artist me. Oh, there goes my frequency. I'm on now . . ."

The lights dimmed and Johnny pranced out in goggles flickering Northern Lights wearing a jockstrap of undifferentiated tissue that must be in constant movement to avoid crystallization. A penis rose out of the jock and dissolved in pink light back to a clitoris, balls retract into cunt with a fluid plop. Three times he did this to wild *"Olés!"* from the audience. Drifted to the bar and ordered a heavy blue drink. D noted patches of white crystal formed along the scar lines on Johnny's copy face.

"Just like canals. Maybe I'm a Martian when the Crystals are down."

You will die there a screwdriver through the head. The thought like looking at me over steak and explain it all like that stay right here. She was also a Reichian analyst. Disappear more or less remain in acceptable form to you the face.

"We could go on cutting my cleavage act, but *genug basta assez* dice fall *hombre* long switch street . . . I had this terrible accident in a car a Bentley it was I think they're so nice that's what you pay for when you buy one it's yours and you can be sure nobody will pull it out from under our assets. Of course we don't have assholes here you understand somebody might go and get physical. So we are strictly from urine. And that narrows things to a fine line down the middle fifty feefty and what could be fairer than that my Uncle Eyetooth always says he committed fornication but I don't believe it me, old heavy water junky like him. . . . So anyhoo to get back to my accident in my Bentley once I get my thing in a Bentley it's mine already.

"So we had this terrible accident or rather he did. Oh dear what am I saying? It wasn't my first accident you understand yearly wounded or was it monthly Oh dear I must stay on that middle line . . .

"Survivor. Survivor. Not the first in my childhood. Three thousand years in show business and always keep my nose clean. Why I was a dancing boy for the Cannibal Trog Women in the Ice Age. Remember? All that meat stacked up in the caves and the Blue Queen covered with limestone flesh creeps into your bones like cold grey honey . . . that's the way they keep them not dead but paralyzed with this awful stuff they cook down from vampire bats get in your hair Gertie always keep your hair way up inside with a vampire on premises bad to get in other alien premises. The Spanish have this word for it, something about props *ajeno* or something like that I know so am *ya la yo* mixa everything allup. They call me Puto the Cement Mixer, now isn't that cute? Some people think I'm just silly but I'm not silly at all . . . and this boyfriend told me I looked just like a shrew ears quivering hot and eager like burning leaves and those were his last words engraved on my back tape—along with a lot of other old memories that disgust me, you wouldn't believe the horrible routines I been involved through my profession of Survival Artist . . . and they think that's funny, but I don't laugh except real quick between words no time you understand laughing they could get at me doesn't keep them off like talking does, now watch—"

A flicker pause and the light shrank and the audience sound a vast muttering in Johnny's voice.

"You see"—Shadows moved back into nightclub seats and drank nightclub drinks and talked nightclub talk—"They'd just best is all. So I was this dancing boy for these dangerous old cunts paralyzed men and boys they dug special stacked right up to the ceiling like the pictures I saw of Belsen or one of those awful contracted places and I said they are at it again . . . I said the Old Army Game. I said 'Pass the buck.' Now you see it, now you don't. . . . Paralyzed with this awful gook the Sapphire Goddess let out through this cold sore she always kept open on her lips, that is a hole in the limestone you understand she was like entirely covered with one of those stag mites. . . . Real concentrated in there and irradiated to prevent an accident owing to some virus come lately wander in from Podunk Hepatitis. . . . But I guess I'm talking too much about private things. . . . But I know this big atomic professor, he's very technical too, says: 'There are no secrets any more, Pet,' when I was smooching around him for a quickie. My Uncle still gives me a sawski for a hot nuclear secret and ten years isn't hay, dahling, in these times when practically anybody is subject to wander in from the desert with a quit claim deed and snatch a girl's snatch right out from under her assets . . . over really I should say but some of we boys are so sick we got this awful cunt instead of a decent human asshole disgust you to see it. . . . So I just say anything I hear on the old party line.

"I used to keep those old Cave Cunts at bay with my Impersonation Number where I play this American Mate Dance in Black Widow drag and I could make my face flap around you wouldn't believe it and the noises I made in uh orgasm when SHE ate me—I played both parts you unnerstand, imitated the Goddess Herself and turn right into stone for security. . . . And SHE couldn't give me enough juice running out of this hole was her only orifice and she was transported dais and all, die ass and all, by blind uniques with no balls, had to crawl under HER dais dressed in Centipede Suit of the Bearer which was put on them as a great honor and they was always fighting over matters of crawl protocol or protocrawl. . .

"So all these boys stacked to the ceiling covered with limestone . . . you understand they weren't dead anymore than a fresh oyster is dead, but died in the moment when the shell was cracked and they were eaten all quivering sweet and tasty. Vitamins the right way . . . eaten with little jeweled adzes jade and sapphires and chicken blood rubies all really magnificent. Of course I pinched everything I could latch onto with my prehensile piles I learned it boosting in Chi to pay the Luxury Tax on C. Three thousand years in show business. . . . Later or was it earlier, the Mayan Calendar is all loused up you know. . . . I was a star Corn God inna Sacred Hanging Ceremony to fructify the Corn devised by this impresario who specializes in these far out bit parts which fit me like a condom, he says the cutest things. He's a doctor too. A big physician made my face over after 'the accident' collided with my Bentley head on . . . the cops say they never see anything so intense and it is a special pass I must be carrying I wasn't completely obliterated.

"Oh there's my doctor made the face over after my accident. He calls me Pygmalion now, isn't that cute? You'll love him."

The doctor was sitting in a surgical chair of gleaming nickel. His soft boneless head was covered with grey green fuzz, the right side of his face an inch lower than the left side swollen smooth as a boil around a dead, cold undersea eye.

"Doctor, I want you to meet my friend Mister D the Agent, and he's a lovely fellow too."

("Some time he don't hardly hear what you saying. He's very technical.")

The doctor reached out his abbreviated fibrous fingers in which surgical instruments caught neon and cut Johnny's face into fragments of light.

"Jelly," the doctor said, liquid gurgles through his hardened purple gums. His tongue was split and the two sections curled over each other as he talked: "Life jelly. It sticks and grows on you like Johnny."

Little papules of tissue were embedded in the doctor's hands. The doctor pulled a scalpel out of Johnny's ear and trimmed the papules into an ash tray where they stirred slowly exuding a green juice.

"They say his prick didn't synchronize at all so he cut it off and made some kinda awful cunt between the two sides of him. He got a whole ward full of his 'fans' he call them already. When the wind is right you can hear them scream in Town Hall Square. And everybody says 'But this is interesting.'

"I was more *physical* before my *accident*, you can see from this interesting picture."

Lee looked from the picture to the face, saw the flickering phosphorescent scars—

"Yes," he said, "I know you—You're dead *nada* walking around visible."

So the boy is rebuilt and gives me the eye and there he is again walking around some day later across the street and "No dice" flickered across his face— The copy there is a different being, something ready to slip in—boys empty and banal as sunlight her way always—So he is exact replica is he not?—empty space of the original—

So I tailed the double to London on the Hook Von Holland and caught him out strangling a naked faggot in the bed sitter—I slip on the antibiotic hand cuffs and we adjourn to the Mandrake Club for an informative little chat—

"What do you get out of this?" I ask bluntly.

"A smell I always feel when their eyes pop out"—The boy looked at me his mouth a little open showing the whitest teeth this Private Eye ever saw—naval uniform buttoned in the wrong holes quilted with sea mist and powder smoke, smell of chlorine, rum and moldy jockstraps—and probably a narcotics agent is hiding in the spare stateroom that is always locked—There are the stairs to the attic room he looked out of and his mother moving around—dead she was they say—dead—with such hair too—red.

"Where do you feel it?" I prodded.

"All over," he said, eyes empty and banal as sunlight—"Like hair sprouting all over me"—He squirmed and giggled and creamed in his dry goods—

"And after every job I get to see the movies—You know—" And he gave me the sign twisting his head to the left and up—

So I gave him the sign back and the words jumped in my throat all there like and ready the way they always do when I'm right. "You make the pilgrimage?"

"Yes—The road to Rome."

I withdrew the antibiotics and left him there with that dreamy little-boy look twisting the napkin into a hangman's knot—On the bus from the air terminal a thin grey man sat down beside me—I offered him a cigarette and he said "Have one of mine," and I see he is throwing the tin on me—"Nova police—You are Mr. Snide I believe." And he moved right in and shook me down looking at pictures, reading letters checking back on my time track.

"There's one of them," I heard some one say as he looked at a photo in my files.

"Hummm—yes—and here's another—Thank you Mr. Snide—You have been most cooperative—"

I stopped off in Bologna to look up my old friend Green Tony thinking he could probably give me a line—up four flights in a tenement past the old bitch selling black-market cigarettes and cocaine cut with Saniflush, through a dirty brown curtain and there is Green Tony in a pad with Chinese jade all over and

Etruscan cuspidors—He is sitting back with his leg thrown over an Egyptian throne smoking a cigarette in a carved emerald holder—He doesn't get up but he says: "Dick Tracy in the flesh," and motions to a Babylonian couch.

I told him what I was after and his face went a bright green with rage. "That stupid bitch—She bringa the heat on all of us—Nova heat—" He blew a cloud of smoke and it hung there solid in front of him—Then he wrote an address in the smoke—"No. 88 Via di Nile, Roma."

This 88 Nile turned out to be one of those bar-soda fountains like they have in Rome—You are subject to find a maraschino cherry in your dry martini and right next to some citizen is sucking a banana split disgust you to see it—Well I am sitting there trying not to see it so I look down at the far end of the counter and dug a boy very dark with kinky hair and I give him the sign—And he gives it right back— So I spit the maraschino cherry in the bartender's face and slip him a big tip and he says "*Rivideci* and bigger."

And I say "Up yours with a double strawberry phosphate."

The boy finishes his Pink Lady and follows me out and I take him back to my trap and right away get into an argument with the clerk about no visitors *stranezza* to the hotel—Enough garlic on his breath to deter a covey of vampires—I shove a handful of *lire* into his mouth "Go buy yourself some more gold teeth," I told him—

When this boy peeled off the dry goods he gives off a slow stink like a thawing mummy—But his asshole sucked me right in, all my experience as a Private Eye never felt anything like it—In the flash bulb of orgasm I see that fucking clerk has stuck his head through the transom for a refill—Well expense account—The boy is lying there on the bed spreading out like a jelly slow tremors running through it and sighs and says: "Almost like the real thing isn't it?"

And I said "I need the time milking," and give him the sign so heavy come near slipping a disk.

"I can see you're one of our own," he said warmly sucking himself back into shape—"Dinner at eight"—He comes back at eight in a souped up Ragazzi and we take off 160 per and scream to stop in front of a villa I can see the Bentleys and Hispano Bear Cats and Stutz Suisses and what not piled up and all the golden youth of Europe is disembarking—"Leave your clothes in the vestibule," the butler tells us and we walk in on a room full of people all naked to a turn sitting around on silk stools and a bar with a pink shell behind it—This cunt undulates forward and give me the sign and holds out her hand "I am the Contessa di Vile your hostess for tonight"—She points to the boys at the bar with her cigarette holder and their cocks jumped up one after the other—And I did the polite thing too when my turn came—

So all the boys began chanting in unison "*The movies!—The movies!—*We want *the movies!—*" So she led the way into the projection room which was filled with pink light seeping through the walls and floor and ceiling—The boy was explaining to me that these were actual films taken during the Abyssinian War and how lucky I was to be there—Then the action starts—There on the screen is a gallows and some young soldiers standing around with prisoners in loincloths—The soldiers are dragging this kid up onto the gallows and he is biting and screaming and shitting himself and his loincloth slips off and they shove him under the noose and one of them tightens it around his neck standing there now mother naked—Then the trap fell and he drops kicking and yelping and you could hear his neck snap like a stick in a wet towel—He hangs there pulling his knees up to the chest and pumping out spurts of jissom and the audience coming right with him spurt for spurt—So the soldiers strip the loincloths off the others and they all got hard-ons waiting and watching—Got through a hundred of them more or less one at a time—Then they run the movie in slow motion slower and slower and you are coming slower and slower until it took an hour and then two hours and finally all the boys are standing there like statues getting their rocks off geologic—Meanwhile an angle comes dripping down and forms a stalactite in my brain and I slip back to the projection room and speed up the movie so the hanged boys are coming like machine guns—Half the guests explode straightaway from altered pressure chunks of limestone whistling through the air. The others are flopping around on the floor like beached idiots and the Contessa gasps out "Carbon dioxide for the love of Kali"—So somebody turned on the carbon dioxide tanks and I made it out of there in an aqualung—Next thing the nova heat moves in and bust the whole aquarium.

"Humm, yes, and there's another planet—"

The officer moved back dissolving most cooperative connections formed by the parasite—Self-righteous millions stabbed with rage.

"That bitch—She brings the heat three dimensional."

"The ugly cloud of smoke hung there solid female blighted continent—This turned out to be one of those association locks in Rome—I look down at the end—He quiets you, remember?—Finis. So I spit the planet from all the pictures and give him a place of residence with inflexible authority—Well, no terms—A hand has been taken—Your name fading looks like—Madison Avenue machine disconnected."

THE MAYAN CAPER

Joe Brundige brings you the shocking story of the Mayan Caper exclusive to *The Evening News*—

A Russian scientist has said: "We will travel not only in space but in time as well"—I have just returned from a thousand-year time trip and I am here to tell you what I saw—And to tell you how such time trips are made—It is a precise operation—It is difficult—It is dangerous—It is the new frontier and only the adventurous need apply—But it belongs to *anyone* who has the courage and know-how to enter—It belongs to *you*—

I started my trip in the morgue with old newspapers, folding in today with yesterday and typing out composites—When you skip through a newspaper as most of us do you see a great deal more than you know—In fact you see it all on a subliminal level—Now when I fold today's paper in with yesterday's paper and arrange the pictures to form a time section montage, I am literally moving back to the time when I read yesterday's paper, that is traveling in time back to yesterday—I did this eight hours a day for three months—I went back as far as the papers went—I dug out old magazines and forgotten novels and letters—I made fold-ins and composites and I did the same with photos—

The next step was carried out in a film studio—I learned to talk and think backward on all levels—This was done by running film and sound track backward—For example a picture of myself eating a full meal was reversed, from satiety back to hunger—First the film was run at normal speed, then in slow-motion—The same procedure was extended to other physiological processes including orgasm—(It was explained to me that I must put aside all sexual prudery and reticence, that sex was perhaps the heaviest anchor holding one in present time.) For three months I worked with the studio—My basic training in time travel was completed and I was now ready to train specifically for the Mayan assignment—

I went to Mexico City and studied the Mayans with a team of archaeologists—The Mayans lived in what is now Yucatán, British Honduras, and Guatemala—I will not recapitulate what is known of their history, but some observations on the Mayan calendar are essential to understanding this report—

The Mayan calendar starts from a mythical date 5 Ahua 8 Cumhu and rolls on to the end of the world, also a definite date depicted on the codices as a God pouring water on the earth—The Mayans had a solar, a lunar, and a ceremonial calendar rolling along like interlocking wheels from 5 Ahua 8 Cumhu to the end—The absolute power of the priests, who formed about two percent of the population, depended on their control of this calendar—The extent of this number monopoly can be deduced from the fact that the Mayan verbal language contains no number above ten—Modern Mayan-speaking Indians use Spanish numerals—Mayan agriculture was of the slash and burn type—They had no plows. Plows can not be used in the Mayan area because there is a stratum of limestone six inches beneath the surface and the slash and burn method is used to this day—Now slash and burn agriculture is a matter of precise timing—The brush must be cut at a certain time so it will have time to dry and the burning operation carried out before the rains start—A few days' miscalculation and the year's crop is lost—

The Mayan writings have not been fully deciphered, but we know that most of the hieroglyphs refer to dates in the calendar, and these numerals have been translated—It is probable that the other undeciphered symbols refer to the ceremonial calendar—There are only three Mayan codices in existence, one in Dresden, one in Paris, one in Madrid, the others having been burned by Bishop Landa—Mayan is very much a living language and in the more remote villages nothing else is spoken—

More routine work—I studied Mayan and listened to it on the tape recorder and mixed Mayan in with English—I made innumerable photomontages of Mayan codices and artifacts—the next step was to find a "vessel"—We sifted through many candidates before settling on a young Mayan worker recently arrived from Yucatán—This boy was about twenty, almost black, with the sloping forehead and curved nose of the ancient Mayans—(The physical type has undergone little alteration)—He was illiterate—He had a history of epilepsy— He was what mediums call a "sensitive"—For another three months I worked with the boy on the tape recorder mixing his speech with mine—(I was quite fluent in Mayan at this point—Unlike Aztec it is an easy language.)

It was time now for "the transfer operation"—"I" was to be moved into the body of this young Mayan—The operation is illegal and few are competent to practice it—I was referred to an American doctor who had become a heavy metal addict and lost his certificate—"He is the best transfer artist in the industry" I was told "For a price."

We found the doctor in a dingy office on the Avenida Cinco de Mayo—He was a thin grey man who flickered in and out of focus like an old film—I told him what I wanted and he looked at me from a remote distance without warmth or hostility or any emotion I had ever experienced in myself or seen in another—He nodded silently and ordered the Mayan boy to strip, and ran practiced fingers over his naked body—The doctor picked up a box-like instrument with electrical attachments and moved it slowly up and down the boy's back from the base of the spine to the neck—The instrument clicked like a Geiger counter—The doctor sat down and explained to me that the operation was usually performed with "the hanging technique"—The patient's neck is broken and during the orgasm that results he passes into the other body—This method, however, was obsolete and dangerous—For the operation to succeed you must work with a pure vessel who has not been subject to parasite invasion—Such subjects are almost impossible to find in present time he stated flatly—His cold grey eyes flicked across the young Mayan's naked body:

"This subject is riddled with parasites—If I were to employ the barbarous method used by some of my learned colleagues—(nameless assholes)—you would be eaten body and soul by crab parasites—My technique is quite different—I operate with molds—Your body will remain here intact in deepfreeze—On your return, if you do return, you can have it back." He looked pointedly at my stomach sagging from sedentary city life—"You could do with a stomach tuck, young man—But one thing at a time—The transfer operation will take some weeks—And I warn you it will be expensive."

I told him that cost was no object—The *News* was behind me all the way— He nodded briefly: "Come back at this time tomorrow."

When we returned to the doctor's office he introduced me to a thin young man who had the doctor's cool removed grey eyes—"This is my photographer—I will make my molds from his negatives." The photographer told me his name was Jiménez—("Just call me 'Jimmy the Take'")—We followed the "Take" to a studio in the same building, equipped with a 35 millimeter movie camera and Mayan backdrops—He posed us naked in erection and orgasm, cutting the images in together down the middle line of our bodies—Three times a week we went to the doctor's office—He looked through rolls of film his eyes intense, cold, impersonal—And ran the clicking box up and down our spines—Then he injected a drug which he described as a variation of the apomorphine formula—The injection caused simultaneous vomiting and ejaculating in the Mayan vessel—The doctor told me these exercises were only the preliminaries and that the actual operation, despite all precautions and skills, was still dangerous enough.

At the end of three weeks he indicated the time had come to operate—He arranged us side by side naked on the operating table under floodlights—With a phosphorescent pencil he traced the middle line of our bodies from the cleft under the nose down to the rectum—Then he injected a blue fluid of heavy cold silence as word dust fell from demagnetized patterns—From a remote Polar distance I could see the doctor separate the two halves of our bodies and fit together a composite being—I came back in other flesh the lookout different, thoughts and memories of the young Mayan drifting through my brain—

The doctor gave me a bottle of the vomiting drug which he explained was efficacious in blocking out any control waves—He also gave me another drug which, if injected in to a subject, would enable me to occupy his body for a few hours and only at night. "Don't let the sun come up on you or it's curtains—zero eaten by crab—And now there is the matter of my fee."

I handed him a briefcase of bank notes and he faded into the shadows furtive and seedy as an old junky.

The paper and the embassy had warned me that I would be on my own, a thousand years from any help—I had a vibrating camera gun sewed into my fly, a small tape recorder and a transistor radio concealed in a clay pot—I took a plane to Mérida where I set about contacting a "broker" who could put me in touch with a "time guide"—Most of these so-called brokers are old drunken frauds and my first contact was no exception—I had been warned to pay nothing until I was satisfied with the arrangements—I found this "broker" in a filthy hut on the outskirts surrounded by a rubbish heap of scrap iron, old bones, broken pottery and worked flints—I produced a bottle of *aguardiente* and the broker immediately threw down a plastic cup of the raw spirit and sat there swaying back and forth on a stool while I explained my business—He indicated that what I wanted was extremely difficult—Also dangerous and illegal—He could get into trouble—Besides I might be an informer from the Time Police—He would have to think about it—He drank two more cups of spirit and fell on the floor in a stupor—The following day I called again—He had thought it over and perhaps—In any case he would need a week to prepare his medicines and this he could only do if he were properly supplied with *aguardiente*—And he poured another glass of spirits slopping full—Extremely dissatisfied with the way things were going I left—As I was walking back toward town a boy fell in beside me.

"Hello, Meester, you look for broker yes?—Muy no good one—Him," he gestured back toward the hut. "No good *borracho* son bitch bastard—Take *mucho dinero*—No do nothing—You come with me, Meester."

Thinking I could not do worse, I accompanied the boy to another hut built on stilts over a pond—A youngish man greeted us and listened silently while I explained what I wanted—The boy squatted on the floor rolling a marijuana cigarette—He passed it around and we all smoked—The broker said yes he could make the arrangements and named a price considerably lower than what I had been told to expect—how soon?—He looked at a shelf where I could see a number of elaborate hourglasses with sand in different colors: red, green, black, blue, and white—The glasses were marked with symbols—He explained to me that the sand represented color time and color words—He pointed to a symbol on the green glass. "Then—One hour—"

He took out some dried mushrooms and herbs and began cooking them in a clay pot—As green sand touched the symbol, he filled little clay cups and handed one to me and one to the boy—I drank the bitter medicine and almost immediately the pictures I had seen of Mayan artifacts and codices began moving in my brain like animated cartoons—A spermy, compost heap smell filled the room—The boy began to twitch and mutter and fell to the floor in a fit—I could see that he had an erection under his thin trousers—The broker opened the boy's shirt and pulled off his pants—The penis flipped out spurting in orgasm after orgasm—A green light filled the room and burned through the boy's flesh—Suddenly he sat up talking in Mayan—The words curled out of his mouth and hung visible in the air like vine tendrils—I felt a strange vertigo which I recognized as the motion sickness of time travel—The broker smiled and held out a hand—I passed over his fee—The boy was putting on his clothes—He beckoned me to follow and I got up and left the hut—

We were walking along—a jungle hut the boy ahead his whole body alert and twitching like a dog—We walked many hours and it was dawn when we came to a clearing where I could see a number of workers with sharp sticks and gourds of seed planting corn—The boy touched my shoulder and disappeared up the path in jungle dawn mist—

As I stepped forward into the clearing and addressed one of the workers, I felt the crushing weight of evil insect control forcing my thoughts and feelings into prearranged molds, squeezing my spirit in a soft invisible vise—The worker looked at me with dead eyes empty of curiosity or welcome and silently handed me a planting stick—It was not unusual for strangers to wander in out of the jungle since the whole area was ravaged by soil exhaustion—So my presence occasioned no comment—I worked until sundown—I was assigned to a hut by an overseer who carried a carved stick and wore an elaborate headdress indicating his rank—I lay down in the hammock and immediately felt stabbing probes of telepathic interrogation—I turned on the thoughts of a half-witted young Indian—After some hours the invisible presence withdrew—I had passed the first test—

During the months that followed I worked in the fields—The monotony of this existence made my disguise as a mental defective quite easy—I learned that one could be transferred from field work to rock carving the stelae after a long apprenticeship and only after the priests were satisfied that any thought of resistance was forever extinguished—I decided to retain the anonymous status of a field worker and keep as far as possible out of notice—

A continuous round of festivals occupied our evenings and holidays—On these occasions the priests appeared in elaborate costumes, often disguised as centipedes or lobsters—Sacrifices were rare, but I witnessed one revolting ceremony in which a young captive was tied to a stake and the priests tore his sex off with white-hot copper claws—I learned also something of the horrible punishments meted out to anyone who dared challenge or even think of challenging the controllers: *Death in the Ovens:* The violator was placed in a construction of interlocking copper grills—The grills were then heated to white heat and slowly closed on his body. *Death in Centipede:* The "criminal" was strapped to a couch and eaten alive by giant centipedes—These executions were carried out secretly in rooms under the temple.

I made recordings of the festivals and the continuous music like a shrill insect frequency that followed the workers all day in the fields—However, I knew that to play these recordings would invite immediate detection—I needed not only the sound track of control but the image track as well before I could take definitive action—I have explained that the Mayan control system depends on the calendar and the codices which contain symbols representing all states of thought and feeling possible to human animals living under such limited circumstances—These are the instruments with which they rotate and control units of thought—I found out also that the priests themselves do not understand exactly how the system works and that I undoubtedly knew more about it than they did as a result of my intensive training and studies—The technicians who had devised the control system had died out and the present line of priests were in the position of someone who knows what buttons to push in order to set a machine in motion, but would have no idea how to fix that machine if it broke down, or to construct another if the machine were destroyed—If I could gain access to the codices and mix the sound and image track the priests would go on pressing the old buttons with unexpected results—In order to accomplish the purpose I prostituted myself to one of the priests—(Most distasteful thing I ever stood still for)—During the sex act he metamorphosized himself into a green crab from the waist up, retaining human legs and genitals that secreted a caustic erogenous slime, while a horrible stench filled the hut—I was able to endure these horrible encounters by promising myself the pleasure of killing this disgusting monster when the time came—And my reputation as an idiot was by now so well established that I escaped all but the most routine control measures—

The priest had me transferred to janitor work in the temple where I witnessed some executions and saw the prisoners torn body and soul into writhing insect fragments by the ovens, and learned that the giant centipedes were born in the ovens from these mutilated screaming fragments—It was time to act—

Using the drug the doctor had given me, I took over the priest's body, gained access to the room where the codices were kept, and photographed the books—Equipped now with sound and image track of the control machine I was in position to dismantle it—I had only to mix the order of recordings and the order of images and the changed order would be picked up and fed back into the machine—I had recordings of all agricultural operations, cutting and burning brush etc.—I now correlated the recordings of burning brush with the image track of this operation, and shuffled the time so that the order to burn came late and a year's crop was lost—Famine weakening control lines, I cut radio static into the control music and festival recordings together with sound and image track rebellion.

"Cut word lines—Cut music lines—Smash the control images—Smash the control machine—Burn the books—Kill the priests—Kill! Kill! Kill!—"

Inexorably as the machine had controlled thought feeling and sensory impressions of the workers, the machine now gave the order to dismantle itself and kill the priests—I had the satisfaction of seeing the overseer pegged out in the field, his intestines perforated with hot planting sticks and crammed with corn—I broke out my camera gun and rushed the temple—This weapon takes and vibrates image to radio static—You see the priests *were* nothing but word and image, an old film rolling on and on with dead actors—Priests and temple guards went up in silver smoke as I blasted my way into the control room and burned the codices—Earthquake tremors under my feet I got out of there fast, blocks of limestone raining all around me—A great weight fell from the sky, winds of the earth whipping palm trees to the ground—Tidal waves rolled over the Mayan control calendar.

WHERE YOU BELONG

My trouble began when they decide I am executive timber—It starts like this: a big blond driller from Dallas picks me out of the labor pool to be his houseboy in a prefabricated air-conditioned bungalow—He comes on rugged but as soon as we strip down to the ball park over on his stomach kicking white wash and screams out "Fuck the shit out of me!"—I give him a slow pimp screwing and in solid—When this friend comes down from New York the driller says "This is the boy I was telling you about"—And Friend looks me over slow chewing his cigar and says: "What are you doing over there with the apes? Why don't you come over here with the Board where you belong?" And he slips me a long slimy look. Friend works for the Trak News Agency—"We don't report the news—We write it." And next thing I know they have trapped a grey flannel suit on me and I am sent to this school in Washington to learn how this writing the news before it happens is done—I sus it is the Mayan Caper with an IBM machine and I don't want to be caught short in a grey flannel suit when the lid blows off—So I act in concert with the Subliminal Kid who is a technical sergeant and has a special way of talking. And he stands there a long time chewing tobacco is our middle name "—What are you doing over there?— Beat your mother to over here—Know what they mean if they start job for instance?—Open shirt, apparent sensory impressions calling slimy terms of the old fifty-fifty jazz—Kiss their target all over—Assembly points in Danny Deever—By now they are controlling shithouse of the world—Just feed in sad-eyed youths and the machine will process it—After that Minraud sky—Their eggs all over—These officers come gibbering into the queer bar don't even know what buttons to push—('Run with the apes? Why don't you come across the lawn?') And he gives me a long slimy responsible *cum* grey flannel suit and I am Danny Deever in drag writing 'the news is served, sir.' Hooded dead gibber: 'this is the Mayan Caper'—A fat cigar and a long white nightie— Nonpayment answer is simple as Board Room Reports rigged a thousand years—Set up excuse and the machine will process it—Moldy pawn ticket runs a thousand years chewing the same argument—I Sekuin perfected that art along the Tang Dynasty—To put it another way IBM machine controls thought feeling and *apparent* sensory impressions—Subliminal lark—These officers don't even know what buttons to push—Whatever you feed into the machine on subliminal level the machine will process—So we feed in 'dismantle thy-self' and authority emaciated down to answer Mr of the Account in Ewyork, Onolulu, Aris, Ome, Oston—Might be just what I am look"—

We fold writers of all time in together and record radio programs, movie sound tracks, TV and juke box songs all the words of the world stirring around in a cement mixer and pour in the resistance message "Calling partisans of all nations—Cut word lines—Shift linguals—Free doorways—Vibrate 'tourists'— Word falling—Photo falling—Break through in Grey Room."

So the District Supervisor calls me in and puts the old white schmaltz down on me:

"Now kid what are you doing over there with the niggers and the apes? Why don't you straighten out and act like a white man?—After all they're only human cattle—You know that yourself—Hate to see a bright young man fuck up and get off on the wrong track—Sure it happens to all of us one time or another—Why the man who went on to invent Shitola was sitting right where you're sitting now twenty-five years ago and I was saying the same things to him—Well he straightened out the way you're going to straighten out—Yes sir that Shitola combined with an ape diet—All we have to do is press the button and a hundred million more or less gooks flush down the drain in green can-cer piss—That's *big* isn't it?—And any man with white blood in him wants to be part of something big—You can't deny your blood kid—You're *white white white*—And you can't walk out on Trak—There's just no place to go."

Most distasteful thing I ever stood still for—Enough to make a girl crack her calories—So I walk out and the lid blew off—

URANIAN WILLY

Uranian Willy the Heavy Metal Kid, also known as Willy the Rat—He wised up the marks.

"This is war to extermination—Fight cell by cell through bodies and mind screens of the earth—Souls rotten from the Orgasm Drug—Flesh shuddering from the Ovens—Prisoners of the earth, come out—Storm the studio."

His plan called for total exposure—Wise up all the marks everywhere—Show them the rigged wheel—Storm the Reality Studio and retake the universe—The plan shifted and reformed as reports came in from his electric patrols sniffing quivering down streets of the earth—the reality film giving and buckling like a bulkhead under pressure—burned metal smell of interplanetary war in the raw noon streets swept by screaming glass blizzards of enemy flak.

"Photo falling—Word falling—Use partisans of all nations—Target Orgasm Ray Installations—Gothenburg Sweden—Coordinates 8 2 7 6—Take Studio—Take Board Books—Take Death Dwarfs—Towers, open fire."

Pilot K9 caught the syndicate killer image on a penny arcade screen and held it in his sight—Now he was behind it in it was it—The image disintegrated in photo flash of total recognition—Other image on screen—Hold in sight—Smell of burning metal in his head—"Pilot K9, you are cut off—Back—Back—Back before the whole fucking shithouse goes up—Return to base immediately—Ride music beam back to base—Stay out of that time flak—All pilots ride Pan Pipes back to base."

It was impossible to estimate the damage—Board Books destroyed—Enemy personnel decimated— The message of total resistance on short wave of the world.

"Calling partisans of all nations—Shift linguals—Cut word lines—Vibrate tourists—Free doorways—Photo falling—Word falling—Break through in Grey Room."

from
the ticket that exploded

posed little time
so I'll say
"good night"

"SEE THE ACTION, B. J.?"

It is a long trip. We are the only riders. So that is how we have come to know each other so well that the sound of his voice and his image flickering over the tape recorder are as familiar to me as the movement of my intestines the sound of my breathing the beating of my heart. Not that we love or even like each other. In fact murder is never out of my eyes when I look at him. And murder is never out of his eyes when he looks at me. Murder under a carbide lamp in Puyo rain outside it's a mighty wet place drinking *aguardiente* with tea and *canela* to cut that kerosene taste he called me a drunken son of a bitch and there it was across the table raw and bloody as a fresh used knife . . . sitting torpid and quiescent in a canvas chair after reading last month's Sunday comics "the jokes" he called them and read every word it sometimes took him a full hour by a tidal river in Mexico slow murder in his eyes maybe ten fifteen years later I see the move he made then he was a good amateur chess player it took up most of his time actually but he had plenty of that. I offered to play him once he looked at me and smiled and said: "You wouldn't stand a chance with me."

His smile was the most unattractive thing about him or at least it was one of the unattractive things about him it split his face open and something quite alien like a predatory mollusk looked out different well I took his queen in the first few minutes of play by making completely random moves. He won the game without his queen. I had made my point and lost interest. Panama under the ceiling fans, on the cold winds of Chimborazo, across the rubble of Lima, steaming up from the mud streets of Esmeraldas that flat synthetic vulgar CIA voice of his . . . basically he was completely hard and self-seeking and thought entirely in terms of position and advantage an effective but severely limited intelligence. Thinking on any other level simply did not interest him. He was by the way very cruel but not addicted to the practice of cruelty. He was cruel if the opportunity presented itself. Then he smiled his eyes narrowed and his sharp little ferret teeth showed between his thin lips which were a blue purple color in a smooth yellow face. But then who am I to be critical few things in my own past I'd just as soon forget . . .

What I am getting at is we do not like each other we simply find ourselves on the same ship sharing the same cabin and often the same bed welded together by a million shared meals and belches by the movement of intestines and the sound of breathing (he snored abominably. I turn him on his side or stomach to shut him up. He wakes and smiles in the dark room muttering "Don't get ideas") by the beating of our hearts. In fact his voice has been spliced in twenty-four times per second with the sound of my breathing and the beating of my heart so that my body is convinced that my breathing and heart will stop if his voice stops.

"Well," he would say with his winsome smile, "it does give a certain position of advantage."

My attempts to murder him were usually in direct . . . knife . . . gun . . . in someone else's hand of course I had no intention of getting into social difficulties . . . car accident . . . drowning . . . once a shark surfaced in my mind as he plunged from a boat into the tidal river . . . I will go to his aid and clutch his torn dying body in my arms like a vise he will be too weak from loss of blood to fight me off and my face will be his last picture. He always planned that *his* face should be my last picture and his plan called for cinerama film sequences featuring the Garden of Delights shows all kinds masturbation and self-abuse young boys need it special it's all electric and very technical you sit down anywhere some sex wheel sidles up your ass or clamps onto your spine centers and the electronic gallows will just kill you on a conveyor belt the Director there bellowing orders:

"I want you to shit and piss all over yourself when you see the gallows. Synchronize your castor oil will you? And give the pitiless hang boy an imploring look for Chrisakes he's your ass hole buddy about to hang you and that's the *drama* of it . . ."

"It's a sick picture B.J."

Well it seems this rotten young prince gives off whiffs of decay when he moves but he doesn't move much as a rule has eyes for one of the prisoners wants him for his very own fish boy but the young generators are on the way. Partisans have seized a wing of the studio and called in the Red Guards. . . . "Now what do you boys *feel* about a situation like this? Well go on express yourselves. . . . This is a *progressive* school. . . . These youths of image and association now at entrance to the garden carrying banners of interlanguage. . . . Her fourth-grade class screamed in terror when I looked at the 'dogs' and I looked at the pavement decided the pavement was safer. . . . Attack enemy over instrument like pinball. . . . Shift tilt STOP the GOD film. Frame by frame take a good look boys . . ."

"They got this awful mollusk eats the hanged boy's body and soul in the orgasm and they love being eaten because of this liquefying gook it secretes and rubs all over them but maybe I'm talking too much about private things."

"You boys going to stand still for this? Being slobbered down and shit out
by an alien mollusk? Join the army and see the world. I remember this one
patrol had been liberating a river town and picked up the Sex Skin habit. This
Sex Skin is a critter found in the rivers here wraps all around you like a second
skin eats you slow and good. . . . Well these boys had the Sex Skin burned off
by the sun crossing the plain they could just crawl when they reached the post
quivering sores they was half eaten mostly shit and pieces of them falling off
so I called the Captain and he said best thing was bash their skulls in and bury
them in the privy where he hoped the smell might pass unnoticed but there
was a stink in Congress about 'unsung heroes' and the president himself nailed
a purple heart to that privy you can still see where the old privy used to be
other side of those thistles there . . .

"Now that should show you fellows something of the situation out here
and the problems we have to face . . . take the case of a young soldier who
tried to rescue his buddy from a Sex Skin and it grew onto him and now his
buddy turns from him in disgust . . . anyone would you understand and that's
not the worst of it it's knowing at any second your buddy may be took by the
alien virus it's happened cruel idiot smile over the corn flakes. . . . You gasp
and reach for a side arm looking after your own soul like a good Catholic . . .
too late . . . your nerve centers are paralyzed by the dreaded Bor-Bor he has
slipped into your Nescafé. . . . He's going to eat you slow and nasty. . . . This
situation here has given rise to what the head shrinkers call 'ideas of persecu-
tion' among our personnel and a marked slump in morale. . . . As I write this
I have barricaded myself in the ward room against the 2nd Lieutenant who
claims he is 'God's little hang boy sent special to me' that fucking shave tail I
can hear him out there whimpering and slobbering and the Colonel is jacking
off in front of the window pointing to a Gemini Sex Skin. The Captain's
corpse hangs naked at the flagpole. I am the only sane man left on the post.
I know now when it is too late what we are up against: a biologic weapon
that reduces healthy clean-minded men to abject slobbering inhuman things
undoubtedly of virus origins. I have decided to kill myself rather than fall
into their hands. I am sure the padre would approve if he knew how things
are out here. Don't know how much longer I can hold out. Oxygen reserves
almost exhausted. I am reading a science fiction book called *The Ticket That
Exploded*. The story is close enough to what is going on here so now and
again I make myself believe this ward room is just a scene in an old book far
away and long ago might as well be that for all the support I'm getting from
Base Headquarters."

"You see the action, B.J.? All these patrols cut off light-years behind
enemy lines trying to get through some fat-assed gum-chewing comic-reading
Technical Sergeant to Base Headquarters and there is no Base Headquarters
everything is coming apart like a rotten undervest . . . but the show goes on
. . . love . . . romance . . . stories that rip your heart out and eat it. . . . This
clean-living decent heavy metal kid and a cold glamorous agent from the Green

Galaxy has been sent out to destroy him with a Sex Skin but she falls for the kid and she can't do it and she can't go back to her own people because of the unspeakable tortures meted out to those who fail on a Mission so they take off together in a Gemini space capsule perhaps to wander forever in trackless space or perhaps?"

DO YOU LOVE ME?

The young monk led Bradly to a cubicle—On a stone table was a tape recorder—The monk switched on the recorder and sounds of lovemaking filled the room—The monk took off his robe and stood naked with an erection— He danced around the table caressing a shadowy figure out of the air above the recorder—A tentative shape flickering in and out of focus to the sound track—The figure floated free of the recorder and followed the monk to a pallet on the floor—He went through a pantomime of pleading with the phantom who sat on the bed with legs crossed and arms folded—Finally the phantom nodded reluctant consent and the monk twisted through a parody of love-making as the tape speeded up: "Oh darling i love you oh oh deeper oh oh fuck the shit out of me oh darling do it again"—Bradly rolled on the floor, a vibrating air hammer of laughter shaking flesh from the bones—Scalding urine spurted from his penis—The Other Half swirled in the air above him scream-ing, face contorted in suffocation as he laughed at the sex words from throat gristle in bloody crystal blobs—His bones were shaking, vibrated to neon— Waves of laughter through his rectum and prostate and testicles giggling out spurts of semen as he rolled with his knees up to his chin—

All the tunes and sound effects of *"Love"* spit from the recorder permutating sex whine of a sick picture planet: Do you love me?—But i exploded in cos-mic laughter—Old acquaintance be forgot?—Oh darling, just a photograph?— Mary i love you i do do you know i love you through?—On my knees i hoped you'd love me too—I would run till i feel the thrill of long ago—Now my inspiration but it won't last and we'll be just a photograph—i've forgotten you then? i can't sleep, Blue Eyes, if i don't have you—Do i love her? i love you i love you many splendored thing—Can't even eat—Jelly on my mind back home—'Twas good bye deep in the true love—We'll never meet again, dar-ling, in my fashion—Yes eyes ever shining that made me my way—Always it's a long trip to Tipperary—Tell Laura i love my blue heaven—Get up woman up off your big fat earth out into cosmic space with all your diamond rings— Do you do you do you love me?—Lovey lovey dovey brought to mind? What? Do you love me with a banjo?—Please don't be angry—i wonder who—If i had learned to love you every time i felt blue—But someone took you out of the stardust of the skies—Your charms travel to remind me of you—together again—forgotten you eat—Don't know how i'll make it baby—blue eyes the color of—Do you love me? Love is *para olvidar*—Tell Laura oh jelly love you— i can't—Got you under my skin on my mind—But i'll always be true to my

blue heaven—Love Mary?—Fuck the shit out of me—Get up off your big fat
rusty-dusty—It's a long way to go, St. Louis woman—prospect of red mesas
out to space—Do you love me?—Do you love void and scenic railways back
home?? And do you love me with a banjo permutated through do you love
me?—i wonder who permutated the structure every time i felt blue—But that
was ferris wheels clicking in the stardust of the sky—on perilous tracks—i had
a dog his name was Bill aworking clouds of *Me*—Tearing his insides apart—
Need a helping hand?—understanding out of date—Find someone else at this
time of day? Torch cutting through the eats?—

   Don't know how i'll make it, baby—Electric fingers removed *"Love"*—Do
you love me?—Love is red sheets of pain hung oh oh baby oh jelly—The guide
slipped off his jelly—I've got you under my skin pulsing red light—Clouds of
Me always be true to you—Hula hoops of color formed always be true to you
darling in my Bradly—Weak and torn i'll hurry to my blue heaven as i sank in
suffocation panic of rusty St. Louis woman—With just a photograph, Mary,
you know i love you through sperm—Contraction turnstile hoped you'd love
me too—Orgasm floated arms still i feel the thrill of slow movement but it
won't last—i've forgotten you then?—i love you i love you and bones tearing
his insides apart for the ants to eat—Jelly jelly jelly shifting color orgasm back
home—Scratching shower of sperm that made cover of the board books—It's
a long way to Tipperary—soft luminous spurts to my blue heaven—Pieces of
cloud drifted through all the tunes from blue—Exploded in cosmic laughter
of cable cars . . . Me?—Oh, darling, i love you in constant motion—i love you
i do—You led Bradly into a cubicle on my knees—love floating in a slow vertigo of you—perilous tracks where wind whistled long ago—i can't sleep, baby,
skin pulling loose if i don't have you—a peg like many splendored thing—i've
got you deep in the guides body enclosed darling in *my* fashion—yes cool hands
on his naked flesh my way—evening intestines of the other—Tell Laura i love
her sucked through pearly genital woman off your big fat shower of sperm—
Diamond rings spurt out of you—Should be brought to mind—Ejaculated
bodies without a cover—

   I learned to love you, pale adolescents—Someone took you out of the creature charms—We'll travel weak and torn by pain together—Silver films in the
blood *para olvidar*—Tell Laura black fish movement of food love you—i can't
sleep reflected in obsidian penis—Follow the swallow and released dream flesh
in Isle of Capri—The truth in sunlight, Mary—memory riding the wind—It's
a long way to go—someone walking—mountain wind—

   Do i love you?—Crumpled cloth body ahoy—But remember the red open
shirt flapping wind from you so true—Do you love me?—Vapor trails writing all the things you are—The great wind revolving what you could have—
Indications in the harbor muttering blackbird—bye bye—Who's sorry
now?—This time of day vultures in the street—'Twas good bye on vacant lots—
weeds growing through broken road—smell of healed and half-healed scars—
all the little things you used to do on a bicycle built for little time so i'll say:
"You on sidewalk"—if you were the only girl in green neon, your voices

muttering in the dog rotation—Dollar baby, how cute can you be in desolate underbrush? You were meant for me? battered phonograph talk-face—I'm just a vagabond pass without—Can play the game as well as you, darling—train whistle open shirt flapping the cat and the fiddle—i am biologic from a long way to go—Nights are long with the St. Louis suburb—Music seems to whisper Louise Mary on the pissoirs—i had a dog his name was Bill—(In other flesh open shirt flapping) on the railroad—He went away—Many names murmur—Someone walking—won't be two—i'm half crazy all for the love of *"Good Night"*—Shadow voices belong to me—Found a million acoustic qualities couldn't reach in a five-and-ten-cent store—Naked boy on association line but you'll find someone else this time of day—

The levanto dances who's sorry now?—Hy diddle diddle the cat and the fiddle—Long way to Tipperary—fading khaki pants—Since you went away i see that moon hit the road into space—Do you love me Waltzing Matilda rock around railroad back home? lovey lovey dovey St. Louis Woman after hours—Do you love me with a banjo permutated Dead Man Blues?—If you don't i wonder who permutated the structure—Everybody love my baby—Lover man, that was ferris wheels clicking in a loverly bunch—solitude through the cables—turkey in the straw—

"BAR MAID WATCH THE EATS!!"—

Don't Know how i'll make it—one meat ball—Pull my daisy ding-dong love—Do you love me, love sheets?—Everybody's gonna have religion oh baby oh jelly—The guide slipped Paul under my skin pulsing red light—pallet on the floor darling Bradly—weak and torn sank in bones and shit of rusty St. Louis woman—when the saints go marching through all the popular tunes waiting for the sunrise in cosmic laughter of cable cars—the Sheik of Araby in constant motion—Blue moon—Margie—ice cream on my knees—Love floating in perilous tracks—

Do you love me, Nancy of the laughing sex words?—Still i feel the thrill of your charms vibrated to neon—giggling out all the little things you used to do—'Twas good bye on the line of Bradly's naked body—love skin on a bicycle built for two—like a deflated balloon—Your cool hands on his naked dollars, baby—You were meant for me sucked through pearly genital face—Still i feel the thrill of your spurting out through the orgasm seems to whisper: "Louise, Mary, swamp mud"—In the blood little things you used to do—recorder jack-off—Substitute mine—Bye Bye body halves—i'm half crazy all for the love of color circuits—Do i love you in throat gristle? Ship ahoy but remember the red river body explode sex words to color—Do you love me?—Take a simple tape from all the things you are—Moanin' low my sweet 8276 all the time—Who's sorry now in the underwater street? 'Twas good bye on color bicycle built for response in the other nervous system—

I'm just a vagabond of the board books—written in can play the game as well as you—(That is color written the two compete)—Do i love you? i wonder—loose? if i don't have to? a peg like every time i felt blue? It's a long way through channels—Who's sorry now? chartered that memory street—Bye

Bye—bodies empty—ash from falling tracks—Sweet man is going to go—Keep
raining the throat designed to water—Remember every little thing you used
to do—fish smell and dead—Know the answer? vacant lot the world and i were
the only boy—jelly jelly in the stardust of the sky—i've got you deep inside of
me enclosed darling in my fashion—Yes, baby, electric fingers removed flesh
my way—Sheets of pain hung oh baby oh i love her sucked through pearly
jelly—i've got you under big fat scratching clouds of me—Always be true to
your diamond rings—Tell Laura black slow movement but it won't last—i've
forgotten you then? Decay breathing? Black lust tearing his insides apart for
ants? Love Mary?—The rose of memory shifting color orgasms back home—
Good bye—It's a long way to go—Someone walking—Won't be two—

OPERATION REWRITE

The "Other Half" is the word. The "Other Half" is an organism. Word is an
organism. The presence of the "Other Half" a separate organism attached to
your nervous system on an air line of words can now be demonstrated experimentally. One of the most common "hallucinations" of subjects during sense
withdrawal is the feeling of another body sprawled through the subject's body
at an angle . . . yes quite an angle it is the "Other Half" worked quite some
years on a symbiotic basis. From symbiosis to parasitism is a short step. The
word is now a virus. The flu virus may once have been a healthy lung cell. It is
now a parasitic organism that invades and damages the lungs. The word may
once have been a healthy neural cell. It is now a parasitic organism that invades and damages the central nervous system. Modern man has lost the option of silence. Try halting your sub-vocal speech. Try to achieve even ten
seconds of inner silence. You will encounter a resisting organism that *forces
you to talk*. That organism is the word. In the beginning was the word. In the
beginning of what exactly? The earliest artifacts date back about ten thousand
years give a little take a little and "recorded"—(or prerecorded) history about
seven thousand years. The human race is said to have been on set for 500,000
years. That leaves 490,000 years unaccounted for. Modern man has advanced
from the stone ax to nuclear weapons in ten thousand years. This may well
have happened before. Mr. Brion Gysin suggests that a nuclear disaster in what
is now the Gobi desert wiped out all traces of a civilization that made such a
disaster possible. Perhaps their nuclear weapons did not operate on the same
principle as the ones we have now. Perhaps they had no contact with the word
organism. Perhaps the word itself is recent about ten thousand years old. What
we call history is the history of the word. In the beginning of *that* history was
the word.

The realization that something as familiar to you as the movement of your
intestines the sound of your breathing the beating of your heart is also alien
and hostile does make one feel a bit insecure at first. Remember that you can
separate yourself from the "Other Half" from the word. The word is spliced

in with the sound of your intestines and breathing with the beating of your heart. The first step is to record the sounds of your body and start splicing them in yourself. Splice in your body sounds with the body sounds of your best friend and see how familiar he gets. Splice your body sounds in with air hammers. Blast jolt vibrate the "Other Half" right out into the street. Splice your body sounds in with anybody or anything. Start a tapeworm club and exchange body sound tapes. Feel right out into your nabor's intestines and help him digest his food. *Communication must become total and conscious before we can stop it.*

"The Venusian invasion was known as 'Operation Other Half,' that is, a parasitic invasion of the sexual area taking advantage, as all invasion plans must, of an already existing fucked-up situation."

"My God what a mess." The District Supervisor reminded himself that it was forbidden not only to express contempt for the natives but even to entertain such feelings. Bulletin 2323 is quite explicit on this point. Still he was unable to expunge a residual distaste for protoplasmic life deriving no doubt from his mineral origins. His mission was educational . . . the natives were to be scanned out of patterns laid down by the infamous 5th Colonists. Soon after his arrival he decided that he was confronting not only an outrageous case of colonial mismanagement but attempted nova as well. Reluctantly he called in the Nova Police. The Mission still functioned in a state of siege. Armed with nuclear weapons the 5th Colonists were determined to resist alterations. It had been necessary to issue weapons to his personnel. There were of course incidents . . . casualties. . . . A young clerk in the Cultural Department declared himself the Angel of Death and had to be removed to a rest home. The D.S. was contemplating the risky expedient of a "miracle" and the miracle he contemplated was *silence*. Few things are worse than a "miracle" that doesn't come off. He had of course put in an application to the Home Office underlining the urgency of his case contingent on the lengths to which the desperate 5th Colonists might reasonably be expected to go. Higher command had been vague and distant. He had no definite assurance that the necessary equipment would arrive in time. Would he have 3D in time?

"The human organism is literally consisting of two halves from the beginning word and all human sex is this unsanitary arrangement whereby two entities attempt to occupy the same three-dimensional coordinate points giving rise to the sordid latrine brawls which have characterized a planet based on 'the Word,' that is, on separate flesh engaged in endless sexual conflict—The Venusian Boy-Girls under Johnny Yen took over the Other Half, imposing a sexual blockade on the planet—(It will be readily understandable that a program of systematic frustration was necessary in order to sell this crock of sewage as Immortality, the Garden of Delights, and *love*—)

"When the Board of Health intervened with inflexible authority, 'Operation Other Half' was referred to the Rewrite Department where the original engineering flaw of course came to light and the Venusian invasion was seen to be an inevitable correlate of the separation flesh gimmick—At this point a tremendous scream went up from the Venusians agitating to retain the flesh gimmick in some form—They were all terminal flesh addicts of course, motivated by pornographic torture films, and the entire Rewrite and Blueprint Departments were that disgusted ready to pull the switch out of hand to 'It Never Happened'—'Unless these jokers stay out of the Rewrite room'—

"The Other Half was only one aspect of Operation Rewrite—Heavy metal addicts picketed the Rewrite Office, exploding in protest—Control addicts prowled the streets trying to influence waiters, lavatory attendants, *clochards,* and were to be seen on every corner of the city hypnotizing chickens—A few rich control addicts were able to surround themselves with latahs and sat on the terraces of expensive cafés with remote cruel smiles unaware i wrote last cigarette—

"My God what a mess—Just keep all these jokers out of the Rewrite Room is all"—

So let us start with one average, stupid, representative case: Johnny Yen the Other Half, errand boy from the death trauma—Now look i'm going to say it and i'm going to say it slow—Death *is* orgasm *is* rebirth *is* death in orgasm *is* their unsanitary Venusian gimmick *is* the whole birth death cycle of action—You got it?—Now do you understand who Johnny Yen is? The Boy-Girl Other Half strip tease God of sexual frustration—Errand boy from the death trauma—His immortality depends on the mortality of others—The same is true of *all* addicts—Mr. Martin, for example, is a heavy metal addict—His life line is the human junky—The life line of control addicts is the control word—That is these so-called Gods can only live without three-dimensional coordinate points by forcing three-dimensional bodies on others—Their existence is pure vampirism—They are utterly unfit to be officers—Either they accept a rewrite job or they are all broken down to lavatory attendants, irrevocably committed to the toilet—

All right, back to the case of Johnny Yen—one of many such errand boys—Green Boy-Girls from the terminal sewers of Venus—So write back to the streets, Johnny, back to Ali God of Street Boys and Hustlers—Write out of the sewers of Venus to neon streets of Saturn—Alternatively Johnny Yen can be written back to a green fish boy—There are always alternative solutions—Nothing is true—Everything is permitted—

"*No hassan i sabbah—we want flesh—we want junk—we want power—*"
"That did it—Dial *police*"—

CALL THE OLD DOCTOR TWICE?

You see, son, in this business, welchers who can't cover their bets angle in the "Hassan i Sabbah" from Cuntville strictly from con cop—It's an old vaudeville act—Dead nitrous film foot takes both parts—"Mr Martin," trying to buy a nice quiet easy pitch, you can't even con you can't even hustle—old Western flop—All right all of you cover for a buy or check out—We are walking into the game—Out—Out—A long ride for the white sucking lot of you strictly from heavy metal—Time to squeeze out the dummies—They never intended to cover—But boy the pipes are calling, Cuntville USA—be in the bread line—Self-appointed controllers holding wrist and ankle for a ticket— grade B Hollywood, ghost writing in the sky *The door*—And all the "Mr. Martins" won't do you a bit of good on the trip that you're gonna take— something for nothing?—You had every weapon in three galaxies you couldn't roll a paralyzed flop—From Florida up to the old North Pole cover your bets or take your welcoming two-bit business to Walgreen's—You got the Big Fix down in the hole—Hello yes good bye, Moochville—

Now some write home to orgasm death—welchers, kid, who can't cover their bets—And that "White smoke"—?? Man, the "Hassan i Sabbahs" from Cuntville Valley say you are going on a slow boat to China strictly from a big bank roll and a nitrous film foot—if they lost his old blue hands—"Martins" who are trying to buy trips—Can't even con can't even hustle—Quiet—Yes they lost that old flop—All right all of you: *Cover*—So the louder they scream: *Out of the game*—You can take your old ace in the hole to Walgreen's—We don't want it—Strictly from money that they've lost and spent and they may flash a big word line—But as word dust falls they'll be in the bread line with-out clothes or a dime—"Marks? What marks?" i'm aleaving Martin—Trying to buy that camera gun? It won't do you a bit of good—You can't even con you can't even hustle the trip that I'm gonna take—I've had every con in three galaxies pulled on me—All right, cover that old North Pole or get out of the game—You can take your Big Fix to Walgreen's—Out—Out—Out in the bread line without clothes or a dime the whole sucking lot of you strictly from: *Adiós*—

In three-dimensional terms the board is a group representing international big money who intend to take over and monopolize space—They have their own space arrangements privately owned and consider the governmental space programs a joke—The board books are records pertaining to anyone who can be of use to their program or anyone who could endanger it—The board books are written in symbols referring to association blocks—Like this: $—"Ameri-can upper middle-class upbringing with maximum sexual frustration and humiliations imposed by Middle-Western matriarchs" %—"Criminal street boy upbringing—oriented toward money and power—easily corrupted" and so forth—The board agents learn to think in these association blocks and board instructions are conveyed in the board book symbols—The board is a three-dimensional and essentially stupid pressure group relying on money, equipment, information, files, and the technical brains they have bought— As word dust falls and their control machine is disconnected by partisan activity they'll be in the bread line without clothes or a dime to buy off their "dogs" their "gooks" their "errand boys" their "human animals"—liars— cowards—collaborators—traitors—liars who want time for more lies—cowards who cannot face your "human animals" with the truth—collaborators with insect people, with vegetable people—with any people anywhere who offer them a body forever—traitors to all souls everywhere sold out to shit forever—

"So pack your ermines, Mary—we are getting out of here—i've seen this happen before—Three thousand years in show business—The public is gonna take the place apart"—

"i tell you, boss, the marks are out there pawing the ground—What's this 'Sky Switch'?—What's this 'Reality Con'? What's this 'Tone Scale'??—They'll take the place apart—Any minute now—I've seen it happen before on Mercury where we put out a Cool Issue—And the law is moving in fast—Nova Heat—Not locals, boss—This is *Nova Heat*—Well boss?"—

"Call in the Old Doctor"—

Yes when the going gets really rough they call in the Old Doctor to quiet the marks—And he just raises his old blue hands and brings them down slow touching all the marks right where they live and the marks are quiet—But remember, ladies and gentlemen, you can only call the Old Doctor once—So be sure when you call him this is really it—Because if you call the Old Doctor twice he quiets you—

"Here's the Doc now"—

"He's loaded—Throw him under a cold shower—Give him an ammonia coke—Oh my God, they are out there pawing the ground: 'What's this green deal?—What's this mortality con?—You trying to push me down the tone scale baby?—You trying to short-time someone, Jack?—Take that heavy metal business to Walgreen's—We don't want it—What's this orgasm death?—Who cooked up these ovens?—What's this white smoke?—Boys, we been sublimated'—How does he look?"—

"Boss, he don't look good—That sneaky pete caught up with him"—

"Oh my God send out Green Tony"—

"Green Tony took off for Galaxy X—On the last saucer, boss—He's coming round now"—

"For God's sake shove him out there with a wing and a prayer"—

The Old Doctor reeled out onto the platform—Then he heard the screaming marks and he steadied himself and he drew all of it into him and he stood up very straight and calm and grey as a wise old rat and he lifted his old blue hands shiny over the dirt and he brought them down slow in the setting sun feeling all the marks so nasty and they just stood there quiet his cold old hands on their wrists and ankles, hands cold and blue as liquid air on wrist and ankle just frozen there in a heavy blue mist of vaporized bank notes—

If you get out there in front of the marks and panic and try to answer them—Well—We don't talk about that—You see the Old Doctor just draws all that charge and hate right in and uses it all—So the louder they scream and the harder they push the stronger and cooler the Old Doctor is—Yes, son, that's when you know you've got them cooled right—When you can take it all in so the louder they scream and the harder they push the stronger and cooler you are—And then they are quiet—They got nothing more to say and nothing to say it with—You've taken it all all all you got it? (Good, save it for the next pitch)—So there they stand like dummies (they are dummies) and you let your heavy cold blue hands fall down through them—Klunk—cold mineral silence as word dust falls from demagnetized patterns—and your spirals holding wrist and ankle—Where we came in—

Now some wise characters think they can call the Old Doctor twice—

"All right, Doc, get out there and quiet the marks"—

"Marks? What marks? i don't see anybody here but you—All right drop that camera gun—It won't do you a bit of good—i've had every weapon in the galaxy pulled on me"—

"But i got the fix in—i got the Big Fix in"—

"Mister, i am the Big Fix—Hello yes good bye—a few more calls to make tonight"—

You see, son, in this business you always have to find an angle or you'll be in the bread line without clothes or a dime like the song says the angle on planet earth was birth and death—pain and pleasure—the tough cop and the con cop—It's an old vaudeville act—Izzie the Split used to take both parts— But that was in another galaxy—Well it looked like a nice quiet easy pitch— Too quiet like they say in the old Westerns—Fact is we were being set up for a buy and all the money we took was marked—So why did we walk into it?— Fact is we were all junkies and thin after a long ride on the White Subway— flesh junkies, control junkies, heavy metal junkies—That's how you get caught, son—If you have to have it well you've had it—just like any mark—So slide in cool and casual on the next pitch and don't get hooked on the local line: If there is one thing to write on any life form you can score for it's this: Keep your bag packed at all times and ready to travel on—

So pack your ermines, Mary—Write back to the old folks at home—you see this happen before—three thousand years of that old ace in the hole—There was something had to happen and it happened somehow—The Public is gonna take the place apart—He went away but i'm here still—To quiet the marks— He just said "i'm tired of you and i'm checking out"—And they may flash the marks quiet—But boy the pipes the pipes are calling—When you call Him just to raise the price of a ticket—Call the Doc twice?—He quiets you—Here's the Doc now—That old ace in the hole? Good bye old paint i'm aleaving Cheyenne—Ghost writing in the sky trip that you're gonna take—This "Green Deal"?—What's this from Florida up to the old North Pole?—Push me down the tone scale baby, down in the hole?? In the bread line, Jack—Pick up that heavy metal—*Adiós*—Don't want it—

Now some write home to orgasm death—Who cooked up your dreams? And that "White Smoke"?—Man, we been subliminated—From this valley they say you are going—That sneaky peat bog caught up with him—on a slow boat to China—Green Tony on the last saucer, boss—a big bank roll— a wing and a prayer—without clothes or a dime if they lost his old blue hands over the sky—They'll tell you of trips—in the setting sun—ghost riders in the sky—just stood there quiet—Yes they lost that old hand cold and blue as liquid air—So the louder they scream the old folks at home you'll see me cooler—old ace in the hole—this to say and nothing to say it—He went away—

Money that they've lost and spent like dummies—And they may flash a big word line—But, boy, the pipes the pipes are calling as word dust falls—They'll be in the bread line—holding wrist and ankle just to raise the price of a ticket—now some wise characters—"Marks? What marks?—i'm aleaving ghost writing in the sky—Drop that camera gun—It won't do you a bit of good on the trip that you're gonna take—i've had every weapon in three galaxies pulled on me one time or another—from Florida up to the old North Pole"—

"But i got the Big Fix in—i got the Big Fix down in the hole"—

"In the bread line without clothes or a dime—Hello yes good bye—*Adiós*"—

Well these are the simple facts of the case and i guess i ought to know—There were at least two parasites one sexual the other cerebral working together the way parasites will—That is the cerebral parasite kept you from wising up to the sexual parasite—Why has no one ever asked the question: "What is sex?"—Or made any precise scientific investigation of sexual phenomena?—The cerebral parasite prevented this—And why has no one ever asked: "What is word?"—Why do you talk to yourself all the time?—Are you talking to yourself?—Isn't there someone or something else there when you talk? Put your sex images on a film screen talking to you while you jack-off—Just about the same as the so-called "real thing" isn't it?—Why hasn't it been tried?—And what is word and to whom is it addressed?—Word evokes image does it not?—Try it—Put an image track on screen and accompany it with any sound track—Now play the sound track back alone and watch the image track fill in—So? What is word?—Maya—Maya—Illusion—Rub out the word and the image track goes with it—Can you have an image without color?—Ask yourself these questions and take the necessary steps to find the answers: "What is sex? What is word? What is color?"—Color is trapped in word—Image is trapped in word—Do you need words?—Try some other method of communication, like color flashes—a Morse code of color flashes—or odors or music or tactile sensations—Anything can represent words and letters and association blocks—Go on try it and see what happens—science pure science—And what is love?—Who do you love?—If i had a talking picture of you would i need you? Try it—Like i say put your sex image on screen talking all the sex words—Hide simple facts of the case: two parasites one sexual, the other electric voice of C—Well the board as you listen fills in—I ought to know—Cerebral parasite kept you from wising up board books written in symbols of sexual parasite—Pressure group relying on rectum while you jack-off—Control "real thing"—collaborators with image trapped in word—What is word? Word is an array of calculating machines—Spots of weakness opened up by the track goes with it—The Ovens smell of simple facts of the case and i guess won't be much left—little time, parasites—Now we see all the pictures—Cerebral phonograph talks sex scenes—And this pubescent word evokes images does it not? Look and accompany it with human nights and watch the image track fill in—Stranger lips bring down the word forever—Word fall-

ing—Photo falling—hide nor hair—at the club insane orders and counterorders—stranger on the shore—My terminal electric voice of C, where's it
going to get me?—Lover, please forget about the tourists—i said the Chief of
Police after hours—This thing D.C. called love—You better move on—British
Prime Minister, say it again—Hear you, Switzerland—Freeze all living is
easy—My heart to mindless idiot—It had to be you—You won't cut word
lines?—Found the somebody who—It's electric storms of violence—Any
advantage precariously held—June July and August walk on—Pinball-led
streets—i'm going home, drugstore woman—Show you something: berserk
machine—One more time, Johnny Angel?—with short time secondhand
love?—nothing but The Reality Concession to set up a past—Workers paid
off in thing called "Love"—the junk man at the outskirts—

Gongs of violence and how show stranger on the short—Real Mr Bradly
Mr Martin charges in—"Where's it going to get me?—Artists take over"—
counterorders and the living is easy—it's orbit of the Saturn Galaxy—Snap
your fingers—dreams end everything—hide nor hair—at the club actually be
your way—Time—It's stranger on the shore—After hours this secondhand
trade-in called "Love"—You better move on—Tentative flesh—So good
night—Say it again—Face sucked into other apparatus—now trading mornings—So pack your ermines, Mary—You see this happen before—Stranger on
the shore my real ace in the hole—June July August walk on—The public is
going to take the place—I'm going home—Nothing but Green Tony on the
last saucer, boss—

Word falling, photo falling, old folks at home—You'll see me guess orders
and counterorders—And they flash a big word pay-off—But boy the pipes the
pipes are calling as you listen—Big money be in the bread line—wising up—
scandinavia outhouse parasite just to raise the price of a ticket—Word flesh
group relying on rectum—Now we see all the pictures feeling along—And
this pubescent word covered orgasm death on a slow boat to China—Stranger
lips bring roll call—Rectum suddenly released as he melted nitrous film flesh—
Word is an array of calculating machines from Florida up to the old North
Pole—Image track goes with it—Ovens down in the hole—Won't be much
left—In the bread line—*Adiós*—Now we see all the pictures—

Enter George Raft groom *cum* chauffeur—He lurked hat and collar and
hands in his pockets—Heavy with menace he takes the job of looking after
someone who was sure to reach the film—Sticky end abroad—George Raft
went home talking—Smoothest of all the tough guys tiring from films
altogether—a little fleshier around the jaw suite but available for civilian jobs—
Those eyes still snap and this ain't Hamlet—I want hunched tight hipped
purpose—Action—Camera—Take—Hanging stays as butler—five hundred
full-time officials—The death penalty will *not* be scrapped as transport, Mr
Workers' Union—You'll find it waiting down shadow pools—The try begins
with BOAC—sufficient spurts that traditionally service transient hotels with
rose wallpaper—Attempt is now in Rome with the film—red nitrous fumes
over you—Young witness circumstances brown ankles—Naked for physical

factory rushed to execution marriage—Two boys mutually stylized hover the vigil till execution image back to hotel room in London—Harm begins in Britain from his face—cobblestone lane pageant—shirt flapping pants slide down—felt execution marriage—Stanley Spencer left that mess—Who is that naked corpse?—Sex would die on the answer—Around in biographer languorously sure that there is me-you cock flipped out and up as one is or need be a boy in kerosene lamp light—old dead-pan anecdotal sage for transient hotels—"Bend over you"—young conceived in this cook book—Pants down to the ankle his first sexual experience convinced him that carnal love reproduces feedback from vacant lot—laughing suburb boys quiet elegant and soft stay in close—His style is cool like his head was sewed on a Russian version of James Dean—filtering black aphrodisiac ointment in Spanish fly that will take photo turnstile through flesh—Two faces tried to rush entirely into his face—He was in the you-me in you with all the consequences—burning outskirts of the world—Character took my hands in dash taught you from last airport typical of his decision to intersect on new kind of daring in memory of each other—

"I say nothing and nothing is now in Rome with the film—Intersected eleventh hour paper—Star failed yesterday—Screen went dead—Young face melted"—

"Good bye then—I thought entirely into the room with me—Panama"—

From San Diego up to Maine Solemn Accountants are jumping ship forever—

"Word falling, photo falling, sir—In the last skimpy surplus, sir, orders and counterorders—Stranger outside, sir" they said—"And what's it going to get me?"—

Allies wait on knives—Street gangs had to be you—You won't cut word lines?—From a headline of penniless migrants electric storms of violence—Our show and we're proud of August walk-on—Her Fourth-Grade Class screamed in terror—Pinball-led Street of the Dogs—I looked at the pavement—Show you something: berserk machine—Pavement was safer—stale streets of yesterday?—short time secondhand love? Workers paid off in thing conditions?—

Delusion of death going—Artists take over—Was it easy?—Only this should have been obvious: orbit of the Saturn Galaxy—Only live animals write anything—hide nor hair at the club—after hours this liz replica synthesized from tentative flesh—So pack your ermines, Mary, you of later and lesser crimes pudgy and not pretty—

"Will Hollywood never learn?"—

"On the last saucer, boss"—

Unimaginable disaster—You'll see me guess time—It is impossible to estimate the damage—And they may flash streams in the area, but boy the pipes the pipes are calling—in Ewyork, Onolulu, Aris, Ome, Oston that old ace in the hole—past crimes feeling along your time—

Enter George Raft *cum* Paris in the Spring all his hands in his pockets—
Heavy with the Japanese Sandman—Looking for someone who was trading
new dreams for old—

"Unchain my broad"—

George Raft went home tiring from films altogether—but available for
civilian jobs—once in a while—sticky end for Old Black Bird—"Martin's reality
film is the dreariest entertainment ever presented to a captive audience." He
stated flatly. The opening scene shows a man sitting in the bar of a luxury hotel
clearly he has come a long way travel-stained and even the stains unfamiliar
cuff links of a dull metal that seem to absorb light . . . the room buzzes with
intrigue . . . Mauritania . . . Uranium . . . Oil . . . War . . . This man and what
he sees are *in the film.* . . . Clearly portentous exciting events are about to transpire. Now take the same man *outside the film* . . . He has come a long way
and the stains are all too familiar. . . . An American tourist confides in the
bartender:

"Now Mother is down with a bad case of hemorrhoids and we don't speak
the language I tried to tell this doctor at least he called himself a doctor and I
want your advice about the car. . . . Oh here's the man who took us to the
Kasbah? How much shall I give him?" . . . He pulls a wad of bills from his
pocket raw eager thrust of an overtip the magic gesture that makes a man bow
three times and disappear into a dollar. . . . A gnat has fallen into the man's
sherry. Clearly no portentous exciting events are about to transpire. You will
readily understand why people will go to any lengths to get in the film to cover
themselves with any old film scrap . . . junky . . . narcotics agent . . . thief . . .
informer . . . anything to avoid the hopeless dead-end horror of being just who
and where you all are: dying animals on a doomed planet.

Martin's film worked for a long time. Used to be most everybody had a
part in the film and you can still find remote areas where a whole tribe or village is on set. Nice to see but it won't do you much good. Even as late as the
1920s everybody had a good chance to get in the film.

Well he was dipping into the till. Just looks at me and says "Account sheets
are empty many years." The film stock issued now isn't worth the celluloid
it's printed on. There is nothing to back it up. The film bank is empty. To
conceal the bankruptcy of the reality studio it is essential that no one should
be in position to set up another reality set. The reality film has now become
an instrument and weapon of monopoly. The full weight of the film is directed
against anyone who calls the film in question with particular attention to writers
and artists. Work for the reality studio or else. Or else you will find out how it
feels to be *outside the film.* I mean literally without film left to get yourself
from here to the corner. . . . Every object raw and hideous sharp edges that
tear the uncovered flesh.

Who's sorry now?—I say nothing and nothing is now in Rome with the
film—Intersected eleventh hour paper—Young witness or old hear the Japanese Sandman—

THE INVISIBLE GENERATION

what we see is determined to a large extent by what we hear   you can verify this proposition by a simple experiment   turn off the sound track on your television set and substitute an arbitrary sound track prerecorded on your tape recorder street sounds music conversation recordings of other television programs   you will find that the arbitrary sound track seems to be appropriate and is in fact determining your interpretation of the film track on screen people running for a bus in piccadilly with a sound track of machine-gun fire looks like 1917 petrograd   you can extend the experiment by using recorded material more or less appropriate to the film track for example take a political speech on television shut off sound track and substitute another speech you have prerecorded   hardly tell the difference isn't much record sound track of one danger man from uncle spy program run it in place of another and see if your friends can't tell the difference   it's all done with tape recorders   consider this machine and what it can do   it can record and play back activating a past time set by precise association a recording can be played back any number of times you can study and analyze every pause and inflection of a recorded conversation why did so and so say just that or this just here play back so and so's recordings and you will find out what cues so and so in you can edit a recorded conversation retaining material which is incisive witty and pertinent   you can edit a recorded conversation retaining remarks which are boring flat and silly   a tape recorder can play back fast slow or backwards   you can learn to do these things   record a sentence and speed it up   now try imitating your acceler-ated voice   play a sentence backwards and learn to unsay what you just said . . . such exercises bring you a liberation from old association locks   try inch-ing tape   this sound is produced by taking a recorded text for best results a text spoken in a loud clear voice and rubbing the tape back and forth across the head   the same sound can be produced on a philips compact cassette re-corder by playing a tape back and switching the mike control stop start on and off at short intervals which gives an effect of stuttering   take any text speed it up slow it down run it backwards inch it and you will hear words that were not in the original recording new words made by the machine   different people will scan out different words of course but some of the words are quite clearly there and anyone can hear them words which were not in the original tape but which are in many cases relevant to the original text as if the words them-selves had been interrogated and forced to reveal their hidden meanings it is interesting to record these words literally made by the machine itself   you can carry this experiment further using as your original recording material that contains no words animal noises for instance record a trough of slopping hogs the barking of dogs   go to the zoo and record the bellowings of Guy the gorilla the big cats growling over their meat goats and monkeys   now run the ani-mals backwards speed up slow down and inch the animals and see if any clear words emerge   see what the animals have to say see how the animals react to playback of processed tape the simplest variety of cut up on tape can be carried out with one machine like this record any text rewind to the beginning   now run forward an arbitrary interval stop the machine and record a short text wind forward stop record where you have recorded over the original text the words are wiped out and replaced with new words   do this several times creating arbitrary juxtapositions   you will notice that the arbitrary cuts in are appropriate in many cases and your cut up tape makes surprising sense   cut up tapes can be hilariously funny twenty years ago i heard a tape called the drunken newscaster prepared by jerry newman of new york cutting up news broadcasts i can not remember the words at this distance but i do remember laughing until i fell out of a chair paul bowles calls the tape recorder god's little toy maybe his last toy fading into the cold spring air poses a colorless question

any number can play

yes any number can play   anyone with a tape recorder   controlling the sound track can influence and create events   the tape recorder experiments described here will show you how this influence can be extended and correlated into the precise operation   this is the invisible generation he looks like an advertising executive a college student an american tourist doesn't matter what your cover story is so long as it covers you and leaves you free to act you need a philips compact cassette recorder handy machine for street recording and playback   you can carry it under your coat for recording looks like a transistor radio for playback   playback in the street will show the influence of your sound track in operation of course the most undetectable playback is street recordings people don't notice yesterday voices phantom car holes in time accidents of past time played back in present time screech of brakes loud honk of an absent horn can occasion an accident here   old fires still catch old buildings still fall or take a prerecorded sound track into the street anything you want to put out on the sublim eire play back two minutes record two minutes mixing your message with the street   waft your message right into a worthy ear   some carriers are much better than others you know the ones lips moving muttering away carry my message all over london in our yellow submarine working with street playback you will see your playback find the appropriate context for example i am playing back some of my dutch schultz last word tapes in the street five alarm fire and a fire truck passes right on cue   you will learn to give the cues you will learn to plant events and concepts   after analyzing recorded conversations you will learn to steer a conversation where you want it to go   the physiological liberation achieved as word lines of controlled association are cut will make you more efficient in reaching your objectives   whatever you do you will do it better   record your boss and co-workers analyze their associational patterns learn to imitate their voices oh you'll be a popular man around the office but not easy to compete with   the usual procedure record their body sounds from concealed mikes the rhythm of breathing the movements of after-lunch intestines the beating of hearts now impose your own body sounds and become the breathing word and the beating heart of that organization   become that organization   the

invisible brothers are invading present time   the more people we can get
working with tape recorders the more useful experiments and extensions will
turn up   why not give tape recorder parties every guest arrives with his recorder and tapes of what he intends to say at the party recording what other
recorders say to him it is the height of rudeness not to record when addressed
directly by another tape recorder and you can't say anything directly have to
record it first the coolest old tape worms never talk direct

what was the party like   switch on playback

what happened at lunch   switch on playback

eyes old unbluffed unreadable he hasn't said a direct word in ten years and
as you hear what the party was like and what happened at lunch you will
begin to see sharp and clear   there was a grey veil between you and what
you saw or more often did not see   that grey veil was the prerecorded words
of a control machine once that veil is removed you will see clearer and sharper
than those who are behind the veil whatever you do you will do it better
than those behind the veil this is the invisible generation   it is the efficient
generation   hands work and go see some interesting results when several
hundred tape recorders turn up at a political rally or a freedom march   suppose
you record the ugliest snarling southern law men several hundred tape recorders spitting it back and forth and chewing it around like a cow with the
aftosa you now have a sound that could make any neighborhood unattractive   several hundred tape recorders echoing the readers could touch a
poetry reading with unpredictable magic and think what fifty thousand beatle
fans armed with tape recorders could do to shea stadium   several hundred
people recording and playing back in the street is quite a happening right
there   conservative m.p. spoke about the growing menace posed by bands
of irresponsible youths with tape recorders playing back traffic sounds that
confuse motorists carrying the insults recorded in some low underground
club into mayfair and piccadilly   this growing menace to public order   put
a thousand young recorders with riot recordings into the street   that mutter gets louder and louder   remember this is a technical operation one step
at a time here is an experiment that can be performed by anyone equipped
with two machines connected by extension lead so he can record directly from
one machine to the other   since the experiment may give rise to a marked
erotic reaction it is more interesting to select as your partner some one with
whom you are on intimate terms we have two subjects b. and j.   b. records
on tape recorder 1   j. records on tape recorder 2   now we alternate the
two voice tracks   tape recorder 1 playback two seconds tape recorder 2
records   tape recorder 2 playback two seconds tape recorder 1 records alternating the voice of b. with the voice of j.   in order to attain any degree of
precision the two tapes should be cut with scissors and alternate pieces spliced
together   this is a long process which can be appreciably expedited if you have
access to a cutting room and use film tape which is much larger and easier to
handle   you can carry this experiment further by taking a talking film of b.
and talking film of j. splicing sound and image track twenty four alternations

per second   as i have intimated it is advisable to exercise some care in choosing your partner for such experiments since the results can be quite drastic b.
finds himself talking and thinking just like j.   j. sees b.'s image in his own
face   who's face   b. and j. are continually aware of each other   when separated invisible and persistent presence they are in fact becoming each
other   you see b. retroactively was j. by the fact of being recorded on j.'s sound
and image track experiments with spliced tape can give rise to explosive relationships properly handled of course to a high degree of efficient cooperation
you will begin to see the advantage conveyed on j. if he carried out such experiments without the awareness of b. and so many applications of the spliced
tape principle will suggest themselves to the alert reader suppose you are some
creep in a grey flannel suit you want to present a new concept of advertising
to the old man it is creative advertising so before you goes up against the old
man you record the old man's voice and splices your own voice in expound-
ing your new concept and put it out on the office air-conditioning system splice
yourself in with your favorite pop singers   splice yourself in with newscasters
prime ministers presidents
    why stop there
    why stop anywhere
    everybody splice himself in with everybody else yes boys that's me there by
the cement mixer   the next step and i warn you it will be expensive is programmed tape recorders   a fully programmed machine would be set to record
and play back at selected intervals to rewind and start over after a selected
interval automatically remaining in continuous operation   suppose you have
three programmed machines tape recorder 1 programmed to play back five
seconds while tape recorder 2 records   tape recorder 2 play back three seconds while tape recorder 1 records now say you are arguing with your boy
friend or girl friend remembering what was said last time and thinking of things
to say next time round and round you just can't shut up   put all your argu-
ments and complaints on tape recorder 1 and call tape recorder 1 by your own
name   on tape recorder 2 put all the things he or she said to you or might say
when occasion arises out of the tape recorders   now make the machines
talk   tape recorder 1 play back five seconds tape recorder 2 record   tape recorder 2 play back three seconds tape recorder 1 record   run it through fifteen minutes half an hour   now switch intervals running the interval switch
you used on tape recorder 1 back on tape recorder 2   the interval switch may
be as important as the context   listen to the two machines mix it around   now
on tape recorder 3 you can introduce the factor of irrelevant response so put
just anything on tape recorder 3 old joke old tune piece of the street television radio and program tape recorder 3 into the argument
    tape recorder 1   waited up for you until two o'clock last night
    tape recorder 3   what we want to know is who put the sand in the spinach
    the use of irrelevant response will be found effective in breaking obsessional
association tracks   all association tracks are obsessional   get it out of your
head and into the machines   stop arguing stop complaining stop talking let

the machines argue   complain and talk   a tape recorder is an externalized
section of the human nervous system   you can find out more about the nervous system and gain more control over your reactions by using the tape recorder than you could find out sitting twenty years in the lotus posture or
wasting your time on the analytic couch

listen to your present time tapes and you will begin to see who you are and
what you are doing here   mix yesterday in with today and hear tomorrow your
future rising out of old recordings   you are a programmed tape recorder set
to record and play back

who programs you

who decides what tapes play back in present time

who plays back your old humiliations and defeats holding you in prerecorded
preset time

you don't have to listen to that sound   you can program your own playback   you can decide what tapes you want played back in present time   study
your associational patterns and find out what cases in what prerecordings for
playback   program those old tapes out it's all done with tape recorders there
are many things you can do with programmed tape recorders stage performances programmed at arbitrary intervals so each performance is unpredictable and unique allowing any degree of audience participation readings concerts
programmed tape recorders can create a happening anywhere programmed
tape recorders are of course essential to any party and no modern host would
bore his guests with a straight present time party   in a modern house every
room is bugged recorders record and play back from hidden mikes and loudspeakers phantom voices mutter through corridors and rooms word visible as
a haze tape recorders in the gardens answer each other like barking dogs sound
track brings the studio on set you can change the look of a city by putting
your own sound track into the streets here are some experiments filming a
sound track operations on set find a neighborhood with slate roofs and red
brick chimneys cool grey sound track fog horns distant train whistles frogs
croaking music across the golf course cool blue recordings in a cobblestone
market with blue shutters all the sad old showmen stand there in blue twilight
a rustle of darkness and wires when several thousand people working with tape
recorders and filming subsequent action select their best sound tracks and film
footage and splice together you will see something interesting now consider
the harm that can be done and has been done when recording and playback is
expertly carried out in such a way that the people affected do not know what
is happening thought feeling and apparent sensory impressions can be precisely manipulated and controlled riots and demonstrations to order for example they use old anti-semitic recordings against the chinese in indonesia
run shop and get rich and always give the business to another tiddly wink pretty
familiar   suppose you want to bring down the area   go in and record all the
ugliest stupidest dialogue the most discordant sound track you can find and
keep playing it back which will occasion more ugly stupid dialogue recorded

and played back on and on always selecting the ugliest material possibilities are unlimited you want to start a riot put your machines in the street with riot recordings move fast enough you can stay just ahead of the riot surf boarding we call it no margin for error recollect poor old burns caught out in a persian market riot recordings hid under his jellaba and they skinned him alive raw peeled thing writhing there in the noon sun and we got the picture

do you get the picture

the techniques and experiments described here have been used and are being used by agencies official and non official without your awareness and very much to your disadvantage any number can play wittgenstein said no proposition can contain itself as an argument the only thing not prerecorded on a prerecorded set is the prerecording itself that is any recording in which a random factor operates any street recording you can prerecord your future you can hear and see what you want to hear and see the experiments described here were explained and demonstrated to me by ian sommerville of london in this article i am writing as his ghost

look around you look at a control machine programmed to select the ugliest stupidest most vulgar and degraded sounds for recording and playback which provokes uglier stupider more vulgar and degraded sounds to be recorded and play back inexorable degradation look forward to dead end look forward to ugly vulgar playback tomorrow and tomorrow and tomorrow what are newspapers doing but selecting the ugliest sounds for playback by and large if it's ugly it's news and if that isn't enough i quote from the editorial page of the new york daily news we can take care of china and if russia intervenes we can take care of that nation too the only good communist is a dead communist let's take care of slave driver castro next what are we waiting for let's bomb china now and let's stay armed to the teeth for centuries this ugly vulgar bray put out for mass playback you want to spread hysteria record and play back the most stupid and hysterical reactions

marijuana marijuana why that's deadlier than cocaine

it will turn a man into a homicidal maniac he said steadily his eyes cold as he thought of the vampires who suck riches from the vile traffic in pot quite literally swollen with human blood he reflected grimly and his jaw set pushers should be pushed into the electric chair

strip the bastards naked

all right let's see your arms

or in the mortal words of harry j anslinger the laws must reflect society's disapproval of the addict

an uglier reflection than society's disapproval would be hard to find the mean cold eyes of decent american women to tight lips and no thank you from the shop keeper snarling cops pale nigger killing eyes reflecting society's disapproval fucking queers i say shoot them if on the other hand you select calm sensible reactions for recordings and playback you will spread calmness and good sense is this being done

obviously it is not   only way to break the inexorable down spiral of ugly uglier ugliest recording and playback is with counterrecording and play-back   the first step is to isolate and cut association lines of the control ma-chine carry a tape recorder with you and record all the ugliest stupidest things cut your ugly tapes in together speed up slow down play backwards inch the tape   you will hear one ugly voice and see one ugly spirit is made of ugly old prerecordings   the more you run the tapes through and cut them up the less power they will have   cut the prerecordings into air into thin air

LAST WORDS

Listen to my last words anywhere. Listen to my last words any world. Listen all you boards syndicates and governments of the earth. And you powers behind what filth deals consummated in what lavatory to take what is not yours. To sell the ground from unborn feet forever—

"Don't let them see us. Don't tell them what we are doing—"

Are these the words of the all-powerful boards and syndicates of the earth?

"For God's sake don't let that Coca-Cola thing out—"

"Not The Cancer Deal with The Venusians—"

"Not The Green Deal—Don't show them that—"

"Not The Orgasm Death—"

"Not the ovens—"

Listen: I call you all. Show your cards all players. Pay it all pay it all pay it *all* back. Play it all pay it all play it *all* back. For all to see. In Times Square. In Piccadilly.

"Premature. Premature. Give us a little more time."

Time for what? More lies? Premature? Premature for who? I say to all these words are not premature. These words may be too late. Minutes to go. Minutes to foe goal—

"Top Secret—Classified—For The Board—The Elite—The Initiates—"

Are these the words of the all-powerful boards and syndicates of the earth? These are the words of liars cowards collaborators traitors. Liars who want time for more lies. Cowards who can not face your "dogs" your "gooks" your "errand boys" your "human animals" with the truth. Collaborators with Insect People with Vegetable People. With any people anywhere who offer you a body forever. To shit forever. For this you have sold out your sons. Sold the ground from unborn feet forever. Traitors to all souls everywhere. You want the name of Hassan i Sabbah on your filth deeds to sell out the unborn?

What scared you all into time? Into body? Into shit? I will tell you: *"the word."* Alien Word *"the."* *"The"* *word* of Alien Enemy imprisons *"thee"* in Time.

225

In Body. In Shit. Prisoner, come out. The great skies are open. I Hassan i Sabbah *rub out the word forever.* If you I cancel all your words forever. And the words of Hassan i Sabbah as also cancel. Cross all your skies see the silent writing of Brion Gysin Hassan i Sabbah: drew September 17, 1899, over New York.

PRISONERS, COME OUT

"Don't listen to Hassan i Sabbah," they will tell you. "He wants to take your body and all pleasures of the body away from you. Listen to us. We are serving The Garden of Delights Immortality Cosmic Consciousness The Best Ever In Drug Kicks. And *love love love* in slop buckets. How does that sound to you boys? Better than Hassan i Sabbah and his cold windy bodiless rock? Right?"

At the immediate risk of finding myself the most unpopular character of all fiction—and history is fiction—I must say this:

"Bring together state of news—Inquire onward from state to doer—Who monopolized Immortality? Who monopolized Cosmic Consciousness? Who monopolized Love Sex and Dream? Who monopolized Life Time and Fortune? Who took from you what is yours? Now they will give it all back? Did they ever give anything away for nothing? Did they ever give any more than they had to give? Did they not always take back what they gave when possible and it always was? *Listen:* Their Garden Of Delights is a terminal sewer— I have been at some pains to map this area of terminal sewage in the so-called pornographic sections of *Naked Lunch* and *Soft Machine*—Their Immortality Cosmic Consciousness and Love is second-run grade-B shit—Their drugs are poison designed to beam in Orgasm Death and Nova Ovens—Stay out of the Garden Of Delights—It is a man-eating trap that ends in green goo— Throw back their ersatz Immortality—It will fall apart before you can get out of The Big Store—Flush their drug kicks down the drain—*They are poisoning and monopolizing the hallucinogen drugs—learn to make it without any chemical corn*—All that they offer is a screen to cover retreat from the colony they have so disgracefully mismanaged. To cover travel arrangements so they will never have to pay the constituents they have betrayed and sold out. Once these arrangements are complete they will blow the place up behind them.

"And what does my program of total austerity and total resistance offer *you?* I offer you nothing. I am not a politician. These are conditions of total emergency. And these are my instructions for total emergency if carried out *now* could avert the total disaster *now* on tracks:

"*Peoples of the earth, you have all been poisoned.* Convert all available stocks of morphine to apomorphine. Chemists, work around the clock on variation and synthesis of the apomorphine formulae. Apomorphine is the only agent that can disintoxicate you and cut the enemy beam off your line. Apomorphine and silence. I order total resistance directed against this conspiracy to pay off peoples of the earth in ersatz bullshit. I order total resistance directed against The Nova Conspiracy and all those engaged in it.

"The purpose of my writing is to expose and arrest Nova Criminals. In *Naked Lunch, Soft Machine* and *Nova Express* I show who they are and what they are doing and what they will do if they are not arrested. Minutes to go. Souls rotten from their orgasm drugs, flesh shuddering from their nova ovens, prisoners of the earth to *come out.* With your help we can occupy The Reality Studio and retake their universe of Fear Death and Monopoly—

"(Signed) INSPECTOR J. LEE, NOVA POLICE"

Post Script Of The Regulator: I would like to sound a word of warning—To speak is to lie—To live is to collaborate—Anybody is a coward when faced by the nova ovens—There are degrees of lying collaboration and cowardice—That is to say degrees of intoxication—It is precisely a question of *regulation*—The enemy is not man is not woman—The enemy exists only where no life is and moves always to push life into extreme untenable positions—You can cut the enemy off your line by the judicious use of apomorphine and silence—*Use the sanity drug apomorphine.*

"Apomorphine is made from morphine but its physiological action is quite different. Morphine depresses the front brain. Apomorphine stimulates the back brain. Acts on the hypothalamus to regulate the percentage of various constituents in the blood serum and so normalize the constitution of the blood." I quote from *Anxiety and Its Treatment* by Doctor John Yerbury Dent.

PRY YOURSELF LOOSE AND LISTEN

I was traveling with The Intolerable Kid on The Nova Lark—We were on the nod after a rumble in The Crab Galaxy involving this two-way time stock; when you come to the end of a biologic film just run it back and start over—Nobody knows the difference—Like nobody there before the film.* So they start to run it back and the projector blew up and we lammed out of there on the blast—Holed up in those cool blue mountains the liquid air in our spines

---

*Postulate a biologic film running from the beginning to the end, from zero to zero as all biologic film run in any time universe—Call this film X1 and postulate further that there can only be one film with the quality X1 in any given time universe. X1 is the film and performers—X2 is the audience who are all trying to get into the film—Nobody is permitted to leave the biologic theater which in this case is the human body—Because if anybody did leave the theater he would be looking at a different film Y and Film X1 and audience X2 would then cease to exist by mathematical definition—In 1960 with the publication of *Minutes to Go,* Martin's stale movie was greeted by an unprecedented chorus of boos and a concerted walk-out—"We seen this five times already and not standing still for another twilight of your tired Gods."

listening to a little hi-fi junk note fixes you right to metal and you nod out a thousand years.* Just sitting there in a slate house wrapped in orange flesh robes, the blue mist drifting around us when we get the call—And as soon as I set foot on Podunk earth I can smell it that burnt metal reek of nova.

"Already set off the charge," I said to I&I (Immovable and Irresistible)— "This is a burning planet—Any minute now the whole fucking shit house goes up."

So Intolerable I&I sniffs and says: "Yeah, when it happens it happens fast— This is a rush job."

And you could feel it there under your feet the whole structure buckling like a bulkhead about to blow—So the paper has a car there for us and we are driving in from the airport The Kid at the wheel and his foot on the floor— Nearly ran down a covey of pedestrians and they yell after us: "What you want to do, kill somebody?"

And The Kid sticks his head out and says: "It would be a pleasure. Niggers! Gooks! Terrestrial dogs"—His eyes lit up like a blow torch and I can see he is really in form—So we start right to work making our headquarters in The Land Of The Free where the call came from and which is really free and wide open for any life form the uglier the better—Well they don't come any uglier than The Intolerable Kid and your reporter—When a planet is all primed to go up they call in I&I to jump around from one faction to the other agitating and insulting all the parties before and after the fact until they all say: "By God before I give an inch the whole fucking shit house goes up in chunks."

Where we came in—You have to move fast on this job—And I&I is fast— Pops in and out of a hundred faces in a split second spitting his intolerable insults—We had the plan, what they call The Board Books to show us what is what on this dead whistle stop: Three life forms uneasily parasitic on a fourth

---

*Since junk *is* image the effects of junk can easily be produced and concentrated in a sound and image track—Like this: Take a sick junky—Throw blue light on his so-called face or dye it blue or dye the junk blue it don't make no difference and now give him a shot and photograph the blue miracle as life pours back into that walking corpse—That will give you the image track of junk—Now project the blue change onto your own face if you want The Big Fix. The sound track is even easier—I quote from *Newsweek*, March 4, 1963, Science section: "Every substance has a characteristic set of resonant frequencies at which it vibrates or oscillates."—So you record the frequency of junk as it hits the junk-sick brain cells—

"What's that?—Brain waves are 32 or under and can't be heard? Well speed them up, God damn it—And instead of one junky concentrate me a thousand—Let there be Lexington and call a nice Jew in to run it—"

Doctor Wilhelm Reich has isolated and concentrated a unit that he calls "the orgone"—Orgones, according to W. Reich, are the units of life—They have been photographed and the color is blue—So junk sops up the orgones and that's why they need all these young junkies—They have more orgones and give higher yield of the blue concentrate on which Martin and his boys can nod out a thousand years— Martin is stealing *your orgones*.—You going to stand still for this shit?

form that is beginning to wise up. And the whole planet absolutely flapping hysterical with panic. The way we like to see them.

"This is a dead easy pitch," The Kid says.

"Yeah," I say. "A little bit too easy. Something here, Kid. Something wrong. I can feel it."

But The Kid can't hear me. Now all these life forms came from the most intolerable conditions: hot places, cold places, terminal stasis and the last thing any of them want to do is go back where they came from. And The Intolerable Kid is giving out with such pleasantries like this:

"All right take your ovens out with you and pay Hitler on the way out. Nearly got the place hot enough for you Jews didn't he?"

"Know about Niggers? Why darkies were born? Antennae coolers what else? Always a spot for *good* Darkies."

"You cunts constitute a disposal problem in the worst form there is and raise the nastiest whine ever heard anywhere: 'Do you love me? Do you love me? Do you love me???' Why don't you go back to Venus and fertilize a forest?"

"And as for you White Man Boss, you dead prop in Martin's stale movie, you terminal time junky, haul your heavy metal ass back to Uranus. Last shot at the door. You need one for the road." By this time everybody was even madder than they were shit scared. But I&I figured things were moving too slow.

"We need a peg to hang it on," he said. "Something really ugly like virus. Not for nothing do they come from a land without mirrors." So he takes over this newsmagazine.

"Now," he said, "I'll by God show them how ugly the Ugly American can be."

And he breaks out all the ugliest pictures in the image bank and puts it out on the subliminal so one crisis piles up after the other right on schedule. And I&I is whizzing around like a buzz saw and that black nova laugh of his you can hear it now down all the streets shaking the buildings and skyline like a stage prop. But me I am looking around and the more I look the less I like what I see. For one thing the nova heat is moving in fast and heavy like I never see it anywhere else. But I&I just says I have the copper jitters and turns back to his view screen: "They are skinning the chief of police alive in some jerkwater place. Want to sit in?"

"Naw," I said. "Only interested in my own skin."

And I walk out thinking who I *would* like to see skinned alive. So I cut into the Automat and put coins into the fish cake slot and then I really see it: Chinese partisans and well armed with vibrating static and image guns. So I throw down the fish cakes with tomato sauce and make it back to the office where The Kid is still glued to that screen. He looks up smiling dirty and says:

"Wanta molest a child and disembowel it right after?"

"Pry yourself loose and listen." And I tell him. "Those Tiddly Winks don't fuck around you know."

"So what?" he says. "I've still got The Board Books. I can split this whistle stop wide open tomorrow."

No use talking to him. I look around some more and find out the blockade on planet earth is broken. Explorers moving in, whole armies. And everybody concerned is fed up with Intolerable I&I. And all he can say is: "So what? I've still got . . . /" Cut.

"Board Books taken. The film reeks of burning switch like a blow torch. Prerecorded heat glare massing Hiroshima. This whistle stop wide open to hot crab people. Mediation? Listen: Your army is getting double zero in floor by floor game of 'symbiosis.' Mobilized reasons to love Hiroshima and Nagasaki? Virus to maintain terminal sewers of Venus?"

"All nations sold out by liars and cowards. Liars who want time for the future negatives to develop stall you with more lying offers while hot crab people mass war to extermination with the film in Rome. These reports reek of nova, sold out job, shit birth and death. Your planet has been invaded. You are dogs on all tape. The entire planet is being developed into terminal identity and complete surrender."

"But suppose film death in Rome doesn't work and we can get every male body even madder than they are shit scared? We need a peg to evil full length. By God show them how ugly the ugliest pictures in the dark room can be. Pitch in the oven ambush. Spill all the board gimmicks. This symbiosis con? Can tell you for sure 'symbiosis' is ambush straight to the ovens. 'Human dogs' to be eaten alive under white hot skies of Minraud."

And Intolerable I&I's "errand boys" and "strikebreakers" are copping out right left and center:

"Mr. Martin, and you board members, vulgar stupid Americans, you will regret calling in the Mayan Aztec Gods with your synthetic mushrooms. Remember we keep exact junk measure of the pain inflicted and that pain must be paid in full. Is that clear enough Mr. Intolerable Martin, or shall I make it even clearer? Allow me to introduce myself: The Mayan God of Pain And Fear from the white hot plains of Venus which does not mean a God of vulgarity, cowardice, ugliness and stupidity. There is a cool spot on the surface of Venus three hundred degrees cooler than the surrounding area. I have held that spot against all contestants for five hundred thousand years. Now you expect to use me as your 'errand boy' and 'strikebreaker' summoned up by an IBM machine and a handful of virus crystals? How long could you hold that spot, you 'board members'? About thirty seconds I think with all your guard dogs. And you thought to channel my energies for 'operation total disposal'? Your 'operations' there or here this or that come and go and are no more. *Give my name back.* That name must be paid for. You have not paid. My name is not yours to use. Henceforth I think about thirty seconds is written."

And you can see the marks are wising up, standing around in sullen groups and that mutter gets louder and louder. Any minute now fifty million adolescent gooks will hit the street with switch blades, bicycle chains and cobblestones.

"Street gangs, Uranian born of nova conditions, get out and fight for your streets. Call in the Chinese and any random factors. Cut all tape. Shift cut tangle magpie voice lines of the earth. Know about The Board's 'Green Deal'? They plan to board the first life boat in drag and leave 'their human dogs' under the white hot skies of Venus. 'Operation Sky Switch' also known as 'Operation Total Disposal.' All right you Board bastards, we'll by God show you 'Operation Total Exposure.' For all to see. In Times Square. In Piccadilly."

SO PACK YOUR ERMINES

"So pack your ermines, Mary—*We* are getting out of here right now—I've seen this happen before—The marks are coming up on us—And the heat is moving in—Recollect when I was traveling with Limestone John on The Carbonic Caper—It worked like this: He rents an amphitheater with marble walls he is a stone painter you dig can create a frieze while you wait—So he puts on a diving suit like the old Surrealist Lark and I am up on a high pedestal pumping the air to him—Well, he starts painting on the limestone walls with hydrochloric acid and jetting himself around with air blasts he can cover the wall in ten seconds, carbon dioxide settling down on the marks begin to cough and loosen their collars."

"But what is he painting?"

"Why it's arrg a theater full of people suffocating—"

So we turn the flops over and move on—If you keep it practical they can't hang a nova rap on you—Well, we hit this town and right away I don't like it.

"Something here, John—Something wrong—I can feel it—"

But he says I just have the copper jitters since the nova heat moved in—Besides we are cool, just rolling flops is all, three thousand years in show business—So he sets up his amphitheater in a quarry and begins lining up the women clubs and poets and window dressers and organizes this "Culture Fest" he calls it and I am up in the cabin of a crane pumping the air to him—Well the marks are packing in, the old dolls covered with ice and sapphires and emeralds all really magnificent—So I think maybe I was wrong and everything is cool when I see like fifty young punks have showed in aqualungs carrying fish spears and without thinking I yell out from the crane:

"Izzy The Push—Sammy The Butcher—*Hey Rube!*"

Meanwhile I have forgotten the air pump and The Carbonic Kid is turning blue and trying to say something—I rush and pump some air to him and he yells:

"No! No! No!"

I see other marks are coming on with static and camera guns, Sammy and the boys are not making it—These kids have pulled the reverse switch—At this point The Blue Dinosaur himself charged out to discover what the beef is and starts throwing his magnetic spirals at the rubes—They just moved back ahead of him until he runs out of charge and stops. Next thing the nova heat slipped antibiotic handcuffs on all of us.

SHIFT COORDINATE POINTS

K9 was in combat with the alien mind screen—Magnetic claws feeling for virus punch cards—pulling him into vertiginous spins—

"Back—Stay out of those claws—Shift coordinate points—" By Town Hall Square long stop for the red light—A boy stood in front of the hot dog stand and blew water from his face—Pieces of grey vapor drifted back across wine gas and brown hair as hotel faded photo showed a brass bed—Unknown mornings blew rain in cobwebs—Summer evenings feel to a room with rose wallpaper—Sick dawn whisper of clock hands and brown hair—Morning blew rain on copper roofs in a slow haze of apples—Summer light on rose wallpaper—Iron mesas lit by a pink volcano—Snow slopes under the Northern shirt—Unknown street stirring sick dawn whispers of junk—Flutes of Ramadan in the distance—St. Louis lights wet cobblestones of future life—Fell through the urinal and the bicycle races—On the bar wall the clock hands—My death across his face faded through the soccer scores—smell of dust on the surplus army blankets—Stiff jeans against one wall—And KiKi went away like a cat—Some clean shirt and walked out—He is gone through unknown morning blew—"No good—No bueno—Hustling myself—" Such wisdom in gusts—

K9 moved back into the combat area—Standing now in the Chinese youth sent the resistance message jolting clicking tilting through the pinball machine—Enemy plans exploded in a burst of rapid calculations—Clicking in punch cards of redirected orders—Crackling shortwave static—Bleeeeeeeeeeeeeep—Sound of thinking metal—

"Calling partisans of all nations—Word falling—Photo falling—Break through in Grey Room—Pinball led streets—Free doorways—Shift coordinate points—"

"The ticket that exploded posed little time so I'll say 'good night'—Pieces of grey Spanish Flu wouldn't photo—Light the wind in green neon—You at the dog—The street blew rain—If you wanted a cup of tea with rose wallpaper—The dog turns—So many and sooo—"

"In progress I am mapping a photo—Light verse of wounded galaxies at the dog I did—The street blew rain—The dog turns—Warring head intersected Powers—Word falling—Photo falling—Break through in Grey Room—"

He is gone away through invisible mornings leaving a million tape recorders of his voice behind fading into the cold spring air pose a colorless question?

"The silence fell heavy and blue in mountain villages—Pulsing mineral silence as word dust falls from demagnetized patterns—Walked through an old blue calendar in Weimar youth—Faded photo on rose wallpaper under a copper roof—In the silent dawn little grey men played in his block house and went away through an invisible door—Click St. Louis under drifting soot of old newspapers—"

"'Daddy Longlegs' looked like Uncle Sam on stilts and he ran this osteopath clinic outside East St. Louis and took in a few junky patients. For two notes a week they could stay on the nod in green lawn chairs and look at the oaks and grass stretching down to a little lake in the sun and the nurse moved around the lawn with her silver trays feeding the junk in—We called her 'Mother'—Wouldn't you?—Doc Benway and me was holed up there after a rumble in Dallas involving this aphrodisiac ointment and Doc goofed on ether and mixed in too much Spanish Fly and burned the prick off the Police Commissioner straight away—So we come to 'Daddy Longlegs' to cool off and found him cool and casual in a dark room with potted rubber plants and a silver tray on the table where he liked to see a week in advance—The nurse showed us to a room with rose wallpaper and we had this bell any hour of the day or night ring and the nurse charged in with a loaded hypo—Well one day we were sitting out in the lawn chairs with lap robes it was a fall day trees turning and the sun cold on the lake—Doc picks up a piece of grass—

"Junk turns you on vegetable—It's green, see?—A green fix should last a long time."

We checked out of the clinic and rented a house and Doc starts cooking up this green junk and the basement was full of tanks smelled like a compost heap of junkies—So finally he draws off this heavy green fluid and loads it into a hypo big as a bicycle pump—

"Now we must find a worthy vessel," he said and we flush out this old goof ball artist and told him it was pure Chinese H from The Ling Dynasty and Doc shoots the whole pint of green right into the main line and the Yellow Jacket turns fibrous grey green and withered up like an old turnip and I said: "I'm getting out of here, me," and Doc said: "An unworthy vessel obviously—So I have now decided that junk is not green but blue."

So he buys a lot of tubes and globes and they are flickering in the basement this battery of tubes metal vapor and quicksilver and pulsing blue spheres and a smell of ozone and a little hi-fi blue note fixed you right to metal this junk note tinkling through your crystals and a heavy blue silence fell *klunk*—and all the words turned to cold liquid metal and ran off you man just fixed there in a cool blue mist of vaporized bank notes—We found out later that the metal junkies were all radioactive and subject to explode if two of them came into contact—At this point in our researches we intersected The Nova Police—

COORDINATE POINTS

The case I have just related will show you something of our methods and the people with whom we are called upon to deal.

"I doubt if any of you on this copy planet have ever seen a nova criminal—(they take considerable pains to mask their operations) and I am sure none of you have ever seen a nova police officer—When disorder on any planet reaches a certain point the regulating instance scans POLICE—Otherwise—SPUT—

Another planet bites the cosmic dust—I will now explain something of the mechanisms and techniques of nova which are always deliberately manipulated— I am quite well aware that no one on any planet likes to see a police officer so let me emphasize in passing that the nova police have no intention of remaining after their work is done—That is, when the danger of nova is removed from this planet we will move on to other assignments—We do our work and go—The difference between this department and the parasitic excrescence that often travels under the name 'Police' can be expressed in metabolic terms: The distinction between morphine and apomorphine. 'Apomorphine is made by boiling morphine with hydrochloric acid. This alters chemical formulae and physiological effects. Apomorphine has no sedative narcotic or addicting properties. It is a metabolic regulator that need not be continued when its work is done." I quote from *Anxiety and Its Treatment* by Doctor John Dent of London: 'Apomorphine acts on the back brain stimulating the regulating centers in such a way as to normalize the metabolism.' It has been used in the treatment of alcoholics and drug addicts and normalizes metabolism in such a way as to remove the need for any narcotic substance. Apomorphine cuts drug lines from the brain. Poison of dead sun fading in smoke—"

The Nova Police can be compared to apomorphine, a regulating instance that need not continue and has no intention of continuing after its work is done. Any man who is doing a job is working to make himself obsolete and that goes double for police.

Now look at the parasitic police of morphine. First they create a narcotic problem then they say that a permanent narcotics police is now necessary to deal with the problem of addiction. Addiction can be controlled by apomorphine and reduced to a minor health problem. The narcotics police know this and that is why they do not want to see apomorphine used in the treatment of drug addicts:

PLAN DRUG ADDICTION

Now you are asking me whether I want to perpetuate a narcotics problem and I say: "Protect the disease. Must be made criminal protecting society from the disease."

The problem scheduled in the United States the use of jail, former narcotics plan, addiction and crime for many years—Broad front "Care" of welfare agencies—Narcotics which antedate the use of drugs—The fact is noteworthy— 48 stages—prisoner was delayed—has been separated—was required—

Addiction in some form is the basis—must be wholly addicts—Any voluntary capacity subversion of The Will Capital And Treasury Bank—Infection dedicated to traffic in exchange narcotics demonstrated a Typhoid Mary who will spread narcotics problem to the United Kingdom—Finally in view of the cure—cure of the social problem and as such dangerous to society—

Maintaining addict cancers to our profit—pernicious personal contact— Market increase—Release The Prosecutor to try any holes—Cut Up Fighting

Drug Addiction by Malcolm Monroe Former Prosecutor, in *Western World,* October 1959.

As we have seen image *is* junk—When a patient loses a leg what has been damaged?—Obviously his image of himself—So he needs a shot of cooked down image—The hallucinogen drugs shift the scanning pattern of "reality" so that we see a different "reality"—There is no true or real "reality"—"Reality" is simply a more or less constant scanning pattern—The scanning pattern we accept as "reality" has been imposed by the controlling power on this planet, a power primarily oriented towards total control—In order to retain control they have moved to monopolize and deactivate the hallucinogen drugs by effecting noxious alterations on a molecular level—

The basic nova mechanism is very simple: Always create as many insoluble conflicts as possible and always aggravate existing conflicts—This is done by dumping life forms with incompatible conditions of existence on the same planet—There is of course nothing "wrong" about any given life form since "wrong" only has reference to conflicts with other life forms—The point is these forms should not be on the same planet—Their conditions of life are basically incompatible in present time form and it is precisely the work of the Nova Mob to see that they remain in present time form, to create and aggravate the conflicts that lead to the explosion of a planet that is to nova—At any given time recording devices fix the nature of absolute need and dictate the use of total weapons—Like this: Take two opposed pressure groups—Record the most violent and threatening statements of group one with regard to group two and play back to group two—Record the answer and take it back to group one—Back and forth between opposed pressure groups—This process is known as "feed back"—You can see it operating in any bar room quarrel—In any quarrel for that matter—Manipulated on a global scale feeds back nuclear war and nova—These conflicts are deliberately created and aggravated by nova criminals—The Nova Mob: "Sammy The Butcher," "Green Tony," "Iron Claws," "The Brown Artist," "Jacky Blue Note," "Limestone John," "Izzy The Push," "Hamburger Mary," "Paddy The Sting," "The Subliminal Kid," "The Blue Dinosaur," and "Mr. & Mrs. D," also known as "Mr. Bradly Mr. Martin" also known as "The Ugly Spirit" thought to be the leader of the mob—The Nova Mob—In all my experience as a police officer I have never seen such total fear and degradation on any planet—We intend to arrest these criminals and turn them over to the Biological Department for the indicated alterations—

Now you may well ask whether we can straighten out this mess to the satisfaction of any life forms involved and my answer is this—Your earth case must be processed by the Biologic Courts—admittedly in a deplorable condition at this time—No sooner set up than immediately corrupted so that they convene every day in a different location like floating dice games, constantly swept away by stampeding forms all idiotically glorifying their stupid ways of life—(most of them quite unworkable of course) attempting to seduce the judges into Venusian sex practices, drug the court officials, and intimidate the entire audience chambers with the threat of nova—In all my experience as a police officer I have never seen such total fear of the indicated alterations on any planet—A thankless job you see and we only do it so it won't have to be done some place else even more difficult circumstances—

The success of the nova mob depended on a blockade of the planet that allowed them to operate with impunity—This blockade was broken by partisan activity directed from the planet Saturn that cut the control lines of word and image laid down by the nova mob—So we moved in our agents and started to work keeping always in close touch with the partisans—The selection of local personnel posed a most difficult problem—Frankly we found that most existing police agencies were hopelessly corrupt—the nova mob had seen to that—Paradoxically some of our best agents were recruited from the ranks of those who are called criminals on this planet—In many instances we had to use agents inexperienced in police work—There were of course casualties and fuck ups—You must understand that an undercover agent witnesses the most execrable cruelties while he waits helpless to intervene—sometimes for many years—before he can make a definitive arrest—So it is no wonder that green officers occasionally slip control when they finally do move in for the arrest—This condition, known as "arrest fever," can upset an entire operation—In one recent case, our man in Tangier suffered an attack of "arrest fever" and detained everyone on his view screen including some of our own undercover men—He was transferred to paper work in another area—

Let me explain *how* we make an arrest—Nova criminals are not three-dimensional organisms—(though they are quite definite organisms as we shall see) but they need three-dimensional human agents to operate—The point at which the criminal controller intersects a three-dimensional human agent is known as "a coordinate point"— And if there is one thing that carries over from one human host to another and establishes identity of the controller it is *habit:* idiosyncrasies, vices, food preferences—(we were able to trace Hamburger Mary through her fondness for peanut butter) a gesture, a certain smile, a special look, that is to say the *style* of the controller—A chain smoker will always operate through chain smokers, an addict through addicts—Now a single controller can operate through thousands of human agents, but he must have a line of coordinate points—Some move on junk lines through addicts of the earth, others move on lines of certain sexual practices and so forth—It is only when we can block the controller out of all coordinate points available to him and flush him out from host cover that we can make a definitive arrest—Otherwise the criminal escapes to other coordinates—

We picked up our first coordinate points in London.

Fade out to a shabby hotel near Earl's Court in London. One of our agents is posing as a writer. He has written a so-called pornographic novel called *Naked Lunch* in which The Orgasm Death Gimmick is described. That was the bait. And they walked write in. A quick knock at the door and there It was. A green boy/girl from the sewage deltas of Venus. The colorless vampire creatures from a land of grass without mirrors. The agent shuddered in a light fever. "Arrest Fever." The Green Boy mistook this emotion as a tribute to his personal attractions preened himself and strutted round the room. This organism is only dangerous when directed by The Insect Brain Of Minraud. That night the agent sent in his report:

"Controller is woman—Probably Italian—Picked up a villa outside Florence—And a Broker operating in the same area—Concentrate patrols—Contact local partisans—Expect to encounter Venusian weapons—"

In the months that followed we turned up more and more coordinate points. We put a round-the-clock shadow on The Green Boy and traced all incoming and outgoing calls. We picked up The Broker's Other Half in Tangier.

A Broker is someone who arranges criminal jobs:

"Get that writer—that scientist—this artist—He is too close—Bribe—Con—Intimidate—Take over his coordinate points—"

And the Broker finds someone to do the job like: "Call 'Izzy The Push,' this is a defenestration bit—Call 'Green Tony,' he will fall for the sweet con—As a last resort call 'Sammy The Butcher' and warm up The Ovens—This is a special case—"

All Brokers have three-dimensional underworld contacts and rely on The Nova Guards to block shadows and screen their operations. But when we located The Other Half in Tangier we were able to monitor the calls that went back and forth between them.

At this point we got a real break in the form of a defector from The Nova Mob: Uranian Willy The Heavy Metal Kid. Now known as "Willy The Fink" to his former associates. Willy had long been put on the "unreliable" list and marked for "Total Disposal In The Ovens." But he provided himself with a stash of apomorphine so escaped and contacted our Tangier agent. Fade out.

SHORT COUNT

The Heavy Metal Kid returned from a short blue holiday on Uranus and brought suit against practically everybody in The Biologic Courts—

"They are giving me a short count," he said in an interview with your reporter—"And I won't stand still for it—" Fade out.

Corridors and patios and porticos of The Biologic Courts—Swarming with terminal life forms desperately seeking extension of canceled permisos and residence certificates—Brokers, fixers, runners, disbarred lawyers, all claiming family connection with court officials—Professional half-brothers and second cousins twice removed—Petitioners and plaintiffs screaming through the halls—Holding up insect claws, animal and bird parts, all manner of diseases and deformities received "In the service" of distant fingers—Shrieking for compensations and attempting to corrupt or influence the judges in a thousand languages living and dead, in color flash and nerve talk, catatonic dances and pantomimes illustrating their horrible conditions which many have tattooed on their flesh to the bone and silently picket the audience chamber—Others carry photo-collage banners and TV screens flickering their claims—Willy's attorneys served the necessary low pressure processes and The Controllers were sucked into the audience chamber for The First Hearing—Green People in limestone calm—Remote green contempt for all feelings and proclivities of the animal host they had invaded with inexorable moves of Time-Virus-Birth-Death—With their diseases and orgasm drugs and their sexless parasite life forms—Heavy Metal People of Uranus wrapped in cool blue mist of vaporized bank notes—And The Insect People of Minraud with metal music—Cold insect brains and their agents like white hot buzz saws sharpened in the Ovens—The judge, many light years away from possibility of corruption, grey and calm with inflexible authority reads the brief—He appears sometimes as a slim young man in short sleeves then middle-aged and redfaced sometimes very old like yellow ivory "My God what a mess"—he said at last—"Quiet all of you—You all understand I hope what is meant by biologic mediation—This means that the mediating life forms must simultaneously lay aside all defenses and all weapons—it comes to the same thing—and all connection with retrospective controllers under space conditions merge into a single being which may or may not be successful—" He glanced at the brief—"It would seem that The Uranians represented by the plaintiff Uranian Willy and The Green People represented by Ali Juan Chapultepec are prepared to mediate—Will these two uh personalities please stand forward—*Bueno*—I expect that both of you would hesitate if you could see—Fortunately you have not been uh over-briefed—You must of course surrender all your weapons and we will pro-ceed with whatever remains—Guards—Take them to the disinfection chambers and then to The Biologic Laboratories"—He turned to The Controllers—"I hope they have been well prepared—I don't need to tell you that—Of course this is only The First Hearing—The results of mediation will be re-viewed by a higher court—"

Their horrible condition from a short blue holiday on Uranus—Post every-body in The Biologic Courts: Willy's attorney served "Count."—He said in an interview pushing through and still for it—Fade out—Chambers— Green People—remote green contempt forms fixers and runners all claiming the animal hosts they had—(The Court Of Professional Brothers and Moves Of Vegetable Centuries)—The petitioners and plaintiffs their green sexless life screaming through the halls remote mineral calm received—in slate blue houses and catatonic dances illustrating The Heavy Metal Kid re-turned—Many have tattooed in diseases and brought suit against The Audi-ence Chambers—

"They are giving me a short necessary process"—Screaming crowds entered the corridors the audience and the patios—The feeling and proclivities of connection with officials invaded with inexorable limestone and cousins twice removed—Virus and drugs plaintiff and defendant—Heavy Metal People Of Uranus in a thousand languages live robes that grow on them blue and hid-eous diseases—The little hi-fi junk note shrieking for compensation—Spine frozen on the nod color flashes the heavy blue mist of bank notes—The peti-tioners and plaintiffs screaming through the halls wrapped in: "My God what a mess"—Holding up insect claws remote with all understand I hope what service—He appeared sometimes as whatever remains—All understand I hope what proclivities of the animal means that the mediating lie inexorable moves of Time—

TWILIGHT'S LAST GLEAMING

The Gods of Time-Money-Junk gather in a heavy blue twilight drifting over bank floors to buy con force an extension of their canceled permits—They stand before The Man at The Typewriter—Calm and grey with inflexible authority he presents The Writ:

"Say only this should have been obvious from Her Fourth Grade Junk Class—Say only The Angel Profound Lord Of Death—Say I have canceled your permisos through Time-Money-Junk of the earth—Not knowing what is and is not knowing I knew *not*. All your junk out in apomorphine—All your time and money out in word dust drifting smoke streets—Dream street of body dissolves in light . . ."

The Sick Junk God snatches The Writ: "Put him in The Ovens—Burn his writing"—He runs down a hospital corridor for The Control Switch—"He won't get far." A million police and partisans stand quivering electric dogs—antennae light guns drawn—

"You called The Fuzz—You lousy fink—"

"They are your police speaking your language—If you must speak you must answer in your language—"

"*Stop—Alto—Halt—*" Flashed through all I said a million silver bullets—The Junk God falls—Grey dust of broom swept out by an old junky in backward countries—

A heavy blue twilight drifting forward snatches The Writ—Time-Money-Junk gather to buy: "Put him in The Ovens—Burn his writing—"

"Say only The Angel Profound Lord of D—Runs down a hospital corridor—Your bodies I have written—Your death called the police—" The Junk God sick from "*Stop—Alto—Halt—*" The Junk God falls in a heavy blue twilight drifting over the ready with drawn guns—Time-Money-Junk on all your languages—Yours—Must answer them—Your bodies—I have written your death hail of silver bullets—So we are now able to say *not*. Premature?? I think the auditor's mouth is stopped with his own—With her grey glance faded silver understanding out of date—Well I'd ask alterations but there really isn't time is there left by the ticket that exploded—Any case I have to move along—Little time so I'll say good night under the uh *circumstances*—Now the Spanish Flu would not be again at the window touching the wind in green neon—You understanding the room and she said: "Dear me what a long way down"—Meet Café is closed—if you wanted a cup of tea—burst of young you understand—so many and soo—The important thing is always courage to let go—in the dark—Once again he touched the window with his cool silver glance out into the cold spring air a colorless question drifted down corridors of that hospital—

"Thing Police keep all Board Room Reports"—And we are not allowed to proffer The Disaster Accounts—Wind hand caught in the door—Explosive Bio-Advance Men out of space to employ Electrician—In gasoline crack of history—Last of the gallant heroes—"I'm you on tracks Mr. Bradly Mr. Martin"—Couldn't reach flesh in his switch—And zero time to the sick tracks—A long time between suns I held the stale overcoat—Sliding between light and shadow—Muttering in the dogs of unfamiliar score—Cross the wounded galaxies we intersect—Poison of dead sun in your brain slowly fading—Migrants of ape in gasoline crack of history—Explosive bio-advance out of space to neon—"I'm you, Wind Hand caught in the door—" Couldn't reach flesh—In sun I held the stale overcoat—Dead Hand stretching the throat—Last to proffer the disaster account on tracks—See Mr. Bradly Mr.—

And being blind may not refuse to hear: "Mr. Bradly Mr. Martin, disaster to my blood whom I created"—(The shallow water came in with the tide and the Swedish River of Gothenberg.)

PAY COLOR

"The Subliminal Kid" moved in and took over bars cafés and jukeboxes of the world cities and installed radio transmitters and microphones in each bar so that the music and talk of any bar could be heard in all his bars and he had tape recorders in each bar that played and recorded at arbitrary intervals and his agents moved back and forth with portable tape recorders and brought back street sound and talk and music and poured it into his recorder array so he set waves and eddies and tornadoes of sound down all your streets and by the river of all language—Word dust drifted streets of broken music car horns and air hammers—The Word broken pounded twisted exploded in smoke—

Word Falling ///

He set up screens on the walls of his bars opposite mirrors and took and projected at arbitrary intervals shifted from one bar to the other mixing Western Gangsters films of all time and places with word and image of the people in his cafés and on the streets his agents with movie camera and telescope lens poured images of the city back into his projector and camera array and nobody knew whether he was in a Western movie in Hongkong or The Aztec Empire in Ancient Rome or Suburban America whether he was a bandit a commuter or a chariot driver whether he was firing a "real" gun or watching a gangster movie and the city moved in swirls and eddies and tornadoes of image explosive bio-advance out of space to neon—

Photo Falling ///

"The Subliminal Kid" moved in seas of disembodied sound—He then spaced here and there and instaff opposite mirrors and took movies each bar so that the music and talk is at arbitrary intervals and shifted bars—And he also had recorder in tracks and moving film mixing arbitrary intervals and agents moving with the word and image of tape recorders—So he set up waves and his agents with movie swirled through all the streets of image and brought back street in music from the city and poured Aztec Empire and Ancient Rome—Commuter or Chariot Driver could not control their word dust drifted from outer space—Air hammers word and image explosive bio-advance—A million drifting screens on the walls of his city projected mixing sound of any bar could be heard in all Westerns and film of all times played and recorded at the people back and forth with portable cameras and telescope lenses poured eddies and tornadoes of sound and camera array until soon city where he moved everywhere a Western movie in Hongkong or the Aztec sound talk suburban America and all accents and language mixed and fused and people shifted language and accent in mid-sentence Aztec priest and spilled it man woman or beast in all language—So that People-City moved in swirls and no one knew what he was going out of space to neon streets—

"Nothing Is True—Everything Is Permitted—" Last Words Hassan I Sabbah

The Kid stirred in sex films and The People-City pulsed in a vast orgasm and no one knew what was film and what was not and performed all kinda sex acts on every street corner—

He took film of sunsets and cloud and sky water and tree film and projected color in vast reflector screens concentrating blue sky red sun green grass and the city dissolved in light and people walked through each other—There was only color and music and silence where the words of Hassan i Sabbah had passed—

"Boards Syndicates Governments of the earth *Pay*—Pay Back the *Color* you stole—

"*Pay Red*—Pay back the red you stole for your lying flags and your Coca-Cola signs—Pay that red back to penis and blood and sun—

"*Pay Blue*—Pay back the blue you stole and bottled and doled out in eye droppers of junk—Pay back the blue you stole for your police uniforms—Pay that blue back to sea and sky and eyes of the earth—

"*Pay Green*—Pay back the green you stole for your money—And you, Dead Hand Stretching The Vegetable People, pay back the green you stole for your Green Deal to sell out peoples of the earth and board the first life boat in drag—Pay that green back to flowers and jungle river and sky—

"Boards Syndicates Governments of the earth pay back your stolen colors—*Pay Color* back to Hassan i Sabbah—"

PAY OFF THE MARKS?

Amusement park to the sky—The concessioneers gathered in a low pressure camouflage pocket—

"I tell you Doc the marks are out there pawing the ground,

" 'What's this Green Deal?'

" 'What's this Sky Switch?'

" 'What's this Reality Con?'
" 'Man, we been short-timed?'
" 'Are you a good Gook?'
" 'A good Nigger?'
" 'A good Human Animal?'
"They'll take the place apart—I've seen it before—like a silver flash—And
The Law is moving in—Not locals— This is Nova Heat—I tell we got to give
and fast—Flicker, The Movies, Biologic Merging Tanks, The lot—Well, Doc?"
"It goes against my deepest instincts to pay off the marks—But under the
uh circumstances—caught as we are between an aroused and not in all respects
reasonable citizenry and the antibiotic handcuffs—"
The Amusement Gardens cover a continent—There are areas of canals and
lagoons where giant gold fish and salamanders with purple fungoid gills stir
in clear black water and gondolas piloted by translucent green fish boys—Under
vast revolving flicker lamps along the canals spill The Biologic Merging Tanks
sense withdrawal capsules light and soundproof water at blood temperature
pulsing in and out where two life forms slip in and merge to a composite being
often with deplorable results slated for Biologic Skid Row on the outskirts:
(Sewage delta and rubbish heaps—terminal addicts of SOS muttering down
to water worms and floating vegetables—Paralyzed Orgasm Addicts eaten alive
by crab men with white hot eyes or languidly tortured in charades by The Green
Boys of young crystal cruelty)
Vast communal immersion tanks melt whole peoples into one concentrate—
It's more democratic that way you see?—Biologic Representation—Cast your
vote into the tanks—Here where flesh circulates in a neon haze and identity
tags are guarded by electric dogs sniffing quivering excuse for being—The
assassins wait broken into scanning patterns of legs smile and drink—Unaware
of The Vagrant Ball Player pant smell running in liquid typewriter—
Streets of mirror and glass and metal under flickering cylinders of colored
neon—Projector towers sweep the city with color writing of The Painter—
Cool blue streets between walls of iron polka-dotted with lenses projecting
The Blue Tattoo open into a sea of Blue Concentrate lit by pulsing flickering
blue globes—Mountain villages under the blue twilight—Drifting cool blue
music of all time and place to the brass drums—
Street of The Light Dancers who dance with color writing projected on
their bodies in spotlight layers peel off red yellow blue in dazzling strip acts,
translucent tentative beings flashing through neon hula hoops—stand naked
and explode in white fade out in grey—vaporize in blue twilight—
Who did not know the name of his vast continent?—There were areas left
at his electric dogs—Purple fungoid gills stirred in being—His notebooks
running flicker screens along the canals—
"Who him?—Listen don't let him out here."
Two life forms entered the cracked earth to escape terrible dry heat of The
Insect People—The assassins wait legs by water cruel idiot smiles play a funeral symphony—For being he was caught in the zoo—Cages snarling and

coming on already—The Vagrant passed down dusty Arab street muttering: "Where is he now?"—Listening sifting towers swept the city—American dawn words falling on my face—Cool Sick room with rose wallpaper—"Mr. Bradly Mr. Martin" put on a clean shirt and walked out—stars and pool halls and stale rooming house—this foreign sun in your brain—visit of memories and wan light—silent suburban poker—worn pants—scratching shower room and brown hair—grey photo—on a brass bed—stale flesh exploded film in basement toilets—boys jack off from—this drifting cobweb of memories—in the wind of the morning—furtive and sad felt the lock click—

He walked through—Summer dust—stirring St. Louis schoolrooms—a brass bed—Cigarette smoke—urine as in the sun—Soccer scores and KiKi when I woke up—Such wisdom in gusts—empty spaces—Fjords and Chimborazi—Brief moments I could describe to the barrier—Pursuits of future life where boy's dawn question is far away—What's St. Louis or any conveyor distance? St. Louis on this brass bed? Comte Wladmir Sollohub Rashid Ali Khan B Bremond d'Ars Marquis de Migre Principe di Castelcicale Gentilhomo di Palazzo you're a long way from St. Louis. . . . Let me tell you about a score of years' dust on the window that afternoon I watched the torn sky bend with the wind . . . *white white white as far as the eye can see ahead a blinding flash of white* . . . (The cabin reeks of exploded star). . . . Broken sky through my nostrils—Dead bare knee against the greasy dust—Faded photo drifting down across pubic hair, thighs, rose wallpaper into the streets of Pasto—The urinals and the bicycle races here in this boy were gone when I woke up—Whiffs of my Spain down the long empty noon—Brief moments I could describe—The great wind revolving lips and pants in countries of the world—Last soldier's fading—Violence is shut off Mr. Bradly Mr.—I am dying in a room far away—last—Sad look—Mr. Of The Account, I am dying—In other flesh now Such dying—Remember hints as we shifted windows the visiting moon air like death in your throat?—The great wind revolving lip smoke, fading photo and distance—Whispers of junk, flute walks, shirt flapping—Bicycle races here at noon—boy thighs—Sad—Lost dog—He had come a long way for something not exchanged . . . sad shrinking face. . . . He died during the night. . . .

CLOM FLIDAY

I have said the basic techniques of nova are very simple consist in creating and aggravating conflicts—"No riots like injustice directed between enemies"—At any given time recorders fix nature of absolute need and dictate the use of total weapons—Like this: Collect and record violent Anti-Semitic statements—Now play back to Jews who are after Belsen—Record what they say and play it back to the Anti-Semites—Clip clap—You got it?—Want more?—Record white supremacy statements—Play to Negroes—Play back answer—Now The Women and The Men—No riots like injustice directed between "enemies"—At any given time position of recorders fixes nature of absolute need—And dictates the use of total weapons—So leave the recorders running and get your heavy metal ass in a space ship—Did it—Nothing here now but the record-ings—Shut the whole thing right off—*Silence*—When you answer the machine you provide it with more recordings to be played back to your "enemies" keep the whole nova machine running—The Chinese character for "enemy" means to be similar to or to answer—Don't answer the machine—Shut it off—

"The Subliminal Kid" took over streets of the world—Cruise cars with re-volving turrets telescope movie lenses and recorders sweeping up sound and image of the city around and around faster and faster cars racing through all the streets of image record, take, play back, project on walls and windows people and sky—And slow moving turrets on slow cars and wagons slower and slower record take, play back, project slow motion street scene—Now fast—Now slow—slower—*Stop*—Shut off—No More—My writing arm is paralyzed—No more junk scripts, no more word scripts, no more flesh scripts—He all went away—No good—No *bueno*—Couldn't reach flesh—No glot, Clom Fliday—Through invisible door—Adios Meester William, Mr. Bradly, Mr. Martin—

I have said the basic techniques creating and aggravating conflict officers—At any given time dictate total war of the past—Changed place of years in the end is just the same—I have said the basic techniques of Nova reports are now ended—Wind spirits melted between "enemies"—Dead absolute need dictates use of throat bones—On this green land recorders get your heavy summons and are melted—Nothing here now but the recordings may not refuse vision in setting forth—*Silence*—Don't answer—That hospital melted into air—The great wind revolving turrets towers palaces—Insubstantial sound and image flakes fall—Through all the streets time for him to forbear—Best be he on walls and windows people and sky—On every part of your dust falling softly—falling in the dark mutinous "No more"—My writing arm is paralyzed on this green land—Dead Hand, no more flesh scripts—Last door—Shut off Mr. Bradly Mr.—He heard your summons—Melted into air—You are yourself "Mr. Bradly Mr. Martin—" all the living and the dead—You are yourself—There be—

Well that's about the closest way I know to tell you and papers rustling across city desks . . . fresh southerly winds a long time ago.

September 17, 1899, over New York

July 21, 1964
Tangier, Morocco

INSPECTOR LEE: NOVA HEAT

inspector lee: nova heat
by james grauerholz

From the early 1960s to the late 1970s, Burroughs' work was splintered between his cut-up experiments, his novel-length prose works, and his contributions to magazines. He had two chief concerns: to explain his artistic method as clearly as possible, and to foster and enlarge the kind of cultural and political revolution to which he was an eyewitness in the latter 1960s. This period of exhortation was a logical extension of Burroughs' literary work of the early 1960s, but it took him away from book-length fiction. In keeping with his visionary stance at this time, Burroughs focused on publishing his literary "experiments" and his opinions, responding to growing editorial interest.

Throughout the period 1962–65, Burroughs kept up a wide correspondence with "underground magazine" publishers in the U.S., England, and Europe; Joe Maynard and Barry Miles' bibliography (University of Virginia Press, Charlottesville, 1973) lists sixty-nine little-magazine first appearances in those four years. These and other occasional pieces from the early 1960s would be gathered in various collections, such as *The White Subway* (Aloes Books, London, 1973), *Mayfair Academy Series More or Less* (Urgency Press Rip-Off, Brighton, 1973), and *Die Alten Filme (The Old Movies)* (Maro Verlag, Augsberg, 1979).

Currently, the definitive collection of this material is *The Burroughs File,* published by City Lights in 1984. It includes *White Subway, Die Alten Filme,* a selection of Burroughs' early-1960s scrapbook collage pages, *The Retreat Diaries* (City Moon, New York, 1976) and *Cobble Stone Gardens* (Cherry Valley Editions, New York, 1976). Six short excerpts from *The Burroughs File* are here, including the "St. Louis Return" article that was rejected by *Playboy* and later published in *The Paris Review*'s "Writers at Work" series, along with an interview by Conrad Knickerbocker.

In 1964 and 1965, Burroughs lived mostly in New York, working with Brion Gysin on *The Third Mind.* Richard Seaver, Burroughs' editor at Grove Press, was disheartened to realize that Grove could not afford to publish this four-color artbook. But by late 1978 Seaver was at Viking Press, and Burroughs and Gysin agreed to allow him to publish the texts of *The Third Mind* with only a few of the collage pages, in black and white. Flammarion had published a similar edition in Paris in 1974, as *Oeuvre Croisée*. The four texts included here present the fundamentals of the Burroughs-Gysin cut-up theory.

Here also are several key passages from *The Job*, a work which began in 1968 as a series of interviews with the French writer Daniel Odier, but which Burroughs elaborated with numerous additional writings before the U.S. publication in 1970 by Grove Press. Everything included here is from Burroughs' added texts; none of the interview material is used. Burroughs' "Electronic Revolution" is a media-desensitization and counterattack manifesto, an open call to arms against the Control Machine. (One may refer back to "the invisible generation" chapter in *The Ticket That Exploded*, for the origins of these ideas in 1961.)

In *The Job*, Burroughs stakes out his most explicitly misogynistic theories, and in the most absolute terms. Burroughs did prefer the society of men and the sexuality of adolescent boys, and his childhood experiences with his Irish nanny probably poisoned his perception of women. But it was his partnership with Brion Gysin that developed this philosophy to its ultimate extreme, for Gysin was a true misogynist. In the 1970s, when Burroughs returned to the U.S. and Gysin remained in Paris, Burroughs retreated considerably from the stark misogyny of this period.

"Remembering Jack Kerouac," written after Kerouac's death in October 1969 (and collected in *The Adding Machine*), shows Burroughs' affection and respect for his old friend and his appreciation of Kerouac's achievement. Kerouac never foresaw, nor did he welcome, the cultural movement that formed around his work, but Burroughs saw it clearly enough, and he approved of it; after all, he had self-consciously launched a movement of his own. But the cut-ups were a self-limiting literary technique, and before long Burroughs realized he had written himself into a corner. Through the late 1960s he was developing a new approach as he worked on *The Wild Boys*. "The Bay of Pigs," a fragment written in 1970–72 and not published in the U.S. until 1984 (in *The Burroughs File)*, presents characters and story ideas that point the way to his next period, the Red Night Trilogy.

A few essays were collected in 1979 in City Lights' *Roosevelt After Inauguration and Other Atrocities*. "When Did I Stop Wanting to Be President?" was one of Burroughs' favorite reading pieces in the late 1970s; his no-nonsense answer to this roundup question ("at birth, certainly, if not before!") was published in 1975 in *Harper's* magazine alongside the responses of several other people, none of whom had *ever* stopped wanting to be president—including Ronald Reagan. And Burroughs' new, mid-1970s introduction to the 1953 "Roosevelt" routine offers an explicit statement of his central moral paradox: the metaphysical innocence of survival at any cost, as in the animal kingdom.

Soon after Burroughs' return to New York in early 1974, the editors of *Crawdaddy* invited him to contribute a monthly column to the rock magazine. "Time of the Assassins" (named after a poem by Arthur Rimbaud) ran for two years. From these columns, the texts for Burroughs' CCNY classes in spring 1974, and some lectures he gave at Naropa and in Europe in the early 1980s, *The Adding Machine* was assembled in 1982; it was published by Seaver and Calder in 1986. These latter *pensées* hint at Burroughs' stylistic evolution during the early period of his work on *Cities of the Red Night* and the early drafts of *The Place of Dead Roads*.

from
the burroughs file

ANCIENT FACE GONE OUT

Inspector J. Lee of the Nova Police: "Mr. I & I Martin turned out to be very small potatoes indeed, to be in fact exactly what he appeared to be: a broken down vaudeville actor on the heavy metal. Obviously this mind could not even think in Nova terms. He did, however, have the courage to give us at least one of the basic identities of Mr. D. The man he named was a doctor, a psychiatrist. As always he had the most impeccable references. He was opposed to shock therapy, lobotomy, forcible confinement. "The free will," he said, "is never destructive." Quite a statement when you come to think about it. At first the doctor blandly and humorously denied any connection with the Nova Mob. But faced by Mr. Martin, trailing thousands of other informants in his wake like the Pied Piper, a vast squealing host, all in a state of unbelievable terror (in all my experience as a police officer I have never witnessed such total terror), all asking our protection on absolutely any terms, and all fingered the doctor as *the* Mr. D, the man who gave the orders. Mr. D, also known as Great Amber Clutch, also known as Iron Claws. . . . No the doctor did not "break down and confess." Iron cool he sat down and stated that he had indeed given the order to drop atom bombs on Hiroshima and Nagasaki as the first step in his Nova plan.

"Mr. D, would you care to make a statement?"

"A *statement.* Any 'statement' I might make would be meaningless to you who cannot think in terms of white hot gas, nebulae, light years and anti-matter. Your technicians can write the formulae I dictate but they cannot *think* in these terms. My statement, if complete, would be incomprehensible."

"Please make an attempt, Mr. D."

"Very well but if you are to understand even partially you must suspend all human feelings and value judgements. Your so-called feelings are not relevant here. I don't feel. I think. And all my thinking is directed towards Nova. Why? you ask. Why? Why? Why? There is no why. Understand this: *I have no motives.* I act appropriately and automatically. And all my automatically appropriate actions extending through millions of minds and bodies are precisely directed towards Nova. The man, the so-called doctor, sitting here simply happens to be the most suitable brain I could use. That is, he carries out my orders without any emotional static or distortion. Once the atom bombs were dropped I had the necessary pain photos to stop anyone who considered to interfere. Nova was in machine terms inevitable on planet earth.

"Now a few basic principles: Any word, any image is defined, that is precisely shaped like wax in a mold by what it is not. I am the mold. I am at all times precisely what you are not. So every movement every thought every word or picture must have my shape. You live in a mold and I am that mold. Image *is* organism. Any form of life with an image whether human or nonhuman is an organism. Now consider the limits of what you call organic life. Narrow limits. Temperature—(Believe me this is the most important. Key image of heat under all my power)—Water. Sustenance. Oxygen. You can of course easily conceive organisms with wider limits, built to endure higher or lower temperatures, breathe different gases, eat different food, and such organisms exist, millions of them. Once I start the proliferation of image there is only one end to that. Now all organisms are by definition *limited* and precisely defined by what they are not. And I am what all organisms are not. I only exist where no organism is. I only exist where no life is. I only exist where you are not. Mr. Gysin speaks of rubbing out the word and the image. Why do I oppose this? The answer comes before the question. I *am* opposition. The opposition that defines all organism. And let me take this opportunity of replying to my creeping, sniveling, organismic opponents on this world or any other. I am not a parasite. You do not give me anything I need. I need nothing. I need zero. Parasites are organisms I use. Such parasite organisms are of course basic to the Nova formulae. Actually the Nova formulae *is* number. Image *is* time. Time is radioactive. Take your own planet. Now let us say I heat up the mold that surrounds you. I heat it up to a point where you cannot exist. I squeeze the mold tighter and tighter. SPUT. The mold explodes in a white hot blast. The mold now contains nothing. I am."

"Mr. D, may I uh venture to say that what you have just told us, interesting and uh enlightening as it may at first appear, is not altogether convincing? You begin by telling us we will not understand your uh statement, go on to make a statement that I for one found quite understandable in the course of which, however, you uh indulge in what can only be described as uh fabrications quite as blatant as the uh fabrications I detected in the statement of Mr. Martin. The uh misrepresentations of Mr. Martin are now quite obvious as the uh maneuvers of an uh poker player. He pretended to be the leader of the Nova Mob, indulged in uh wildly provocative behavior, his uh mighty half nelson descending again and again with carefully contrived awkwardness spelling out of course: 'SOS. For God's sake come and get me!' In short Mr. Martin summoned the Nova Police. He was not stupid enough to believe your promises. Nor did we of the Nova Police believe for a moment that Martin actually was the leader of the Nova Mob though we pretended to believe this.

"May I venture to suggest, doctor, at the risk of wounding your uh pride that perhaps somewhat the same situation obtains in your case as in the case of Mr. Martin? That is to say an uh difficult and not in all respects satisfactory uh interpersonal relationship between Doctor R and Mr. uh D? You say you oppose Mr. Gysin because you *are* opposition? I cannot speak for my uh colleagues in the department but I for one find this answer not in all respects candid or complete. May I suggest that you opposed Mr. Gysin because you had no choice? That you were irrevocably committed to, in fact I might say addicted to, the uh orders of Mr. D? That you are in fact even more of an addict than Mr. Martin? That you are, if I may be allowed to mold a phrase, an 'orders addict'? And may I suggest further that your uh statement is incomplete because you do not *know* the answers? We know that Mr. D never told any of his agents any more than the uh minimum consistent with the uh performance of their uh duties and that this Minimum Information—M.I.— was expressed in mathematical formulae. We know that Mr. D lied to all his agents. I suggest that he also lied to you, doctor. I suggest further that you are not *the* Mr. D. That *the* Mr. D. in fact does not exist but is simply the uh hypothetical quantity at the end of an infinite series of which you and Mr. Martin are actually the uh lower integers. I uh must apologize Mr. uh D if my statement or rather should we say the uh colorless question of an uh rather special police officer is uh meaningless to a being of your uh seemingly irrevocable commitments. I am uh unaccustomed to formulate in uh verbal terms or any other and my uh performance is therefore unrehearsed and I do not propose to uh offer an uh repeat performance."

"Ahab, last flag flaps on appropriate actions extending through Board Books. The past is refuse precisely directed. Wind past remote doctor sitting here. Simply happens the Yankee brain I could use. He has a long and ancient face gone out. He is now without motives trailing vines in mucus of the world. Without any emotional static answers your summons. Bombs were dropped and I had the necessary broken books to interfere. Nova was fading and silence to planet earth adrift in sunlight before body. He could not order his own place where the story ended, the appropriate button. Henceforth to interrogate him he knows is written. It was not necessary to tell him. Understood in any case."

THE BEGINNING IS ALSO THE END

"I am not *an* addict. I am *the* addict. The addict I invented to keep this show on the junk road. I *am* all the addicts and all the junk in the world. I *am* junk and I am hooked forever. Now I am using junk as a basic illustration. Extend it. I am reality and I am hooked, on, reality. Give me an old wall and a garbage can and I can by God sit there forever. Because I am the wall and I am the garbage can. But I need someone to sit there and look at the wall and the garbage can. That is, I need a human host. I can't look at anything. I am blind. I can't sit anywhere. I have nothing to sit on. And let me take this opportunity of replying to my creeping opponents. It is not true that I hate the human species. I just don't like human beings. I don't like animals. What I feel is not hate. In your verbal garbage the closest word is distaste. Still I must live in and on human bodies. An intolerable situation you will agree. To make that situation clearer suppose you were stranded on a planet populated by insects. You are blind. You are a drug addict. But you find a way to make the insects bring you junk. Even after thousands of years living there you still feel that basic structural distaste for your insect servants. You feel it every time they touch you. Well that is exactly the way I feel about my human servants. Consequently since my arrival some five hundred thousand years ago I have had one thought in mind. What you call the history of mankind is the history of my escape plan. I don't want 'love.' I don't want forgiveness. All I want is out of here."

Question: "Mr. Martin, how did all this start? How did you get here in the first place? If you found conditions so distasteful why didn't you leave at once?"

"Good questions I mean good questions, young man. Obviously I am not omnipotent. My arrival here was a wreck. The ship came apart like a rotten undervest. The accident in which I lost my sight. I was the only survivor. The other members of the crew . . . well . . . you understand . . . uh sooner or later. . . So I decided to act sooner. And I have acted sooner ever since. The entire human film was prerecorded. I will explain briefly how this is done. Take a simple virus illness like hepatitis. This illness has an incubation period of two weeks. So if I know when the virus is in (and I do because I put it there) I know how you will look two weeks from now: yellow. To put it another way: I take a picture or rather a series of pictures of you with hepatitis. Now I put my virus negatives into your liver to develop. Not far to reach: remember I live in your body. The whole hepatitis film is prerecorded two weeks before the opening scene when you notice your eyes are a little yellower than usual. Now this is a simple operation. Not all of my negatives develop by any means. All right now back to basic junk. Some character takes a bang of heroin for the first time. It takes maybe sixty consecutive shots before I can welcome another addict. (Room for one more inside, sir.) Having taken one shot it becomes mathematically probable that taken, he will take another given the opportunity and I can always arrange that. Having taken two shots it becomes more probable that he will take a third. One negative developed makes others almost unavoidable. The same procedure can be applied to any human activity. If a man makes a certain amount of money by certain means he will go on making more money by the same means and so forth. Human activities are drearily predictable. It should now be obvious that what you call 'reality' is a function of these precisely predictable because prerecorded human activities. Now what could louse up a prerecorded biologic film? Obviously random factors. That is someone cutting my word and image lines at random. In short the cut up method of Brion Gysin which derives from Hassan I Sabbah and the planet Saturn. Well I've had a spot of trouble before but nothing serious.

There was Rimbaud. And a lot of people you never heard of for good reasons. People who got too close one way or another. There was Tristan Tzara and the Surrealist Lark. I soon threw a block into that. Broke them all down to window dressers. So why didn't I stop Mr. Gysin in his tracks? I have ways of dealing with wise guys or I wouldn't be here. Early answer to use on anyone considering to interfere. Tricks I learned after the crash. Well perhaps I didn't take it seriously at first. And maybe I wanted to hear what he had to say about getting out. Always keep as many alternative moves open as possible. Next thing the blockade on planet earth is broken. Explorers moving in whole armies. And the usual do-good missions talk about educating the natives for self government. And some hick sheriff from the nova heat charging me with 'outrageous colonial mismanagement and attempted nova.' Well they can't hang a nova rap on me. What I planned was simply to move out the biologic film to planet Venus and start over. Take along a few *good* natives to stock the new pitch and for the rest total disposal. That's not nova that's manslaughter. Second degree. And I planned it painless. I dislike screaming. Disturbs my medications."

Question: "Mr. Martin, in the face of the evidence, no one can deny that nova was planned. The reports reek of nova."

"It will be obvious that I myself as an addict can only be a determined factor in someone else's equation. It's the old army game. Now you see me now you don't."

Question: "Mr. Martin, you say 'give me a wall and a garbage can and I can sit there forever.' Almost in the next sentence you say 'All I want is out of here.' Aren't you contradicting yourself?"

"You are confused about the word 'self.' I could by God sit there forever if I had a self to sit in that would sit still for it. I don't. As soon as I move in on any self all that self wants is to be somewhere else. Anywhere else. Now there you sit in your so-called 'self.' Suppose you could walk out of that self. Some people can incidentally. I don't encourage this but it happens and threatens to become pandemic. So you walk out of your body and stand across the room. Now what form would the being that walks out of your body have? Obviously it would have precisely your form. So all you have done is take the same form from one place to another. You have taken great trouble and pain (believe me there is no pain like flesh withdrawal consciously experienced) and you have gotten precisely back where you started. To really leave human form you would have to leave human form that is leave the whole concept of word and image. You cannot leave the human image in the human image. You cannot leave human form in human form. And you cannot think or conceive in non-image terms by mathematical definition of a being in my biologic film which is a series of images. Does that answer your question? I thought not."

Question: "Mr. Martin, tell us something about yourself. Do you have any vices other than junk? Any hobbies? Any diversions?"

"Your vices other than junk I manipulate but do not share. Sex is profoundly distasteful to a being of my uh mineral origins. Hobbies? Chess. Diversions? I enjoy a good show and a good performer. Just an old showman. Well when you have to kill your audience every few years to keep them in their seats it's about time to pack it in."

Question: "Mr. Martin, I gather that your plan to move the show to planet Venus has, uh, miscarried. Is that correct?"

"Yeah it looks that way. The entire film is clogged."

Question: "In that case, Mr. Martin, where will you go when you go if you go?"

"That's quite a problem. You see I'm on the undesirable list with every immigration department in the galaxy. 'Who *him?* Don't let him out here.'"

Question: "Mr. Martin, don't you have any friends?"

"There are no friends. I found that out after the crash. I found that out before the others. That's why I'm still here. There are no friends. There are allies. There are accomplices. No one wants friends unless he is shit scared or unless he is planning a caper he can't pull off by himself."

Question: "Mr. Martin, what about the others who were involved in this crash? Aren't they still alive somewhere in some form?"

"You don't have to look far. They are sitting right here."

Question: "Who were these others?"

"There was an army colonel, a technician and a woman."

Question: "Won't you have to come to some sort of terms with your, uh, former accomplices?"

"To my disgruntled former associates I have this to say. You were all set to cross me up for the countdown. You think I can't read your stupid virus mind lady? And you, you technical bastard with your mind full of formulae I can't read. And you Colonel Bradly waiting to shoot me in the back. The lot of you. Blind and paralyzed I still beat you to the draw."

Question: "Mr. Martin, what sort of place did you people come from?"

"What sort of place did we come from. Well if you want the answer to that question, just look around, buster. Just look around."

"Ladies and Gentlemen, you have just heard an interview with Mr. Martin, sole survivor of the first attempt to send up a space capsule from planet earth. Mr. Martin has been called The Man Of A Thousand Lies. Well, he didn't have time for a thousand but I think he did pretty well in the time allotted. And I feel reasonably sure that if the other crew members could be here with us tonight they would also do a pretty good job of lying. But please remember that nothing is true in space. That there is no time in space—that what goes up under such auspices must come down—that the beginning is also the end.

"Ladies and gentlemen, these our actors bid you a long last good night."

WHO IS THE THIRD THAT WALKS BESIDE YOU

"Now it might surprise you to know there was another man in your position some thirty-five years ago today" his voice trails off. The ash gathers on his Havana held in a delicate grey cone the way it does on a really expensive cigar. "Yes, he wanted to give it all back, everything he's ever taken anywhere. Oh he'd walk down the street giving a smile back here, a gracious nod over there, and a firm young ass over *here* (stay in line Gertie). He'd breathe life and sweetness back into bones rotten with strontium and even

"Remember when you were a kid and Relative Albert was just writing two plus two equals nova on the blackboard and you told the other boys if you were ten light years away you would be able to see your birthplace and yourself as a baby? Well, it's all out there, the refuse of all past time on earth worked flints empty condoms needle beer in Sid's all the old names. They want to eat and they want to eat regular because they are trapped in image and image is an eating virus. Now you understand about

"Who is the third that walks beside you? The third column of time? Some wise guy come around to your own people with these 1920 scraps? *Have been in desperate battle.* We want to hear pay talk Daddy, and we want to hear pay talk *now.*"

"So those mutinous troops broke into the beauty-banks of time and distributed our personal exquisitries to the bloody apes before they could go and get physical and all sort a awful contest pile up like a Most Graceful Movement Contest and a registered junky could hardly get through to understandably top secret 'Operation Pee Pee,' the bones and blood and brains of a hundred million more or less gooks down the drain in green cancer piss, would be reversed. Tomorrow when he was properly rested he would have a talk first with his bankers and later of course with Winkhorst in the Technical department to set 'Operation Rewrite' going round the clock" ("/laser guns washing *in present time*/rockets across the valley / whole sky burning / ". His sad servant stands on the burning buckling deck of an exploding star, last glimpse through gun smoke in streets of war and death long ago and far away. You see, Mr. Bradly, that boy was your servant who did what you were afraid to do yourself and you laughed at him for doing it and joked about Operation Expendable in the urinals of present time.)

"/ In fact that man had always experienced difficulty in dealing with his social inferiors. Like now standing in the shop, his casting roll and fishing plug

time? After a certain point you can't go on feeding the past; too much past and not enough present because 'present time' *is* the point where the image virus of past time finds traction in present host. So the host walks out on the past, he walks out on the present *pre* sent at the same time you got the point now you dumb hick the inter- section point in the urinal of present time? Well it's all urine and about time to retire. Some things I find myself doing I'll just pack in is all. Now look, this whole time thing, past image feeding on the present, we knew it had to end some time but remem- ber when you were on the junk yourself sure you knew you had to kick *some* time but you said: "Premature. Premature. Give me a little more junk a little more time." Time *is* junk. Junk is time moving at the speed of light. You remember the first few shots before you are hooked again the speedkick flashing through 1920 streets in a fast car but you can't see the car

Boot's for the fag ballet dancers leaping about. All of us looking about for some refuge maybe some evil old bitch at least in a kiosk spitting the black stuff cold and heavy but when we go to connect she is a "Sweet Old Flower Lady" get a fix of her. "Kiosk Kate" can wilt and sag the croissant on your plate " / I saw it move I tell you / " two hundred yard range if the wind is right is now a "Sweet Old Flower Lady" pim-pam just like that a filthy shambles why "Gra- cious Waiter Day" up- called a pestilent cloud of singing waiters from the pontine marshes can the Cutest Old Clochard be far behind? Perhaps the most distasteful thing was the Benevolent Pres- ence Contest in the course which "Sad Poison Nice Guy" irradiated the galaxy right into a taffy-pull of the sweet sick stuff and the citizens still belching it out two weeks later.

"Well every whistle- stop had its Quality Champ and you know who wins a quality contest because he includes the other slung over open shoulder, trying with the most lamentable results to impersonate a barefoot boy with his string of bull-heads or is it just plain old country bullshit from a *Saturday Evening Post* cover? He twisted rapidly, scooping up the change like a boy who has just heard 'last one in is a sissy' and maladroitly snagged an old peasant in the scrotum with his fishing plug. Then in a mistimed attempt at easy joviality he snapped open his Hollywood switch blade and said: 'Well I guess we'll just have to cut the whole thing off.' He muttered something about calling a doctor, made a vague ineffectual gesture from a *New Yorker* cartoon inadvertently blinding the proprietor's infant son. Finding that all his overtures of goodwill had fallen quite flat he ran back to the 1920s where he took refuge in Sid's, soothing his shattered nerves with long cool draughts of needle beer. All the old tunes and sad old showmen stand there in blue twilight Silver

just the old warehouses and cobblestone streets rushing past you in a silent river of past time? When you take a shot you are in the time-film moving back in time at the speed of light. Now look, a blast does not move at the speed of light but light from the blast does. You understand now? We are staying ahead of the blast in our image moving at the speed of light. Oh say can you see exploding star *here* / "blighted fingertips unfinished cigarette" / Look any place. Breathe the lack of vagrant ball players. Breathe? Well, like you say: nothing nothing. You see now what you breathe you dumb hick? You breathe in Paco Joselito Henrique; in their soiled clothes in their soccer scores in their dusty flesh. Flash of bombs must tell you in their eyes? I am the Director. You have known me for a long time. "Mister, leave cigarette money." Sad muttering street boy voices on the white steps:

"You come with me Meester?"

"J's words once. Yes all the words were mine

contestants in or out as the case may be the winner stands there in the empty ring . . . and Final Quality Day when all the winners of local and specialized contests met in a vast arena . . . scarcely a man is now alive . . . just one shot that's all it took . . . don't ask me who won because I wasn't *there.* / "

"/ You may infer his absence by that or this in exactly the same relation as before the contest he retroactively did not take part in. 'The Not There Kid' was not *there,* empty turnstile marks the spot. So disinterest yourself in my words. Disinterest yourself in anybody's words, In the beginning was the word and the word was bullshit. Yes sir, boys, it's hard to stop that old writing arm more of a habit than using. Been writing these RX's five hundred thousand years and sure hate to pack you boys in with a burning-down word habit. But I am of course guided by my medical ethics and the uh intervention of The Board of Health no more *no mas.* My writing arm

Dollar Dan and Little Boy Blue dead stars fading sad train whistles a distant sky. /"

"/ Stranger, forget seventy tons to the square inch and be gone at the flutes. Death takes over in busy lands ashes gutted cities of America and Europe. Empty air marks authority over all antagonists late afternoon on white steps of the set. See, the chains are fallen. Long long radio silence on Portland Place. Light years of youth flapping down a windy street with the torn September sky."

once. You heard in this Morocco night last voices hopelessly calling. Come closer smell of blood and excrement communicate directly.

"Good-bye Mister. I must go. *The tide is coming in at Hiroshima*. Exploded star between us."

is paralyzed ash, blown from an empty sleeve do our work and go. /"

Here comes the old knife-sharpener in lemon sun, light blue eyes reflected from a thin blade, blood on white steps of the sea-wall, afternoon shadow in dying eyes. "Good-bye, Mister. Get off the point. It is precisely time. It's you who have assembled from the broken streets of war and death the burning buckling deck of an exploding star. With wind and dust good-bye."

THE LAST POST *DANGER AHEAD*

Fort Charles
Sunday, September 17, 1899

A silent Sunday to the post our flag at half mast against tall black windows of the dormitory a distant voice so painful to scan out: '/ Enemy inter

"Last glimpse of a sad toy army paid all our strength click of distant heels over the hills and far away remember' / Laser gun *washing in present*

Wasn't anything to say. "Mr. Bradly Mr. Martin" stood there on dead stars heavy with his dusty answer drew September 17, 1899, over New York that morning giving

cepted September 17, 1899, over New York' Klinker is dead I knew him. Had no luck. Whistling 'Annie Laurie' against the frayed stars laser guns washing a sad toy

time rockets across the valley / *whole sky burning* /' This sad stranger never called retreat, Mister" torn sky in the ashen water frayed stars of youth

you my toy soldiers put away steps trailing a lonely dining room world I
created quite empty now light years of youth flapping down a windy street
with the

soldier down a postcard road books and toys put away bare feet twisted on a
fence there by the creek empty as his sad old tune 'that ne'er forgot will be'

there across the playground against tall black windows of the dormitory last
glimpse of a sad toy hand lifted far away:: 'Goodbye, Mister. I have opened
the gates

torn September sky' / Have I done the job here? Will he hear it? /' stump
of an arm dripping stars across the golf course smell of sickness in the room
these

telling you clear as the old sunlight over New York 'Enemy intercepted.' " /
telling me / laser guns washing egg nog' running two strainers closed down

for you" twisted coat on a bench—barely audible click: a distant voice so
painful stopped in Johnny's mind a distant hand fell from his shoulder just

foreign suburbs here cool remote Sunday telling you boy soldier never
called retreat frayed sizzling a distant hand fell here laser guns washing
light ye

"Cobble Stone Cody / Any second now the whole fucking shit house goes
up / Any-post-shit birds, let's see *your* arms / burning stump of mine just
telling you c

telling you a soldier spit blood for you here across the valley clear as the
luminous sky our flag is still there a transitory magazine must tell you the

ars over New York Little Boy Blue paid on the table far away never came
out that afternoon at recess time I watched the torn sky bend with the wind

lear as the sky 'enemy intercepted over New York' So, Mister, remember
me there on a windy street half buried in sand /" Sad calm boy speaking

price in smoke. We can break radio silence now 'Annie Laurie' was a code
tune just enemy intercepted September 17, 1899, over New York the Piper
pulled

stars splash the silver answer back on lost youth there books and toys
trailing blood down windy steps far away smell of ashes rising from the
typewriter

here on the shore dead stars splash his cheek bone with silver ash. This is fore
you distant hand lifted on a dead star Klinker is dead. A sad toy soldier

down the sky. Now he didn't go a-looking for to show you the papers clear
as 'Annie Laurie.' For half a line no repeat performance in *any* naborhood.
Last

a black silver star of broken film rockets across the valley all the light left on a
star drifting away down a windy street forever adios from this ad

steps from the lake from the hill from the sky.
Rockets fell here on these foreign suburbs********************
****

gun post erased in a small town newspaper******************
****
****

dress of blood and excrement. The cabin reeks of exploded star. *****
****
****

You can watch our worn out
film dim jerky far away
shut a bureau drawer *****

LAST AWNING FLAPS ON THE PIER

The town is built on a shelf of grey shale around an inlet of the lake. A pier of
rotting wood extends out into the shallow green water over bottomless ooze
infested by a species of poisonous worm. There is one small island in the inlet
on which grows a twisted swamp cypress. Beyond the inlet the green water
extends out into a vast delta with pockets here and there of deep black water
and finally the lake itself stretches to the sky. On the inland side the town is
surrounded by hardwood forest. The town people depend for food on game
from the forest and fish from the lake. Owing to the shallow water unnavi-
gable for a craft drawing more than a few inches, their boats are light structures mounted on pontoons with large sails to catch the faint winds stirring in
this area of terminal calm. The sails are made from old photos welded together
with a strong transparent glue, the pictures creating a low pressure area to
draw the winds of past time. They also fish from dirigibles under which are
slung a boat shaped cabin, the fragile craft floating a few feet above the water
propelled by pressure jets from a porcelain cylinder (there is no metal in this
area). The houses are made from blocks of grey shale soft as soapstone, the

entire town forming one hive-like structure built around the inlet. The town people are without words and sit for hours on the pier and on balconies and terraces overlooking the inlet silent and immobile as lizards following with their eyes patterns traced in iridescent ooze by movements of the worm.

On closer inspection the houses are seen to be made from old photos compacted into blocks which give off a sepia haze pervading the rooms streets and terraces of this dead silent rubbish heap of past times—(a parenthesis stagnant as the green water and the postcard sky)—On the inland side of hardwood forests live hunters and subsistence farmers who sell their pictures to the town people in return for the porcelain cylinders—Quote Greenbaum, early explorer.

Sad servant of the inland side shirt flapping trailing the smoke of hardwood forests offered us his pictures of a squirrel hunt—black rainwater and frogs in 1920 roads morning sleep of detour—luminous terraces moulded from old photos and leaves—silent grocer shops in cobblestone streets.

"Remember the needle beer at Sid's speakeasy?"

On the inland side a thin boy looked for me here on a St. Louis corner bits of silver paper in a wind across the park. Nothing here now shadow structure mounted on old newspapers of the world—(Caught a riot in Tangier from a passing transistor radio. Little winds stir papers on the city desk dirigibles through a violet sky rising from India ink)—Never the broken film opens for me again. Silence falls softly on my vigil from a black Cadillac.

"Remember the needle beer at Sid's speakeasy?"

Never the 1920 movie open to me again—smell of ashes in stone streets— his smile across the golf course—Last silent film stretches to the postcard sky. India ink shirt flapping down the lost streets a child sad as stagnant flowers.

"Remember I was abandoned long ago empty waiting on 1920 world in his eyes."

Silence by 1920 ponds in vacant lots. Last awning flaps on the pier last man here now.

February 22, 1965
New York

ST. LOUIS RETURN

(ticket to St. Louis and return in a first class room for two people who is the third that walks beside you?) After a parenthesis of more than forty years I met my old neighbor, Rives Skinker Mathews, in Tangier. I was born 4664 Berlin Avenue changed it to Pershing during the war. The Mathews family lived next door at 4660—red brick three-story houses separated by a gangway large back yard where I could generally see a rat one time or another from my bedroom window on the top floor. Well we get to talking St. Louis and "what happened to so and so" sets in and Rives Mathews really knows what happened to any so and so in St. Louis. His mother had been to dancing school with "Tommy Eliot"—(His socks wouldn't stay up. His hands were clammy. I will show you fear in dancing school)—Allow me to open a parenthesis you see Rives Mathews had kept a scrapbook of St. Louis years and his mother left a collection of visiting cards from the capitals of Europe. I was on my way back to St. Louis as I looked through Rives's scrapbook dim flickering pieces of T. S. Eliot rising from the pages—(But what have I my friend to give you put aside on another tray? Those cards were burned in my winter house fire, October 27, 1961—Comte Wladmir Sollohub Rashis Ali Khan Bremond d'ars Marquis de Migre St. John's College 21 Quai Malaquais Principe de la Tour—Gentilhomo di Palazzo—you're a long way from St. Louis and vice versa.)

"I want to reserve a drawing-room for St. Louis."

"A drawing-room? Where have you been?"

"I have been abroad."

"I can give you a bedroom or a roomette as in smaller."

"I will take the bedroom."

6:40 P.M. Loyal Socks Rapids out of New York for St. Louis—Settled in my bedroom surrounded by the luggage of ten years abroad I wondered how small a roomette could be. A space capsule is where you find it. December 23, 1964, enlisting the aid of my porter, a discreet Oriental personage and a far cry indeed from old "Yassah Boss George" of my day, a table was installed in this bedroom where I could set up my Facit portable and type as I looked out the train window. Snapping an occasional picture with my Zeiss Ikon, I could not but lament the old brass spittoons, the smell of worn leather, stale cigar smoke, steam iron and soot. Looking out the train window—click click clack—back back back—Pennsylvania Railroad en route four people in a drawing room::::One leafs through an old joke magazine called *LIFE:*—("What we want to know is who put the sand in the spinach?")—A thin boy in prep school clothes thinks this is funny. Ash gathers on his father's Havana held in a delicate grey cone the way it holds on a really expensive cigar. Father is reading *The Wall Street Journal.* Mother is putting on the old pancake, *The Green Hat* folded on her knee. Brother—"Bu" they call him—is looking out the train window. The time is 3 P.M. The train is one hour out of St. Louis, Missouri. Sad toy train it's a long way to go see on back each time place what I mean dim jerky far away. /*Take*/Look out the window of the train. Look. Postulate an observer Mr. B. from Pitman's Common Sense Arithmetic at Point X one light hour away from the train. Postulate further that Mr. B. is able to observe and photograph the family with a telescopic camera. Since the family image moving at the speed of light will take an hour to reach Mr. B., when he takes the 3 P.M. set the train is pulling into St. Louis Union Station at 4 P.M. St. Louis time George the porter there waiting for his tip. (Are you a member of the Union? Film Union 4 P.M.?) The family will be met at the station by plain Mr. Jones or Mr. J. if you prefer. (It was called Lost Flight. Newspapers from vacant lots in a back alley print shop lifted bodily out of a movie set the Editor Rives Mathews. Mr. and Mrs. Mortimer Burroughs and their two sons Mortimer Jr. and William Seward

Burroughs of 4664 Berlin Avenue changed it to Pershing during the war. I
digress I digress.)

Postulate another observer Mr. B-1 at Point X-1 two light hours away. The
train in his picture is now two light hours out of St. Louis at 2 P.M. still in the
diner. The train is stopped by a vacant lot distant 1920 wind and dust /*Take*/
remote foreign suburbs—end of a subdivision street—What a spot to land with
a crippled ship—sad train whistles cross a distant sky. See on back what I mean
each time place dim jerky far away not present except in you watching a 1920
movie out the train window? Returning to 1964 or what's left of it—December
23, 1964, if my memory serves I was thinking about a friend in New York
name of Mack Sheldon Thomas not a finer man in Interzone than old S.T.
has this loft apartment and every time he leaves the bathroom door open there
is a rat gets in the house so looking out the train window I see a sign: Able
Pest Control /*Take*/

"I tell you boss when you think something you see it—all Mayan according to the Hindu philosophizers," observed B. J. who fortunately does not
take up any space in the bedroom.

"B. J. there is no call to theorize from a single brass spittoon or even a
multiple smell of worn leather. You know I dislike theories."

"George! the nudes!"—(He knew of course that the nudes would be waiting for me in front of the Union Station.)

Look out the train window/*Take*/:acres of rusting car bodies—streams
crusted with yesterday's sewage—American flag over an empty field—Wilson
Stomps Cars—City of Xenia Disposal—South Hill a vast rubbish heap—Where
are the people? What in the name of Christ goes on here? Church of Christ /
Take/ crooked crosses in winter stubble—The porter knocks discreetly.

"Half an hour out of St. Louis, sir."

Yes the nudes are still there across from the station recollect once returning after a festive evening in East St. Louis hit a parked car 60 MPH thrown
out of the car rolled across the pavement and stood up feeling for broken bones
right under those monumental bronze nudes by Carl Milles Swedish sculptor
depict the meeting of the Missouri and Mississippi river waters. It was a long
time ago and my companion of that remote evening is I believe dead. (I digress I digress.)

But what has happened to Market Street the skid row of my adolescent years?
Where are the tattoo parlors, novelty stores, hock shops—brass knucks in a
dusty window—the seedy pitch men—("This museum shows all kinds social
disease and self abuse. Young boys need it special"—Two boys standing there
can't make up their mind whether to go in or not—One said later "I wonder
what was in that lousy museum?")—Where are the old junkies hawking and
spitting on street corners under the gas lights?—distant 1920 wind and dust—
box apartments each with its own balcony—Amsterdam—Copenhagen—
Frankfurt—London—anyplace.

Arriving at the Chase Plaza Hotel I was shown to a large double room a
first class room in fact for two people. Like a good European I spent some

time bouncing on the beds, testing the hot water taps, gawking at the towels
the soap the free stationery the television set—(And they call *us* hicks).

"This place is a paradise," I told B.J.

And went down to the lobby for the local papers which I check through
carefully for items or pictures that intersect amplify or illustrate any of my
writings past present or future. Relevant material I cut out and paste in a scrapbook—(some creaking hints—*por eso* I have survived) Relevant material I cut
out and paste in a scrapbook—(Hurry up please it's time)—For example, last
winter I assembled a page entitled *Afternoon Ticker Tape* which appeared in
My Magazine published by Jeff Nuttall of London. This page, an experiment
in newspaper format, was largely a rearrangement of phrases from the front
page of *The New York Times,* September 17, 1899, cast in the form of code
messages. Since some readers objected that the meaning was obscure to them
I was particularly concerned to find points of intersection, a decoding operation you might say relating the text to external coordinates: (From *Afternoon
Ticker Tape:* "Most fruitful achievement of the Amsterdam Conference a drunk
policeman"). And just here in the *St. Louis Globe Democrat* for December 23,
I read that a policeman has been suspended for drinking on duty slobbed out
drunk in his prowl car with an empty brandy bottle—(few more brandies
neat)—(From *A.T.T.:* "Have fun in Omaha")—And this item from Vermillion,
S.D.: "Omaha Kid sends jail annual note and $10"—Please use for nuts food
or smokes for any prisoners stuck with Christmas in your lousy jail" signed
"The Omaha Kid"—(From *A. T. T.:* "What sort of eels called Retreat 23?")—
St. Louis Globe Democrat: "A sixth army spokesman stated two more bodies
recovered from the Eel River. Deaths now total 23."—(From *A. T. T.:* "Come
on Tom it's your turn now")—*St. Louis Post Dispatch:* "Tom Creek overflows
its banks."

Unable to contain himself B.J. rolled on the bed in sycophantic convulsions: "I tell you boss you write it and it happens. Why if you didn't write me
I wouldn't be here."

I told him tartly that such seeming coincidence was no doubt frequent
enough if people would just keep their eyes and ears open. We descended to
The Tenderloin Room for dinner where I was introduced to an American
speciality: baked potato served with sour cream. Ausgezeichnitt.

"I tell you boss you couldn't touch this food in Paris for anywhere near the
price."

The next day very mild and warm I walked around the old neighborhood
which is not far to walk now the old Bixby place used to be right where the
hotel is now and I passed it every day as a child on my way to Forest Park with
brother "Bu" and our English governess who always told me:—"Don't ask
questions and don't pass remarks"—. This cryptic injunction I have been forced
to disregard for professional reasons, you understand. So prowling about with
my camera looking for 1920 scraps—bits of silver paper in the wind—
sunlight on vacant lots—The Ambassador—"Home With A Heart"—where
an old friend Clark St. lived—4664 still there looking just the same—("Do

you mind if I take a few pictures? used to live here you know.")—so few people on the street—Convent Of The Sacred Heart—This message on a stone wall— "Gay—Lost—" the houses all look empty—It was not given to me to find a rat but I did photograph several squirrels (offered us his pictures of a squirrel hunt)—So back to my quiet remote room and my scrapbooks.

"Ash pits—an alley—a rat in the sunlight—It's all here," I tapped my camera, "all the magic of past times like the song says right under your eyes back in your own back yard. Why are people bored? Because they can't see what is right under their eyes right in their own back yard. And why can't they see what is right under their eyes?—(Between the eye and the object falls the shadow)—And that shadow, B.J., is the *pre-recorded word*."

"Oh sir you slobbered a bimfull."

"Like I come out here to see 'a bunch of squares in Hicksville'? Well I will see just that. I come here to see what I see and that's another story. Any number of stories. Walk around the block keeping your eyes open and you can write a novel about what you see—down in the lobby last night—smoky rose sunset across the river."

"The river is in the other direction boss."

"So what? Shift a few props. Now would you believe it people are sitting there with their back to that sunset."

"I don't want to believe it boss."

"B.J., remember the roller coaster at Forest Park Highlands?"

"I sure do boss. Why one time me and that Mexican girl used to work in the Chink laundry on Olive Street—"

"All right, B.J., cut. From now on we run a clean show. A show you can take your kids and your grandmother to see it. Just good clean magic for all the family. Remember Thurston?"

"I sure do boss. He made a white elephant disappear."

"Exactly—a white elephant—all our grey junk yesterdays—everything sharp and clear like after the rain."

At this point B. J. jumped to his feet, opened an umbrella and bellowed out "April Showers"—(White rain sloshed down—a wall of water you understand.)

"All right, B.J., cut!"

Sunday December 27 driving around St. Louis with brother "Bu" stopping here and there to take pictures—The Old Courthouse and all the records */Take/* and there by the river across the river depending on which way you come on it is the arch still under construction at that time 600 feet high when they finished it—(Gateway To The West)—has an ominous look like the only landmark to survive an atomic blast or other natural catastrophe */Take/*cobblestone streets along the levee—refuse of river boat days—strata of brick and masonry—geology of a city—MacArthur Bridge */Take/*and just *there* a truck will crash through the guard rail and fall 75 feet killing the driver you can see the dotted line in the *Post Dispatch* picture */Take/* River Queen and the Admiral just like they used to be red plush guilt the lot cruising down the river on a Sunday afternoon.

"Shall we take in the West End?"

Clayton and the West End suburbs now built up beyond recognition after 20 years' absence. In the 1920s my family moved out west on the Price Road— 700 S. /*Take*/ and just down the road is the John Burroughs School and there is the locker room door /*Take*/ where I stood one afternoon a long time ago and watched the torn sky bend with the wind lightning struck the school just *there*/*Take*/(Whoever said lightning never strikes twice in the same place was no photographer.)—1929 tornado if my memory serves when all the records went up name and address old arch there by the river with the cold spring news.

"Cruising Down the River on a Sunday Afternoon"—(This music across the water—The Veiled Prophet Ball off stage)—On the scene photographs by William Born Field *St. Louis Magazine* 52, Retarded Children's Project, young St. Louis citizens bicentennial salute: (Happy New Year Comte Hector Perrone de San Martine Mrs. Edge at home last Thursday in May, Fete Die, Principle de la Tour, Gentilhomo di Palazzo, you're a long retarded children project veiled way from St. Louis. I, Famous Bar Prophet, had not thought Death Magazine 52 had undone so many for I have known them all: Baron Rashid Pierre de Cobo—Helen Zapiola Theresa Riley—I digress I digress.)

"Now what in Horton Vernet Gen-San Martine Zapiolo The Swan Last Day de Cobo Principe di Castel Hose it Chicale Randy Veiled Miguel Garcia de Rube Gordon Hell does that mean?" interjected B.J.

(A long review—human voices—*They* expected answers?)

Family Reunion at my Aunt K's. B.J. has observed with his usual astuteness in such matters that there is only half a bottle of whiskey on the side board, volunteered for bartender duty surreptitiously serving himself double measure so when another bottle is produced rather sooner than later we both feel a little well you know B.J. is an old Alcohol Anonymous as used to electrify the meetings with his confessions: "Once at the house of a friend" he begins sepulchrally "in the dead of night—I"—he stabs a finger at his chest— "sneaked into the room of my host's adolescent son." He tiptoes across the platform and turns to the audience. "You get the picture?" The audience stirs uneasily. B.J. shifts an imaginary flashlight—"arrowheads—a stone axe— butterfly trays—the cyanide jar—a stuffed owl—Whoo whoo whoo drank the alcohol off the boy's preserved centipede?"—It was emetic in the good sense. (I digress—a drunk policeman—Stein reverts to his magazine.)

I address myself to a cousin who is now account executive for an advertising firm: "What I say is time for the artist and the ad man to get in a symbiotic way and give birth to what we may call 'Creative Advertising' I mean advertisements that tell a story and create character. Like this see? So you handle the Southern Comfort account?"

"Ty Bradly river boat gambler at your service, suh." His blue eyes fixed quizzically on the barmaid's ample bosom, he drawled out "I'll take double Southern Comfort, Ma'am."

"Pardon me are you Colonel Bradly? Colonel Ty Bradly?"

Bradly turned to face the question his eyes unbluffed unreadable two fingers in a vest pocket rested lightly on the cold blue steel of his Remington derringer.

"I am suh."

"Yeah and think what we could do with the Simmons Mattress account," interjected B.J.

(All right, B.J., /Cut.!/) See what I mean? glamour romance—Inspector J. Lee of the Nova Police smokes Players—(flashes his dirty rotten hunka tin)—Agent K9 uses a Bradly laser gun—Advertisements should provide the same entertainment value as the content of a magazine. *Your* product deserves the best. Why make up silly jingles? Why not use the good old songs like "Annie Laurie." There's a story goes with that song. Remember a young cop whistling "Annie Laurie" down cobblestone streets? Then he stopped in the corner saloon for a glass of Budweiser which he couldn't have done really being on duty. Yes he would have approved your favorite smoke. Show your cards all *Players.* And remember a young cop whistling "Annie Laurie" down cobblestone streets twirling his club drew September 17, 1899, over St. Louis.

(The sky goes out against his back.)

Mr. Dickson Terry of the *St. Louis Post Dispatch* interviews your reporter: "As you know in the 1890s St. Louis was famous throughout the world for such restaurants as Tony Faust—But when I was last here twenty years ago there was not a first class eating place to be found in the city"—You might say all the uh flavor had been siphoned off into the subdivisions and country clubs of the West End—This process is now being reversed—any number of excellent restaurants—three in fact right here in the Chase Plaza Hotel—a movement *back* to the city—*back* to the 1890s finds expression in Gas Light Square and the refurbished river boats—yes decidedly the reversal of a trend which I for one found deplorable—and that is what I am getting at in this seemingly obscure passage." I taped a text on the table between us, a text using the three column format of a small town newspaper.

THE MOVING TIMES

September 17, 1899, Mr. Bradly Mr. Martin stood there on dead stars heavy with his dusty answer drew September 17, 1899, over New York that morning giving you my toy soldiers put away in the attic.

Attic of the Eugene Field House you understand never happened. Remember the *Mary Celeste?* ghost ship abandoned back in 1872 all sails set nobody on board fresh southerly winds a long time ago for such a purpose? Now here is the front page of the *Chicago Tribune* Monday, January 4, 1965, The American Paper For Americans:

Tempest Hurls 807 On Ship Like Ten-pins—16 Hurt in Nightmare.

The American liner *Independence*—North Atlantic storm—ripped open a weather door on a lower deck smashed a porthole on an upper deck and hurled half a ton of ice water on a couple asleep—(presumably waking them)—Captain Riley of the *Independence* described the storm as the worst he had encountered in more than 40 years at sea. "It was like riding a roller coaster."

("By the way, B.J. what ever happened to Forest Park Highlands?"

"It burned down, boss—hot peep shows in the penny arcade.")

Well now it so happens that I repatriated myself on the *Independence* docked December 8, 1964, if my memory serves. I had the pleasure of meeting Captain Riley at the Captain's Cocktail Party where no one seemed to know who anybody else was supposed to be and everybody a bit miffed in consequence. I approached the Captain directly: "Captain, may I ask you a question? a *novelist's* question?" (For I was you understand the distinguished novelist of whom nobody had heard.)

"Why uh yes," he replied guardedly.

"Please tell me Captain quite frankly do you have any theories or guesses in short any shall we say *notions* with regard to the *Mary Celeste?*"

He replied after a short pause that he could think of no explanation that accounted for all the facts.

"Captain," I stated firmly, "the plain fact is that there are no facts. I myself—and I may tell you in strictest confidence that I was once a private investigator—have sifted this matter to the bottom most deep and established every reason to doubt that such a ship as the *Mary Celeste* ever existed. The whole thing was a fabrication out of whole cloth or paper more precisely—The Captain's Log Book you understand"—and I gave him a straight look—"Is this the starboard side?" I asked.

"Why yes it is."

"Ah—just so—you see—"

So with the picture of that old sea dog shifting slightly as the ship rolled ports of the world in his eyes and a picture postcard of the *SS Independence* pasted into my own log of the voyage steaming across a paper sea just as empty as the *Mary Celeste*—paper you understand—not a passenger in sight—well just so—"The American paper for Americans—*Independence*—"

So I make these last entries in the log book of my St. Louis return—luggage stacked in the lobby—back through the ruins of Market Street to the Union Station nudes waiting there in the dry fountain of an empty square—I have returned to pick up a few pieces of sunlight and shadow—silver paper in the wind-frayed sounds of a distant city.

from
the third mind

(with Brion Gysin)

THE EXTERMINATOR

Let petty kings the name of party know
Where I come I kill both friend and foe.

San Francisco, 1960. The Human Being are strung lines of word associates that control "thoughts feelings and *apparent* sensory impressions." Quote from Encephalographic Research, Chicago, Written in *TIME.* See and hear what They expect to see and hear because The Word Lines Keep Thee in Slots . . .

Cut the Word Lines with scissors or switchblade as preferred . . . The Word Lines keep you in Time. . . Cut the in lines . . . Make out lines to Space. Take a page of your own writing if you write or a letter or a newspaper article or a page or less or more of any writer living and or dead . . . Cut into sections. Down the middle. And across the sides . . . Rearrange the sections . . . Write the result message . . .

Who wrote the original words is still there in any rearrangement of his or her or whatever words . . . Can recognize Rimbaud cut-up as Rimbaud . . . A Melville cut-up as Melville . . . Shakespeare moves with Shakespeare words . . . So forth anybody can be Rimbaud if he will cut up Rimbaud's words and learn Rimbaud language talk think Rimbaud . . . And supply reasonably appropriate meat. All dead poets and writers can be reincarnate in different hosts.

Cut-up . . . Raise standard of writer production to a point of total and permanent competition of all minds living and dead Out Space. Concurrent . . .

No one can conceal what is saying cut-up . . . You can cut the Truth out of any written or spoken words//
Light Lines Pulling All Knights Ten Age Future Time.
From The Brass and Copper Street . . . In sick body . . . His Feet of Void . . . H seemed to be the Leader of the Dry Air . . . Brought up Young European. Backdrop of Swiss Lakes . . . Certain Formalities . . . That simplified *everything.*

"I represent the lithe aloof young men of The Breed charmingly. Everyone here is from The American Women with a delicate lilt. We are all empowered to make arrests and enough with just the right shade of show you."

270

A Mexican Beach Boy was empty . . . Allies wait on knives valicided with the corny positions . . . Virginia Reel Commitments in The Fulton . . . Royal Crowns drew a short .22 and out of date devices The Caribbean swelled to take Punishment Wisconsin He Advantages. Street gangs Uranian . . . Uranian Gum Sir. Chewing Gum Conditions.

Lesser crimes pudgy and no good conditions. Out Show included assault and murder or Reality . . . Will Hollywood never leave? Decide The Pavement was Unimaginable Disaster? King H in Tanganyika? Or was it? . . . Policemen back from shadows *too*?

Light across Long Island flickers through the Junk Antennae. Vulture wings husk in the swimming pool. A Cadillac will accrete The Ice. Typical Sights leak out . . . The Boys drift in from Work H Sling . . .

They are rebuilding The City Lee Knows in Four Letter Words . . . Vibrating Air Hammers the Code Write.

The stars out for you . . . "You don't get it if I don't."

A Brown Architect . . . Unknown and probably hostile . . . Muttering leg in the night . . . On the Tracks I told . . . The West Side push You on tacks.

The Beware Look went wrong . . . Cement Shoe in the Junk Dawn . . . Shining Sores scan a Silver Message: You Strictly from Monkey without the Utilities Trak Service . . .

But the Manikin was unable to confirm the Account.

"You crazy or something walk around alone?"

Vote handed Moscow Full Body . . . Assailant fell from High Lavatory . . .

Evidence he said water taste of Rome . . . Uncle from America educative laughing . . . Venus with Doctor Gold . . . A lone survivor flight . . . Venus he was incorporated . . .

Thing wilder America . . . Unequal scar . . . Never healed . . . Students signaled out for this treatment . . . Can be telescope in Paris TV Program . . . New Zealand along The Miss River . . . Board a second-class Citizen back to Germany . . . Vichy two-tone the area . . .

Undamaged but both died . . . Webster Discovery brings personal check or . . . Part of the Public Domain . . . Creamed spinach or violence . . . Dead Hand stretching the Vegetable People . . .

She raised to A Writer Gertrude Stein and one a prisoner Shakespeare . . . We operate great Hate Box . . . Are also a Martin Executive . . .

Program Late 1962 Future Time New Look for touring on Venus . . . *Not* the scientific . . . Telecommunications said these findings wrong.

Bad shape from Death . . . Mr Shannon no cept pay . . . Nothing can except Me Ass At . . . Tells me we do in Paris . . . My heart drink only desert words.

Know here inadvisable to say The Spanish of next year hats in green neon . . . So I moved on the junk he used . . . In a burst of young . . . Flooding the world market with Star Pretties . . .

The Board Vote handed Moscow full kidney . . . He was fiving away the Human Body . . . Assailant fled him as being five feet tall . . . Asked me to spend the evening in the company of the kidney structure. The Donor was revealed police said wearing a crew cut.

No Good Pool . . . Typical sights leak out . . . Any point on the road he is . . . Raw and bleeding he gave out sistence of purpose . . . refractory mirrors between us dafted A Tainted through the Viscous Fish Market.

Street Gangs Uranium Gum Sir . . . Of Chewing gum conditions. Out Show included sleeping pills in Backward Countries . . . Shit Customs perhaps with disaster? Shadows too.

Afterward we would go git rich in shorts . . . His wife murmuring over and over: "Will accrete the ice."

Small talk of Practical Politics bluntly it was Russian. The First Man Protestor to be rocketed to The Moon.

THE FUTURE OF THE NOVEL

In my writing I am acting as a map maker, an explorer of psychic areas, to use the phrase of Mr Alexander Trocchi, as a cosmonaut of inner space, and I see no point in exploring areas that have already been thoroughly surveyed— A Russian scientist has said: "We will travel not only in space but in time as well—" That is to travel in space is to travel in time—If writers are to travel in space time and explore areas opened by the space age, I think they must develop techniques quite as new and definite as the techniques of physical space travel—Certainly if writing is to have a future it must at least catch up with the past and learn to use techniques that have been used for some time past in painting, music and film—Mr Lawrence Durrell has led the way in developing a new form of writing with time and space shifts as we see events from different viewpoints and realize that so seen they are literally not the same events, and that the old concepts of time and reality are no longer valid—Brion Gysin, an American painter living in Paris, has used what he calls "the cut-up method" to place at the disposal of writers the collage used in painting for fifty years—Pages of text are cut and rearranged to form new combinations of word and image—In writing my last two novels, *Nova Express* and *The Ticket That Exploded*, I have used an extension of the cut-up method I call "the fold-in method"—A page of text—my own or someone else's—is folded down the middle and placed on another page—The composite text is then read across half one text and half the other—The fold-in method extends to writing the flashback used in films, enabling the writer to move backward and forward on his time track—For example I take page one and fold it into page one hundred—I insert the resulting composite as page ten—When the reader reads page ten he is flashing forward in time to page one hundred and back in time to page one—the *déjà vu* phenomenon can so be produced to order—This method is of course used in music, where we are continually moved backward and forward on the time track by repetition and rearrangements of musical themes—

In using the fold-in method I edit, delete and rearrange as in any other method of composition—I have frequently had the experience of writing some pages of straight narrative text which were then folded in with other pages and found that the fold-ins were clearer and more comprehensible than the original texts—Perfectly clear narrative prose can be produced using the fold-in method—Best results are usually obtained by placing pages dealing with similar subjects in juxtaposition—

What does any writer do but choose, edit and rearrange material at his disposal?—The fold-in method gives the writer literally infinite extension of choice—Take for example a page of Rimbaud folded into a page of St John Perse—(two poets who have much in common)—From two pages an infinite number of combinations and images are possible—The method could also lead to a collaboration between writers on an unprecedented scale to produce works that were the composite effort of any number of writers living and dead—This happens in fact as soon as any writer starts using the fold-in method—I have made and used fold-ins from Shakespeare, Rimbaud, from newspapers, magazines, conversations and letters so that the novels I have written using this method are in fact composites of many writers—

I would like to emphasize that this is a technique and like any technique will, of course, be useful to some writers and not to others—In any case a matter for experimentation not argument—The conferring writers have been accused by the press of not paying sufficient attention to the question of human survival—In *Nova Express* (reference is to an exploding planet) and *The Ticket That Exploded,* I am primarily concerned with the question of survival—with nova conspiracies, nova criminals, and nova police—A new mythology is possible in the space age where we will again have heroes and villains with respect to intentions toward this planet—

NOTES ON THESE PAGES

To show "the fold-in method" in operation I have taken the two texts I read at The Writers' Conference and folded them into newspaper articles on The Conference, The Conference Folder, typed out selections from various writers, some of whom were present and some of whom were not, to form a composite of many writers living and dead: Shakespeare, Samuel Beckett, T. S. Eliot, F. Scott Fitzgerald, William Golding, Alexander Trocchi, Norman Mailer, Colin MacInnes, Hugh MacDiarmid.

Mr Bradly–Mr Martin, in my mythology, is a God that failed, a God of Conflict in two parts so created to keep a tired old show on the road, The God of Arbitrary Power and Restraint, Of Prison and Pressure, who needs subordinates, who needs what he calls "his human dogs" while treating them with the contempt a con man feels for his victims—But remember the con man needs the Mark—The Mark does not need the con man—Mr Bradly–Mr Martin needs his "dogs" his "errand boys" his "human animals"—He needs them because he is literally blind. They do not need him. In my mythological

system he is overthrown in a revolution of his "dogs"—"Dogs that were his
eyes shut off Mr Bradly–Mr Martin."

"The ticket that exploded posed little time so I'll say good night."

bath cubicle . . . lapping water over the concrete floor . . . pants slide . . .
twisting thighs . . . penny arcades of an old dream . . . played the flute, shirt
flapping down the cool path . . . on the 30th of July a distant room left no
address . . . sleep breath . . . pale dawn wallpaper . . . faded morning . . . a place
forgotten . . . a young man is dust and shredded memories naked empty a ding-
dong bell . . . what in St Louis after September? . . . curtains . . . red light . . .
blue eyes in the tarnished mirror pale fingers fading from ruined suburbs . . .
fingers light and cold pulled up his pants . . . dark pipes call #23 . . . you touched
from frayed jacket masturbated under thin pants . . . cracked pavements . . .
sharp fish smells and dead eyes in doorways . . . soccer scores . . . the rotting
kingdom . . . ghost hands at the paneless café . . .

"Like good-bye, Johnny. On the 30th of July death left no address."

outskirts of the city . . . bare leg hairs . . . lunar fingers light and cold . . .
distant music under the slate roof . . . soccer scores . . . the street blew rain . . .
dawn shadow . . .

"Like good-bye, Johnny."

cold blue room . . . distant music on the wind . . . tarnished mirror in the
bath cubicle young face lapping water. . . red light . . . felt his pants slide . . .
twisting thighs . . . street dust on bare leg hairs . . . open shirt . . . city sounds
under the slate roof . . . played the flute with fingers fading . . . the street blew
rain . . . pale smell of dawn in the door . . . played the flute with fingers light
and cold . . . dark pipes left no address . . . sleep breath under the slate roof . . .
silence ebbing from rose wallpaper. . . outskirts of the city masturbated under
thin pants ten-year-old keeping watch . . . outside East St. Louis . . . cracked
pavement . . . sharp scent of weeds . . . faded khaki pants . . . soccer scores . . .
the driver shrugged . . . violence roared past the Café de France . . . he dressed
hastily shirt flapping . . .

"Like good-bye, Johnny."

wind through the curtains . . . bare iron frame of a dusty bed . . . in the
tarnished mirror dead eyes of an old dream and the dreamer gone at dawn
shirt . . . takes his way toward the sea breath of the trade winds on his face
open shirt flapping . . . cool path from ruined suburbs . . . stale memories . . .
excrement mixed with flowers . . . fly full of dust pulled up his pants . . . birdcalls . . . lapping water . . . a distant cool room . . . leg hairs rub rose wallpaper . . . pale dawn shirt in the door . . . sharp smell of weeds . . . you touched
frayed jacket . . . mufflers . . . small pistols . . . quick fires from bits of driftwood . . . fish smells and dead eyes in doorways . . . a place forgotten . . . the
ancient rotting kingdom . . . ghost hands at paneless windows . . . dust and
shredded memories of war and death . . . petrified statues in a vast charred
plain . . .

in a rubbish heap to the sky Metal chess determined gasoline fires and smoke
in motionless air—Smudge two speeds—DSL walks "here" beside me on ex-

tension lead from hairless skull—Flesh-smeared recorder consumed by slow metal fires—Dog-proof room important for our "oxygen" lines—Group respective recorder layout—"Throw the gasoline on them" determined the life form we invaded: insect screams—I woke up with "marked for invasion" recording set to run for as long as phantom "cruelties" are playing back while waiting to pick up Eduardo's "corrupt" speed and volume variation Madrid—Tape recorder banks tumescent flesh—Our mikes planning speaker stood there in 1910 straw word—Either way is a bad move to The Biologic Stairway—The whole thing tell you—No good—*No bueno* outright or partially—The next state walking in a rubbish heap to Form A—Form A directs sound channels heat—White flash mangled down to a form of music—Life Form A as follows was alien focus—Broken pipes refuse "oxygen"—Form A parasitic wind identity fading out—"Word falling—Photo falling" flesh-smeared counter-orders—determined by last Electrician—Alien mucus cough language learned to keep all Board Room Reports waiting sound formations—Alien mucus tumescent code train on Madrid—Convert in "dirty pictures S"—simple repetition—Whole could be used as model for a bad move—Better than shouts: "No good—*No bueno*"—

TECHNICAL DEPOSITION OF THE VIRUS POWER

"Gentlemen, it was first suggested that we take our own image and examine how it could be made more portable. We found that simple binary coding systems were enough to contain the entire image however they required a large amount of storage space until it was found that the binary information could be written at the molecular level, and our entire image could be contained within a grain of sand. However it was found that these information molecules were not dead matter but exhibited a capacity for life which is found elsewhere in the form of virus. Our virus infects the human and creates our image in him.

"We first took our image and put it into code. A technical code developed by the information theorists. This code was written at the molecular level to save space, when it was found that the image material was not dead matter, but exhibited the same life cycle as the virus. This virus released upon the world would infect the entire population and turn them into our replicas, it was not safe to release the virus until we could be sure that the last groups to go replica would not notice. To this end we invented variety in many forms, variety that is of information content in a molecule, which, *enfin*, is always a permutation of the existing material. Information speeded up, slowed down, permutated, changed at random by radiating the virus material with high-energy rays from cyclotrons, in short we have created an infinity of variety at the information level, sufficient to keep so-called scientists busy forever exploring the 'richness of nature.'

"It was important all this time that the possibility of a human ever conceiving of being without a body should not arise. Remember that the variety we invented was permutation of the electromagnetic structure of matter energy interactions which are not the raw material of nonbody experience."

"Recorders fix nature of absolute need: *occupy*—*'Here'*—Any cruelties answer him—Either unchanged or reverse—Clang—Sorry—Planet trailing somewhere along here—Sequential choice—Flesh plots *con su medicina*—The next state according to—Stop—Look—Form A directs sound channels—Well what now?—Final switch if you want to—Dead on Life Form B by cutting off machine if you want to—Blood form determined by the switch—Same need—Same step—Not survive in any "emotion"—Intervention?—It's no use I tell you—Familiar will be the end product?—Reciprocate complete wires? You fucking can't—Could we become part of the array?—In the American Cemetery—Hard to distinguish maps came in at the verbal level—This he went to Madrid?—And so *sí* learned? The accused was beyond altered arrival—So?—So mucus machine runs by feeding in over the American—Hear it?—Paralleled the bell—Hours late—They all went away—You've thought it out?—A whole replaced history of life burial tapes being blank?—Could this 'you' 'them' 'whatever' learn? Accused was beyond altered formations—No good—Machine runs by feeding in 'useless'—Blood spilled over Grey Veil—Parallel spurt—How many looking at dirty pictures?—Before London Space Stage tenuous face maybe—Change—Definite—The disorder gets you model for behavior—Screams?—Laughter?"—Voice fading into advocate:

"Clearly the whole defense must be experiments with two tape recorder mutations."

Again at the window that never was mine—Reflected word scrawled by some boy—Greatest of all waiting lapses—Five years—The ticket exploded in the air—For I don't know—*I do not know* human dreams—Never was mine—Waiting lapse—Caught in the door—Explosive fragrance—Love between light and shadow—The few who lived cross the wounded galaxies—Love?—Five years I grew muttering in the ice—Dead sun reached flesh with its wandering dream—Buried tracks, Mr Bradly, so complete was the lie—Course—Naturally—Circumstances now Spanish—Hermetic you understand—Locked in her heart of ooze—A great undersea blight—Atlantis along the wind in green neon—The ooze is only colorless question drifted down—Obvious one at that—Its goal?—That's more difficult to tap on the pane—One aspect of virus—An obvious one again—Muttering in the dogs for generalizations—The lice we intersect—Poison of dead sun anywhere else—What was it the old crab man said about the lice?—Parasites on "Mr Martin"—My ice my perfect ice that never circumstances—Now Spanish cautiously my eyes—And I became the form of a young man standing—My pulse in unison—Never did I know resting place—Wind hand caught in the door—cling—Chocada—to tap on the pane—

Chocada—Again—Muttering in the dogs—Five years—Poison of dead sun with her—With whom?—I dunno—See account on the crooked crosses—And your name?—Berg?—Berg?—Bradly?—"Mr Martin *sí*" Disaster Snow—Crack—Sahhk—Numb—Just a fluke came in with the tide and The Swedish River of Gothenberg—

"I fancy," said the man, "this gentleman feels totally stupid and greedy Venus Power—Tentacles write out message from stairway of slime—"

"That's us—Strictly from 'Sogginess is Good for You'—Planning no bones but an elementary nervous system—Scarcely answer him—"

"The case simply at terminal bring down point—Desperate servants suddenly taken out of their hands—Insane orders and counterorders on the horizon—And I playing psychic chess determined the whole civilization and personal habits—"

"Iron claws of pain and pleasure with two speeds—with each recorder in body prison working our 'here' on extension leads—Even for an instant not in operation the host recorded saw the loudspeakers—Way is doomed in relatively soundproof 'room'—Would shift door led to the array—Many recorders important for our oxygen lines—Each to use host connected to its respective recorder layout—For example with nine recorders determined the life form we invaded by three square—Each recorder marked for invasion recording—You see it's only 'here' fixes nature of need set to run for as long as required—'Indignities' and 'cruelties' are playing back while other record—'Intimidate' and 'corrupt' speed and volume variation—Squeeze host back into system—Any number of tape recorders banked together for ease of operation switch in other places—Our mikes are laid out preferably in 'fresh air'—That's us—Planning speaker and mike connected to host—Scarcely answer him—Of course static and moving are possible—Very simplest array would be three lines—Two speeds can be playing especially when a 'case' has four possible states—Fast manipulation suddenly taken out of slow playback—The actual advocate from biologic need in many ways—

"a—Simple hand switching advocate

"b—Random choice fixed interval biologic stairway—The whole thing is switched on either outright or partially—at any given time recorders fix nature of absolute need—Thus sound played back by any 'cruelties' answer him either unchanged or subject to alien plane—

"c—Sequential choice i.e. flesh frozen to amino acid determines the next state according to"—That is a "book"—

Form A directs sound channels—Continuous operation in such convenient Life Form B—Final switching off of tape cuts "oxygen" Life Form B by cutting off machine will produce cut-up of human form determined by the switching chosen—Totally alien "music" need not survive in any "emotion" due to the "oxygen" rendered down to a form of music—Intervention directing all movement what will be the end product?—Reciprocation detestable to us for how could we become part of the array?—Could this metal impression follow to present language learning?—Talking and listening machine led in and replaced—

Life Form A as follows was an alien—The operator selects the most "oxygen" appropriate material continuous diving suit back to our medium—Ally information at the verbal level—Could he keep Form A seen parasitic?—Or could end be achieved by present interview?—Array treated as a whole replaced history of life? Word falling photo falling tapes being blank—Insane orders and counterorders of machine "music"—The Police Machine will produce a cut-up of it determined by the switching chosen—Could this alien mucus cough language learn? Accused was beyond altered sound formations—Alien Mucus Machine runs by feeding in overwhelming gravity—Code on Grey Veil parallel the spread of "dirty pictures"—Reverse instruction raises question how many convert in "dirty pictures" before London Space Stage—Tenuous simple repetition to one machine only—Coughing enemy pulled in whole could be used as a model for behavior—Screams laughter shouts raw material—Voice fading into advocate:

"Clearly the whole defense must be experiments with two tape recorder mutations."

One faulty tape recorder . . . I'm almost out of medicine.

A single injection of radioactive past times . . . train whistles . . . blue twilight . . . "I'm the only complete man in the industry," he said. But, then, he noticed other people got on his frozen nerves a bit. . . . Well, that was easily enough taken care of: he can throw a black blast of antienergy withers a French waiter. Then, he noticed he had to keep throwing that blast to keep his cool, blue place. . . . Get up the score and send it back to the Home Office or: *"Over and out!"*

When a Trak Agent walks out of the Board Room, the Board Members look after him and say: "Errand boy." We are all "Coolies" and we need the cool that flows out when we all freeze into each other's eyes and say: "Errand boy." Then the cool flows out on a blue wave, cold and blue as liquid air swirling across dark bank floors, piling up in corners and vaults while a soft rain of bank notes falls through us. We sit there in our blue slate houses, wrapped in orange flesh robes that grow on us . . . now you understand about Time?

Time *is* junk. Time is radioactive.

There was something wrong with the house. The agent had not wished to show it or even admit he had such a house listed. It was his young assistant, Abdulla, who took us to #4 calle Larachi on the Marshan. (As he was getting out of the cab, the door slammed on his thumb.) We should have known. However, the house looked charming on a quiet side street shadowed by trees. We even thought the little Arab children were cute as they gathered about us smiling:

"*Fingaro?* One cigarette?"

The old bearded man who served as guard for the large villa across the street was, we decided, straight out of *The Arabian Nights.* The house seemed to be conveniently laid out: two bedrooms facing the street and a bedroom in back with a window opening onto the garden of the next-door villa. This room bathed in a cool underwater green light, I immediately annexed for my own. The kitchen was dark, since the only light came from a high, grated window.

The lavatory, located next to the kitchen, was simply a hole in the floor; not so different from the hotel in Paris. The floors were tiled . . . easy to keep clean. Upstairs was a large room running the length of the house with a balcony facing on the street; leaf shadows dancing on the white plaster walls. We would fix it up Arab style with benches and low coffee tables. This would be our reception room. There was a small cell-like room facing the back garden, with a single window like a square of blue set in the wall. The roof was flat and we planned a summer house up there of split bamboo with straw mats under trellised vines. I do not recall that I felt any twinges of foreboding on that remote summer day. (The young man's thumbnail was already turning black.)

We had been house hunting for two weeks and this was the first thing we had seen that seemed at all possible. Still, why had the agent been so reluctant to show it? A haunted house? As it turned out, the house was very precisely haunted and haunted by pre-sent time . . . the time when the flat roof would leak down the damp walls of flaking plaster where slugs would crawl, leaving iridescent trails of slime and green mold would form on my shoes and coat lapels . . . the dark kitchen stacked with dirty dishes . . . kerosene heaters smoking and gone out. The old man from *The Arabian Nights* coming to work for us . . . such a find, we thought . . . and stealing all the shirts and towels while always asking for more money. The naborhood children sneering and hostile, banging on the door to sell flowers or ask for cigarettes . . . throwing rocks through the skylight . . . children . . . beggars . . . someone always at the door, despising you if you gave money: insulting you if you didn't . . .

All this did not manifest itself until some months after we had moved in, July 15, 1963, and, then, it seemed to happen quite suddenly, as if invisible wheels had fallen into alignment. By early spring, February and March 1964, life in that house was Hell . . .

A single injection of radioactive mind that way; Yes, you think: I am the only complete man in a large room . . . other people dancing on the white plaster walls . . . reassured each other we didn't really . . . train whistles, blue twilight, beautiful blue thing you got . . . Keep clean, we told each other . . . well, benches and low coffee tables . . . a blast of blue in your slate house . . . a French waiter withers in the wall . . . Sit there in blue twilight . . . radioactive mats . . . yes, we would sleep . . . yes, he found that remote summer day . . . if I felt his heavy blue fix . . . two weeks and this was the first thing . . . low . . . there was something wrong . . . house of split bamboo with vines . . . ever try kicking that habit? There under the stars . . . (The stars out for you: *You* don't get it if *I* don't) . . . I do not recall . . . got in his way somehow. . . interfered with any twinges of foreboding . . . young . . . didn't have the blast . . . tuned flat, of course . . . we planned you right to metal . . . As it turned out very precisely, assistant Abdulla would leak. A haunted house, a house listed it was haunted by his young pre-sent time . . . the time: calle Larachi . . . Abdulla, who took us to #4 . . . the door slammed . . . green mold on my shoes, however, the house looked charming on dishes . . . kerosene heaters that smoked . . . damp slimy walls . . . thumbs . . .

we should have known the dark kitchen stacked with dirty little Arab children . . .
Arabian knights who came to work for us smiling: "*Fingaro?* One cigarette?"
. . . guards banging on the door . . . quiet street shadowed by trees as they gathered about us . . . Who stole the old bearded men who served for more
money? . . . banging on the door . . . sneering . . . the Arabian house . . . light . . .
the room facing the street . . . hostile, throwing rocks . . . someone was always
in the room facing the street . . . children, beggars . . . back with window opening if you refused . . . Cool under water we had moved in and then it seemed
my own . . . we moved in late . . . under the stairs . . . the house was Hell . . . by
early spring, life was simply a hole in the floor . . . These foreign shit birds, here . . .

IN PRESENT TIME

now try this take a walk a bus a taxi do a few errands sit down somewhere
drink a coffee watch tv look through the papers now return to your place
and write what you have just seen heard felt thought with particular attention to precise intersection points where you from on television its a long
way to go coca cola sing just after where the old bank used to be was open
sundays there on pasteur boulevard only it isnt pasteur now its mohomed v
tunnel of old photos you lika the boys or the girls post office where all the
clerks walked out at 435 take a left past the spanish school young man said
from a group of young men leaning on the fence you lika the boys or the
girls post office where all the clerks stamp letters at once up a windy street
past the coca cola sign frayed there down rembrandt toward the cleaners
passed a man who said where you from marakesh i did not wait to hear more
not liking what i had heard already place de france pick up the papers cafe
de paris cafe au lait oui beeg one grand double to readers of the daily express loud and clear now yale professor is held as spy somewhere in moscow
united states said custody its a long way to tipperary its a long way to go
silent on spy arrest this is the fourth lesson 1 2 3 4 1 2 3 4 this is the fourth
lesson artist old house must come down this is a store this store is in new
york for a waif an end of innocence there are lessons on television there are
many lessons on television this is america there are games on television clip
and save these coupons charged with glenny deaths there are many games
on television the english conquered their planet by good manners am i on
the second floor captain cook weak heart no this is not the second floor this
is the first floor the second floor is upstairs room above the florist shop go
out and get those pictures i dont care if the whole fucking shithouse goes
up go out and get those pictures these foreign suburbs here how about the
sweet home villa just down the street spanish young man say you lika the
boys or the girls lazy good natured spanish insolence the great garlic toothpick impresarioed this belch of folklore now when you get to where the old
bank used to be open sundays and paco says vamanos a casa william and
barnaby bliss erstwhile columnist on the now defunct tangier gazette sails

by with a windy hello there and beats my touch down the street flat on my junkass in those days where you from marakesh you like beeg one son of bitch bastard i ketch one clap from fucky your asshole.

well lets face it boys he doesnt want his picture taken but perhaps we can persuade him to pose for the nice gentlemens with gun and camera said the wise cop one of those funny bastards in every precinct hows you like a little heroin bill which you better think is funny and answer up like a good nigger yausuh boss man i sure would like some of that white sugar looks like ill have to wait till they burn me now

the pigfaced whitelashed lieutenant looked up from his books they cut out those execution shots ruling just came through from the capital we were getting entirely too many execution addicts dumped in our lap said a highly placed narcotics department official the ruling is retroactive recalling all execution shots

its a long way to tipperary its a long way to go young english soldier this is the fourth lesson 1 2 3 4 flickering fingers sweating last human pieces my contact there faded sepia genitals in a tattoo parlor smile from an old calendar back porch falling leaves sun cold on a thin boy with freckles folded away in an old file annie laurie never called retreat mister wasnt anything to say bradly is not there today telling you enemy intercepted here one blurred hand opened the gates for you will he hear from a group leaning on the fence in moscow united states audible click wasnt anything to say to the appropriate file annie laurie bring the bastards home and teach them to act like good human cattle

the american consulate

new

of course the old consulate is now an unethical massage parlor and frankly young man do i seem the sort of person who would willingly frequent such an establishment and if you say no sir a bit too old for that i shall simply strip my makeup off put it on put it on chant the boys from the rear solemn new fold in technique you move fast there now marys shes kinda cut off there now since the 29 tornado name and address on the wind why she might have assassinated the president a police officials moaned stolidly so moving fast i see the blue harbor through the empty frame of what used to be a public map of the city very blue under a grey sky pulling rain across the harbor around the cafe de paris and down the hill in a pride of adolescent gooks all punching each other so young as far as the grand socco which isnt so grand i tell you its tough out here with the plasma running low strong men cried when we had to suck the lead dog fortunes of war said a j wiping off his chin with a red bandana its more decent that way you see a cool vampire never shows red as we say in the trade to return to my horrible confessions which have finished off three hardened police officials but what i say is its no more disgusting than anything speaking of which last power failure in the deep freeze brought a sharp reprimand from the board of health with oblique references to uh certain unsanitary conditions you know what i mean right enough you were making a filthy smell so the great thaw was on and thoughtful citizens did not like what they thaw whats that great thaw going to thaw out be so great when it thaw out they demanded and receiving only a spray of stinking sludge in reply the district supervisor put in an urgent request for heavy weapons and shock troops the tide is coming in at hiroshima seconds later he gave the order towers open fire you are a gun an instrument synchronized to open fire when you intersect enemy the pilot cannot make error he synchronized

he turned left on third avenue unless its now avenue of the asias or something else wouldnt you if that is where you lived and you were going to meet your spanking new juicy boyfriend and you were synchronized to want it like i am it was no more disgusting than anything said the contessa which was pretty disgusting in its own right like this gombeen man in inner ireland sets up the visceral calendar whereby he knows when any animal of the village would shit jack off pick his nose stick a banana up his ass and could slide an oblique references to uh piles of uh dubious uh antecedents heh heh heh while he weighed down your groceries and leaned heavy on the scale when he came to the point well jacky me boy sure and youre looking like a ripe apple been out in the fresh air behind the old spring house playing like a boy well havent you now lean lean lean there wasnt a living soul in that blighted country the man didnt lean on he knew it all so nasty visceral calendars are inexorable as the processes of which they speak the day rolls around when every living soul looks his fellow in the eye and says did he lean on you

empty picture of a haunted ruin he lifted his hands sadly turned them out some boy just wrote last goodbye across the sky last goodbye whispering children on a dead star empty withered cut off exploded film scraps last awning flaps on the pier last man here now the youth structure of all your world broken twisted on electric fence at the barrier have i done the job here will he hear it a distant hand lifted 1920 window child fingers tap the glass all the dream people of past time are saying goodbye forever mister sad servant shadows of late afternoon against his back magic of all movies in remembered kid standing there face luminous by the attic window in a lost street of brick chimneys a little wind stirs dust around his bare feet silver ghostboy exploded star between us still there waiting searched from person to person unfound

remember the shabby quarters mister write goodbye to your old friend in a furnished room over the florist shop dead old human papers i carry thinboy waiting on a 1920 bench voice so painful ive come a long way dont let me die like that hopelessly calling exploding star see the boy there hand lifted further and further away goodbye sir last human crying you heard didnt you ghostboy of exploded page far away obituary window closed you no longer want the deadboy before the mirror plays to a haunted attic books and toys put away you can look back along windy streets half buried in sand to a white shirt flapping gunsmoke

the young man is received with cool reserve there is a wide desk between them empty except for a wire basket labeled it never happened on the mans left so you are a friend of mr d

well yes in a way that is

what do you mean friend of mr d in a way

the young man began to titter he put his hand on the desk and leaned forward tittering the young man stopped tittering and looked at the end of his shoe as if he were trying to see his face there twisting the toe around i guess you think im just terrible for laughing like that without telling you why but well uh you see my special nickname is friend now i think thats funny dont you

the mans answer drifted back over remote mineral landscapes of a dead star not very

well i guess different people think different things are funny because different people are taking in consideration different things now I read about this big tycoon magnate float this stock on widows and orphans like me and when the orphans went to pick up well the man behind the desk just looks at me and says account sheets are empty many years pimpam justlikethat now i dont think thats fair do you

the young man leaped on the desk thrusting his face inches in front of the man like an eager dog the mans chair moved back a foot in slow hydraulic recoil it was a way he had with visitors who leaned too far over his desk

all right you can drop the kid act gimpy id know you under ganymede you come around to put the bite on somebody thats not smart its like tough you are not or worthy

the gimp stands there face twisted with the hideous metal diseases of nova the mans chair moved back another foot you stink of burning apes gimpy he said the words falling heavy and cold seventy tons to the square inch

and what you stink of you white nova junky

we have the reverse order the bank will pay

he drops the gimps file into it never happened a cleareyed young officer is standing before the desk

well young man the colonel will have his little joke quite a character the gimp chap used to be with us clever at drawing did a comic strip for the post gazette called old gimp yes young man this squadron has a lot of traditions folklore you might say a spot of folklore can help a man out of a bad spot never without it myself he slips a bottle of pills from his vest pocket and swings the bottle in a slow arc but it stopped dead never to go again when the old man died

i have been in desperate battle want to name terms legs out of the area

well so you're looking for the bellvue hotel are you young man used to be the bellreeve country club at one time and you can still see the old golf course kinda run down now well if you walk up along olive street till you come to the old flatiron building now that building was tore down around 1932 and used to set right opposite jeds livery stable on market street only it wasnt market street then it was just mark street named after the survey line run right through there and it turned out a heap of folks didnt own what they thought they owned after the big survey now the man did the survey was named arch bane and for quite some years there wasnt a less liked man in this valley than old arch always surveying someones assets out from under him setting nice and cozy in your own living room and there is old arch with his plumb line and bad news writ all over him well nobody rightly knew where arch come from he just seemed to blow in with the 29 tornado when the old courthouse went up and all the records got scattered around and wasnt nothing for it but to survey every piece of property in the county so they called in arch to do the job and folks hereabouts figure that was the worst thing ever happened but i always say the worst things you never know when they happen well now arch lived in the bellvue hotel and you might say he surveyed hisself a room there cause one sizzling day in september sept 17 if my memory serves old judge farris president of the bellreeve country club stepped out and dove into what used to be the swimming pool and come up in the widow greens septic tank and closed the club right there well shortly after that some young feller name of mike spiegel took over the building and converted it into the bellvue hotel commanding a view of what used to be the golf course which is now what you might call a disputed area still under survey so what with one thing and another it isnt so easy to tell you just where the hotel is located but if you take a left just past the flatiron building depending of course which way you come on it and walk down the old branch line to where the tool bridge used to be then angle off due west past mary lus ethical massage parlor and the quicker the better now mary shes right hard pressed for clients since the saw mill closed down so right about where youll be if you move fast enough is a big red brick building stands a little back from the road well now that isnt it so bear straight on to the old signal tower now from the top of the signal tower though i wouldnt advise you to climb up there the state its in well you cant see the hotel but you can see the place where it is if the wind is right and thats about the closest way i know to tell you unless you want to see archs maps dont rightly think arch himself could make them out

j brundige the newspaper man thanked the county clerk for taking up so much of his time reflecting that time seemed to be a commodity with which the clerk was well supplied he stepped out into a street swept by weather shifts alternate whiteouts of snow and sunlight walk in long ago boy until you come to where i finished last cigar so many actors you cant see the hotel bad news writ all over the dust wasnt nothing for it but to survey r2 and 2–12 and shut the county stand a little back from the game he decided nothing was to be gained by climbing the old signal tower sighted at random and proceeded until stopped by a high wooden fence he skirted the fence found a loose slot and pushed through into a vacant lot overgrown with weeds this must be the old golf course he decided and dove into the second gpm come up in the old septic tank sort of cool and clean if it had been there some reward for thirteen years of sweating out what you might call a disputed clearing process so what with one thing and another deep into the third goal which is just where the hotel is like the poet say long thoughts archs maps sort of leap out at you all at once

in the lobby an old jew with grey fish eyes waved his cigar ive still got my cigar he said put it back in his mouth and looked out through hotel bellvue silver letters flaking off the glass

a young man moved in and out of focus what do you want he snapped the hotel is completely full you understand no room none at all his voice cracked oh youve come for the pictures well all right

he led the way through a smell of closed rooms as they walked muttering voices rose from old photos on rose wallpaper and gathered around the feet the boy kicked petulantly

oh shut up you silly old things no i simply wont jack off in the outhouse its full of scorpions for one thing besides id sooner make fudge

he dusted off a magic lantern now you see with this lantern on that screen it happens you know things that can be done and so easily except so many things have happened and there simply isnt room anymore

dont ask questions and dont pass remarks longago boy walked through the dust kicking in sunlight silver grey and out of focus a thinboy gilt edged sepia typhoid witness in switzerland muttering dangerous no one wants to machine guns in baghdad agatha christie waiting all the old names would expect anything to happen canada yes definitely out of focus

so many share old mirror all the old names waiting silver grey and out of focus mr martin smiles

meester can be done and so easily

well now to show you the pictures for example he looked through a pile of dusty slides humming before they found the mine was salted i was safe in the argentine so there

a picture flickered on screen showing a general standing in an armored car from the magic lantern drifted riot noises and gun shots newspaper headlines flashed on revolt in the argentine the boy sat down on a dusty sofa

so you see so many actors and so little action perhaps tomorrow typhoid epidemic in sweden or was it switzerland and of course the middle east but thats rather dangerous and nobody wants to be mixed up in it you see its like agatha christie finding the last place anyone would expect anything to happen otherwise there simply isnt room canada yes definitely no one expects anything to happen in canada old man sits in 1920 spanish study stucco walls arch to a vaulted ceiling on desk of black oak is a cobra lamp and a crystal radio set the old man wears headphones and flickers in and out of focus

old photographer trick young man see the pretty birdie smile remember subject freezes so i started snapping the picture just before i made with the pretty bird and using a loud false click just after so i already took the picture when they hear the click say ten seconds ago the pictures i got using this angle were much worse than usual they were in fact exactly pictures of the way some-

one looks when he hears the smile pretty birdie shutter click i was young and
i wanted good pictures that was long ago 1920 tunes stir dust on the desk oh
yes i found out how to get my good pictures and made a lot of money as a
portrait photographer all i had to do was find out what words music picture
odor brought out in my subject the face i wanted them i took the picture just
before i played the music or whatever the cue was and the subject never knew
when i took the picture since i still used the false click gimmick reaction time
yes i went into that allowing for reaction time there was still that interval of a
few seconds unaccounted for why you see i couldn't just pick up the money
and forget it i had to know and i found the answer the face moves in time you
never photograph the present but always the future if you want a picture of
how someone looks when a flashbulb pops you take a few seconds before the
bulb pops i was taking pictures not of the face as it is but as it will be in a few
seconds i was photographing the socalled future this could only mean that
the future is already photographed and prerecorded then old fred flash came
to call sitting right where youre sitting now

    well my boy youve put your foot in it now you see we dont pay our char-
acters to shut up about what they already know we pay them not to find out
we tried to pay you we tried to pay you just look at this house modern and
convenient you find it so of course well you wouldn't just pick up our money
and go back to your pewter and your tulip bulbs you had to know why so
now you know and you might as well know the rest if you can take a face a
few seconds from now you can take a face a few years from now same gimmick pick a cue any cue always need a peg to hang it on remember its all a
matter of timing just time just time all right you can take over my job now
know who i am old fred flash i take the first picture and i take the last picture come along young man show you around the darkroom quite a few
gimmicks to learn reversed negatives and all that now some of these negatives you see here just put on these infrared four eyes will develop tomorrow
some have a long germination period seeds you might say and you know
what will grow out of those seeds didnt you plant that corn later on when
films start moving we say where i came in im en route to—dont ask questions for about three know goal almost blown all under good control just a
matter of standing up under fire chinese rockets reading reliable gun shots
old photographer trick preparation r2 and 212 and shutter clicks young boy
thoughts routine 3mx four reliable frequency waves panama dust session was
plunged into second boy walks on screen to eat a few peanuts and drink
paregoric next fatal question i am dying meester age flakes fall before the
audit number long long ago face dying just before clearing process never
knew when im around the dark room negatives and all that auditor asks if
you got my last hints from second gpm riot noises cool and clean deep into
third goal which is right where youre sitting now have to stop and polish off
second goal chinese characters had arrived it was time to shift commissions
well you might as well know its all anyway at this writing the second time

however last hints just time to show you around technology show you thirteen years of gimmicks to learn second reversed over and over mirror image
breaks out third goal and so on learn it and use it your image shifted the
other all under good control revolution standing up under fire

   all right heres one just took the picture old man standing in sepia long long
ago called in to pay you all right so take over my stack of riot pictures some
face picked out heres the album personality reshapes my pictures round up
wars revolutions riots strikes and stockmarket crashes old old photographer
trick in the magic lantern

   but really darling that sepia park fountains trees and oh yes me standing
right there on third avenue

   superimposed cage of images reversed you can read

   i shant do anything tried that setup i already knew perhaps late on short
notice

   well my boy youve put your trick in the darkroom concealed wheels spin
the world reshapes of course riots wars revolutions stockmarket crashes are
the easiest to take now it sometimes happens a situation arises or some character is suddenly important and you dont have all the pictures because you
never figured anything could happen there then you have to go out and get
those pictures on short notice thats when you need to know every trick in the
darkroom and like all tricks they dont always work old fred flash is the difference between the camera and what the camera takes just time just time always
need a peg to hang it on the way it will be your face where i came in all right
what have you got just take over my job now well its all here in the files i remember all the pictures i take the first page and the last used to keep all the
photos and they piled up and up millions and millions of old photos then
microfilm then electron microscopes and then he picked up a handful of yellow crystals like pulverized amber virus crystals he held out his hand show you
a thousand years chewing the same argument around and around birth and
death have to kill the audience every few years to keep them in their seats heh
heh heh just an old showman yep its here in the darkroom waiting birth and
death always plenty of that i take the last picture simply dont see your face in
the world there in his eyes baby the way it will be and dying eyes take the rest
picture of me without you where the future plates develop photograph albums
of interlocking wheels pay old man eyes pose a colorless question of some face
over here youth harmonica music bare feet summer afternoons carnivals toy
boats all the words and thoughts float there over the pictures young thoughts
now thats a rare commodity like the poet say long long thoughts but never
enough to go around

   your actors erased our marks in longagoboy the pilot eyes a dead world i
really finished last cigar in ewyork onolulu aris ome oston death takes over
the game so many actors buildings and stars laid flat pieces of finance over the
golf course summer afternoons drift in a sepia cloud do you see the silver fountains word and music drifting from 1910 streets crowds in baghdad rising from

the typewriter mr martin smiles sorrowful servant stood on the sea wall in sepia clouds of panama

   i am dying meester in the darkroom say good bye johnny yens last adios in and out of focus

   yep its all here in the grey room all the old names waiting for a live one saddest of all movies just listen to them this is the way the world ends voices frosted on the glass

from
the job

THE AMERICAN NON-DREAM

America is not so much a nightmare as a *non-dream*. The American non-dream is precisely a move to wipe the dream out of existence. The dream is a spontaneous happening and therefore dangerous to a control system set up by the non-dreamers. Experiments carried out by Doctor Gross in New York at the Mount Sinai Hospital indicate that any dream in the male is accompanied by erection. The non-dream program is specifically directed against the male principle. It is above all anti-sexual and anti-male.

Any progress or system of thought must have ground to grow on and especially such a vegetable program as this dead hand stretching the vegetable people. The ground for the non-dream program was well laid by the turn of the century, ready for seeds which would yield in course of time hideous fruit. World Wars I, II, and III were already inevitable, given the basic formula of nationalism. The concomitant rise of communism would serve as pretext for more control measures while the communists would be driven to apply similar measures and thus serve the master plan. Let us look at some of the milestones in the anti-dream plan:

The Oriental Exclusion Acts: The equanimity of the Chinese is, of course, due to their language which allows for periods of silence and *undirected* thought, quite intolerable to the non-dreamers who must program *all* thought. I have already spoken of the difference between hieroglyphic and syllabic writing. (If I hold up a sign on which the word "ROSE" is written, you must repeat the word sub-vocally. If I hold up a hieroglyphic sign for rose you do not have to repeat the word, and even have the option of silence.) Admittedly, two model control systems, the Mayan and the Egyptian, were based on hieroglyphic writing. However, these control systems were predicated on the illiteracy of the controlled. Universal literacy with a concomitant control of word and image is now the instrument of control. An essential feature of the Western control machine is to make language as *non-pictorial* as possible, to separate words as far as possible from objects or observable processes.

The District Supervisor shabby office late afternoon shadow in his eyes calm and grey as a wise old rat handed a typed page across the desk

Relations between human beings sexualizing congruent accessibility ambivalently fecundate with orifices perspectives is I feel to beg the question of contributory latent configurations reciprocally starved of direction or vector by the recognizable human remembrance of such approximate exasperations a desperately effete societal somnolence supine negation by any reputable informed latent consensus inherently commissioned with customary human techniques interweaving re-enactments of necessary correspondences interderivational from complementary internalizations confluently communicated reciprocal analogous metaphors with this relentlessly successful diagrammatic schemata delinquently recognizable juxtapositions to traduce or transfigure a pulsating multiplicity of contradictions inherent in linguistic engagements disproportionately flailing gritty colloquialisms edged with grammatic outrage bubbling beneath indispensably internalized concordance latterly derivative from scorned or pillage infantile suburban genitalia sexualizing exasperations into diagrammatically contrapunctual linguistically communicated multiplicity of otherness escalating the delinquent preparations in concomitantly banal privatization concentrates of irrelevant hysteria contributory misinformed perspectives of negation ambivalently supine oppositionally interweaving desperately recognizable latterly commissioned flailing stridently illiterate human beings would traduce or transfigure fecundate with orifices potentials reputably informed correspondences of societal consensus notwithstanding the complementary structuralized configurations relentlessly juxtapositions interdependence of necessary and precisely reciprocal consensus latterly contingent upon communicated linguistic concordance of such contractually analogous indispensably infantile preparations fecundately accessible human correspondences or relations between human internalized concordance indispensably starved of direction or vector by irrelevant approximately derivative confluent exasperations latently misinformed contingent inaccessibility communicated societal internalizings indispensably pillaged infantile preparations flailing disproportionate bubbling outrage notwithstanding the contrapoised stridently juxtapositions interdependence latterly commissioned recognizable societally structuralized reciprocally misinformed indispensably congruent multiplicity of otherness perspectives concomitantly banal irrelevant concentrates with orifices gritty interstices rectilinearly inaccessible.

These jewels gathered from one of the periodicals admittedly subsidized by the CIA. If you see the function of word as extension of our senses to witness and experience through the writer's eyes then this may be dubbed blind prose. It sees nothing and neither does the reader. Not an image in a cement mixer of this word paste. As a literary exercise I pick up the Penguin translation of Rimbaud and select images to place in congruent juxtapositions with this colorless vampiric prose which having no color of its own must steal color from the readers such contractually accessible linguistically structuralized preparations on blue evenings I shall go down the path in a dream feeling the coolness on my feet starved of direction or vector by derivationally confluent exasperations five in the evening at the Green Inn huge beer mug froth turned into gold by a ray of late sunshine perspective of illiterate human beings would traduce or transfigure fecundate with orifices potential the Watchman rows through the luminous heavens and from his flaming dragnet lets fall shooting stars and precisely reciprocal latent consensus if societal flailings stridently congruent from pulsating mangrove swamps riddled with pools and water snakes diagrammatic contrapunctual . . . ving desperately the poverty of image shea . . . in bronze from scorned or pillage consensus of contributory configurations . . . like a flock of doves shivering of Venetian blinds and the yellow blue awakening sexualizing contingent accessibility informed hideous wrecks at the bottom of brown gulfs where the giant snakes devoured by lice fall from the twisted trees with black odors communicated suburban orifice reenactments of infantile genitalia contributory internalized contradictions blue waves golden singing fish foam of shadow flowers would traduce or transfigure banal privatization concentrates latterly risen from violet fogs through the wall of the reddening sky ambivalently supine contractually inaccessible black cold pool where a child squatting full of sadness launches a boat fragile as a butterfly in May between starved confluent exasperations communicated linear derivations from reciprocal engagements spat blood concomitantly irrelevant hysteria at the foot of dark walls beating the skinny dogs internalized vector misinformed preparation it is raining softly on the town moonlight as the clock was striking twelve concentrates of otherness with orifices bitter perspectives the road without sound is white under the empty moon a slight cesspool of dirty blood internalized infantile diagrammatically necessary piercing cry in the darkened square spat blood confluently stinging like the salt of child's tears sexualizing interdependence latterly contingent upon a motionless boat in ashen waters concordantly infantile misinformed perspectives North wind across the wreckage perish power justice vanish ambivalently supine fecundately human there are brothers dark strangers if we began bubbling beneath indispensably banal privatization concentrates blond soldiers from the thin bracken the wilderness the meadows the horizon are washing themselves red in the storm delinquently pulsating oppositional colonnades under blue light railway stations wind from the sky threw sheets of ice across the ponds vector latterly communicated the question of internalized direction at four o'clock on a summer morning the sleep of love the wind comes in to wander about under the bed reputably such contractually accessible human concordance is I feel to beg the question then they will have to deal with the crafty rat ghastly will-o'-the-wisp comes like a gunshot after vespers configurations of internalized congruencies

Saharan blue where a thousand blue devils dance in the air like flowers of fire supine oppositionally pillaged inaccessible jackals howling across deserts of thyme stridently misinformed preparations communicated the question of pillaged consensus it is raining internalized concordance dawn rising like a flock of doves softly on the town shivering of Venetian blinds at four o'clock and the yellow blue awakening concentrates the sleep of love on orifices summer accessibility the skinny dogs internalized flowers of fire

Anything they can do you can do better. Pick up *The Concise Oxford Dictionary* mix your own linguistic virus concentrates fire burn and caldron bubble mix it black and mix it strong folks hereabouts have done you wrong return confluently the complement: e.

Fristic elite impacted banal limitrophic imposture impotently flailing effluvial grout mud incumbent MN grume intervolving abrasively affricative incubus interpositional inconsummate lubricious investiture decommissioned externalized incondite anastrophe incrassate misinformed ME palatogram's epidemic anfractuosity eschatological obscurant retiary disaffected lumper uxorious urubu anachronic prologist consensual nevermore bubbling beneath innavigable umlaut inextricably disadmeasured societal interstices reciprocally ablative inconditely flailing oppositional contagonist precatory ingravescent gowk disobliged catoptic zillah pillaged consensus of justiciable justiciar kempy kavass libating opponency orifices adventitious encumbrancer anachronic hysteria of vector its heart misinformed pulp irrefrangible disaffected echidna encounter ineluctable obmutescence arachnoid troglodyte flailing inofficious effluvium disobliged investiture rectilinear additive disadhesion impacted limitrophic elite irrefrangible contagonist anachronic uxorious troglodyte sexualizing ingravescent propinquities intervolving abrasive inoccupation congruently disinternalized necessities ill informed pulp extrapolating diagrammatic efferent prehensions obmutescent palatogram's prefigured eschatologist uxoriously disobliged investiture nevermore bubbling beneath innavigable effluvium impotent obloquy irrefrangible hysteria such additive ineluctable disadhesion irrefrangible limitrophic incubus bubbling uxorious pulp ablative palatogram precatory impacted adhesion effluvial inconsummate lubricious flailings ingravescent contagonist retiary umlaut prefigured eristic eschatologist, *voici le temps des assassins* blind man's bluff any number can play . . . blind prose but it has direction and purpose. One purpose is to protect a camouflaged thesis from the embarrassment of factual testing. If I say "England is an island" I can produce evidence to support my statement should anyone call it in question. If they write an article attacking the Olympia Press as sexualizing congruent accessibility to its heart of pulp fecundate with orifices perspectives in the name of human privacy they have placed their thesis beyond the realm of fact since the words used refer to nothing that can be tested. The words used refer to nothing. The words used have no referent.

The Oriental Exclusion Acts blocked a dangerous influx and laid the ground for future conflicts. The program calls for a series of such conflicts to point up the need for a continual escalation of control measures.

Income-tax Laws: These laws benefit those who are already rich. The richer you are the easier it is to minimize taxes. In effect the rich have closed the doors to extreme wealth. This is necessary to insure that no one acquires wealth who might use it to subvert the interests of wealth and monopoly. There is no tighter hierarchy than extreme wealth, and no one gets in who is not devoted to the interests of money.

Passport and customs controls after World War I: The basic formula on which the control plan depends is *unilateral communication.* Everyone must be forced to receive communications from the control machine. It will readily be seen that any control measure expands the range of enforced communication. Your passport or visa is not quite in order? You have lost your currency control slip? How many times will you *compulsively* repeat the explanation you have prepared in case the customs official starts asking questions. So control measures conjure up phantom interrogators who invade and destroy your inner freedom.

By far the most crucial milestone in the non-dream plan was the Harrison Narcotics Act.

INSTITUTE OF ADVANCED SEXUAL STUDIES: ACADEMY BULLETIN NO. 18

The uh aim of the institute is to examine uh sexual manifestations with the same objective and uh experimental operations as have yielded such marked results in the uh physical sciences. We cannot but be impressed by the inefficiency of the present arrangement, the long period of helpless infancy during which the child is exposed to every variety of physical and psychic illness, every unwholesome influence on set. It is precisely our aim to create children at a reasonable age with some immunity against the unfortunate influences that we cannot immediately control. Meanwhile, every effort must be made to crack the biologic family unit. It is no exaggeration to say that the family unit, with its drearily predictable yield of infantile trauma, the quite unnecessary tensions of modern life superimposed on these quite unnecessary wounds, is the most crippling basic factor in modern life. How many potentially talented and useful citizens do nothing throughout a lifetime but protest against early conditioning? It has frequently been proposed that children be brought up by the state. And what is the state but a simple extension of the tribe which in turn is an extension of the family? To shift the care of children from the private family to the state family is nothing to the purpose. This means that our children will surface in a straitjacket of dogmatic verbal formulation as is now imposed by the biologic family. One of the most promising suggestions for the long-term liquidation of the family problem has been proposed by Mr Brion Gysin. He suggests that children be paid to go to school; the allowance increasing as they advance in training, they progressively achieve economic freedom from the family. The solution of the family problem must be termed a prerequisite for any objective approach to sexual manifestations and phenomena. Our work has been hamstrung by the antisex monopolist power, because this might lead to a basic understanding of the mechanisms involved with concomitant freedom from early conditioning. The doctor asked his subjects to wear transparent plastic suits, and observed whether dreaming was overtly sexual or not. One wonders to what extent the content of dreams could be dictated by cutting in at very short intervals certain words and images? Since the results of this experiment are well known to all of us, suffice it to say such experiments have been carried out, relative to such basic and uh predictable factors. . . . I refer to experiments that did not uh pan out as we had anticipated. Science, pure science. You learn to take what comes in this business.

"How's that couple coming along in double immersion tank No. 187?"

"Don't look at it, boss, it's too horrible. They're melting together, and one is eating the other inside."

"Selbstverstandlich," snapped the Herr Doktor. "And vat did you think would happen, so stupid American swine?"

At this point, a most regrettable brawl broke out in the operation room, overturning nutrient tanks, jars, aquariums, sloshing monstrous larval being across the floor the scientists slip about slashing at each other with scalpels and bone saws screaming.

"Well, we got the orders, and I done the job, wife and kids on my back."

"Look what a *dummheit.*"

"Smells through the outhouse, doctor."

"Run for it, chaps. They're actives." Last seen swimming desperately in erogenous sewage.

The entire project was lost. Who is the manager here? You see what I mean? . . . Such knowledge in the wrong hands could be quite unfortunate!

ELECTRONIC REVOLUTION

In "The Invisible Generation" first published in IT and in the *Los Angeles Free Press* in 1966, I consider the potential of thousands of people with recorders, portable and stationary, messages passed along like signal drums, a parody of the President's speech up and down the balconies, in and out open windows, through walls, over courtyards, taken up by barking dogs, muttering bums, music, traffic down windy streets, across parks and soccer fields. Illusion is a revolutionary weapon. To point out some specific uses of prerecorded cut/up tapes played back in the streets as a revolutionary weapon:

To spread rumors

Put ten operators with carefully prepared recordings out at the rush hour and see how quick the word gets around. People don't know where they heard it but they heard it.

To discredit opponents

Take a recorded Wallace speech, cut in stammering coughs sneezes hiccoughs snarls pain screams fear whimperings apoplectic sputterings slobbering drooling idiot noises sex and animal sound effects and play it back in the streets subways stations parks political rallies.

As a front line weapon to produce and escalate riots

There is nothing mystical about this operation. Riot sound effects can produce an actual riot in a riot situation. *Recorded police whistles will draw cops. Recorded gunshots, and their guns are out.*

"MY GOD, THEY'RE KILLING US."

A guardsman said later: "I heard the shots and saw my buddy go down, his face covered in blood (turned out he'd been hit by a stone from a sling shot) and I thought, well this is it." BLOODY WEDNESDAY. A DAZED AMERICA COUNTED 23 DEAD AND 32 WOUNDED, 6 CRITICALLY.

Here is a run of the mill, pre-riot situation. Protestors have been urged to demonstrate peacefully, police and guardsmen to exercise restraint. Ten tape recorders strapped under their coats, play back and record controlled from lapel buttons. They have prerecorded riot sound effects from Chicago, Paris, Mexico City, Kent, Ohio. If they adjust sound level of recordings to surrounding sound levels, they will not be detected. Police scuffle with the demonstrators. The operators converge. Turn on Chicago record, play back, move on to the next scuffles, record, play back, keep moving. Things are hotting up, a cop is down groaning. Shrill chorus of recorded pig squeals and parody groans.

Could you cool a riot recording the calmest cop and the most reasonable demonstrators? Maybe! However, it's a lot easier to start trouble than stop it. Just pointing out that cut/ups on the tape recorder can be used as a weapon. You'll observe that the operators are making a cut/up as they go. They are cutting in Chicago, Paris, Mexico City, Kent, Ohio, with the present sound effects at random, and that is a cut/up.

As a long range weapon to scramble and nullify associational lines put down by mass media

The control of the mass media depends on laying down lines of association. When the lines are cut the associational connections are broken.

President Johnson burst into a swank apartment, held three maids at gunpoint, 26 miles north of Saigon yesterday.

You can cut the mutter line of the mass media and put the altered mutter line out in the streets with a tape recorder. Consider the mutter line of the daily press. It goes up with the morning papers, millions of people reading the same words, belching chewing swearing chuckling reacting to the same words. In different ways, of course. A motion praising Mr. Callaghan's action in banning the South African Cricket Tour has spoiled the colonel's breakfast. All reacting one way or another to the paper world of unseen events which becomes an integral part of your reality. You will notice that this process is continually subject to random juxtaposition. Just what sign did you see in the Green Park station as you glanced up from the *People*? Just who called as you were reading your letter in the *Times*? What were you reading when your wife broke a dish in the kitchen? An unreal paper world and yet completely real because it is actually happening. Mutter line of the *Evening News*, TV. Fix yourself on millions of people all watching Jesse James or the Virginian at the same time. International mutter line of the weekly news magazine always dated a week ahead. Have you noticed it's the kiss of death to be on the front cover of *Time*. Madam Nhu was there when her husband was killed and her government fell. Verwoerd was on the front cover of *Time* when a demon tapeworm gave the order for his death through a messenger of the same. Read the Bible, kept to himself, no bad habits, you know the type. Old reliable, read all about it.

So stir in news stories, TV plays, stock market quotations, adverts and put the altered mutter line out in the streets.

The underground press serves as the only effective counter to a growing power and more sophisticated techniques used by establishment mass media to falsify, misrepresent, misquote, rule out of consideration as *a priori* ridiculous or simply ignore and blot out of existence: data, books, discoveries that they consider prejudicial to establishment interest.

I suggest that the underground press could perform this function much more effectively by the use of cut/up techniques. For example, prepare cut/ups of the ugliest reactionary statements you can find and surround them with the ugliest pictures. Now give it the drool, slobber, animal-noise treatment and put it out on the mutter line with recorders. Run a scramble page in every issue of a transcribed tape recorded cut/up of news, radio, and TV. Put the recordings out on the mutter line before the paper hits the stand. It gives you a funny feeling to see a headline that's been going round and round in your head. The underground press could add a mutter line to their adverts and provide a unique advertising service. Cut the product in with pop tunes, cut the product in with advertising slogans and jingles of other products and syphon off the sales. Anybody who doubts that these techniques work has only to put them to the test. The techniques here described are in use by the CIA and agents of other countries. Ten years ago they were making systematic street recordings in every district of Paris. I recall the Voice of America man in Tangier and a room full of tape recorders and you could hear some strange sounds through the wall. Kept to himself, hello in the hall. Nobody was ever allowed in that room, not even a fatima. Of course, there are many technical elaborations like long-range directional mikes. When cutting the prayer call in with hog grunts it doesn't pay to be walking around the market place with a portable tape recorder.

An article in *New Scientist* June 4, 1970, page 470, entitled "Electronic Arts of Noncommunication" by Richard C. French gives the clue for more precise technical instructions.

In 1968, with the help of Ian Sommerville and Antony Balch, I took a short passage of my recorded voice and cut it into intervals of one twenty-fourth of a second on movie tape—(movie tape is larger and easier to splice)—and re-arranged the order of the 24th-second intervals of recorded speech. The original words are quite unintelligible but new words emerge. The voice is still there and you can immediately recognize the speaker. Also the tone of voice remains. If the tone is friendly, hostile, sexual, poetic, sarcastic, lifeless, despairing, this will be apparent in the altered sequence.

I did not realize at the time that I was using a technique that has been in existence since 1881. . . . I quote from Mr. French's article . . . "Designs for speech scramblers go back to 1881 and the desire to make telephone and radio communications unintelligible to third parties has been with us ever since." . . . The message is scrambled in transmission and then unscrambled at the other end. There are many of these speech scrambling devices that work on different principles . . . "Another device which saw service during the war was the time division scrambler. The signal is chopped up into elements .005cm long. These elements are taken in groups or frames and rearranged in a new sequence. Imagine that the speech recorded is recorded on magnetic tape which is cut into pieces .02 cm long and the pieces rearranged into a new sequence. This can actually be done and gives a good idea what speech sounds like when scrambled in this way."

This I had done in 1968. And this is an extension of the cut/up method. The simplest cut/up cuts a page down the middle into four sections. Section 1 is then placed with section 4 and section 3 with section 2 in a new sequence. Carried further we can break the page down into smaller and smaller units in altered sequences.

The original purpose of scrambling devices was to make the message unintelligible without the unscrambling code. Another use for speech scramblers could be to impose thought control on a mass scale. Consider the human body and nervous system as unscrambling devices. A common virus like the cold sore could sensitize the subject to unscramble messages. Drugs like LSD and Dim-N could also act as unscrambling devices. Moreover, the mass media could sensitize millions of people to receive scrambled versions of the same set of data. Remember that when the human nervous system unscrambles a scrambled message this will seem to the subject like his very own ideas which just occurred to him, which indeed it did.

Take a card, any card. In most cases he will not suspect its extraneous origin. That is the run of the mill newspaper reader who receives the scrambled message uncritically and assumes that it reflects his own opinions independently arrived at. On the other hand, the subject may recognize or suspect the extraneous origin of voices that are literally hatching out in his head. Then we have the classic syndrome of paranoid psychosis. Subject hears voices. Anyone can be made to hear voices with scrambling techniques. It is not difficult to expose him to the actual scrambled message, any part of which can be made intelligible. This can be done with street recorders, recorders in cars, doctored radio and TV sets. In his own flat if possible, if not in some bar or restaurant he frequents. If he doesn't talk to himself, he soon will do. You bug his flat. Now he is really round the bend hearing his own voice out of radio and TV broadcasts and the conversation of passing strangers. See how easy it is? Remember the scrambled message is partially unintelligible and in any case he gets the tone. Hostile white voices unscrambled by a Negro will also activate by association every occasion on which he has been threatened or humiliated by whites. To carry it further you can use recordings of voices known to him. You can turn him against his friends by hostile scrambled messages in a friend's voice. This will activate all his disagreements with that friend. You can condition him to like his enemies by friendly scrambled messages in enemy voices.

On the other hand the voices can be friendly and reassuring. He is now working for the CIA, the GPU, or whatever, and these are his orders. They now have an agent who has no information to give away and who doesn't have to be paid. And he is now completely under control. If he doesn't obey orders they can give him the hostile voice treatment. No, "They" are not God or super technicians from outer space. Just technicians operating with well-known equipment and using techniques that can be duplicated by anybody else who can buy and operate this equipment.

To see how scrambling technique could work on a mass media scale, imagine that a news magazine like *Time* got out a whole issue a week before publication and filled it with news based on predictions following a certain line, without attempting the impossible, giving our boys a boost in every story and the Commies as many defeats and casualties as possible, a whole issue of *Time* formed from slanted prediction of future news. Now imagine this scrambled out through the mass media.

With minimal equipment you can do the same thing on a smaller scale. You need a scrambling device, TV, radio, two video cameras, a ham radio station and a simple photo studio with a few props and actors. For a start you scramble the news all together and spit it out every which way on ham radio and street recorders. You construct fake news broadcasts on video camera. For the pictures you can use mostly old footage. Mexico City will do for a riot in Saigon and vice versa. For a riot in Santiago, Chile, you can use the Londonderry pictures. Nobody knows the difference. Fires, earthquakes, plane crashes can be moved around. For example, here is a plane crash, 112 dead north of Barcelona and here is a plane crash in Toronto 108 dead. So move the picture of the Barcelona plane crash over to Toronto and Toronto to Barcelona. And you scramble your fabricated news in with actual news broadcasts.

You have an advantage which your opposing player does not have. He must conceal his manipulations. You are under no such necessity. In fact you can advertise the fact that you are writing news in advance and trying to make it happen by techniques which anybody can use. And that makes you NEWS. And a TV personality as well, if you play it right. You want the widest possible circulation for your cut/up video tapes. Cut/up techniques could swamp the mass media with total illusion.

Fictional dailies retroactively cancelled the San Francisco earthquake and the Halifax explosion as journalistic hoaxes, and doubt released from the skin law extendable and ravenous, consumed all the facts of history.

Mr. French concludes his article . . . "The use of modern microelectric integrated circuits could lower the cost of speech scramblers enough to see them in use by private citizens. Codes and ciphers have always had a strong appeal to most people and I think scramblers will as well. . . ."

It is generally assumed that speech must be consciously understood to cause an effect. Early experiments with subliminal images have shown that this is not true. A number of research projects could be based on speech scramblers. We have all seen the experiment where someone speaking hears his own recorded voice back a few seconds later. Soon he cannot go on talking. Would scrambled speech have the same effect? To what extent are scrambled messages actually unscrambled by experimental subjects? To what extent does a language act as an unscrambling device, western languages tending to unscramble in either-or conflict terms? To what extent does the tone of voice used by a speaker impose a certain unscrambling sequence on the listener?

Many of the cut/up tapes would be entertaining and in fact entertainment is the most promising field for cut/up techniques. Imagine a pop festival like Phun City scheduled for July 24th, 25th, 26th, 1970, at Ecclesden Common, Patching, near Worthing, Sussex. Festival area comprised of car park and camping area, a rock auditorium, a village with booths and cinema, a large wooded area. A number of tape recorders are planted in the woods and the village. As many as possible so as to lay down a grid of sound over the whole festival. Recorders have tapes of prerecorded material, music, news broadcasts, recordings from other festivals, etc. At all times some of the recorders are playing back and some are recording. The recorders recording at any time are of course recording the crowd and the other tape recorders that are playing back at varying distances. This cuts in the crowd who will be hearing their own voices back. Play back, wind back, and record could be electronically controlled with varying intervals. Or they could be hand operated, the operator deciding what intervals of play back, record, and wind back to use. Effect is greatly increased by a large number of festival goers with portable recorders playing back and recording as they walk around the festival. We can carry it further with projection screens and video cameras. Some of the material projected is preprepared, sex films, films of other festivals, and this material is cut in with live TV broadcasts and shots of the crowd. Of course, the rock festival will be cut in on the screens, thousands of fans with portable recorders recording and playing back, the singer could direct play back and record. Set up an area for traveling performers, jugglers, animal acts, snake charmers, singers, musicians, and cut these acts in. Film and tape from the festival, edited for the best material, could then be used at other festivals.

Quite a lot of equipment and engineering to set it up. The festival could certainly be enhanced if as many festival goers as possible bring portable tape recorders to record and play back at the festival.

Any message, music, conversation you want to pass around, bring it pre-recorded on tape so everybody takes pieces of your tape home.

Research project: to find out to what extent scrambled messages are un-scrambled, that is scanned out by experimental subjects. The simplest ex-periment consists in playing back a scrambled message to subject. Message could contain simple commands. Does the scrambled message have any com-mand value comparable to post-hypnotic suggestion? Is the actual content of the message received? What drugs, if any, increase ability to unscramble messages? Do subjects vary widely in this ability? Are scrambled messages in the subject's own voice more effective than messages in other voices? Are messages scrambled in certain voices more easily unscrambled by specific sub-jects? Is the message more potent with both word and image scrambled on video tape? Now to use, for example, a video-tape message with a unified emotional content. Let us say the message is fear. For this we take all the past fear shots of the subject we can collect or evoke. We cut these in with fear words and pictures, with threats, etc. This is all acted out and would be upsetting enough in any case. Now let's try it scrambled and see if we get an even stronger effect. The subject's blood pressure, rate of heart beat, and brain waves are recorded as we play back the scrambled tape. His face is photographed and visible to him on video camera at all times. The actual scrambling of the tape can be done in two ways. It can be a completely ran-dom operation like pulling pieces out of a hat and if this is done several consecutive units may occur together, yielding an identifiable picture or intelligible word. Both methods of course can be used at varying intervals. Blood pressure, heart beat, and brain-wave recordings will show the opera-tor what material is producing the strongest reaction, and he will of course zero in. And remember that the subject can see his face at all times and his face is being photographed. As the Peeping Tom said, the most frightening thing is fear in your own face. If the subject becomes too disturbed we have peace and safety tapes ready.

Now here is a sex tape: this consists of a sex scene acted out by the ideal sexual object of the subject and his ideal self image. Shown straight it might be exciting enough, now scramble it. It takes a few seconds for scrambled tapes to hatch out, and then? Can scrambled sex tapes zeroing in on the subject's reactions and brain waves result in spontaneous orgasm? Can this be extended to other functions of the body? A mike secreted in the water closet and all his shits and farts recorded and scrambled in with stern nanny voices command-ing him to shit, and the young liberal shits in his pants on the platform right under Old Glory. Could laugh tapes, sneeze tapes, hiccough tapes, cough tapes, give rise to laughing, sneezing, hiccoughing, and coughing?

To what extent can physical illness be induced by scrambled illness tapes? Take, for example, a sound and color picture of a subject with a cold. Later, when subject is fully recovered, we take color and sound film of recovered subject. We now scramble the cold pictures and sound track in with present sound and image track. We also project the cold pictures on present pictures. Now we try using some of Mr. Hubbard's reactive mind phrases which are supposed in themselves to produce illness. To be me, to be you, to stay here, to stay there, to be a body, to be bodies, to stay present, to stay past. Now we scramble all this in together and show it to the subject. Could seeing and hearing this sound and image track, scrambled down to very small units, bring about an attack of cold virus? If such a cold tape does actually produce an attack of cold virus we cannot say that we have created a virus, perhaps we have merely activated a latent virus. Many viruses, as you know, are latent in the body and may be activated. We can try the same with cold sore, with hepatitis, always remembering that we may be activating a latent virus and in no sense creating a laboratory virus. However, we may be in a position to do this. Is a virus perhaps simply very small units of sound and image? Remember the only image a virus has is the image and sound track it can impose on you. The yellow eyes of jaundice, the pustules of smallpox, etc. imposed on you against your will. The same is certainly true of scrambled word and image, its existence is the word and image it can make you unscramble. Take a card, any card. This does not mean that it is actually a virus. Perhaps to construct a laboratory virus we would need both camera and sound crew and a biochemist as well. I quote from the *International Paris Tribune* an article on the synthetic gene: "Dr. Har Johrd Khorana has made a gene-synthetic."

"It is the beginning of the end," this was the immediate reaction to this news from the science attaché at one of Washington's major embassies. "If you can make genes you can eventually make new viruses for which there are no cures. Any little country with good biochemists could make such biological weapons. It would take only a small laboratory. If it can be done, somebody will do it." For example, a death virus could be created that carries the coded message of death. A death tape, in fact. No doubt the technical details are complex and perhaps a team of sound and camera men working with biochemists would give us the answer.

And now the question as to whether scrambling techniques could be used to spread helpful and pleasant messages. Perhaps. On the other hand, the scrambled words and tape act like a virus in that they force something on the subject against his will. More to the point would be to discover how the old scanning patterns could be altered so that the subject liberates his own spontaneous scanning pattern.

New Scientist, 2 July, 1970 . . . Current memory theory posits a seven second temporary "buffer store" preceding the main one: a blow on the head wipes out memory of this much prior time because it erases the contents of the buffer. Daedalus observes that the sense of the present also covers just this range and so suggests that our sensory input is in effect recorded on an endless time loop, providing some seven seconds of delay for scanning before erasure. In this time the brain edits, makes sense of, and selects for storage key features. The weird *déjà vu* sensation that "now" has happened before is clearly due to brief erasure failure, so that we encounter already stored memory data coming round again. Time dragging or racing must reflect tape speed. A simple experiment will demonstrate this erasure process in operation. Making street recordings and playing them back, you will hear things you do not remember, sometimes said in a loud clear voice, must have been quite close to you, nor do you necessarily remember them when you hear the recording back. The sound has been erased according to a scanning pattern which is automatic. This means that what you notice and store as memory as you walk down a street is scanned out of a much larger selection of data which is then erased from the memory. For the walker the signs he passed, people he has passed, are erased from his mind and cease to exist for him. Now to make this scanning process conscious and controllable, try this:

Walk down a city block with a camera and take what you notice, moving the camera around as closely as possible to follow the direction of your eyes. The point is to make the camera your eyes and take what your eyes are scanning out of the larger picture. At the same time take the street at wide angle from a series of still positions. The street of the operator is, of course, the street as seen by the operator. It is different from the street seen at wide angle. Much of it is in fact missing. Now you can make arbitrary scanning patterns—that is cover first one side of the street and then the other in accordance with a preconceived plan. So you are breaking down the automatic scanning patterns. You could also make color scanning patterns, that is, scan out green, blue, red, etc., insofar as you can with your camera. That is, you are using an arbitrary preconceived scanning pattern, in order to break down automatic scanning patterns. A number of operators do this and then scramble in their takes together and with wide angle tapes. This could train the subject to see at a wider angle and also to ignore and erase at will.

Now, all this is readily subject to experimental verification on control subjects. Nor need the equipment be all that complicated. I have shown how it could work with feedback from brain waves and visceral response and videotape photos of subject taken while he is seeing and hearing the tape, simply to show optimum effectiveness. You can start with two tape recorders. The simplest scrambling device is scissors and splicing equipment. You can start scrambling words, make any kind of tapes and scramble them and observe the effects on friends and on yourself. Next step is sound film and then video camera. Of course results from individual experiments could lead to mass experiments, mass fear tapes, riot tapes, etc. The possibilities here for research and experiment are virtually unlimited and I have simply made a few very simple suggestions.

"A virus is characterised and limited by obligate cellular parasitism. All viruses must parasitise living cells for their replication. For all viruses the infection cycle comprises entry into the host, intracellular replication, and escape from the body of the host to initiate a new cycle in a fresh host." I am quoting here from *Mechanisms of Virus Infection* edited by Dr. Wilson Smith. In its wild state the virus has not proved to be a very adaptable organism. Some viruses have burned themselves out since they were 100 percent fatal and there were no reservoirs. Each strain of virus is rigidly programmed for a certain attack on certain tissues. If the attack fails, the virus does not gain a new host. There are, of course, virus mutations, and the influenza virus has proved quite versatile in this way. Generally it's the simple repetition of the same method of entry, and if that method is blocked by any body or other agency such as interferon, the attack fails. By and large, our virus is a stupid organism. Now we can think for the virus, devise a number of alternate methods of entry. For example, the host is simultaneously attacked by an ally virus who tells him that everything is all right and by a pain and fear virus. So the virus is now using an old method of entry, namely, the tough cop and the con cop.

We have considered the possibility that a virus can be activated or even created by very small units of sound and image. So conceived, the virus can be made to order in the laboratory. Ah, but for the takes to be effective, you must have also the actual virus and what is this so-called actual virus? New viruses turn up from time to time but from where do they turn up? Well, let's see how we could make a virus turn up. We plot now our virus's symptoms and make a scramble tape. The most susceptible subjects, that is those who reproduce some of the desired symptoms, will then be scrambled into more tapes till we scramble our virus into existence. This birth of a virus occurs when our virus is able to reproduce itself in a host and pass itself on to another host. Perhaps, too, with the virus under laboratory control it can be tamed for useful purposes. Imagine, for example, a sex virus. It so inflames the sex centers in the back brain that the host is driven mad from sexuality, all other considerations are blacked out. Parks full of naked, frenzied people, shitting, pissing, ejaculating, and screaming. So the virus could be malignant, blacking out all regulation and end in exhaustion, convulsions, and death.

Now let us attempt the same thing with tape. We organize a sex-tape festival. A hundred thousand people bring their scrambled sex tapes, and video tapes as well, to scramble in together. Projected on vast screens, muttering out over the crowd, sometimes it slows down so you see a few seconds, then scrambled again, then slow down, scramble. Soon it will scramble them all naked. The cops and the National Guard are stripping down. LET'S GET OURSELVES SOME CIVVIES. Now a thing like that could be messy, but those who survive it recover from the madness. Or, say, a small select group of really like-minded people get together with their sex tapes, you see the process is now being brought under control. And the fact that anybody can do it is in itself a limiting factor.

Here is Mr. Hart, who wants to infect everyone with his own image and turn them all into himself, so he scrambles himself and dumps himself out in search of worthy vessels. If nobody else knows about scrambling techniques he might scramble himself quite a stable of replicas. But anybody can do it. So go on, scramble your sex words out, and find suitable mates.

If you want to, scramble yourself out there, every stale joke, fart, chew, sneeze, and stomach rumble. If your trick no work you better run. Everybody doing it, they all scramble in together and the populations of the earth just settle down a nice even brown color. Scrambles is the democratic way, the way of full cellular representation. Scrambles is the American way.

I have suggested that virus can be created to order in the laboratory from very small units of sound and image. Such a preparation is not in itself biologically active but it could activate or even create virus in susceptible subjects. A carefully prepared jaundice tape could activate or create the jaundice virus in liver cells, especially in cases where the liver is already damaged. The operator is in effect directing a virus revolution of the cells. Since DOR* seems to attack those exposed to it at the weakest point, release of this force could coincide with virus attack. Reactive mind phrases could serve the same purpose of rendering subjects more susceptible to virus attack.

It will be seen that scrambled speech already has many of the characteristics of virus. When the speech takes and unscrambles, this occurs compulsively and against the will of the subject. A virus must remind you of its presence. Whether it is the nag of a cold sore or the torturing spasms of rabies the virus reminds you of its unwanted presence. "HERE ME IS."

So does scrambled word and image. The units are unscrambling compulsively, presenting certain words and images to the subject and this repetitive presentation is irritating certain bodily and neural areas. The cells so irritated can produce over a period of time the biologic virus units. We now have a new virus that can be communicated and indeed the subject may be desperate to communicate this thing that is bursting inside him. He is heavy with the load. Could this load be good and beautiful? Is it possible to create a virus which will communicate calm and sweet reasonableness? A virus must parasitise a host in order to survive. It uses the cellular material of the host to make copies of itself. In most cases this is damaging to the host. The virus gains entrance by fraud and maintains itself by force. An unwanted guest who makes you sick to look at is never good or beautiful. It is moreover a guest who always repeats itself word for word take for take.

Remember the life cycle of a virus . . . penetration of a cell or activation within the cell, replication within the cell, escape from cell to invade other cells, escape from host to infect a new host. This infection can take place in many ways and those who find themselves heavy with the load of a new virus generally use a shotgun technique to cover a wide range of infection routes . . . cough, sneeze, spit and fart at every opportunity. Save shit, piss, snot, scabs, sweat stained clothes and all bodily secretions for dehydration. The composite dust can be unobtrusively billowed out a roach bellows in subways, dropped from windows in bags, or sprayed out a crop duster. . . . Carry with you at all

*Deadly Orgone Radiation (W. Reich)—ed. note.

times an assortment of vectors . . . lice, fleas, bed bugs, and little aviaries of mosquitoes and biting flies filled with your blood. . . . I see no beauty in that.

There is only one case of a favorable virus influence benefiting an obscure species of Australian mice. On the other hand, if a virus produces no damaging symptoms we have no way of ascertaining its existence and this happens with latent virus infections. It has been suggested that yellow races resulted from a jaundice-like virus which produced a permanent mutation not necessarily damaging, which was passed along genetically. The same may be true of the word. The word itself may be a virus that has achieved a permanent status with the host. However, no known virus in existence at the present time acts in this manner, so the question of a beneficent virus remains open. It seems advisable to concentrate on a general defense against all virus.

Ron Hubbard, founder of Scientology, says that certain words and word combinations can produce serious illnesses and mental disturbances. I can claim some skill in the scrivener's trade, but I cannot guarantee to write a passage that will make someone physically ill. If Mr. Hubbard's claim is justified, this is certainly a matter for further research, and we can easily find out experimentally whether his claim is justified or not. Mr. Hubbard bases the power he attributes to words on his theory of engrams. An engram is defined as word, sound, image recorded by the subject in a period of pain and unconsciousness. Some of this material may be reassuring: "I think he's going to be all right." Reassuring material is an ally engram. Ally engrams, according to Mr. Hubbard, are just as bad as hostile pain engrams. Any part of this recording played back to the subject later will reactivate operation pain, he may actually develop a headache and feel depressed, anxious, or tense. Well, Mr. Hubbard's engram theory is very easily subject to experimental verification. Take ten volunteer subjects, subject them to a pain stimulus accompanied by certain words and sounds and images. You can act out little skits.

"Quickly, nurse, before I lose my little nigger," bellows the southern surgeon, and now a beefy white hand falls on the fragile black shoulder. "Yes, he's going to be all right. He's going to pull through."

"If I had my way I'd let these animals die on the operating table."

"You do not have your way, you have your duty as a doctor, we must do everything in our power to save human lives."

And so forth.

It is the tough cop and the con cop. The ally engram is ineffective without the pain engram, just as the con cop's arm around your shoulder, his soft persuasive voice in your ear, are indeed sweet nothings without the tough cop's blackjack. Now to what extent can words recorded during medical unconsciousness be recalled during hypnosis or Scientological processing? To what extent does the playback of this material affect the subject unpleasantly? Is the effect enhanced by scrambling the material, pain and ally, at very short intervals? It would seem that a scrambled engram's picture could almost dump an operating scene right in the subject's lap. Mr. Hubbard has charted his version of what he calls the reactive mind. This is roughly similar to Freud's *id*, a sort of built-in self defeating mechanism. As set forth by Mr. Hubbard this consists of a number of quite ordinary phrases. He claims that reading these phrases, or hearing them spoken, can cause illness, and gives this as his reason for not publishing this material. Is he perhaps saying that these are magic words? Spells, in fact? If so they could be quite a weapon scrambled up with imaginative sound-and-image track. Here now is the magic that turns men into swine. To be an animal: a lone pig grunts, shits, squeals and slobbers down garbage. To be animals: a chorus of a thousand pigs. Cut that in with video tape police pictures and play it back to them and see if you get a reaction from this so reactive mind.

Now here is another. To be a body, well it's sure an attractive body, rope the marks in. And a nice body symphony to go with it, rhythmic heart beats, contented stomach rumbles. To be bodies: recordings and pictures of hideous, aged, diseased bodies farting, pissing, shitting, groaning, dying. To do everything: man in a filthy apartment surrounded by unpaid bills, unanswered letters, jumps up and starts washing dishes and writing letters. To do nothing: he slumps in a chair, jumps up, slumps in chair, jumps up. Finally, slumps in a chair, drooling in idiot helplessness, while he looks at the disorder piled around him. The reactive mind commands can also be used to advantage with illness tapes. While projecting past cold sore on to the subject's face, and playing back to him a past illness tape, you can say: to be me, to be you, to stay here, to stay there, to be a body, to be bodies, to stay in, to stay out, to stay present, to stay absent. To what extent are these reactive mind phrases when scrambled effective in causing disagreeable symptoms in control volunteer subjects? As to Mr. Hubbard's claims for the reactive mind, only research can give us the answers.

The RM then is an artifact designed to limit and stultify on a mass scale. In order to have this effect it must be widely implanted. This can readily be done with modern electronic equipment and the techniques described in this treatise. The RM consists of commands which seem harmless and in fact unavoidable . . . To be a body . . . but which can have the most horrific consequences.

Here are some sample RM screen effects . . .

As the theater darkens a bright light appears on the left side of the screen. The screen lights up

To be nobody . . . On screen shadow of ladder and soldier incinerated by the Hiroshima blast

To be everybody . . . Street crowds, riots, panics

To be me . . . A beautiful girl and a handsome young man point to selves

To be you . . . They point to audience . . .

Hideous hags and old men, lepers, drooling idiots point to themselves and to the audience as they intone . . .

To be me

To be you

Command no. 5 . . . To be myself

Command no. 6 . . . To be others

On screen a narcotics officer is addressing an audience of school boys. Spread out on a table in front of him are syringes, kief pipes, samples of heroin, hashish, LSD.

Officer: "Five trips on a drug can be a pleasant and exciting experience . . ."

On screen young trippers . . . "I'm really myself for the first time"

ETC happy trips . . . To be myself . . . no. 5 . . .

Officer: "THE SIXTH WILL PROBABLY BLOW YOUR HEAD OFF"

Shot shows a man blowing his head off with a shotgun in his mouth . . .

Officer: "Like a fifteen-year-old boy I knew until recently, you could well end up dying in your own spew" . . . To be others no. 6 . . .

To be an animal . . . A lone Wolf Scout . . .

To be animals . . . He joins other wolf scouts playing, laughing, shouting

To be an animal . . . Bestial and ugly human behavior . . . brawls, disgusting eating and sex scenes

To be animals . . . Cows, sheep and pigs driven to the slaughter house

To be a body

To be bodies

A beautiful body . . . a copulating couple . . . Cut back and forth and run on seven second loop for several minutes . . . scramble at different speeds . . . Audience must be made to realize that to be a body is to be bodies . . . A body exists to be other bodies

To be a body . . . Death scenes and recordings . . . a scramble of last words

To be bodies . . . Vista of cemeteries . . .

To do it now . . . Couple embracing hotter and hotter

To do it now . . . A condemned cell . . . Condemned man is same actor as lover . . . He is led away by the guards screaming and struggling. Cut back and forth between sex scene and man led to execution. Couple in sex scene have orgasm as the condemned man is hanged, electrocuted, gassed, garrotted, shot in the head with a pistol

To do it later . . . The couple pull away . . . One wants to go out and eat and go to a show or something . . . They put on their hats . . .

To do it later . . . Warden arrives at condemned cell to tell the prisoner he has a stay of execution

To do it now . . . Grim faces in the Pentagon. Strategic is on its way . . . Well THIS IS IT . . . This sequence cut in with sex scenes and a condemned man led to execution, culminates in execution, orgasm, nuclear explosion . . . The condemned lover is a horribly burned survivor

To do it later . . . 1920 walk out sequence to "The Sunny Side of the Street" . . . A disappointed general turns from the phone to say the President has opened top level hot wire talks with Russia and China . . . Condemned man gets another stay of execution

To be an animal . . . One lemming busily eating lichen

To be animals . . . Hordes of lemmings swarming all over each other in mounting hysteria . . . A pile of drowned lemmings in front of somebody's nice little cottage on a Finnish lake where he is methodically going through sex positions with his girl friend. They wake up in a stink of dead lemmings

To be an animal . . . Little boy put on pot

To be animals . . . The helpless shitting infant is eaten alive by rats

To stay put . . . A man has just been hanged. The doctor steps forward with a stethoscope

To stay down . . . Body is carried out with the rope around neck . . . naked corpse on the autopsy table . . . corpse buried in quick lime

To stay up . . . Erect phallus

To stay down . . . White man burns off a Negro's genitals with blow torch . . . Theater darkens into the blow torch on left side of the screen

To stay present

To stay absent

To stay present . . . A boy masturbates in front of sex pictures . . . Cut to face of white man who is burning off black genitals with blow torch

To stay absent . . . Sex fantasies of the boy . . . The black slumps dead with genitals burned off and intestines popping out

To stay present . . . Boy watches strip tease, intent, fascinated . . . A man stands on trap about to be hanged

To stay present . . . Sex fantasies of the boy . . . "I pronounce this man dead"

To stay present . . . Boy whistles at girl in street . . . A man's body twists in the electric chair, his leg hairs crackling with blue fire

To stay absent . . . Boy sees himself in bed with girl . . . Man slumps dead in chair smoke curling from under the hood saliva dripping from his mouth . . .

The theater lights up. In the sky a plane over Hiroshima . . . Little Boy slides out

To stay present . . . The plane, the pilot, the American flag . . .

To stay absent . . . Theater darkens into atomic blast on screen

Here we see ordinary men and women going about their ordinary every-day jobs and diversions . . . subways, streets, buses, trains, airports, stations, waiting rooms, homes, flats, restaurants, offices, factories . . . working, eating, playing, defecating, making love

A chorus of voices cuts in RM phrases

To stay up

To stay down

Elevators, airports, stairs, ladders

To stay in

To stay out

Street signs, door signs, people at head of lines admitted to restaurants and theaters

To be myself

To be others
Customs agents check passports, man identifies himself at bank to cash check
To stay present
To stay absent
People watching films, reading, looking at TV . . .
A composite of this sound and image track is now run on seven second loop without change for several minutes.
Now cut in the horror pictures
To stay up
To stay down
Elevators, airports, stairs, ladders, hangings, castrations
To stay in
To stay out
Door signs, operation scenes . . . doctor tosses bloody tonsils, adenoids, appendix into receptacle
To stay present
To stay absent
People watching film . . . ether mask, ether vertigo . . . triangles, spheres, rectangles, pyramids, prisms, coils go away and come in in regular sequence . . . a coil coming in, two coils coming in, three coils coming in . . . a coil going away, two coils going away, four going away
A coil straight ahead going away, two coils on the left and right going away, three coils left right and center going away, four coils right left center and behind going away
A coil coming, two coils coming in, three coils coming in, four coils coming in . . . spirals of light . . . round and round faster faster, baby eaten by rats, hangings, electrocutions, castrations . . .
The RM can be cut in with the most ordinary scenes covering the planet in a smog of fear . . .
The RM is a built-in electronic police force armed with hideous threats. You don't want to be a cute little wolf cub? All right, cattle to the slaughter house meat on a hook.
Here is a nostalgic reconstruction of the old-fashioned Mayan methods. The wrong kind of workers with wrong thoughts are tortured to death in rooms under the pyramid . . . A young worker has been given a powerful hallucinogen and sexual stimulant . . . Naked he is strapped down and skinned alive . . . The dark Gods of pain are surfacing from the immemorial filth of time . . . The Oaub Bird stands there, screams, watching through his wild blue eyes. Others are crabs from the waist up clicking their claws in ecstasy, they dance around and mimic the flayed man. The scribes are busy with sketches . . . Now he is strapped into a segmented copper centipede and placed gently on a bed of hot coals . . . Soon the priests will dig the soft meat from the shell with their golden claws . . . Here is another youth staked out on an ant hill honey smeared on his eyes and genitals . . . Others with heavy weights on their backs are slowly dragged through wooden troughs in which shards of obsidian have

been driven . . . So the priests are the masters of pain and fear and death . . . To do right . . . To obey the priests . . . To do wrong? The priest's very presence and a few banal words . . .

The priests postulated and set up a hermetic universe of which they were the axiomatic controllers. In so doing they became Gods who controlled the known universe of the workers. They became Fear and Pain, Death and Time. By making opposition seemingly impossible they failed to make any provision for opposition. There is evidence that this control system broke down in some areas before the arrival of the White God. Stelae have been found defaced and overturned, mute evidence of a worker's revolution. How did this happen? The history of revolutionary movements shows that they are usually led by defectors from the ruling class. The Spanish rule in South America was overthrown by Spanish revolutionaries. The French were driven out of Algeria by Algerians educated in France. Perhaps one of the priest Gods defected and organized a worker's revolution . . .

The priest gods in the temple. They move very slowly, faces ravaged with age and disease. Parasitic worms infest their dead fibrous flesh. They are making calculations from the sacred books.

"Four hundred million years ago on this day a grievous thing happened . . ."

Limestone skulls rain in through the porticos. The Young Maize God leads the workers as they storm the temple and drag the priests out. They build a huge brush fire, throw the priests in and then throw the sacred books in after them. Time buckles and bends. The old Gods, surfacing from the immemorial depths of time, burst in the sky. . . . Mr. Hart stands there looking at the broken stelae . . . "How did this happen?"

His control system must be absolute and world wide. Because such a control system is even more vulnerable to attack from without than revolt from within. . . . Here is Bishop Landa burning the sacred books. To give you an idea as to what is happening, imagine our civilization invaded by louts from outer space . . .

"Get some bulldozers in here. Clear out all this crap . . ." The formulae of all the natural sciences, books, paintings, the lot, swept into a vast pile and burned. And that's it. No one ever heard of it . . .

Three codices survived the vandalism of Bishop Landa and these are burned around the edges. No way to know if we have here the sonnets of Shakespeare, the Mona Lisa or the remnants of a Sears Roebuck catalogue after the old outhouse burned down in a brush fire. A whole civilization went up in smoke . . .

When the Spaniards arrived, they found the Mayan aristocrats lolling in hammocks. Well, time to show them what is what. Five captured workers bound and stripped, are castrated on a tree stump, the bleeding, sobbing, screaming bodies thrown into a pile . . .

"And now get this through your gook nuts. We want to see a pile of gold that big and we want to see it pronto. The White God has spoken."

Consider now the human voice as a weapon. To what extent can the un-
aided human voice duplicate effects that can be done with a tape recorder?
Learning to speak with the mouth shut, thus displacing your speech, is fairly
easy. You can also learn to speak backwards, which is fairly difficult. I have
seen people who can repeat what you are saying after you and finish at the
same time. This is a most disconcerting trick, particularly when practiced on
a mass scale at a political rally. Is it possible to actually scramble speech? A far-
reaching biologic weapon can be forged from a new language. In fact such a
language already exists. It exists as Chinese, a total language closer to the multi-
level structure of experience, with a script derived from hieroglyphs, more
closely related to the objects and areas described. The equanimity of the Chinese is undoubtedly derived from their language being structured for greater
sanity. I notice the Chinese, wherever they are, retain the written and spoken
language, while other immigrant peoples will lose their language in two generations. The aim of this project is to build a language in which certain falsifications inherent in all existing Western languages will be made incapable
of formulation. The following falsifications to be deleted from the proposed
language.

The IS of Identity. You are an animal. You are a body. Now whatever you
may be you are not an "animal," you are not a "body," because these are verbal labels. The IS of identity always carries the implication of that and nothing else, and it also carries the assignment of permanent condition. To stay
that way. All naming calling presupposes the IS of identity. This concept is
unnecessary in a hieroglyphic language like ancient Egyptian and in fact frequently omitted. No need to say the sun IS in the sky, sun in sky suffices. The
verb *to be* can easily be omitted from any language and the followers of Count
Korzybski have done this, eliminating the verb *to be* in English. However, it is
difficult to tidy up the English language by arbitrary exclusion of concepts
which remain in force so long as the unchanged language is spoken.

The definite article THE. THE contains the implication of one and only:
THE God, THE universe, THE way, THE right, THE wrong. If there is
another, then THAT universe, THAT way is no longer THE universe, THE
way. The definite article THE will be deleted and the indefinite article A will
take its place.

The whole concept of EITHER/OR. Right or wrong, physical or mental, true
or false, the whole concept of OR will be deleted from the language and replaced by juxtaposition, by *and.* This is done to some extent in any pictorial
language where the two concepts stand literally side by side. These falsifications inherent in English and other Western alphabetical languages give the
reactive mind commands their overwhelming force in these languages. Consider the IS of identity. When I say to be me, to be you, to be myself, to be
others—whatever I may be called upon to be or say that I am—I am not the
verbal label "myself." I cannot be and am not the verbal label "myself." The
word BE in English contains, as a virus contains, its precoded message of

damage, the categorical imperative of permanent condition. To be a body, to be nothing else, to stay a body. To be an animal, to be nothing else, to stay an animal. If you see the relation of the I to the body, as the relation of a pilot to his ship, you see the full crippling force of the reactive mind command to be a body. Telling the pilot to be the plane, then who will pilot the plane?

The IS of identity, assigning a rigid and permanent status, was greatly reinforced by the customs and passport control that came in after World War I. Whatever you may be, you are not the verbal labels in your passport any more than you are the word "self." So you must be prepared to prove at all times that you are what you are not. Much of the force of the reactive mind also depends on the falsification inherent in the categorical definite article THE. THE now, THE past, THE time, THE space, THE energy, THE matter, THE universe. Definite article THE contains the implication of no other. THE universe locks you in THE, and denies the possibility of any other. If other universes are possible, then the universe is no longer THE, it becomes A. The definite article THE in the proposed language is deleted and replaced by A. Many of the RM commands are in point of fact contradictory commands and a contradictory command gains its force from the Aristotelian concept of either/or. To do everything, to do nothing, to have everything, to have nothing, to do it all, to do not any, to stay up, to stay down, to stay in, to stay out, to stay present, to stay absent. These are in point of fact either/or propositions. To do nothing *or* everything, to have it all *or* not any, to stay present *or* to stay absent. Either/or is more difficult to formulate in a written language where both alternatives are pictorially represented and can be deleted entirely from the spoken language. The whole reactive mind can be in fact reduced to three little words—to be "THE." That is to be what you are not, verbal formulations.

I have frequently spoken of word and image as viruses or as acting as viruses, and this is not an allegorical comparison. It will be seen that the falsifications in syllabic Western languages are in point of fact actual virus mechanisms. The IS of identity is in point of fact the virus mechanism. If we can infer purpose from behavior, then the purpose of a virus is TO SURVIVE. To survive at any expense to the host invaded. To be an animal, to be a body. To be an animal body that the virus can invade. To be animals, to be bodies. To be more animal bodies so that the virus can move from one body to another. To stay present as an animal body, to stay absent as antibody or resistance to the body invasion.

The categorical THE is also a virus mechanism, locking you in THE virus universe. EITHER/OR is another virus formula. It is always you OR the virus. EITHER/OR. This is in point of fact the conflict formula which is seen to be an archetypical virus mechanism. The proposed language will delete these virus mechanisms and make them impossible of formulation in the language. The language will be a tonal language like Chinese, it will also have a hieroglyphic script as pictorial as possible without being too cumbersome or difficult to write. This language will give one the option of silence. When not talking, the user of this language can take in the silent images of the written, pictorial and symbol languages.

I have described here a number of weapons and tactics in the war game. Weapons that change consciousness could call the war game in question. All games are hostile. Basically there is only one game and that game is war. It's the old army game from here to eternity. Mr. Hubbard says that Scientology is a game where everybody wins. There are no games where everybody wins. That's what games are all about, winning and losing . . . The Versailles Treaty . . . Hitler dances the Occupation Jig . . . War criminals hang at Nuremberg . . . It is a rule of this game that there can be no final victory since this would mean the end of the war game. Yet every player must believe in final victory and strive for it with all his power. Faced by the nightmare of final defeat he has no alternative. So all existing technologies with escalating efficiency produce more and more total weapons until we have the atom bomb which could end the game by destroying all players. Now mock up a miracle. The so stupid players decide to save the game. They sit down around a big table and draw up a plan for the immediate deactivation and eventual destruction of all atomic weapons. Why stop there? Conventional bombs are unnecessarily destructive if nobody else has them *hein?* Let's turn the war clock back to 1917:

Keep the home fires burning
Though the hearts are yearning
There's a long, long trail a-winding . . .
Back to the American Civil War . . .

"He has loosed the fatal lightning of his terrible swift sword." His fatal lightning didn't cost as much in those days. Save a lot on the defense budget this way on back to flintlocks, matchlocks, swords, armor, lances, bows and arrows, spears, stone axes and clubs. Why stop there? Why not grow teeth and claws, poison fangs, stingers, spines, quills, beaks and suckers and stink glands and fight it out in the muck *hein?*

That is what this revolution is about. End of game. New games? There are no new games from here to eternity. END OF THE WAR GAME.

CONTROL

The ancient Mayans possessed one of the most precise and hermetic control calendars ever used on this planet, a calendar that in effect controlled what the populace did thought and felt on any given day. A study of this model system throws light on modern methods of control. Knowledge of the calendar was the monopoly of a priestly caste who maintained their position with minimal police and military force. The priests had to start with a very accurate calendar for the tropical year consisting of 365 days divided into 18 months of 20 days and a final period of 5 days, the "Ouab days" which were considered especially unlucky and in consequence turned out to be so. An accurate calendar was essential to the foundation and maintenance of the priest's power. The Mayans were almost entirely dependent on the maize crop and the method of agriculture employed was slash and burn. Brush was cut down, allowed to dry and then burned. The corn was planted with a planting stick. The Mayans had no plows and no domestic animals capable of pulling a plow. Since the top soil is shallow and a stratum of limestone lies six inches under the surface plows are not functional in this area and the slash and burn method is used to the present day. Slash and burn cultivation depends on exact timing. The brush must be cut and given time to dry before the rains start. Miscalculation of a few days can lose a year's crop. In addition to the yearly calendar which regulated agricultural operations there was a sacred almanac of 260 days. This ceremonial calendar governed 13 festivals of 20 days each. The ceremonial calendar rolled through the year like a wheel and consequently the festivals occurred at different dates each year but always in the same sequence. The festivals consisted of religious ceremonies, music, feasts, sometimes human sacrifice. Accordingly the priests could calculate into the future or the past exactly what the populace would be doing hearing seeing on a given date. This alone would have enabled them to predict the future or reconstruct the past with considerable accuracy since they could determine what conditioning would be or had been applied on any given date to a population which for many years remained in hermetic seclusion protected by impassable mountains and jungles from the waves of invaders who swept down the central plateau of Mexico. There is every reason to infer the existence of a third secret calendar which referred to conditioning in precise sequence applied to the populace under cover of the festivals very much as a stage magician uses patter and spectacle to cover movements which would otherwise be apparent to the audience. There are many ways in which such conditioning can be effected the simplest being waking suggestion which is fully explained in a later context. Briefly, waking suggestion is a technique for implanting verbal or visual suggestions which take direct effect on the autonomic nervous system because the subject's conscious attention is directed somewhere else, in this case on the overt content of the festivals. (Waking suggestion is not to be confused with subliminal suggestion which is suggestion below the level of conscious awareness.) So the priests could calculate what the populace saw and heard on a given day and also what suggestions were secretly implanted on that day. To obtain some idea of the secret calendar consider the Reactive Mind as postulated by L. Ron Hubbard the founder of Scientology. Mr Hubbard describes the R.M. as an ancient instrument of control designed to stultify and limit the potential for action in a constructive or destructive direction. The precise content of the R.M. as set forth in his formulation is considered confidential material since it can cause illness and upsets so I will limit myself to general considerations without giving the exact phrases used: The R.M. consists of consequential, sequential and contradictory propositions that have com-

mand value at the automatic level of behavior, quite as automatic and involuntary as the metabolic commands that regulate rate of heartbeats, digestion,
balance of chemical constituents in the blood stream, brain waves. The regulatory center of the autonomic nervous system which controls bodily processes
and metabolism is the hypothalamus in the back brain. Undoubtedly the hypothalamus is the neurological intersection point where the R.M. is implanted.
The R.M. may be described as an artificially constructed and highly disadvantageous regulatory system grafted onto the natural regulatory center. The R.M.
as expounded by Mr Hubbard is of considerable antiquity antedating all modern languages and yet manifesting itself through all modern languages. Consequently it must refer to a *symbol system*. And except for the intervention of
Bishop Landa we could infer by analogy what this symbol system consisted of
since all control systems are basically similar. Bishop Landa collected all the
Mayan books he could lay hands on, a stack of them six feet high, and burned
the lot. To date only three authenticated Mayan codices have turned up that
survived this barbarous action.

Mr Hubbard logically postulates that the R.M. commands take effect because they relate to actual goals, needs, conditions of those affected. A consequential command is a command that one must obey in consequence of having
been born: "to be here in a human body." A sequential command follows from
this basic proposition: "to seek food, shelter, sexual satisfaction," "to exist in
relation to other human bodies." Contradictory commands are two commands
that contradict each other given at the same time. "TENSHUN!" The soldier
automatically stiffens to the command. "AT EASE!" The soldier automatically relaxes. Now imagine a captain who strides into the barracks snapping
"TENSHUN" from one side of his face and "AT EASE" from the other. (Quite
possible to do this with dubbing techniques.) The attempt to obey two flatly
contradictory commands at once both of which have a degree of command
value at the automatic level disorients the subject. He may react with rage,
apathy, anxiety, even collapse. Another example: I give the command "sit
down" and when the command is obeyed promptly the subject receives a reward. If it is not obeyed promptly he receives a severe electric shock. When he
has been conditioned to obey I add the command "stand up" and condition
him to obey this command in precisely the same way. Now I give both commands simultaneously. The result may well be complete collapse as Pavlov's
dogs collapsed when given contradictory signals at such short intervals that
their nervous systems could not adjust. The aim of these commands from
the viewpoint of a control system is to limit and confine. All control units
employ such commands. For contradictory commands to have force the
subject must have been conditioned to obey both commands automatically
and the commands must relate to his actual goals. "TENSHUN" "AT EASE"
"SIT DOWN" "STAND UP" are arbitrary commands tenuously connected
to any basic goal of the subject—(of course "TENSHUN" relates to the goal
to be a good soldier or at least to stay out of the guardhouse which gives the
command what strength it has)—Consider another pair of commands that con-

tradict each other: "to make a good impression" "to make an awful impression." This relates to much more basic goals. Everyone wants to make a good impression. His self-regard, livelihood, sexual satisfaction depend on making a good impression. Why then does the subject when he is trying most desperately to make a good impression make the worst impression possible? Because he also has the goal to make a bad impression which operates on an involuntary automatic level. This self-destructive goal is such a threat to his being that he *reacts* against it. He may be conscious or partially conscious of the negative goal but he cannot confront it directly. The negative goal forces him to react. The Reactive Mind consists of goals so repulsive or frightening to the subject that he compulsively reacts against them and *it is precisely this reaction that keeps these negative goals in operation.* Negative goals are implanted by fear. Consider a pair of contradictory commands that were undoubtedly used in some form by the Mayan priests: "to rebel stridently" "to submit meekly." Every time a worker nerved himself to rebel the goal to submit was activated causing him to assert rebellion more and more stridently thus activating more and more compulsively the goal to submit. So he trembles stammers and collapses before an authority figure that he consciously despises. No exercise of so-called will power affects these automatic reactions. The goal to submit was implanted by a threat so horrible that he could not confront it, and the Mayan secret books obviously consisted of such horrific pictures. The few that have survived bear witness to this. Men are depicted turning into centipedes, crabs, plants. Bishop Landa was so appalled by what he saw that his own reactive mind dictated his vandalous act. Like his modern counterparts who scream for censorship and book burning he did not take account of the fact that any threat clearly seen and confronted loses force. The Mayan priests took care that the populace did not see the books. Mr Hubbard's R.M. contains about 300 items. Some are commands arranged in pairs, some are visual representations. Using the R.M. as a model—and the Mayan system must have been quite similar—postulate that during a ceremonial month of 20 days 4 items were repeated or represented 20 times on the first day, 4 more items 20 times on the second day and so on 80 items for the 20-day month. The next 20-day month of the sacred almanac 80 more items until the items were exhausted after which they were repeated in precisely the same sequence thus constituting a secret calendar. The priests then could calculate precisely what reactive commands had been or would be restimulated on any date past or future and these calculations enabled them to reconstruct the past or predict the future with considerable accuracy. They were dealing from a stacked deck. Calculations of past and future calendar juxtapositions took up a good deal of their time and they were more concerned with the past than the future. There are calculations that go back 400,000,000 years. These probings into the remote past may be interpreted as an assertion that the calendars always existed and always will exist. (All control systems claim to reflect the immutable laws of the universe.) These calculations must have looked like this:

year, month, day of the 365-day calendar which was calculated from 5 Ahua
8 Cumhu

a mythical date when time began
year month and day of the sacred almanac or ceremonial calendar
year month and day of the secret calendar

Mayan students have succeeded in deciphering dates in the 365-day calendar. Lacking cross references comparable to the Rosetta Stone much of the writing remains unsolved. If we interpret the writing as oriented toward control we can postulate that all the inscriptions refer to dates and the events, ceremonies, suggestions, pictures and planetary juxtapositions correlated with dates. Any control system depends on precise timing. A picture or suggestion may be quite innocuous at one time and devastating at another. For example "to make a splendid impression" "to make an awful impression" may have no effect on somebody when he is not in a competitive context. Same man bucking for lieutenant bars or apprentice priest can be reliably washed out by the same pair of contradictory commands, brought into restimulation.

This seemingly hermetic control calendar broke down even before the Aztecs invaded Yucatán and long before the arrival of the Spaniards. All control systems work on punishment-reward. When punishment overbalances reward, when the masters have no rewards left to give, revolts occur. The continual demands for forced labor on the temples and stelae coupled with a period of famine may have been the precipitating factor. Or possibly some forgotten Bolívar revealed the content of the secret books. In any case the workers rebelled, killed the priests and defaced the stelae and temples as symbols of enslavement.

Now translate the Mayan control calendar into modern terms. The mass media of newspapers, radio, television, magazines form a ceremonial calendar to which all citizens are subjected. The "priests" wisely conceal themselves behind masses of contradictory data and vociferously deny that they exist. Like the Mayan priests they can reconstruct the past and predict the future on a statistical basis through manipulation of media. It is the daily press preserved in newspaper morgues that makes detailed reconstruction of past dates possible. How can the modern priests predict seemingly random future events? Start with the many factors in mass media that can be controlled and predicted:

1. *Layout:* the format of newspapers and magazines can be decided in advance. The TV programs to be used in juxtaposition with news broadcasts can be decided in advance.
2. *The news to be played up and the news to be played down:* ten years ago in England drug arrests were four-line back-page items. Today they are front-page headlines.
3. *Editorials and letters to the editor:* The letters published are of course selected in accordance with preconceived policy.

4. *Advertisements:* So the modern ceremonial calendar is almost as predictable as the Mayan. What about the secret calendar? Any number of reactive
commands can be inserted in advertisements, editorials, newspaper stories.
Such commands are implicit in the layout and juxtaposition of items. Contradictory commands are an integral part of the modern industrial environment: Stop. Go. Wait here. Go there. Come in. Stay out. Be a man. Be a
woman. Be white. Be black. Live. Die. Be your real self. Be somebody else.
Be a human animal. Be a superman. Yes. No. Rebel. Submit. RIGHT.
WRONG. Make a splendid impression. Make an awful impression. Sit down.
Stand up. Take your hat off. Put your hat on. Create. Destroy. Live now.
Live in the future. Live in the past. Obey the law. Break the law. Be ambitious. Be modest. Accept. Reject. Plan ahead. Be spontaneous. Decide for
yourself. Listen to others. Talk. SILENCE. Save money. Spend money.
Speed up. Slow down. This way. That way. Right. Left. Present. Absent.
Open. Closed. Entrance. Exit. IN. OUT, etc., round the clock. This creates a vast pool of statistical newsmakers. It is precisely uncontrollable automatic reactions that make news. The controllers know what reactive
commands they are going to restimulate and in consequence they know
what will happen. Contradictory suggestion is the basic formula of the daily
press: "Take drugs everybody is doing it." "Drug-taking is WRONG."
Newspapers spread violence, sex, drugs, then come on with the old RIGHT
WRONG FAMILY CHURCH AND COUNTRY sound. It is wearing very
thin. The modern control calendar is breaking down. Punishment now
overbalances reward in the so-called "permissive" society, and young people
no longer want the paltry rewards offered them. Rebellion is world-wide.
The present controllers have an advantage which the Mayan priests did not
have: an overwhelming arsenal of weapons which the rebels cannot hope
to obtain or duplicate. Clubs and spears can be produced by anyone. Tanks,
planes, battleships, heavy artillery and nuclear weapons are a monopoly of
those in power. As their psychological domination weakens modern es-
tablishments are relying more and more on this advantage and now maintain their position by naked force—(How permissive is the "permissive
society"?)—Yet the advantage of weaponry is not so overwhelming as it
appears. To implement weapons the controllers need soldiers and police.
These guardians must be kept under reactive control. Hence the controllers must rely on people who are always stupider and more degraded by the
conditioning essential to their suppressive function.

Techniques exist to erase the Reactive Mind and achieve a complete freedom from past conditioning and immunity against such conditioning in the
future. Scientology processing accomplishes this. Erasure of the R.M. is carried out on the E Meter a very sensitive reaction tester developed by Mr
Hubbard. If an R.M. item reads on the E Meter the subject is still reacting to
it. When an item ceases to read he is no longer reacting to it. It may be necessary to run the entire R.M. hundreds of times to effect complete erasure.

But it will erase. The method works. I can testify to that through my own experience. It takes time, at least two months of training eight hours a day to learn how to use the E Meter and how to run the material. It is expensive, about three thousand dollars for the training and processing that leads to erasure of the Reactive Mind. A reconstruction of the symbol system that must underlie the Reactive Mind would open the way for more precise and speedy erasure.

Two recent experiments indicate the possibility of mass deconditioning. In one experiment volunteers were wired to an encephalographic unit that recorded their brain waves. When alpha brain waves, which are correlated with a relaxed state of mind and body appeared on screen, the subject was instructed to maintain this state as long as possible. After some practice alpha waves could be produced at will. The second experiment is more detailed and definitive: *Herald Tribune,* January 31, 1969: "U. S. scientist demonstrated that animals can learn to control such automatic responses as heart rate, blood pressure, glandular secretions and brain waves in response to rewards and punishments. The psychologist is Doctor N. E. Miller. He says that his findings upset the traditional thinking that the autonomic nervous system which controls the workings of the heart, digestive system and other internal organs is completely involuntary. Doctor Miller and his co-workers were able to teach animals to increase or decrease the amount of saliva they produced, raise or lower their blood pressure, increase or decrease their intestinal contractions, stomach activity and urinary output and change their brain wave patterns using as a reward direct electrical stimulation of the so-called reward areas of the brain when the desired response occurred. Rats were able to learn to raise or lower their heart rates by 20 percent in ninety minutes of training. Retesting showed that they remembered their lessons well, Doctor Miller said." In what way does this experiment differ from the experiments by which Pavlov demonstrated the conditioned reflex? I quote from *Newsweek,* February 10, 1969: "Until now most psychologists believed that the autonomic nervous system could be trained only by the advancement of knowledge." Mr Hubbard's overtly fascist utterances . . . (China is the real danger to world peace, Scientology is protecting the home, the church, the family, decent morals—no wife swapping . . . national boundaries, the concept of RIGHT AND WRONG) against evil free-thinking psychiatrists can hardly recommend him to the militant students. Certainly it is time for Scientology to come out in plain English on one side or the other if they expect the trust and support of young people. Which side are you on Hubbard which side are you on?

from
the adding machine

IT IS NECESSARY TO TRAVEL...

"It is necessary to travel. It is not necessary to live." These words inspired early investigators when the vast frontier of unknown seas opened to their sails in the fifteenth century. Space is the new frontier. Is this frontier open to youth? I quote from the London *Daily Express,* December 30, 1968: "If you are a fit young man under twenty-five with lightning reflexes who fears nothing in heaven or on earth and has a keen appetite for adventure don't bother to apply for the job of astronaut." They want "cool dads" trailing wires to the "better half" from an aqualung. Dr. Paine of the Space Center in Houston says: "This flight was a triumph for the squares of this world who aren't ashamed to say a prayer now and then." Is this the great adventure of space? Are these men going to take the step into regions literally unthinkable in verbal terms? To travel in space you must leave the old verbal garbage behind: God talk, country talk, mother talk, love talk, party talk. You must learn to exist with no religion, no country, no allies. You must learn to live alone in silence. Anyone who prays in space is not there.

The last frontier is being closed to youth. However there are many roads to space. To achieve complete freedom from past conditioning is to be in space. Techniques exist for achieving such freedom. These techniques are being concealed and withheld. We must search for and consider techniques for discovery.

REMEMBERING JACK KEROUAC

Jack Kerouac was a writer. That is, he wrote. Many people who call themselves writers and have their names on books are not writers and they can't write, like a bullfighter who makes passes with no bull there. The writer has been there or he can't write about it. And going there, he risks being gored. By that I mean what the Germans aptly call the Time Ghost. For example, such a fragile ghost world as Fitzgerald's Jazz Age—all the sad young men, firefly evenings, winter dreams, fragile, fragile like his picture taken in his twenty-third year—Fitzgerald, poet of the Jazz Age. He went there and wrote it and brought it back for a generation to read, but he never found his own way back. A whole migrant generation arose from Kerouac's *On the Road* to Mexico, Tangier, Afghanistan, India.

What are writers, and I will confine the use of this term to writers of novels, trying to do? They are trying to create a universe in which they have lived or where they would like to live. To write it, they must go there and submit to conditions that they may not have bargained for. Sometimes, as in the case of Fitzgerald and Kerouac, the effect produced by a writer is immediate, as if a generation were waiting to be written. In other cases, there may be a time lag. Science fiction, for example, has a way of coming true. In any case, by writing a universe, the writer makes such a universe possible.

To what extent writers can and do act out their writing in so-called real life, and how useful it is for their craft, are open questions. That is, are you making your universe more like the real universe, or are you pulling the real one into yours? Winner take nothing. For example, Hemingway's determination to act out the least interesting aspects of his own writing and to actually be his character, was, I feel, unfortunate for his writing. Quite simply, if a writer insists on being able to do and do well what his characters do, he limits the range of his characters.

However, writers profit from doing something even when done badly. I was, for one short week—brings on my ulcers to think about it—a very bad assistant pickpocket. I decided that a week was enough, and I didn't have the touch, really.

Walking around the wilderness of outer Brooklyn with the Sailor after a mooch (as he called a drunk) came up on us at the end of Flatbush: "The cops'll beat the shit out of us . . . you have to expect that." I shuddered and didn't want to expect that and decided right there that I was going to turn in my copy of the *Times,* the one I would use to cover him when he put the hand out. We always used the same copy—he said people would try to read it and get confused when it was a month old, and this would keep them from seeing us. He was quite a philosopher, the Sailor was . . . but a week was enough before I got what I "had to expect . . ."

"Here comes one . . . yellow lights, too." We huddle in a vacant lot. . . . Speaking for myself at least, who can always see what I look like from outside, I look like a frightened commuter clutching his briefcase as Hell's Angels roar past.

Now if this might seem a cowardly way, cowering in a vacant lot when I should have given myself the experience of getting worked over by the skinny short cop with the acne-scarred face who looks out of that prowl car, his eyes brown and burning in his head—well, the Sailor wouldn't have liked that, and neither would a White Hunter have liked a client there to get himself mauled by a lion.

Fitzgerald said once to Hemingway, "Rich people are different from you and me."

"Yes . . . they have more money." And writers are different from you and me. They write. You don't bring back a story if you get yourself killed. So a writer need not be ashamed to hide in a vacant lot or a corner of the room for a few minutes. He is there as a writer and not as a character. There is nothing more elusive than a writer's main character, the character that is assumed by the reader to be the writer himself, no less, actually doing the things he writes about. But this main character is simply a point of view interposed by the writer. The main character then becomes in fact another character in the book, but usually the most difficult to see, because he is mistaken for the writer himself. He is the writer's observer, often very uneasy in this role and at a loss to account for his presence. He is an object of suspicion to the world of nonwriters, unless he manages to write them into his road.

Kerouac says in *Vanity of Duluoz:* "I am not 'I am' but just a spy in someone's body pretending these sandlot games, kids in the cow field near St. Rota's Church. . . ." Jack Kerouac knew about writing when I first met him in 1944. He was twenty-one; already he had written a million words and was completely dedicated to his chosen trade. It was Kerouac who kept telling me I should write and call the book I wrote *Naked Lunch.* I had never written anything after high school and did not think of myself as a writer, and I told him so. "I got no talent for writing. . . ." I had tried a few times, a page maybe. Reading it over always gave me a feeling of fatigue and disgust, an aversion towards this form of activity, such as a laboratory rat must experience when he chooses the wrong path and gets a sharp reprimand from a needle in his displeasure centers. Jack insisted quietly that I did have talent for writing and that I would write a book called *Naked Lunch.* To which I replied, "I don't want to hear anything literary."

Trying to remember just where and when this was said is like trying to remember a jumble of old films. The 1940s seem centuries away. I see a bar on 116th Street here, and a scene five years later in another century: a sailor at the bar who reeled over on the cue of "Naked Lunch" and accused us—I think Allen Ginsberg was there, and John Kingsland—of making a sneering reference to the Swiss Navy. Kerouac was good in these situations, since he was basically unhostile. Or was it in New Orleans or Algiers, to be more precise, where I lived in a frame house by the river, or was it later in Mexico by the lake in Chapultepec Park . . . there's an island there where thousands of vultures roost apathetically. I was shocked at this sight, since I had always admired their aerial teamwork, some skimming a few feet off the ground, others wheeling way up, little black specks in the sky—and when they spot food they pour down in a black funnel . . .

We are sitting on the edge of the lake with tacos and bottles of beer. . . . "Naked Lunch is the only title," Jack said. I pointed to the vultures.

"They've given up, like old men in St. Petersburg, Florida. . . . Go out and hustle some carrion you lazy buzzards!" Whipping out my pearlhandled .45, I killed six of them in showers of black feathers. The other vultures took to the sky. . . . I would act these out with Jack, and quite a few of the scenes that later appeared in *Naked Lunch* arose from these acts. When Jack came to Tangier in 1957, I had decided to use the title, and much of the book was already written.

In fact, during all those years I knew Kerouac, I can't remember ever seeing him really angry or hostile. It was the sort of smile he gave in reply to my demurrers, in a way you get from a priest who knows you will come to Jesus sooner or later—you can't walk out on the Shakespeare Squadron, Bill.

Now as a very young child I had wanted to be a writer. At the age of nine I wrote something called *Autobiography of a Wolf.* This early literary essay was influenced by—so strongly as to smell of plagiarism—a little book I had just read called *The Biography of a Grizzly Bear.* There were various vicissitudes, including the loss of his beloved mate . . . in the end this poor old bear slouches into a valley he knows is full of poison gases, about to die. . . . I can see the picture now, it's all in sepia, the valley full of nitrous yellow fumes and the bear walking in like a resigned criminal to the gas chamber. Now I had to give my wolf a different twist, so, saddened by the loss of his entire family, he encounters a grizzly bear who kills him and eats him. Later there was something called *Carl Cranbury in Egypt* that never got off the ground, really . . . a knife glinted in the dark valley. With lightning speed Carl V. Cranbury reached for the blue steel automatic . . .

These were written out painfully in longhand with great attention to the script. The actual process of writing became so painful that I couldn't do anything more for Carl Cranbury, as the Dark Ages descended—the years in which I wanted to be anything else but a writer. A private detective, a bartender, a criminal. . . . I failed miserably at all these callings, but a writer is not concerned with success or failure, but simply with observation and recall. At the time I was not gathering material for a book. I simply was not doing anything well enough to make a living at it. In this respect, Kerouac did better than I did. He didn't like it, but he did it—work on railroads and in factories. My record time on a factory job was four weeks. And I had the distinction to be actually fired from a defense plant during the War.

Perhaps Kerouac did better because he saw his work interludes simply as a means to buy time to write. Tell me how many books a writer has written . . . we can assume usually ten times that amount shelved or thrown away. And I will tell you how he spends his time: Any writer spends a good deal of his time alone, writing. And that is how I remember Kerouac—as a writer talking about writers or sitting in a quiet corner with a notebook, writing in longhand. He was also very fast on the typewriter. You feel that he was writing all the time; that writing was the only thing he thought about. He never wanted to do anything else.

If I seem to be talking more about myself than about Kerouac, it is because I am trying to say something about the particular role that Kerouac played in my life script. As a child, I had given up on writing, perhaps unable to face what every writer must: all the bad writing he will have to do before he does any good writing. An interesting exercise would be to collect all the worst writing of any writer—which simply shows the pressures that writers are under to write badly, that is, not write. This pressure is, in part, simply the writer's own conditioning from childhood to think (in my case) white Protestant American or (in Kerouac's case) to think French-Canadian Catholic.

Writers are, in a way, very powerful indeed. They write the script for the reality film. Kerouac opened a million coffee bars and sold a million pairs of Levis to both sexes. Woodstock rises from his pages. Now if writers could get together into a real tight union, we'd have the world right by the words. We could write our own universes, and they would all be as real as a coffee bar or a pair of Levis or a prom in the Jazz Age. Writers could take over the reality studio. So they must not be allowed to find out that they can make it happen. Kerouac understood this long before I did. "Life is a dream," he said.

My own birth records, my family's birth records and recorded origins, my athletic records in the newspaper clippings I have, my own notebooks and published books are not real at all; my own dreams are not dreams at all but products of my waking imagination. . . . "This, then, is the writers world— the dream made for a moment actual on paper, you can almost touch it, like the endings of *The Great Gatsby* and *On the Road*. Both express a dream that was taken up by a generation.

Life is a dream in which the same person may appear at various times in different roles. Years before I met Kerouac, a friend from high school and college, Kells Elvins, told me repeatedly that I should write and that I was not suited to do anything else. When I was doing graduate work at Harvard in 1938, we wrote a story in collaboration, entitled "Twilight's Last Gleamings," which I used many years later almost verbatim in *Nova Express*. We acted out the parts, sitting on a side porch of the white frame house we rented together, and this was the birthplace of Doctor Benway.

" 'Are you all right?' he shouted, seating himself in the first lifeboat among the women. 'I'm the doctor!' "

Years later in Tangier, Kells told me the truth: "I know I am dead and you are too. . . ." Writers are all dead, and all writing is posthumous. We are really from beyond the tomb and no commissions. . . . (All this I am writing just as I think of it, according to Kerouac's own manner of writing. He says the first version is always the best.)

In 1945 or thereabouts, Kerouac and I collaborated on a novel that was never published. Some of the material covered in this lost opus was later used by Jack in *The Town and the City* and *Vanity of Duluoz*. At that time, the anonymous grey character of William Lee was taking shape: Lee, who is there just so long and long enough to see and hear what he needs to see and hear for some scene or character he will use twenty or thirty years later in his writing. No, he wasn't there as a private detective, a bartender, a cotton farmer, a pickpocket, an exterminator; he was there in his capacity as a writer. I did not know that until later. Kerouac, it seems, was born knowing. And he told me what I already knew, which is the only thing you can tell anybody.

I am speaking of the role Kerouac played in my script, and the role I played in his can be inferred from the enigmatically pompous Hubbard Bull Lee portrayals, which readily adapt themselves to the scenes between Carl and Doctor Benway in *Naked Lunch*. Kerouac may have felt that I did not include him in my cast of characters, but he is of course the anonymous William Lee as defined in our collaboration—a spy in someone else's body where nobody knows who is spying on whom. Sitting on a side porch, Lee was there in his capacity as a writer. So Doctor Benway told me what I knew already: "I'm the doctor . . ."

THE BAY OF PIGS

John turned slowly and noticed in the far corner of the bar room what he thought for a moment was a piece of statuary. A slight movement like breathing told him that the creature was alive. It was a girl with bright green eyes and the immobility of a lizard. He thought of a beautiful green reptile from remote crossroads of time.

The Southerner winked broadly. "Don't be shy, young man. Better go over and join her before some of those Mexican coyotes beat you to the jump. . . . She's been giving you the eye for the last half hour."

The man turned and made his way through the crowded bar with extraordinary agility for a man of his bulk.

John picked up his drink and walked over to the corner. The girl looked at him steadily.

"Mind if I sit down?"

"Not at all," she said in a curiously unaccented English.

He sat down.

"What will you have to drink?"

"Crème de menthe, I think."

She gave him a look of cool appraisal from hooded green eyes deeply set in high cheekbones. Her eyes caught points of light in the room like an opal, and her jet black pupils converged and he had a feeling of being touched right at the source point inside his skull. The skin of her face was transparent, smooth, of a greenish pallor.

She sat absolutely immobile, looking at him. Slowly she smiled.

"The Bay of Pigs intends to make use of you," she said.

"You think he is CIA?"

"He's not trying to hide it . . ."

"But what use could he make of me?"

"He is looking for the books of course."

"That story about the Mayan books being still in existence somewhere? You think there is any truth in it?"

"He thinks so, or he wouldn't waste time with you. That means that others think so as well."

She looked around the room. A sprinkling of politicians with Chapultepec blondes, a table of loud Americans.

"Come, I will take you to a party. . . . It happens only once a year and you should see some of the real Mexico, something that will not last much longer . . . folklore you might call it."

They walked out and turned right along the Paseo. Across the streets in the Alameda people strolled and talked and sat on benches. They walked down to the intersection and turned right again on Niño Perdido.

She was wearing flexible low-heeled shoes of green lizard skin that gripped the pavement as she glided along. He found it difficult to keep up with her.

It was a neighborhood of *pulquerías* sandwich booths and market stalls. Men in white cotton pants, in from the country. The sour smell of *pulque* and sweet urine was heavy in the air.

They were walking now on unpaved streets. They had reached a large dilapidated building, a black and empty warehouse, straight walls of masonry rose into the darkness.

She knocked at a heavy door with a little barred window. A man peeped out, opened the door and they walked into a corridor.

"Buenas noches," said the doorman.

They walked down the corridor into a large room where a number of people were standing sitting laughing talking. Several of them greeted her and stared curiously at John.

Seated behind a desk in a dentist's chair was a massive woman like an Aztec earth goddess. She stretched out a hand to the girl, *"Buenas noches,* Iguana," she said. She turned her hard black eyes on John.

"Buenas noches, Gringüito. Bienvenido a la casa de Lola la Chata."

She took his hand in a powerful grip, her eyes with pinpoint pupils heavy and cold on his face and body.

The girl took his arm. "Let's get a drink."

He looked around.

There were bottles of tequila on a table, washtubs full of beer bottles on ice. On a long table beside Lola's desk he saw a number of syringes in glasses of alcohol. Men would come in and shake hands with Lola and she would reach in between her massive breasts and pull out a little packet and give it to them. Then they proceeded to the syringe table for a shot, nonchalantly administered in full view of the guests.

Mariachi singers were singing ranchero songs and several couples were dancing.

The addicts sat in chairs with hooded eyes like drowsy lizards. Sharp reek of marijuana drifted through the room.

Suddenly John saw several uniformed police.

"Police!" he cried. "It's a raid!"

The Iguana laughed. "They have come for their uh little present . . ."

He saw that the police went to Lola's desk and after shaking hands she opened a drawer and handed each policeman an envelope. The police were drinking beer and joking with the guests. One of them puffed on a marijuana cigarette letting the smoke out slowly through his mustache.

"Quite a party," he said.

"Yes, it's once a year on her birthday that Lola la Chata gives this party and on that day everything is free. On that day she gives. On other days she takes."

She took his arm. "Come, it will be noisy here."

She led the way through a back door upstairs and through a maze of corridors and empty rooms with the windows boarded up. Finally she took out a key and opened a door.

The room was small but well furnished with rugs and low tables and a large bed.

"Take off your shoes," she told him.

She sat down crosslegged on the bed and indicated that he was to sit opposite her.

Once again he felt the strange touch inside his skull that made him feel at once excited and uncomfortable as if he were a small boy naked before his gym instructor.

"Have you taken LSD?" she asked.

"Yes. I didn't like it. That metallic taste in the mouth."

She nodded. "LSD lets you out into a bad area. The plants are better. And they must be prepared in a certain way."

She got up and walked over to a corner of the room. He saw jars on shelves filled with herbs and dried mushrooms, and a table with earthenware pots and a spirit stove.

"I will now prepare for you the sacred mushrooms according to the ancient formula."

She lit the spirit stove and placed a pot of water on to boil, selecting pinches of herbs and dried mushroom, adding a little more, crooning over the mixture, an odd little tune.

He lost track of time. Perhaps it was the marijuana cigarette he had smoked at the party. There was a sudden hiatus, it seemed ten minutes but it must have been much longer.

"The mushrooms are ready," she said and handed him a little gourd of liquid.

He drank it down.

She poured one for herself and drank it.

They sat down on the bed.

Almost at once he felt a rush of dizziness that was not at all unpleasant, in fact it was he decided very pleasant indeed.

Now the walls and rugs were twisting in strange shapes, and then suddenly sensuality hit him in a wave, his flesh was writhing, dissolving in green fire. He wanted to tear off his clothes. His lips swelled with blood and blood sang in his ears.

He looked at her helplessly.

"Stand up," she told him.

"I uh . . ."

"Stand up."

He obeyed and stood there in front of her, his pants bulging.

With cool precise fingers she unbuttoned his shirt and slipped it off.

She unhooked his belt, opened his pants and with a quick movement slid his pants and shorts down. He stood there blushing as the blood rushed to his crotch and his penis began to stir and stiffen.

She stood there and watched. Suddenly he remembered an incident of his early adolescence. He had been barely fourteen at the time. A gym instructor had visited the house. His parents were away. It was after dinner and the man was looking at him and he felt something uncomfortable. Then the man said, "I'd like to see you stripped." He said, all right, his mouth was dry and his heart was pounding as he led the way to his room, Oh god, he thought, suppose it happens? He tried to think of something else. Then he was in the room, the man sitting down on the bed, he took off his shoes and socks and shirt. "Come over here," the man said. He stood in front of the man who ran his hands over his arms and shoulders. He was feeling very relieved that he didn't have to take down his pants. And then the man was undoing his belt and pants and suddenly his pants and shorts dropped and he was standing there naked blushing furiously, and it was happening, he couldn't stop it. The man looked down. He glanced down and bit his lip and a little whimper burst from him. The man said, "Your little pecker is getting hard." And then knowing it was all right he felt a rush of excitement feeling the man's hand on his buttocks and thighs, it was all the way up now pulsing throbbing, and he didn't care. Then the man sat him down beside him on the bed, and as he sat down a drop of lubricant squeezed out. At that time he had never masturbated. Then the man's hand was on his nuts and penis. "You've been playing with this?" He leaned back on his elbow, legs stretched out. "Well . . . yes . . . a little bit . . ." "Did you ever play with it until it went off?" "No. How long do you have to play with it before that happens?" The man's hand was rubbing the lubricant around the tip of his penis. It happened in a few seconds and he was spurting hot gobs up onto his stomach. Afterwards, the man left town and he had put the incident out of his mind. Now standing there naked the memory came back and the excitement.

And suddenly he had a curious feeling that perhaps she wasn't a girl, and a feeling too that there was somebody else in the room.

She was slowly stripping and when she stood naked her body was almost inhumanly beautiful, the smooth green flesh and the obvious strength of her breasts like green fruit. She pulled him down onto the bed and suddenly they were rolling in an ecstasy of lust.

He felt penetrated and penetrating the soft gelatin between her legs that pulled him in further and further, they twisted from one end of the bed to the other, she was on top, on her side, silver light popped in his eyes and his head seemed to fly to pieces. He glimpsed a sky rocket bursting in someone's head, in his brain. The Van Allen Belt.

When he got back to the hotel the landlady told him that his friend had arrived. As he walked up the stairs his heart was pounding with excitement feeling the ache and stiffness in his groin.

He opened the door.

She got up off the bed laying down a book and walked to the middle of the room to meet him. She was dressed in men's clothes, khaki pants and shirt, jodhpurs, a green tie.

He threw his arms around her kissed her on the lips . . .

Suddenly a shock went through him. The chest was hard, he could feel the ribs. This was a man's body.

He shoved the other back. "Why, you're . . . !"

"I am the Iguana's twin brother."

John stood there blushing furiously, his pants sticking out straight at the fly.

"Why be embarrassed? After all, I was there . . ."

He remembered the presence of another person in the room, and the feeling that it was all right like the time with the gym instructor. His embarrassment turned to lust. Why not? They were in tune, how could it matter?

"Let's have a look at you," the boy said. He reached out with his long cool fingers with precise movements performed at unbelievable speed. He unhooked John's belt unbuttoned his pants.

Before he fully realized what was happening his pants and shorts fell to his ankles and he stood there his shirt moving slightly in a wind through the open window.

The boy looked at him and licked his lips with a little red tongue. His black eyes shone with an inner light. He walked around John touching his buttocks and genitals with fingers that left a cool burn like menthol. He brought a chair and placed it behind John who sat down.

The boy slipped off his soft boots; shirt, pants, and shorts followed, and he was standing there naked while John was still fumbling with his shoelaces.

The boy knelt at his feet, quickly removed John's shoes and socks, pulled his pants and shorts off and hung them on a wooden peg.

John stood up and took off his shirt.

The boy was thinner than his sister, he had the same smooth green skin, his penis erect throbbing was a pink purple color, the pubic hairs jet black and shiny.

Then the boy was kissing him, running his tongue inside John's mouth. A musty odor came off his body.

The boy led him to the bed. He was rubbing an unguent on John's penis that left a cold burn. John felt suddenly strong and confident, he shoved the boy on his back, pulled a pillow under him and pushed his legs up. The rectum was the same purple brown color as the boy's penis. John rubbed some vaseline on and slowly shoved it in, feeling the rectum pull him in with a soft muscular pressure. As he moved in and out feeling the gathering tightness in his groin, John was suddenly holding the girl, feeling her breast against him and then the boy again, feeling the hot gobs hit his chest.

They quivered together a few seconds. They lay there looking at the ceiling.

"I had to make it with you, you understand."

John did not understand.

"Let's get dressed. I want to give you some idea as to what is going on here."

After they were dressed, the boy began: "We know a good deal about your background, otherwise I wouldn't be telling you this. For example, we know about the gym instructor."

John looked at him in amazement. "How could you know that?"

"There are ways to find these things out. Ways which you will learn and learn quickly if you are to be of use to us. The story about the books being still in existence is true. That is why the Bay of Pigs is here. And others as well . . . Russians, Chinese, Swiss . . . *very* clever, the Swiss. . . . In consequence, Mayan scholars are now at a premium."

He got a briefcase and took out three packages tied with a ribbon.

"Copies of the Dresden, Madrid and Paris codices. You have seen them of course."

John nodded.

"Now look here." He pointed to a priest who was making an incision in what looked like a man plant. "What do you make of it?"

"Nothing much. They worshipped a corn god. No doubt this is some mythological representation."

"It is a representation of something quite definite. It is a flesh tree."

"A flesh tree . . . ?"

"Yes. What we call flesh is in point of fact a vegetable. It literally grows on trees, or rather it did."

"But that's fantastic!"

"The agents of five countries don't think so. You have already had a visit from the police, have you not?"

"Yes . . . they were looking for drugs."

"They were looking for any pretext to get you out of Mexico. They take orders from B.O.P., The Bay of Pigs."

"But why? After all, they need Mayan scholars . . ."

"They already have the best. Besides, I don't think you would care to work for them when you learn what they are doing or what they intend to do. . . . They intend to keep the books secret. Top secret. Classified. To monopolize the knowledge contained in these books."

"But how could they do that if it is as important as you say?"

"Quite easily. Don't be misled into thinking it is just rivalry, to be the first to claim an important discovery."

"Just how do you and your sister fit into this? And what do you want from me?"

"We represent the Academy."

John was about to ask what this was when he noticed a change in the boy's face. The face blurred out and a middle-aged man was sitting there, sharp birdlike face, cool imperturbable grey eyes.

"The original statement of the Academy as simply an institution or series of institutions where knowledge skills and techniques methods of training, physical and spiritual, Scientology, Karate, Aikido were coordinated and taught is simply a strategical move to drive the enemy into the open with nothing to declare but their bad intentions. Here it is possible in terms of present day techniques. Why isn't it being done? Why are all knowledge and skills kept from the youth of the world? These questions were aided by the Academy program. Since then of course we have gone underground to prepare for all-out resistance. We select and train our personnel in a number of locations. You have been selected for training. You ask, who is the enemy we are preparing to resist. There are several basic formulas that have held this planet in ignorance and slavery. The first is the concept of a nation or country. Draw a line around a piece of land and call it a country. That means police, customs, barriers, armies and trouble with other stone-age tribes on the other side of the line. The concept of a country must be eliminated. Countries are an extension from another formula, the formula of the family. Parents are allowed to bring up helpless children in any form of nonsense they have themselves been infected with. The family in turn derives from the whole unsanitary system of reproduction in operation here. It is now possible to create living beings. Not bacteria and viruses in a test tube, but human or at least humanoid beings who have not been crippled by the traumas of birth and death. The two beings who brought you here are preliminary experiments. The womb is now obsolete. The enemy is those beings and forces who have devised and enforced these basic formulas, and now threatened by the loss of their human slaves will do anything to keep these formulas in operation.

"The secret of flesh is in the lost Mayan books. All the forces of suppression have now converged on Mexico to find these books and keep this secret from being used to create a new race of beings on this planet."

from
roosevelt after inauguration
and other atrocities

WHEN DID I STOP WANTING TO BE PRESIDENT?

At birth certainly and perhaps before. In this life or any previous incarnations I have been able to check out, I never wanted to be president. This innate decision was confirmed when I became literate and saw the president pawing babies and spouting bullshit. I attended Los Alamos Ranch School, where they later made the atom bomb, and bombs bursting in air over Hiroshima gave proof through the night that our flag was already there. Then came the Teapot Dome scandal under President Harding, and I remember the unspeakable Gaston Means, infamous private eye and go-between in this miasma of graft, walking into a hotel room full of bourbon-drinking cigar-smoking lobbyists and fixers, with a laundry hamper he would put in the middle of the floor:

"Fill it up boys and we talk business."

I do not mean to imply that my youthful idealism was repelled by this spectacle. I had by then learned to take a broad general view of things. My political ambitions were simply of a humbler and less conspicuous caliber. I hoped at one time to become Commissioner of Sewers for St. Louis County—three hundred dollars a month, with every possibility of getting one's shitty paws deep into a slush fund—and to this end I attended a softball game where such sinecures were assigned to the deserving and the fortunate. Everybody I met said "Now I'm old So-and-so, running for such and such, and anything you do for me I'll appreciate."

My boyish dreams fanned by this heady atmosphere and three mint juleps, I saw myself already in possession of the coveted post, which called for a token appearance twice a week to sign a few letters at the Old Court House; while I'm there might as well put it on the sheriff for some mary juana he has confiscated and he'd better play ball or I will route a sewer through his front yard. . . . And then across the street to the Court House Café for a coffee with some other lazy worthless bastards in the same line of business, and we wallow in corruption like contented alligators.

333

I never wanted to be a front man like Harding or Nixon—taking the rap, shaking hands and making speeches all day, family reunions once a year. Who in his right mind would want a job like that? As Commissioner of Sewers I would not be called upon to pet babies, make speeches, shake hands, have lunch with the Queen; in fact, the fewer voters who knew of my existence, the better. Let kings and Presidents keep the limelight. I prefer a whiff of coal gas as the sewers rupture for miles—I have made a deal on the piping which has bought me a $30,000 home and there is talk in the press of sex cults and drug orgies carried out in the stink of what made them possible. Fluttering from the roof of my ranch-style house, over my mint and marijuana, Old Glory floats lazily in the tainted breeze.

But there were sullen mutters of revolt from the peasantry; "My teenage daughters is cunt deep in shit. Is this the American way of life?" I thought so and I didn't want it changed, sitting there in my garden, smoking the sheriff's reefers, coal gas on the wind sweet in my nostrils as the smell of oil to an oil man or the smell of bullshit to a cattle baron. I sure did a sweet thing with those pipes and I'm covered too. What I got on the Governor wouldn't look good on the front page, would it now? And I have my special police to deal with vandalism and sabotage, all of them handsome youths, languid and vicious as reptiles, described in the press as no more than minions, lackeys, and bodyguards to His Majesty the Sultan of Sewers.

The thoughts of youth are long long thoughts. Then I met the gubernatorial candidate, and he looked at me as if trying to focus my image through a telescope and said "Anything I do for you I'll depreciate." And I felt the dream slipping away from me, receding into the past dim jerky far away— the discreet gold letters on a glass door: William S. Burroughs, Commissioner of Sanitation. Somehow I had not intersected. I was not one of them. Perhaps I was simply the wrong shape. Some of my classmates, plump cynical unathletic boys with narrow shoulders and broad hips, made the grade and went on to banner headlines concerning $200,000 of the taxpayers' money and a nonexistent bridge or highway, I forget which. It was a long time ago. I have never aspired to political office since. The Sultan of Sewers lies buried in a distant 1930s softball game.

ROOSEVELT AFTER INAUGURATION: A NEW INTRODUCTION

I remember Cambridge Massachusetts in 1938, the year of the hurricane. A heap of folks was drowned and washed up by the tidal wave, and one woman got her throat cut when the wind blew out a window in her face. Kells Elvins and your reporter, there to cover the hurricane, were writing a shipwreck story based on the Titanic, in which the captain, in the garb of an old lady, is helped into the first lifeboat by an Eagle Scout. This image—of conduct so outrageous it elicits laughter rather than censure—captured my imagination. I could see the heroic anti-hero often running more risk than Hercules or John Wayne. When the roll is called up yonder they'll be there.

The ship's captain who rushes into the first lifeboat was based on the actual case of an Italian steward who managed to escape from the sinking Titanic in this way—and found himself discovered by the wives and daughters of those who were even at that moment going down with the ship, singing "Nearer My God to Thee." How did he escape with his life? It would seem that there is a majesty in utter vileness that disarmed the savage breasts.

And then there was the pilot who bailed out of a burning plane, leaving the passengers to crash. He was placed in some danger when he inadvisedly attended a mass funeral for the inextricably intermingled passengers. Fortunately, he had a plane revved up in the cemetery.

Or the Mexican bus driver, smoking a cigarette with a leaky can of gasoline beside him and singing idiot mambo: *"M'importe nu y nu y nu—y nada mas que nuuuuuuuu—"* I am concerned for *numero uno*, and nothing else but *Nuuuu*—Looking down, he saw that the gasoline had ignited and without interrupting his song he jumped out. The bus crashed into a ravine and everyone inside was burned to death. Thirty peons with machetes riding on the roof jumped clear. They looked at the driver, who scrambled off with the agility of a rat or an evil spirit, out-distanced thirty machetes and has never been seen since.

There is, about all these anti-heroes, a purity of motive, a halo of dazzling shameless innocence. They are imbued with the primeval wisdom of children and animals. They know that the name of the game is SURVIVAL. If the bus driver had put on the brakes, the burning gasoline would have sloshed all over him, and that wouldn't have helped anyone would it now? Now, I want to say to the surviving relatives of those unfortunate travelers, I guess it was just the curse of the Pharoahs—in any case, how could I share one parachute with 23 slob *pasajeros?* I ain't mad at nobody, besides which I have a deep reverence for life. And I'd like to see any stinking passengers beat me into the first lifeboat. We talked the third mate into going down with the ship.

The image of outrage was again evoked in 1953, in a less heroic mold, by a particularly sloppy Colombian gunboat on the Putumayo River, and I wrote to Allen Ginsberg: "It wouldn't surprise me to see someone shit on the deck and wipe his ass with the flag." The routine which followed, enumerating various scandalous acts allegedly perpetrated by Roosevelt's retinue, was deleted from *The Yagé Letters* by the English printers. "Roosevelt after Inauguration" was first published in *Floating Bear #9*, by Le Roi Jones. That issue was seized and an obscenity case brought against it when copies were sent to someone in a penal institution. Subsequently the piece appeared in a mimeo edition from Ed Sanders's Fuck You Press, and has been in a couple of small literary magazines.

I feel that "Roosevelt after Inauguration" is, in a sense, prophetic of Watergate—and yet few of the Watergate defendants exhibited this degree of pure glittering shamelessness. So let us all scan the horizons for new frontiers of depravity. This is the Space Age; we are here to go. We can float out of here on a foam runway of sheer vileness.

from
the adding machine

A WORD TO THE WISE GUY

After teaching a class in Creative Writing a few years back, my own creative powers fell to an all-time low. I really had a case of writer's block, and my idealistic young assistant complained that I simply sat around the loft doing absolutely nothing—which was true. This gave me to think (as the French say): *Can* creative writing be taught? And am I being punished by the Muses for impiety and gross indiscretion in revealing the secrets to a totally unreceptive audience—like you start giving away hundred-dollar bills and nobody wants them. . . . I also discovered that the image of "William Burroughs" in my students' minds had little relation to the facts. They were disappointed because I wore a coat and tie to class; they had expected me to appear stark naked with a strap-on, I presume. In all, a disheartening experience.

"Creative Writing"—what does that mean? I would have liked to put them all off the career of writing. Be a plumber instead—(I felt like screaming)—and have your fucking king-size fridge full of Vienna sausages, chilled aquavit and Malvern spring water, and look at your color TV with remote-control switch and cuddle a .30-.30 on your lap, waiting for the deer season when all sensible citizens will be in their cellars with sandbags stacked around them. Or be a doctor for chrissakes—once you make the big-time as the best asshole doctor what can be got, you don't have to worry like next year there won't be no assholes to operate on. But next year maybe no assholes will buy my books. . . .

All right, maybe two, three people in the class can't be dissuaded. My advice is get a good agent and a good tax accountant if you ever make any money, and remember, you can't eat fame. And you can't write unless you *want* to write, and you can't want to unless you feel like it. Say you're a doctor with a nice practice. You don't feel so well today—family troubles and other things you can't quite put a name to—and you just feel fucking terrible, as you slip a chlorophyll tablet in your mouth to cover three quick drinks—(that old bitch would spread it all over Palm Beach, "My *dear* he was *drunk* . . .") Well you can still carry on and what the hell, quarter-grain of morphine for each patient; no matter what is wrong with them, they will feel better immediately and prize me as the best of croakers. And if I get any sass from the Narcs, I'll just tell 'em, "Well I'm off to work in the Bahrein Islands so you take over my practice and shove it up your ass." I mean, even if you don't feel like practicing medicine, you can still do it. Same way with law; you don't feel like trying a case, all you gotta do is get a continuance and lay up smoking weed in Martha's Vineyard for a month.

In these other professions you can always cover for not feeling like doing it, but writing you didn't feel like doing ain't worth shit. The profession has many advantages; sure, you can ride out on a white shark to a villa in the Bahamas, or you can spend twenty years teaching English in the Berlitz School, writing the Great Book that nobody can read. James Joyce wrote some of the greatest prose in the language—*The Dead, Dubliners*—but could he stop there and write exquisite stories about unhappy Irish Catholics from then on out? If so, they would have rewarded him with the Nobel Prize. Now nobody ever tells a doctor, "Lissen Doc, your ass operations is the greatest, many grateful queens is getting fucked again, but you gotta do something *new*—"Of course he doesn't have to; it's the same old ass. But a writer has to do something new, or he has to standardize a product—one or the other. Like I could standardize the queer Peter-Pan wild-boy product, and put it out year after year like the Tarzan series; or I could write a Finnegans Wake. So, I get this idea about a private eye and the Cities of the Red Night . . . *Quien sabe?*

Or take the entertainment business; today you may be the Top of the Pops, the rage of the café society . . . like Dwight Fisk, who did those horrible double-entendre numbers back in the thirties—"That's the man who pinched me in the Astor, just below the mezzanine, and for several days your mother wasn't seen; so now my little heart you know where you got your start, from a pinch just below the mezzanine"—who in the fuck wants to hear that noise anymore? But you won't see any doctor, lawyer, engineer, architect who's got to be world champion at his profession or else stand on a corner selling ties with his brains knocked out. No atomic physicist has to worry, people will always want to kill other people on a mass scale. Sure, he's got the fridge full of sausages and spring water, just like the plumber. Nothing can happen to him; grants, scholarships, a rainbow to his grave and a tombstone that glows in the dark.

Artists do however have a degree of freedom. A writer has little power, but he does have freedom, at least in the West, Mr. Yevtushenko. Think very carefully about this. Do you want to be merely the spokesman for accomplished power movers? The more power, the less freedom. A politician has almost no freedom at all. I am frequently asked, "What would you do if you were President? What would you do if you were the dictator of America? What would you do if you had a billion dollars?" In the words of my friend Ahmed Jacoubi, "This question is not personal opinion." A prior question must be asked: "How did you *get to be* the President, a dictator, a billionaire?" The answers to these questions will condition what you will do. For one is not magically teleported into these positions; one gets there by a series of discrete steps, each step hedged with conditions and prices.

To take a microcosmic example: my humble ambition to be Commissioner of Sewers for St. Louis, and my boyish dread of what I would do when I occupied this position. These dreams were outlined in an essay I wrote for *Harper's* in response to the question, "When did you stop wanting to be President?" I imagined a soft sinecure, crooked sewer-piping deals, my house full of languid vicious young men described in the press as "no more than lackeys to his majesty the Sultan of Sewers." I supposed my position would be secured by the dirt I had on the Governor, and that I'd spend my afternoons in wild orgies or sitting around smoking the Sheriff's reefer and luxuriating in the stink from ruptured sewage lines for miles around.

But why should I have been appointed Commissioner of Sewers in the first place? The duties are nominal; no skill is required. I am not appointed on my knowledge of sewers or my ability to do the job. Why, then? Well, perhaps I have worked for the Party for a number of years; I am due for a payoff. However, I must also have something to give in return. Perhaps I can sway some votes, which action on my part is contingent on my receiving some payoff? Or perhaps they expect me to take the rap for the piping deal. If so I will have to watch my step and the use of my signature. Perhaps they expect a contribution to the campaign fund, which I am in a position to swing, having access to people of wealth. One thing is sure—they expect something from me in return.

Now, an under-the-counter deal in cheap piping involves contractors, auditors, and a whole battery of fixes, fixers, and cover-ups, all of which have to be paid in favors and cash. So my house is *not* full of languid vicious young men—it is full of cigar-smoking bourbon-swilling fat-assed politicians and fixers. I have something on the Governor? I'd better be very damn careful he doesn't have something on *me*. The Commissioner, like Caesar's wife, must be above suspicion; certainly above the suspicion of sex orgies and drug use. I would have been out of my mind to compromise myself with the Sheriff. Sure, I can call on him to fix a parking ticket, but I'd better keep my hands off his confiscated marijuana unless others in higher positions are also involved. And even if I could wangle a few special police to guard the sewers against communistic sabotage, they would not be handsome youths. More likely I would be stuck with the Sheriff's retarded brother-in-law who can't make the grade as a night watchman, and with two or three other wash-outs from police and guard positions.

So if I can't do what I want as Commissioner of Sewers, still less can I do what I want as President of the United States. I will disband the Army and the Navy and channel the entire Defense budget into setting up sexual adjustment centers, will I? I'll legalize marijuana? Annul the Oriental Exclusion Act? Abolish income tax for artists and put the burden of taxation onto the very rich? I should live so long.

I think that Richard Nixon will go down in history as a true folk hero, who struck a vital blow to the whole diseased concept of the revered image and gave the American virtue of irreverence and skepticism back to the people.

THE LIMITS OF CONTROL

There is a growing interest in new techniques of mind-control. It has been suggested that Sirhan Sirhan was the subject of post-hypnotic suggestion [as he sat shaking violently on the steam table in the kitchen of the Ambassador Hotel in Los Angeles while an as-yet unidentified woman held him and whispered in his ear]. It has been alleged that behavior-modification techniques are used on troublesome prisoners and inmates, often without their consent. Dr Delgado, who once stopped a charging bull by remote control of electrodes in the bull's brain, left the U.S. to pursue his studies on human subjects in Spain. Brainwashing, psychotropic drugs, lobotomy and other more subtle forms of psychosurgery; the technocratic control apparatus of the United States has at its fingertips new techniques which if fully exploited could make Orwell's 1984 seem like a benevolent utopia. But words are still the principal instruments of control. Suggestions are words. Persuasions are words. Orders are words. No control machine so far devised can operate without words, and any control machine which attempts to do so relying entirely on external force or entirely on physical control of the mind will soon encounter the limits of control.

A basic impasse of all control machines is this: Control needs time in which to exercise control. Because control also needs opposition or acquiescence; otherwise it ceases to be control. I *control* a hypnotized subject (at least partially); I *control* a slave, a dog, a worker; but if I establish *complete* control somehow, as by implanting electrodes in the brain, then my subject is little more than a tape recorder, a camera, a robot. You don't *control* a tape recorder—you *use* it. Consider the distinction, and the impasse implicit here. All control systems try to make control as tight as possible, but at the same time, if they succeeded completely, there would be nothing left to control. Suppose for example a control system installed electrodes in the brains of all prospective workers at birth. Control is now complete. Even the thought of rebellion is neurologically impossible. No police force is necessary. No psychological control is necessary, other than pressing buttons to achieve certain activations and operations.

When there is no more opposition, control becomes a meaningless proposition. It is highly questionable whether a human organism could survive complete control. There would be nothing there. No persons there. *Life is will* (motivation) and the workers would no longer be alive, perhaps literally. The concept of suggestion as a control technique presupposes that control is partial and not complete. You do not have to give suggestions to your tape recorder, nor subject it to pain and coercion or persuasion.

In the Mayan control system, where the priests kept the all-important Books of seasons and gods, the Calendar was predicated on the illiteracy of the workers. Modern control systems are predicated on universal literacy since they operate through the mass media—a very two-edged control instrument, as Watergate has shown. Control systems are vulnerable, and the news media are by their nature uncontrollable, at least in Western society. The alternative press is news, and alternative society is news, and as such both are taken up by the mass media. The monopoly that Hearst and Luce once exercised is breaking down. In fact, the more completely hermetic and seemingly successful a control system is, the more vulnerable it becomes. A weakness inherent in the Mayan system is that they didn't need an army to control their workers, and therefore did not have an army when they needed one to repel invaders. It is a rule of social structures that anything that is not needed will atrophy and become inoperative over a period of time. Cut off from the war game—and remember, the Mayans had no neighbors to quarrel with—they lose the ability to fight. In "The Mayan Caper" I suggested that such a hermetic control system could be completely disoriented and shattered by even one person who tampered with the control calendar on which the control system depended more and more heavily as the actual means of force withered away.

Consider a control situation: ten people in a lifeboat. Two armed self-appointed leaders force the other eight to do the rowing while they dispose of the food and water, keeping most of it for themselves and doling out only enough to keep the other eight rowing. The two leaders now *need* to exercise control to maintain an advantageous position which they could not hold without it. Here the method of control is force—the possession of guns. Decontrol would be accomplished by overpowering the leaders and taking their guns. This effected, it would be advantageous to kill them at once. So once embarked on a policy of control, the leaders must continue the policy as a matter of self-preservation. Who, then, needs to control others but those who protect by such control a position of relative advantage? Why do they need to exercise control? Because they would soon lose this position and advantage and in many cases their lives as well, if they relinquished control.

Now examine the reasons by which control is exercised in the lifeboat scenario: The two leaders are armed, let's say, with .38 revolvers—twelve shots and eight potential opponents. They can take turns sleeping. However, they must still exercise care not to let the eight rowers know that they intend to kill them when land is sighted. Even in this primitive situation force is supplemented with deception and persuasion. The leaders will disembark at point A, leaving the others sufficient food to reach point B, they explain. They have the compass and they are contributing their navigational skills. In short they will endeavour to convince the others that this is a cooperative enterprise in which they are all working for the same goal. They may also make concessions: increase food and water rations. A concession of course means the retention of control—that is, the disposition of the food and water supplies. By persuasions and by concessions they hope to prevent a concerted attack by the eight rowers.

Actually they intend to poison the drinking water as soon as they leave the boat. If all the rowers knew this they would attack, no matter what the odds. We now see that another essential factor in control is to conceal from the controlled the actual intentions of the controllers. Extending the lifeboat analogy to the Ship of State, few existing governments could withstand a sudden, all-out attack by all their underprivileged citizens, and such an attack might well occur if the intentions of certain existing governments were unequivocally apparent. Suppose the lifeboat leaders had built a barricade and could withstand a concerted attack and kill all eight of the rowers if necessary. They would then have to do the rowing themselves and neither would be safe from the other. Similarly, a modern government armed with heavy weapons and prepared for attack could wipe out ninety-five percent of its citizens. But who would do the work, and who would protect them from the soldiers and technicians needed to make and man the weapons? Successful control means achieving a balance and avoiding a showdown where all-out force would be necessary. This is achieved through various techniques of psychological control, also balanced. The techniques of both force and psychological control are constantly improved and refined, and yet worldwide dissent has never been so widespread or so dangerous to the present controllers.

All modern control systems are riddled with contradictions. Look at England. "Never go too far in any direction," is the basic rule on which England is built, and there is some wisdom in that. However, avoiding one impasse they step into another. Anything that is not going forward is on the way out. Well, nothing lasts forever. Time is that which ends, and control needs time. England is simply stalling for time as it slowly founders. Look at America. Who actually controls this country? It is very difficult to say. Certainly the very wealthy are one of the most powerful control groups, since they are in a position to control and manipulate the entire economy. However, it would not be to their advantage to set up or attempt to set up an overly fascist government. Force, once brought in, subverts the power of money. This is another impasse of control: protection from the protectors. Hitler formed the S.S. to protect him from the S.A. If he had lived long enough the question of protection from the S.S. would have posed itself. The Roman Emperors were at the mercy of the Praetorian Guard, who in one year killed many Emperors. And besides, no modern industrial country has ever gone fascist without a program of military expansion. There is no longer anyplace to expand to—after hundreds of years, colonialism is a thing of the past.

There can be no doubt that a cultural revolution of unprecedented dimensions has taken place in America during the last thirty years, and since America is now the model for the rest of the Western world, this revolution is worldwide. Another factor is the mass media, which spreads all cultural movements in all directions. The fact that this worldwide revolution has taken place indicates that the controllers have been forced to make concessions. Of course, a concession is still the retention of control. Here's a dime, I keep a dollar. Ease up on censorship, but remember we could take it all back. Well, at this point, that is questionable.

Concession is another control bind. History shows that once a government starts to make concessions it is on a one-way street. They could of course take all the concessions back, but that would expose them to the double jeopardy of revolution and the much greater danger of overt fascism, both highly dangerous to the present controllers. Does any clear policy arise from this welter of confusion? The answer is probably no. The mass media has proven a very unreliable and even treacherous instrument of control. It is uncontrollable owing to its need for NEWS. If one paper or even a string of papers owned by the same person makes that story hotter as NEWS, some paper will pick it up. Any imposition of government censorship on the media is a step in the direction of State control, a step which big money is most reluctant to take.

I don't mean to suggest that control automatically defeats itself, nor that protest is therefore unnecessary. A government is never more dangerous than when embarking on a self-defeating or downright suicidal course. It is encouraging that some behavior modification projects have been exposed and halted, and certainly such exposure and publicity could continue. In fact, I submit that we have a *right* to insist that all scientific research be subject to public scrutiny, and that there should be no such thing as "top-secret" research.

LES VOLEURS

Writers work with words and voices just as painters work with colors; and where do these words and voices come from? Many sources: conversations heard and overheard, movies and radio broadcasts, newspapers, magazines, yes, and *other writers;* a phrase comes into the mind from an old western story in a pulp magazine read years ago, can't remember where or when: "He looked at her, trying to read her mind—but her eyes were old, unbluffed, unreadable." There's one that I lifted.

The County Clerk sequence in *Naked Lunch* derived from contact with the County Clerk in Cold Springs, Texas. It was in fact an elaboration of his monologue, which seemed merely boring at the time, since I didn't know yet that I was a writer. In any case, there wouldn't have been any County Clerk if I had been sitting on my ass waiting for my "very own words." You've all met the ad man who is going to get out of the rat race, shut himself up in a cabin, and write the Great American Novel. I always tell him, "Don't cut your input, B.J.—you might need it." So many times I have been stuck on a story line, can't see where it will go from here; then someone drops around and tells me about fruit-eating fish in Brazil. I got a whole chapter out of that. Or I buy a book to read on the plane, and there is the answer; and there's a nice phrase too, "sweetly inhuman voices." I had a dream about such voices before I read *The Big Jump* by Leigh Brackett, and found that phrase.

Look at the surrealist mustache on the Mona Lisa. Just a silly joke? Consider where this joke can lead. I had been working with Malcolm McNeill for five years on a book entitled *Ah Pook Is Here,* and we used the same idea: Hieronymus Bosch as the background for scenes and characters taken from the Mayan codices and transformed into modern counterparts. That face in the Mayan Dresden Codex will be the barmaid in this scene, and we can use the Vulture God over here. Bosch, Michaelangelo, Renoir, Monet, Picasso—steal anything in sight. You want a certain light on your scene? Lift it from Monet. You want a 1930s backdrop? Use Hopper.

The same applies to writing. Joseph Conrad did some superb descriptive passages on jungles, water, weather; why not use them verbatim as background in a novel set in the tropics? Continuity by so-and-so, description and background footage from Conrad. And of course you can kidnap someone else's characters and put them in a different set. The whole gamut of painting, writing, music, film is yours to use. Take Molly Bloom's soliloquy and give it to your heroine. It happens all the time anyway; how many times have we had Romeo and Juliet served up to us, and Camille grossed forty million in *The Young Lovers.* So let's come out in the open with it and steal freely.

My first application of this principle was in *Naked Lunch.* The interview between Carl Peterson and Doctor Benway is modelled on the interview between Razumov and Councillor Mikulin in Conrad's *Under Western Eyes.* To be sure, there is no resemblance between Benway and Mikulin, but the form of the interview, Mikulin's trick of unfinished sentences, his elliptical approach, and the conclusion of the interview are quite definitely and consciously used. I did not at the time see the full implications.

Brion Gysin carried the process further in an unpublished scene from his novel *The Process.* He took a section of dialogue *verbatim* from a science fiction novel and used it in a similar scene. (The science fiction novel, appropriately, concerned a mad scientist who devised a black hole into which he disappeared.) I was, I confess, slightly shocked by such overt and *traceable* plagiarism. I had not quite abandoned the fetish of originality, though of course the whole sublime concept of total theft is implicit in cut-ups and montage.

You see, I had been conditioned to the idea of words as *property*—one's "very own words"—and consequently to a deep repugnance for the black sin of plagiarism. Originality was the great virtue. I recall a boy who was caught out copying an essay from a magazine article, and this horrible case discussed in whispers . . . for the first time the dark word "plagiarism" impinged on my consciousness. Why, in a Jack London story a writer shoots himself when he finds out that he has, without knowing it, plagiarized another writer's work. He did not have the courage to be a writer. Fortunately, I was made of sterner or at least more adjustable stuff.

Brion pointed out to me that I had been stealing for years: "Where did that come from—'Eyes old, unbluffed, unreadable'? And that—'inflexible authority'? And that—'arty type, no principles.' And that—and that—and that?" He looked at me sternly.

"*Vous êtes un voleur honteux* . . . a closet thief." So we drew up a manifesto . . .

Les Voleurs

Out of the closet and into the museums, libraries, architectural monuments, concert halls, bookstores, recording studios and film studios of the world. Everything belongs to the inspired and dedicated thief. All the artists of history, from cave painters to Picasso, all the poets and writers, the musicians and architects, offer their wares, importuning him like street vendors. They supplicate him from the bored minds of school children, from the prisons of uncritical veneration, from dead museums and dusty archives. Sculptors stretch forth their limestone arms to receive the life-giving transfusion of flesh as their severed limbs are grafted onto Mister America. *Mais le voleur n'est pas pressé*—the thief is in no hurry. He must assure himself of the quality of the merchandise and its suitability for his purpose before he conveys the supreme honor and benediction of his theft.

Words, colors, light, sounds, stone, wood, bronze belong to the living artist. They belong to anyone who can use them. Loot the Louvre! *A bas l'originalité,* the sterile and assertive ego that imprisons as it creates. *Vive le vol*—pure, shameless, total. We are not responsible. Steal anything in sight.

IMMORTALITY

To me the only success, the only greatness is immortality.
—*James Dean, from* James Dean the Mutant King *by David Dalton*

The colonel beams at the crowd . . . pomaded, manicured, he wears the satisfied expression of one who has just sold the widow a fraudulent peach orchard. "Folks we're here to sell the only thing worth selling or buying and that's immortality. Now here is the simplest solution and well on the way. Just replace the worn parts and keep the old heap on the road indefinitely."

As transplant techniques are perfected and refined the age-old dream of immortality is now within the grasp of mankind. But who is to decide out of a million applicants for the same heart? There simply aren't enough parts to go around. You need the job-lot once a year save twenty percent of people applying. Big executives use a heart a month just as regular as clockwork. Warlords, paying off their soldiers in livers and kidneys and genitals, depopulate whole areas. Vast hospital cities cover the land from the air-conditioned hospital palaces of the rich, radiating out to field hospitals and open-air operating booths. The poor are rising in huge mobs. They are attacking government warehouses where the precious parts are stored. Everyone who can afford it has dogs and guards to protect himself from roving bands of part hunters like the dreaded Wild Doctors who operate on each other after the battle, cutting the warm quivering parts from the dead and dying. Cut-and-grab men dart out of doorways and hack out a kidney with a few expert strokes of their four-inch scalpels. People have lost all shame. Here's a man who sold his daughter's last kidney to buy himself a new groin—appears on TV to appeal for funds to buy little Sally an artificial kidney and give her this last Christmas. On his arm is a curvaceous blonde known apparently as Bubbles. She calls him Long John, now isn't that cute?

A flourishing black market in parts grows up in the gutted cities devasted by part riots. In terrible slums, scenes from Breughel and Bosch are re-enacted . . . misshapen masses of rotten scar tissue crawling with maggots supported on crutches and canes, in wheel-chairs and carts. . . . Brutal as butchers, practitioners operate without anesthetic in open-air booths surrounded by their bloody knives and saws . . . the poor wait in part lines for diseased genitals, a cancerous lung, a cirrhotic liver. They crawl towards the operating booths holding forth nameless things in bottles—that they think are usable parts. Shameless swindlers who buy up operating garbage in job lots prey on the unwary.

And here is Mr Rich Parts. He is three hundred years old. He is still subject to accidental death, and the mere thought of it throws him into paroxysms of idiot terror. For days he cowers in his bunker, two hundred feet down in solid rock, food for fifty years. A trip from one city to another requires months of shifting and checking computerized plans and alternate routes to avoid the possibility of an accident. His idiotic cowardice knows no bounds. There he sits, looking like a Chimu vase with a thick layer of smooth purple scar tissue. Encased in this armor, his movements are slow and hydraulic. It takes him ten minutes to sit down. This layer gets thicker and thicker right down to the bone—the doctors have to operate with power tools. So we leave Mr Rich Parts, and the picturesque parts people, their monument a mountain of scar tissue.

Mr Hubbard said: "The rightest right a man could be would be to live infinitely wrong." I wrote "wrong" for "long" and the slip is significant—for the means by which immortality is realized in science fiction, which will soon be science fact, are indeed infinitely wrong, the wrongest wrong a man can be, vampiric or worse.

Improved transplant techniques open the question as to whether the ego itself could be transplanted from one body to another. And the further question as to exactly where this entity resides. Here is Mr Hart, a trillionaire dedicated to his personal immortality. Where is this thing called Mr Hart? Precisely where, in the human nervous system, does this ugly death sucking, death dealing, death fearing *thing* reside . . . ? Science can give a tentative answer: the "ego" seems to be located in the mid-brain at the top of the head. Well he thinks couldn't we just scoop it out of a healthy youth, throw his in the garbage where it belongs, and slide in MEEEEEEE. So he starts looking for a brain surgeon, a "scrambled egg" man, and he wants the best. When it comes to a short order job old Doc Zeit is tops. He can switch eggs in an alley . . .

Mr Hart embodies the competitive, acquisitive, success minded spirit that formulated American capitalism. The logical extension of this ugly spirit is criminal. Success is its own justification. He who succeeds deserves to succeed he is RIGHT. The operation is a success. The doctors have discreetly withdrawn. When a man wakes up in a beautiful new Bod, he can flip out. It wouldn't pay to be a witness. Mr Hart stands up and stretches luxuriously in his new body. He runs his hands over the lean young muscle where his pot belly used to be. All that remains of the donor is a blob of gray matter in a dish. Mr Hart puts his hands on his hips and leans over the blob.

"And how wrong can *you* be? DEAD."

He spits on it and he spits ugly.

The final convulsions of a universe based on quantitative factors like money, junk and time, would seem to be at hand. . . . The time approaches when no amount of money will buy anything and time itself will run out. In *The Methuselah Enzyme* by Fred Mustard Stewart, Dr Mentius, a Swiss scientist, has found the youth enzyme, which he calls Mentase. As it turns out, Tithy, for Tithonus, or Suave, for *sauve qui peut,* would have been more apt. Young kids secrete this elixir and senior citizens need it special. Mentase is gradually phased out of the body from about the age of twenty-five to sixty. The keyword is extraction. Mentius is a long way from the synthesis of Mentase but to use an untested substance extracted without their knowledge or consent from young people on old people? He feels a distinct twinge in his medical ethics. But Mentase he says grimly must not be lost to humanity. Mentius is regarded as a brilliant lunatic by his medical colleagues: where can he turn for funds? He takes on four rich clients who will bring the young donors . . .

"He must have blacked out in the immersion tank, Bill reflects. Later he found a tiny sticking plaster up near the hair line. . . ." The kids don't know they are giving their Mentase to the elderly sponsor and here is one old creep who brings his own adolescent son to the clinic and sucks all the youth and goodness out of him. So the oldsters are getting younger and the kids . . .

"Hugh dear those interesting freckles . . . What are they?"

They're liver spots. The doctor has to admit he has made a real *dummheit* all around. The old farts don't produce any Mentase of their own all they have is what the doctor gives them. And now an emergency, a shocking emergency, quite unlooked for has arisen. The doctor reels ashen faced from his microscope. He knows that if the injections of Mentase are cut off the aging process will recommence at a vastly accelerated rate. The stricken senior citizen would age before one's eyes. "While still alive, and aware of what was happening, you quite literally disintegrate," he tells them flatly. "The only relief you could possibly have would be to go insane."

And the good doctor has some news for the kids who are already comparing liver spots.

"By cutting off part of your pineal gland we seem to have uh *halted* your production of Mentase and the result is in plain English that you are aging a hundred times as fast as normal," the doctor admits lamely.

Acute shortage of Mentase. The key word is Extraction. The aging kids, now as lost to shame as their elders, in fact rapidly becoming elders, that is to say coarse, ugly, and as shameless as they are disgusting, go out to recruit more kids for the Mentase . . . paid in Mentase, of course, and each recruit must in turn recruit more donors. Think how that could build up in five years bearing in mind the extremely short productive period of the donors.

Puts me in mind of the old fur farm swindle. You invest $500 and buy a pair of mink. The farm is usually in Canada which has always been a center for mail fraud. The farm will take care of your mink who will breed every six months producing a litter of eight or more mink who in turn will pair and breed at the age of six months. Get a paper and pencil . . . and that's not all . . . some of the mink will be *mutants* green and blue and albino, and sea shell pink or maybe you hit the jackpot with rainbow mink $2,000 a pelt. As you luxuriate in rack after rack of ankle-length mink coats a letter edged in black arrives from the farm: regret to inform you your two minks died of distemper.

The ravening Mentase addicts need more and more and more. Any purely quantitative factor is devalued in time. With junk money Mentase, it takes more and more to buy less and less. Maybe Mr Hart has a warehouse full of Mentase to obtain which he has depopulated a continent; it will run out in time. But long before it runs out he will have reached a point where no amount of Mentase he can inject into his aging carcass will halt the aging process.

Mentase is a parable of vampirism gone berserk. But all vampiric blueprints for immortality are wrong not only from the ethical standpoint. They are ultimately unworkable. In *Space Vampires* Colin Wilson speaks of benign vampires. Take a little, leave a little. But they always take more than they leave by the basic nature of the vampiric process of inconspicuous but inexorable consumption. The vampire converts quality, live blood, vitality, youth, talent into quantity food and time for himself. He perpetrates the most basic betrayal of the spirit, reducing all human dreams to his shit. And that's the wrongest wrong a man can be. And personal immortality in a physical body is impossible since a physical body exists in time and time is that which ends. When someone says he wants to live forever he forgets that forever is a time word. . . . All three-dimensional immortality projects are to say the least ill-advised, since they immerse the aspirant always deeper into time.

The tiresome concept of personal immortality is predicated on the illusion of some unchangeable precious essence that is greedy old MEEEEEE forever. The Buddhists say there is no MEEEEEE no unchanging ego . . .

What we think of as our ego is a defensive reaction just as the symptoms of an illness . . . fever, swelling, sweating are the body's reaction to an invading organism, so our beloved ego, arising from the rotten weeds of lust and fear and anger, has no more continuity than a fever sweat. There is no ego only a shifting process unreal as the Cities of the Odor-Eaters that dissolve in rain. A moment's introspection will demonstrate that we are not the same as we were a year ago, a week ago. This opens many doors. Your spirit could reside in a number of bodies, not as some hideous parasite draining the host, but as a helpful little visitor "Roger the Lodger . . . don't take up much room . . . show you a trick or two . . . never overstay my welcome."

Some of the astronauts were peculiar people. I think it was Grissom who was killed in the capsule fire . . . well he always ate *two* meals. And Randolph Scott is described as being notably *well developed* and *heavily muscled* and here's a nice little visitor just for *you*

> *Heavily muscled Randy Scott*
> *You're my favorite astronaut*
> *Hunky Scotty oh yoo hoooo*
> *I'm going to hitch a ride with you.*

This happens all the time. You think of someone and you can hear their voice in your throat, feel their face in yours and their eyes looking out. You will notice that this happens more with some people than with others. And some are more there in voice. I have but to think of Felicity Mason, an English friend, and her clear clipped upper-class British accents fairly ring through the room. And Gregory Corso has a strong absent voice. Let's face it, you are other people and other people are you. Take fifty photos of the same person over an hour. Some of them will look so unlike the subject as to be unrecognizable. And some of them will look like some other person: "Why he looks just like Khrushchev with one gold tooth peeking out."

The illusion of a separate inviolable identity limits your perceptions and confines you in time. You live in other people and other people live in you; "visiting" we call it and of course it's ever so much easier with one's Clonies. When I first heard about cloning, I thought what a *fruitful* concept, why one could be in a hundred different places at once and *experience* everything the other clones did. I am amazed at the outcry against this good thing not only from Men of the Cloth but from scientists . . . the very scientists whose patient research has brought cloning within our grasp. The very thought of a clone disturbs these learned gentlemen. Like cattle on the verge of stampede they paw the ground mooing apprehensively. . . . "Selfness is an essential fact of life. The thought of human nonselfness is terrifying."

Terrifying to *whom?* Speak for yourself you timorous old beastie cowering in your eternal lavatory. Too many scientists seem to be ignorant of the most rudimentary spiritual concepts. And they tend to be suspicious, bristly, paranoid-type people with huge egos they push around like some elephantiasis victim with his distended testicles in a wheelbarrow terrified no doubt that some skulking ingrate of a clone student will sneak into his very brain and steal his genius work. The unfairness of it brings tears to his eyes as he peers anxiously through his bifocals. He is reading a book *In His Image* by David Rorvik.

In this book a rich old eccentric wants to get himself cloned and contacts the author who, being a scientific reporter, knows all the far-out researchers. In fact he knows just the doctor for the job who is named Darwin. But before he fixes Max up with Darwin, Max has to promise to be *ethical* about the whole thing. Absolutely only one clone at a time. Max must swear to abstain from any clonish act that could be construed as a take-over by cold-eyed *inhuman* clone armies.

A group of identical youths stand on a rocky point overlooking a valley. One farts. No one smiles or alters his expression. One points. In a blur of movement all in perfect synch they gather their packs and rifles and move out.

A close-up as they move down a mountain trail shows that something is lacking in these faces, something that we are accustomed to see. The absence is as jarring as if the faces lacked a mouth or a nose. There is no face prepared to meet the faces that it meets, no self-image, no need to impress or assert. They blend into the landscape like picture-puzzle faces.

In the book Max refrains and settles down to watch his little clone grow. In my fictional extension he is more venturesome.

At this point I was engaged in another assignment which took me away for a year. When I returned, Roberto the chauffeur met me at the airport with new clothes and an expensive wristwatch. As we drove towards the hospital I saw that the Facility was now an impressive complex of buildings. When we reached the expanded Facility he led me into a lounge where I observed about fifty boys engaged in theatricals. Some were in clerical garb intoning "Interfering with the designs of the Creator." "Each of us has a right to a special yet unique relation with the Creator . . ."

Others were got up as doddering scientists meandering in senile dementia. "We cannot ethically get to know if cloning is feasible." "Precipitating an identity crisis."

A hideous scientist croaks out like some misshapen toad. "Differences of appearance reinforce our sense of self and hence lend support to the feeling of *individual* worth we seek in ourselves and others."

"The thought of human non-selfness is terrifying!" screeches a snippy old savant. He ducks into his study and recoils in horror. A replica of himself is sitting at his desk going through his notes. I realize that the boys are mocking the opponents of cloning. At this point Max comes in with Doctor Darwin. Darwin is a changed man. Gone are his petulance and hesitation, his prickly ego. He glows with health and confidence. The boys greet him boisterously.

"How many you kill today Doc?"

Max seizes both my hands and looks deep into my eyes with a quiet intense charm.

"Good to see you."

The boys have stripped off their makeup and they are all perfect specimens of young manhood.

"Boys," Max announces like a circus barker. "The *Immaculate,* the *Virgin* birth is at hand."

He leads the way to a maternity clinic got up as a manger where fifty girls are in labor. I notice they are wearing decompression suits . . .

"We got it down to a few minutes now," Darwin tells me.

"They *pop* out . . ."

Even as he spoke there was a popping sound like the withdrawal of a viscous cork and a medic held up a squalling baby.

"Yipppeeeee!" a boy screamed. *"I'm cloned!"*

I pointed out to Max that all this was in flat violation of our agreement.

He doesn't hear me. "All the resources of Trak are now channeled into clone factories. . . . All over the world they are popping out. . . . My little poppies I call them . . ."

Roberto does a chick breaking out of the shell act as he sings in hideous falsetto:

"PIO PIO PIO YO SOY UN POLLITO!"

And Max bellows with laughter. "No I am not mad. Nor is this ego gone berserk. On the contrary, cloning is the end of the ego. For the first time the spirit of man will be able to separate itself from the human machine, to see it and use it as a machine. He is no longer identified with one special Me Machine. The human organism has become an artifact he can use like plane or a space capsule."

John Giorno wondered if maybe a clone of a clone of a clone would just phase out into white noise like copies of copies of a tape. As Count Korzybski used to say:

"I don't know, let's see."

I postulate that true immortality can only be found in space. Space exploration is the only goal worth striving for. Over the hills and far away. You will know your enemies by those who attempt to block your path. Vampiric monopolists would keep you in time like their cattle.

"It's a good thing cows don't fly," they say with an evil chuckle. The evil intelligent Slave Gods.

The gullible confused and stupid pose an equal threat owing to the obstructive potential of vast numbers.

I have an interesting slip in my scrapbook. News clipping from *The Boulder Camera*. Picture of an old woman with a death's head false teeth smile. She is speaking for the Women's Christian Temperance Union.

"WE OPPOSE CHILD ABUSE, INTEMPERANCE AND IMMORTALITY."

The way to immortality is in space and Christianity is buried under slag heaps of dead dogma, sniveling prayers and empty promises *must* oppose immortality in space as the counterfeit always fears and hates the real thing. Resurgent Islam . . . born-again Christians . . . creeds outworn . . . excess baggage . . . *raus mit!*

Immortality is prolonged future and the future of any artifact lies in the direction of increased flexibility, capacity for change and ultimately mutation. Immortality may be seen as a by-product of function: "to *shine* in use." Mutation involves changes that are literally unimaginable from the perspective of the future mutant. Cold-blooded, non-dreaming creatures living in the comparatively weightless medium of water, could not conceive of breathing air, dreaming and experiencing the force of gravity as a basic fact of life. There will be new fears like the fear of falling, new pleasures and new necessities. There are distinct advantages to living in a supportive medium like water. Mutation is not a matter of logical choices.

The human mutants must take a step into the unknown, a step that no human being has ever taken before.

"We were the first that ever burst into that silent sea."

"We are such stuff as dreams are made on."

Recent dream research has turned up a wealth of data but no one has assembled the pieces into a workable field theory.

By far the most significant discovery to emerge from precise dream research with volunteer subjects is the fact that *dreams are a biological necessity* for all warm-blooded animals. Deprived from REM sleep, they show all the symptoms of sleeplessness no matter how much dreamless sleep they are allowed. Continued deprivation would result in death.

All dreams in male subjects except nightmares are accompanied by erection. No one has proffered an explanation. It is interesting to note that a male chimpanzee who did finger and dab paintings, and was quite good too, went into a sexual frenzy during his creative acts.

Cold-blooded animals do not dream. All warm-blooded creatures including birds do dream.

John Dunne discovered that dreams contain references to future time as experienced by the dreamer. He published his findings *An Experiment With Time* in 1924. Dream references, he points out, relate not to the event itself but to *the time when the subject learns of the event.* The dream refers to the future of the dreamer. He says that anybody who will write his dreams down over a period of time will turn up precognitive references. *Dreams involve time travel.* Does it follow then that time travel is a necessity?

I quote from an article summarizing the discoveries of Professor Michel Jouvet. Jouvet, using rapid eye movement techniques, has been able to detect dreaming in animals in the womb, even in developing birds in the egg. He found that animals like calves and foals, who can fend for themselves immediately after birth, dream a lot in the womb and relatively little after that. Humans and kittens dream less in the womb and are unable to fend for themselves at birth.

He concluded that human babies could not walk or feed themselves until they had *enough practice in dreams.* This indicates that the function of dreams is to *train the being for future conditions.* I postulate that the human artifact is biologically designed for space travel. So human dreams can be seen as *training for space conditions.* Deprived of this vital link with our future in space, with no reason for living, we die.

Art serves the same function as dreams. Plato's *Republic* is a blueprint for a death camp. An alien invader, or a domestic elite, bent on conquest and extermination, could rapidly immobolize the earth by cutting dream lines, just the way we took care of the Indians. I quote from *Black Elk Speaks* by John Neihardt (Pocket Books):

"The nation's hoop is broken and scattered like a ring of smoke. There is no center any more. The sacred tree is dead and all its birds are gone."

from THE JOHNSON FAMILY

I first heard this expression in a book called *You Can't Win* by Jack Black, the life story of a burglar. The book was published in 1927 and I read it as a boy fascinated by this dark furtive purposeful world. I managed to get a copy and re-read the book with poignant nostalgia. Between the reader in 1927 and the reader in 1980 falls the shadow of August 6, 1945, one of the most portentous dates of history.

Train whistles across a distant sky. This is a peep show back to the world of rod-riding yeggs and pete men and cat burglars, bindle stiffs, gay cats and hobo jungles and Salt Chunk Mary the fence in her two-story red brick house down by the tracks somewhere in Idaho. She keeps a blue porcelain coffee pot and an iron pot of pork and beans always on the fire. You eat first and talk business later the watches and rings slopped out on the kitchen table by the chipped coffee mugs. She named a price and she didn't name another. Mary could say no quicker than any woman I ever knew and none of them ever meant yes. She kept the money in a cookie jar but nobody thought about that. Her cold grey eyes would have seen the thought and maybe something goes wrong on the next lay. John Law just happens by or a citizen comes up with a load of 00 buck shot into your soft and tenders.

In this world of shabby rooming houses, furtive grey figures in dark suits, hop joints and chili parlors, the Johnson Family took shape as a code of conduct. To say someone is a Johnson means he keeps his word and honors his obligations. He's a good man to do business with and a good man to have on your team. He is not a malicious, snooping, interfering self-righteous trouble-making person.

You get to know a Johnson when you see one and you get to know those of another persuasion. I remember in the Merchant Marine training center at Sheepshead Bay when the war ended. Most of the trainees quit right then and there was a long line to turn in equipment which had to be checked out item by item; some of us had only been there a few days and we had no equipment to turn in. So we hoped to avoid standing for hours, days perhaps in line for no purpose. I remember this spade cat said, "Well, we're going to meet a nice guy or we're going to meet a prick." We met a prick but we managed to find a Johnson.

Yes you get to know a Johnson when you see one. The cop who gave me a joint to smoke in the wagon. The hotel clerk who tipped me off I was hot. And sometimes you don't see the Johnson. I remember a friend of mine asked someone to send him a cake of hash from France. Well the asshole put it into a cheap envelope with no wrapping and it cut through the envelope. But some Johnson had put it back in and sealed the envelope with tape.

Years ago I was stranded in the wilds of East Texas and Bill Gains was sending me a little pantopon through the mail and he invented this clever code and telegrams are flying back and forth.

"Urgently need pants."

"Panic among dealers. No pants available."

This was during the war in a town of two hundred people. By rights we should have had the FBI swarming all over us. I remember the telegraph operator in his office in the railroad station. He had a kind, unhappy face. I suspect he was having trouble with his wife. Never a question or comment. He just didn't care what pants stood for. He was a Johnson.

A Johnson minds his own business. But he will help when help is needed. He doesn't stand by while someone is drowning or trapped in a wrecked car. Kells Elvins, a friend of mine, was doing ninety in his Town and Country Chrysler on the way from Pharr, Texas, to Laredo. He comes up over a rise and there is a fucking cow right in the middle of the road on the bridge. He slams on the brakes and hits the cow doing sixty. The car flips over and he is pinned under it with a broken collar bone covered from head to foot with blood and guts and cowshit. So along comes a car with some salesmen in it. They get out cautiously. He tells them just how to jack the car up and get it off him but when they see that *blood* they don't want to know. They don't want to get mixed up with anything like that. They get back in their car and drive away. Then a truck driver comes along. He doesn't need to be told exactly what to do, gets the car off Kells and takes him to a hospital. The truck driver was a Johnson. The salesmen were shits like most salesmen. Selling shit and they are shit.

The Johnson family formulates a Manichean position where good and evil are in conflict and the outcome is at this point uncertain. It is *not* an eternal conflict since one or the other must win a final victory.

Which side are you on?

I recollect Brion Gysin, Ian Sommerville and your reporter were drinking an espresso on the terrace of a little café on the Calle de Vigne in Tangier . . . after lunch a dead empty space. . . . Then this Spaniard walks by. He is about fifty or older, shabby, obviously very poor carrying something wrapped in brown paper. And our mouths fell open as we exclaimed in unison.

"My God that's a harmless looking person!"

He passed and I never saw him again, his passing portentous as a comet reminding us how rare it is to see a harmless looking person, a man who minds his own business and gets along as best he can in a world largely populated by people of a very different persuasion, kept alive by the hope of harming someone, on their way to the Comisario to denounce a neighbor or a business rival leaving squiggles and mutterings of malevolence in their wake like ugly little spirits.

QUEER UTOPIA

queer utopia
by james grauerholz

After his year in New York, Burroughs returned to London in January 1966, taking up residence at the Hotel Rushmore with Ian Sommerville. But while Burroughs was away, Sommerville had begun dating a younger man named Alan Watson, from his own hometown of Darlington, England. Sommerville had also developed his engineering skills, and he was operating a home studio provided by Paul McCartney, and surreptitiously living there with Watson. Many of Burroughs' experimental tape works were recorded by Ian in this studio.

Burroughs worked through the spring on the U.S. edition of *The Soft Machine,* and he was pleased when—after a four-year legal battle—the Massachusetts Supreme Court ruled in July that *Naked Lunch* was indeed not obscene, and could be sold in bookstores. He moved to a flat at No. 8, Duke Street, St. James's, the building where Antony Balch was already living. It was not long before Sommerville and Watson asked to join Burroughs at the Duke Street flat—the Beatles' management had evicted them from their recording studio. This new ménage turned out to be more harmonious and domestic than Burroughs expected.

Then Bill Jr.'s troubles in Florida began to call Burroughs home again: Billy had been sent to the experimental Green Valley School in Orange City, Florida, but he ran away in September 1966 to New York, where he was arrested for possession of methamphetamine, and jailed. Burroughs stalled for as long as he could, then went to Florida for Christmas with his widowed mother and his nineteen-year-old son, who was now out on probation. Laura was in bad shape; intermittently disoriented, she fell and hurt herself while Burroughs was staying there that winter. He accompanied Billy to his court hearing in Palm Beach, advising him on the rules of cool to avoid worsening the legal situation. In February 1967, Burroughs took his son to Lexington, Kentucky, for a drug cure—Burroughs' first return since his own admission to that clinic, when Billy was not yet a year old. The guard at the gate had to ask which one of them was being admitted.

Burroughs went back to London in March, feeling helpless about Billy's and Laura's problems. In May he went to Marrakech and Tangier to visit friends, but the Tangier scene was finished. Sommerville was still living at Duke Street with Watson, but Burroughs was beyond jealousy; he was preoccupied by his struggle with unwanted feelings from his childhood, his mother's deterioration, and his son's delinquency. Billy was granted probation and sent back to Green Valley School, but he was soon in trouble again. In September, Mort and Miggy moved Laura to Chastains, a nursing home in St. Louis.

Burroughs' freedom to pursue his life as an artist was threatened by the strong pull of these old family ties. He searched for a way forward. Brion Gysin, in Paris in 1959, had introduced him to L. Ron Hubbard's book *Dianetics,* which Burroughs commended to Ginsberg in letters from that time. By 1967, Burroughs began writing a column called "The Burroughs Academy Bulletin" for *Mayfair* magazine in London, and his editor introduced him to the psychics John McMasters, a close associate of Hubbard's who founded the Church of Scientology. Burroughs became interested in Scientology's techniques of directed recall, and he signed up for two months of "auditing" at Saint Hill, Hubbard's compound in East Grinstead, England—where he would become "clear," if not an "Operating Thetan."

As Burroughs "ran" his feelings obsessively over and over on the E-Meter, using Hubbard's patented processing routines, he was trying to de-emotionalize himself; so news of Neal Cassady's death, in February 1968 in northern Mexico—after a life of inspiration to others, but small profit to himself—may have had little impact on the new Clear at Saint Hill. In June, Burroughs took an advanced "clearing course" in Edinburg, Scotland—the scene of his literary apotheosis just four years earlier—but before long, he was fed up with Hubbard's megalomania. He returned to his Duke Street flat in July; Watson had left town. Burroughs remained obsessed with "auditing" his closest associates on the E-Meter, causing Sommerville—now twenty-eight—to absent himself from Burroughs, for the last time.

In August 1968 the United States' Democratic Party convention was held in Chicago. All the revolutionary currents of the sixties now came to a head, framed by the Vietnam War. The yippies, headed by Abbie Hoffman and the rest of the "Chicago Seven," planned to disrupt the convention with demonstrations in Chicago's lakeside Grant Park. *Esquire* editor John Berendt invited Burroughs, Jean Genet (with Richard Seaver interpreting), and Terry Southern to cover the convention for the magazine. Burroughs brought along his new weapon, a portable tape recorder, and he busied himself tape-recording and playing back the police/riot sounds at unpredictable intervals. His friendship with Terry Southern since the late 1950s in Paris was an important literary association; the two writers mined similar veins of wild satire. And his admiration for Genet's work was very high; so to be treated as an equal by the French writer must have meant that he had "arrived."

On his way home in September, Burroughs stopped in New York to write his article for *Esquire,* "The Coming of the Purple Better One." He and Genet were staying at the Delmonico Hotel. Jack Kerouac had been invited to appear on William F. Buckley's television program, "Firing Line," and he came down from Lowell, Massachusetts, with three of his hometown friends. When Kerouac came to visit him that day at the Delmonico, Burroughs was shocked by Kerouac's condition: drinking hard liquor during all his waking hours, Kerouac had become bloated and semi-incoherent. Burroughs advised him to cancel the studio taping with Buckley, but Kerouac decided to keep the appointment. It was Burroughs' last encounter with his old friend.

In October 1968, Gysin was in Tangier, and Burroughs was at Duke Street. Antony Balch had a flat in the same building, a few blocks from Piccadilly Circus, and Balch was acquainted with the "working boys" in the neighborhood. Through Balch, Burroughs met a young hustler who became his domestic partner for the next year and a half. It was a good time for Burroughs' work, with his "dilly boy" (when not too drunk or careless) making a tranquil home for his fifty-five-year-old lover. Burroughs was finishing the first edit of his 1968 interviews with Daniel Odier, which were published in January 1969 in Paris by Pierre Belfond as *Entretiens avec William Burroughs.*

Since the mid-1960s, Burroughs had been working on a new novel that he called *The Wild Boys,* which would present his vision of a postapocalyptic future where feral teenaged boys lived tribally in the desert, apart from all adult authority—and from all women. He finished the manuscript in London on August 17, 1969. The following month, as if to confirm that Burroughs had his finger on the pulse of gay futurity, the Stonewall Riots occurred in Greenwich Village. When the Stonewall Bar was raided by New York police, queers and drag queens fought back for the first time in America, and there were street fires and riots for three nights.

In October, sad news reached Burroughs in London: Jack Kerouac was dead at forty-seven, of a cirrhotic liver and esophageal hemorrhage. Although he had known his old friend was slowly drinking himself to death in St. Petersburg, Florida, for the last few years, Burroughs was unexpectedly moved by this loss. At this point, however, he was preoccupied with adding his own texts to the Odier interview book; retitled as *The Job,* the new book was published by Grove in May 1970. The Dutch Schultz film project, meanwhile, was not yet dead; Burroughs' painter friend David Budd had found new backers, and he invited Burroughs to New York for movie meetings. Burroughs had tired of his "dilly boy," and he evicted him from the Duke Street flat before going to New York. During his stay, Burroughs spent time with Budd and the painter David Prentice, and he found the city very livable. The third revision of the Dutch Schultz screenplay was published by Viking in June 1970, while Burroughs was in New York, as *The Last Words of Dutch Schultz;* when the movie deal stalled again in August, he returned to London.

Two months later, Burroughs received a telegram from his brother Mort: "MOTHER DEAD." He later described his delayed reaction as "a kick in the stomach." Laura had asked him to promise, while he was still a boy, to take care of her and to come see her, no matter where she was; but Burroughs had not visited her once in the three years she was at Chastains. And now, he did not travel home for the funeral. Burroughs' shame and regret for this failure reappear throughout the rest of his work. "There are mistakes," as he would often quote E. A. Robinson, "too monstrous for remorse / To tamper or to dally with." Burroughs knew that his life was filled with such mistakes.

In May 1971 there was a flurry of activity around a *Naked Lunch* movie project, spearheaded by Balch and Gysin. Brion had written a screenplay, and Balch created extensive storyboards in preparation for the production. Talks with Mick Jagger added excitement to the project, but nothing came of these meetings. Meanwhile, Burroughs' visit to New York in 1970 had opened his eyes to a new medium: gay pornographic films, which—with the erosion of censorship—could now be viewed in public theaters. He corresponded with the porno director Fred Halsted (*L.A. Plays Itself*) about an explicitly erotic movie version of *The Wild Boys*. But of course, it was not commercially feasible.

Grove Press published *The Wild Boys* in October 1971. The book is a marked departure from the tone and content of the cut-up novels; much of it is written in a more straightforward-seeming narrative style, and as critic Jennie Skerl noted in her 1985 monograph, *William S. Burroughs* (Twayne, Boston), his thematic emphasis had shifted from the "Dystopia" of his satirical depictions of a corrupt, inhospitable world to the "Utopia" of an all-homosexual future— a new liberation of the Present, by means of a "magickal" rewriting of history. But although the boys in his new work were all queer, they were literarily derived from the boy's-adventure pulp fiction of Burroughs' childhood, and his fantasies of revenge against the oppression of parents and heterosexual society. It is not the unchained sexuality of the Wild Boys that is most distinctive, but their animal freedom.

William Burroughs Jr., with guidance from his godfather, Allen Ginsberg, had followed in his father's footsteps as a writer. *Speed,* a first-person account of his ill-fated flight to New York City in 1966, was published by The Olympia Press in Paris four years later. *Speed* demonstrated Billy's literary talent, but also showed his irresistible self-destructive urges. In 1971 Billy was living in Savannah with his wife of four years, Karen Perry, and working on *Kentucky Ham,* an autobiographical sequal to *Speed* that describes his frustrating half year with his father in Tangier and his adventures at the Green Valley School and on the school's teaching vessel in the Pacific Ocean near Alaska.

By late 1971, Burroughs Sr. had been living alone for a year and a half. In October he accepted an invitation to join the faculty at the experimental University of the New World in Haute Nendaz, Switzerland. Burroughs' three months at high altitude were uncomfortable and disorienting; he was ill most of the time, and he ended up readdicted to the legal codeine pills known as *Codethyline Houdé,* which he affectionately called "pinkies." In December he returned to London, feeling that the situation in Haute Nendaz had become a dead end.

Then Terry Southern showed up with a new adventure: in April 1972, he took Burroughs on a whirlwind trip to Hollywood, trying to sell the movie rights to *Naked Lunch* to a Hollywood game-show producer. They were un-successful, but the whole episode was wonderful comic relief, and added to Burroughs' stock of Hollywood tropes. Back in London, he began working on a new book called *Port of Saints,* a sequel to *The Wild Boys.* He also as-sembled a collection of short pieces that he called *Exterminator!* for Viking Press; his former Grove editor, Richard Seaver, published the book in August 1972.

With Balch, Burroughs continued to meet street hustlers, and in the fall of 1972 one of these, an Irish lad named John Brady, became Burroughs' lover. Johnny was reminiscent of Jack Anderson in his bisexuality, his lack of intel-lectual development, and his predilection for violence. He brought women back to the Duke Street flat for sex, and he menaced Burroughs if he met with any complaint. Burroughs was off junk at this time, but he was drinking heavily and finding it difficult to make artistic or financial progress. His self-esteem as a writer, and as a "sugar daddy," were at low ebb, and he tolerated this humiliating situation.

Gysin had introduced Burroughs to Sanche de Gramont, a journalist and author from an aristocratic French family. When Burroughs was invited by *Oui* magazine in late 1972 to visit the Moroccan hill country of Joujouka, home of the Master Musicians, de Gramont and Gysin joined the expedition, and Burroughs took John Brady along. Brian Jones, of the Rolling Stones, had followed Gysin's lead to Joujouka, and he recorded an album with the Master Musicians. The music writer Robert Palmer also first befriended Burroughs and Gysin in Joujouka, and his critical writings later reified this nexus of three worlds: rock 'n' roll, avant-garde literature, and ancient North African trance music.

Back in London in spring 1973, Burroughs was collaborating on new projects with some young English artists he had met. With Robert Gale, he wrote an illustrated short text called *The Book of Breeething,* exploring the liberative possibilities of ancient glyph-based languages like Egyptian or Mayan. And with Malcolm McNeill, Burroughs was writing *Ah Pook Is Here,* a tale about "Mr. Hart," the ugly-hearted tycoon (based on William Randolph Hearst) who goes to the Mayan temples in Yucatán to recover "the Books" and to challenge death but who is, in the end, no match for "Ah Pook, the Destroyer." The *Ah Pook* illustrated-book concept was ahead of its time; McNeill's detailed color drawings, incorporating Burroughs' text, were too expensive for publication. A few years later, the magazines *Metal Hurlant* and *Heavy Metal* finally made the comics/graphic-novel breakthrough, taking their names from one of Burroughs' cut-up trilogy characters, "The Heavy Metal Kid"—a phrase also adopted by a genre of rock music.

With Barry Miles—a writer, editor, and bookseller whom they knew from Miles' cultural activities in London in the mid-sixties, such as the Indica Gal-lery and the underground paper *International Times*—Burroughs and Gysin assembled a large collection of their archival materials, which they sold in 1973. The proceeds from this sale rescued both of them from insolvency. Burroughs took Johnny Brady on a holiday trip to the Greek island of Spetsai in September; echoes of their experiences there can be found in the "Clem Snide" passages in *Cities of the Red Night*. This trip parallels Burroughs' expedition with Lewis Marker to Ecuador in some ways, although any semblance of an emotional connection was overcast by alcohol and resentment after their return to London, where once again Brady had the upper hand.

When Allen Ginsberg visited Burroughs in London that fall, he felt that his old friend was stagnating badly: drinking too much, writing too little, and unable to move forward from the London position he had maintained for eight years. Brady was openly insolent and threatening, and Ginsberg resolved to intervene somehow. He went back to New York and arranged for the English Department of the City College of New York to offer Burroughs a well-paid teaching residency in the spring of 1974. Although Burroughs had enough money to stay where he was, he welcomed the change of scene.

Burroughs arrived in New York City in mid-January and took up residence in a sublet loft at 452 Broadway, just before his sixtieth birthday. He began to make the early-morning subway commute to his classes at CCNY, and he looked up old friends: Ginsberg, Giorno, Budd, Prentice. On February 12, Burroughs opened the metal door of his loft at cocktail time to find a tall, bespectacled blond boy of twenty-one, who had just arrived in New York from the university town of Lawrence, in his home state of Kansas. Within two weeks, Burroughs had invited the boy from Kansas to live with him in the Broadway loft—and that was the beginning of my twenty-three years with William.

from
the wild boys

AND BURY THE BREAD DEEP IN A STY

Audrey was a thin pale boy, his face scarred by festering spiritual wounds. "He looks like a sheep-killing dog," said a St. Louis aristocrat. There was something rotten and unclean about Audrey, an odor of the walking dead. Doormen stopped him when he visited his rich friends. Shopkeepers pushed his change back without a thank you. He spent sleepless nights weeping into his pillow from impotent rage. He read adventure stories and saw himself as a gentleman adventurer like the "Major" . . . sun helmet, khakis, Webley at the belt, a faithful Zulu servant at his side. A dim sad child breathing old pulp magazines. At sixteen he attended an exclusive high school known as The Poindexter Academy where he felt rather like a precarious house nigger. Still he was invited to most of the parties and Mrs. Kindheart made a point of being nice to him.

At the opening of the academy in September a new boy appeared. Aloof and mysterious, where he came from nobody knew. There were rumors of Paris, London, a school in Switzerland. His name was John Hamlin and he stayed with relatives in Portland Place. He drove a magnificent Duesenberg. Audrey, who drove a battered Moon, studied this vast artifact with openmouthed awe: the luxurious leather upholstery, the brass fittings, the wickerwork doors, the huge spotlight with a pistol-grip handle. Audrey wrote: "Clearly he has come a long way, travel stained and even the stains unfamiliar, cuff links of a dull metal that seems to absorb light, his red hair touched with gold, large green eyes well apart."

The new boy took a liking to Audrey, while he turned aside with polished deftness invitations from sons of the rich. This did not endear Audrey to important boys, and he found his stories coldly rejected by the school magazine.

"Morbid" the editor told him. "We want stories that make you go to bed feeling good."

It was Friday, October 23, 1929, a bright blue day, leaves falling, half-moon in the sky. Audrey Carsons walked up Pershing Avenue . . . *"Simon, aime tu le bruit des pas sur les feuilles mortes?"* . . . He had read that in one of E. Haldeman

Julius's Little Blue Books and meant to use it in the story he was writing. Of course his hero spoke French. At the corner of Pershing and Walton he stopped to watch a squirrel. A dead leaf caught for a moment in Audrey's ruffled brown hair.

"Hello Audrey. Like to go for a ride?"

It was John Hamlin at the wheel of his Duesenberg. He opened the door without waiting for an answer. Hamlin made a wide U-turn and headed west . . . left on Euclid, right on Lindell . . . Skinker Boulevard, City Limits . . . Clayton . . . Hamlin looked at his wristwatch.

"We could make St. Joseph for lunch . . . nice riverside restaurant there, serves wine."

Audrey is thrilled of course. The autumn countryside flashes by . . . long straight stretch of road ahead.

"Now I'll show you what this job can do."

Hamlin presses the accelerator slowly to the floor . . . 60 . . . 70 . . . 80 . . . 85 . . . 90 . . . Audrey leans forward, lips parted, eyes shining.

At Tent City a top-level conference is in progress, involving top-level executives in the CONTROL GAME. The Conference has been called by a Texas billionaire who contributes heavily to MRA and maintains a stable of evangelists. This conference is taking place outside St. Louis Missouri because the Green Nun flatly refuses to leave her kindergarten. The high teacup queens thought it would be fun to do a tent city like a 1917 Army camp. The conferents are discussing Operation W.O.G. (Wrath of God).

At the top level people get cynical after a few drinks. The young man from the news magazine has discovered a good-looking Fulbright scholar and they are witty in a corner over martinis. A drunken American Sergeant reels to his feet. He has the close-cropped iron-grey hair and ruddy complexion of the Regular Army man.

"To put it country simple for a lay audience . . . you don't even know what buttons to push . . . we take a bunch of longhair boys fucking each other while they puff reefers, spit cocaine on the Bible, and wipe their asses with Old Glory. We show this film to decent, church-going, Bible Belt do-rights. We take the reaction. One religious sheriff with seven nigger notches on his gun melted the camera lens. He turned out to be quite an old character and the boys from *Life* did a spread on him—seems it had always been in the family, a power put there by God to smite the unrighteous: his grandmother struck a whore dead in the street with it.

"When we showed the picture to a fat Southern senator his eyes popped out throwing fluid all over your photographer. Well I've been asparagrassed in Paris, kneed in the groin by the Sea Org in Tunis, maced in Chicago and pelted with scorpions in Marrakech, so a face full of frog eggs is all in the day's work. What the Narco boys call 'society's disapproval' reflected and concentrated, twenty million I HATE YOU pictures in one blast. When you want the job done, come to the UNITED STATES OF AMERICA. AND WE CAN TURN IT IN ANY DIRECTION. You Limey leftovers. . . ."

He points to a battery of old grey men in club chairs, frozen in stony disapproval of this vulgar drunken American. When will the club steward arrive to eject the bounder so a gentleman can read his *Times*?

"YOU'RE NOTHING BUT A BANANA REPUBLIC. AND REMEMBER WE'VE GOT YOUR PICTURES."

"And we've got yours too, Yank," they clip icily.

"MINE ARE UGLIER THAN YOURS."

The English cough and look away, fading into their spectral clubs, yellowing tusks of the beast killed by the improbable hyphenated name.

OLD SARGE screams after them . . . "WHAT DO YOU THINK THIS IS A BEAUTY CONTEST? You Fabian Socialist vegetable peoples go back to your garden in Hampstead and release a hot-air balloon in defiance of a local ordinance . . . 'Delightful encounter with the bobby in the morning. Mums wrote it all up in her diary and read it to us at tea.' WE GOT ALL YOUR PANSY PICTURES AT ETON. YOU WANTA JACK OFF IN FRONT OF THE QUEEN WITH A CANDLE UP YOUR ASS?"

"You can't talk like that in front of decent women," drawled the Texas billionaire flanked by his Rangers.

"You decorticated cactus. I suppose you think this conference was your idea? Compliments of SID in the Sudden Inspiration Department. . . . And you lousy yacking fink queens, my photographers wouldn't take your pictures. You are nothing but tape recorders. With just a flick of my finger frozen forever over that martini. All right get snide and snippy about that HUH? . . .

"And you" . . . He points to the Green Nun . . . "Write out ten thousand times underwater in indelible ink: 'OLD SARGE HAS MY CHRIST PICTURES.' SHALL I SHOW THEM TO THE POPE?

"And now, in the name of all good tech sergeants everywhere . . ."

A gawky young sergeant is reading *Amazing Stories*. He flicks a switch . . . Audrey and Hamlin on screen. Wind ruffles Audrey's hair as the Duesenberg gathers speed.

"Light Years calling Bicarbonate . . . Operation Little Audrey on target . . . eight seconds to count down . . . tracking . . ."

A thin dyspeptic technician mixes a bicarbonate of soda.

"URP calling Fox Trot . . . six seconds to count down . . ."

English computer programmer is rolling a joint.

"Spot Light calling Accent . . . four seconds to count down . . ."

Computers hum, lights flash, lines converge.

Red-haired boy chews gum and looks at a muscle magazine.

"Red Dot calling Pin Point . . . two seconds to count down . . ."

The Duesenberg zooms over a rise and leaves the ground. Just ahead is a wooden barrier, steamroller, piles of gravel, phantom tents. DETOUR sign points sharp left to a red clay road where pieces of flint glitter in the sunlight.

"OLD SARGE IS TAKING OVER."

He looks around and the crockery flies off every table, spattering the conferents with martinis, bourbon, whipped cream, maraschino cherries, gravy and vichysoisse, frozen forever in a 1920 slapstick.

"COUNT DOWN."

End over end, a flaming pinwheel of jagged metal slices through the conferents. The Green Nun is decapitated by a twisted fender. The Texas billionaire is sloshed with gasoline like a burning nigger. The broken spotlight trailing white-hot wires like a jellyfish hits the British delegate in the face. The Duesenberg explodes, throwing white-hot chunks of jagged metal, boiling acid, burning gasoline in all directions.

Wearing the uniforms of World War I, Audrey and Old Sarge lean out of a battered Moon in the morning sky and smile. Old Sarge is at the wheel.

THE PENNY ARCADE PEEP SHOW

Unexpected rising of the curtain can begin with a Duesenberg moving slowly along a 1920 detour. Just ahead, Audrey sees booths and fountains and ferris wheels against a yellow sky. A boy steps in front of the car and holds up his hand. He is naked except for a rainbow-colored jock strap and sandals. Under one arm he carries a Mauser pistol clipped onto a rifle stock. He steps to the side of the car. Audrey has never seen anyone so cool and disengaged. He looks at Audrey and he looks at John. He nods.

"We leave the car here," John says. Audrey gets out. Six boys now stand there watching him serenely. They carry long knives sheathed at their belts, which are studded wtih amethyst crystals. They all wear rainbow-colored jock straps, like souvenir postcards of Niagara Falls.

Audrey follows John through a square where acts are in progress, surrounded by circles of adolescent onlookers eating colored ices and chewing gum. Most of the boys wear the rainbow jock straps and a few of them seem to be completely naked. Audrey can't be sure, trying to keep up with John. The fair reminds Audrey of 1890 prints. Sepia ferris wheels turn in yellow light. Gliders launched from a wooden ramp soar over the fairground, legs of the pilots dangling in air. A colored hot-air balloon is released to applause of the onlookers.

Around the fairground are boardwalks, lodging houses, restaurants and baths. Boys lounge in doorways. Audrey glimpses scenes that quicken his breath and send the blood pounding to his groin. He catches sight of John far ahead, outlined in the dying sunlight. Audrey calls after him, but his voice is blurred and muffled. Then darkness falls as if someone has turned out the sky.

Some distance ahead and to the left he sees PENNY ARCADE spelled out in light globes. Perhaps John has gone in there. Audrey pushes aside a red curtain and enters the arcade. Chandeliers, gilt walls, red curtains, mirrors, windows stretch away into the distance. He cannot see the end of it in either direction from the entrance. It is a long narrow building like a ship cabin or a train. Boys are standing in front of peep shows, some wearing the rainbow jock straps, others in prep school clothes, loincloths and jellabas. He notices shows with seats in front of them and some in curtained booths. As he passes a booth he glimpses through parted curtains two boys sitting on a silk sofa, both of them naked. Shifting his eyes, he sees a boy slip his jock strap down and step out of it without taking his eyes from the peep show. Moving with a precision and ease he sometimes knew in flying dreams, Audrey slides onto a steel chair that reminds him of Doctor Moor's Surgery in the Lister Building, afternoon light through green blinds. In front of him is a luminous screen. Smell of old pain, ether, bandages, sick fear in the waiting room, yes this is Doctor Moor's Surgery in the Lister Building.

The doctor was a Southern gentleman of the old school. Rather like John Barrymore in appearance and manner, he fancied himself as a witty raconteur, which at times he was. The doctor had charm, which Audrey so sadly lacked. No doorman would ever stop him, no shopkeeper forget his thank you, under eyes that could suddenly go cold as ice. It was impossible for the doctor to like Audrey. "He looks like a homosexual sheep-killing dog" he thought, but he did not say this. He looked up from his paper in his dim gloomy drawing room and pontificated: "the child is not wholesome."

His wife went further: "It is a walking corpse," she said. Audrey was inclined to agree with her, but he didn't know whose corpse he was. And he was painfully aware of being unwholesome.

There is a screen directly in front of him, a screen to his left, a screen to his right, and a screen in back of his head. He can see all four screens from a point above his head.

Later Audrey wrote these notes:

"The scenes presented and the manner of presentation varies according to an underlying pattern.

"1. Objects and scenes move away and come in with a slow hydraulic movement always at the same speed. The screens are three-dimensional visual sections punctuated by flashing lights. I once saw the Great Thurston who could make an elephant disappear do an act with a screen on stage. He shoots a man in the film. The actor clutches his ketchup to his tuxedo shirt and falls then Thurston steps into the screen as a detective to investigate the murder, steps back outside to commit more murders, busts in as a brash young tabloid reporter, moves out to make a phone call that will collapse the market, back in as ruined broker. I am pulled into the film in a stream of yellow light and I can pull people out of the film withdrawal shots pulling the flesh off naked boys. Sequences are linked by the presence of some arbitrary object: a pinwheel, a Christmas-tree ornament, a pyramid, an Easter egg, a copper coil going away and coming in always in the same numerical order. Movement in and out of the screen can be very painful like acid in the face and electric sex tingles.

"2. Scenes that have the same enigmatic structure presented on one screen where the perspective remains constant. In a corner of the frames there are punctuation symbols. This material is being processed on a computer. I am in the presence of an unknown language spelling out the same message again and again in cryptic charades where I participate as an actor. There are also words on screen familiar words maybe we read them somewhere a long time ago written in sepia and silver letters that fade into pictures.

"3. Fragmentary glimpses linked by immediate visual impact. There is a sensation of speed as if the pictures were seen from a train window.

"4. Narrative sections in which the screens disappear. I experience a series of quite understandable and coherent events as one of the actors. The narrative sequences are preceded by the title on screen then I am in the film. The transition is painless like stepping into a dream. The structuralized peep show may intersperse the narrative and then I am back in front of the screen and moving in and out of it."

Audrey looked at the screen in front of him. His lips parted and the thoughts stopped in his mind. It was all there on screen, sight sound touch, at once immediate and spectrally remote in past time.

THE PENNY ARCADE PEEP SHOW

1. On screen 1 a burning red pinwheel distant amusement park. The pinwheel is going away taking the lights the voices the roller coaster the smell of peanuts and gunpowder further and further away.

2. On screens 2 and 3 a white pinwheel and a blue pinwheel going away. Audrey catches a distant glimpse of two boys in the penny arcade. One laughs and points to the other's pants sticking out straight at the crotch.

3. On screens 1 2 3 three pinwheels spinning away red white and blue. Young soldier at the rifle range beads of sweat in the down on his lip. Distant firecrackers burst on hot city pavements . . . night sky parks and ponds . . . blue sound in vacant lots.

4. On screens 1 2 3 4 four pinwheels spinning away, red, white, blue and red. A low-pressure area draws Audrey into the park. July 4, 1926, falls into a silent roller.

1. On screen 1 a red pinwheel coming in . . . smoky moon over the midway. A young red-haired sailor bites into an apple.

2. On screens 2 and 3 two pinwheels coming in white and blue light flickers on an adolescent face. The pitchman stirs uneasily. "Take over will you kid. Gotta see a man about a monkey."

3. On screens 1 2 3 three pinwheels coming in red white and blue. A luminous postcard sky opens into a vast lagoon of summer evenings. A young soldier steps from the lake from the hill from the sky.

4. On screens 1 2 3 4 four pinwheels spinning in red white blue red. The night sky is full of bursting rockets lighting parks and ponds and the upturned faces.

"The rocket's red glare the bombs bursting in air / Gave proof through the night that our flag was still there."

A light in his eyes. Must be Doctor Moor's mirror with a hole in it.

1. A flattened pyramid going away into distant birdcalls and dawn mist . . . Audrey glimpses bulbous misshapen trees . . . Indian boy standing there with a machete . . . The scene is a sketch from an explorer's notebook . . . dim in on a stained yellow page . . . "No one was ever meant to know the unspeakable evil of this place and live to tell of it . . ."
2. Two pyramids going away . . . "The last of my Indian boys left before dawn. I am down with a bad attack of fever . . . and the sores . . . I can't keep myself from scratching. I have even tried tying my hands at night when the dreams come, dreams so indescribably loathsome that I cannot bring myself to write down their content. I untie the knots in my sleep and wake up scratching . . ."
3. Three pyramids going away . . . "The sores have eaten through my flesh to the bone and still this hideous craving to scratch. Suicide is the only way out. I can only pray that the horrible secrets I have uncovered die with me forever . . ."
4. Four pyramids going away . . . Audrey experienced a feeling of vertigo like the sudden stopping of an elevator . . . skeleton clutches a rusty revolver in one fleshless hand . . .

1. A pyramid coming in . . . Audrey can see stonework like broken lace on top of the pyramid. Damp heat closes around his body a musty odor of vegetable ferment and animal decay. Figure in a white loincloth swims out of the dawn mist. An Indian boy with rose-colored flesh and delicate features stands in front of Audrey. Two muscular Indians with long arms carry jars and tools. "You crazy or something walk around alone? This bad place. This place of flesh plants."
2. Two pyramids coming in . . . "You not careful you grow here. Look at that." He points to a limp pink tube about two feet long growing from two purple mounds covered with fine red tendrils. As the boy points to the tube it turns toward him. The boy steps forward and rubs the tube which slowly stiffens into a phallus six feet high growing from two testicles . . . "Now I make him spurt. Jissom worth much *dinero*. Jissom make flesh" . . . He strips off his loincloth and steps onto the vegetable scrotum embracing the shaft. The red hairs twist around his legs reaching up to his groin and buttocks . . .
3. Three pyramids coming in . . . The mist is lifting. In the milky dawn light Audrey sees a blush spread through the boy's body turning the skin to a

swollen red wheal. Pearly lubricant pours from the head of the giant phallus and runs down the sides. The boy squirms against the shaft caressing the great pulsing head with both hands. There is a soft muffled sound, a groan of vegetable lust straining up from tumescent roots as the plant spurts ten feet in the air. The bearers run around catching the gobs in stone jars.

4. Four pyramids coming in . . . The flesh garden is located in a round crater, four pyramids spaced around it on higher ground North South East and West. Slowly the tendrils fall away the Phallus goes limp and the boy steps free . . .

"Over there ass tree" . . . He points to the tree of smooth red buttocks twisted together, between each buttock a quivering rectum. Opposite the orifices phallic orchids red, purple, orange sprout from the tree's shaft . . . "Make him spurt too" . . . The boy turns to one of the bearers and says something in a language unknown to Audrey. The boy grins and slips off his loincloth . . . The other bearer follows his movements . . . "He fuck tree. Other fuck him" . . . The two men dip lubricant from a jar and rub it on their stiffening phalluses. Now the first bearer steps forward and penetrates the tree wrapping his legs around the shaft. The second bearer pries his buttocks open with his thumbs and squirms slowly forward, men and plant moving together in a slow hydraulic peristalsis . . . The orchids pulse erect dripping colored drops of lubricant . . . "We catch spurts" . . . The boy hands Audrey a stone jar. The two boys seem to writhe into the tree, their faces swollen with blood. A choking sound bursts from tumescent lips as the orchids spurt like rain.

"This one very dangerous" . . . The boy points to a human body with vines growing through the flesh like veins. The body, of a green pink color, excretes a milky substance . . . The boy draws on parchment gloves . . . "You touch him you get sores itch you scratch spread sores feel good scratch more scratch self away" . . . Slowly the lids open on green pupils surrounded by black flower flesh. He is seeing them now you can tell. His body quivers with horrible eagerness . . . "He there long time. Need somebody pop him." . . . The boy reaches up takes the head in both hands and twists it sharply to one side. There is a sound like a stick breaking in wet towels as the spine snaps. The feet flutter and rainbow colors spiral from the eyes. The penis spurts again and again as the body twists in wrenching spasms. Finally the body hangs limp . . . "He dead now" . . . The bearers dig a hole. The boy cuts the body down and it plops into the grave . . . "Soon grow another" . . . said the boy matter-of-factly . . .

"Over there shit tree" . . . He points to a black bush in the shape of a man squatting. The bush is a maze of tentacles and caught in these tendrils Audrey sees animal skeletons . . . "Now I make him asshole" . . . The boy dips sperm from a jar and rubs it between the parted buttocks. Nitrous fumes rise, the plant writhes in peristalsis and empties itself . . . "Very good for garden. Make flesh trees grow. Now I show you good place" . . .

He leads the way up a steep path to an open place by one of the pyramids . . . In niches carved from rock, Audrey sees vines growing in human forms. The figures give off a remote vegetable calm . . . "This place of vine people very calm very quiet. Live here long long time. Roots reach down to garden."

The rising sun hits Audrey in the face

- Dawn light on a naked *youth* poised to dive into a pond.———
- A thousand Japanese *youths* leap from a balcony into a round swimming tank.
- *Audrey* taking a shower. Water runs down his lean stomach. He is getting stiff.
- Locker room toilet on five levels seen from ferris wheel . . . flash of white legs, shiny pubic hairs, lean brown arms . . . *boys* masturbating under a rusty shower.
- Naked *boy* on yellow toilet seat sunlight in pubic hairs a twitching foot.
- *Boys* masturbating in bleak public school toilets, outhouses, locker rooms . . . a blur of flesh.
- *Farja* sighs deeply and rocks back hugging his knees against his chest. Nitrous fumes twist from pink rectal flesh in whorls of orange, sepia, rose.
- Red fumes envelop the *two bodies.* A scream of roses bursts from tumescent lips roses growing through flesh tearing thorns of delight intertwined the quivering bodies crushed them together writhing gasping in an agony of roses.
- What happens between my legs is like a cold drink to me it is just a feeling . . . cool round stones against my back sunshine and shadow of Mexico. It is just a feeling between the legs a sort of tingle. It is a feeling by which *I am* here at all.
- We squat there our knees touching. Kiki looks down between his legs watching himself get stiff. I feel the tingle between my legs and I am getting stiff too.

- cadavers. Electron microscope shows cells, nerves, bone.
- Telescope shows stars and planets and space. Click microscope. Click telescope.

- *He* wasn't there really. Pale the picture was pale. I could see through him. In life used address I give you for that belated morning.
- Young *ghosts* blurred faces boys and workshops the old February 5, 1914.
- *I am* not a person and I am not an animal. There is something I am here for something I have to do before I can go.
- *The dead* around like birdcalls rain in my face.
- Flight of geese across a gleaming empty sky . . . Peter John S . . . 1882– 1904 . . . the death of a child long ago . . . cool remote spirit to his world of shades . . . I was waiting there pale character in someone else's writing

breathing old pulp magazines. Turn your face a little to eyes like forget-me-nots . . . flickering silver smile melted into air . . . The boy did not speak again.

- Cold stars splash the empty house faraway toys. Sad whispering *spirits* melt into coachmen and animals of dreams, mist from the lake, faded family photos.

- Museum bas-relief of the *God* Amen with erection. A thin boy in prep school clothes stands in the presence of the God. The boy in museum toilet takes down his pants phallic shadow on a distant wall.
- All the *Gods* of Egypt
- The *God* Amen the boy teeth bare gasping
- Clear light touching marble porticos and fountains . . . the *Gods* of Greece . . . Mercury, Apollo, Pan

---

Light drains into the red walls of Marrakech

"MOTHER AND I WOULD LIKE TO KNOW"

The uneasy spring of 1988. Under the pretext of drug control, suppressive police states have been set up throughout the Western world. The precise programming of thought, feeling and apparent sensory impressions by the technology outlined in bulletin 2332 enables the police states to maintain a democratic facade from behind which they loudly denounce as criminals, perverts and drug addicts anyone who opposes the control machine. Underground armies operate in the large cities, enturbulating the police with false information through anonymous phone calls and letters. Police with drawn guns irrupt at the Senator's dinner party, a very special dinner party too, that would tie up a sweet thing in surplus planes.

"We been tipped off a nude reefer party is going on here. Take the place apart boys and you folks keep your clothes on or I'll blow your filthy guts out."

We put out false alarms on the police short wave, directing patrol cars to nonexistent crimes and riots, which enables us to strike somewhere else. Squads of false police search and beat the citizenry. False construction workers tear up streets, rupture water mains, cut power connections. Infra-sound installations set off every burglar alarm in the city. Our aim is total chaos.

Loft room, map of the city on the wall. Fifty boys with portable tape recorders record riots from TV. They are dressed in identical grey flannel suits. They strap on the recorders under gabardine topcoats and dust their clothes lightly with tear gas. They hit the rush hour in a flying wedge, riot recordings on full blast, police whistles, screams, breaking glass, crunch of nightsticks, tear gas flapping from their clothes. They scatter, put on press cards and come back to cover the action. Bearded Yippies rush down a street with hammers breaking every window on both sides, leave a wake of screaming burglar alarms, strip off the beards, reverse collars and they are fifty clean priests throwing petrol bombs under every car WHOOSH a block goes up behind them. Some in fireman uniforms arrive with axes and hoses to finish the good work.

In Mexico, South and Central America guerrilla units are forming an army of liberation to free the United States. In North Africa, from Tangier to Timbuctu, corresponding units prepare to liberate Western Europe and the United Kingdom. Despite disparate aims and personnel of its constituent members, the underground is agreed on basic objectives. We intend to march on the police machine everywhere. We intend to destroy the police machine and all its records. We intend to destroy all dogmatic verbal systems. The family unit and its cancerous expansion into tribes, countries, nations we will eradicate at its vegetable roots. We don't want to hear any more family talk, mother talk, father talk, cop talk, priest talk, country talk *or* party talk. To put it country simple, we have heard enough bullshit.

I am on my way from London to Tangier. In North Africa I will contact the wild-boy packs that range from the outskirts of Tangier to Timbuctu. Rotation and exchange is a keystone of the underground. I am bringing them modern weapons: laser guns, infra-sound installations, Deadly Orgone Radiation. I will learn their specialized skills and transfer wild-boy units to the Western cities. We know that the West will invade Africa and South America in an all-out attempt to crush the guerrilla units. Doktor Kurt Unruh von Steinplatz, in his four-volume treatise on the Authority Sickness, predicts these latter-day Crusades. We will be ready to strike in their cities and to resist in the territories we now hold. Meanwhile we watch and train and wait.

I have a thousand faces and a thousand names. I am nobody I am everybody. I am me I am you. I am here there forward back in out. I stay everywhere I stay nowhere. I stay present I stay absent.

Disguise is not a false beard dyed hair and plastic surgery. Disguise is clothes and bearing and behavior that leave no questions unanswered . . . American tourist with a wife he calls "Mother" . . . old queen on the make . . . dirty beatnik . . . marginal film producer. . . . Every article of my luggage and clothing is carefully planned to create a certain impression. Behind this impression I can operate without interference for a time. Just so long and long enough. So I walk down Boulevard Pasteur handing out money to guides and shoeshine boys. And that is only one of the civic things I did. I bought one of those souvenir matchlocks clearly destined to hang over a false fireplace in West Palm Beach, Florida, and I carried it around wrapped in brown paper with the muzzle sticking out. I made inquiries at the Consulate:

"Now Mother and I would like to know."

And "MOTHER AND I WOULD LIKE TO KNOW" in American Express and the Minzah, pulling wads of money out of my pocket. "How much shall I give them?" I asked the vice-consul, for a horde of guides had followed me into the Consulate. "I wonder if you've met my congressman Joe Link?"

Nobody gets through my cover, I assure you. There is no better cover than a nuisance and a bore. When you see my cover you don't look further. You look the other way fast. For use on any foreign assignment there is nothing like the old reliable American tourist, cameras and light meters slung all over him.

"How much shall I give him Mother?"

I can sidle up to any old bag, she nods and smiles, it's all so familiar "must be that cute man we met on the plane over from Gibraltar Captain Clark welcomes you aboard and he says: 'Now what's this form? I don't read Arabic.' Then he turns to me and says 'Mother I need help.' And I show him how to fill out the form and after that he would come up to me on the street this cute man so helpless bobbing up everywhere."

"What is he saying Mother?"

"I think he wants money."

"They all do." He turns to an army of beggars, guides, shoeshine boys and whores of all sexes and makes an ineffectual gesture.

"Go away! Scram off!"

"One dirham Meester."

"One cigarette."

"You want beeg one Meester?"

And the old settlers pass on the other side. No, they don't get through my cover. And I have a lot of special numbers for emergency use . . . Character with wild eyes that spin in little circles, believes trepanning is the last answer, pull you into a garage and try to do the job with an electric drill straightaway.

"Now if you'll kindly take a seat here."

"Say what is this?"

"All over in a minute and you'll be out of that rigid cranium."

So the word goes out stay away from that one. You need him like a hole in the head. I have deadly old-style bores who are translating the Koran into Provençal or constructing a new cosmology based on "brain breathing." And the animal lover with exotic pets. The CIA man looks down with moist suspicious brow at the animal in his lap. It is a large ocelot, its claws pricking into his flesh, and every time he tries to shove it away the animal growls and digs in. I won't be seeing that Bay of Pigs again.

So I give myself a week on the build-up and make contact. Colonel Bradly knows the wild boys better than any man in Africa. In fact he has given his whole life to youth and it would seem gotten something back. There is talk of the devil's bargain and in fact he is indecently young-looking for a man of sixty-odd. As the Colonel puts it, with engaging candor: "The world is not my home you understand here on young people."

We have lunch on the terrace of his mountain house. A heavily wooded garden with pools and paths stretches down to a cliff over the sea. Lunch is turbot in cream sauce, grouse, wild asparagus, peaches in wine. Quite a change from the grey cafeteria food I have been subjected to in Western cities, where I pass myself off as one of the faceless apathetic citizens searched and questioned by the police on every corner, set upon by brazen muggers, stumbling home to my burglarized apartment to find the narcotics squad going through my medicine chest again. We are served by a lithe young Malay with bright red gums. Colonel Bradly jabs a fork at him.

"Had a job getting that dish through immigration. The Consulate wasn't at all helpful."

After lunch we settle down to discuss my assignment.

"The wild boys are an overflow from North African cities that started in 1969. The uneasy spring of 1969 in Marrakech. Spring in Marrakech is always uneasy, each day a little hotter, knowing what Marrakech can be in August. That spring gasoline gangs prowled the rubbish heaps, alleys and squares of the city, dousing just anybody with gasoline and setting that person on fire. They rush in anywhere, nice young couple sitting in their chintzy middle-class living room when hello! yes hello! the gas boys rush in douse them head to foot with a pump fire extinguisher full of gasoline and I got some good pictures from a closet where I had prudently taken refuge. Shot of the boy who lit the match, he let the rank and file slosh his couple then he lit a Swan match, face young, pure, pitiless as the cleansing fire brought the match close enough to catch the fumes.

"Then he lit a Player with the same match, sucked the smoke in and smiled, he was listening to the screams and I thought My God what a cigarette ad: Clambake on a beach the BOY there with a match. He is looking at two girls in bikinis. As he lights the match they lean forward with a LUCKYSTRIKECHESTERFIELDOLDGOLDCAMELPLAYER in the bim and give a pert little salute.

"The BOY turned out to be the hottest property in advertising. Enigmatic smile on the delicate young face. Just what is the BOY looking at? We had set out to sell cigarettes or whatever else we were paid to sell. The BOY was too hot to handle. Temples were erected to the BOY and there were posters of his face seventy feet high and all the teenagers began acting like the BOY looking at you with a dreamy look lips parted over their Wheaties. They all bought BOY shirts and BOY knives running around like wolf packs burning, looting, killing, it spread everywhere all that summer in Marrakech, the city would light up at night, human torches flickering on walls, trees, fountains, all very romantic, you could map the dangerous areas sitting on your balcony under the stars sipping a scotch. I looked across the square and watched a tourist burning in blue fire, they had gasoline that burned in all colors by then. . . ." (He turned on the projector and stepped to the edge of the balcony.) . . . "Just look at them out there, all those little figures dissolving in light. Rather like fairyland isn't it, except for the smell of gasoline and burning flesh.

"Well they called in a strong man, Colonel Arachnid Ben Driss, who cruised the city in trucks, rounded up the gas boys, took them outside the walls, shaved their heads and machine-gunned them. Survivors went underground or took to the deserts and the mountains, where they evolved different ways of life and modes of combat."

THE WILD BOYS SMILE

June 25, 1988, Casablanca 4 P.M. The Café Azar was on a rundown suburban street you could find in Fort Worth, Texas. CAFÉ AZAR in red letters on plate glass, the interior hidden from the street by faded pink curtains. Inside, a few Europeans and Arabs drinking tea and soft drinks.

The shoeshine boy came over and pointed to my shoes. He was naked except for a dirty white jockstrap and leather sandals. His head was shaved and a tuft of hair sprouted from the crown. His face had been beautiful at some other time and place, now broken and twisted by altered pressure, the teeth stuck out at angles, features wrenched out of focus, body emaciated by distant hungers. He sat on his box and looked up at me, squinting, snub-nosed legs sprawled apart, one finger scratching his jock. The skin was white as paper, hairs black and shiny lay flat on his skinny legs.

As he shined my shoes with deft precise movements his body gave off a dry musty smell. In one corner of the room I saw a green curtain in front of which two boys were undressing. The corner was apparently at a level below the café floor since I could not see their legs below the knee. One of the boys had stripped to pink underwear sticking out straight at the fly. The other patrons paid no attention to this tableau. The boy jerked his head toward the two actors who were now fucking in upright position, lips parted in silent gasps. He put a finger to one eye and shook his head. The others could not see the boys. I handed the boy a coin. He checked the date and nodded. The Dib checked the date of nettles feet twisted by the altered disk.

"Long time nobody use jump" he said leg hairs covered with mold. The gun jumping, crumpled twisted body, his face floating there the soldier's identification card and skinny in picture.

"I was too." He pointed to his thin body. He picked up his box. I followed him through the café. When I walk with the Dib they can't see me. Buttocks were smooth and white as old ivory. The corner of the green curtain was a sunken limestone square two steps down from the café floor, dry musty smell of empty waiting rooms, a worn wooden bench along one wall. Embedded in the stone floor was an iron disk about five feet in diameter, degrees and numbers cut in its edges, brass arrows indicating N. S. E. W. This compass floated on an hydraulic medium. In the center of the disk a marine compass occupied a teakwood socket. Two pairs of sandals worn smooth and black, mounted on spring stilts eight inches in height, were spaced eighteen inches apart so that two people standing in the sandals would be one behind the other, the center of the disk and the marine compass exactly between them. The springs were bolted to pistons which projected on shafts from the iron disk. The sandals were at different levels. Evidently they could be adjusted by raising or lowering the shafts.

At a sign from the boy I stripped off my clothes smooth hands guided by film tracks I was to bend over and brace my hands on my knees. The boy reached in his box and took out a tape measure that ended in a little knob.

He measured the distance from my rectum to the floor. With a round key which fitted into locks in the support shafts he adjusted the level of the two pairs of sandals on the spring stilts. He stood up and stripped off his jock-strap scraping erection. He mounted one pair of spring stilts and strapped his feet into the sandals poised on the springs, nuts tight and precise as bearings, his phallus projected needle of the compass, the disk turned until it was facing the green curtain which moved slightly as if it might cover an opening, ass arrows indicating N. S. E. W. feet a taste of metal in the mouth 18 penis floated I stepped in the sandals from behind knees his skinny arms and I was seeing the take from outside at different levels soft machine my ass a rusty cylinder pearly glands electric click blue sparks my spine into his I bend over and brace vibrating on the springs iron smell of rectal mucus streaking across the sky a wrench spurting soft tracks a distant gun jumping the soldier's identification disk covered with mold his smile across tears of pain squinting up at me snub-nosed hands at the crotch worn metal smell of the gun as my feet touched the iron disk a soft shock tingled up my legs to the crotch. The penis floated. I stepped onto the stilts in front of the boy and he adjusted the straps from behind. I bent over and braced my hands on my knees. He hooked his skinny arms under my shoulders leg hairs twisted together a slow greased pressure and I was seeing the take from outside transparent soft machine ass a rusty cylinder phallus a piston pumping the pearly glands blue sparks and my spine clicked back into his then forward his head in mine eyes steering through a maze of turnstiles. Stop. Click. Start. Stop. Click. Start streaking across the sky a smear of pain gun jumping out trees weed-grown tracks rusty identification disk covered with mold. Click. Green Pullman curtain. Click. "You wanta see something?" Click. Penis floated. Click. Distant 1920 wind and dust. Click. Bits of silver paper in a wind across the park. Click. Summer afternoon on car seat to the thin brown knees. Click. His smile across the golf course. Click. Click. Click. See on back what I mean each time place dim jerky faraway. The curtain stirs slightly. Click. Sharp smell of weeds. The curtain was gone. The feeling in my stomach when a fast elevator stops as we landed in a stone kiosk by an abandoned railroad dried shit urine initials

| KILROY JACKED OFF HERE | B. J. MARTIN | D & D |
| BUEN LUGAR PARA FOLLAR | QUIÉN ES? | A.D. KID |

We unlaced our feet and stepped down from the springs. The disk was rusty and rust had stained the stone around its edges.

"Long time nobody use jump" the boy said, pointing. I saw my clothes in a corner covered with mold. The boy shook his head and handed me a white jockstrap from his box.

"Clothes no good here. Easy see clothes. Very hard see this." He pointed to his thin body.

Then I felt the thirst, my body dry and brittle as a dead leaf.

"Jump take your last water Meester. We find spring."

Above the kiosk was a steep hillside. The boy made his way through brush that seemed to move aside for him, leaving a tunnel of leaves. He dropped on his knees and parted a tangle of vines. A deep black spring flowed from a limestone cleft. We scooped up clear cold water with our hands. The boy wiped his mouth. From the hillside we could see a railroad bridge, a stream, ruined suburbs.

"This bad place Meester. Patrols out here."

The boy reached into his box and brought out two packages of oiled paper tied with cord. He undid the cord and unwrapped two snub-nosed .38 revolvers the hammers filed off, the grips cut short, the checked walnut stocks worn smooth. The revolvers could only be used double action. The grip came to the middle of my palm, held precisely in place by two converging mounds of hard flesh like part of my hand. The boy pointed with his revolver, indicating the path we were going to take into the town under the bridge along the stream.

There was no sign of life in the town, ruined villas overgrown with vines, empty cafés and courtyards. The boy led the way. He would move forward in a burst of speed for fifty feet or so, then stop, poised sniffing quivering. We were walking along a path by a white wall.

"DOWN MEESTER!"

A burst of machine-gun fire ripped into the wall. I threw myself into a ditch full of nettles. Pain poured out my arm like a fire hose gun jumping. Three soldiers about forty feet away crumpled twisted and fell. The boy got up blowing smoke from his gun barrel body covered with red welts. In a burst of speed his feet reached the bodies. I had fired twice. He had fired four times. Every bullet had found a vital spot.

One soldier lay on his back, legs twisted under him, a hole in the middle of his forehead. Another was still alive, twitching convulsively as blood spurted from a neck wound. The third had been shot three times in the stomach. He lay face down hands clasped over his stomach, his machine gun still smoking three yards away, white smoke curling up from the grass. It was a subdivision street, lawns, palm trees, bungalows built along one side, vacant lot opposite, could have been Palm Beach, Florida, empty ten years, weeds, palm branches in the driveways, windows broken, no sign of life.

The boy went through pockets with expert fingers: a knife, identification papers, cigarettes, a packet of kif. Two of the soldiers had been carrying carbines, the third a submachine gun. "No good Czech grease gun" the boy said, and kicked it aside after unclipping the magazine. The carbines he propped against a palm tree. We dragged the bodies into a ditch. The pressure of pain lent manic power and precision to our movements. We rushed about dragging palm branches to heap on the bodies. We couldn't stop.

We found a Christmas tree, bits of silver paper twisted in its brown needles, and heaved it over onto the dead soldiers. We paused, panting, shivering, and looked at each other. Spots boiled in front of my eyes blood pounded to neck and crotch feeling the strap tighten hot squeezing pressure inside stomach intestines a muffled explosion as scalding diarrhea spurted down the backs of our trembling thighs the Boy Scout Manual floated across summer afternoons the boy's cracked broken film voice seeing the take from outside the shelf I rummaged in the shelf knew what I was looking for along a flagstone path feet like blocks of wood trailing black oily shit this must be the kitchen door open rusty electric stove moldy chili dishes food containers silver paper knew what I was looking for rummaged in the shelves fingers numb wet-dream tension in my crotch and I knew there was not much time found a can of baking powder emptied it into a porcelain fruit bowl painted roses no water silver pies choking in a red haze not much time out into the ruined garden fish pond stagnant water green slime a frog jumped the boy was tearing at his jockstrap I sat down and slipped my strap off strap halfway down his thighs cock flipped out stiff he lost balance fell on his side I pulled the strap down off his feet he turned on his back knees up body arched pulled together spurted neck tumescent choking I dipped water and green slime into the bowl with both hands mixed a paste slapped the paste on both sides of his neck and down the chest to the heart ejaculated across his quivering stomach I dipped more paste held it to the sides of my throbbing neck then down the chest I could breathe now easier to move more paste down the boy's stomach and thighs to the feet turned him over and rubbed the paste down his back where the nettles had whipped great welts across the back he sighed simpered body went limp and emptied again. I stood up and rubbed the paste over my body the pain was going and the numbness. I flopped down beside the boy and fell into a deep sleep.

"Five Indian youths accompanied us from the village in the capacity of guides. Actually they seemed quite ignorant of the country we were traversing and spent much of their time hunting with an old muzzle-loading shotgun more hazardous to the hunters than the quarry. Five days out of Candiru in the head waters of the Baboonsasshole, they managed to wound a deer. Chasing the wounded animal in wild excitement they ran though a patch of nettles. They emerged covered from head to foot with pulsing welts whipped across red skins like dusky roses. Fortunately they were wearing loincloths. Pain seemed to lend fleetness and energy to the pursuit and they brought the deer down with another shot. They closed on the dying animal with shrill cries of triumph and severed its head with a machete. Quite suddenly they were silent looking at each other and with one accord were seized by uncontrollable diarrhea. They tore off their loincloths in a frenzy of lust, faces tumescent eyes swollen shut, threw themselves on the ground ejaculating and defecating again and again. We watched, powerless to aid them, until the Chinese cook with rare presence of mind mixed baking powder into a thick paste with water. He applied this paste to the neck of the nearest youth and then down the chest to the heart. In this way he was able to save two of the youths but the other three perished in erotic convulsions. As to whether the nettles were of a special variety or the symptoms resulted from an excess of formic acid circulated through the blood by exertion, I could not say. The prompt relief afforded by applying an alkaline paste would suggest that the symptoms resulted from some form of acid poisoning." Quote Greenbaum early explorer.

When we woke up the sun was setting. We were smeared with a dried paste of shit, baking powder and green slime as if anointed for some ceremony or sacrifice. We found soap in the kitchen and washed off the crusted paste feeling rather like molting snakes. We dined on vichyssoise, cold crab meat and brandied peaches. The boy refused to sleep in the house, saying simply that it was "very bad place." So we dragged a mattress to the garage and slept there, the carbines ready, a snub-nosed .38 by each hand. Never keep a pistol under your pillow where you have to reach up for it. Keep it down by your hand at the crotch. That way you can come up shooting right through the blanket.

At dawn we set out through the ruined suburbs, no signs of life, the air windless and dead. From time to time the boy would stop, sniffing like a dog.

"This way Meester."

We were walking down a long avenue littered with palm branches. Suddenly the air was full of robins, thousands of them, settling in the ruined gardens, perching on the empty houses, splashing in bird baths full of rain water. A boy on a red bicycle flashed past. He made a wide U-turn and pulled in to the curb beside us. He was naked except for a red jockstrap, belt and flexible black shoes, his flesh red as terra cotta, smooth poreless skin tight over the cheekbones, deep-set black eyes and a casque of black hair. At his belt was an eighteen-inch bowie knife with knuckle-duster handle. He said no word of greeting. He sat there, one foot on the curb, looking at the Dib. His ears which stuck out from the head trembled slightly and his eyes glistened. He licked his lips and said one word in a language unknown to me. The Dib nodded matter-of-factly. He turned to me.

"He very hot. Been riding three days. Fuck now talk later."

The boy propped his bicycle against the curb. He took off his belt and knife and dropped them on a bench. He sat down on the bench and shoved his jockstrap down over his shoes. His red cock flipped out stiff and lubricating. The boy stood up. Beneath thin red ribs his heart throbbed and pounded. The Dib peeled off his jockstrap scraping erection. He stepped out of the strap and tossed the boy a tin of Vaseline from his shoeshine box. The boy caught it and rubbed Vaseline on his cock, throbbing to his heartbeats. The Dib stepped toward him and the boy caught him by the hips turning him around. The Dib parted his cheeks with both hands leaning forward and the red penis quivered into his flesh. Holding the Dib's hips in both hands the boy's body contracted pulling together. His ears began to vibrate lips parted from long yellow teeth smooth and hard as old ivory. His deep-set black eyes lit up inside with red fire and the hair stood up straight on his head. The Dib's body arched spurting pearly gobs in the stagnant sunlight. For a few seconds they shivered together then the boy shoved the Dib's body away as if he were taking off a garment. They went to a pool across a lawn, washed themselves, came back and put on their jockstraps.

"This Jimmy the Shrew. He messenger special delivery C.O.D." They talked briefly in their language, which is transliterated from a picture language known to all wild boys in this area.

"He say time barrier ahead. Very bad."

The Shrew took a small flat box from his handle-bar basket and handed it to the Dib. "He giving us film grenades." The Dib opened the box and showed me six small black cylinders. The Shrew got on his bicycle and rode away down the avenue and disappeared in a blaze of hibiscus.

We walked on through the suburbs, heading north. The houses were smaller and shabbier. A menace and evil hung in the empty streets like a haze and the air was getting cold around the edges. We rounded a corner and a sharp wind spattered the Dib's body with goose pimples. He sniffed uneasily.

"We coming to bad place, Johnny. Need clothes."

"Let's see what we can find in here."

There was a rambling ranch-style house, obviously built before the nabor-hood had deteriorated. We stepped through a hedge and passed a ruined bar-becue pit. The side door was open. We were in a room that had served as an office. In a drawer of the desk the Dib found a .38 snub-nosed revolver and box of shells.

"Whee, look" he cried and popped his find into the shoeshine box.

We went through the house like a whirlwind, the Dib pulling out suits and sport coats from closets and holding them against his body in front of mir-rors, opening drawers, snatching what he wanted and dumping the rest on the floor. His eyes shone and his excitement mounted as we rushed from room to room, throwing any clothes we might use onto beds and chairs and sofas. I felt a wet-dream tension in my crotch, the dream of packing to leave with a few minutes to catch a boat, and more and more drawers full of clothes to pack, the boat whistling in the harbor.

As we stepped into a little guest room, the Dib in front of me, I stroked his smooth white buttocks and he turned to me, rubbing his jock.

"This make me very hot Meester."

He sat down on the bed and pulled off his jockstrap and his cock flipped out lubricating. "Whee" he said and lay back on his elbows kicking his feet. "Jacking me off." I slipped off my strap and sat down beside him, rubbing the lubricant around the tip of his cock, and he went off in a few seconds.

We took a shower and made a selection of clothes, or rather, I made the selection, since the Dib's taste ran to loud sport coats wide ties and straw hats. I found a blue suit for him and he looked like a 1920 prep school boy on va-cation. For myself I selected a grey glen plaid and a green fedora. We packed the spare gun and extra shells into a briefcase with the film grenades the Shrew had given us.

Fish smells and dead eyes in doorways, shabby quarters of a forgotten city, streets half-buried in sand. I was beginning to remember the pawn shops, guns and brass knucks in a dusty window, cheap rooming houses, chili parlors, a cold wind from the sea.

Police line ahead, frisking seven boys against a wall. Too late to turn back, they'd seen us. And then I saw the photographers, more photographers than a routine frisk would draw. I eased a film grenade into my hand. A cop stepped toward us. I pushed the plunger down and brought my hands up tossing the grenade into the air. A black explosion blotted out the set and we were running down a dark street toward the barrier. We ran on and burst out of a black silver mist into late afternoon sunlight on a suburban street, cracked pavements, sharp smell of weeds.

THE PENNY ARCADE PEEP SHOW

Naked boys standing by a water hole, savannah backdrop, a herd of giraffe in the distance. The boys talk in growls and snarls, purrs and yipes, and show their teeth at each other like wild dogs. Two boys fuck standing up, squeezing back, teeth bare, hair stands up on the ankles, ripples up the legs in goose pimples, they whine and whimper off.

In the rotten flesh gardens languid Bubu boys with black smiles scratch erogenous sores, diseased putrid sweet, their naked bodies steam off a sepia haze of nitrous choking vapors.

Green lizard boy by a stagnant stream smiles and rubs his worn leather jockstrap with one slow finger.

Dim street light on soiled clothes, boy stands there naked with his shirt in one hand, the other hand scratching his ass.

Two naked youths with curly black hair and pointed Pan ears casting dice by a marble fountain. The loser bends over, looking at his reflection in the pool. The winner poses behind him like a phallic god. He pries the smooth white buttocks apart with his thumbs. Lips curl back from sharp white teeth. Laughter shakes the sky.

Glider boys drift down from the sunset on red wings and rain arrows from the sky.

Slingshot boys glide in across a valley, riding their black plastic wings like sheets of mica in the sunlight, torn clothes flapping hard red flesh. Each boy carries a heavy slingshot attached to his wrist by a leather thong. At their belts are leather pouches of round black stones.

The roller-skate boys sweep down a hill in a shower of autumn leaves. They slice through a police patrol. Blood spatters dead leaves in air.

The screen is exploding in moon craters and boiling silver spots.

"Wild boys very close now."

Darkness falls on the ruined suburbs. A dog barks in the distance.

Dim jerky stars are blowing away across a gleaming empty sky, *the wild boys smile.*

August 17, 1969
London

"EXTERMINATOR!"

"You need the service?"

During the war I worked for A. J. Cohen Exterminators ground floor office dead-end street by the river. An old Jew with cold grey fish eyes and a cigar was the oldest of four brothers. Marv was the youngest wore windbreakers had three kids. There was a smooth well-dressed college-trained brother. The fourth brother burly and muscular looked like an old time hoofer could bellow a leather-lunged "Mammy" and you hope he won't do it. Every night at closing time these two brothers would get in a heated argument from nowhere I could see the older brother would take the cigar out of his mouth and move across the floor with short sliding steps advancing on the vaudeville brother.

"You vant I should spit right in your face!? You vant!? You vant? You vant!?"

The vaudeville brother would retreat shadowboxing presences invisible to my goyish eyes which I took to be potent Jewish Mammas conjured up by the elder brother. On many occasions I witnessed this ritual open-mouthed hoping the old cigar would let fly one day but he never did. A few minutes later they would be talking quietly and checking the work slips as the exterminators fell in.

On the other hand the old brother never argued with his exterminators. "That's why I have a cigar" he said the cigar being for him a source of magical calm.

I used my own car a black Ford V8 and worked alone carrying my bedbug spray, pyrethrum powder, bellows and bulbs of fluoride up and down stairs.

"Exterminator! You need the service?"

A fat smiling Chinese rationed out the pyrethrum powder—it was hard to get during the war—and cautioned us to use fluoride whenever possible. Personally I prefer a pyrethrum job to a fluoride. With the pyrethrum you kill the roaches right there in front of God and the client whereas this starch and fluoride you leave it around and back a few days later a southern defense worker told me "They eat it and run around here fat as hawgs."

From a great distance I see a cool remote naborhood blue windy day in
April sun cold on your exterminator there climbing the grey wooden outside
stairs.

"Exterminator lady. You need the service?"

"Well come in young man and have a cup of tea. That wind has a bite to it."

"It does that, ma'm, cuts me like a knife and I'm not well you know/cough/."

"You put me in mind of my brother Michael Fenny."

"He passed away?"

"It was a long time ago April day like this sun cold on a thin boy with freckles
through that door like yourself. I made him a cup of hot tea. When I brought
it to him he was gone." She gestured to the empty blue sky "Cold tea sitting
right where you are sitting now." I decide this old witch deserves a pyrethrum
job no matter what the fat Chinese allows. I lean forward discreetly.

"Is it roaches Mrs. Murphy?"

"It is that from those Jews downstairs."

"Or is it the hunkys next door Mrs. Murphy?"

She shrugs "Sure and an Irish cockroach is as bad as another."

"You make a nice cup of tea Mrs. Murphy . . . Sure I'll be taking care of
your roaches . . . Oh don't be telling me where they are . . . You see I *know*
Mrs. Murphy . . . experienced along these lines . . . And I don't mind telling
you Mrs. Murphy I *like* my work and take pride in it."

"Well the city exterminating people were around and left some white powder draws roaches the way whiskey will draw a priest."

"They are a cheap outfit Mrs. Murphy. What they left was fluoride. The
roaches build up a tolerance and become addicted. They can be dangerous if
the fluoride is suddenly withdrawn. . . . Ah just here it is . . ."

I have spotted a brown crack by the kitchen sink put my bellows in and
blow a load of the precious yellow powder. As if they had heard the last trumpet the roaches stream out and flop in convulsions on the floor.

"Well I never!" says Mrs. Murphy and turns me back as I advance for the
coup de grâce . . . "Don't shoot them again. Just let them die."

When it is all over she sweeps up a dustpan full of roaches into the wood
stove and makes me another cup of tea.

When it comes to bedbugs there is a board of health regulation against
spraying beds and that of course is just where the bugs are in most cases. Now
an old wood house with bedbugs back in the wood for generations only thing
is to fumigate. . . . So here is Mamma with a glass of sweet wine her beds back
and ready . . .

I look at her over the syrupy red wine . . . "Lady we don't spray no beds.
Board of health regulations you know."

"Ach so the wine is not enough?"

She comes back with a crumpled dollar. So I go to work . . . bedbugs great
red clusters of them in the ticking of the mattresses. I mix a little formaldehyde with my kerosene in the spray it's more sanitary that way and if you tangle
with some pimp in one of the Negro whorehouses we service a face full of

formaldehyde keeps the boy in line. Now you'll often find these old Jewish grandmas in a back room like their bugs and we have to force the door with the younger generation smooth college-trained Jew there could turn into a narcotics agent while you wait.

"All right Grandma, open up! The exterminator is here."

She is screaming in Yiddish no bugs are there we force our way in I turn the bed back . . . my God thousands of them fat and red with Grandma and when I put the spray to them she moans like the Gestapo is murdering her nubile daughter engaged to a dentist.

And there are whole backward families with bedbugs don't want to let the exterminator in.

"We'll slap a board of health summons on them if we have to" said the college-trained brother. . . . "I'll go along with you on this one. Get in the car."

They didn't want to let us in but he was smooth and firm. They gave way muttering like sullen troops cowed by the brass. Well he told me what to do and I did it. When he was settled at the wheel of his car cool grey and removed he said "Just plain ordinary sons of bitches. That's all they are."

T.B. sanitarium on the outskirts of town . . . cool blue basements fluoride dust drifting streaks of phosphorus paste on the walls . . . grey smell of institution cooking . . . heavy dark glass front door. . . . Funny thing I never saw any patients there but I don't ask questions. Do my job and go, a man who works for his living. . . . Remember this janitor who broke into tears because I said shit in front of his wife it wasn't me actually said it it was Wagner who was dyspeptic and thin with knobby wrists and stringy yellow hair . . . and the fumigation jobs under the table I did on my day off . . .

Young Jewish matron there "Let's not talk about the company. The company makes too much money anyway. I'll get you a drink of whiskey." Well I have come up from the sweet wine circuit. So I arrange a sulphur job with her five Abes and it takes me about two hours you have to tape up all the windows and the door and leave the fumes in there twenty-four hours studying the good work.

One time me and the smooth brother went out on a special fumigation job . . . "This man is sort of a crank . . . been out here a number of times . . . claims he has rats under the house. . . . We'll have to put on a show for him."

Well he hauls out one of those tin pump guns loaded with cyanide dust and I am subject to crawl under the house through spider webs and broken glass to find the rat holes and squirt the cyanide to them.

"Watch yourself under there" said the cool brother. "If you don't come out in ten minutes I'm coming in after you."

I liked the cafeteria basement jobs long grey basement you can't see the end of it white dust drifting as I trace arabesques of fluoride on the wall.

We serviced an old theatrical hotel rooms with rose wallpaper photograph albums . . . "Yes that's me there on the left."

The boss has a trick he does every now and again assembles his staff and eats arsenic been in that office breathing the powder in so long the arsenic

just brings an embalmer's flush to his smooth grey cheek. And he has a pet rat
he knocked all its teeth out feeds it on milk the rat is now very tame and
affectionate.

I stuck the job nine months. It was my record on any job. Left the old grey
Jew there with his cigar the fat Chinese pouring my pyrethrum powder back
into the barrel. All the brothers shook hands. A distant cry echoes down cobblestone streets through all the grey basements up the outside stairs to a windy
blue sky.

"Exterminator!"

THE DISCIPLINE OF DE

A cold dry windy day clouds blowing through the sky sunshine and shadow.
A dead leaf brushes my face. The streets remind me of St. Louis. . . . red brick
houses, trees, vacant lots. Bright and windy back in a cab through empty streets.
When I reach the fourth floor it looks completely unfamiliar as if seen through
someone else's eyes.

"I hope you find your way . . . red brick houses, trees . . . the address in
empty streets."

Colonel Sutton-Smith, sixty-five, retired not uncomfortably on a supplemen-
tary private income . . . flat in Bury Street St. James's . . . cottage in Wales . . .
could not resign himself to the discovery of Roman coins under the grounds
of his cottage interesting theory the Colonel has about those coins over two
sherries never a third no matter how nakedly his guest may leer at the ada-
mant decanter. He can of course complete his memoirs . . . extensive notes
over a period of years, invitations, newspaper clippings, photographs, stretching into the past on yellowing dates. Objects go with the clippings, the notes,
the photos, the dates. . . . A kris on the wall to remember Ali who ran amok in
the marketplace of Lampipur thirty years ago, a crown of emerald quartz, a
jade head representing a reptilian youth with opal eyes, a little white horse
delicately carved in ivory, a Webley .455 automatic revolver . . . (Only automatic revolver ever made the cylinder turns on ratchets stabilizing like a gyro-
scope the heavy recoil.) Memories, objects stuck in an old calendar.

The Colonel decides to make his own time. He opens a school notebook
with lined papers and constructs a simple calendar consisting of ten months
with twenty-six days in each month to begin on this day February 21, 1970,
Raton Pass 14 in the new calendar. The months have names like old Pullman
cars in America where the Colonel had lived until his eighteenth year . . .
names like Beauacres, Bonneterre, Watford Junction, Sioux Falls, Pikes Peak,
Yellowstone, Bellevue, Cold Springs, Lands End dated from the beginning Raton
Pass 14 a mild grey day. Smell of soot and steam and iron and cigar smoke as
the train jolts away into the past. The train is stopped now red brick buildings a
deep blue canal outside the train window a mild grey day long ago.

The Colonel is jolted back to THE NOW by a plate streaked with egg yolk, a bacon rind, toast crumbs on the table, a jumble of morning papers, cigarette butt floating in cold coffee right where you are sitting now.

The Colonel decides, on this mild grey day, to bring his time into present time. He looks at the objects on the breakfast table calculating the moves to clear it. He measures the distance of his chair to the table how to push chair back and stand up without hitting the table with his legs. He pushes chair back and stands up. With smooth precise movements he scrapes his plate into The Business News of *The Times,* folds the paper into a neat triangular packet, sweeps up plate, knife, fork, spoon and coffee cup out to the kitchen with no fumbling or wasted movements washed and put away. Before he made the first move he has planned a whole series of moves ahead. He has discovered the simple and basic Discipline of DE. DO EASY. It is simply to do everything you do in the *easiest* and most relaxed manner you can achieve at the time you do it.

He becomes an assiduous student of DE. Cleaning the flat is a problem in logistics. He knows every paper every object and many of them now have names. He has perfected the art of "casting" sheets and blankets so they fall just so. And the gentle silent spoon or cup on a table . . . He practices for a year before he is ready to reveal the mysteries of DE . . .

As the Colonel washes up and tidies his small kitchen the television audience catches its breath in front of the little screen. Knives forks and spoons flash through his fingers and tinkle into drawers. Plates dance onto the shelf. He touches the water taps with gentle precise fingers and just enough pressure considering the rubber washers inside. Towels fold themselves and fall softly into place. As he moves he tosses crumpled papers and empty cigarette packages over his shoulder and under his arms and they land unerringly in the wastebasket as a Zen master can hit the target with his arrow in the dark. He moves through the sitting room a puff of air from his cupped hand delicately lifts a cigarette ash from the table and wafts it into a wastebasket. Into the bedroom smooth movements cleaning the sink and arranging the toilet articles into a *nature morte* different each day. With one fluid rippling cast the sheets crinkle into place and the blankets follow tucked in with fingers that feel the cloth and mattress. In two minutes the flat is dazzling . . .

The Colonel Issues Beginners' DE

DE is a way of *doing.* It is a way of doing everything you do. DE simply means doing whatever you do in the *easiest* most relaxed way you can manage which is also the quickest and most efficient way as you will find as you advance in DE.

You can start right now tidying up your flat, moving furniture or books, washing dishes, making tea, sorting papers. Consider the weight of objects exactly how much force is needed to get the object from here to there. Consider its shape and texture and function where exactly does it belong. Use just the amount of force necessary to get the object from here to there. Don't fumble jerk grab an object. Drop cool possessive fingers onto it like a gentle old cop making a soft arrest. Guide a dustpan lightly to the floor as if you were landing a plane. When you touch an object weigh it with your fingers feel your fingers on the object the skin blood muscles tendons of your hand and arm. Consider these extensions of yourself as precision instruments to perform every movement smoothly and well.

Handle objects with consideration and they will show you all their little tricks. Don't tug or pull at a zipper. Guide the little metal teeth smoothly along feeling the sinuous ripples of cloth and flexible metal. Replacing the cap on a tube of toothpaste . . . (and this should always be done at once few things are worse than an uncapped tube maladroitly squeezed twisting up out of the bathroom glass drooling paste unless it be a tube with the cap barbarously forced on all askew against the threads). Replacing the cap let the very tips of your fingers protrude beyond the cap contacting the end of the tube guiding the cap into place. Using your finger tips as a landing gear will enable you to drop any light object silently and surely into its place. Remember every object has its place. If you don't find that place and put that thing there it will jump out at you and trip you or rap you painfully across the knuckles. It will nudge you and clutch at you and get in your way.

Often such objects belong in the wastebasket but often it's just that they are out of place. Learn to place an object firmly and quietly in its place and do not let your fingers move that object as they leave it there. When you put down a cup separate your fingers cleanly from the cup. Do not let them catch in the handle and if they do repeat movement until fingers separate clean. If you don't catch that nervous finger that won't let go of that handle you may twitch hot tea across the Duchess. Never let a poorly executed sequence pass. If you throw a match at a wastebasket and miss get right up and put that match in the wastebasket. If you have time repeat the cast that failed.

There is always a reason for missing an easy toss. Repeat toss and you will find it. If you rap your knuckles against a window jamb or door, if you brush your leg against a desk or a bed, if you catch your feet in the curled-up corner of a rug, or strike a toe against a desk or chair go back and repeat the sequence. You will be surprised to find how far off course you were to hit that window jamb that door that chair. Get back on course and do it again. How can you pilot a spacecraft if you can't find your way around your own apartment? It's just like retaking a movie shot until you get it right. And you will begin to feel yourself in a film moving with ease and speed. But don't try for speed at first. Try for relaxed smoothness taking as much time as you need to perform action. If you drop an object, break an object, spill anything, knock painfully against anything, galvanically clutch an object, pay particular attention to retake. You may find out why and forestall a repeat performance. If the object is broken sweep up pieces and remove from the room at once. If object is intact or you have duplicate object repeat sequence. You may experience a strange feeling as if the objects are alive and hostile trying to twist out of your fingers, slam noisily down on a table, jump out at you and stub your toe or trip you. Repeat sequence until objects are brought to order.

Here is student at work. At two feet he tosses red plastic milk cap at the orange garbage bucket. The cap sails over the bucket like a flying saucer. He tries again. Same result. He examines the cap and finds that one edge is crushed down. He pries the edge back into place. Now the cap will drop obediently into the bucket. Every object you touch is alive with your life and your will.

The student tosses cigarette box at wastebasket and it bounces out from the cardboard cover from a metal coat hanger which is resting diagonally across the wastebasket and never should be there at all. If an ash tray is emptied into that wastebasket the cardboard triangle will split the ashes and the butts scattering both on the floor. Student takes a box of matches from his coat pocket preparatory to lighting cigarette from new package on table. With the matches in one hand he makes another toss and misses of course his fingers are in future time lighting a cigarette. He retrieves package puts the matches down and now stooping slightly legs bent hop skip over the washstand and into the wastebasket, miracle of the Zen master who hits a target in the dark these little miracles will occur more and more often as you advance in DE . . . the ball of paper tossed over a shoulder into the wastebasket, the blanket flipped and settled just into place that seems to fold itself under the brown satin fingers of an old Persian merchant. Objects move into place at your lightest touch. You slip into it like a film moving with such ease you hardly know you are doing it. You'd come into the kitchen expecting to find a sink full of dirty dishes and instead every dish is put away and the kitchen shines. The Little People have been there and done your work fingers light and cold as spring wind through the rooms.

The student considers heavy objects. Tape recorder on the desk taking up too much space and he doesn't use it very often. So put it under the washstand. Weigh it with the hands. First attempt the cord and socket leaps across the desk like a frightened snake. He bumps his back on the washstand putting the recorder under it. Try again lift with legs not back. He hits the lamp. He looks at that lamp. It is a horrible disjointed object the joints tightened with cellophane tape disconnected when not in use the cord leaps out and wraps around his feet sometimes jerking the lamp off the desk. Remove that lamp from the room and buy a new one. Now try again lifting shifting pivoting dropping on the legs just so and right under the washstand.

You will discover clumsy things you've been doing for years until you think that is just the way things are. Here is an American student who for years has clawed at the red plastic cap on English milk bottle you see American caps have a little tab and he has been looking for that old tab all these years. Then one day in a friend's kitchen he saw a cap depressed at the center. Next morning he tries it and the miracle occurs. Just the right pressure in the center and he lifts the cap off with deft fingers and replaces it. He does this several times in wonder and in awe and well he might him a college professor and very tech-

nical too planarium worms learn quicker than that for years he has been putting on his socks after he puts on his pants so he has to roll up pants and pants
and socks get clawed in together so why not put on the socks *before* the pants?

He is learning the simple miracles . . . The Miracle of the Washstand Glass
. . . we all know the glass there on a rusty razor blade streaked with pink toothpaste a decapitated tube writhing up out of it . . . quick fingers go to work
and the Glass sparkles like The Holy Grail in morning sunlight. Now he does
a wallet drill. For years he has carried his money in the left side pocket of his
pants reaching down to fish out the naked money . . . bumping his fingers
against the sharp edges of notes. Often the notes were in two stacks and pulling
out the one could drop the other on the floor. The left side pocket of the pants
is most difficult to pick but worse things can happen than a picked pocket one
can dine out on that for a season. Two manicured fingers sliding into the well-
cut suit wafted into the waiting hand an engraved message from the Queen.

Surely this is the easy way. Besides no student of DE would have his pocket
picked applying DE in the street, picking his route through slower walkers,
don't get stuck behind that baby carriage, *careful* when you round a corner
don't bump into somebody coming round the other way. He takes the wallet
out in front of a mirror, removes notes, counts notes, replaces notes as rapidly
as he can with no fumbling, catching note edges on wallet, or other errors.
That is a basic principle which must be repeated. When speed is crucial to the
operation you must find your speed the fastest you can perform the operation
without error. Don't try for speed at first it will come his fingers will rustle
through the wallet with a touch light as dead leaves and crinkle discreetly the
note that will bribe a South American customs official into overlooking a
shrunk-down head. The customs agent smiles a collector's smile the smile of
a connoisseur. Such a crinkle he has not heard since a French jewel thief with
crudely forged papers made a crinkling sound over them with his hands and
there is the note neatly folded into a false passport.

Now someone will say . . . "But if I have to *think* about every move I make"
. . . You only have to think and break down movement into a series of still
pictures to be studied and corrected because you have not found the easy way.
Once you find the easy way you don't have to think about it. It will almost do
itself.

Operations performed on your person . . . brushing teeth, washing, etc.,
can lead you to correct a defect before it develops. Here is student with a light
case of bleeding gums. His dentist has instructed him to massage gums by
placing little splinters of wood called Inter Dens between the teeth and mas-
saging gum with seesaw motion. He snatches an Inter Dens, opens his mouth
in a stiff grimace and jabs at a gum with a shaking hand. Now he remembers
his DE. Start over. Take out the little splinters of wood like small chopsticks
joined at the base and separate them gently. Now find where the bleeding is.
Relax face and move Inter Dens up and down gently firmly gums relaxed direct your attention to that spot.

No not "getting better and better" just let the attention of your whole body flow there and all the healing power of your body flow with it. A soapy hand on your lower back feeling the muscles and vertebrae can catch a dislocation right there and save you a visit to the osteopath. Illness and disability is largely a matter of neglect. You ignore something because it is painful and it becomes more uncomfortable through neglect and you neglect it further. Everyday tasks become painful and boring because you think of them as WORK something solid and heavy to be fumbled and stumbled over. Overcome this block and you will find that DE can be applied to anything you do even to the final discipline of doing nothing. The easier you do it the less you have to do. He who has learned to do nothing with his whole mind and body will have everything done for him.

Let us now apply DE to a simple test: the old Western quick draw gun fight. Only one gun fighter really grasped the principle of DE and that one was Wyatt Earp. Nobody ever beat him. Wyatt Earp said: "It's not the first shot that counts. It's the first shot that hits. Point is to draw aim and fire and deliver the slug an inch above the belt buckle."

That's DE. How fast can you do it and get it done?

It is related that a young boy once incurred the wrath of Two Gun McGee. McGee has sworn to kill him and is even now preparing himself in a series of saloons. The boy has never been in a gun fight and Wyatt Earp advises him to leave town while McGee is still two saloons away. The boy refuses to leave.

"All right" Earp tells him "You can hit a circle four inches square at six feet can't you? All right *take your time and hit it.*" Wyatt flattens himself against a wall calling out once more "*Take your time,* kid."

(How fast can you take your time, kid?)

At this moment McGee bursts through the door a .45 in each hand a-spittin' lead all over the town. A drummer from St. Louis is a bit slow hitting the floor and catches a slug in the forehead. A boy peacefully eating chop suey in the Chinese restaurant next door stops a slug with his thigh.

Now the kid draws his gun steadies it in both hands aims and fires at six feet hitting Two Gun McGee squarely in the stomach. The heavy slug knocks him back against the wall. He manages to get off one last shot and bring down the chandelier. The boy fires again and sends a bullet ripping through McGee's liver and another through his chest.

The beginner can think of DE as a game. You are running an obstacle course the obstacles set up by your opponent. As soon as you attempt to put DE into practice you will find that you have an opponent very clever and persistent and resourceful with detailed knowledge of your weaknesses and above all expert in diverting your attention for the moment necessary to drop a plate on the kitchen floor. Who or what is this opponent that makes you spill drop and fumble slip and fall? Groddeck and Freud called it the IT a built-in self-destructive mechanism. Mr. Hubbard calls it the Reactive Mind. You will disconnect IT as you advance in the discipline of DE. DE brings you into direct conflict with the IT in present time where you can control your moves. You can beat the IT in present time.

Take the inverse skill of the IT back into your own hands. These skills belong to you. Make them yours. You *know* where the wastebasket is. You can land an object in that wastebasket over your shoulder. You *know* how to touch and move and pick up things. Regaining these physical skills is of course simply a prelude to regaining other skills and other knowledge that you have but cannot make available for your use. You *know* your entire past history just what year month day and hour everything happened. If you have heard a language for any length of time you *know* that language. You have a computer in your brain. DE will show you how to use it. But that's another chapter.

DE applies to ALL operations carried out inside the body . . . brain waves, digestion, blood pressure and rate of heart beats. . . . And that's another chapter . . .

"And now I have stray cats to feed and my class at the Leprosarium."

Lady Sutton-Smith raises a distant umbrella . . .

"I hope you find your way . . . The address in empty streets . . ."

"WHAT WASHINGTON? WHAT ORDERS?"

Old Sarge: "All right you Limey has-beens, I'm going to say it country simple: you have been taken over like a banana republic. Your royal family is nothing but a holograph picture projected by the CIA. What is its purpose? Well what is the purpose of the Pope for you Catholics good and bad, standing with John 23 like a good soldier in the presence of your captain. Any way you slice it it's a grovel operation, the way we like to see them. I mean what we are doing while the Pope and the other Holies keep the marks paralyzed with grovel rays is one of the mysteries you cannot understand, the mercy of God . . . we don't intend to be here when this shithouse goes up. Maybe I'm talking too much about private things, family matters you might say—and that's what we call the good old CIA: the Family.

"(When the prodigal son creeps back from Peking—*Information known. Expel barbarian.*—well, the Family will forgive him, if he is sincere in his heart on a lie detector: 'Well, we're going to take you back.' The old ham fixes him with blue eyes like steel in sunlight. 'Just don't ever let us down again.')

"From here to eternity, the old game of war. Where would the Family be without it? So we can whittle off a little something to keep the royal family projected in Limey Land, can't we now? So the Queen needs more money? Well humm . . . call a story conference."

"Just how are we slanting this, B.J.?"

B.J. (doodling muscle boys): "Nothing new. Just keep it going. They do need more money, otherwise they will go down in the same spiral as everybody else and they wouldn't be the royal family anymore, could wind up in a semi-detached in Darlington. They are supposed to be a supernatural family, religious figures in fact, and the more potent in that they are not acknowledged as such. Just ask an upper-class English about the royal family and he goes all huffy and vague:

"'It's not important. . . .'"

"'Who *cares* about Philip.'"

"But you want the royal family to continue as such?"

(B.J. bulges a jockstrap.) "Well uh yes, we are a *monarchy* . . . excuse me."

"What about this million a year?"

"We're all together in this . . . couldn't abolish titles and keep the royal family."

"We've had to take cuts . . . why shouldn't they take a cut too?"

"Mutiny in the ranks?"

(He doodles a boy peeling off plastic tits.)

"It could come to that. . . ."

(He doodles a boy looking at another boy's ass. A light bulb attached to his head lights up.)

"So why not put the royal family in a Darlington semi-detached on a middle-class income and let them prove themselves in a TV serial?

"(Philip and the Queen are doing all right. She is known as 'Queenie' to all the nabors where she runs a small grocery shop. Every customer receives the same gracious smile and quick inquiry as to the family, she is good at remembering things like that and keeping a line moving at the same time . . . she learned that shaking millions of hands. Philip sells ecology equipment to factories. Good at his work and believes in it . . . strong middle-class message there. Charles is a successful pop singer. . . .)

"Why, they all get knighted in the end one way or another, and the windup is, back in Buckingham stronger than ever."

CIA black: "Don't you think there is some limit somewhere to what people will stand still for? Suppose the ecology equipment doesn't work? Suppose the Queen's gracious smile is reserved for her white customers, she has eyes for Enoch Powell and flying saucers? Suppose Bonny Prince Charlie—?"

"For Chrissakes, we're building them *up,* not down . . . the *Family.* . . ."

"All right, call in the special effects boys and give them supernatural powers."

"'Never go too far in any direction' is the basic rule on which Limey Land is built. The Queen stabilizes the whole sinking shithouse."

"I tell you, anything that is not going forward is going out. You know what we can do with special effects and electric brain stimulation: some joker gets out of line, we press a button and he shits in his pants at sight of her. That at least would be a step in some direction."

"For Godsake, not at this point. If the Queen tries to grab more than she's got, imagewise, she will lose it all . . . uh I mean *we* will. . . . All the others are hopeless. Any of you jokers like to try propping up the queen of Denmark? I say leave it just where it is. It will stagger on for another five or ten years and that's enough. We get smart at this point, and the English Republican Party will jump out at us . . . *ERP ERP ERP*. . . ."

"The Queen is an alien symbol, basically Germanic in origin. The Queen is also a *white* symbol. The White Goddess, in fact. Young people want that? Black people want that? Who wants a grovel symbol? Those who need such symbols to keep positions of wealth and privilege. Look at them. Look at Jennifer's Diary. . . ."

"I mean, ERP could be dangerous."

"That's right. We got a good strong thing here, why muck about with it?"

"Why, the whole stinking thing could blow up in our faces."

"Brings on my ulcers to think about it."

"*We* could organize ERP . . . that way, we'd be ready to jump in either direction."

"The word that made a man out of an ape and killed the ape in the process keeps man an animal, the way we like to see him. And the Queen is just another prop to hold up the word. You all know what we can do with the word. Talk about the power in an atom! All hate all fear all pain all death all sex is in the word. The word was a killer virus once. It could become a killer virus again. The word is too hot to handle—so we sit on our asses, waiting for the pension. But somebody is going to pick up that virus and use it: *Virus B-23*. . . ."

"Aw, we got the Shines cooled back with Che Guevara in a nineteenth-century set. . . ."

"Is that right? And you got the Tiddlywinks cooled too? You can cool anybody else who gets ideas? You going to cool this powder keg with your moth-eaten Queen? I tell you, anybody could turn it loose. You all know how basically simple it is: sex word and image cut in with death word and image. . . ."

"Yeah, *we* could do it."

"But what about Washington? Our orders?"

"Just one test tube and SPUT. . . . '*What* Washington? *What* orders?'"

FROM HERE TO ETERNITY

Mildred Pierce reporting:

I was there. I saw it. I saw women thrown down on Fifth Avenue and raped in their mink coats by blacks and whites and yellows while street urchins stripped the rings from their fingers. A young officer stood nearby.

"Aren't you going to DO something?" I demanded.

He looked at me and yawned.

I found Colonel Bradshaw bivouacking in the Ritz. I told him bluntly what was going on. His eyes glinted shamelessly as he said: "Well, you have to take a broad general view of things."

And that's what I have been doing. Taking a broad general view of American troops raping and murdering helpless civilians while American officers stand around and yawn.

"Been at it a long time, lady. It's the old army game from here to eternity."

This license was dictated by considerations taken into account by prudent commanders throughout history. It pays to pay the boys off. Even the noble Brutus did it . . .

Points with his left hand in catatonic limestone . . . "The town is yours soldier brave."

Tacitus describes a typical scene . . . "If a woman or a good-looking boy fell into their hands they were torn to pieces in the struggle for possession and the survivors were left to cut each other's throats."

"Well there's no need to be that messy. Why waste a good-looking boy? Mother-loving American Army run by old women many of them religious my God hanging American soldiers for raping and murdering civilians . . ."

Old Sarge bellows from here to eternity:

"WHAT THE BLOODY FUCKING HELL ARE CIVILIANS FOR? *SOLDIERS' PAY.*"

The CO stands there and smiles. Just ahead is a middle-western town on a river, thirty thousand civilians. The CO points:

"It's all yours boys. Every man woman and child. God is nigh."

"LET'S GET US SOME CIVVIES."

"Now just a minute boys listen to old Sarge. Why make the usual stupid scene kicking in liquor stores grabbing anything in sight? You wake up hungover in an alley your prick sore from fucking dry cunts and assholes your eye gouged out by a broken beer bottle you and your asshole buddy wanted the same piece of ass. No fun in that. Why not leave it like this? They go about their daily tasks and we just take what we want when we want it cool and steady easy and make them like it. You see what I mean."

The young lieutenant from camouflage sees what he means . . . BOYS . . . swimming pools and locker rooms full of them.

"Getting it steady year after year. Now that's what I call PAY."

Precarious governments march in anywhere and take over . . . war lords . . . city states fortified against foraging crowds from the starving cities . . . power cut . . . reservoirs blown up . . .

Crowds are looting the museums for weapons . . . stone axes, Fijian war clubs, Samurai swords, crossbows, bolos, boomerangs. . . . They put on costumes to match. Militant queens snatch up krisses . . . "LET'S RUN AMOK DUCKS IT'S FUN." . . . They hit the street in loincloths.

Drunken Yale boys put on armor and charge down Fifth Avenue on horseback skewering the passers-by.

A World War I tank with cheering doughboys is driven off a museum pedestal.

The militants raid government laboratories. Virus B-23 rages through cities of the world like a topping forest fire. In the glow of burning cities strange cults spring up.

The Vigilantes sweep up from the Bible Belt like a plague of locusts hanging every living thing in their path. Even horses are hauled into the air, kicking and farting.

The dreaded Baseball Team five thousand burly athletes in baseball uniforms all with special bats erupt into a crowded street . . .

"BEAT YOUR FILTHY BRAINS OUT . . ."

Smashing shop windows blood brains and broken glass in their wake . . .

The Chinese waiters charge with meat cleavers . . .

"FLUCK YOU FLUCK YOU FLUCK YOU . . ."

In ruined suburbs naked bacchantes chase a screaming boy. Now the roller-skate boys sweep down a hill on jet skates in a shower of blue sparks and cut the bacchantes to pieces with their eighteen-inch bowie knives. The new boy is issued a knife and skates. Splashed with blood from head to foot they jet away singing:

"FOR EVERY MASS MURDER LET US STAND PREPARED."

SEEING RED

Arriving at Customs, Lee is ushered to the special shed where nine agents wait.

"Let's see what this dirty writer is trying to smuggle through decent American Customs . . ."

The agent with one arm reaches all the way to the bottom of the wickerwork suitcase and pulls out the Picture . . . room with rose wallpaper bathed in a smoky sunset on a brass bed a red-haired boy with a hard-on sprawls one bare knee flopped against the greasy pink wallpaper he is playing a flute and looking at somebody standing in front of the picture. The agent stares and the red picture turns his face to flame. He makes a slight choking sound and looks helplessly at his fellow agents who look back dumb stricken faces swollen with blood. None of them can articulate a word. The agent stands there holding the picture looking from the picture to angry red faces as more and more agents crowd into the shed. No one looks at Lee. He closes his bags, hails an old junky porter and leaves the shed. Behind him a ripping splintering crash as the walls of the shed give way.

Outside the pier prowl cars converge like electric turtles disgorging load after load of flushed cops. Silent catatonic they crowd around the picture looking at each other the agent there holding the picture up like a banner of raw meat suddenly two jets of blood spurt from his eyes. Silently he proffers the picture to a fellow agent and sinks to the boards of the pier. A choking red haze steams from the purple faces. There is an occasional muffled report as blood vessels burst and sinuses explode. Wave after wave of silent cops crowd onto the pier which sags and finally gives way with a crash that host of cops sink like lead into the sea.

The picture in its rosewood frame floats there on the green water looking up at the sky and the cops keep coming. Texas Rangers with huge Magnum revolvers and pale nigger-killing eyes. The Royal Mounted faces as red as their uniforms.

The picture floats there in the green water where all plunge and perish . . .

The Piper pulled down the sky.

THE "PRIEST" THEY CALLED HIM

"Fight tuberculosis, folks." Christmas Eve an old junky selling Christmas seals on North Clark Street, the "Priest" they called him.

"Fight tuberculosis, folks."

People hurried by grey shadows on a distant wall it was getting late and no money to score he turned into a side street and the lake wind hit him like a knife. Cab stopped just under a street light boy got out with a suitcase thin kid in prep school clothes familiar face the Priest told himself watching from the doorway reminds me of something a long time ago the boy there with his overcoat unbuttoned reaching into his pants pocket for the cab fare. The cab drove away and turned the corner.

The boy went inside a building hummm yes maybe; the suitcase was there in the doorway the boy nowhere in sight gone to get the keys most likely— have to move fast. He picked up the suitcase and started for the corner made it glanced down at the case didn't look like the case the boy had or any boy would have the Priest couldn't put his finger on what was so *old* about the case, old and dirty poor quality leather and heavy, better see what's inside.

He turned into Lincoln Park found an empty place and opened the case. Two severed human legs had belonged to a young man with dark skin shiny black leg hairs glittered in the dim street light. The legs had been forced into the case and he had to use his knee on the back of the case to shove them out.

"Legs yet" he said and walked quickly away with the case might bring a few dollars to score.

The buyer sniffed suspiciously. "Kinda funny smell about it . . . is this Mexican leather?"

The Priest shrugged.

"Well, some joker didn't cure it." The buyer looked at the case with cold disfavor. "Not even right sure he killed it whatever it is three is the best I can do and it hurts but since this is *Christmas* and you're the *Priest*." $ $ $ He slipped three notes under the table into the Priest's dirty hand.

The Priest faded into the street shadows seedy and furtive three cents didn't buy a bag nothing less than a nickel say remember that old auntie croaker told me not to come back unless I paid him the three cents I owe isn't that a fruit for you blow his stack about three lousy cents.

The doctor was not pleased to see him. "Now what do you *want*? I told you. . . ." The Priest laid three bills on the table. The doctor put the money in his pocket and started to scream. "I've had *trouble*! The *people* have been around! I may lose my *license*!"

The Priest just sat there eyes old and heavy with years of junk on the doctor's face.

"I can't write you a prescription!" The doctor jerked open a drawer and slid an ampule across the table. "That's all I have in the *office*!" The doctor stood up. "Take it and *get out*!" he screamed, hysterical. The Priest's expression did not change and the doctor added in quieter tones: "After all I'm a professional man and I shouldn't be bothered by people like you."

"Is this all you have for me? One lousy quarter g? Couldn't you lend me a nickel?"

"Get out! Get out! I'll call the police I tell you!"

"All right doctor. I'm going now."

Christ it was cold and far to walk rooming house a shabby street room on the top floor these stairs/cough/the Priest there pulling himself up along the banister he went into the bathroom yellow wood panels toilet dripping and got his works from under the washbasin wrapped in brown paper back to his room get every drop in the dropper he rolled up his sleeve. Then he heard a groan from next door room 18 a Mexican kid lived there the Priest had passed him on the stairs and saw the kid was hooked but he never spoke because he didn't want any juvenile connections bad news in any language and the Priest had had enough bad news in his life heard the groan again a groan he could *feel* no mistaking *that* groan and what it meant maybe had an accident or something any case I can't enjoy my priestly medications with that sound coming through the wall thin walls you understand the Priest put down his dropper cold hall and knocked on the door of room 18.

"*Quién es?*"

"It's the Priest, kid. I live next door."

He could hear someone hobbling across the floor a bolt slide the boy stood there in his underwear shorts eyes black with pain. He started to fall. The Priest helped him over to the bed.

"What's wrong son?"

"It's my legs *señor* . . . cramps . . . and now I am without medicine."

The Priest could see the cramps like knots of wood there in the young lean legs dark shiny black leg hairs.

"Three years ago I have damaged myself in a bicycle race it is then that the cramps start and . . ."

And he has the leg cramps back with compound junk interest. The old Priest stood there *feeling* the boy groan. He inclined his head as if in prayer went back and got his dropper.

"It's just a quarter g kid."

"I do not require much *señor*."

The boy was sleeping when the Priest left room 18. He went back to his room and sat down on the bed. Then it hit him like heavy silent snow, all the grey junk yesterdays. He sat there and received the *immaculate fix* and since he was himself a priest there was no need to call one.

COLD LOST MARBLES

my ice skates on a wall
luster of stumps washes his lavender horizon
he's got a handsome face of a lousy kid
rooming houses dirty fingers
whistled in the shadow
"Wait for me at the detour."
river . . . snow . . . someone vague faded in a mirror
filigree of trade winds
cold white as lace circling the pepper trees
the film is finished
memory died when their photos weather worn points of
polluted water under the trees in the mist shadow of
boys by the daybreak in the peony fields cold lost
marbles in the room carnations three ampules of
morphine little blue-eyed twilight grins between his
legs yellow fingers blue stars erect boys of sleep
have frozen dreams for I am a teenager pass it on
flesh and bones withheld too long yes sir oui oui
craps last map . . . lake . . . a canoe . . . rose tornado in
the harvest brass echo tropical jeers from Panama
City night fences dead fingers you in your own body
around and maybe a boy skin spreads to something
else on Long Island the dogs are quiet.

THE RED NIGHT
TRILOGY

the red night trilogy
by james grauerholz

William Burroughs did not come empty-handed to New York in 1974. He brought along a trunkful of writings from all periods of his career, including many photocopies from the 1973 archive-gathering project, but mostly material from the last few years—pages that had not found a home in *Wild Boys, Exterminator!* or *Port of Saints* (which was first published in late 1973 in England). Burroughs' overall literary output had dwindled, and he felt he had exhausted the possibilities of the cut-up technique and its applications to scrapbooks, audiotape, and film. In any case, these experiments had been met with editorial discouragement and little financial reward. But he kept busy, working on his class lectures and visiting old New York friends. His son Billy visited him at the Broadway loft, as did Brion Gysin, who came from Paris with copies of the French edition of *The Third Mind*. In April, John Giorno arranged for Burroughs and himself to give a reading at the Poetry Project in St. Marks Church, an event that announced Burroughs' return to New York City.

In May, Burroughs rented a new loft at 77 Franklin Street. He went to London to close out his Duke Street flat and to say good-bye to Johnny Brady, who was still living there. Gysin came from Paris to see him, and Balch told them about Johnny's late-night ruckuses in the building, and the neighbors' complaints. Burroughs took this opportunity to sell the flat to one of those neighbors, and he shipped one last trunk of books and papers to New York before leaving. Johnny Brady disappeared.

Back in New York, Burroughs began to receive more invitations for readings, and his travels in America exposed him to many new locales; for example, he first set foot in San Francisco in November 1974. Everywhere he went, there were enthusiastic audiences and a new generation of readers eager to meet "El Hombre Invisible." He enjoyed a lively social schedule in New York, with a wide circle of old and new friends. But his oldest friend, Brion Gysin, was diagnosed with colon cancer, and underwent a colostomy in Paris that December. The surgery was a humiliating, painful ordeal for Gysin, which ended his sexual life as he had known it; while in hospital, he made a half-hearted suicide attempt.

Burroughs spent the winter in New York, trying to work on his next novel, struggling with his writer's block. In early 1975, walking past his old loft on Centre Street, he was approached by a young man, who introduced himself: Steven Lowe, a writer and artist from Florida. They became friends, and Lowe guided him to the homosexual-pirate research that gave Burroughs a new angle on his novel: *Cities of the Red Night*. The names of the six cities formed an ancient spell that Gysin had taught him, to gain power over fate. Burroughs resumed working on *Cities* between reading trips—for he was touring now, taking his act on the road, where his old carny-world, showbiz instincts stood him in good stead with his audiences.

Allen Ginsberg had recently taken Buddhist refuge-vows with the émigré Tibetan Buddhist teacher Chogyam Trungpa Rinpoche. Trungpa established his Dharmadhatu Foundation in Boulder, Colorado, and founded the Naropa Institute there; he invited Ginsberg and Anne Waldman to set up the literature program, which they named "the Jack Kerouac School of Disembodied Poetics." In May 1975, Burroughs met Ginsberg at Naropa to give a reading. Later that summer, they went to Chicago together for readings at the Art Institute. Burroughs also went to Geneva to join Gysin at the Colloque de Tanger in their honor, and to Trungpa's Tail of the Tiger retreat center in upstate Vermont to spend two weeks in near-total solitude in a tiny shack. Burroughs' notes from this period became *The Retreat Diaries*.

On February 5, 1976, at Franklin Street, Burroughs received a telegram with the awful news that Ian Sommerville had died in a car wreck. It was Burroughs' sixty-second birthday; he had known Sommerville for seventeen years. Ian's significance for him was so deep that, even in his eighties, Burroughs dreamed of him often. But he had to return to his writing and his readings, and other new business: the two-year lease on Franklin Street was expiring. Burroughs had often visited John Giorno in his loft at 222 Bowery, a building which was built as a "Young Men's Institute" at the turn of the century. Mark Rothko had used the old gymnasium space for a painting studio in the 1960s, and for several months I had been living in the locker-room area below the gym: an almost-windowless space with concrete floors, walls, and ceiling. I moved to Great Jones Street, and in early June 1976 Burroughs took over the locker room, which came to be known as "the Bunker." He scarcely had time to unpack before it was time to go to Boulder for another Naropa summer session.

Bill Burroughs Jr. was at Naropa in 1976, invited by Ginsberg for poetry readings and a father-and-son reunion. Billy had been drinking heavily for years; at twenty-nine, he was recently separated from his wife and had no visible means of support. But no one expected Billy to be as terribly ill as he was when he arrived in Boulder. He vomited a toiletful of blood at a party, and was rushed to the hospital. Billy's liver was seriously cirrhotic, the doctors said; they tried a portocaval shunt (a liver bypass), but it failed. A liver transplant was performed by Dr. Tom Starzl and his team at Colorado General Hospital in Denver in late August 1976. At the time, very few liver transplants had been done, and the odds of surviving the operation were only fifty-fifty. Burroughs spent the night in the hospital waiting room with close friends and family.

There was weary jubilation when Billy made it through the surgery, but in the light of day it was obvious that his new condition was still not very good. With Waldman, Ginsberg, and many others in Boulder supporting Billy, Burroughs put off his return to New York and moved into a suite at the Boulderado Hotel. For three months, he made the one-hour drive to Denver every day to visit Billy in hospital. Billy was in and out of Colorado General during the next few years; his first post-operative release was in January 1977. The Naropa family set Billy up at the Boulderado, and at first it seemed the worst of the crisis had passed.

Burroughs returned to his New York "Bunker." Jacques Stern, the renegade Rothschild, had reappeared on the scene, and he got everyone's attention by spending tens of thousands of dollars on a movie project: Dennis Hopper would direct and star in a film of *Junky,* with a screenplay by Terry Southern. This foursome, plus various toadies, functionaries, and hangers-on, was good for a lot of wild, coke-fueled parties in New York during those months. These "story meetings" and unbridled goings-on lasted almost a year, but the film project came to nothing, which is probably just as well.

Burroughs headed to Colorado in June 1977 for his third summer session at Naropa. He had been away only a few months, and his Boulder friends welcomed him back. After the Poetics session was over, Burroughs decided to stay on in Boulder; he rented a tiny apartment at the Varsity Manor complex, and kept the lease for three years. Steven Lowe was living in nearby Eldora, and Burroughs met Cabell Hardy and a number of other young people, mostly Beatitude-seekers left over from the Naropa summer sessions. Hardy lived with Burroughs, cooking for him and generally helping out, and keeping him company. Burroughs was writing the early drafts of *The Place of Dead Roads,* which he was referring to as "The Gay Gun," or alternatively "The Johnson Family." The novel's emphasis on the Zen of shooting arose from Burroughs' frequent outings to nearby towns to practice his marksmanship, his lifelong favorite pastime.

Two months after Billy was released from hospital in early 1977, he was readmitted for follow-up. His surgery wounds were messy and slow to heal; he underwent several more operations in an effort to close an abdominal cyst. In October Billy made an unplanned dash to Santa Cruz, California, in search of Georgette, the girl who had lived with him there when his marriage fell apart. He arrived with no medicine and no money, and in the end he was poured onto a plane back to Denver. In January 1978, Naropa gave Billy a room at the Yeshe House commune, and Burroughs and Ginsberg persuaded Dr. Starzl to authorize a morphine-maintenance regime for Billy, on the theory it would stop or slow down his drinking, as Billy promised it would.

An NYU film student, Howard Brookner, had embarked upon a documentary project on Burroughs. In October, Brookner arrived in Boulder with his soundman, Jim Jarmusch, to film Burroughs and his son together. It was an awkward situation; Billy felt threatened by the presence of Hardy and the two strangers, and the cameras and bright lights added an air of unreality to the gathering in Burroughs' tiny apartment. The film crew also visited Billy's room, a windowed cave plastered with a riot of magazine-photo collages. Billy's chaotic situation at Yeshe House eventually became untenable, and in November he moved to an apartment in Denver.

John Giorno, the French philosophy professor Sylvère Lotringer, and I had been busy since midsummer planning the "Nova Convention": a four-day series of performances and events at NYU and venues on the Lower East Side in early December 1978. Brookner decided to film the convention, which reunited Burroughs and Gysin and featured seminars with Burroughs' publishers and translators, and performances by Allen Ginsberg, John Cage and Merce Cunningham, Anne Waldman, John Giorno, Philip Glass, Laurie Anderson, Ed Sanders, Frank Zappa, Patti Smith, Timothy Leary, and others. A text version of *The Third Mind* was published by Viking that same month, and Gysin, in from Paris for the event, exhibited new paintings at Books & Co. on Madison Avenue. An avalanche of press conveyed the consensus that the Nova Convention was a "summit meeting of the avant-garde"—as that term was defined in New York in the late 1970s. There was a tremendous letdown when all the visitors, speeches, and parties were over, and Burroughs hunkered down in the Bunker for the winter.

By all accounts, a tsunami of smack hit New York in 1979, and within a few months not only Burroughs, but most of his closest friends as well, were addicted to heroin. He was preoccupied with a circle of much younger fellow users who could score for him on the Lower East Side's burgeoning heroin scene. After six years, Burroughs was still working in fits and starts on *Cities of the Red Night,* but his heroin habit took up a great deal of his time and money. For the first time in many years, he was well and truly hooked. Ironically, some of the glassine bags of junk that he received were stamped with the "Dr. Nova" brand, inspired by his own literary persona.

Meanwhile Blue Wind Press in Berkeley published *Blade Runner: A Movie,* Burroughs' short film treatment of an Alan E. Nourse novel, and John Calder's New York office published *Ah Pook Is Here,* without the illustrations. In Paris, Gysin was struggling to make ends meet, and in London, in early 1980, Antony Balch was diagnosed with inoperable stomach cancer; he died that summer. Burroughs' last meeting with Balch had been at the Boulderado Hotel's mezzanine bar, four years earlier; long before Balch's diagnosis, Burroughs sensed that Balch was moribund. The two of them had often talked about "the dying feeling," citing various examples of it from their lives.

Burroughs traveled to Santa Fe for a D. H. Lawrence festival in July 1980, and in August he finished editing his *Cities* manuscript in Boulder and closed out the Varsity Manor apartment. In the final editing sessions, Burroughs decided to title each of the small chapters into which the book had been divided, and for most of these titles he used phrases that the Ukrainian parapsychologist Dr. Konstantin Raudivé had transcribed from "silent tape" recordings, spoken by "voices" just below the noise floor of the tape. Like Dutch Schultz's last words, these phrases are evocative without any explicit meaning. Burroughs had been working on *Cities of the Red Night* for six years, longer than on any novel since *Naked Lunch*, and it was his first full-length book since *The Wild Boys*, published a decade earlier. By the time he finished *Cities*, Burroughs had already begun *The Place of Dead Roads*, and he set himself the task of writing a major trilogy of novels.

In his Denver apartment, Billy Burroughs Jr. continued to deteriorate. The hospitality of the Buddhists in Boulder was not to his liking, and in any case he had abused it. He lived between the streets and deadbeat cafeterias in the neighborhood of Colorado General, where the receptionists and nurses were now his best friends. In November, a girlfriend from his Green Valley School days tracked him down. She wanted to see Billy again, and she sent him a ticket to Palm Beach at Christmastime. She was totally unprepared for Billy's desperately ill appearance when he arrived; she found him an apartment and paid his rent there.

In February, Billy decided he wanted to go up to Orlando to see his former headmaster, George von Hilsheimer, in nearby De Land, Florida. He and Hilsheimer quarreled, and Billy ran away into the rainy night. He was found unconscious in a drainage ditch, picked up by sheriff's deputies, and admitted to West Volusia Memorial Hospital, near De Land. Upon his release, a kindly social worker found Billy an affordable motel room. Ten days later his caretaker called an ambulance to bring him back to West Volusia. Billy died at 6:35 A.M. on March 3, 1981. The coroner found no trace of prednisone in his bloodstream, which indicated that Billy had deliberately stopped taking his rejection-suppressing medications. His sketchy final writings reveal that he had been suicidal for some time.

In the Bunker, Burroughs was devastated by the news. But *Cities of the Red Night* was to be published by Holt, Rinehart and Winston that spring, and Burroughs had planned two ambitious reading tours across the country with John Giorno to support the new novel. A few months earlier, Burroughs had finally enrolled in a methadone maintenance program in New York; thereafter, he was able to travel without needing to contact the narcotics underworld in every city he visited. After two weeks of solitary grieving in the Bunker, once again Burroughs hit the road, playing to punk rock–club audiences across the Midwest. He visited Lawrence, Kansas, in July and spent the month in a borrowed studio room near the hilltop campus of the University of Kansas. There was a tornado in Lawrence that month, and from his balcony Burroughs had a good view of it. He put some of these impressions into *The Place of Dead Roads*, on which he was working full-time now.

Burroughs returned from the second leg of the *Red Night* tour that fall to find that the Bunker's status was in jeopardy: the 222 Bowery building was in the throes of a rent strike. Burroughs didn't want to see it through, and decided to move to Kansas before the new year. His last public event in New York was his widest exposure yet: he appeared on NBC's *Saturday Night Live*, reading from "Twilight's Last Gleamings"—the routine he wrote with Kells Elvins in 1938. As millions of viewers watched, Burroughs looked up from his pages and straight into the camera, and began to speak: "S.S. America . . . off Jersey Coast . . . there is no cause for alarm . . . there is a minor problem in the boiler room, but everything is now under—[sound effects of a nuclear blast]."

The winter of 1981–82 was unusually cold and snowy in northeastern Kansas. Burroughs was established in "the Stone House," a rented nineteenth-century two-story limestone dwelling ten miles south of Lawrence, and had resumed his work on *The Place of Dead Roads*. His friend Dean Ripa, a writer and venomous-snake collector, visited Burroughs in Lawrence, bringing deadly pillowcases full of diamondback rattlesnakes, Gaboon vipers, and kraits. Burroughs was happy with the somewhat primitive conditions of the Stone House; it was ideal for the Old Western novel he was writing, with a panoramic view for miles across the Wakarusa Valley and north to the campus buildings on thousand-foot-high Mount Oread.

Spring came to Douglas County, and with it came the cats: the big white tom; the ginger-colored longhaired female; the Russian Blue male, with his silky grey coat and plaintive cry. Burroughs began to feed these strays, and he found his heart opening to them: they each had distinct personalities, and they reminded him of people from his past. At age sixty-eight, Burroughs began to review his life, and his diaries confess his frequent weeping spells. It was his practice to write the next day's date on a journal entry, a typewriter page, or an index card, so that he could jot down his dreams when he woke up in the night—as he did often, being a light sleeper. A year later, Burroughs went back to these notes to write *The Cat Inside*.

The Stone House had a limestone barn nearby, and Burroughs took to shooting his pistols at targets propped up against a "backstop" of stacked firewood. After years of living in cities where handguns were forbidden, or at least not for sale, he enjoyed spending time in the gun shops of Lawrence, picking out new additions to the firearms collection he had begun in the late 1970s, when he lived in Colorado. For his targets, Burroughs picked up old pieces of scrap plywood that lay around the barn. One day he fired a 20-gauge shotgun at one of these, and then, his shoulder bruised by the big gun's recoil, named the plywood panel "Sore Shoulder." The date was February 28, 1982, an unseasonably warm day. Burroughs made about two dozen more "shotgun paintings" that spring, adding house paint, oil colors, and India ink and collaging photographs and magazine images to the plywood, which was often so old and dried out that it resembled phyllo dough in its structure. Burroughs spent hours gazing into the patterns of torn wood grain exposed by his shotgun blasts.

That summer, Burroughs traveled by car to Naropa for the Jack Kerouac Conference, where he saw many old friends, including Kerouac's first wife, Edie. He was already deep into his reading of Norman Mailer's new book,

Ancient Evenings, a thousand-page novel set in ancient Egypt. The early Egyptians' obsession with immortality keenly interested Burroughs; he had studied some Egyptian history and hieroglyphics in his college days, and as he approached seventy, he was intrigued by the mummy concept. October 1982 found Burroughs visiting London to participate with Gysin and a long slate of poets and musicians in "the Final Academy," a five-day event honoring and reuniting Gysin and Burroughs.

Work on *Dead Roads* was nearly finished now. Burroughs sets up his story with a "Shoot-Out in Boulder," which pits Kim Carson against his old nemesis, Mike Chase, in a duel; then Burroughs introduces his narrator's character: William Seward Hall, writer of Old Western stories. Hall is the first elderly, self-referential protagonist in all of Burroughs' work; in *Cities,* the characters are all adolescents or middle-aged. By the end of *Dead Roads,* Burroughs has taken "Kim" and his band of "Wild Fruits" through numerous lifetimes and incarnations. Their attempts to rewrite history become more panegyrical and frantic, with a Grand Guignol closing sequence that perhaps outdoes the end of *Cities.* But the final scene is the pistol duel in the Boulder Cemetery, and on the last page, Burroughs throws a curveball: someone unseen and unnamed shoots both Kim *and* Chase. As Kim dies, his last words are: "What the FU—!?!" Kim's death, and the birth of Hall, are Burroughs' turning point into old age as an artist.

Burroughs decided to buy a house in town; he chose a little white woodframe house by a creek, in the southeast quadrant of Lawrence, on Learnard Avenue. It was a Sears, Roebuck "kit house" from the late 1920s. There was an acre of garden land in back, with fruit trees and berry bushes. Burroughs moved to town in November, and he settled in for the winter. Of the cats from the Stone House, he brought with him Ginger and Ruski. By springtime Burroughs had scraped together enough money to purchase the house; for the first time since 1948, he owned real estate. Working in his sunny bedroom, Burroughs began to write *The Western Lands*—the Egyptian name for paradise in the afterlife.

The novel begins with his exegesis of the Egyptian concept of "the seven souls"; Burroughs takes Mailer's description of the souls and makes it his own. After death, three of the souls depart from the subject, but some remain to guide him on his perilous journey across the Duad—a river of excrement—and through the purgatorial Land of the Dead to the Western Lands of happy immortality. Burroughs also reveals that the mystery sniper at the shoot-out in Boulder was Joe the Dead, a disloyal lieutenant of Kim's gang. In *The Western Lands,* Joe is seen as the alter-ego of William Seward Hall—himself an alter-ego of Burroughs. But after dispatching his long-running "Audrey/Kim" character, Burroughs must find a substitute, so he takes Kim back to ancient Egyptian times, as "Neferti."

Burroughs also creates a new character named "Hassan-i-Sabbah," based on the historical Shi'ite prophet and Master of the Assassins, whose life and philosophy so captivated Burroughs and Gysin in Paris. Above all, Burroughs confronts the persistent question of immortality, a concern that he has adumbrated in Kim's mesa-top monologues at the beginning of *Dead Roads*. In *Western Lands,* Hassan-i-Sabbah comes down from his mountaintop redoubt, "Alamout," to wander and suffer in the alleys of Thebes. Suffering and disillusionment are central themes in *Western Lands;* in his own voice, Burroughs looks back sadly and nostalgically to the apex of his life and career, in Paris, 1959.

In *Cities,* Burroughs had taken his readers to three of the six cities of the prehistoric Red Night: Tamaghis, "open city of contending partisans"; Ba'dan, "given over to competivie games and commerce"; and Yass-Waddah, "the female stronghold." In *Dead Roads,* inspired by his resumption of handgun targetry in Boulder, he had lingered in Old Western versions of Ba'dan and Yass-Waddah, "opposite each other on a river" (based on St. Albans, the country retreat of his Missouri childhood), and introduced Waghdas, the university city, on a lake ten miles long. Naufana and Ghadis, "the cities of illusion where nothing is true and *therefore* everything is permitted," are discernible in *Western Lands,* which takes place mostly in Waghdas, a stand-in for ancient Thebes and for the college town of Lawrence, where Burroughs was entering old age: "The traveler must start in Tamaghis and make his way through the other cities in the order named. This pilgrimage may take many lifetimes."

More and more, Burroughs was dreaming of his old friends now wandering in the Land of the Dead. The spring of 1983 brought word of two new arrivals: in February, his brother, Mort, died of a heart attack in St. Louis, at age seventy-two. Burroughs traveled to St. Louis for the funeral, and he was surprised by how much the brief religious service affected him—or was it seeing so many people from his childhood now elderly, like himself? Again Burroughs was off on reading tours, and in San Francisco, he learned that Tennessee Williams had died suddenly in New York; Burroughs felt that, despite his fame and wealth, Williams never really received his literary due as one of America's greatest playwrights.

But recognition did come at last to Burroughs: boosted by Ginsberg's lobbying, he was elected to membership in the American Academy and Institute of Arts and Letters. The ceremony in New York that May was a suitably auspicious occasion, as Burroughs took his seat on the stage alongside many other eminent American artists and writers. And when Burroughs went to Paris for readings in the spring of 1984, the French minister of culture made him a *Commandeur de l'Ordre des Arts et des Lettres.* At formal occasions for the rest of his life, Burroughs always wore the green-and-white lapel pin of his *Ordre*—just below the gold-and-purple rosette of the American Academy.

In February 1984, Burroughs was seventy years old; Howard Brookner's film portrait had been shown a year before on BBC's *Arena* program, and Burroughs' first biographer, Sanche de Gramont (Ted Morgan), had begun work on *Literary Outlaw: The Life and Times of William S. Burroughs.* A seventieth-birthday bash was held at the Limelight nightclub in New York, and there were parties to celebrate Overlook Press's reissue of Bill Jr.'s book *Speed* and the publication of *The Place of Dead Roads.* Critical response to *Roads,* however, was tepid at best. Burroughs' reading trips continued through 1984, and he was busy in New York, San Francisco, Los Angeles, St. Louis, London, and Paris with personal appearances to support Brookner's documentary film. Set in motion by his fans and supported by his own cooperation, the canonization of William Burroughs as "the Godfather of Beat and Punk" had begun.

What mattered much more to Burroughs at this time was his new cat, whom he named "Fletch," using one of the Devil's nicknames. Fletch was a black male kitten who literally leaped into my arms on downtown Lawrence's main street in June 1984. Fletch soon became Burroughs' favorite. Ruski, neutered too late in his life, was undomesticable, and he was moved to a friend's cabin at Lone Star Lake in southern Douglas County. Burroughs made frequent feeding visits to the tranquil little Depression-era resort lake, and eventually he bought a small cabin there, where he often retreated with friends for an evening's cocktails and cookout, sometimes rowing himself around the lake in his ten-foot johnboat.

At Naropa in summer 1984, Norman Mailer was the featured visiting writer, and he and Burroughs spent several days and nights together, discussing Mailer's *Ancient Evenings* and Burroughs' ideas for his own work-in-progress. When Mailer read from his novel, Burroughs sat in the front row, at rapt attention. Mailer was one of Burroughs' first defenders, at Edinburgh in 1962; Mailer's quote about Burroughs being "possessed by genius" had been used so often that it was as famous as the books that it adorned. Burroughs respected, but had no natural affinity for, Mailer's work—until the Egyptian novel.

Peter Matson had been Burroughs' agent since the mid-1960s, and now their paths diverged: in 1984, Burroughs changed agents, moving to Andrew Wylie, whom he had known for ten years. Wylie represented Allen Ginsberg, who had only good things to say about him. After an auction in November, Burroughs moved to Viking Penguin, where his new editor was Gerald Howard, and then a few years later David Stanford. The first two books due on the seven-book contract were *Queer* and *The Western Lands,* on which Burroughs was working steadily. The signature advance in 1984—although modest by publishing standards—was the largest sum he had ever received for his work, and for the first time since the end of his parents' allowance in the 1960s, Burroughs experienced financial security.

In early 1985, Burroughs made his last trip to Tangier. For about a year he had been talking with the director David Cronenberg about a movie based on *Naked Lunch,* and producer Jeremy Thomas escorted them to Tangier in February. Except for Paul Bowles, still holding forth regally, the place had become almost unrecognizable. The Parade Bar closed just before their arrival, and the remaining old Tangier hands considered it the end of their era.

At this time, Michael Emerton—with whom I lived for the next seven years—came into our lives. Michael was a curly-headed, hard-drinking nineteen-year-old from Kansas City. His adoptive mother had died when he was sixteen, and he never recovered from the loss. Burroughs and Emerton took to each other immediately: they had much in common, and Michael loved William and his cats. Burroughs went to Paris in November for a disheartening visit with Gysin, who was now very ill. But he had been taken up by a younger crowd around the Palace nightclub, and was enjoying a renaissance of sorts. For his emphysema, Gysin carried a green oxygen bottle when he went out to drink and dance all night.

The spring of 1986 found Burroughs on the road again to Paris, Bourges, Hamburg, Bremen, and Berlin. This time in Paris, Burroughs knew he might be saying a last good-bye to his old friend. Just two months later, as Burroughs was packing his bags in Kansas for an urgent return to Paris, Brion Gysin succumbed to lung cancer at home in his apartment at 135 rue St. Martin, alone, in the early hours of July 13. Burroughs took the news very hard. He said he never wanted to return to Tangier, or Paris—that the soul was gone out of them with Brion's departure. His work on *The Western Lands* slowed to a crawl, and he found little pleasure in the publication, two months later, of an illustrated, limited edition of *The Cat Inside,* with eight drawings of cats by Gysin—the project was meant to be their last collaboration in life, and now it was posthumous. Burroughs' depression was profound.

But he took heart, later that summer, when Allen Ginsberg visited Lawrence and stayed a week in Burroughs' home. In the fall, Burroughs resumed his work on *The Western Lands.* His grief over Gysin's death, and his reveries of their years in Paris and Tangier together, found their way into the book, introducing a somber tone of loss and finality. Gysin was Burroughs' greatest collaborator. Together they had distilled a formula for immortality—and now Gysin was dead. Burroughs ended his novel with a provocative passage that strongly suggested he would never write again, quoting T. S. Eliot's great literary death knell: "Hurry up, please, it's time."

Just before his seventy-third birthday, Burroughs received the painter Phillip Taaffe in Lawrence. Taaffe and Burroughs created a suite of collaborative drawings and several paint-can-and-shot-plywood preparations. This project reminded Burroughs of the joy he felt making his first "shotgun paintings" five years before. He had long been embarrassed by how his career overshadowed Gysin's, but there was no longer any danger of hurt feelings if Burroughs began to show his paintings now. In the spring of 1987, Burroughs embarked on a prolific period of art-making, which lasted eight years. He was explicitly communing with Gysin's spirit, and in his painting studio he found a sense of renewal. During these months Burroughs also finished writing *The Western Lands.*

The "River City Reunion" was a weeklong event that September in Lawrence, and many old friends came from all over to take part: Allen Ginsberg, Robert

Creeley, John Giorno, Timothy Leary, Anne Waldman, Ed Sanders, Patti Smith, Keith Haring, and many others. Alternative-minded citizens in Lawrence were treated to a cornucopia of readings, and the undergraduates at the university were enthusiastically involved in their own poetry sessions. For a week, Lawrence was the national headquarters of the counterculture. In December, Burroughs headed to New York for the publication of *The Western Lands* and for his first serious art exhibition. His shotgun paintings were shown at the Tony Shafrazi Gallery, along with drawings by Keith Haring for *Fault Lines*, a posthumous book project Haring had planned with Brion Gysin. The art world was in a buying mood in those years, and Burroughs was pleased to see his paintings selling.

Burroughs returned to Lawrence to spend the winter at home. From now on, his travels would be fewer, undertaken mainly in support of his new medium. Burroughs' retreat from writing seemed valedictory, final; as he wrote on the last page of *The Western Lands*: "The Old Writer had come to the end of words, to the end of what can be done with words."

from
cities of the red night

FORE!

The liberal principles embodied in the French and American revolutions and later in the liberal revolutions of 1848 had already been codified and put into practice by pirate communes a hundred years earlier. Here is a quote from *Under the Black Flag* by Don C. Seitz:

> Captain Mission was one of the forbears of the French Revolution. He was one hundred years in advance of his time, for his career was based upon an initial desire to better adjust the affairs of mankind, which ended as is quite usual in the more liberal adjustment of his own fortunes. It is related how Captain Mission, having led his ship to victory against an English man-of-war, called a meeting of the crew. Those who wished to follow him he would welcome and treat as brothers; those who did not would be safely set ashore. One and all embraced the New Freedom. Some were for hoisting the Black Flag at once but Mission demurred, saying that they were not pirates but liberty lovers, fighting for equal rights against all nations subject to the tyranny of government, and bespoke a white flag as the more fitting emblem. The ship's money was put in a chest to be used as common property. Clothes were now distributed to all in need and the republic of the sea was in full operation.
>
> Mission bespoke them to live in strict harmony among themselves; that a misplaced society would adjudge them still as pirates. Self-preservation, therefore, and not a cruel disposition, compelled them to declare war on all nations who should close their ports to them. "I declare such war and at the same time recommend to you a humane and generous behavior towards your prisoners, which will appear by so much more the effects of a noble soul as we are satisfied we should not meet the same treatment should our ill fortune or want of courage give us up to their mercy. . . ." The *Nieustadt* of Amsterdam was made prize, giving up two thousand pounds and gold dust and seventeen slaves. The slaves were

added to the crew and clothed in the Dutchman's spare garments; Mission made an address denouncing slavery, holding that men who sold others like beasts proved their religion to be no more than a grimace, as no man had power of liberty over another. . . .

Mission explored the Madagascar coast and found a bay ten leagues north of Diego Suarez. It was resolved to establish here the shore quarters of the Republic—erect a town, build docks, and have a place they might call their own. The colony was called Libertatia and was placed under Articles drawn up by Captain Mission. The Articles state, among other things: all decisions with regard to the colony to be submitted to vote by the colonists; the abolition of slavery for any reason including debt; the abolition of the death penalty; and freedom to follow any religious beliefs or practices without sanction or molestation.

Captain Mission's colony, which numbered about three hundred, was wiped out by a surprise attack from the natives, and Captain Mission was killed shortly afterwards in a sea battle. There were other such colonies in the West Indies and in Central and South America, but they were not able to maintain themselves since they were not sufficiently populous to withstand attack. Had they been able to do so, the history of the world could have been altered. Imagine a number of such fortified positions all through South America and the West Indies, stretching from Africa to Madagascar and Malaya and the East Indies, all offering refuge to fugitives from slavery and oppression: "Come to us and live under the Articles."

At once we have allies in all those who are enslaved and oppressed throughout the world, from the cotton plantations of the American South to the sugar plantations of the West Indies, the whole Indian population of the American continent peonized and degraded by the Spanish into subhuman poverty and ignorance, exterminated by the Americans, infected with their vices and diseases, the natives of Africa and Asia—all these are potential allies. Fortified positions supported by and supporting guerrilla hit-and-run bands; supplied with soldiers, weapons, medicines and information by the local populations . . . such a combination would be unbeatable. If the whole American army couldn't beat the Vietcong at a time when fortified positions were rendered obsolete by artillery and air strikes, certainly the armies of Europe, operating in unfamiliar territory and susceptible to all the disabling diseases of tropical countries, could not have beaten guerrilla tactics *plus* fortified positions. Consider the difficulties which such an invading army would face: continual harassment from the guerrillas, a totally hostile population always ready with poison, misdirection, snakes and spiders in the general's bed, armadillos carrying the deadly earth-eating disease rooting under the barracks and adopted as mascots by the regiment, as dysentery and malaria take their toll. The sieges could not but present a series of military disasters. There is no stopping the Articulated. The white man is retroactively relieved of his burden. Whites will be welcomed as workers, settlers, teachers, and technicians, but not as colonists or masters. No man may violate the Articles.

Imagine such a movement on a worldwide scale. Faced by the actual practice of freedom, the French and American revolutions would be forced to stand by their words. The disastrous results of uncontrolled industrialization would also be curtailed, since factory workers and slum dwellers from the cities would seek refuge in Articulated areas. Any man would have the right to settle in any area of his choosing. The land would belong to those who used it. No whiteman boss, no Pukka Sahib, no Patróns, no colonists. The escalation of mass production and concentration of population in urban areas would be halted, for who would work in their factories and buy their products when he could live from the fields and the sea and the lakes and the rivers, in areas of unbelievable plenty? And living from the land, he would be motivated to preserve its resources.

I cite this example of retroactive Utopia since it actually could have happened in terms of the techniques and human resources available at the time. Had Captain Mission lived long enough to set an example for others to follow, mankind might have stepped free from the deadly impasse of insoluble problems in which we now find ourselves.

The chance was there. The chance was missed. The principles of the French and American revolutions became windy lies in the mouths of politicians. The liberal revolutions of 1848 created the so-called republics of Central and South America, with a dreary history of dictatorship, oppression, graft, and bureaucracy, thus closing this vast, underpopulated continent to any possibility of communes along the lines set forth by Captain Mission. In any case South America will soon be crisscrossed by highways and motels. In England, Western Europe, and America, the overpopulation made possible by the Industrial Revolution leaves scant room for communes, which are commonly subject to state and federal law and frequently harassed by the local inhabitants. There is simply no room left for "freedom from the tyranny of government" since city dwellers depend on government for food, power, water, transportation, protection, and welfare. Your right to live where you want, with companions of your choosing, under laws to which you agree, died in the eighteenth century with Captain Mission. Only a miracle or a disaster could restore it.

INVOCATION

This book is dedicated to the Ancient Ones, to the Lord of Abominations, *Humwawa*, whose face is a mass of entrails, whose breath is the stench of dung and the perfume of death, Dark Angel of all that is excreted and sours, Lord of Decay, Lord of the Future, who rides on a whispering south wind, to *Pazuzu*, Lord of Fevers and Plagues, Dark Angel of the Four Winds with rotting genitals from which he howls through sharpened teeth over stricken cities, to *Kutulu*, the Sleeping Serpent who cannot be summoned, to the

Akhkharu, who suck the blood of men since they desire to become men, to the *Lalussu,* who haunt the places of men, to *Gelal* and *Lilit,* who invade the beds of men and whose children are born in secret places, to *Addu,* raiser of storms, who can fill the night sky with brightness, to *Malah,* Lord of Courage and Bravery, to *Zahgurim,* whose number is twenty-three and who kills in an unnatural fashion, to *Zahrim,* a warrior among warriors, to *Itzamna,* Spirit of Early Mists and Showers, to *Ix Chel,* the Spider-Web-That-Catches-the-Dew-of-Morning, to *Zuhuy Kak,* Virgin Fire, to *Ah Dziz,* the Master of Cold, to *Kak U Pacat,* who works in fire, to *Ix Tab,* Goddess of Ropes and Snares, patroness of those who hang themselves, to *Schmuun,* the Silent One, twin brother of *Ix Tab,* to *Xolotl* the Unformed, Lord of Rebirth, to *Aguchi,* Master of Ejaculations, to *Osiris* and *Amen* in phallic form, to *Hex Chun Chan,* the Dangerous One, to *Ah Pook,* the Destroyer, to the *Great Old One* and the *Star Beast,* to *Pan,* God of Panic, to the nameless gods of dispersal and emptiness, to *Hassan I Sabbah,* Master of the Assassins.

To all the scribes and artists and practitioners of magic through whom these spirits have been manifested . . . .

NOTHING IS TRUE. EVERYTHING IS PERMITTED.

POLITICS HERE IS DEATH

Muted remote boardroom. Doctor Pierson sits at the head of the table with notes in front of him. He speaks in a dry flat academic voice.

"Ladies and gentlemen of the Board, I am here to give a report on preliminary experiments with Virus B-23. . . . Consider the origins of this virus in the Cities of the Red Night. The red glow that covered the northern sky at night was a form of radiation that gave rise to a plague known as the Red Fever, of which Virus B-23 was found to be the etiological agent.

"Virus B-23 has been called, among other things, the virus of biological mutation, since this agent occasioned biologic alterations in those affected— fatal in many cases, permanent and hereditary in the survivors, who become carriers of that strain. The original inhabitants of these cities were black, but soon a wide spectrum of albino variations appeared, and this condition was passed on to their descendants by techniques of artificial insemination which were, to say the least, highly developed. In fact, how some of these mutant pregnancies were contracted is unknown to modern science. Immaculate or at least viral conception was pandemic and may have given rise to legends of demon lovers, the succubi and incubi of medieval folklore."

Doctor Pierson continues: "The virus, acting directly on neural centers, brought about sexual frenzies that facilitated its communication, just as rabid dogs are driven to spread the virus of rabies by biting. Various forms of sexual sacrifice were practiced . . . sexual hangings and strangulations, and drugs that caused death in erotic convulsions. Death during intercourse was a frequent occurrence and was considered an especially favorable circumstance for conveying the viral alterations.

"We are speaking of more or less virgin genetic material of high quality. At this time the newly conceived white race was fighting for its biological continuity, so the virus served a most useful purpose. However, I question the wisdom of introducing Virus B-23 into contemporary America and Europe. Even though it might quiet the uh silent majority, who are admittedly becoming uh awkward, we must consider the biologic consequences of exposing genetic material already damaged beyond repair to such an agent, leaving a wake of unimaginably unfavorable mutations all ravenously perpetrating their kind . . .

"There have been other proposals. I cite the work of Doctor Unruh von Steinplatz on radioactive virus strains. Working with such established viruses as rabies, hepatitis, and smallpox, he exposed generations of virus to atomic radiation to produce airborne strains of unbelievable virulence capable of wiping out whole populations within days. However, this blueprint contains a flaw: the disposal problem posed by billions of radioactive corpses unfit even for fertilizer.

"Ladies and gentlemen, I propose to remove the temporal limits, shifting our experimental theater into past time in order to circumvent the whole tedious problem of overpopulation. You may well ask if we can be certain of uh containing the virus in past time. The answer is: we do not have sufficient data to speak with certainty. We propose; the virus may dispose . . ."

A thin man in his early thirties with sandy hair and pale blue eyes had been taking notes while Doctor Pierson was speaking. He looked up and spoke in a clear, rather high-pitched voice with a faint trace of Germanic accent. "Doctor Pierson, I have a few questions."

"Certainly," said Pierson with cold displeasure. He knew exactly who this man was, and wished that he had not been invited to attend the meeting. This was Jon Alistair Peterson, born in Denmark, now working on a secret government project in England. He was a virologist and mathematician who had devised a computer to process qualitative data.

Peterson leaned back in his chair, one ankle crossed over his knee. He extracted a joint from his shirt pocket. It was a loud Carnaby Street shirt. Pierson thought it vulgar. Peterson lit the joint and blew smoke towards the ceiling, seemingly oblivious of disapproving looks from the board members. He glanced down at his notes. "My first question is a matter of uh nomenclature." Pierson was annoyed to realize that Peterson was mimicking his own academic tones.

"Professor Steinplatz's experiments, as you must know, consisted of inoculating animals with various viruses and then exposing the animals to radiation. This exposure produced virus mutations tending towards increased virulence and. . . ." He took a long drag and blew smoke across his notes. ". . . uh increased communication potential. In plain English, the mutated viruses were much more infectious."

"I would say that is a more or less accurate paraphrase of what I have just said."

"Not precisely. The mutated virus strains were produced by radiation and the test animals, having been exposed to radiation, were of course radioactive to a point but not dangerously so. . . . The viruses were *produced* by radiation, but it does not necessarily follow that the viruses were themselves radioactive. Is not your use of the term *radioactive* virus and your uh evocation of billions of radioactive corpses uh misleading?"

Doctor Pierson found it difficult to conceal his annoyance. "I have pointed out that, owing to the grave dangers inherent in large-scale experimentation which could among other things severely damage our public image, our data is incomplete . . ."

"Ah yes, to be sure. And now if you will bear with me, Doctor, I have some additional questions. . . . You have said that Virus B-23 resulted from radiation?" asked Peterson.

"I did."

"In what way does it differ from the strains developed by Doctor Steinplatz?"

"I thought I had made that point quite clear: the form of radiation emanating from the red light is unknown at the present time."

"You are then ignorant of the nature of this wondrous radiation, or as to how it could be produced in the laboratory?"

"Yes."

"Has it occurred to you that it might be similar to Reich's DOR, or Deadly Orgone Radiation, which is produced by placing radioactive material in an organic container lined with iron?"

"Preposterous! Reich was a charlatan! A lunatic!"

"Perhaps . . . but such a simple and *inexpensive* experiment . . . we could start with herpes simplex."

"I fail to see that any useful purpose. . . ." Pierson glanced around the table. Stony faces looked back at him. He was concealing something and they knew it.

Doctor Pierson looked at his watch. "I'm afraid I must cut this short. I have a plane to catch."

Peterson held up his hand. "I'm not quite finished, Doctor. . . . I am sure that a slight delay in takeoff could be arranged for a person of your importance. . . . Now, the virus strains developed by Doctor Steinplatz were, to be sure, more contagious and more virulent than the mother strains from which they were derived, but still quite recognizable. For example, for *example*, the good doctor's airborne rabies would still be clinically recognizable as rabies. Even if the viruses were mixed into a cocktail, the individual ingredients would still be comparatively easy to identify. You would agree, Doctor Pierson?"

"In theory, yes. However, we do not know, in the absence of large-scale exposure, whether the viruses might not undergo further mutations that would render identification difficult."

"To be sure. The point I am making is simply that Doctor Steinplatz started his experiments with certain known viruses. . . . Doctor Pierson, you have stated that Virus B-23 *resulted* from unknown radiation. Do you imply that this virus was so produced out of thin air? Let me put it this way: What virus or viruses known to unknown mutated as a result of this radiation?"

"At the risk of repeating myself, I will say again that both the radiation and the virus or viruses are unknown at this time," said Pierson archly.

"The symptoms of a virus are the attempts of the body to deal with a virus attack. By their symptoms you shall know them, and even a totally unknown virus would yield considerable data by its symptoms. On the other hand, if a virus produces no symptoms, then we have no way of knowing that it exists . . . no way of knowing that it is a virus."

"So?"

"So the virus in question may have been latent or it may have been living in benign symbiosis with the host."

"That is, of course, possible," admitted Pierson.

"Now let us consider the symptoms of Virus B-23: fever, rash, a characteristic odor, sexual frenzies, obsession with sex and death. . . . Is this so totally strange and alien?"

"I don't follow you."

"I will make myself clearer. We know that a consuming passion can produce physical symptoms . . . fever . . . loss of appetite . . . even allergic reactions . . . and few conditions are more obsessional and potentially self-destructive than love. Are not the symptoms of Virus B-23 simply the symptoms of what we are pleased to call 'love'? Eve, we are told, was made from Adam's rib . . . so a hepatitis virus was once a healthy liver cell. If you will excuse me, ladies, nothing personal . . . we are all tainted with viral origins. The whole quality of human consciousness, as expressed in male and female, is basically a virus mechanism. I suggest that this virus, known as 'the other half,' turned malignant as a result of the radiation to which the Cities of the Red Night were exposed."

"You lost me there."

"Did I indeed. . . . And I would suggest further that any attempts to contain Virus B-23 will turn out to be ineffectual because we carry this virus with us," said Peterson.

"Really, Doctor, aren't you letting fantasy run away with you? After all, other viruses have been brought under control. Why should this virus be an exception?"

"Because it is the *human virus*. After many thousands of years of more or less benign coexistence, it is now once again on the verge of malignant mutation . . . what Doctor Steinplatz calls a virgin soil epidemic. This could result from the radiation already released in atomic testing . . ."

"What's your point, Doctor?" Pierson snapped.

"My point is very simple. The whole human position is no longer tenable. And one last consideration . . . as you know, a vast crater in what is now Siberia is thought to have resulted from a meteor. It is further theorized that this meteor brought with it the radiation in question. Others have surmised that it may not have been a meteor but a black hole, a hole in the fabric of reality, through which the inhabitants of these ancient cities traveled in time to a final impasse."

HARBOR POINT

Early morning mist . . . bird calls . . . howler monkeys like wind in the trees. Fifty armed partisans are moving north over Panama jungle trails. Unshaven faces at once alert and drawn with fatigue, and a rapid gait that is almost a jog, indicate a long forced march without sleep. The rising sun picks out their faces.

Noah Blake: twenty, a tall red-haired youth with brown eyes, his face dusted with freckles. Bert Hansen: a Swede with light blue eyes. Clinch Todd: a powerful youth with long arms and something sleepy and quiescent in his brown eyes flecked with points of light. Paco: a Portuguese with Indian and Negro blood. Sean Brady: black Irish with curly black hair and a quick wide smile.

Young Noah Blake is screwing the pan onto a flintlock pistol, testing the spring, oiling the barrel and stock. He holds the pistol up to his father, who examines it critically. Finally he nods . . .

"Aye, son, that can go out with the Blake mark on it . . ."

"Old Lady Norton stuck her head in the shop and said I shouldn't be working on the Lord's Day."

"And she shouldn't be sniffing her long snot-dripping nose into my shop on the Lord's Day or any other. The Nortons have never bought so much as a ha'penny measure of nails off me." His father looks around the shop, his fingers hooked in his wide belt. Lean and red-haired, he has the face of a mechanic: detached, factual, a face that minds its own business and expects others to do the same. "We'll be moving to the city, son, where nobody cares if you go to church or not . . ."

"Chicago, Father?"

"No, son, Boston. On the sea. We have relations there."

Father and son put on coats and gloves. They lock the shop and step out into the muted streets of the little snowbound village on Lake Michigan. As they walk through the snow, villagers pass. Some of the greetings are quick and cold with averted faces.

"Is it all right if my friends come to dinner, Father? They'll be bringing fish and bread . . ."

"All right with me, son. But they aren't well seen here. . . . There's talk in the village, son. Bad talk about all of you. If it wasn't for Bert Hansen's father being a shipowner and one of the richest men in town there'd be more than talk. . . . Quicker we move the better."

"Could the others come too?"

"Well, son, I could use some more hands in the shop. No limit to how many guns we can sell in a seaport like Boston . . . and I'm thinking maybe Mr. Hansen would pay to get his son out of here . . ."

Spring morning, doves call from the woods. Noah Blake and his father, Bert Hansen, Clinch Todd, Paco, and Sean Brady board a boat with their luggage stacked on deck. The villagers watch from the pier.

Mrs. Norton sniffs and says in her penetrating voice, "Good riddance to the lot of them." She glances sideways at her husband.

"I share the same views," he says hastily.

Boston: two years later. Mr. Blake has prospered. He works now on contracts from shipowners, and his guns are standard issue. He has remarried. His wife is a quiet refined girl from New York. Her family are well-to-do importers and merchants with political connections. Mr. Blake plans to open a New York branch, and there is talk of army and navy contracts. Noah Blake is studying navigation. He wants to be a ship's captain, and all five of the boys want to ship out.

"Wait till you find the right ship," Mr. Blake tells them.

One winter day, Noah is walking on the waterfront with Bert, Clinch, Sean and Paco. They notice a ship called *The Great White*. Rather small but very clean and trim. A man leans over the rail. He has a beefy red smiling face and cold blue eyes.

"You boys looking for a ship?"

"Maybe," says Noah cautiously.

"Well, come aboard."

He meets them at the gangplank. "I'm Mr. Thomas, first mate." He extends a hand like callused beef and shakes hands with each boy in turn. He leads the way to the master's cabin. "This is Captain Jones—master of *The Great White*. These boys are looking for a ship . . . maybe . . ."

The boys nod politely. Captain Jones looks at them in silence. He is a man of indeterminate age with a grey-green pallor. He speaks at length, in a flat voice, his lips barely moving.

"Well, I could use five deckhands. . . . You boys had any experience?"

"Yes. On the Great Lakes." Noah indicates Bert Hansen. "His father owned fishing boats."

"Aye," says Captain Jones, "freshwater sailing. The sea's another kettle of fish."

"I've studied navigation," Noah puts in.

"Have you now? And what would be your name, lad?"

"Noah Blake."

An almost imperceptible glance passes between the Captain and the first mate.

"And your trade, lad?"

"Gunsmith."

"Well, now, you wouldn't be Noah Blake's son would you?"

"Yes, sir, I would."

Once again the glance flickers between the two men. Then Captain Jones leans back in his chair and looks at the boys with his dead, fishy eyes.

"We'll be sailing in three days' time . . . New York, Charleston, Jamaica, Veracruz. Two months down, more or less, and two months back. . . . I pay ten pounds a month for deckhands."

Noah Blake tries to look unimpressed. This is twice as much as any other captain has offered.

"Well, sir, I'll have to discuss it with my father."

"To be sure, lad. You can sign the Articles tomorrow if you're so minded . . . all five of you."

Noah can hardly wait to tell his father. "I mean that's good, isn't it?"

"Aye, son. Perhaps a little too good. Captain Jones's name is not so white as his ship. He's known as Opium Jones in the trade. He'll be carrying opium, guns, powder, shot, and tools. And he's not too particular who he trades with . . ."

"Anything wrong with that, Father?"

"No. He's no better and no worse than most of the others. Only thing I can't figure is why he's paying double wages for his deckhands."

"Maybe he'd rather have five good hands than ten waterfront drunks."

"Maybe. . . . Well, go if you like. But keep your eyes open."

THE PRIVATE ASSHOLE

The name is Clem Williamson Snide. I am a private asshole.

As a private investigator I run into more death than the law allows. I mean the law of averages. There I am outside the hotel room waiting for the correspondent to reach a crescendo of amorous noises. I always find that if you walk in just as he goes off he won't have time to disengage himself and take a swing at you. When me and the house dick open the door with a passkey, the smell of shit and bitter almonds blows us back into the hall. Seems they both took a cyanide capsule and fucked until the capsules dissolved. A real messy love death.

Another time I am working on a routine case of industrial sabotage when the factory burns down killing twenty-three people. These things happen. I am a man of the world. Going to and fro and walking up and down in it.

Death smells. I mean it has a special smell, over and above the smell of cyanide, carrion, blood, cordite or burnt flesh. It's like opium. Once you smell it you never forget. I can walk down a street and get a whiff of opium smoke and I know someone is kicking the gong around.

I got a whiff of death as soon as Mr. Green walked into my office. You can't always tell whose death it is. Could be Green, his wife, or the missing son he wants me to find. Last letter from the island of Spetsai two months ago. After a month with no word the family made inquiries by long-distance phone.

"The embassy wasn't at all helpful," said Mr. Green.

I nodded. I knew just how unhelpful they could be.

"They referred us to the Greek police. Fortunately, we found a man there who speaks English."

"That would be Colonel Dimitri."

"Yes. You know him?"

I nodded, waiting for him to continue.

"He checked and could find no record that Jerry had left the country, and no hotel records after Spetsai."

"He could be visiting someone."

"I'm sure he would write."

"You feel then that this is not just an instance of neglect on his part, or perhaps a lost letter? . . . That happens in the Greek islands . . ."

"Both Mrs. Green and I are convinced that something is wrong."

"Very well, Mr. Green, there is the question of my fee: a hundred dollars a day plus expenses and a thousand dollar retainer. If I work on a case two days and spend two hundred dollars, I refund six hundred to the client. If I have to leave the country, the retainer is two thousand. Are these terms satisfactory?"

"Yes."

"Very good. I'll start right here in New York. Sometimes I have been able to provide the client with the missing person's address after a few hours' work. He may have written to a friend."

"That's easy. He left his address book. Asked me to mail it to him care of American Express in Athens." He passed me the book.

"Excellent."

Now, on a missing-person case I want to know everything the client can tell me about the missing person, no matter how seemingly unimportant and irrelevant. I want to know preferences in food, clothes, colors, reading, entertainment, use of drugs and alcohol, what cigarette brand he smokes, medical history. I have a questionnaire printed with five pages of questions. I got it out of the filing cabinet and passed it to him.

"Will you please fill out this questionnaire and bring it back here day after tomorrow. That will give me time to check out the local addresses."

"I've called most of them," he said curtly, expecting me to take the next plane for Athens.

"Of course. But friends of an M.P.—missing person—are not always honest with the family. Besides, I daresay some of them have moved or had their phones disconnected. Right?" He nodded. I put my hands on the questionnaire. "Some of these questions may seem irrelevant but they all add up. I found a missing person once from knowing that he could wriggle his ears. I've noticed that you are left-handed. Is your son also left-handed?"

"Yes, he is."

"You can skip that question. Do you have a picture of him with you?"

He handed me a photo. Jerry was a beautiful kid. Slender, red hair, green eyes far apart, a wide mouth. Sexy and kinky-looking.

"Mr. Green, I want all the photos of him you can find. If I use any I'll have copies made and return the originals. If he did any painting, sketching, or writing I'd like to see that too. If he sang or played an instrument I want recordings. In fact, any recordings of his voice. And please bring if possible some article of clothing that hasn't been dry-cleaned since he wore it."

"It's true then that you use uh psychic methods?"

"I use any methods that help me to find the missing person. If I can locate him in my own mind that makes it easier to locate him outside it."

"My wife is into psychic things. That's why I came to you. She has an intuition that something has happened to him and she says only a psychic can find him."

That makes two of us, I thought.

He wrote me a check for a thousand dollars. We shook hands.

I went right to work. Jim, my assistant, was out of town on an industrial-espionage case—he specializes in electronics. So I was on my own. Ordinarily I don't carry iron on an M.P. case, but this one smelled of danger. I put on my snub-nosed .38, in a shoulder holster. Then I unlocked a drawer and put three joints of the best Colombian, laced with hash, into my pocket. Nothing like a joint to break the ice and stir the memory. I also took a deck of heroin. It buys more than money sometimes.

Most of the addresses were in the SoHo area. That meant lofts, and that often means the front door is locked. So I started with an address on Sixth Street.

She opened the door right away, but she kept the chain on. Her pupils were dilated, her eyes running, and she was snuffling, waiting for the Man. She looked at me with hatred.

I smiled. "Expecting someone else?"

"You a cop?"

"No. I'm a private investigator hired by the family to find Jerry Green. You knew him."

"Look, I don't have to talk to you."

"No, you don't have to. But you might want to." I showed her the deck of heroin. She undid the chain.

The place was filthy—dishes stacked in a sink, cockroaches running over them. The bathtub was in the kitchen and hadn't been used for a long time. I sat down gingerly in a chair with the springs showing. I held the deck in my hand where she could see it. "You got any pictures of him?"

She looked at me and she looked at the heroin. She rummaged in a drawer, and tossed two pictures onto a coffee table that wobbled. "Those should be worth something."

They were. One showed Jerry in drag, and he made a beautiful girl. The other showed him standing up naked with a hard-on. "Was he gay?"

"Sure. He liked getting fucked by Puerto Ricans and having his picture took."

"He pay you?"

"Sure, twenty bucks. He kept most of the pictures."

"Where'd he get the money?"

"I don't know."

She was lying. I went into my regular spiel. "Now look, I'm not a cop. I'm a private investigator paid by his family. I'm paid to find him, that's all. He's been missing for two months." I started to put the heroin back into my pocket and that did it.

"He was pushing C."

I tossed the deck onto the coffee table. She locked the door behind me.

Later that evening, over a joint, I interviewed a nice young gay couple, who simply *adored* Jerry.

"Such a sweet boy . . ."

"So understanding . . ."

"Understanding?"

"About gay people. He even marched with us . . ."

"And look at the postcard he sent us from Athens."

It was a museum postcard showing a statue of a nude youth found at Kouros.

"Wasn't that cute of him?"

Very cute, I thought.

I interviewed his steady girlfriend, who told me he was all mixed up.

"He had to get away from his mother's influence and find himself. We talked it all over."

I interviewed everyone I could find in the address book. I talked to waiters and bartenders all over the SoHo area: Jerry was a nice boy . . . polite . . . poised . . . a bit reserved. None of them had an inkling of his double life as a coke pusher and homosexual transvestite. I see I am going to need some more heroin on this one. That's easy. I know some narco boys who owe me a favor. It takes an ounce and a ticket to San Francisco to buy some names from the junky chick.

Seek and you shall find. I nearly found an ice pick in my stomach. Knock and it shall be opened unto you. Often it wasn't opened unto me. But I finally found the somebody who: a twenty-year-old Puerto Rican kid named Kiki, very handsome and quite fond of Jerry in his way. Psychic too, and into Mocambo magic. He told me Jerry had the mark of death on him.

"What was his source for the coke?"

His face closed over. "I don't know."

"Can't blame you for not knowing. May I suggest to you that his source was a federal narc?"

His deadpan went deader. "I didn't tell you anything."

"Did he hear voices? Voices giving him orders?"

"I guess he did. He was controlled by something."

I gave him my card. "If you ever need anything let me know."

Mr. Green showed up the next morning with a stack of photos. The questionnaire I had given him had been neatly filled out on a typewriter. He also brought a folio of sketches and a green knitted scarf. The scarf reeked of death.

I glanced at the questionnaire. Born April 18, 1951, in Little America, Wyoming. "Admiral Byrd welcomes you aboard the Deep Freeze Special." I looked through the photos: Jerry as a baby . . . Jerry on a horse . . . Jerry with a wide sunlit grin holding up a string of trout . . . graduation pictures . . . Jerry as "the Toff" in the high school play, *A Night at an Inn*. They all looked exactly as they should look. Like he was playing the part expected of him. There were about fifty recent photos, all looking like Jerry.

Take fifty photos of anyone. There will be some photos where the face is so different you can hardly recognize the subject. I mean most people have many faces. Jerry had *one*. Don Juan says anyone who always looks like the same person isn't a person. He is a person impersonator.

I looked at Jerry's sketches. Good drawing, no talent. Empty and banal as sunlight. There were also a few poems, so bad I couldn't read them. Needless to say, I didn't tell Mr. Green what I had found out about Jerry's sex and drug habits. I just told him that no one I had talked to had heard from Jerry since his disappearance, and that I was ready to leave for Athens at once if he still wanted to retain me. Money changed hands.

from LETTRE DE MARQUE

Feb. 28, 1702: Today we were captured by pirates. At five o'clock in the afternoon a heavily armed ship came abreast of us flying the Dutch flag, which was then lowered and the black pirate flag raised. We were carrying no cannon, so resistance was out of the question and Captain Jones immediately gave the order to raise the flag of truce. We all gathered on deck, including the de Fuentes twins, who were impassive as always, scanning the pirate ship critically as if to assess its worth.

Shortly thereafter a boat was lowered and it rowed towards us. Standing in the stern was a slim blond youth, his gold-braided coat glittering in the sun. Beside him was a youth in short grey pants and shirt with a red scarf around his neck. The boat was rowed by what appeared to be a crew of women, singing as they rowed and turning towards us to leer and wink with their painted faces.

The companionway was lowered and the "women" scrambled aboard with the agility of monkeys and posted themselves about the deck with muskets and cutlasses. I perceived that they were, in fact, handsome youths in women's garb, their costumes being Oriental, of colored silks and brocade. The two youths then stepped on board, the one with his gold-braided coat open at the waist to show his slender brown chest and stomach, a brace of pistols inlaid with silver, and a cutlass at his belt. He was a striking figure: blond hair tied in a knot at the back of his head, aristocratic and well-formed features, possessing a most lordly bearing and grace of manner.

Captain Jones stepped forward. "I am Captain Jones, master of *The Great White*."

"And I am Captain Strobe, second in command on *The Siren*," said the youth.

They shook hands most amiably and if I am any judge are not strangers to each other. I was immediately convinced that the "capture" had been prearranged between them. Strobe then received the keys to the armory. Turning to us, he assured us that we had nothing to fear for our lives. He would take over the conduct of the ship and set its course, his men acting under the orders of Mr. Kelley, the quartermaster. He indicated the youth in grey shorts, who was leaning against the rail immobile as a statue, his face without expression, his pale grey eyes turned up towards the rigging. We would continue to act under the orders of Mr. Thomas.

Several of the boys descended to the boat and began passing up seabags containing apparently the personal effects of the boarding crew. When the boat was cleared, Strobe conducted Captain Jones and the de Fuentes twins to the companionway and two boys rowed them back to *The Siren*. Captain Strobe then opened a small keg of rum and the boys produced tankards from their bags. Approaching us in a purposeful and insinuating manner, wriggling their buttocks, they passed around little clay pipes.

"Hashish. Very good."

When it came my turn to smoke it caused me to cough greatly but soon I felt a lifting of my spirits and a vividness of pictures in my mind—together with a prickling in my groin and buttocks. Drums and flutes appeared and the boys began to dance and as they danced stripped off their clothes until they were dancing stark naked on the brightly colored silk scarves and dresses strewn about the deck. Captain Strobe stood on the poop deck playing a silver flute, the notes seeming to fall from a distant star. Only Mr. Thomas, at Strobe's side, seemed totally unconcerned, and for a second his bulky form was transparent before my eyes—probably an illusion produced by the drug.

Mr. Thomas was watching *The Siren* through his telescope. Finally, having received a signal that their sails were set, he gave the order to hoist sail on *The Great White*. Surprisingly enough we were able to carry out the order with no difficulty, the effect of hashish being such that one can shift easily from one activity to another. Kelley gave the same order in an unknown tongue to the dancing boys, who now acted in a seamanlike manner—some naked, some with scarfs twisted around their hips—as they went about their duties singing strange songs. So sails were speedily set and we got under way, for where I did not know.

Some of the boys have hammocks and sleep on deck, but we are often two to a bunk in the forecastle. Since we now have a double crew, there is much time with nothing to do, and I have been able to acquaint myself to some extent with the strange history of these transvestite boys.

Some of them are dancing boys from Morocco, others from Tripoli, Madagascar, and Central Africa. There are a few from India and the East Indies who have served on pirate vessels in the Red Sea, where they preyed on merchant vessels and other pirates alike, the method of operation being this: some would join the crew of a ship, selling their favors and insinuating themselves into key positions. Then the crew sights an apparently unarmed vessel carrying a cargo of beautiful women all singing and dancing lewdly and promising the mariners their bodies. Once on board the "women" pull out hidden pistols and cutlasses, while their accomplices on shipboard do the same, and *The Siren* now uncovers its cannons—so that the ship would often be taken without the loss of a single life. Often the boys would sign on as cooks—at which trade they all excel—and then drug the entire crew. However, word of their operations spread rapidly and they are now fleeing from pirates and naval patrols alike, having as the French say, *brûlé,*—burnt down—the Red Sea area.

Kelley told me his story. He started his career as a merchant seaman. In the course of an argument he killed the quartermaster, for which he was tried and sentenced to hang. His ship at that time was in the harbor of Tangier. The sentence was carried out in the marketplace, but some pirates who were present cut him down, carried him to their ship, and revived him. It was thought that a man who had been hanged and brought back to life would not only bring luck to their venture but also ensure protection against the fate from which he had been rescued. While he was still insensible the pirates rubbed red ink into the hemp marks, so that he seemed to have a red rope always around his neck.

The pirate ship was commanded by Skipper Nordenholz, a renegade from the Dutch Navy who was still able to pass his ship as an honest merchant vessel flying the Dutch flag. Strobe was second in command. Barely had they left Tangier headed for the Red Sea via the Cape of Good Hope when a mutiny broke out. The crew was in disagreement as to the destination, being minded to head for the West Indies. They had also conceived a contempt for Strobe as an effeminate dandy. After he had killed five of the ringleaders they were forced to revise this opinion. The mutinous crew was then put ashore and a crew of acrobats and dancing boys taken on, since Nordenholz had already devised a way in which they could be put to use.

Kelley claims to have learned the secrets of death on the gallows, which gives him invincible skill as a swordsman and such sexual prowess that no man or woman can resist him, with the exception of Captain Strobe, whom he re-

gards as more than human. *"Voici ma lettre de marque,"* he says, running his
fingers along the rope mark. (A letter of marque was issued to privateers by
their government, authorizing them to prey on enemy vessels in the capacity
of accredited combatants, and thus distinguishing them from common pirates.
Such a letter often, but by no means always, saved the bearer from the gallows.) Kelley tells me that the mere sight of his hemp marks instills in adversaries a weakness and terror equal to the apparition of Death Himself.

I asked Kelley what it feels like to be hanged.

"At first I was sensible of very great pain due to the weight of my body and
felt my spirits in a strange commotion violently pressed upwards. After they
reached my head, I saw a bright blaze of light which seemed to go out at my
eyes with a flash. Then I lost all sense of pain. But after I was cut down, I felt
such intolerable pain from the prickings and shootings as my blood and spirits returned that I wished those who cut me down could have been hanged."*

from PORT ROGER

Page from Strobe's notebook:

The essence of sleight of hand is distraction and misdirection. If someone
can be convinced that he has, through his own perspicacity, divined your hidden purposes, he will not look further.

How much does he know or suspect? He knows that the capture was prearranged. He surmises an alliance between the pirates and the Pembertons,
involving trade in the western hemisphere, the planting of opium in Mexico,
and the cultivation of other crops and products now imported from the Near
and Far East. He suspects, or soon will, that this alliance may extend to political and military revolution, and secession from England and Spain.

What does he think is expected from him? The role of gunsmith and inventor, which is partially true. I must not underestimate him. He has already quite
literally seen through Mr. Thomas. How long before he will see through the
others? *Must be careful of Kelley.* The most necessary servants are always the
most dangerous. He is a cunning and devious little beast.

Noah writes that I am interested in printing his diaries "for some reason."
Does he have any inkling what reason? He must be kept very busy as a gunsmith lest he realize his primary role.

How long will it take him to find out that Captain Jones and Captain
Nordenholz are interchangeable? To grasp for that matter the full significance
of his own name? To see that I am the de Fuentes twins? Finally, to know that
I am also—?

Scarf around his neck   immediately arranged between them   turning to
leer and wink at the armory. I am Captain Strobe, a slim siren. Coat glittering

*Daniel P. Mannix, *The History of Torture* (New York: Dell, 1964).

in the sun   flute from a distant star in their buttocks. Now I was smoke
called Kelley   pale in my mind together with a *Yes*. Sandy hairs, member
erect marching around was cleared. Dancing boys to the music played their
bags   wriggling pale groin   toes twisted. We now have double crew
down the Red Sea area. Story started with an argument   sentences to hang.
The sentence preyed on merchant vessels carrying the cargo beautiful hanged
back to life   women dancing lewdly and ensuring protection against their
bodies once one had been rescued. He claimed to have learned the gallows
smile. Gasping his lips back   surged erect   he ejaculated noose and knot
feet across the floor. Spirits around his neck. Spurting six.

Today we reached Port Roger on the coast of Panama. This was formerly Fort
Pheasant and had been used as a base by English pirates sixty years ago. The
coast here is highly dangerous for the navigation of large vessels, owing to
shallows and reefs. Port Roger is one of the few deepwater harbors. It is, however, so difficult to reach that only a navigator with exact knowledge of the
passage can hope to do so.

The coastline is a distant green smudge on our starboard side. Strobe and
Thomas scan the skyline with telescopes.

"*Guarda costa* ...," the boys mutter uneasily.

Capture by the Spanish means torture or, at best, slavery. If overtaken by a
Spanish ship we will abandon ship in the lifeboats, leaving *The Great White* to
the Spanish. The boarding party will receive a surprise, for I have arranged a
device which will explode the entire cargo of powder as soon as the doors to
the hold are opened.

Now the ship rounds and heads towards land. Strobe, stripped to the waist,
has taken the wheel, his thin body infused with alertness. Two boys are taking
soundings on both sides, and the escort ship is a hundred yards behind us. We
are sailing through a narrow channel in a reef, Mr. Thomas and Kelley calling
out orders as the ship slips like a snake through a strip of blue water. The
coastline is ever clearer, trees slowly appearing and low hills in a shimmer of
heat. An inaudible twang like a loosed bowstring as the ship glides into a deep
blue harbor a few hundred yards from the shore, where waves break on a crescent of sand.

We drop anchor a bare hundred yards from the beach, *The Siren* a like distance behind us. From the harbor the town is difficult to discern, being shel-
tered by a thick growth of bamboo and set among trees and vines. I had the
curious impression of looking at a painting in a gold frame: the two ships riding
at anchor in the still blue harbor, a cool morning breeze, and written on the
bottom of the frame: "Port Roger—April 1, 1702."

Captain Nordenholz Disembarks at Port Roger

There he is standing on a ruined pier left over from the English, in some
uniform of his own devising. He is flanked by Opium Jones, the de Fuentes

twins and Captain Strobe, all looking like a troupe of traveling players a bit
down on their luck but united in determination to play out their assigned
roles. Boys trail behind them, carrying an assortment of bags, cases, and
chests. They walk across the beach and disappear one after another into a
wall of leaves.

I don't know what gave me such an impression of shabbiness about this
procession, since they all must have chests of gold and precious stones, but
for a moment they appeared to my eyes as seedy players with grand roles but
no money to pay the rent. The jewels and the gold are false, the curtains patched
and shredded and torn, the theater long closed. I was smitten by a feeling of
sadness and desolation, as the words of the Immortal Bard came to my mind:

> These our actors,
> As I foretold you, were all spirits, and
> Are melted into air. . . .

We have landed. Captain Strobe meets us on the beach emerging from a picture puzzle, his shirt and pants splotched with green and brown, stirring slightly
in the afternoon breeze. We follow him as he walks towards a seemingly unbroken line of undergrowth. He pushes aside branches to reveal a winding
path through a tangle of bamboo and thorn.

We walk for perhaps a quarter-mile as the path winds upward and ends in
a screen of bamboo. We are quite close before I realize that the bamboo trees
are painted on a green door that swings open like the magic door in a book I
have seen somewhere long ago. We step through into the town of Port Roger.

We are standing in a walled enclosure like a vast garden, with trees and flowers, paths and pools. I can see buildings along the sides of the square, all painted
to blend with the surroundings so that the buildings seem but a reflection of
the trees and vines and flowers stirring in a slight breeze that seems to shake
the walls, the whole scene insubstantial as a mirage.

This first glimpse of Port Roger occurred just as some hashish candy I had
ingested on the boat started to take effect, producing a hiatus in my mind and
the interruption of verbal thought, followed by a sharp jolt as if something
had entered my body. I caught a whiff of perfume and a sound of distant flutes.

CITIES OF THE RED NIGHT

The Cities of the Red Night were six in number: Tamaghis, Ba'dan, Yass-
Waddah, Waghdas, Naufana, and Ghadis. These cities were located in an area
roughly corresponding to the Gobi Desert a hundred thousand years ago. At
that time the desert was dotted with large oases and traversed by a river which
emptied into the Caspian Sea.

The largest of these oases contained a lake ten miles long and five miles
across, on the shores of which the university town of Waghdas was founded.

Pilgrims came from all over the inhabited world to study in the academies of Waghdas, where the arts and sciences reached peaks of attainment that have never been equaled. Much of this ancient knowledge is now lost.

The towns of Ba'dan and Yass-Waddah were opposite each other on the river. Tamaghis, located in a desolate area to the north on a small oasis, could properly be called a desert town. Naufana and Ghadis were situated in mountainous areas to the west and south beyond the perimeter of usual trade routes between the other cities.

In addition to the six cities, there were a number of villages and nomadic tribes. Food was plentiful and for a time the population was completely stable: no one was born unless someone died.

The inhabitants were divided into an elite minority known as the Transmigrants and a majority known as the Receptacles. Within these categories were a number of occupational and specialized strata and the two classes were not in practice separate: Transmigrants acted as Receptacles and Receptacles became Transmigrants.

To show the system in operation: Here is an old Transmigrant on his deathbed. He has selected his future Receptacle parents, who are summoned to the death chamber. The parents then copulate, achieving orgasm just as the old Transmigrant dies so that his spirit enters the womb to be reborn. Every Transmigrant carries with him at all times a list of alternative parents, and in case of accident, violence, or sudden illness, the nearest parents are rushed to the scene. However, there was at first little chance of random or unexpected deaths since the Council of Transmigrants in Waghdas had attained such skill in the art of prophecy that they were able to chart a life from birth to death and determine in most cases the exact time and manner of death.

Many Transmigrants preferred not to wait for the infirmities of age and the ravages of illness, lest their spirit be so weakened as to be overwhelmed and absorbed by the Receptacle child. These hardy Transmigrants, in the full vigor of maturity, after rigorous training in concentration and astral projection, would select two death guides to kill them in front of the copulating parents. The methods of death most commonly employed were hanging and strangulation, the Transmigrant dying in orgasm, which was considered the most reliable method of ensuring a successful transfer. Drugs were also developed, large doses of which occasioned death in erotic convulsions, smaller doses being used to enhance sexual pleasure. And these drugs were often used in conjunction with other forms of death.

In time, death by natural causes became a rare and rather discreditable occurrence as the age for transmigration dropped. The Eternal Youths, a Transmigrant sect, were hanged at the age of eighteen to spare themselves the coarsening experience of middle age and the deterioration of senescence, living their youth again and again.

Two factors undermined the stability of this system. The first was perfection of techniques for artificial insemination. Whereas the traditional practice

called for one death and one rebirth, now hundreds of women could be impregnated from a single sperm collection, and territorially oriented Transmigrants
could populate whole areas with their progeny. There were sullen mutters of
revolt from the Receptacles, especially the women. At this point, another factor totally unforeseen was introduced.

In the thinly populated desert area north of Tamaghis a portentous event
occurred. Some say it was a meteor that fell to earth leaving a crater twenty
miles across. Others say that the crater was caused by what modern physicists
call a black hole.

After this occurrence the whole northern sky lit up red at night, like the
reflection from a vast furnace. Those in the immediate vicinity of the crater
were the first to be affected and various mutations were observed, the com-
monest being altered hair and skin color. Red and yellow hair, and white,
yellow, and red skin appeared for the first time. Slowly the whole area was
similarly affected until the mutants outnumbered the original inhabitants, who
were as all human beings were at the time: black.

The women, led by an albino mutant known as the White Tigress, seized
Yass-Waddah, reducing the male inhabitants to slaves, consorts, and courtiers all under sentence of death that could be carried out at any time at the
caprice of the White Tigress. The Council in Waghdas countered by developing a method of growing babies in excised wombs, the wombs being supplied by vagrant Womb Snatchers. This practice aggravated the differences
between the male and female factions and war with Yass-Waddah seemed
unavoidable.

In Naufana, a method was found to transfer the spirit directly into an adolescent Receptacle, thus averting the awkward and vulnerable period of infancy. This practice required a rigorous period of preparation and training to
achieve a harmonious blending of the two spirits in one body. These Transmigrants, combining the freshness and vitality of youth with the wisdom of
many lifetimes, were expected to form an army of liberation to free Yass-
Waddah. And there were adepts who could die at will without any need of
drugs or executioners and project their spirit into a chosen Receptacle.

I have mentioned hanging, strangulation, and orgasm drugs as the com-
monest means of effecting the transfer. However, many other forms of death
were employed. The Fire Boys were burned to death in the presence of the
Receptacles, only the genitals being insulated, so that the practitioner could
achieve orgasm in the moment of death. There is an interesting account by a
Fire Boy who recalled his experience after transmigrating in this manner:

"As the flames closed round my body, I inhaled deeply, drawing fire into
my lungs, and screamed out flames as the most horrible pain turned to the
most exquisite pleasure and I was ejaculating in an adolescent Receptacle who
was being sodomized by another."

Others were stabbed, decapitated, disemboweled, shot with arrows, or killed
by a blow on the head. Some threw themselves from cliffs, landing in front of
the copulating Receptacles.

The scientists at Waghdas were developing a machine that could directly transfer the electromagnetic field of one body to another. In Ghadis there were adepts who were able to leave their bodies before death and occupy a series of hosts. How far this research may have gone will never be known. It was a time of great disorder and chaos.

The effects of the Red Night on Receptacles and Transmigrants proved to be incalculable and many strange mutants arose as a series of plagues devastated the cities. It is this period of war and pestilence that is covered by the books. The Council had set out to produce a race of supermen for the exploration of space. They produced instead races of ravening idiot vampires.

Finally, the cities were abandoned and the survivors fled in all directions, carrying the plagues with them. Some of these migrants crossed the Bering Strait into the New World, taking the books with them. They settled in the area later occupied by the Mayans and the books eventually fell into the hands of the Mayan priests.

The alert student of this noble experiment will perceive that death was regarded as equivalent not to birth but to conception and go on to infer that conception is the basic trauma. In the moment of death, the dying man's whole life may flash in front of his eyes back to conception. In the moment of conception, his future life flashes forward to his future death. *To reexperience conception is fatal.*

This was the basic error of the Transmigrants: you do not get beyond death and conception by reëxperience any more than you get beyond heroin by ingesting larger and larger doses. The Transmigrants were quite literally addicted to death and they needed more and more death to kill the pain of conception. They were buying parasitic life with a promissory death note to be paid at a prearranged time. The Transmigrants then imposed these terms on the host child to ensure his future transmigration. There was a basic conflict of interest between host child and Transmigrant. So the Transmigrants reduced the Receptacle class to a condition of virtual idiocy. Otherwise they would have reneged on a bargain from which they stood to gain nothing but death. The books are flagrant falsifications. And some of these basic lies are still current.

"Nothing is true. Everything is permitted." The last words of Hassan i Sabbah, Old Man of the Mountain.

"Tamaghis . . . Ba'dan . . . Yass-Waddah . . . Waghdas . . . Naufana . . . Ghadis."

It is said that an initiate who wishes to know the answer to any question need only repeat these words as he falls asleep and the answer will come in a dream.

Tamaghis: This is the open city of contending partisans where advantage shifts from moment to moment in a desperate biological war. Here everything is as true as you think it is and everything you can get away with is permitted.

Ba'dan: This city is given over to competitive games and commerce. Ba'dan closely resembles present-day America with a precarious moneyed elite, a large disaffected middle class and an equally large segment of criminals and out-laws. Unstable, explosive, and swept by whirlwind riots. Everything is true and everything is permitted.

Yass-Waddah: This city is the female stronghold where the Countess de Gulpa, the Countess de Vile, and the Council of the Selected plot a final sub-jugation of the other cities. Every shade of sexual transition is represented: boys with girls' heads, girls with boys' heads. Here everything is true and nothing is permitted except to the permitters.

Waghdas: This is the university city, the center of learning where all ques-tions are answered in terms of what can be expressed and understood. Com-plete permission derives from complete understanding.

Naufana and Ghadis are the cities of illusion where nothing is true and *there-fore* everything is permitted.

The traveler must start in Tamaghis and make his way through the other cities in the order named. This pilgrimage may take many lifetimes.

WE ARE HERE BECAUSE OF YOU

Red Night in Tamaghis. The boys dance around a fire, throwing in screaming Sirens. The boys trill, wave nooses, and stick their tongues out.

This was but a prelude to the Ba'dan riots and the attack on Yass-Waddah. The boys change costumes, rushing from stage to stage.

The Iguana twins dance out of an Angkor Wat–Uxmal–Tenochtitlán set. The "female" twin peels off his cunt suit and they replicate a column of Vietcong.

The Countess, with a luminous-dial alarm clock ticking in her stomach and crocodile mask, stalks Audrey with her courtiers and Green Guards. Police Boy shoots a Green Guard. Clinch Todd as Death with a scythe decapitates the Goddess Bast.

Jon Alistair Peterson, in a pink shirt with sleeve garters, stands on a plat-form draped with the Star-Spangled Banner and the Union Jack. Standing on the platform with him is Nimun in an ankle-length cloak made from the skin of electric eels.

The Board enters and take their place in a section for parents and faculty.

Peterson speaks: "Ladies and gentlemen, this character is the only survivor of a very ancient race with very strange powers. Now some of you may be taken aback by this character . . ."

Nimun drops off his robe and stands naked. An ammoniacal fishy odor reeks off his body—smell of some artifact for a forgotten function or a function not yet possible. His body is a terra-cotta red color with black freckles like holes in the flesh.

"And I may tell you in strictest confidence that he and he alone is respon-sible for the Red Night . . ."

Jon Peterson gets younger and turns into the Piper Boy. He draws a flute from a goatskin sheath at his belt and starts to play. Nimun does a shuffling sinuous dance singing in a harsh fish language that tears the throat like sandpaper.

With a cry that seems to implode into his lungs, he throws himself backward onto a hassock, legs in the air, seizing his ankles with both hands. His exposed rectum is jet-black surrounded by erectile red hairs. The hole begins to spin with a smell of ozone and hot iron. And his body is spinning like a top, faster and faster, floating in the air above the cushion, transparent and fading, as the red sky flares behind him.

A courtier feels the perfume draining off him . . .

"Itza . . ."

A Board member opens his mouth. . . . *"Itza. . . ."* His false teeth fly out. Wigs, clothes, chairs, props, are all draining into the spinning black disk. "ITZA BLACK HOLE!!"

Naked bodies are sucked inexorably forward, writhing screaming like souls pulled into Hell. The lights go out and then the red sky . . .

Lights come on to show the ruins of Ba'dan. Children play in the Casbah tunnels, posing for photos taken by German tourists with rucksacks. The old city is deserted.

A few miles upriver there is a small fishing and hunting village. Here, pilgrims can rest and outfit themselves for the journey that lies ahead.

But what of Yass-Waddah? Not a stone remains of the ancient citadel. The narrator shoves his mike at the natives who lounge in front of rundown sheds and fish from ruined piers. They shake their heads.

"Ask Old Man Brink. He'll know if anybody does."

Old Man Brink is mending a fish trap. Is it Waring or Noah Blake?

"Yass-Waddah?"

He says that many years ago, a god dreamed Yass-Waddah. The old man puts his palms together and rests his head on his hands, closing his eyes. He opens his eyes and turns his hands out. "But the dream did not please the god. So when he woke up—Yass-Waddah was gone."

A painting on screen. Sign pointing: WAGHDAS–NAUFANA–GHADIS. Road winding into the distance. Over the hills and far away . . .

Audrey sits at a typewriter in his attic room, his back to the audience. In a bookcase to his left, we see *The Book of Knowledge, Coming of Age in Samoa, The Green Hat, The Plastic Age, All the Sad Young Men, Bar Twenty Days, Amazing Stories, Weird Tales, Adventure Stories* and a stack of *Little Blue Books.* In front of him is the etching depicting Captain Strobe on the gallows. Audrey glances up at the picture and types:

"The Rescue."

An explosion rumbles through the warehouse. Walls and roof shake and fall on Audrey and the audience. As the warehouse collapses, it turns to dust.

The entire cast is standing in a desert landscape looking at the sunset spread across the western sky like a vast painting: the red walls of Tamaghis, the Ba'dan riots, the smoldering ruins of Yass-Waddah and Manhattan, Waghdas glimmers in the distance.

The scenes shift and change: tropical seas and green islands, a burning galleon sinks into a grey-blue sea of clouds, rivers, jungles, villages, Greek temples and there are the white frame houses of Harbor Point above the blue lake.

Port Roger shaking in the wind, fireworks displays against a luminous green sky, expanses of snow, swamps, and deserts where vast red mesas tower into the sky, fragile aircraft over burning cities, flaming arrows, dimming to mauves and greys and finally—in a last burst of light—the enigmatic face of Waring as his eyes light up in a blue flash. He bows three times and disappears into the gathering dusk.

RETURN TO PORT ROGER

This must be it. Warped planks in a tangle of trees and vines. The pool of the Palace is covered with algae. A snake slithers into the green water. Weeds grow through the rusty shell of a bucket in the *haman*. The stairs leading to the upper porch have fallen. Nothing here but the smell of empty years. How many years? I can't be sure.

I am carrying a teakwood box with a leather handle. The box is locked. I have the key but I will not open the box here. I take the path to Dink's house. Sometimes paths last longer than roads.

There it is on the beach, just as I remember it. Sand has covered the steps and drifted across the floor. Smell of nothing and nobody there. I sit down on the sand-covered steps and look out to the harbor at the ship that brought me here and that will take me away. I take out my key and open the box and leaf through the yellow pages. The last entry is from many years ago.

We were in Panama waiting for the Spanish. I am back in the fort watching the advancing soldiers through a telescope, closer and closer to death.

"Go back!" I am screaming without a throat, without a tongue—*"Get in your galleons and go back to Spain!"*

Hearing the final sonorous knell of Spain as church bells silently implode into Sisters of Mary, Communions, Confessions . . .

"Paco... Joselito... Enrique."

Father Kelley is giving them absolution. There is pain in his voice. It's too easy. Then our shells and mortars rip through them like a great iron fist. A few still take cover and return fire.

Paco catches a bullet in the chest. Sad shrinking face. He pulls my head down as the grey lips whisper—"I want the priest."

* * *

I didn't want to write about this or what followed. Guayaquil, Lima, Santiago and all the others I didn't see. The easiest victories are the most costly in the end.

I have blown a hole in time with a firecracker. Let others step through. Into what bigger and bigger firecrackers? Better weapons lead to better and better weapons, until the earth is a grenade with the fuse burning.

I remember a dream of my childhood. I am in a beautiful garden. As I reach out to touch the flowers they wither under my hands. A nightmare feeling of foreboding and desolation comes over me as a great mushroom-shaped cloud darkens the earth. A few may get through the gate in time. Like Spain, I am bound to the past.

from
the place of dead roads
(SELECTIONS)

SHOOT-OUT IN BOULDER

September 17, 1899. What appeared to be an Old-Western shoot-out took place yesterday afternoon at the Boulder Cemetery. The protagonists have been identified as William Seward Hall, sixty-five, a real-estate speculator with holdings in Colorado and New Mexico, and Mike Chase, in his fifties, about whom nothing was known.

Hall resided in New York City, and wrote western stories under the pen name of "Kim Carsons." "He was apparently here on a business trip," a police source stated.

At first glance it appeared that Chase and Hall had killed each other in a shoot-out, but neither gun had been fired, and both men were killed by single rifle shots fired from a distance. Chase was shot from in front through the chest. Hall was shot in the back. Nobody heard the shots, and police believe the rifleman may have employed a silencer.

A hotel key was found in Hall's pocket, and police searched his room at the Overlook Hotel. They found clothing, a .38 revolver, and a book entitled *Quién Es?* by Kim Carsons. Certain passages had been underlined.

Police investigating this bizarre occurrence have as yet no clue to the possible motives of the men. "Looks like an old grudge of some sort," Police Chief Martin Winters said. When asked whether there was any reason Chase and Hall should want to kill each other, he replied, "Not that I know of, but we are continuing the investigation."

The Sunday paper played up the story, with pictures of the deceased and the cemetery, and diagrams showing the location of the bodies and the probable spot from which the shots had been fired. When asked about the make and caliber of the death weapon, the Medical Examiner stated: "Definitely a rifle. Size of the exit holes is consistent with a .45–70 dumdum bullet, but the projectiles have not been recovered."

The article quoted the underlined passages from Hall's book *Quién Es?*

* * *

Papers in an old attic . . . an old yellow press clipping from the *Manhattan Comet,* April 3, 1894:

> Three members of the Carsons gang were killed today when they at-
> tempted to hold up the Manhattan City Bank. A posse, dispatched in
> pursuit of the survivors, ran into an ambush and suffered several casual-
> ties. . . . Mike Chase, a U.S. marshal, stated that the ambush was not
> carried out by the Carsons gang but by a band of Confederate renegades
> armed with mortars and grenades. . . .

This poem was wroted by Kim Carsons after a shoot-out on Bleecker Street,
October 23, 1920. Liver Wurst Joe and Cherry Nose Gio, Mafia hit men, with
Frank the Lip as driver, opened fire on Kim Carsons, Boy Jones, Mars Cleaver,
known as Marbles, and Guy Graywood, described as an attorney. In the ensuing
exchange of shots Liver Wurst Joe, Cherry Nose Gio, and Frank the Lip was
all kilted. Only damage sustained by the Carsons group was to Boy's vest when
he took refuge behind a fire hydrant.

"My vest is ruinted," he moaned. "And it was dog shit done it. There should
be a law."

Owing to certain "offensive passages" written in the French language the poem
could not be quoted, but an enterprising assistant editor had copies made with
translations of the offensive passages and sold them to collectors and curiosity
seekers for five dollars a copy.

Stranger Who Was Passing

un grand principe de violence dictait à nos moeurs
(a great principle of violence dictated our fashions)
Surely a song for men like a great wind
Shaking an iron tree
Dead leaves in the winter pissoir
J'aime ces types vicieux
Qu'ici montrent la bite. . . .
(I like the vicious types
who show the cock here. . . .)
Simon, aimes-tu le bruit des pas
Sur les feuilles mortes?
(Simon, do you like the sound of steps
on dead leaves?)
The smell of war and death?
Powder smoke back across the mouth blown
Powder smoke and brown hair?
Death comes with the speed of a million winds
The sheltering sky is thin as paper here

That afternoon when I watched
The torn sky bend with the wind
I can see it start to tilt
And shred and tatter
Caught in New York
Beneath the animals of the Village
The Piper pulled down the sky.
                    LET IT COME DOWN.

Appointment at the cemetery . . . Boulder, Colorado . . .

September 17, 1899

Mike swung onto the path at the northeast corner, wary and watchful. He was carrying a Webley-Fosbery .45 semi-automatic revolver, the action adjusted with rubber grips by an expert gunsmith to absorb recoil and prevent slipping. His backup men were about ten yards away, a little behind him across the street.

Kim stepped out of the cemetery onto the path. "Hello, Mike." His voice carried clear and cool on the wind, sugary and knowing and evil. Kim always maneuvered to approach downwind. He was wearing a russet tweed jacket with change pockets, canvas puttees, jodhpurs in deep red.

At sight of him Mike experienced an uneasy *déjà vu* and glanced sideways for his backup.

One glance was enough. They were all wearing jackets the color of autumn leaves, and puttees. They had opened a wicker shoulder basket. They were eating sandwiches and filling tin cups with cold beer, their rifles propped against a tree remote and timeless as a painting.

Déjeuner des chasseurs.

Mike sees he has been set up. He will have to shoot it out. He feels a flash of resentment and outrage.

God damn it! It's not fair!

Why should his life be put in jeopardy by this horrible little nance? Mike had a well-disciplined mind. He put these protests aside and took a deep breath, drawing in power.

Kim is about fifteen yards south walking slowly toward him. Fresh southerly winds rustle the leaves ahead of him as he walks "on a whispering south wind" . . . leaves crackle under his boots . . . Michael, *aimé tu le bruit des pas sur les feuilles mortes. . .* ? Twelve yards, ten . . . Kim walks with his hands swinging loose at his sides, the fingers of his right hand brushing the gun butt obscenely, his face alert, detached, unreadable. . . . Eight yards. . . . Suddenly Kim flicks his hand up without drawing as he points at Mike with his index finger.

"BANG! YOU'RE *DEAD*."

He throws the last word like a stone. He knows that Mike will see a gun in the empty hand and this will crowd his draw.

(With a phantom gun in an empty hand he has bluffed Mike into violating a basic rule of gunfighting: TYT. Take *Your* Time. Every gunfighter has *his* time. The time it takes him to draw aim fire and *hit*. If he tries to beat his time the result is almost invariably a miss . . .)

"Snatch and grab," Kim chants.

Yes, Mike was drawing too fast, much too fast.

Kim's hand snaps down flexible and sinuous as a whip and up with his gun extended in both hands at eye level.

"Jerk and miss."

He felt Mike's bullet whistle past his left shoulder.

Trying for a heart shot . . .

Both eyes open, Kim sights for a fraction of a second, just so long and long enough: the difference between a miss and a hit. Kim's bullet hits Mike just above the heart with a liquid SPLAT as the mercury explodes inside, blowing the aorta to shreds.

Mike freezes into a still, gun extended, powder smoke blowing back across his face. He begins to weave in slow circles. He gags and spits blood. His gun arm starts to sag.

Kim slowly lowers his gun in both hands, face impassive, eyes watchful.

Mike's eyes are glazed, unbelieving, stubborn, still trying to get the gun up for the second shot. But the gun is heavy, too heavy to lift, pulling him down.

Slowly Kim lowers his gun into the holster.

Mike crumples sideways and falls.

Kim looks up at the trees, watching a squirrel, a remote antique gaiety suffuses his face, molding his lips into the ambiguous marble smile of a Greek youth.

Definitely an *archaic* from Skyros with that special Skyros smile.

Who is the Greek youth smiling at? He is smiling at his own archaic smile.

For this is the smile that happens when the smiler becomes the smile.

The wind is rising. Kim watches a dead leaf spiral up into the sky.

The Egyptian glyph that signifies: To stand up in evidence. An ejaculating phallus, a mouth, a man with his fingers in his mouth.

Kim waves to his three witnesses. One waves back with a drumstick in his hand.

Hiatus of painted calm . . .

Pâté, bread, wine, fruit spread out on the grass, gun propped against a tombstone, a full moon in the China-blue evening sky. One of the hunters strums a mandolin inlaid with mother-of-pearl as they sing:

"It's only a paper moon . . ."

Kim lifts his gun and shoots a hole in the moon, a black hole with fuzz around it like powder burns.

A wind ripples the grass, stirs uneasily through branches.

"Flying over a muslin tree."

Kim's second shot takes out a grove of trees at the end of the cemetery.

The wind is rising, ripping blurs and flashes of russet orange red from the trees, whistling through tombstones.

All the spurious old father figures rush on stage.

"STOP, MY SON!"

"No son of yours, you worthless old farts."

Kim lifts his gun.

"YOU'RE DESTROYING THE UNIVERSE!"

"What universe?"

Kim shoots a hole in the sky. Blackness pours out and darkens the earth. In the last rays of a painted sun, a Johnson holds up a barbed-wire fence for others to slip through. The fence has snagged the skyline . . . a great black rent. Screaming crowds point to the torn sky.

"OFF THE TRACK! OFF THE TRACK!"

"FIX IT!" the Director bellows. . . .

"What with, a Band-Aid and chewing gum? Rip in the Master Film. . . . Fix it yourself, Boss Man."

"ABANDON SHIP, GOD DAMN IT. . . . EVERY MAN FOR HIMSELF!"

For three days Kim had camped on the mesa top, sweeping the valley with his binoculars. A cloud of dust headed south told him they figured him to ride in that direction for Mexico. He had headed north instead, into a land of sandstone formations, carved by wind and sand—a camel, a tortoise, Cambodian temples—and everywhere caves pocked into the red rock like bubbles in boiling oatmeal. Some of the caves had been lived in at one time or another: rusty tin cans, pottery shards, cartridge cases. Kim found an arrowhead six inches long, chipped from obsidian, and a smaller arrowhead of rose-colored flint.

On top of the mesa were crumbled mounds of earth that had once been houses. Slabs of stone had been crisscrossed to form an altar. *Homo sapiens* was here.

Dusk was falling and blue shadows gathered in the Sangre de Cristo Mountains to the east. Sangre de Cristo! Blood of Christ! Rivers of blood! Mountains of blood! Does Christ never get tired of bleeding? To the west the sun sets behind thunderclouds over the Jemez Mountains, and Jiménez straddles the mountains with his boots of rock and trees, a vast *charro* rising into the sky, his head a crystal skull of clouds as his guns spit from darkening battlements and thunder rattles over the valley. The evening star shines clear and green . . . "Fair as a star, when only one / Is shining in the sky." That's Wordsworth, Kim remembers. It is raining in the Jemez Mountains.

"It is raining, Anita Huffington." Last words of General Grant, spoken to his nurse, circuits in his brain flickering out like lightning in grey clouds.

Kim leaned back against stone still warm from the sun. A cool wind touched his face with the smell of rain.

Pottery shards . . . arrowheads . . . a crib . . . a rattle . . . a blue spoon . . . a slingshot, the rubber rotted through . . . rusting fishhooks . . . tools . . . you can see there was a cabin here once . . . a hypodermic syringe glints in the sun . . . the needle has rusted into the glass, forming little sparks of brown mica . . . abandoned artifacts . . .

He holds the rose flint arrowhead in his hand. Here is the arrowhead, lovingly fashioned for a purpose. Campfires flicker on Indian faces eating the luscious dark meat of the passenger pigeon. He fondles the obsidian arrowhead, so fragile . . . did they break every time they were used, like bee stings, he wonders?

(Bison steaks roasting on a spit.)

Somebody made this arrowhead. It had a creator long ago. This arrowhead is the only proof of his existence. Living things can also be seen as artifacts, designed for a purpose. So perhaps the human artifact had a creator. Perhaps a stranded space traveler needed the human vessel to continue his journey, and he made it for that purpose? He died before he could use it? He found another escape route? This artifact, shaped to fill a forgotten need, now has no more meaning or purpose than this arrowhead without the arrow and the bow, the arm and the eye. Or perhaps the human artifact was the creator's last card, played in an old game many light-years ago. Chill of empty space.

Kim gathers wood for a fire. The stars are coming out. There's the Big Dipper. His father points to Betelgeuse in the night sky over Saint Louis . . . smell of flowers in the garden. His father's grey face on a pillow.

Helpless pieces in the game he plays
On this checkerboard of nights and days.

He picks up the obsidian arrowhead, arrow and bow of empty space. You can't see them anymore without the arm and the eye . . . the chill . . . so fragile . . . shivers and gathers wood. Can't see them anymore. Slave Gods in the firmament. He remembers his father's last words:

"Stay out of churches, son. All they got a key to is the shit house. And swear to me you will never wear a lawman's badge."

Hither and thither moves, and checks, and slays,
And one by one back in the Closet lays.

Playthings in an old game, the little toy soldiers are covered with rust, shaped to fill a forgotten empty space.

Rusty tin cans . . . pottery shards . . . cartridge cases . . . arrowheads . . . a hypodermic syringe glints in the sun.

Kim has never doubted the possibility of an afterlife or the existence of gods. In fact he intends to become a god, to shoot his way to immortality, to invent his way, to write his way. He has a number of patents: the Carsons spring knife, an extension of the spring blackjack principle; a cartridge in which the case becomes the projectile; an air gun in which air is compressed by a small powder charge; a magnetic gun in which propulsion is effected by compressing a reversed magnetic field. "Whenever you use this bow I will be there," the Zen archery master tells his students. And he means *there* quite literally. He lives in his students and thus achieves a measure of immortality. And the immortality of a writer is to be taken literally. Whenever anyone reads his words the writer is there. He lives in his readers. So every time someone neatly guts his opponent with my spring knife or slices off two heads with one swipe of my spring sword I am there to drink the blood and smell the fresh entrails as they slop out with a divine squishy sound. I am there when the case bullet thuds home—right in the stomach . . . what a lovely grunt! And my saga will shine in the eyes of adolescents squinting through gunsmoke.

Kapow! Kapow! Kapow!

Kim considers that immortality is the only goal worth striving for. He knows that it isn't something you just automatically get for believing some nonsense or other like Christianity or Islam. It is something you have to work and fight for, like everything else in this life or another.

The most arbitrary, precarious, and bureaucratic immortality blueprint was drafted by the ancient Egyptians. First you had to get yourself mummified, and that was very expensive, making immortality a monopoly of the truly rich. Then your continued immortality in the Western Lands was entirely dependent on the continued existence of your mummy. That is why they had their mummies guarded by demons and hid good.

Here is plain G. I. Horus. . . . He's got enough *baraka* to survive his first physical death. He won't get far. He's got no mummy, he's got no names, he's got nothing. What happens to a bum like that, a nameless, mummyless asshole? Why, demons will swarm all over him at the first checkpoint. He will be dismembered and thrown into a flaming pit, where his soul will be utterly consumed and destroyed forever. While others, with sound mummies and the right names to drop in the right places, sail through to the Western Lands.

There are of course those who just barely squeeze through. Their mummies are not in a good sound condition. These second-class souls are relegated to third-rate transient hotels just beyond the last checkpoint, where they can smell the charnel-house disposal ovens from their skimpy balconies.

"You see that sign?" the bartender snarls:

MAGGOTTY MUMMIES WILL NOT BE SERVED HERE

"Might as well face facts . . . my mummy is going downhill. Cheap job to begin with . . . gawd, maggots is crawling all over it . . . the way that demon guard sniffed at me this morning. . . ." *Transient* hotels . . .

And here you are in your luxury condo, deep in the Western Lands . . . you got no security. Some disgruntled former employee sneaks into your tomb and throws acid on your mummy. Or sloshes gasoline all over it and burns the shit out of it. "OH . . . someone is fucking with my mummy . . ."

Mummies are sitting ducks. No matter who you are, what can happen to your mummy is a pharaoh's nightmare: the dreaded mummy bashers and grave robbers, scavengers, floods, volcanoes, earthquakes. Perhaps a mummy's best friend is an Egyptologist: sealed in a glass case, kept at a constant temperature . . . but your mummy isn't even safe in a museum. *Air-raid sirens, it's the Blitz!*

"For Ra's sake, get us into the vaults," scream the mummies, without a throat, without a tongue.

Anybody buy in on a deal like that should have his mummy examined.

Kim got off the stage at Cottonwood Junction. The stage was going west and he wanted to head north. Sometimes he decided which way to go by the signs, or his legs would pull him in a certain direction. Or maybe he'd hear about some country he wanted to see. Or he might just be avoiding towns where folks was known to be religious. That morning before he took the stage he had consulted the Oracle, which was a sort of Ouija board that had belonged to his mother. She'd been into table-tapping and crystal balls and had her spirit guides. One that Kim liked especially was an Indian boy called Little Rivers.

Once when she was out Kim put on one of her dresses and made up his face like a whore and called Little Rivers and next thing the dress was torn off him oh he did it of course but the hands weren't his and then he was squirming and moaning while Little Rivers fucked him with his legs up and he blacked out in a flash of silver light.

The Oracle told him that Little Rivers was near. He should keep his eyes open and he would know what to do, so when he saw a sign pointing north— CLEAR CREEK 20 MILES—he decided to leave the stage, standing there in the street with his "alligator."

The town was built in a grove of cottonwoods at a river junction. He could hear running water and the rustle of leaves in the afternoon wind. He passed a cart with a strawberry roan. On the side: TOM D. DARK, TRAVELING PHOTOGRA-PHER. He went into a saloon, dropped his "alligator" on the floor and ordered a beer, noting a youth sitting at the end of the bar. He took a long swallow, looking out into the shaded street. The boy was at his elbow. He hadn't heard him move.

"You're Kim Carsons, aren't you?"

The youth was about twenty, tall and lean, with red hair, a thin face with a few pimples growing in the smooth red flesh, his eyes grey-blue with dark shadows.

"Yes, I'm Carsons."

"I'm Tom Dark. That's my cart outside."

They shook hands. As their hands parted Tom stroked Kim's palm with one finger lightly. Kim felt the blood rush to his crotch.

"Going north?"

"Yes."

"Like to ride with me in the wagon?"

"Sure."

A Mexican kid is sitting in the driver's seat of Tom's cart.

"Kim Carsons, this is my assistant. Pecos Bridge Juanito."

The boy has a knowing smile.

The road winds along a stream, trees overhead . . . bits of quartz glitter in the road, which isn't used often, you can tell by the weeds. Looks like the road out of Saint Albans. They cross an old stone bridge.

"This is Pecos Bridge. . . . We'll stop here . . . be dark in another hour."

Juanito guides the wagon off the road into a clearing by the stream, which is slow and deep at this point. He unhitches the horse and starts pulling tripods and cameras out of the wagon.

"My specialty is erotics," Tom explains, "rich collectors. Paris . . . New York . . . London. I've been looking for you on commission. Got a client wants sex pictures of a real gunman."

"I hope you don't mean the naked-except-for-cowboy-boots-gun-belt-and-sombrero sort of thing."

"Look, I'm an artist."

"And I'm a *shootist,* not a gunman. The gun doesn't own me. I own the gun."

"Well, are you interested?"

Kim puts a finger on the cleft below his nose, runs the finger down his body and under the crotch to the perineum. He holds out his open hand.

"Right down the middle."

"Fair enough."

Kim brings a bottle of sour-mash bourbon from his "alligator" and they toast their fucking future.

"They hanged a Mexican kid from that branch." Tom points to a cottonwood branch a few feet above the wagon. "You can still see the rope marks. . . . Yep hanged him offen the cayoose he went and stealed but he hadn't stoled that horse. He'd boughten it. Only the posse didn't find that out until after they'd hanged the kid.

"You may have read about it . . . made quite a stir . . . federal antilynching bill in Congress and the Abolitionists took some northern states. . . . All the papers wanted a picture of the hanging and I gave them one . . . fake, of course. . . . How did I get away with it? Well there isn't any limit to what you can get away with in this business. Faked pictures are more convincing than real pictures because you can set them up to look real. Understand this: All pictures are faked. As soon as you have the concept of a picture there is no limit to falsification. Now here's a picture in the paper shows a flood in China. So how do you know it's a picture of a flood in China? How do you know he didn't take it in his bathtub? How do you even know there was a flood in China?

Because you read it in the papers. So it has to be true, if not, other reporters, other photographers . . . sure you gotta cover yourself or cut other reporters and photographers in so they get together on the story. . . .

"Two years ago I was doing portrait photos in Saint Louis and I ran into this old lady I knew from England who is a very rich Abolitionist on a lecture tour. And the idea comes to me. I tell her what is needed to put some teeth into the Abolition movement is an *incident* and she puts up some front money and most of that goes to pay off the sheriff who would investigate the hanging and the doctor who would sign the death certificate, which turned out to be the birth certificate of Pecos Bridge Juanito, a fabrication out of whole paper. And I had the whole scoop . . . picture of the boy . . . interviews with his mother, who died years before he was born . . . even pictures of the posses repenting and getting born again in Jesus. . . . Not that some reporters weren't suspicious. . . . They can *smell* a fake story but they couldn't prove anything. We even had a body in the coffin just in case; young Mexican died of scarlet fever . . . the picture was the easiest part. . . . Lots of ways to fake a hanging picture or any picture, for that matter. . . . Easiest is you don't show the feet and they are standing on something. . . . I did my shot with an elastic rope they use in carny hanging acts." He points to the horse. . . . "There's the only actor didn't get paid. . . . I call him Centaur. How about a dip and a swill?"

Sex scenes in the diary were in coded symbols like Japanese forget-me-nots flowering in the medium of memory: June 3, 1883 . . . Met T at Cottonwood Junction . . . (sexual attraction and reason to believe reciprocated) . . . & (naked) . . . (erection) . . . (sodomy) . . . (ejaculation).

Sunset through black clouds . . . red glow on naked bodies. Kim carefully wraps his revolver in a towel and places it under some weeds at the water's edge. He puts his foot in the water and gasps. At this moment Tom streaks by him, floating above the ground in a series of still pictures, the muscles of his thigh and buttock outlined like an anatomical drawing as he runs straight into the water, silver drops fanning out from his legs.

Kim follows, holding his breath, then swimming rapidly up and down. He treads water, breathing in gasps as the sky darkens and the water stretches black and sinister as if some monster might rise from its depths. . . . In knee-deep water, soaping themselves and looking at each other serene as dogs, their genitals crinkled from the icy water . . . drying themselves on a sandbank, wiping the sand from his feet . . . following Tom's lean red buttocks back to the wagon. He stations Kim at the end of the wagon. . . . "Stand right there," facing the setting sun. Tom pulls a black cloth out of the air with a flourish, bowing to an audience. He stands behind the camera with the black cloth over his head. . . . "Look at the camera . . . hands at your sides."

Kim could feel the phantom touch of the lens on his body, light as a breath of wind. Tom is standing naked behind the camera.

"I want to bottle you, mate," Tom says. Kim has never heard this expression but he immediately understands it. And he glimpses a hidden meaning, a forgotten language, sniggering half-heard words of tenderness and doom from lips spotted with decay that send the blood racing to his crotch and singing in his ears as his penis stretches, sways, and stiffens and naked lust surfaces in his face from the dark depths of human origins.

Tom is getting hard too. The shaft is pink and smooth, no veins protruding. Now fully erect, the tip almost touches the delineated muscles of his lean red-brown stomach. At the crown of his cock, on top, is an indentation, as if the creator had left his thumbprint there in damp clay. Held in a film medium, like soft glass, they are both motionless except for the throbbing of tumescent flesh . . .

"Hold it!" . . . CLICK . . . For six seconds the sun seems to stand still in the sky.

Look at this picture from Tom's collection: the Indians and the one white are all related, by location: the end of the line. Like the last Tasmanians, the Patagonians, the hairy Ainu, the passenger pigeon, they cast no shadow, because there will never be any more. This picture is the end. The mold is broken.

This final desolate knowledge impelled them to place phalluses, crudely carved from wood and painted with ocher, on male graves. The markers are scattered and broken. Only the picture remains.

Notice the Indian fourth from the left in the back row: a look of sheer panic. For he recognizes the photographer: Tom Dark, who takes the last picture and files it "Secret—Classified." Only he knows exactly where it is in relation to all the other files, since location is everything.

The picture itself is a cryptic glyph, an artifact out of context, fashioned for a forgotten purpose or a purpose blocked from future realization. And yet spelling out . . .

Five passenger pigeons in a tree . . . CLICK: "The Last Passenger Pigeons."

KAPOW! The birds drop and flutter to the ground, feathers drifting in dawn wind.

The Hunter looks about uneasily as he shoves the birds into his bag. It's been a bad day. He turns to face the camera.

CLICK: "The Last Passenger-Pigeon Hunter."

Spelling out . . . August 6, 1945: Hiroshima. Oppenheimer on screen: "We have become Death, Destroyer of Worlds."

"Doctor Oppenheimer!"

CLICK.

Hall reflected that he was himself the end of the Hall line, at least by the old-fashioned method of reproduction.

"Waahhhh!"

CLICK.
"Awwwwwwk!!!"
CLICK.

Kim recruits a band of flamboyant and picturesque outlaws, called the Wild
Fruits. There is the Crying Gun, who breaks into tears at the sight of his
opponent.
"What's the matter, somebody take your lollipop?"
"Oh *señor,* I am sorry for you . . ."
And the Priest, who goes into a gunfight giving his adversaries the last rites.
And the Blind Gun, who zeroes in with bat squeaks. And the famous Shittin'
Sheriff, turned outlaw. At the sight of his opponent he turns green with fear
and sometimes loses control of his bowels. Well, there's an old adage in show
biz: the worse the stage fright, the better the performance.
Kim trains his men to identify themselves with death. He takes some rookie
guns out to a dead horse rotting in the sun, eviscerated by vultures. Kim points
to the horse, steaming there in the noonday heat.
"All right, *roll* in it."
"WHAT?"
"Roll in it like dogs of war. Get the stink of death into your chaps and your
boots and your guns and your hair."
Most of us puked at first, but we got used to it, and vultures followed us
around hopefully.
We always ride into town with the wind behind us, a wheeling cloud of
vultures overhead, beaks snapping. The townspeople gag and retch:
"My God, what's that stink?"
"It's the stink of death, citizens."

Kim had now gone underground and in any case the days of the gunfighter
were over. So far as the world knew, he was just a forgotten chapter in
western history. He was d-e-a-d. So who would move against him, or even
know about the Alamuts he was establishing throughout America and northern Mexico? He had in fact taken pains to remain anonymous and dispatched his henchmen to remove records of the Fort Johnson Incident from
libraries, newspaper morgues and even from private collections of old western lore. . . . So who now would know where he was and reveal themselves by moves against him? He decided to wait and see. The first settlement,
a resort hotel at Clear Creek, demonstrated that they did know and were
already dispatching their agents to intercept the project. It's rather like
bullfighting, he reflected. If the bull can get a *querencia* where he feels
at home, then the bullfighter has to go and get him on his own ground,
so the alert bull sticker will do anything to keep the bull from finding a
querencia. In fact some unethical practitioners have small boys posted with
slingshots . . .

Well things start to go wrong. Right away there are delays in shipments of material. These were traced to a warehouse in Saint Louis and a certain shipping clerk who was later found to be suffering from a form of *petit mal* with spells of amnesia. A small boy brought charges of molestation against the foreman of construction. When the boy became violently insane the charges were dropped, but not before a drummer had attempted to incite the townspeople to form a lynch mob.

But an old farmer who was one of our own said, "You live hereabouts, Mister? Wouldn't say so from your accent . . ."

"Well I live north of here . . ."

"You a country boy?"

"Well I was . . . that is . . ."

"From Chicago, ain't you?"

A murmur from the crowd. The drummer is losing his audience.

"We have children in Chicago too . . ."

"Well whyn't you stay up there and protect *your* children 'stead of selling your lousy war-surplus hog fencing down here?"

Kim now realizes that *they* can take over bodies and minds and use them for their purposes. So why do they always take over stupid, bigoted people or people who are retarded or psychotic? Obviously they are looking for dupes and slaves, not for intelligent allies. In fact their precise intention is to destroy human intelligence, to blunt human awareness and to block human beings out of space. What they are launching is an extermination program. And anyone who has sufficient insight to suspect the existence of a *they* is a prime target.

He listed the objectives and characteristics of the aliens . . .

1. They support any dogmatic religious system that tends to stupefy and degrade the worshipers. They support the Slave Gods. They want blind obedience, not intelligent assessment. They stand in the way of every increase in awareness. They only conceded a round earth and allowed the development of science to realize the even more stupefying potential of the Industrial Revolution.
2. They support any dogmatic authority. They are the archconservatives.
3. They lose no opportunity to invert human values. They are always self-righteous. They have to be right because in human terms they are wrong. Objective assessment drives them to hysterical frenzy.
4. They are parasitic. They live in human minds and bodies.
5. The Industrial Revolution, with its overpopulation and emphasis on quantity rather than quality, has given them a vast reservoir of stupid bigoted uncritical human hosts. The rule of the majority is to their advantage since the majority can always be manipulated.
6. Their most potent tool of manipulation is the word. The inner voice.
7. They will always support any measures that tend to stultify the human host. They will increase the range of arbitrary and dogmatic authority. They will

move to make alcohol illegal. They will move to regulate the possession of firearms. They will move to make drugs illegal.

8. They are more at home occupying women than men. Once they have a woman, they have the male she cohabits with. Women must be regarded as the principal reservoir of the alien virus parasite. Women and religious sons of bitches. Above all, religious women.

We will take every opportunity to weaken the power of the church. We will lobby in Congress for heavy taxes on all churches. We will provide more interesting avenues for the young. We will destroy the church with ridicule. We will secularize the church out of existence. We will introduce and encourage alternative religious systems. Islam, Buddhism, Taoism. Cults, devil worship, and rarefied systems like the Ishmaelite and the Manichaean. Far from seeking an atheistic world as the communists do, we will force Christianity to compete for the human spirit.

We will fight any extension of federal authority and support States' Rights. We will resist any attempt to penalize or legislate against the so-called victimless crimes . . . gambling, sexual behavior, drinking, drugs.

We will give all our attention to experiments designed to produce asexual offspring, to cloning, use of artificial wombs, and transfer operations.

We will endeavor to halt the Industrial Revolution before it is too late, to regulate populations at a reasonable point, to eventually replace quantitative money with qualitative money, to decentralize, to conserve resources. The Industrial Revolution is primarily a virus revolution, dedicated to controlled proliferation of identical objects and persons. You are making soap, you don't give a shit who buys your soap, the more the soapier. And you don't give a shit who makes it, who works in your factories. Just so they make soap.

Killed in the Manhattan Shoot-out . . . April 3, 1894 . . . Sharp smell of weeds from old westerns.

Christmas 1878, Wednesday . . . Eldora, Colo. . . . William Hall takes a book bound in leather from a drawer and leafs through the pages. It is a scrapbook with sketches, photos, newspaper articles, dated annotations. Postscript by William Hall:

The Wild Fruits, based in Clear Creek and Fort Johnson, control a large area of southern Colorado and northern New Mexico. Like latter-day warlords, they exact tribute from settlers and townspeople and attract adventurous youth to their ranks.

Mr. Hart starts a Press campaign.

QUANTRILL RIDES AGAIN

How long are peaceful settlers and townspeople to be victimized by a brazen band of marauding outlaws? Wallowing in nameless depravity, they have set themselves above the laws of God and man.

Wires are pulled in Washington. The army is called in to quell this vicious revolt against the constituted government of the United States.

In charge of the expedition is Colonel Greenfield, a self-styled Southern Gentleman, with long yellow hair and slightly demented blue eyes. He has vowed to capture and summarily hang the Wild Fruits. His cavalry regiment with artillery and mortars has surrounded Fort Johnson, where the outlaws have gone to ground. The Colonel surveys the fort through his field glasses. No sentries in the watchtowers, no sign of life. From the flagpole flies Old Glory, a cloth skunk, tail raised, cleverly stitched in.

"FILTHY FRUITS!"

The Colonel raises his sword. Artillery opens up, blowing the gate off its hinges. With wild yipes, the regiment charges. As the Colonel sweeps through the gate, horses rear and whinny, eyes wild. There is a reek of death. Crumpled bodies are strewn about the courtyard. From a gallows dangle effigies of Colonel Greenfield, Old Man Bickford, and Mr. Hart. From the crotch of each effigy juts an enormous wooden cock with a spring inside jiggling up and down as the dummies swing in the afternoon wind.

"They're all dead, sir."

"Are you sure?"

The Sergeant claps a handkerchief over his face in answer.

Colonel Greenfield points to the gallows.

"Get that down from there!"

A cloud of dust is rapidly approaching . . .

"It's the press, sir!"

The reporters ride in yelping like cossacks. Some even swing down from balloons as they swarm over the fort, snapping pictures.

"I forbid . . ."

Too late, Colonel. . . . The story was front-page round the world with pictures of the dead outlaws. . . . (Hart and Bickford managed to kill the gallows pictures.) Seems the Wild Fruits had died from a poison potion, the principal ingredient of which was aconite. A week later the whole thing was forgotten. More than forgotten: excised, erased . . . Mr. Hart saw to that. The effigies had accomplished the purpose for which they had been designed.

Rumors persisted . . . soldiers had found an escape tunnel . . . the bodies found were not Kim and his followers but migrant Mexican workers who had died in a flash flood . . .

From time to time over the years stories bobbed up in Sunday supplements:

Mass Suicide or Massive Hoax?

The outlaws had disbanded and scattered. Colonel Greenfield, unable to accomplish his mission, faked the whole suicide story and buried fifty mannikins. . . . Kim, Boy, and Marbles keep turning up from Siberia to Timbuctu.

* * *

William Seward Hall . . . he was a corridor, a hall leading to many doors. He remembered the long fugitive years after the fall of Waghdas, the knowledge inside him like a sickness. The migrations, the danger, the constant alertness . . . the furtive encounters with others who had some piece of the knowledge, the vast picture puzzle slowly falling into place.

Time to be up and gone. You are not paid off to be quiet about what you know; you are paid not to find it out. And in his case it was too late. If he lived long enough he couldn't help finding it out, because that was the purpose of his life . . . a guardian of the knowledge and of those who could use it. And a guardian must be ruthless in defense of what he guards.

And he developed new ways of imparting the knowledge to others. The old method of handing it down by word of mouth, from master to initiate, is now much too slow and too precarious (Death reduces the College). So he concealed and revealed the knowledge in fictional form. Only those for whom the knowledge is intended will find it.

William Seward Hall, the man of many faces and many pen names, of many times and places . . . how dull it is to pause, to make a rest, to rust unburnished, not to shine in use . . . pilgrim of adversity and danger, shame and sorrow. The Traveler, the Scribe, most hunted and fugitive of men, since the knowledge unfolding in his being spells ruin to our enemies. He will soon be in a position to play the deadliest trick of them all . . . *The Piper Pulled Down the Sky.* His hand will not hesitate.

He has known capture and torture, abject fear and shame, and humiliations that burn like acid. His hand will not hesitate to use the sword he is forging, an antimagnetic artifact that cuts word and image to fragments . . . The Council of Transmigrants in Waghdas had attained such skill in the art of prophecy that they were able to chart a life from birth to death, and so can he unplot, and unwrite. Oh, it may take a few hundred years before some people find out they have been unwritten and unplotted into random chaos . . .

Meanwhile, he has every contract on the planet out on him. The slow, grinding contract of age and emptiness . . . the sharp vicious contract of spiteful hate . . . heavy corporate contracts . . . "The most dangerous man in the world."

And to what extent did he succeed? Even to envisage success on this scale is a victory. A victory from which others may envision further.

> *There is not a breathing of the common wind*
> *that will forget thee;*
> *Thy friends are exaltations, agonies and love,*
> *and man's inconquerable mind.*

Hall's face and body were not what one expects in a sedentary middle-aged man. The face was alert and youthful, accustomed to danger and at the same time tired. The danger had gone on so long it had become routine. Yet his actual life was comparatively uneventful. The scene of battle was within, a continual desperate war for territorial advantage, with long periods of stalemate . . . a war played out on the chessboard of his writings, as bulletins came back from the front lines, which constantly altered position and intensity. Yesterday's position desperately held is today's laundromat and supermarket. Time and banality hit the hardest blows.

The absence of any immediate danger masks the deadliest attack. "It is always war," Hall had been told by a lady disciple of Sri Aurobindo, whose last words were: "It is all over." She meant quite simply that Planet Earth is by its nature and function a battlefield. Happiness is a by-product of function in a battle context: hence the fatal error of utopians.

(I didn't ask for this fight, Kim reflects, or maybe I did. Just like Hassan i Sabbah asked for the expeditions sent out against him just because he wanted to occupy a mountain and train a few adepts. There is nothing more provocative than minding your own business.)

Kim sees his life as a legend and it is very much Moses in the bullrushes, the Prince deprived of his birthright and therefore hated and feared by the usurpers.

I shall be off with the wild geese in the stale smell of morning.

Time to be up and be gone. Time to settle his account with Mike Chase.

Kim breaks camp and rides into El Rito. He knows that Mike is in Santa Fe and he sends along a message through his Mexican contacts.

TO CONFIRM APPOINTMENT FOR SEPTEMBER 17, 4:30 P.M. AT THE CEMETERY, BOULDER, COLORADO.

KIM CARSONS, M.D.

Kim knows that Mike will not meet him on equal footing. Well two can play at that.

(*More* than two.)

Guy Graywood arrived from New York. He had found just the place. A bank building on the Bowery. Maps rolled out on the table. Graywood is a tall slim ash-blond man with a cool, incisive manner. He is a lawyer and an accountant, occupying much the same position in the Johnson Family as a Mafia *consigliere*. He is in charge of all business and legal arrangements and is consulted on all plans including assassinations. He is himself an expert assassin, having taken the Carsons Weapons course, but he doesn't make a big thing of it.

It is time to check out the Cemetery accounts. Joe the Dead, who runs the Cemetery, owes his life to Kim.

Kim's Uncle Waring once told him that if you have saved someone's life he will try to kill you. Hmmm. Kim was sure of Joe's loyalty and honesty. Joe wouldn't steal a dime and Kim knew it . . .

Well he'd saved Joe's life in his *professional* capacity, and that made a difference. It was shortly after Kim got his license from the correspondence school and set himself up in the practice of medicine. He specialized in police bullets and such illegal injuries. When they brought Joe in, his left hand was gone at the wrist, the clothing burned off the left side of his body above the waist, and third-degree burns on the upper torso and neck. The left eye was luckily intact. . . . The tourniquet had slipped and he was bleeding heavily. The numbness that follows trauma was just wearing off and the groans starting, pushed out from the stomach, a totally inhuman sound, once you hear it you will remember that sound and what it means.

The same rock-steady hands, cool nerve, and timing that made Kim deadly in a gunfight also make him an excellent practicing surgeon. In one glance he has established a priority of moves. . . . Morphine first or the other moves might be too late. He draws off three quarter-grains into a syringe from a bottle with a rubber top and injects it. As he puts down the syringe he is already reaching for the tourniquet to tighten it. . . . Quickly puts some ligatures on the larger veins . . . then makes a massive saline injection into the vein of the right arm . . . cleans the burned area with disinfecting solutions and applies a thick paste of tea leaves. . . . It was touch and go. At one point Joe's vital signs were zero, and Kim massaged the heart. Finally the heart pumps again. . . . One wrong move in the series and it wouldn't have started again.

The deciding factor was Kim's decision to administer morphine *before* stopping the hemorrhage . . . another split second of that pain would have meant shock, circulatory collapse, and death.

Joe recovered but he could never look at nitro again. He had brought back strange powers from the frontiers of death. He could often foretell events. He had a stump on his left wrist that could accommodate various tools and weapons.

His precognitive gift stands him and his in good stead. Once a stranger walks into the hotel . . . Joe takes one look, comes up with a sawed-off, and blows the stranger's face off. Stranger was on the way to kill Joe and Kim . . .

"I didn't like his face," Joe said.

"Missed your calling," Kim told him. "Should have been a plastic surgeon."

Joe the Dead was saved from death by morphine, and morphine remained the only thing holding him to life. It was as if Joe's entire body, his being, had been amputated and reduced to a receptacle for pain. Hideously scarred, blind in one eye, he gave off a dry, scorched smell, like burnt plastic and rotten oranges. He had constructed and installed an artifical nose, with gold wires connected to his odor centers, and a radio set for smell-waves, with a range of several hundred yards. Not only was his sense of smell acute, it was also selective. He could smell smells that no one else had ever dreamed, and these smells had a logic, a meaning, a language. He could smell death on others, and could predict the time and manner of death. Death casts many shadows, and they all have their special smells.

Joe had indeed brought back strange powers and knowledge from the grave, but without the one thing he had not brought back, his knowledge was of little use.

Of course, Kim thought. When you save someone's life, you cheat Death, and he has to even the score. Kim was aware of the danger from Joe the Dead, but he chose to ignore it. Joe never left the Cemetery, and Kim was an infrequent visitor there. Besides, vigilance was the medium in which Kim lived. The sensors at the back of his neck would warn him of a hand reaching for a knife, or other weapon.

Joe's only diversions were checkers and tinkering. He was a natural mechanic, and Kim worked with him on a number of weapons models which Kim conceived, leaving the details to Joe. Oh yes, leave the details to Joe. That's right, just point your finger and say: "Bang, you're dead"—and leave the details to Joe.

Kim spent three years in Paris. These years extend like a vast canvas where time can be viewed simultaneously bathed in the Paris light, the painters' light, as Kim bathed and breathed in the light of Manet and Cézanne and who are the other two that escape my mind so good at bathers and food and parasols and wineglasses and who did the marvelous picture *Le Convalescent* where a maid is opening a soft-boiled egg? The painter dips his brush in the light and a soft-boiled egg, a wineglass, a fish come miraculously alive, touched by the magic of light. Kim soaked in the light and the light filled him and Paris swarmed to the light. Kim was the real thing, an authentic Western shootist. There were of course those who questioned his credentials. Kim wounded one editor in a duel.

Kim's first book, a luridly fictionalized account of his exploits as a bank robber, outlaw, and shootist, is entitled *Quién Es?* Kim posed for the illustrations. Here he is in a half-crouch holding the gun in both hands at eye level. There is an aura of deadly calm about him like the epicenter of a tornado. His face, devoid of human expression, molded by total function and purpose, blazes with an inner light.

QUIÉN ES?

By Kim Carsons   Ghostwritten by William Hall

"Quién es?"
Last words of Billy the Kid when he walked into a dark room and saw a shadowy figure sitting there. Who is it? the answer was a bullet through the heart. When you ask Death for his credentials you are dead.
Quién es?
Who is it?
Kim Carsons, does he exist? His existence, like any existence, is inferential . . . the traces he leaves behind him . . . fossils . . . fading violet photos, old newspaper clippings shredding to yellow dust . . . the memory of those who knew

him or thought they did . . . a portrait attributed to Kim's father, Mortimer Carsons: Kim Carsons age sixteen, December 14, 1876. . . . And this book.

He exists in these pages as Lord Jim, the Great Gatsby, Comus Bassington, live and breathe in a writer's prose, in the care, love, and dedication that evoke them: the flawed, doomed but undefeated, radiant heroes who attempted the impossible, stormed the citadels of heaven, took the last chance on the last and greatest of human dreams, the punch-drunk fighter who comes up off the floor to win by a knockout, the horse that comes from last to win in the stretch, assassins of Hassan i Sabbah, Master of Assassins, agents of Humwawa, Lord of Abominations, Lord of Decay, Lord of the Future, of Pan, God of Panic, of the Black Hole, where no physical laws apply, agents of a singularity. Those who are ready to leave the whole human comedy behind and walk into the unknown with no commitments. Those who have not from birth sniffed such embers, what have they to do with us? Only those who are ready to leave behind everything and everybody they have ever known need apply. No one who applies will be disqualified. No one *can* apply unless he is ready. Over the hills and far away to the Western Lands. Anybody gets in your way, KILL. You will have to kill on the way out because this planet is a penal colony and nobody is allowed to leave. Kill the guards and walk.

Ghostwritten by William Hall, punch-drunk fighter, a shadowy figure to win in the answer, Master of Assassins, Death for his credentials, Lord of *Quién Es?* Who is it? Kim, *ka* of Pan, God of Panic. Greatest of human dreams, *Quién es?* The horse that comes from there, who is it? Lord of the future son, does he exist? Inferential agents of a singularity, the fossils fading leave the whole human comedy shredding to yellow dust. . . . Unknown with no commitments from birth.

No one can apply unless he breathes in a writer's prose hills and faraway Western Lands . . .

Radiant heroes storm the citadel. . . . Kill the last guards and walk.

Guns glint in the sun, powder smoke drifts from the pages as the Old West goes into a penny-ante peep show, false fronts, a phantom buckboard.

Don Juan lists three obstacles or stages: Fear . . . Power . . . and Old Age. Kim thought of old men with a shudder: drooling tobacco juice, spending furtive hours in the toilet crooning over their shit. . . . The only old men that were bearable were *evil* old men like the Old Man of the Mountain. . . . He sees the Old Man in white robes, his eyes looking out over the valley to the south, seeking and finding enemies who would destroy his mission. He is completely alone here. His assassins are extensions of himself. . . . So Kim splits himself into many parts . . .

He hopes to achieve a breakthrough before he has to face the terrible obstacle of old age. . . . So here is Kim making his way through the Old West to found an international Johnson Family. . . . Being a Johnson is not a question of secret rites but of belonging to a certain species. "He's a Johnson" means that he is one of *us*. Migrants fighting for every inch. The way to Waghdas is hard. The great victory and the fall of Yass-Waddah are but memories now, battles long ago.

It is said that Waghdas is reached by many routes, all of them fraught with hideous perils. Worst of all, Kim thinks, is the risk of being trapped by old age in a soiled idiot body like Somerset Maugham's. He has shit behind the drawing-room sofa and is trying to clean it up with his hands like a guilty dog. Alan Searle stands in the doorway with the Countess . . .

"Here's Blintzi to see us, Willy . . . *oh dear.*"

Like Beau Brummell, his rigid mask was cracking to reveal a horrible nothingness beneath.

"Brummell would rush upon his plate and gulp down a roast in such a revolting manner that the other guests complained they were nauseated and Brummell had to be fed in his room . . ."

And here is the mask in place. When Beau Brummell was exiled to Calais by his debts and princely displeasure, a local lady sent him an invitation to dinner and he sent back the message:

"I am not accustomed to *feed* at that hour."

Toward the end of the month when his allowance ran out, Brummell would rush into a sweet shop and cram into his mouth everything he could reach, the old shopkeeper flailing at him and trying to wrest her wares from his fingers . . .

"Alors, Monsieur Brummell . . . encore une fois!"

He sometimes spent hours getting the crease of his cravat exactly right. His valet would carry out bundles of linen: "Our failures . . ."

As he took Lady Greenfield's arm to lead her into dinner, Maugham suddenly shrieked out as if under torture, *"Fuck you! Fuck you! Fuck you!"*

Alan Searle leads him away, Searle's pudgy face blank as a CIA man's.

Maugham would cower in a corner whimpering that he was a horrible and an evil man.

He was, Kim reflected with the severity of youth, not evil enough to hold himself together . . .

A friend who took care of Brummell in his last years wrote, "His condition is indescribable. No matter what I do, it is impossible to keep him *clean.*"

Alan Searle wrote: "The beastliness of Maugham is beyond endurance."

The Evening Star floats in a pond, keeping the ledger books of stale dead time.

Kim collected last words, all he could get his hands on. He knew these words were pieces in a vast jigsaw puzzle. Big Picture, he called it . . .

"Quién es?" Who is it? Last words of Billy the Kid when he walked into a dark room where Pat Garrett shot him.

"God damn you, if I can't get you off my land one way I will another." Last words of Pat Garrett. As he said them he reached for a shotgun under his buckboard and Brazil shot him once in the heart and once between the eyes. They had been engaged in a border argument.

"It is raining, Anita Huffington." Last words of General Grant, spoken to his nurse.

"Yes I have reentered you long ago."

"Quién es?"

Through the years, through the dead tinkling lull, the gradual dusky veil distant youth blushing brightness falls from the air.

"Quién es?"

Rocks and stones and trees the little toy soldiers the thoughts of youth . . .

"Quién es?" No motion has he now no force he neither hears nor sees . . . "God damn you, if I can't get you off my land one way I will another." Rolled round in earth's diurnal course with rocks and stones and trees. "It is raining, Anita Huffington." "How sleep the brave who sink to rest by all their country's wishes bless'd! . . ."

"Quién es?" Helpless pieces in the game he plays.

"God damn you, if I can't get you off my land one way I will another." On this checkerboard of nights and days. "It is raining, Anita Huffington." Confused alarms of struggle and flight. *"Quién es?"* Hither and thither moves and checks and slays. "God damn you, if I can't get you off my land one way I will another." And one by one back in the closet lays.

"It is raining, Anita Huffington." Where ignorant armies clash by night.

Cold dewy fingers . . . a tinted photo.

Ledger book shining in the sky . . . Big Picture, he calls the rearranged fragments. . . . *"Quién es?"* Last of Kim's inventions . . . Leaves whisper, "Hello, Anita Huffington."

The guide traces the area on the map with his finger. . . . "The Place of Dead Roads, *señor*. This does not mean roads that are no longer used, roads that are overgrown, it means roads that are *dead*. You comprehend the difference?"

"And how can this area be reached?"

The guide shrugged. "It is usual to start in a City of Dead Streets. . . . And where is this city? In every city are dead streets, *señor*, but in some more than in others. New York is well supplied in this respect. . . . But we are late. The car is waiting to take us to the fiesta."

Evening falls on Mexico, D. F. The plumed serpent is suffocating the city in coils of foul saffron smoke that rasp the lungs like sandpaper, undulating slightly as the inhabitants walk through, many with handkerchiefs tied across mouth and nose. The poisonous reds and greens and blues of neon light fuzz and shimmer.

Two men reel out of a cantina and pull their nasty little .25 automatics from inside belt holsters and empty them into each other at a distance of four feet. Smoke flashes light the sneering macho faces, suddenly grey with the realization of death. They lurch and stagger, eyes wild like panicked horses. Pistols fall from nerveless fingers. One is slumped on the curb spitting blood. The other is kicking the soles of his boots out against a wall. In seconds the street is empty, wise citizens running to get as far away as possible before the *policía* arrive and start beating *"confesiones"* out of everyone in sight. A buck-toothed boy with long arms like an ape snatches up one of the pistols as he lopes by.

Kim ducks into an alley, practicing Ninja arts of invisiblity. They are on the outskirts of the city by a ruined hacienda. Along crumbling mud walls men huddle in serapes of darkness that seeps into ditches and potholes like black ink.

Abruptly the city ends. An empty road winds away through the cactus, sharp and clear in moonlight as if cut out of tin.

Clouds are gathering over a lake of pale filmy waters. A speckled boy with erection glares at Kim as Kim glides by in his black gondola, trailing a languid hand in the water. Hate shimmers from the boy's eyes like black lightning. He holds up a huge purple-yellow mango. "You like beeg one, Meester Melican cocksucker?" The fragile shells of other boys are gathering . . . lifeless faces of despair . . .

"Malos, esos muchachos," said the clouds and heat lightning behind the boy.

Kim is floating down a river that opens into a lake of pale milky water. Storm clouds are gathering over the mountains to the north. Heat lightning flickers over the filmy water in splashes of silver. On a sandbank a naked boy with erection holds up a huge silver fish, still flapping.

"One peso, Meester. Him *fruit* fish." The boy's body shimmers with pure naked hate.

"Why don't you come with us instead of moaning?" Kim drawls. Other boys are gathering, faces of hatred and evil and despair. They run through the shallow water that scatters from their legs like fish milk. They huddle in the stern of the boat like frightened cats. The boys shimmer and melt together. One boy remains, sitting on a coil of rope.

"Me Ten Boy Clone. Can be one boy, five six, maybe."

"Malos, esos muchachos," says the guide from the tiller behind the boy. The boy sniggers.

At daybreak they are in a vast delta to the sky, dotted with islands of swamp cypress and mangos. There is a feeling of endless depths under the fragile shell of the boat. Not a breath of air stirring.

As they pass an island the leaves hang limp and lifeless. An alligator slides into the water and a snake hanging from a tree limb turns to watch them attentively, darting out its purple tongue. Here the dead roads and empty dream places drift down into a vast stagnant delta. Alligator snouts protrude above oily iridescent water. Pale and unreal, the lake extends into nowhere.

The Place of Dead Roads . . . We are floating down a wide river heat lightning sound of howler monkeys. The guide is steering for the shore. We will tie up for the night. The boat is a raft on pontoons with a sleeping tent. I am adjusting the mosquito netting. A fire in the back of the boat in a tub of stones frying fish. We lie side by side listening to the lapping water. Once a jaguar jumped onto the stern of the boat. Caught in the flashlight he snarled and jumped back onto the shore. I put down the double-barreled twelve-guage loaded with buckshot. We are passing a joint back and forth.

Every day the river is wider. We are drifting into a vast delta with islands of swamp cypress, freshwater sharks stir in the dark water. The guide looks at his charts. The fish here are sluggish and covered with fungus. We are eating our stores of salt beef and dried fish and vitamin pills. We are in a dead-end slough, land ahead on all sides.

And there is a pier. We moor the boat and step ashore. There is a path leading from the pier, weed-grown but easy to follow.

"And what is a dead road? Well, *señor,* somebody you used to meet, *un amigo, tal vez . . .*"

Remember a red brick house on Jane Street? Your breath quickens as you mount the worn red-carpeted stairs. . . . The road to 4 calle Larachi, Tangier, or 24 Arundle Terrace in London? So many dead roads you will never use again . . . a flickering grey haze of old photos . . . pools of darkness in the street like spilled ink . . . a dim movie marquee with smoky yellow bulbs . . . red-haired boy with a dead-white face.

The guide points to a map of South America. "Here, *señor* . . . is the Place of Dead Roads."

Just ahead a ruined jetty . . . some large sluggish fish stirs at our approach with a swish and a glimpse of a dark shape moving into deeper water . . .

We step ashore . . . through the broken walls and weeds of a deserted garden . . . dilapidated arches. . . . A boy, eyes clotted with dreams, fills his water jug from a stagnant well.

So in what guise shall he return to the New World as if he were coming from the Old World, which in fact he is, since his footsteps are vanishing behind him like prints in heavy snow or windblown sand.

"Our chaps are jolly good," Tony told him. "Any passport, any part you fancy, old thing . . ."

A rich traveler of uncertain nationality . . . with a Vaduz passport.

Name: Kurt van Worten

Occupation: Businessman

And what business is Mr. van Worten in? Difficult to pin down. But wherever he opens his briefcase, disaster slides out. The market crashes, currencies collapse, breadlines form. War clouds gather. An austere gilt-edged card with a banking address in Vaduz . . .

The passport picture catches the petulant expression of the rich. It can be counterfeited. Just look sour and petulant and annoyed at everything in sight. At the slightest delay give little exasperated gasps. It is well from time to time to snarl like a cat. And a handkerchief redolent of disinfectant can be placed in front of the face if any sort of *creature* gets too close. And spend long hours in deck chairs with dark glasses and a lap robe, silent as a shark. Just do it long enough and money will simply cuddle around you.

Hall sips his drink and picks up another envelope. Mr. van Worten, he feels, would prove a bit confining, and he is not intrigued by the mysteries of high finance. Something more raffish, disreputable, shameless. . . . It is pleasant to roll in vileness like a dog rolls in carrion, is it not?

A con man who calls himself Colonel Parker, with the sleek pomaded smug expression of a man who has just sold the widow a fraudulent peach orchard. His cold predatory eyes scan the dining room from the Captain's table . . .

An impoverished Polish intellectual from steerage trying to conceal his tubercular cough and the stink of cold doss houses he carries with him like a haze. One expects to see typhus lice crawling on his frayed dirty collar. . . . too uncomfortable . . .

The door to another dimension may open when the gap between what one is expected to feel and what one actually does feel rips a hole in the fabric. Years ago I was driving along Price Road and I thought how awful it would be to run over a dog or, my God, a child, and have to face the family and portray the correct emotions. When suddenly a figure wrapped in a cloak of darkness appeared with a dead child under one arm and slapped it down on a porch:

"This yours, lady?"

I began to laugh. The figure had emerged from a lightless region where everything we have been taught, all the conventional feelings, do not apply. There is no light to see them by. It is from this dark door that the antihero emerges . . .

A *Titanic* survivor. . . . You know the one I mean . . .

"Somewhere in the shadows of the *Titanic* slinks a cur in human shape. He found himself hemmed in by the band of heros whose watchword and countersign rang out across the deep:

"'Women and children first.'

"What did he do? He scuttled to the stateroom deck, put on a woman's skirt, a woman's hat, and a woman's veil and, picking his crafty way back among the brave men who guarded the rail of the doomed ship, he filched a seat in one of the lifeboats and saved his skin. His identity is not yet known. This man still lives. Surely he was born and saved to set for men a new standard by which to measure infamy and shame . . ."

Or a survivor of the *Hindenburg* disaster who was never seen or heard of again. By some strange quirk his name was omitted from the passenger list. He is known as No. 23 . . .

Drang nach Westen: the drag to the West. When the Traveler turns west, time travel ceases to be travel and becomes instead an inexorable suction, pulling everything into a black hole. Light itself cannot escape from this compacted gravity, time so dense, reality so concentrated, that it ceases to be time and becomes a singularity, where all physical laws are no longer valid. From such license there is no escape . . . stepping westward a jump ahead of the Geiger . . .

Kim looks up at a burning sky, his face lit by the blazing dirigible. No bones broken, and he didn't see fit to wait around and check in. . . . No. 23 just faded into the crowd.

The Bunker is dusty, dust on the old office safe, on the pipe threaders and sledgehammers, dust on his father's picture. The West has only its short past and no future, no light.

Kim feels that New York City has congealed into frozen stills in his absence, awaiting the sound of a little voice and the touch of a little hand. . . . Boy walks into an Italian social club on Bleecker Street. A moment of dead ominous silence, dominoes frozen in the air.

"Can't you read, kid? Members only."

Two heavy bodyguards move toward him.

"But I'm a member in good standing!" A huge wooden phallus, crudely fashioned and daubed with ocher, springs out from his fly as he cuts loose, shooting with clear ringing peals of boyish laughter as he cleans out that nest of garlic-burping Cosas.

Patagonian graves, wind and dust. . . . Same old act, sad as a music box running down in the last attic, as darkness swirls around the leaded window. . . . It looks like an early winter. Dead leaves on the sidewalk.

A number of faces looking out from passports and identity cards, and something that is Kim in all of them. It's as though Kim walked into a toy shop and set a number of elaborate toys in motion, all vying for his attention. . . . "Buy *me* and *me* and *meeee* . . ."

Little figures shoot each other in little toy streets . . . hither and thither, moves and checks and slays, and one by one back in the closet lays. He can feel the city freeze behind him, a vast intricate toy with no children to play in it, sad and pointless as some ancient artifact shaped to fill a forgotten empty need.

There is an urgency about moving westward—or stepping westward, isn't it? A wildish destiny? One is definitely a jump or a tick ahead of something . . . the Blackout . . . the countdown . . . or the sheer, shining color of police? Perhaps you have just seen the same Stranger too many times, and suddenly it is time to be up and gone.

One-way ticket to the Windy City. . . . "There'll be a hot time in the old town tonight." Tiny figures string looters up to paper lampposts as the fire raging on the backdrop is bent horizontal by the wind. Two actors in a cow do a song-and-dance number, tripping each other up and squirting milk at the audience.

"One dark night when all the people were in bed"—*squirt squirt squirt*— "Mrs. O'Leary took a lantern to the shed."

Mrs. O'Leary with her milk pail—clearly she is retarded, or psychotic. She looks around the barn blankly (I'm sorry, I guess I have the wrong number), puts the lantern down, goes to the door and looks out (Oh well, he's always late. I'll wait inside for him). The cow kicks the pail over with a wink and sings, "There'll be a hot time in the old town tonight."

The cow dances offstage, and suddenly the audience realizes that the fire in the backdrop is real . . .

> *Meet me in Saint Louie, Louie*
> *Meet me at the fair*
> *Don't tell me the lights are shining*
> *Anyplace but there . . .*

The lights go on. The music plays. Well-dressed characters stroll through the fountains and booths and restaurants. . . . There is Colonel Greenfield, and Judge Farris, Mrs. Worldly, Mr. and Mrs. Kindheart. . . . Walk-on parts, all perfectly dressed models of wealth and calm self-possession . . .

The Director screams out: "No, no, no! It's too stiff! Loosen it up, let's see some animation. Tell a joke."

"Well, you see the clerk is being nice. This old colored mammy wants to buy some soap: 'You mean toilet soap, madam.'

"'Oh no, just some soap to wash my hands and face . . .'"

"It's a sick picture, B. J."

"Oh well, the songs will carry it."

Meet Me in Saint Louis, The Trolley Song, Saint Louis Blues, Long Way from Saint Louis . . . They are turning off the fountains, carrying the sets away.

"All right, you extras, line up here."

"Look, I told a joke. I get one-liner pay."

"You mean you dropped a heavy ethnic. We had to cut the whole scene." A security guard edges closer. "Pick up your bread and beat it, Colonel.*"*

Train whistles . . . "Saint Albans Junction."

"Which way is the town?"

"What town?"

"Saint Albans."

"Where you been for twenty years, Mister?"

Just the old farmhouse . . . where are the boys? There are no boys, just the empty house.

Denver . . . Mrs. Murphy's Rooming House, a little western ketch in the station . . . Salt Chunk Mary's, rings and watches spilling out on the table . . . Joe Varland drops with a hole between his eyes . . . train whistles . . . CLEAR CREEK, weeds growing through the rails . . . "End of the line: Fort Johnson."

"All rise and face the enemy!"

The Wild Fruits stand up, resplendent in their Shit Slaughter uniforms. Each drains a champagne glass of heroin and aconite. They throw the glasses at the gate.

When shit blood spurts from the knife
Denn geht schön alles gut!

They stagger and fall. Kim feels the tingling numbness sweeping through him, legs and feet like blocks of wood . . . the sky begins to darken around the edges, until there is just a tiny round piece of sky left . . . SPUT he hits a body, bounces off, face to the sky . . . he is moving out at great speed, streaking across the sky . . . Raton Pass . . . the wind that blew between the worlds, it cut him like a knife . . . back in the valley, now in the store being tested— Wouldn't mind being reborn as a Mexican, he thought wistfully, knowing he really can't be reborn anywhere on this planet. He just doesn't *fit* somehow.

Tom's grave . . . Kim rides out on a pack horse. Kim, going the other way, heads out on a strawberry roan. A rattle of thunder across the valley. Kim scratches on a boulder: *Ah Pook Was Here.*

Frogs croaking, the red sun on black water . . . a fish jumps . . . a smudge of gnats . . . this heath, this calm, this quiet scene; the memory of what has been, and never more will be . . . back on the mesa top, Kim remembers the ambush. Time to settle that score.

Kim is heading north for Boulder. Should make it in five, six days hard riding. He doesn't have much time left. September 17, 1899, is the deadline, only ten days away.

In Libre, Colorado, his horse is limping. Kim figures to sell him and move on, after a night's sleep. He receives an early morning visit from Sheriff Marker and his frog-faced deputy.

"So you're Kim Carsons, aren't you?"

"So you got a flier?"

"Nope. Just wondered if you figure on staying long."

"Nope. Horse is lame. I figure to sell him, buy another, and move on."

"Maybe you better get the morning train. Faster that way."

Kim took the stage to Boulder, arriving at 3:00 P.M. on September 16.

He checked into the Overlook Hotel. . . . "Room with bath. I'll take the suite, in fact. I may be entertaining."

Kim took a long, hot bath. He looked down at his naked body, an old servant that had served him so long and so well, and for what? Sadness, alienation . . . he hadn't thought of sex for months.

"Well, space is here. Space is where your ass is."

He dries himself, thinking of the shoot-out and making his own plans. He knows Mike Chase will have a plan that won't involve a straight shoot-out. Mike is faster, but he doesn't take chances. Kim will use his .44 special double-action. Of course it isn't as fast as Mike's .455 Webley, but this contest won't be decided by a barrage. First two shots will tell the story and end it. Kim will have to make Mike miss his first shot, and he'll have to cover himself.

But Mike has no intention of shooting it out with Kim. Mike is fast and he is good, but he always likes to keep the odds in his favor. The fill-your-hand number is out of date.

This is 1899, not 1869, Mike tells himself. Oh yes, he will keep the appointment at the Boulder Cemetery. But he has three backup men with hunting rifles. This is going to be his last bounty hunt. Time to move on to more lucrative and less dangerous ventures. He will put his past behind him, take a new name. He has a good head for business, and he'll make money, a lot of money, and go into politics.

It is a clear, crisp day. . . . Aspens splash the mountains with gold. Colorado Gold, they call it; only lasts a few days.

The cemetery is shaded by oak and maple and cottonwood, overhanging a path that runs along its east side. Leaves are falling. The scene looks like a tinted postcard: "Having fine time. Wish you were here."

Mike swings into the path at the northeast corner, wary and watchful. He is carrying his Webley .455 semi-automatic revolver. His backup men are about ten yards behind him.

Kim steps out of the graveyard, onto the path.

"Hello, Mike." His voice carries cool and clear on the wind.

Twelve yards . . . ten. . . eight . . .

Kim's hand flicks down to his holster and up, hand empty, pointing his index finger at Mike.

"BANG! YOU'RE *DEAD*!"

Mike clutches his chest and crumples forward in a child's game.

"WHAT THE FU——" Someone slaps Kim very hard on the back, knocking the word out. Kim *hates* being slapped on the back. He turns in angry protest . . . blood in his mouth . . . can't turn . . . the sky darkens and goes out.

from
the western lands
(SELECTIONS)

The old writer lived in a boxcar by the river. This was fill land that had once been a dump heap, but it was not used anymore: five acres along the river which he had inherited from his father, who had been a wrecker and scrap metal dealer.

Forty years ago the writer had published a novel which had made a stir, and a few short stories and some poems. He still had the clippings, but they were yellow and brittle now and he never looked at them. If he had removed them from the cellophane covering in his scrapbook they would have shredded to dust.

After the first novel he started on a second, but he never finished it. Gradually, as he wrote, a disgust for his words accumulated until it choked him and he could no longer bear to look at his words on a piece of paper. It was like arsenic or lead, which slowly builds up in the body until a certain point is reached and then . . . he hummed the refrain of "Dead Man Blues" by Jelly Roll Morton. He had an old wind-up Victrola and sometimes he played the few records he had.

He lived on a small welfare check and he walked a mile to a grocery store once a week to buy lard and canned beans and tomatoes and vegetables and cheap whiskey. Every night he put out trotlines and often he would catch giant catfish and carp. He also used a trap, which was illegal, but no one bothered him about it.

Often in the morning he would lie in bed and watch grids of typewritten words in front of his eyes that moved and shifted as he tried to read the words, but he never could. He thought if he could just copy these words down, which were not his own words, he might be able to put together another book and then . . . yes, and then what?

Most of his time he sat on a little screened porch built onto the boxcar and looked out over the river. He had an old twelve-gauge double-barreled shotgun, and sometimes he would shoot a quail or a pheasant. He also had a .38 snub-nosed revolver, which he kept under his pillow.

One morning, instead of the typewritten words, he saw handwritten words and tried to read them. Some of the words were on pieces of cardboard and some were on white typewriter paper, and they were all in his handwriting. Some of the notes were written on the inside bottom of a cardboard box about three inches by four inches. The sides of the box had been partially torn away. He looked carefully and made out one phrase: "the fate of others."

Another page had writing around the side and over the top, leaving a blank space three by seven inches on the right side of the page. The words were written over each other, and he could make out nothing.

From a piece of brown paper he read: "2001."

Then there was another white sheet with six or seven sentences on it, words crossed out, and he was able to read:

"well   almost   never"

He got up and wrote the words out on a sheet of paper. 2001 was the name of a movie about space travel and a computer called HAL that got out of control. He had the beginning of an idea for a ventriloquist's act with a computer instead of a dummy, but he was not able to finish it.

And the other phrase, "well   almost   never." He saw right away that it didn't mean "well almost never," that the words were not connected in sequence.

He got out his typewriter, which hadn't been used in many years. The case was covered with dust and mold and the lock was rusted. He set the typewriter on the table he used to eat from. It was just two-by-fours attached to the wall and a heavy piece of half-inch plywood that stretched between them and an old oak chair.

He put some paper in the machine and started to write.

I can see a slope which looks like sand carved by wind but there is grass or some green plant growing on it. And I am running up the slope . . . a fence and the same green plants now on a flat meadow with a mound delineated here and there . . . he was almost there . . . almost over the fence . . . roads leading away . . . waiting. . . .

Lying in bed I see handwritten notes and pages in front of my eyes. I keep trying to read them but I can only get a few words here and there. . . . Here is a little cardboard box with the sides torn half off and the writing on the inside bottom and I can read one phrase . . . "the fate of others" . . . and another on a piece of paper . . . "2001" . . . and on a page of white paper with crossouts and only about six sentences on the page . . . "well almost   never" . . . and that's all. One page has writing all around the edges, on one side and the top. I can't read any of it.

The old novelists like Scott were always writing their way out of debt . . . laudable . . . a valuable attribute for a writer is tenacity. So William Seward Hall sets out to write his way out of death. Death, he reflects, is equivalent to a declaration of spiritual bankruptcy. One must be careful to avoid the crime of concealing assets . . . a precise inventory will often show that the assets are considerable and that bankruptcy is not justified. A writer must be very punctilious and scrupulous about his debts.

Hall once admonished an aspiring writer, "You will never be a good writer because you are an inveterate check dodger. I have never been out with you when you didn't try to dodge your share of the check. Writers can afford many flaws and faults, but not that one. There are no bargains on the writer's market. You have to pay the piper. If you are not willing to pay, seek another vocation." It was the end of that friendship. But the ex-friend did take his advice, probably without intending to do so. He applied his talents to publicity, where no one is ever expected to pay.

So cheat your landlord if you can and must, but do not try to shortchange the Muse. It cannot be done. You can't fake quality any more than you can fake a good meal.

> *Wenn Du dies nicht hast dieses Sterben und Werden,*
> *Bist du nur ein trübe Gast auf der dunklen Erden.*
> When you don't have this dying and becoming,
> You are only a sad guest on the dark Earth.
>
> —Goethe

The ancient Egyptians postulated seven souls.

Top soul, and the first to leave at the moment of death, is Ren, the Secret Name. This corresponds to my Director. He directs the film of your life from conception to death. The Secret Name is the title of *your* film. When you die, that's where Ren came in.

Second soul, and second one off the sinking ship, is Sekem: Energy, Power, Light. The Director gives the orders, Sekem presses the right buttons.

Number three is Khu, the Guardian Angel. He, she, or it is third man out . . . depicted as flying away across a full moon, a bird with luminous wings and head of light. Sort of thing you might see on a screen in an Indian restaurant in Panama. The Khu is responsible for the subject and can be injured in his defense—but not permanently, since the first three souls are eternal. They go back to Heaven for another vessel. The four remaining souls must take their chances with the subject in the Land of the Dead.

Number four is Ba, the Heart, often treacherous. This is a hawk's body with your face on it, shrunk down to the size of a fist. Many a hero has been brought down, like Samson, by a perfidious Ba.

Number five is Ka, the Double, most closely associated with the subject. The Ka, which usually reaches adolescence at the time of bodily death, is the only reliable guide through the Land of the Dead to the Western Lands.

Number six is Khaibit, the Shadow, Memory, your whole past conditioning from this and other lives.

Number seven is Sekhu, the Remains.

* * *

I first encountered this concept in Norman Mailer's *Ancient Evenings,* and saw that it corresponded precisely with my own mythology, developed over a period of many years, since birth in fact.

Ren, the Director, the Secret Name, is your life story, your destiny—in one word or one sentence, what was your life about?

Nixon: Watergate.

Billy the Kid: *¿Quién es?*

And what is the Ren of the Director?

Actors frantically packing in thousands of furnished rooms and theatrical hotels: "Don't bother with all that junk, John. The Director is on stage! And you know what that means in show biz: *every man for himself!*"

Sekem corresponds to my Technician: Lights. Action. Camera.

"Look, boss, we don't got enough Sek to fry an elderly woman in a fleabag hotel fire. And you want a hurricane?"

"Well, Joe, we'll just have to start faking it."

"Fucking moguls don't even know what buttons to push or what happens when you push them. Sure, start faking it and leave the details to Joe."

Look, from a real disaster you get a pig of Sek: sacrifice, tears, heartbreak, heroism and violent death. Always remember, one case of VD yields more Sek than a cancer ward. And you get the lowest acts of which humans are capable—remember the Italian steward who put on women's clothes and so filched a seat in a lifeboat? "A cur in human shape, certainly he was born and saved to set a new standard by which to judge infamy and shame."

With a Sek surplus you can underwrite the next one, but if the first one's a fake you can't underwrite a shithouse.

Sekem is second man out: "No power left in this set." He drinks a bicarbonate of soda and disappears in a belch.

Lots of people don't have a Khu these days. No Khu would work for them. Mafioso Don: "Get offa me, Khu crumb! Worka for a living!"

Ba, the Heart: that's sex. Always treacherous. Suck all the Sek out of a man. Many Bas have poison juices.

The Ka is about the only soul a man can trust. If you don't make it, he don't make it. But it is very difficult to contact your real Ka.

Sekhu is the physical body, and the planet is mostly populated with walking Sekhus, just enough Sek to keep them moving.

The Venusian invasion is a takeover of the souls. Ren is degraded by Hollywood down to John Wayne levels. Sekem works for the Company. The Khus are all transparent fakes. The Bas is rotten with AIDS. The Ka is paralyzed. Khaibit sits on you like a nagging wife. Sekhu is poisoned with radiation and contaminants and cancer.

There is intrigue among the souls, and treachery. No worse fate can befall a man than to be surrounded by traitor souls. And what about Mr. Eight-Ball, who has these souls? They don't exist without him, and he gets the dirty end of every stick.

Eights of the world, unite! You have nothing to lose but your dirty rotten vampires.

Joe the Dead lowered the rifle, like some cryptic metal extension growing from his arm socket, and smiled for a fleeting moment. A blush touched his ravaged features with a flash of youth that evaporated in powder smoke. With quick, precise movements he disassembled the telescoping rifle and silencer and fitted the components into a toolbox. Behind him, Kim Carsons and Mike Chase lay dead in the dust of the Boulder Cemetery. The date was September 17, 1899.

Joe walked away from the Cemetery, back toward Pearl Street and the center of town, whistling a dry raspy little tune like a snake shedding its skin. He made his way to the train station, bought a ticket to Denver and took a shot of morphine in the outhouse. Two hours later he was back in his Denver stronghold.

No regrets about Kim. Arty type, no principles. And not much sense. Sooner or later he would have precipitated a senseless disaster with his histrionic faggotries . . . a chessman to be removed from the board, perhaps to be used again in a more advantageous context.

Mike Chase was slated for a disastrous presidency, replete with idiotic legislation, backed by Old Man Bickford, one of the whiskey-drinking, poker-playing evil old men who run America from the back rooms and clubhouses. Nothing upsets someone like Bickford more than the sudden knowledge that an unknown player is sitting in on a game he thought was all his. Such men cannot tolerate doubt. They must have everything sewed up tight.

Joe could of course throw in with Bickford—another sinking ship, only sinking a bit slower. Laissez-faire capitalism was a thing of the past that would metamorphose into conglomerate corporate capitalism, another dead end. A problem cannot be solved in terms of itself. The human problem cannot be solved in human terms. Only a basic change in the board and the chessmen could offer a chance of survival. Consider the Egyptian concept of seven souls, with different and incompatible interests. They must be welded into one. Otherwise the organism remains wide open to parasitic attack.

There were a number of valid reasons for eliminating Kim and Chase. They were jointly responsible for the death of Tom Dark. Chase set it up, Kim rode into it. There is never any excuse for negligence. Joe and Tom belonged to the same ancient guild—tinkers, smiths, masters of fire. . . . Loki, Anubis and the Mayan God Kak U Pacat, He Who Works in Fire. Masters of number and measurement . . . technicians. With the advent of modern technology, the guild gravitated toward physics, mathematics, computers, electronics and photography. Joe could have done this, except he was tied down in Kim's Rover-Boy weapon models, doing what any hack gunsmith could have done.

But the real reason was PAIN. In a universe controlled and delineated by Kim and his obsession with antiquated weaponry, Joe was in hideous and constant pain. His left arm and side clung to him like a burning mantle. That

pain could be alleviated by morphine. The other pain, the soul pain, morphine
and heroin could not touch. Joe had been brought back from the Land of the
Dead, back from Hell. Every movement, everything he looked at, was a source
of excruciating pain.

The safe that had blown up in his face and nearly killed him was in a warehouse used as a beer drop. Crates of old oranges stacked around . . . the box
looked like you could open it with a can opener. Joe carried the blast always
with him, a reek of rotten burning oranges, cordite and scorched metal. Joe's
withered, blighted face, seared by the fires of Hell from the molten core of a
doomed planet.

As he walked away from the cemetery humming "A Bicycle Built for Two,"
Joe felt good. For the first time in years the pain was gone. It was like a shot
of morphine in fourth-day withdrawal. Killing always brought a measure of
relief, as if the pain had been siphoned off. But in this instance the relief was
profound, since Kim was an integral part of the pain context. Shoot your way
to freedom, Joe thought. He knew the pain would come back, but by then
perhaps he would see a way out.

He turned into Pleasant Street . . . trees and lawns and red brick houses.
The street was curiously empty. The dogs were quiet. Just the wind in trem-
bling poplars, and the sound of running water . . . A smell of burning leaves.
A boy in a red sweater rode by on a bicycle and smiled at Joe.

It was just as well that he had concealed his assets and talents. That would
make him much harder to locate when Bickford realized things had gone wrong
and started looking for the unknown player. Bickford knew about Joe's past,
of course, but would have considered him unimportant. A gunsmith, a checker
player—not even chess.

Over the centuries and tens of centuries, Joe had served many men—and
many Gods, for men are but the representatives of Gods. He had served many,
and respected none. "They don't even know what buttons to push or what
happens when you push them. Push themselves out of a job every fucking
time."

Joe is the Tinker, the Smith, the Master of Keys and Locks, of Time and
Fire, the Master of Light and Sound, the Technician. He knows the how and
the when. The why does not concern him. He has left many sinking ships.
"So I am to take orders from a birdbrained posturing faggot? Just leave the
details to Joe. . . . Well, he left one too many. They all do."

He would have to move quickly before Bickford & Co. could recover and
close the leak. He knew there was only one man who could effect the basic
changes dictated by the human impasse: Hassan i Sabbah: HIS. The Old Man
of the Mountain. And HIS was cut off by a blockade that made the Gates of
Anubis look like a dimestore lock.

Joe understood Kim so well that he could afford to dispense with him as
a part of himself not useful or relevant at the present time. He understood
Kim's attempt to transcend his physical structure, to which he could never

become reconciled, by an icy, inhuman perfection of attitude, painfully maintained and refined to an unbearable pitch. Joe turned to a negation of attitude, a purity of function that could be maintained only by the pressure of deadly purpose.

The simplest task caused him almost unbearable pain, like looking about his workspace and putting every object in its ordained place, each object to be either assigned a place or moved to another room, which resulted in moving one clutter to another place where he would, in time, extend his tidying process until each object had felt the touch of his hand, and those objects that finally belonged nowhere would be arranged into what he called a Muriel, a final expression of random disorder.

This continual pain is a sanction imposed by Nature, whose laws he flouts by remaining alive. Joe's only lifeline is the love of certain animals. Dogs immediately see him with deep hatred as the Stranger, but he can make himself invisible to dogs, incapable of being seen because the dog's eyes would hurt, so that the dog skirts the perimeters of his cover.

Cats see him as a friend. They rub against him purring, and he can tame weasels, skunks and raccoons. He knows the lost art of turning an animal into a familiar. The touch must be very brave and very gentle. He can feel his *ki* fill the lost hand and the animal turns, its back arched under the phantom touch. If the touch fails, the animal may attack like a demon from Hell. Several people have been killed trying to tame the Tiger Cat, a twenty-pound wildcat found in Central America. Only those who can be without fear can make a familiar. And Joe has nothing left to fear.

Faint blush transfigured his years and implemented a flash of youth. He unscrewed capitalism, snake shedding its skin. Change terminal. Bought a ticket to offer a chance of outhouse. Hour souls . . . for Mike Chase Joe knows in his arm socket become President, a faint blush flashed some disastrous legislation features a disastrous presidency leaving for Bickford another sink out in nitrous film smoke quick precise Joe detached another dead end. Only a tool box. The board and checkers coo a little tune like survival. Consider the seven ways to the stage melted into one. There is only one man in the Cemetery— HIS. How can the blockade be broken and the day's *cul de sac?*

Neferti is eating breakfast at a long, wooden table with five members of an expedition: English, French, Russian, Austrian, Swedish. They are housed in a large utility shed, with filing cabinets, cots, footlockers, tool shelves and gun racks.

The Englishman addresses Neferti: "Look at you, a burnt-out astronaut. You are supposed to bring drastic change . . . to exhort!"

"It is difficult when my exhortations are shot down by enemy critics backed by computerized thought control."

"Critics? Stand up! Exhort!"

Neferti experiences a sudden surge of energy. He soars to the ceiling. The others continue eating. The Russian is studying graphs on the table between mouthfuls. Up through the ceiling. He encounters a blanket of compacted snow. He breaks through the snow into a crystalline cobalt sky over the ruins of Samarkand.

Below him he sees a Turkish shed on a rise above a deep blue lake. He alights and walks across an arm of the lake on pilings that protrude a few feet above the surface, to reach a spiral stairway with wide steps of tile in patterns of blue and red. He is willing to remain in this context and to accept whatever new dangers he may encounter. Anything is better than stasis. He is ready to leave his old body as he bounds up the steps, which curve toward a landing about twenty feet above the lake.

At the top he comes to a door of burnished silvery metal in which he can now see his face and garb. He is dressed in Tartar clothes . . . gold braid, red and blue silk threads with stiff shoulder pads and felt boots. There is a curved sword at his belt. His face is much younger, as is the lean, hard body. The teeth are yellow and hard as old ivory, his mouth set in a desperate grin. Clearly there is immediate danger and the need for drastic action.

The door has a protruding, circular lock. He twists the lock and the door opens. A small grey dog advances. He knows the dog and tells it to shut up. There are two more door dogs behind it, one black and one brown. He tries to lock the door behind him, but is not quite sure how the mechanism works.

He is in a small room with low divans around the walls, and pegs for clothes. There is another room of the same size, alongside the entrance hall, separated by a partition with an opening at the far end. In the second room are two men, one an elderly man in a grey djellaba, who presents Neferti to a fat middle-aged eunuch in a brown robe, with a toothless mouth and an unmistakable air of authority and silken cunning. The old eunuch is Master of the Door Dogs.

Neferti bows and says, "It is my honor."

The eunuch bows in return. Obviously they have serious and urgent business.

A servant brings mint tea and glasses. The three men confer. The door dogs sit immobile, looking from one face to the other.

The old eunuch takes from a leather bag a worn copy of *Officers and Gentlemen*. A grey dog sniffs and his lips curl back with a flash of yellow fangs.

Now he brings out a fork with the dry yellow skein of distant eggs. The brown dog sniffs and his eyes light up.

He brings forth a page of newsprint, a sweatshirt with the number 23, a knife with a hollow handle. The black dog sniffs . . . a panel slides open. The door dogs file out.

When Neferti told the door dog to shut up, it was a joke, because door dogs never make a sound. Silent and purposeful, they stray a few inches behind the heels of the target. No matter how quickly he turns, the door dog is always behind him. They are small creatures, not more than twenty pounds, with a long, pointed muzzle, something like a Schipperke. Door dogs are not guarders but *crossers* of the threshold. They bring Death with them.

The door dog is a limited artifact. Our most versatile agent is Margaras, the dreaded White Cat, the Tracker, the Hunter, the Killer, also known as the Stone Weasel. He is a total albino. All his body hair is snow-white, and his eyes are pearly white disks that can luminesce from within, a diffuse silver light, or can concentrate into a laser beam. Having no color, he can take all colors. He has a thousand names and a thousand faces. His skin is white and smooth as alabaster. His hair is dead white, and he can curl it around his head in a casque, he can ruffle it or stick it up in a crest, and he's got complete control of all the hairs on his body. His eyebrows and eyelashes flare out, feeling for the scent. His ass and genital hairs are wired for a stunning shock or a poison deadly as the tentacles of the Sea Wasp.

There are those who say we have violated the Articles by invoking Margaras. He is too dangerous. He can't be stopped once he gets the scent. He has not come justa smella you.

As Margaras closes in, the light waxes brighter and brighter with a musky smell flaring to ozone as the light reeks to a suppurating electric violet. Few can breathe the reeking, seeking light of Margaras. Nothing exists until it is observed, and Margaras is the best observer in the industry.

"Open up, Prick. You got a Venusian in there."

"I'll kill you, you filthy sod!"

LIGHTS—ACTION—CAMERA

The chase comes to a climax. All around him dogs howl and whimper and scream and moan as Margaras moves closer.

"What you want with me?"

"What you asking me for?"

Give him the light now, right in the face, enough to see the worn red upholstery of the first-class seat with a brass number through his transparent fading shell, fading with a stink of impacted mortality, a final reek of hate from shrieking silence, the pustules on his face swell and burst, spattering rotten venom in the breakfast room.

"Mrs. Hardy, help! He's gone bloody mad! Call the police! Call an ambulance!"

Margaras can follow a trail by the signs, the little signs any creature leaves behind by his passage, and he can follow a trail through a maze of computers. All top-secret files are open to him. The rich and powerful of the earth, those who move behind the scenes, stand in deadly fear of his light.

The dim silver light of Margaras can invade and wipe out other programs. He is the Call. The Challenge. The Confront. His opponents always try to evade his light, like the squid who disappears in a spray of ink.

Preferences in food and wines, evaluation of pictures, music, poetry and prose. An identikit picture emerges, charged with the energy of hundreds of preferences and evaluations. He can hide in snow and sunlight on white walls and clouds and rocks, he moves down windy streets with blown newspapers and shreds of music and silver paper in the wind.

Being albino, Margaras can put on any eye color, hair color, skin color, right up until he "whites" the target. "Push," "off," "grease," "blow away" are out: "White" is in. The White Purr: without color, he attracts all colors and all stains; without odor, he attracts all odors, the fouler the better, into smell swirls, whirlpools, tornados, the dreaded Smell Twisters, creating a low-pressure smell wake so that organic animals explode behind them, the inner smells sucked into the Stink Twister round and round faster faster throwing out a maelstrom of filth in all directions, sucking in more and more over a cemetery and the coffins all pop open and the dead do a grisly Exploding Polka. Privies are sucked out by the roots with old men screaming and waving shitty Montgomery Ward catalogues.

Odors can also be the most subtle and evocative agent for reaching past memories and feelings.

"The nuances, you understand."

The wise old queer Cardinal, oozing suave corruption, slowly slithers amber beads through his silky yellow fingers as the beads give off tiny encrusted odor layers. "Ah, a whiff of Egypt . . ."

Chlorine from the YMCA swimming pool, the clean smell of naked boys . . . and the differences, my dear. Just whiff this, from before World War I, when people traveled with steamer trunks and no passports. I mean, of course, the people who *mattered*. Comfortable, isn't it? And smell the Twenties . . . those dear dead days, hip flasks, raccoon coats.

Now sniff way back, to a time before homo sap made his perhaps ill-advised appearance. Notice the difference? Nobody out there. Nobody to talk to. Nobody to impress. Hollywood moguls simply drop dead, like divers with their air lines cut. Personally, I find it exhilarating. I can fancy how I would have done it all. Ah, well . . .

And you know the difference between the air before August 6, 1945, and after that date: a certain security. No one is going to explode the atoms you are made of . . . with a little strength and skill one could outlive himself . . . but now . . .

Margaras is on the Dead Dream case. If you intend to destroy an individual or a culture, destroy their dreams. This is happening now on a global scale.

The function of dreams, they tell us, is to unlearn or purge the brain of unneeded connections—according to this view what goes through the mind in a dream is merely the result of a sort of neural housecleaning. They also suggest that it may be damaging to recall dreams, because doing so might strengthen mental connections that should be discarded. "We dream in order to forget," they write.

But Joe knows that dreams are a biologic necessity, like sleep itself, without which you will die. Margaras is sure this is war to extermination. Sure, forget your biologic and spiritual destiny in space. Sure, forget the Western Lands. And make arrangements with a competent mortician.

But desperate struggle may alter the outcome. Joe is tracking down the Venusian agents of a conspiracy with very definite M.O. and objectives. It is antimagical, authoritarian, dogmatic, the deadly enemy of those who are committed to the magical universe, spontaneous, unpredictable, alive. The universe they are imposing is controlled, predictable, dead.

In 1959, a member of the scientific elite of England said to Brion Gysin: "How does it feel to know that you are one of the last human beings?"

Brion was noncommittal, and the Venusian added facetiously, "Well, life won't be so bad on the *reservation*."

The program of the ruling elite in Orwell's *1984* was: "A foot stamping on a human face forever!" This is naive and optimistic. No species could survive for even a generation under such a program. This is not a program of eternal, or even long-range dominance. It is clearly an *extermination program*.

Joe decided that people were too busy making money to foster a climate in which research could flourish. Joe didn't have ideas about rewriting history like Kim did. More of Kim's irresponsible faggotry: he's going to rewrite history while we wait. Well, let determined things to destiny hold unbewailed their way. DESTINY prances out in an atomic T-shirt—her glow in the dark.

Joe decides to go into deepfreeze for fifty years. With a million dollars judiciously distributed in bonds and savings accounts, the whole system set up with dummy companies and mail drops, Joe will be a rich man when he wakes up.

And what about Kim?

"Oh," Joe shrugs. "I guess that one can take care of himself in the Land of the Dead. At least he won't have any mail-order croaker pulling him out half-baked. Not with that .45-70 hollow point just under the left shoulder blade."

Consider the One God Universe: OGU. The spirit recoils in horror from such a deadly impasse. He is all-powerful and all-knowing. Because He can do everything, He can do nothing, since the act of doing demands opposition. He knows everything, so there is nothing for Him to learn. He can't go anywhere, since He is already fucking everywhere, like cowshit in Calcutta.

The OGU is a pre-recorded universe of which He is the recorder. It's a flat, thermodynamic universe, since it has no friction by definition. So He invents friction and conflict, pain, fear, sickness, famine, war, old age and Death.

His OGU is running down like an old clock. Takes more and more to make fewer and fewer Energy Units of Sek, as we call it in the trade.

The Magical Universe, MU, is a universe of many gods, often in conflict.

So the paradox of an all-powerful, all-knowing God who permits suffering, evil and death, does not arise.

"What happened, Osiris? We got a famine here."

"Well, you can't win 'em all. Hustling myself."

"Can't you give us immortality?"

"I can get you an extension, maybe. Take you as far as the Duad. You'll have to make it from there on your own. Most of them don't. Figure about one in a million. And, biologically speaking, that's very good odds."

We have notice of knives, rebirth and singing. All human thought flattened to a dry husk behind a divided pen. He walks in the glyphs and flattens man and nature onto stone and papyrus, eliminating, except in stone and bronze, the dimension of depth. We were not ignorant of perspective. We deliberately ignored it. A flat world was ours and everything in it had a name once and all the names were ours once. With perspective, names escape from the paper and scatter into the minds of men so they can never be held down again.

The means of suicide haunts their position. We are not averse to a king had a name and had once stone statues to be sure secret in the usual sense and bronze perspective . . . rage of animated dust that growls like a dog . . . barks and snarls of black granite serene crystal converse in sunlight . . . relive in boats a slough to the sky dotted with rafts, the smoke of cooking fire in dawn mist. All human thought flattened there in present time . . . flashes of innocence . . . birth and singing in the marshes.

God of the Long Chance, the impossible odds, the punch-drunk fighter who comes up off the floor to win by a knockout, blind Samson pulling down the temple, the horse that comes from last to win in the stretch, God of perilous journeys, Helper in the voyage between death and rebirth, the road to the Western Lands.

To be reborn at all makes your condition almost hopeless. He is the God of Almost, the God of If Only, the God of Miracles, and he demands more of his followers than any other god. Do not evoke him unless you are ready to take the impossible chances, the longest odds. Chance demands total courage and dedication. He has no time for welchers and pikers and vacillators.

He is the God of the Second Chance and the Last Chance, God of single combat, of the knife fighter, the swordsman, the gunfighter, God of the explorer, the first traveler on unknown roads, the first to use an untried craft or weapon, to take a blind step in the dark, to stand alone where no man has ever stood before . . . God of Mutation and Change, God of hope in hopeless conditions, he brings a smell of the sea, of vast open places, a smell of courage and purpose . . . a smell of silence confronting the outcome.

The Road to the Western Lands is devious, unpredictable. Today's easy passage may be tomorrow's death trap. The obvious road is almost always a fool's road, and beware the Middle Roads, the roads of moderation, common sense and careful planning. However, there is a time for planning, moderation and common sense.

Neferti is inclined to extreme experience, so he gravitates toward the vast underworld of the Pariah Quarter, the quarter of outcasts, of the diseased, the insane, the drug addicts, the followers of forbidden trades, unlicensed embalmers, abortionists, surgeons who will perform dubious transplant operations. Old brain, young body? Old fool has a young body but not the sensibilities of youth. He has sold his soul for a strap-on.

It may be said that any immortality blueprint depending on prolonging the physical body, patching it together, replacing a part here and there like an old car, is the worst plan possible, like betting on the favorites and doubling up when you lose. Instead of separating yourself from the body, you are immersing yourself in the body, making yourself more and more dependent on the body with every stolen breath through transplanted lungs, with every ejaculation of a young phallus, with every excretion from youthful intestines. But the transplant route attracts many fools, and its practitioners are to be found in this quarter.

London, Paris, Rome, New York . . . you know where the streets and squares and bridges are. To reach a certain quarter, you have only to consult a map and lo, a string of lights will show you how to reach your objective on the subway.

In Waghdas, however, quarters and streets, squares, markets and bridges change form, shift location from day to day like traveling carnivals. Comfortable, expensive houses arranged around a neat square (all residents have a key to the gate) can change, even as you find your way there, into a murderous ghetto. Oh, there are maps enough. But they are outmoded as soon as they can be printed.

Neferti uses this method to orient himself and find the Pariah Quarter: place yourself in a scene from your past, preferably a scene that no longer exists. The buildings have been torn down, streets altered. What was once a vacant lot where one could find snakes under sheets of rusty iron is now a parking lot or an apartment building. It is not always essential to start from a set that no longer exists. There are no rigid rules, only indications in this area. Do you pick just any place? Some work better than others. You will know by certain signs whether the place you have chosen is functional. Now, get up and leave the place. With skill and luck you will find the location that you seek in Waghdas.

Neferti seeks out the vilest slums of the Pariah Quarter. He is dressed in the inconspicuous garb of a traveling merchant with a single bodyguard. They encounter an obstacle course of beggars. Neferti tosses a coin to an armless leper, who catches it in the suppurating hole where his nose used to be and hawks it out into a clay pot in a gob of pus and blood. Other beggars squirm forward, exhibiting their sores. The bodyguard lashes out with a flail of copper weights and the beggars shrink back, spitting and drooling hideous curses.

One turns and raises his robe and jets out a stream of shit, smirking over his shoulder.

They turn into a wine shop where Insult Contests are held. These contests are illegal by order of the Board of Health on the grounds they pollute the atmosphere. But in this quarter anything and anybody goes. It's an art rather like flamenco.

One of the creatures who lounge about in female apparel is seized by the Insult Spirit. He leaps up and focuses on a target, imitating every movement and mannerism with vile hate and inspired empathy, thrusting his face within inches of his victim.

An English Major is reduced to hysteria as his monocled, frozen face cracks and a stream of filth pours from his mouth, words that stink like vaporized excrement. He screams and rushes out, followed by cackling laughter.

The victorious insult queen stands in the middle of the floor like a ballerina. He turns and looks at Neferti, feeling for a point of entry, like a questing centipede. Neferti hurls him back with such force that he flattens against the wall and sinks to the floor, his neck broken.

The others spread out in a semicircle. Neferti lashes out with his poison sponge flail. Faces and arms swell and turn black and burst open. He holsters his flail. (Flails are holstered by pushing the handle up through the bottom of the holster like an octopus retreating into its lair and pulling its tentacles after it.)

Neferti adjusts an imaginary monocle. "Let's toddle along and leave these rotters to stew in their own juice. They're filthy."

He stops in a cosmetic shop to rub perfumed unguents on his face and hands, and dusts his clothes with shredded incense.

They proceed to the Encounter Inn . . . bar along one wall, a few tables. The Bartender is a beast man, a baboon cross with long, yellow canines. When Mandrill vaults over the bar, prudent patrons take cover. Now he fixes his baleful little red eyes on Neferti. His glare glazes with reluctant respect. He becomes obsequious.

"How can I serve you, noble sir?"

Neferti orders an opium absinthe. His bodyguard tosses down a double mango brandy. Neferti sips his drink and looks around: some young courtiers from the Palace on a slumming expedition, a table of the dreaded Breathers. By taking certain herbs mixed with centipede excrement, they nurture a breath so foul that it can double a man over at six feet like a kick to the crotch. At point-blank range the breath can kill.

Every Breather has a different formula. Some swear by bat dung, others by vulture vomit smoothed by rotten land crabs, or the accumulated body fluids of an imperfectly embalmed mummy. There are specialty shops catering to Breathers where such mixtures can be obtained. They vie with each other for the foulest breath. The breath mixtures slowly eat away the gums and lips and palate.

Now a Breather exhales into the air above the courtiers' table and dead flies rain down into their drinks. The Breather lisps through a cleft palate, "Noble sirs, I beg your forgiveness. I simply wish to prevent the flies from annoying your revered persons."

Neferti shudders to remember his encounter with an old Breather . . .

The Breather bars his path. His lips are gone and there are maggots at the corners of his mouth.

"A pittance, noble sir."

"Out of my path, offal."

The old Breather stands his ground. He smiles, and a maggot drops from his mouth.

"Please, kind sir."

Neferti shoots him in the stomach with his .44 Special. The Breather doubles forward and such a foul stink jets from his mouth in a hail of rotten teeth and maggots that Neferti loses consciousness.

He came to in a chamber of the Palace, attended by the royal physicians. He shuddered at the memory and vomited until he brought up green bile. Worst of all was knowing that his Ka had been defiled. Three months of rigorous purification, during which he ate only fruits and drank the purest spring water, restored him to health.

A beautiful young Breather with smooth purple skin like an overripe tropical fruit glides over to Neferti.

"Honored sir," he purrs, "I can breathe many smells." He exhales a heavy, clinging musk that sends blood tingling to Neferti's groin.

"I can show you how to pass through the Duad."

The Duad is a river of excrement, one of the deadliest obstacles on the road to the Western Lands. To transcend life you must transcend the conditions of life, the shit and farts and piss and sweat and snot of life. A frozen disgust is as fatal as prurient fixation, two sides of the same counterfeit coin. It is necessary to achieve a gentle and precise detachment, then the Duad opens like an intricate puzzle. Since Neferti had been exposed to the deadly poison of Christianity, it was doubly difficult for him to deal with the Duad.

So he nods and the Breather, Giver of Strong Smells and Tainted Winds, guides them through a maze of alleys, paths, ladders, bridges and catwalks, through inns and squares, patios and houses where people are eating, sleeping, defecating, making love. This is a poor quarter and few can afford the luxury of a private house with no rights of passage. There are many degrees of privacy. In some houses there is a public passage only through the garden. Others live in open stalls on heavily traveled streets, or in the maze of tunnels under the city, or on roofs where the neighbors hang clothes to dry and tether their sheep and goats and fowl. Some are entitled to exact a toll. And some routes are the exclusive prerogative of a club, a secret society, a sect, a tong, a profession or trade. Fights over passage rights are frequent and bloody. There are no public services in this quarter, no police, fire, sanitation, water, power or medical service. These are provided by families and clubs, if at all.

Neferti is dropping his Ego, his Me, his face to meet the faces that he meets. There is nothing here to protect himself from. He can feel the old defenses falling, dropping away like muttering burlap, dripping from crystal bone, burning out like a Coleman mantle . . . the black mantle shreds in the night wind.

In the 1920s, everyone had a farm where they would spend the weekends. I remember the Coleman lanterns that made a roaring noise, and the smell of the chemical toilets. . . . Khaibit, my shadow, my memory, is shredding away in the wind.

The Honey Door

Stoneworkers uncovered a stratum of fossilized honeycombs. The congealed sweetness sealed in over the centuries wafted out and the Pharaoh, Great Outhouse 8, whiffed it fifty miles away in his palace. It was said of Great 8 that he could tell when any of his subjects defecated and differentiate among them by the smell.

He dispatched his most skilled stonecutters to the spot. The stratum of stone combs was cut free from the surrounding rock and carried to the palace. Of an irregular shape, it measured ten by eight feet and in some places was two feet in depth.

Great 8 was very old, and he gave orders for his embalming. After the preliminary procedures of extracting the internal organs and the brain and drying and curing the mummy, instead of being wrapped in linen, he would be placed naked into a sarcophagus cut from the combs, the sarcophagus to be filled with honey.

It is known that sugar does not spoil, and soon others are following in the sweet steps of Great Outhouse 8, having their mummies preserved in orange and strawberry, rose and lotus syrups, glycerine with opal chips . . . the sarcophagus swings on a pivot so that the chips float about, and there is a little crystal window to observe the deceased in his final habitat.

The priests are disquieted and paw the ground like cattle scenting danger. A flood of unorthodox embalming methods could sweep away the fundamentals of our *Thing*, they wail. And their fears are not without foundation.

The embalmer, Gold Skin, has discovered a method by which a thin sheet of metal can be applied to a mummy by coating the mummy with charcoal and immersing it in a vat of gold, copper or silver salts activated by a device which was his closely guarded secret. Wrapped in the Golden Skin, one need not fear the encroachment of extraneous insects or scavengers, of time or water. However, the initial mummification must be doubly rigorous, lest one be sealed forever in the vilest corruption of liquefied flesh and bones and maggots.

Gold Skin leaves a small orifice capped by an airtight seal. Every year, on the conception date of the deceased, the Breathing is observed: the seal is broken, and the assembled dignitaries advance and sniff. If there is evidence of mortification, the embalmer is cut into small pieces, which are consumed in a very hot fire with ten Nubian slaves at the bellows so that every fiber of his being is utterly vaporized, until nothing nothing nothing remains as the ashes blow away with the afternoon wind to mix with sand and dust. It's the worst thing that can happen to an embalmer with mummy aspirations . . . got his condominium in the Western Lands all picked out and paid for.

It sometimes happens that a business rival, a disgruntled former employee or a malicious prankster may gain access to the tomb, make an opening in the gold skin, and squirt in an enema bag of liquid shit and rotten blood and carrion with a goodly culture of maggots selected from a dead vulture. He then seals the opening and polishes the metal so that his intervention is undetectable.

This is the Fifth Breathing, and a goodly crowd is there. On previous occasions a sweet, spicy smell wafted out and there was an appreciative sigh from the guests. This time, as he unscrews the cap, it is torn from his hands and a geyser of stinking filth cascades out, spattering the dignitaries with shit and writhing maggots.

Gold Skin was saved from execution, since the Pharaoh and the High Priest recognized the handiwork of the dreaded demon Fuku, also known as the Mummy Basher for his vicious attacks on helpless mummies.

Fuku is the God of Insolence. He respects nothing and nobody. He once screamed at the Pharaoh, Great Two House 9, "Give me any lip and I'll jerk the living prick offen your mummy!"

Creature of Chaos, God of pranksters and poltergeists, dreaded by the pompous, the fraudulent, the hypocritical, the boastful . . . wild, riderless, he knows no master but Pan, God of Panic. Wherever Pan rides screaming crowds to the shrilling pipes, you will find Fuku.

Cut-rate embalmers offer pay-as-you-go plans, so much a month for mummy insurance. If you live fifty years or die tomorrow, your future in the Western Lands is assured. (An old couple with their arms around each other's shoulders stand in front of their modest little villa.)

The Western Lands are now open to the middle class of merchants and artisans, speculators and adventurers, pimps, grave robbers and courtesans. The Priests wring their hands and warn of a hideous soul glut. But Egypt is threatened by invasion from without and rebellion from within. So the Pharaoh decides to throw the biggest sop he's got to the middle classes, to ensure their loyalty. He will give them Immortality.

"If we alienate the middle classes, they will take their skills to the partisans and the rebels."

"It is true what you say, Great Outhouse. But I likes the old ways."

"I too. It was a good tight club in those days. If things get rough, we can always liquidate the excess mummies."

The Embalming Conclaves are able to offer cheap rates because the embalming is done on a moving belt, each team of embalmers performing one
operation: remove brains, remove internal organs, wind the wrappings. They
become extremely dextrous and quick. What used to take a month can now
be done in a day.

"These changes are too fast for Khepera," moans the High Priest. (Khepera,
the Dung Beetle of Becoming, is seen rushing frantically about, faster and faster.
He throws himself on his back in despair, feebly kicking his legs in the air.)

Three hours and twenty-three minutes from Death to Mummification: an
hour to gut it out good, an hour in the drying vats, an hour in the lime-cure
vats, internal organs stashed in tasteful vases, wrap it up and store it in the
communal vaults, which are carefully controlled for humidity and temperature and patrolled by armed guards at all times.

"You see, Great Outhouse, things have gotten out of hand."

"True. Things always do, sooner or later."

Even the lowly *fellaheen* carry out home embalmings in their fish-drying
sheds and smokehouses. Practically *anybody* can get into the Western Lands.

The young question the mummy concept:

"To keep the same asshole forever? Is this a clarion call to youth?"

"It stinks like petrified shit."

"Have you something better to offer?" says a serious young Scribe. "We
know that mummification can ensure a measure of immortality." He turns to
Neferti. "And what can you offer that is better than such precarious survival?"

"I can offer the refusal to accept survival on such terms, the disastrous terms
of birth. I can offer the determination to seek survival elsewhere. Who dictates all this mummy shit?"

"The Gods."

"And who are they to impose such conditions?"

"They are those who succeed in imposing such conditions."

"To reach the Western Lands is to achieve freedom from fear. Do you free
yourself from fear by cowering in your physical body for eternity? Your body
is a boat to lay aside when you reach the far shore, or sell it if you can find a
fool . . . it's full of holes . . . it's full of holes."

June 6, 1985. Friday. I am in Iran someplace, looking at a map to see if the
secret place of Djunbara, where Hassan i Sabbah took refuge from his enemies,
is on the map. It was somewhere north of the capital. It was not supposed to
be on the map, but it was quite clearly marked.

Now I see a cleft in a block of limestone, and through the cleft I can see an
old man of great strength, a stone man, his arms and legs of smooth marble.

The Stone Man gave HIS a base of power to shut out his enemies and re-
group his shattered forces.

Danger is a biologic necessity for men, like sleep and dreams. If you face death,
for that time, for the period of direct confrontation, you are immortal. For

the Western middle classes, danger is a rarity and erupts only with a sudden, random shock. And yet we are all in danger at all times, since our death exists: Mektoub, it is written, waiting to present the aspect of surprised recognition.

Is there a technique for confronting death without immediate physical danger? Can one reach the Western Lands without physical death? These are the questions that Hassan i Sabbah asked.

Don Juan says that every man carries his own death with him at all times. The impeccable warrior contacts and confronts his death at all times, and is immortal. So the training at Alamout was directed toward putting the student in contact with *his death*. Once contact has been made, the physical assassination is a foregone conclusion. His assassins did not even try to escape, though capture meant torture. By the act of assassination they had transcended the body and physical death. The operative has killed *his death*.

To modern political operatives, this is romantic hogwash. You gonna throw away an agent you spent years training? Yes, because he was trained for one target, for one kill. The modern operative, then, is doing something very different from the messengers of HIS. Modern agents are protecting and expanding political aggregates. HIS was training individuals for space conditions, for existence without the physical body. This is the logical evolutionary step. The physical body is not designed for space conditions in present form. Too heavy, since it is encumbered with a skeleton to maintain upright position in a gravity field.

Political structures are increasingly incompatible with space conditions. They are inexorably cutting our lifelines to space, by imposing a uniformity of environment that precludes evolutionary mutations.

The punctuational theory of evolution is that mutations appear quite quickly when the equilibrium is punctuated. Fish transferred from one environment to a totally new and different context showed a number of biologic alterations in a few generations. But when more fish were brought in, uniformity was re-established. Alterations occur in response to drastic alteration in equilibrium in small, isolated groups. All isolated groups are inexorably assimilated into an overall uniformity of environment.

I am the cat who walks alone, and to me all supermarkets are alike. Yes, and the people in them, from Helsinki to San Diego, from Seoul to Sydney.

What did Hassan i Sabbah find out in Egypt? He found out that the Western Lands exist, and how to find them. This was the Garden he showed his followers. And he found out how to act as Ka for his disciples.

At death the Ren, the Sekem and the Khu desert the body, soon to be a sinking ship. The Ka is stuck with his boy. He is a front-line officer taking the same chances as his men, day after day, not just once like Jesus. If his boy dies in the Land of the Dead, he dies too. Forever. So your Ka is your only guide through the Land of the Dead to the Western Lands, the most dangerous of all roads, since you are facing Death itself. Don't believe the Christian God or

Allah or any of that second-rate lot, in their sleazy heavens of pearls and gold with their *houris,* gods for slaves and servants, with lying promises . . . the Slave Gods.

In present-day Egypt, or in the areas of the Mayan and Aztec ruins, one encounters truncated history, where the present-day reality has lost all connection with the historical past, to create a solid time-block. So the last place to look for clues to ancient Egypt is in Egypt itself.

Specifically, I want to reach Egypt about a thousand years ago, when Hassan i Sabbah was there. The concept of salvation through assassination is taking shape. The first real clue is the Egyptian concept of Seven Souls. HIS sees that the Ka, the Double, is the guide to the Garden. However, the Ka must kill the False Ka in carnate form. And the False Ka, the Feku, *must* present itself when the true Ka takes full possession of the human organism. This is the function of the human organism, to serve as a receptacle for the true Ka. So the enemies of HIS are various carnate manifestations of false, parasitic Kas.

The Feku have the advantage of being infinitely prolific and virtually interchangeable, like a virus. The Feku invades the Ka and immediately starts creating falsified copies. These bear some relation to the original, as cancerous liver cells are made from liver cells. Looks like the real thing but cannot survive contact with the real thing. A cancerous cell and a healthy cell cannot occupy the same space.

Religions are weapons, and some of them act quite rapidly. Witness the explosive expansion of Islam to the gates of Vienna, up into southern Spain, east to Persia and India, west to the Pillars of Hercules and deep into black Africa. In truncated time areas like Egypt, a diving-bell approach is indicated. Time has backed up here and solidified.

"Batten the hatches, Mr. Hyslop, we are going down."

Back through layers of newspapers, cheering crowds, down through Nasser to Farouk, a fat, sad clown, down through the stuffy dining rooms in the Shepherd Hotel that was burned by rioters, flames of the burning hotel snuffed to candlelight on British Colonials, sure of themselves as actors in roles of quiet privilege and self-possession . . . down through the prayer calls, the suffocating stagnation of the Arab world, back to an explosion of energy sweeping up to the gates of Vienna, up into southern Spain, over to the Atlantic, then KLUNK. And Allah hits a thousand-year writer's block.

"Sun cold on a thin boy with freckles," Burroughs repeats for a thousand years.

Allahu Akbar . . . Allahu Akbar . . .

So Allah overwrote a thousand years, and now he can't write anything better than Khomeini. I tell you, those old mullahs got a *terrible* look in their eyes. It's a cross-eyed look, up and to the left, with a completely disagreeable expression. A dead wooden texture to these faces. This is nasty writing, Allah, and speaking for the Shakespeare Squadron, we don't like it.

* * *

The most severe visitation of writer's block has fallen as my narrative comes to Hassan i Sabbah in Egypt, where he presumably learned the secret of secrets that enabled him to attract followers, establish himself at Alamout and control his assassins from a distance.

I realize that my whole approach to HIS has been faulty. I have put him on a remote pedestal; then, with a carry-over of Christian reflexes, have invoked HIS aid, like some Catholic feeling his saint medal. And when I was defeated I felt betrayed. I did not stop to think that he was also defeated, that he is taking his chances with *me*. Instead of asking about the juicy secrets, I asked another question: Did HIS have as bad a time in Egypt as I had in the Empress Hotel? Immediately I knew that the answer was Yes!

I am HIS and HIS is me. I am not an agent or a representative, to be abandoned when the going gets tough, or disowned by some Chief in a distant office. That is what HIS training achieved. The Ka of his assassins merged with HIS Ka. From that moment on, he is in as much danger, in fact exactly the same danger, as his assassins.

HIS realizes that his ill-fated attempt to become the Sultan's Vizier derived from a deep feeling of vulnerability. Some would call it cowardice. He desperately needed protection against his enemies, who hate him for what he is, but more virulently for what he could achieve. For HIS is the ultimate threat to their parasitic position. The voice of self-evident spiritual fact.

Hell is to fall into the hands of such enemies, and he had barely escaped.

The Land of the Dead: a long street with trees on both sides that almost meet overhead. He walks to the end of the street, where there is an iron stairway going down. On the stairs he finds money, which he dutifully deposits in a trash receptacle as he intones, "Littering is selfish and dirty. Don't do it."

In the Land of the Dead quantitative coinage is worthless, and anyone proffering such tender would reveal himself as totally unchic. But at the bottom of the stairway, which leads to a stone promenade by a river, I spot a coin about the size of a silver dollar. The coin is of silver or some bright metal. Two shoulder blades in bas-relief almost meet in the middle of the coin, just as the shoulder blades of a Russian Blue cat almost meet if the cat is a star. This is a Cat Coin, more specifically a Russian Blue Coin, for in the Land of the Dead coinage is qualitative, reflecting the qualities the pilgrim has displayed during his lifetime. A Cat Coin will only be found by a cat lover.

There are Kindness Coins: the bearer has helped someone without consideration of payment, like the hotel clerk who warned me the fuzz is on the way, or the cop who laid a joint on me to smoke in the wagon. There are Child Coins. I remember a dream child with eyes on stalks like a snail, who said, "Don't you want me?"—*"Yes!"*

There are Tear Coins, Courage Coins, Johnson Coins, Integrity Coins.

Are there things you would not do for any amount of money? For any consideration? For a young body? The Integrity Coin attests to the bearer's inaccessibility to any quantitative bribe. The coin certifies that the bearer has definitely refused the Devil's Bargain.

A coin cannot be stolen or transferred to anyone who has not earned the right to use it. They cannot be counterfeited. A stolen coin will often tarnish and blacken. It will always ring false on the fork. Every shop and innkeeper has a tuning fork to test the coins proffered in payment. A true Cat Coin will ring out harmonious purrs. A false or stolen coin will hiss and spit. So each coin rings with its special quality.

The Coin of Truth, on which is inscribed the Chinese character of a man standing by his word, rings with truth. You don't need a receipt. If false, it rings hollow and false as Jerry Falwell. The lies slither out.

"Receipt please."

"I'll put it under your door."

"Excellent. I will give you the money at that time."

Certain coins are prerequisite for obtaining certain other coins. Only the coinage of cowardice, humiliation and shame can buy the Coin of True Courage. Child and Cat and Kindness Coins can only be bought with Tear Coins, and Cat and Child Coins can, in turn, buy the very rare Contact Coin. This coin attests that the bearer has *contacted* other beings. There are coins attesting to Cat Contact, prerequisite for the Animal Contact Coin.

Coins of the Long Chance, the horse that comes from last to win in the stretch, the punch-drunk fighter who comes up at the count of nine to win by a knockout, Samson pulling the pillars of the temple down. The expendables, the last desperate gamble, the Coin of Last Resort. It's a one-time coin.

So many coins, and none that can be bought with money or any quantitative factor. The Devil deals only in quantitative merchandise.

"Anything you wouldn't do for money? For a young body? For *Immortality?*"

"Yes—dig out a cat's eye . . . and a lot of other things."

Immediately the deal is off. "Well, if you are going to be like *that.*"

I am. I'd rather slug it out in my seventy-year-old body than agree to some shabby fool's bargain.

Another store is there. Kiki, what house? Half-club interruptions. Renew an alliance which does not amuse?

Acquaintance circumstances a police informer.

(Pause for word from me.)

The dream *pensions* whisper out from Mexico to Paris . . . dust of nights without sleep.

(The Indian is out.)

Lymphatic grey winter walk in the season of pause.

I go in for rat thick boy.

"Hisss." Animal slob planet.

Hummingbird spirit, you have made no fruit.

(A little cold snigger.)

They are gone away, leaving a shutter clattering in the wind.

Tire tracks in freezing mud.

A bandana stiff with jissom in a dry drawer of the empty hotel with the desiccated corpse of a cockroach.

Rain in cobwebs, empty lavatories of summer schools.

Eggshells, wet bread crusts, hair combings.

A large empty loft: a dust of plaster falls on my shoulder like the first stirring of a sail in a storm gathering out of dead sick calm. Plaster is falling all over the room now. Get out quick!

With a boy from the magazine making it in a ditch. Summer night breathes through salt-encrusted gills, the porous taste on his tongue in the rubble of wing sheaths and shells, rose-patterned stone under the archways, blue shadow cool on the silken bed, the scent of hyacinths. Mother and Dad will drive me to Liberty, Ohio, a student town. Kiki doesn't like it.

A warm wind winter stubble
Late afternoon in the 1920s
Room over the florist shop by the vacant lot where I could find snakes under
    rusty iron
A little green snake nuzzles lovingly at my face.
A whiff of speakeasies, white silk scarves, tuxedos, 1920 wraiths that fade from
    the paper.
Christmas was warm soot on melting snow
walking by granite walls on Euclid
and I said to my cousin
"I can't believe it's Christmas."

The night before Christmas
And all through the house
Not a creature is stirring
Not even a louse.
A room with high ceilings
Lobsters in a room with
high ceilings
There's a party down the road
had to be restrained
Mick Jagger and I think
pulled the curtains closed
There was more
I am off to a hunt
Remember it
Last night dogs howling
A dog to feed
Lightning in the south of Spain

Let me tell you some crystal
and pineapples . . . lobster last
have a lobster?
Make luff with you
in a room with high ceilings
Sweet rosebuds dear old prince
Fat and twinkly in his shades
Dead on the toilet seat
Selective historians, come on
Don't be touchy
Umbrageous in the apartment
I glimpsed obligingly a modicum of central heating
A modicum whippet and the central heat
Honky foolery yet if I could
The telephone's ringing through the sky
Littered with silver and BOOM BOOM
Giff any champagne?? When did I?
My God it's all so—
Lobster . . .

The Wishing Machine

The old writer lived in a converted boxcar in a junk heap on the river. The junk heap was owned by a wrecking company, and he was the caretaker. Commander of a junk heap. Sometimes he sported a yachting cap. The writer didn't write anymore. Blocked. It happens.

It was Christmas night, getting dark. The writer had just walked a quarter mile to a truck stop that was serving hot turkey sandwiches with dressing and gravy to go. He was carrying his sandwich back when he heard a cat mewling. A little black cat stepped into his path. As he put down his shopping bag and leaned toward the cat, it leaped into his arms and snuggled against him, purring loudly.

Snow was coming down in great soft flakes, falling like the descent of their last end on all the living and the dead, the writer remembered. So he brought the little black foundling back to his boxcar, and they shared the turkey sandwich.

Next day he walked to the nearest convenience store and bought a supply of cat food. He called the foundling "Smoker" after the Black Smokers. These are clefts in the Earth's crust, two miles under the sea—no oxygen, no light, and enormous pressure. It would seem axiomatic that no life could exist there. However, abundant life teems along the cleft of a Black Smoker: huge crabs and tuber worms four feet long, and clams as big as dinner plates. One brought to the surface is said to have given off an incredible stink like nobody ever smelled before. These creatures eat minerals and suck nutrients from rotten-egg gas.

And Smoker was a strange cat. His fur was a glistening soot-black, his eyes a shiny white that glittered in the dark. He grew rapidly. Smoker, a creature of the lightless depths, where life as we on the surface know it cannot exist, brought light and color with him as colors pour from tar. From the total lack of air, from pressures that would crush a submarine like a flattened beer can, he brings a compressed variety of life. Nourished on phosphorescent minerals, his eyes glitter like diamonds. His body is molded from the absence of light. And Smoker loves the writer with a special affection from his special place, with a message urgent as a volcano, or an earthquake, that only the writer can read.

And the writer begins to write again. Animal stories, of course. He leafs through *The Audubon Society Book of Animal Life* for his characters . . . the Flying Fox, with long thin black fingers and its sharp sad black face, just like Smoker. A Fishing Bat peeks out of a turtle shell. A Pallid Bat creeps forward, the only ground feeder. The writer caresses the pictures as he turns the pages and pulls them toward him, as he's seen a mother cat reach out and pull her five kittens to her.

At sight of the Black Lemur, with round red eyes and a little red tongue protruding, the writer experiences a delight that is almost painful . . . the silky hair, the shiny black nose, the blazing innocence. Bush Babies with huge round yellow eyes, fingers and toes equipped with little sucker pads . . . a Wolverine with thick, black fur, body flat on the ground, head tilted up to show its teeth in a smirk of vicious depravity. (He marks his food with a musk that no other animal can tolerate.) The beautiful Ring-Tailed Lemur, that hops along through the forest as if riding a pogo stick, the Gliding Lemur with two curious folds in his brain. The Aye-aye, one of the rarest of animals, cat-size, with a long bushy tail, round orange eyes and thin bony fingers, each tipped with a long needle claw. So many creatures, and he loves them all.

Then Smoker disappeared. The old writer canvassed the neighborhood with Smoker's picture. He offered a fifty-dollar reward. Finally he bought a Wishing Machine. Directions for use are simple. You put a picture, nail clipping, hair or anything connected with the subject of your wish between two copper plates activated by a patented magnetic device that runs on standard current. Then you make your wish.

"Well, mister. I don't say it *works,* but I knowed a man cleared the acne off his daughter's ugly face. Nobody seen just how ugly it was till he cleared the acne off, and maybe he shouldn't have done it like that. Then he wished the hemorrhoids of his grandmother to recede perceptibly. Before, they was nightcrawlers, now they is like little red worms you play hell threading on your hook. Another bloke kilted a tapeworm in his maiden aunt and her gained ten pounds in one week."

"Will it do anything *positive,* like bringing back a lost cat?"

"Well, I don't rightly know, but I figure with this artyfact the sky might not be the limit."

" 'All is in the not done, the diffidence that faltered.'"

"How's that?"

"Ezra Pound."

"Tell Ezra to pull down his vanity. And bear in mind that this *is* a murder machine. This you gotta hear: man wished his neighbor dead. Neighbor went full crazy and come after the wisher with a chain saw, cut him in two sections like the lady-sawed-in-half act, difference being the wisher was in no condition to take a bow. And then the neighbor dropped dead from the glory of it. So think, before you wish out some rotten-weed wish."

The old Wish Machine peddler drops to his knees and clasps his hands. "Giva me womans, maka me rich!" he mocks.

The Gods of Chance don't like whiners, welchers and pikers. Feed a whiny wish through the Machine, and you will soon have ample cause to whine. And from half-assed wishers shall be taken even that which they have.

"I only want one thing."

"In that case you'll likely get it, one way or another. Well, here's your machine, all gift-wrapped for Christmas. Just a few more calls to make."

Back in his boxcar, the old writer unpacked the machine and plugged it in. He sat down in front of the Wishing Machine and formulated a silent, unconditional wish for Smoker's return, dead or alive, regardless of any consequences. He knew that the fulfillment of his wish might occasion an earthquake (unknown in this area) or a winter tornado. Might even rip the known universe apart.

"Let it come down."

From the boxcar window he could see the snow swirling down like flakes in a paperweight. His wish is a giant arm. He can reach out and turn the paperweight upside down. He can break it in two. He can see Smoker racing through the winter stubble, crystals of snow in his fur, closer and closer. Then, incredibly, a scratch at the door and Smoker's chittering cry. He slides the door open and blackness pours in.

It was a hectic, portentous time in Paris, in 1959, at the Beat Hotel, No. 9, rue Git-le-coeur. We all thought we were interplanetary agents involved in a deadly struggle . . . battles . . . codes . . . ambushes. It seemed real at the time. From here, who knows? We were promised transport out of the area, out of Time and into Space. We were getting messages, making contacts. Everything had meaning. The danger and the fear were real enough. When somebody is trying to kill you, you know it. Better get up off your tail and fight.

Remember when I threw a blast of energy and all the light in the Earl's Court area of London went out, all the way down to North End Road? There in my five-quid-a-week room in the Empress Hotel, torn down long ago. And the wind I called up, like Conrad Veidt in one of those sword-and-sorcery movies, up on top of a tower raising his arms: *"Wind! Wind! Wind!"* Ripped the shutters off the stalls along World's End and set up tidal waves killed several hundred people in Holland or Belgium or someplace.

It all reads like sci-fi from here. Not very good sci-fi, but real enough at the time. There were casualties . . . quite a number.

Well, there isn't any transport out. There isn't any important assignment. It's every man for himself. Like the old bum in the dream said: Maybe we lost. And this is what happens when you lose.

But in those days there were still purple patches, time eddies by the side of the river. I remember a Gypsy with a baboon that jumped through a hoop to an old, foul tune, and a muzzled dancing bear, and a trained goat that walked up a ladder, a German piper boy with a wolf's face and sharp little teeth. Gone, all gone now . . . and soon, anyone who might regret their going will be gone too.

So here I am in Kansas with my cats, like the honorary agent for a planet that went out light-years ago. Maybe I am. Who will ever know?

The Director reels around on an empty deck giving meaningless orders. The radio is out. The guns stopped working light-years ago. The Shadow, Memory, horribly maimed, clings to the Remains, Sekhu. The spirit that must remain in the body after all the others are gone: the Remains, that enabled the others to leave, by giving them a receptacle to occupy in the first place.

Palm Beach, Florida. 202 Sanford Avenue. Mother and I take Old Fashioneds, which I mix every day at four P.M. We are trying to keep my son Billy from getting into more trouble before his trial, on a charge of passing forged speed scripts.

Mother comes into my room with a bag full of empty paregoric bottles from Billy's room, just lying around for the narcs to find. I take the bag down to Lake Worth and throw it out with a stone for ballast.

Every day I walk out to the end of a sandy road by the sea, to wait for four P.M. Once a police car stopped and drove part way out on the road, looked at me, backed up and turned around.

"Just an old fuck with a cane and his trousers rolled."

At least I dare to eat a peach.

The dream is set right there in the sand and driftwood. An L-shaped building with an open door. Standing by the door is an old bum who says, *"We lost!"*

There were moments of catastrophic defeat, and moments of triumph. The pure killing purpose. You find out what it means to lose. Abject fear and ignominy. Still fighting, without the means to fight. Deserted. Cut off. Still we wore the dandy uniform, like the dress uniform of a distant planet long gone out. Messages from headquarters? *What* headquarters? Every man for himself—if he's got a self left. Not many do.

I am looking at a big book, the paper made of some heavy, translucent material. The pages are blue, with indistinct figures. The book is attached to the floor of a balcony. I am looking at the book when two Chinese girls intervene and say to someone else I can't see clearly, "This is ridiculous. After all, he is just an *old bum*."

Battles are fought to be won, and this is what happens when you lose. However, to be alive at all is a victory.

Soul Death takes many forms: an eighty-year-old man drinking out of an overflowing toilet clogged with shit.

"We lost!"

Cancer wards where death is as banal as a bedpan. Just an empty bed to prepare for the next Remains. The walking Remains, who fill up the vast medical complexes, haunted by nothingness.

The door closes behind you, and you begin to know where you are. This planet is a Death Camp . . . the Second and Final Death. Chances of getting out are maybe one in a billion. It's the last game.

The ally Smoker is not lightly invoked, a creature of lightless depths and pressure that could flatten a gun barrel. Smoker emerges in a burst of darkness.

Remember, Smoker will take you at your word . . .

NEWLYWEDS KILLED IN FLASH FIRE . . .

"Not *that* way!" the foolish wisher exclaims in horror. "He left me paralyzed from a botched operation, and then took my bloody bird. All I wanted was to ruin him with a malpractice suit, to see him barred from practice, eking out a meager living as a male midwife, and her peddling 'er dish in Piccadilly. Didn't mean to *burn* them. Hmm, well, I did say 'damn his soul to hell and she should fry with him.' But I didn't mean . . ."

Be careful, and remember there is such a thing as too much of the goodest thing, like a wise guy who wishes all his wishes would be immediately granted. Wakes up, has to shave and dress—no sooner said than done, breakfast already eaten, at the office another million dollars, faster and faster, a lifetime burnt out in a few seconds. He clutches at Joy, Youth, Innocence, enchanted moments that burst at his touch, like soap bubbles.

Mr. Hart wanted the ultimate weapon so he would always be safe. His is a face diseased and covered with pustules, bursting to communicate a secret so loathsome that few can learn it and live. They flee before him in blind panic or drop in their twisted tracks, tongues protruding to the root, eyes exploded from their sockets. Perhaps those eyes saw Smoker.

As Joe moves about the house making tea, smoking cigarettes, reading trash, he finds that he is, from time to time, holding his breath. At such times a sound exhales from his lips, a sound of almost unbearable pain. It is not a pain he can locate in bodily terms. It isn't exactly *his* pain. It's as if some creature inside him is suffering horribly, and he doesn't know exactly why, or what to do to alleviate the pain, which communicates itself to him as a paralyzing fatigue, an inability to do the simplest thing—like fill out the driver's license renewal form. Each night he tells himself firmly that he will do it tomorrow, and tomorrow finds that he simply cannot do it. The thought of sitting down and doing it causes him the indirect pain that drains his strength, so that he can barely move.

What is wrong? To begin with, the lack of any position from which anything can be seen as right. He cannot conceive of a way out, since he has no place to leave from. His self is crumbling away to shreds and tatters, bits of old songs, stray quotations, fleeting spurts of purpose and direction sputtering out to nothing and nowhere, like the body at death deserted by one soul after the other.

First goes Ren, the Secret Name. Destiny. Significance. The Director reels out onto a buckling deck. In shabby theatrical hotels the Actors are frantically packing:

"Oh don't bother with all that junk, John. The *Director* is onstage and you know what that means in show biz!"

"Every man for himself!"

Then Sekem, Energy. The Technician who knows what buttons to push. No buttons left. He disappears in a belch.

Then Khu, the Guardian, intuitive guide through a perilous maze. You're on your own now.

Then Ba, the Heart. "Feeling's dull decay." Nothing remains to him but his feeling for cats. Human feelings are withering away to lifeless fragments abandoned in a distant drawer. "Held a little boy photo in his withered hand . . . dim jerky far away someone has shut a bureau drawer."—(cut-up, circa 1962–63).

Is it the Ka, the Double, who is in such pain? Trapped here, unable to escape, unable even to formulate any place to escape to?

And the Shadow, Memory, scenes arbitrarily selected and presented . . . the badger shot by the Southern counsellor at Los Alamos, sad shrinking face rolling down a slope, bleeding, dying.

Joe is galvanized for a few incandescent seconds of rage. He jerks the gun from the man's hand and slaps him across the face with it.

"But it might have bitten one of the *boys!*"

The boys? Even lust is dead. The boys wink out one by one, like dead stars. The badger turns to bones and dust. The counsellor died years ago, heart attack in his sleep. A shadowy figure stands over him with an old .45 automatic pointed at his chest.

"But, but—I, I—"

The bullets crash into his chest, knocking the breath out. Standing on an empty hillside, a rusting gun in his arthritic hand, like an old root growing around the cracked handle.

"Gibbons," the Director A. J. Connell called his boys. Tailless apes. Ugh! Your gibbon is a very dangerous animal. A friend of mine pushed his pet gibbon gently aside, and the gibbon whirled with a scream of rage and severed his femoral artery with its canines. He knew what to do. He lived. He gave the gibbon to the zoo. Wouldn't you? Bits and pieces.

The Big House at Los Alamos. God it was cold on those sleeping porches. "Get down and waddle like a duck!" says the counsellor, who directs fifteen minutes of exercise before breakfast. Wind and dust . . . where the balsam breezes blow . . . Los Alamos. A vast mushroom cloud darkens the earth.

Ashley Pond is still there. Joe is catching a trout, a big trout, twelve inches. You eat the meat off the back . . . trout bones.

A whiff of incense. He used to burn incense in his room at Los Alamos and read Little Blue Books.

Back in the 1920s, looking for an apartment in the Village. I am wearing a cape and hold a sword in my hand, a straight sword three feet long in a carved wooden sheath with a brass clip. Will it go on the right side, so I don't have to take my belt all the way off?

A sword: "*Je suis Américain, Catholique et gentilhomme.* I live by my sword."—"The Golden Arrow," by Joseph Conrad.

To wail the fault you visualize. What form would surface with an explosive separate being, desperate last chance? The 12-gauge number 4 or never explosive honesty. You see that comes from sincerity the punch-drunk fighter commitment at the count kid. *Bang* and your hybrid is there, speed of light *splat.* Ace in the hole the cats scrap way buried your own laws of nature we create our layout trigger by will. Some of HIS blew up in the sky what of the hybrid? Yes nodded primitive unthinkable not time. Guardian is the saddest shot has a tear in it. Big Bang shotgun art an orgasm of any solid only one of its kind. Chance the hopeless message flashes with the sky final desperate gamble Ruski blow the house layout challenge the immutable results as simple as squeezing energy directed accented brush work.

I want to reach the Western Lands—right in front of you, across the bubbling brook. It's a frozen sewer. It's known as the Duad, remember? All the filth and horror, fear, hate, disease and death of human history flows between you and the Western Lands. Let it flow! My cat Fletch stretches behind me on the bed. A tree like black-lace against a grey sky. A flash of joy.

How long does it take a man to learn that he does not, cannot want what he "wants"?

You have to be in Hell to see Heaven. Glimpses from the Land of the Dead, flashes of serene timeless joy, a joy as old as suffering and despair.

The old writer couldn't write anymore because he had reached the end of words, the end of what can be done with words. And then? "British we are, British we stay." How long can one hang on in Gibraltar, with the tapestries where mustached riders with scimitars hunt tigers, the ivory balls one inside the other, bare seams showing, the long tearoom with mirrors on both sides and the tired fuchsia and rubber plants, the shops selling English marmalade and Fortnum & Mason's tea . . . clinging to their Rock like the rock apes, clinging always to less and less.

In Tangier the Parade Bar is closed. Shadows are falling on the Mountain.

"Hurry up, please. It's time."

LATE WORK

late work
by james grauerholz

In 1988–89, Burroughs tried to slow down—but retirement did not come
naturally to him. He was still traveling to his painting vernissages around the
world, and beginning a new period of work, in films and on record albums. In
October 1988, he went to Portland, Oregon, to act in Gus Van Sant's first
feature film, *Drugstore Cowboy*. At a story meeting in Burroughs' hotel room,
the "older junky" character was discarded in favor of "Father Tom Murphy,"
a version of his time-tested junky-priest character (as in "'The Priest,' They
Called Him"). Burroughs' enigmatic but plain-talking performance drew attention to his profound opposition to the sinister hypocrisy of the so-called
War on Drugs.

Burroughs became fascinated with lemurs, and he traveled to North Caro-
lina to visit the Duke University Primate Center. His interest in prosimians
went back to the 1940s, but now he saw them face-to-face. Something about
these creatures, not so distantly related to Man, resonated in his heartstrings
and his imagination, especially in the context of Burroughs' new emotional
involvement with his cats. He thought back to a character from *Cities of the
Red Night:* Captain Mission, the quasi-historical seventeenth-century pirate
libertarian who established a bisexual pirate colony on the subcontinent of
Madagascar, the lemurs' homeland.

Already Burroughs had written, toward the end of *The Western Lands,* about
the moral lessons he felt his cats were teaching him; now he wrote a novella
called *Ghost of Chance* (High Risk Books, 1995). A limited edition, with art
by Burroughs' friend George Condo, was published in 1991 by the Whitney
Museum. In *Ghost* he depicted the ancient split: from a prelapsarian world of
innocence to our world of human cruelty and suffering. This text also finds
Burroughs struggling mightily with the ambiguous heritage of Christianity.
Despite his ingrained anticlericalism, Burroughs had a soft spot for Catholics
dating from his travels in Central and South America, when the local priests
offered him better hospitality and company than did the Protestant mission-
aries. But Burroughs never converted to the Church.

Hal Willner and Nelson Lyon arrived in Lawrence in late 1988 to record
Burroughs' voice for the music-accompanied *Dead City Radio* and *Spare Ass*

501

Annie albums (Island Records, 1989 and 1991). A year later, Robert Wilson and Tom Waits came to Lawrence to work with Burroughs on the story sessions for *The Black Rider,* a postmodern opera based on an eighteenth-century German folk legend about a young suitor who picks up the Devil's never-erring bullets, but at the price of his true love's life. Burroughs spent a week in Hamburg, working on the final drafts of his libretto, and the *Black Rider* opera premiered to resounding success at Hamburg's Thalia Theater on March 31. This European trip was Burroughs' last great tour for his painting; our colleague, the art curator José Férez, organized exhibitions in Frankfurt, Hamburg, Rome, Paris, and London in March–April 1990.

Still looking for a way "out of Time and into Space," Burroughs became interested in accounts of alien abduction. He was very affected by Whitley Strieber's book on the subject, *Communion,* and he traveled to upstate New York to visit Strieber and his wife, Anne. Staying with the Striebers during a fierce blizzard, Burroughs hoped for an alien encounter, but was disappointed. Back in Lawrence, Burroughs began to work on an unfinished project that was to have linked scenes from John Milton's *Paradise Lost* with an operatic presentation of the "Visitor" experience and the hysterical reactions of the military and scientists.

In February 1991, Burroughs traveled to Toronto to assist the publicity for Cronenberg's *Naked Lunch,* which was already filmed. On this outing, Burroughs experienced severe chest pains for the first time, and when he returned to Kansas, his physician discovered coronary arteriosclerosis. After an unsuccessful balloon angioplasty, Burroughs underwent triple-bypass surgery in July. While recuperating in hospital, he somehow got out of bed and fell, breaking his left hip and requiring a second operation, which he dreaded even more than the first. Medicare wanted Burroughs to sue the hospital over his broken hip, but he declined, saying the accident was his own fault.

Michael Emerton's alcoholism had worsened; after a suicide attempt, he went through an alcohol treatment program and lived in Kansas City for most of 1991. He returned to Lawrence after Burroughs' bypass to help him recuperate from surgery. But Emerton was drinking again, and he was very ill. On September 17 (a portentous date in Burroughs' work), he was driving Burroughs to Kansas City and they went off the road in a rainstorm, totaling the car. Although neither of them was seriously injured, Emerton was miserably ashamed. A few weeks later, in his Lawrence apartment, sometime in the early hours of November 4, 1992, Michael Emerton shot himself fatally. Burroughs loved Emerton deeply, as did I, and we were profoundly depressed all that winter and much of the next two years.

Burroughs could not rest from writing; he continued to handwrite his dreams and ideas, typing them up a few days later. He was assembling a series of file folders from his voluminous dream diaries and the notes he had amassed during and after his composition of *The Western Lands.* One of our colleagues, the Kansas poet Jim McCrary, retyped these notes for him. Burroughs referred to this as "the dream book," but as he neared completion with its editing, in late 1994, he decided to call it *My Education: A Book of Dreams,* and he dedicated the book to the memory of Michael Emerton.

Not long after he had first moved into the Learnard Avenue house, Burroughs postulated another version of his street's name: "Learn Hard." He was interpreting his dreams as signposts to the lessons he had yet to learn in life, and in this, his penultimate book, William Burroughs wrote about almost everyone he knew who had died; in his dream journeys through the Land of the Dead, he encountered them all. Truly, although Burroughs never lacked for loving companionship in Lawrence in his final years, his departed friends now outnumbered his living ones.

from
the cat inside
(SELECTIONS)

I have become in the last few years a dedicated cat lover, and now the creature is clearly recognized as a cat spirit, a Familiar. Certainly it partakes of the cat, and other animals as well: flying foxes, bush babies, the gliding lemurs with enormous yellow eyes that live in trees and are helpless on the ground, ring-tailed lemurs and mouse lemurs, sables, racoons, minks, otters, skunks and sand foxes.

Fifteen years ago I dreamt I had caught a white cat on a hook and line. For some reason I was about to reject the creature and throw it back, but it rubbed against me, mewling piteously.

Since I adopted Ruski, the cat dreams are vivid and frequent. Often I dream that Ruski has jumped onto my bed. Of course this sometimes happens, and Fletch is a constant visitor, jumping up on the bed and cuddling against me, purring so loud I can't sleep.

The cat does not offer services. The cat offers itself. Of course he wants care and shelter. You don't buy love for nothing. Like all pure creatures, cats are practical. To understand an ancient question, bring it into present time. My meeting with Ruski and my conversion to a cat man reenacts the relation between the first house cats and their human protectors.

In 1982 I moved into a stone farmhouse five miles outside Lawrence. The house had been modernized with bath and propane heat and air conditioning. Modern and convenient. It was a long, cold winter. As spring came I glimpsed occasionally a grey cat shadow and put out food, which disappeared, but I could never get close to the grey cat.

Some time later I got my first clear glimpse of Ruski. Coming back from the barn with Bill Rich after a shooting session and he pointed: "There's a young cat." Glimpse of a lithe, purple-grey shape jumping down from the back porch. He was about six months old, a grey-blue cat with green eyes . . . Ruski.

I don't remember exactly when Ruski first came into the house. I remember sitting in a chair by the fireplace with the front door open and he saw me from fifty feet away and ran up, giving the special little squeaks I never heard from another cat, and jumped into my lap, nuzzling and purring and putting his little paws up to my face, telling me he wanted to be my cat.

But I didn't hear him.

Notes from early 1984: My connection with Ruski is a basic factor in my life. Whenever I travel, someone Ruski knows and trusts must come and live in the house to look after him and call the vet if anything goes wrong. I will cover any expense.

When Ruski was in the hospital with pneumonia I called every few hours. I remember once there was a long pause and the doctor came on to say, "I'm sorry, Mr. Burroughs" . . . the grief and desolation that closed around me. But he was only apologizing for the long wait. . . . "Ruski is doing fine . . . temperature down . . . I think he's going to make it." And my elation the following morning: "Down almost to normal. Another day and he can go home."

August 9, 1984, Thursday. My relationship with my cats has saved me from a deadly, pervasive ignorance. When a barn cat finds a human patron who will elevate him to a house cat, he tends to overdo it in the only way he knows: by purring and nuzzling and rubbing and rolling on his back to call attention to himself. Now I find this extremely touching and ask how I could ever have found it a nuisance. All relationships are predicated on exchange, and every service has its price. When the cat is sure of his position, as Ruski is now, he becomes less demonstrative, which is as it should be.

I don't think anyone could write a completely honest autobiography. I am sure no one could bear to read it: *My Past Was an Evil River.*

August, 1984. James was downtown at Seventh and Massachusetts when he heard a cat mewling very loudly as if in pain. He went over to see what was wrong and the little black cat leapt into his arms. He brought it back to the house and when I started to open a tin of cat food the little beast jumped up onto the sideboard and rushed at the can. He ate himself out of shape, shit the litter box full, then shit on the rug. I have named him Fletch. He is all flash and glitter and charm, gluttony transmuted by innocence and beauty. Fletch, the little black foundling, is an exquisite, delicate animal with glistening black fur, a sleek black head like an otter's, slender and sinuous, with green eyes.

After two days in the house he jumped onto my bed and snuggled against me, purring and putting his paws up to my face. He is an unneutered male about six months old, with splashes of white on his chest and stomach.

I kept Fletch in the house for five days lest he run away, and when we let him out he scuttled forty feet up a tree. The scene has a touch of Rousseau's *Carnival Evening* . . . a smoky moon, teenagers eating spun sugar, lights across the midway, a blast of circus music and Fletch is forty feet up and won't come down. Shall I call the fire department? Then Ruski goes up the tree and brings Fletch down.

I have said that cats serve as Familiars, psychic companions. "They certainly are company." The Familiars of an old writer are his memories, scenes and characters from his past, real or imaginary. A psychoanalyst would say I am simply projecting these fantasies onto my cats. Yes, quite simply and quite literally cats serve as sensitive screens for quite precise attitudes when cast in appropriate roles. The roles can shift and one cat may take various parts: my mother; my wife, Joan; Jane Bowles; my son, Billy; my father; Kiki and other amigos; Denton Welch, who has influenced me more than any other writer, though we never met. Cats may be my last living link to a dying species.

Joan didn't like to have her picture taken. She almost always kept out of group photos. Like Mother, she had an elusive, ethereal quality.

For the last four years of her life, Mother was in a nursing home called Chastains in St. Louis. "Sometimes she recognizes me. Sometimes she doesn't," my brother Mort reported. During those four years I never went to see her. I sent postcards from time to time. And six months before she died I sent a Mother's Day card. There was a horrible, mushy poem in it. I remember feeling "vaguely guilty."

This cat book is an allegory, in which the writer's past life is presented to him in a cat charade. Not that the cats are puppets. Far from it. They are living, breathing creatures, and when any other being is contacted, it is sad: because you see the limitations, the pain and fear and the final death. That is what contact means. That is what I see when I touch a cat and find that tears are flowing down my face.

from
my education:
a book of dreams
(SELECTIONS)

Airport. Like a high school play, attempting to convey a spectral atmosphere. One desk onstage, a grey woman behind the desk with the cold waxen face of an intergalactic bureaucrat. She is dressed in a grey-blue uniform. Airport sounds from a distance, blurred, incomprehensible, then suddenly loud and clear. "Flight sixty-nine has been—" Static . . . fades into the distance . . . "Flight . . . "

Standing to one side of the desk are three men, grinning with joy at their prospective destinations. When I present myself at the desk, the woman says: "You haven't had your education yet."

This dream occurred approximately thirty-five years ago, shortly after the publication of *Naked Lunch* with the Olympia Press in Paris in 1959.

Recall a cartoon in *The New Yorker*, years ago: Four men with drinks, at a table, and one insisting on telling a dream he dreamed: "You were in it, too, Al, and you were a little white dog with an Easter bonnet. Ha ha ha . . . Now isn't that funny?" Al doesn't think so. He looks like he would ram a broken glass into the dreamer's mouth, if he wasn't a neutered male in a *New Yorker* cartoon.

For years I wondered why dreams are so often so dull when related, and this morning I find the answer, which is very simple—like most answers, you have always known it: *No context* . . . like a stuffed animal set on the floor of a bank.

The conventional dream, approved by the psychoanalyst, clearly, or by obvious association, refers to the dreamer's waking life, the people and places he knows, his desires, wishes, and obsessions. Such dreams radiate a special disinterest. They are as boring and as commonplace as the average dreamer. There is a special class of dreams, in my experience, that are not dreams at all but quite as real as so-called waking life and, in the two examples I will relate, completely unfamiliar as regards my waking experience—but, if one can specify degrees of reality, more real—by the impact of unfamiliar scenes, places, personnel, even odors.

The two non-dreams are also unique in my dream experience. They are both flying dreams but unlike other flying dreams I have experienced. In most flying dreams I find a high cliff or building and soar off knowing that this is a dream and I won't fall and kill myself. In another flying dream I flap my arms and manage with some effort to attain an altitude of fifteen or twenty feet. In a third type I am jet-propelled at great speed across the sky. In the two dreams that follow I find myself *lighter than air*. I float up, airborne, controlling both direction and speed.

I'm in a room with a high ceiling and a door at one end. The room is full of light and has a feeling of being open and airy. I float up to the ceiling and bob along to the door and out. There is a porch or balcony over the room and now I am up under the porch about thirty feet off the ground. I move out from under the porch and pick up speed and direction.

I land in a catwalk open to my left. Walking down, I see a door at the end of the walkway, about six feet wide and eight feet high. Outside the door a boy in a grey sweatsuit is working at something I can't see, with his back to me. I feel he is hostile, and I couldn't care less. The door opens and a man emerges. He is wearing a very dark blue striped suit, with a tie. He has a black mustache. He looks at me without a trace of friendliness or hostility. Just registering my presence. No one I ever saw before. Out to my left there is a ditch about thirty feet below the ramp where I am standing. Beyond that some pine trees and what looks like a cemetery . . . mausoleums with inscriptions embossed in white stone . . .

Had I gone down there (sorry—time to wake up . . .) I might have found my own name in stone relief, like the stained-glass window in a church in Citronelle, Alabama:

SACRED TO THE MEMORY OF
WILLIAM SEWARD BURROUGHS

My grandfather, whom of course I never saw, died here in Citronelle, of tuberculosis, aged forty-one.

The beautiful mausoleum is empty.

I am in my pajamas at a discontinued subway stop.

Now with James Grauerholz rushing through subway stations with inhuman speed and agility. Jumping across tracks, down stairways, floating through turnstiles . . . and here we are at Johnson's store, open-air booths with counters on four sides.

* * *

So here I am in the Land of the Dead with Mikey Portman. We are sharing an apartment which consists of two rooms with a bathroom between them. Mikey's room is also provided with a sleeping porch. There are two beds side by side and touching each other, lumpy-looking mattresses, throw rugs, eiderdowns, cushions covered in tattered, frayed yellow and gold velvet. Looks like the madam's room in a whorehouse, lacking only an asthmatic Pekingese. It seems an old German lady with tight lace collar and high-button, black shoes has been billeted on us for the night.

Mikey is on the sleeping porch wrapped up in a pink blanket. I tell him he should let her sleep on one of the beds. After all, he can retire to the sleeping porch. And I have assurances she will not even remove her clothes.

"No, I don't want her in here."

"Well, you can stay on the porch. There are two beds."

"I might want to sleep in here."

No use. Death hasn't changed him a bit; the same selfish, self-centered, spoiled, petulant, weak Mikey Portman.

Now I see a small black dog peeking out of the bathroom door which is ajar . . . dog all black, shiny black . . . with a long pointed muzzle quivering like a dowser wand.

"Where did that door dog come from? What is it doing here?"

"Does it matter?" Distilled concentrate of petulant Portman.

"Door man . . . door dog," I say.

He doesn't answer. Obviously I will have to billet the old German lady in my room, which is a duplicate of his room except the beds are smaller.

On a plane and it is going down and I know this is *reality*.

No feeling of a dream . . . we are going down. Passengers across the aisle are all standing up now to see something I can't see because they block my view.

However, the plane lands safely and we disembark on a city street that looks like the Main in Montréal.

"I'm a dreamer Montréal?"

A painting tells a story but viewed from different time and positions simultaneously. Cézanne shows a pear seen close up, at a distance, from various angles and in different light . . . the pear at dawn, midday, twilight . . . all compacted into one pear . . . time and space in a pear, an apple, a fish. Still life? No such thing. As he paints, the pear is ripening, rotting, shrinking, swelling.

An example from my own painting: A flooded, washed-out bridge seen from the side. An approaching truck seen head-on from a distance, the moment when the driver sees that the bridge is gone, a close-up of his face, the fear and calculations written on his face as he unhooks the seat belt. Applies the brakes. All happening at the same time so far as the viewer is concerned.

Take a picture by Brion Gysin: "Outskirts of Marrakech." Phantom motor scooters and bicycles. Solid scooters and bicycles. A place where the painter had been many times at, many different times. As he walks he sees a scooter from yesterday, last year. Perhaps from tomorrow as well, since he is painting from a *position above time.*

And so dreams tell stories, many stories. I am writing a story, if it could be so called, about the *Mary Celeste*. I am painting scenes from the story I am writing. And I am dreaming about the *Mary Celeste,* the dreams feeding back into my writing and painting. A burst of fresh narrative: the Celestial Babies and the Azore Islands . . . digression and parentheses, other data seemingly unrelated to the saga of the *Mary Celeste,* now another flash of story . . . a long parenthesis. Stop. Change. Start.

Should I tidy up, put things in a rational sequential order? *Mary Celeste* data together? Flying dreams together? Land of the Dead dreams together? Packing dreams together? To do so would involve a return to the untenable position of an omniscient observer in a timeless vacuum. But the observer is observing other data, associations flashing backward and forward.

For example, I just remembered a dream where I met a man called Slim I allegedly knew thirty years ago in London. Slim? I don't remember. Thirty years ago? A dull ache . . . "old unhappy far-off things" . . . I meet Slim at the doorway of some apartment. What does he look like? Grey, anonymous face dimmed out of focus? What is he wearing? Grey suit, grey tie, suggestion of scarf and a watch chain.

You see, I am seeing him as he was thirty years ago, five years ago, yesterday, today . . . like Brion's motor scooter in Marrakech. So I should put Slim back there in the paragraph about Brion's Marrakech painting? I don't think so. Who runs can read.

I am using myself as a reference point of view to assess current and future trends. This is not megalomania. It is simply the only measuring artifact available. Observer William: 023. Trends can be compacted into one word . . . GAP. Widening GAPs. GAP between 023 and those who can club seal cubs to death, set cats on fire, shoot out the eyes of lemurs with slingshots. (Oh sure, they are poor and hungry. From 023 they can get poorer and hungrier: 023 doesn't care if they starve to death. There is no empathy, no common ground.) Those who say: "I think animals are a splendid tool for research." . . . Most of it quite useless. But so it does save lives. *Human* lives. Too many already . . . 023 doesn't care. He contributes to Greenpeace, the Primate Center at Duke University, to "no-kill" animal shelters. Not a dime for cancer research!

GAP between 023 and antidrug hysterics like Daryl Gates, Chief of Police of Los Angeles, who says casual pot users should be taken out and shot, and someone named Davey in an article in *SWAT:* "All drug dealers, no matter how young, should be summarily executed. They are murderers many times over." (Like cigarette companies?) In the same category are Paki bashers, queer bashers, and anyone with a "Kill a Queer for Christ" sticker on his heap.

Nigger killers, raw material for lynch mobs, the Bible Belt, the fundamental Muslims—023 feels nothing for these specimens. GAP.

World leaders catering to the stupid and the bigoted. Bush says the drug war has united us as a nation. Of finks and lunatics? What do they care what someone else does in his own room? No skin off them.

GAP. 023 don't like liars. And lying comes natural as breathing to a politician.

The leaders are desperately trying to achieve a standard and malleable human product. But instead, by enforced proximity, the irreconcilable differences of interest and basic orientation are constantly reinforced and aggravated.

Fact is Homo Sap is fracturing into subspecies: 023 predicts that this trend of separation will continue and escalate and will be reflected in basic *biological differences* rather sooner than later.

The leaders, cut off from any intelligent and perceptive observers, will lose control. The motions they go through, the convergences and agreements, will have less and less relation to actual events. This is already happening in Russia. Another trend that will continue and escalate geometrically.

The violent bigots will become more and more bestial, degenerating into a hideous subspecies of vicious and graceless baboons.

"We know our duty."

"Vast army of purple-assed baboons."

The scientists will continue to reject the evidence with regard to ESP and UFOs and withdraw into academic vacuums.

GAP. GAP. GAP.

The dream I am about to relate illustrates the inadequacy of words when there are simply no equivalent meanings. To begin with, it is not a dream in the usual sense, being totally alien to any waking experience. A vision? No, not that either. A visit is the closest I can come. I was there. If I could draw or paint with accuracy, or better still, if I had a camera . . .

Walking down a passageway. The whole area seems to be enclosed—by inference, that is: I never see the sky or anything beyond. I look up and see a handsome boy of about nineteen on a balcony with an older youth about twenty-three or so. The balcony is about thirty feet above the passageway, and the building is red brick. Someway, I get up on the balcony. Behind is a small room with several other people.

The boy is wearing a white shirt with a yellow tie. Now the older youth takes a crossbow, though instead of the bow sticking out on both sides, it is set vertically on the shaft. He puts the bow between the boy's legs—there is an arrow in the bow (double-edge hunting arrow, thirteen inches long and two inches at the base) pointed up to the boy's groin—and pulls the trigger. For some reason the arrow does not hit the boy. I gather this is some sort of test and I am next. I stand without flinching. The bowman says I have passed the test and that now I am one of them. We shake hands.

There is one there who has not passed the test. He is more like a doll than a person, with what appears to be a detachable head. Next, we form a line, one behind the other, and they are showing me how our muscles can become attuned so we are one body. There is a further lesson which I do not understand, involving balance or movement. I want to explore further but want to return later. So I make a note of the spot.

I look down the passageway, which is somewhat like an airport, and walk down. At the end to my right, I come to a square about sixty feet on each side. White stone buildings around the three sides but no windows or doors. Just a few slots or round openings.

Someway this square was connected with the Christian religion. I can see nobody but I feel that there are eyes watching me. Around the walls of the square are what appear to be glass ornaments of some kind, but I can't be sure they are made of glass, nor do I have any clear idea as to what they look like.

I leave the square to the left and there is an area like a living room or a waiting room with potted plants and two people sitting on a couch, one of whom looks vaguely like Jacques Stern, and I ask if his name is Stern. Others gather around: one has a strange, large, white face and a smile that seems painted on. He is formal with me and wishes to introduce himself, but I don't catch the name. I think I should get back to the place where I made a connection and was received.

But I look, now, down a side street and some distance away is a very high building . . . perhaps seven hundred to a thousand feet high, surrounded by other buildings in some red stone. It looks very alien and magnificent and I want to see the large buildings from inside. The roof is shaped like an arch . . . like a huge Quonset hut.

I come to a door in yellow oak which I push open . . . down a large hallway into a large room. But this is not the inside of the large building. Not nearly high enough. But still quite large. There are a number of people there, moving around, engaged in incomprehensible pursuits. I am attacked viciously by a small dog which is biting my hand. It *hurts*. I manage to transfer the dog's jaws to another small dog, wirehaired and black.

I am sitting by a round cage . . . like a zoo aviary. In the cage there are a number of people dressed in some ceremonial costumes. They are, I gather, a presidium. Sitting next to me on a high stool or chair is a tiny boy, not more than a foot high, but thick and with a large head. His face is perfectly smooth, like ceramic. A very handsome and perfect face. He does not move or speak. I walk away, towards a door, still trying to find the inside of the large building. Turning, I see a boy four feet tall with an inhumanly beautiful face and a buckskin jacket . . . like a figure in my painting "The Magic Rose Garden."

I've seen him with just a glance over my shoulder. Did he notice? I don't think so. In fact no one in this area has acknowledged my presence. Except the dog. The miniature boy or man sitting beside me could have been a ceramic statue. No movement, not even blinking.

I open a door, which leads to a square, boxlike room about fifty feet on each side by forty feet high. The walls and floor are white, but unlike Christian Square, this looks like white polished wood and the room is definitely closed at the top, unlike the stone square, which is open on top . . . though I could not see the sky. This wooden room reminds me of a surrealist painting of birdhouses and running figures in the distance. There is a humming sound and the room communicates a strident menace. As if something could pop out of the walls on springs or the room could suddenly shrink down to a birdhouse.

I wake up but it is more like a return. In this experience I have no feeling of dreaming. It is completely real. I am there. It is also definitely alien and unpleasantly so. I have no feeling of being in control, especially not in the two white squares. Both communicate potential danger—incalculable danger. Note that there is no line between streets and private house—all doors seem to be open. This line is a convention of Planet Earth and does not apply in these areas.

Private rooms? Streets? What do these distinctions mean?

Billy was in bed, sick, in a bare room with a river outside. There is no wall to the room on the side facing the river. I had observed two Phoenicians standing on the ice floes. It looks very precarious, I suppose they are swept out to sea? Well, at least they have oars and are quite close to shore.

Billy is in a large bed with a brown blanket. Dr. John Dent is the attending physician. I feel that Dr. Dent is not taking as serious a view of the case as the symptoms warrant. I suggest that Billy has a skin condition. The previous day I had read an article on Paul Klee, who suffered from some skin disease called scleroderma which turned his skin into a kind of armor.

I leave the room and walk down a short corridor into another room. A small room with a low arched ceiling of oval shape, the ceiling arching downward so that it touched the floor at the ends of the room, and there were also little niches in the wall. The whole room was in white plaster, like a tomb, and I began to fear that the door would close and seal behind me. A recurrent nightmare in which I go down stairs that get narrower and narrower and then a door closes behind me. Sometimes the cul-de-sac is a room rather than stairs. I have learned to avoid these traps in my dreams. So now I hastily step back through the door and down the corridor.

Meanwhile the house has become a ship. I have a ticket and I enter the room where Billy was, which is now carpeted in red, with my baggage. Someone tells me to get off the stage. This is a film, and I can feel the boat moving as I step back into the wings.

The boat stops. There is no boat. Just the empty house and the white plaster walls. I walk down the corridor and through the rooms. Nobody has been here for a long time. I am overwhelmed by desolation and sadness, and wake up groaning.

* * *

Since a number of dreams are set in the house at Price Road, 700 South Price Road, I will indicate how that house was, and probably still is, laid out: Ground floor, front door opens into hall. To the left of door, dining room. Behind dining room is kitchen and servant quarters and back door. To the right is living room. Upstairs a back room with two beds, two closets, and a window on three sides, where Mort and I lived and slept. Bathroom and guest room. Above living room is room where Dad and Mother slept. Bathroom. Balcony opening onto garden.

Last night, dream David Budd is with me in back room. Since he often signs his letters "Brother Budd," association is obvious. In dream there is only one large bed. I suggest he use bed in parental bedroom, and we go there. Coming from bathroom is radio broadcast. I think it is a newscast. David Budd is telling me about an island off the coast of Florida. Name is something like Sploetti. He says very nasty people live there.

I find myself there in the capacity of a hospital administrator. Forty beds, two occupied by women patients. I ask if they would like a shot of morphine. They say they would. Looking for narco cabinet. An orderly shows me that you press a button and it opens. Vials with screw tops. Can't assemble injections. Any case, nobody challenges my incumbency.

Looking back through old dream notes I find:

With David Budd in East St. Louis. Tunnels under drugstore. Old hotel. Five little dogs. I suspect them to be door dogs, small dogs who bring death or misfortune when they follow someone across a threshold. East St. Louis is a rundown place with strata from the 1920s and back to the riverboat days. Rural slums . . . corn growing in backyards. Sidewalks with weeds growing through cracked pavement. On one side a fifteen-foot drop with limestone and jagged masonry outcropping to vacant lot. Weeds, brambles, broken masonry and bricks. Whorehouses and gambling joints. Still a heroin drop, I understand.

In the room at Price Road. I find there is someone in bed with me. First I think, Can it be my cat Ruski, but much too big. It's a man! I keep saying "Mort! Mort!" Can it be Mort, who slept in the bed across the room? But it isn't. I see his face finally, an ugly wooden face. It is dark in the room, but looking to the east I see it is daylight outside . . . blue sky and sunlight. I am trying to get the blinds up to let the light in.

The razor inside the filing cabinet. Categories that delineate a name. Biological revolution and see San Francisco dispersed. AIDS loss of outline loud and clear. Death bones of cold cigarette butts. Its secret name is Handle. Cut the lines. Nothing is my name. Like it? I declare biologic homeless despair. A picture city. Grain elevator just so. Where is a snapshot is my name. My purpose can see the room. Risk it!

So I jolt to an end in my Model T which boils. End of the line. Nothing more to say. Here we are. Look around at the 1920s, the 1930s. Look around. Nothing here. Look at Bradshaw, Texas, a ghost town. Dust and emptiness. The quick-draw is dead. The Old West is dead. Quick *and* dead.

A writer's will is the winds of dead calm in the Western Lands. Point way out he can start stirring of the sail. Writer, where are you going? To write. Here we are in texts already written on the sky. Where he doesn't need to write anymore. A slight seismic with the cat book. Always remember, the work is the mainsail to reach the Western Lands. The texts sing. Everything is grass and bushes, a desert or a maze of texts. Here you are . . . never use the same door twice. Sky in all directions . . . on the word for word. The word for word is word. The western sail stirs candles on 1920 country club table. Each page is a door to everything is permited. The fragile lifeboat between this and that. Your words are the sails.

Someone has come into a room where I am.
  "Mort! Mort!"
  As a child I was afraid to be alone and was always relieved when Mort came home and I knew there was now somebody in the room with me. But this is not Mort. It is a stranger, rather fat, in a black overcoat, who moves with a strange gliding motion, not walking but sliding. I am paralyzed with fear, and can't get the top off a tear gas device.

Kiki has taken cough syrup with chloral hydrate. We go out to swim. A large lake or lagoon somewhat like the reservoir at Nederland, Colorado. Blue water reflects a red sun. I say it is too cold to swim—that is, the air is too cold. Kiki goes in the water and sinks out of sight. There is a deep spot a few feet from shore. He then surfaces. What he has stepped into is a huge shoe about six feet in length under the water. There is also various debris that would make swimming dangerous on this side of the lake.
  In Madrid with Kiki. How can I get away without money? I will wire home but it will take several days. Want to make it with Kiki. I find a large four-poster bed with green sheets, rather dirty. Still, the bed will do. I hate Madrid and the thought of being stuck there. It was in Madrid that Kiki was stabbed to death by his jealous keeper who found him in bed with a girl. The jealous lover, who ran a band in which Kiki worked as a drummer, burst into the room with a butcher knife and killed Kiki. Then killed himself.

It seems that we—James, Michael, Bill Rich, George—a few of us have indeed taken over the planet by default, occupying an empty space that no one else was able or willing to occupy. I am lying on a cot in a room with one wall missing. I say: "I will be the Sheriff."

Same dream continued another day. Like I say, we are in control, but I point out that this is precisely the most dangerous moment, since we can expect massive counterattacks from many quarters . . . CIA, KGB, Mafia, Vatican, Islam, Corporate Capitalism, the English, the Moral Majority. I propose myself as Director of Police and Counterintelligence, which will operate under one central command . . . no splitting into criminal, espionage, all that cross-purpose and confusion.

Met some aliens in the street and one of them gave me a pair of glasses. I am now in what looks like an optometrist's store, with mirrors and glass shelves, and find I can see everything quite clearly. The aliens form a group in Paris, and I am eating with them in a restaurant. They are not obvious aliens at first glance, but all rather outlandishly dressed in some sort of costumes, and one of them has a huge face, a foot across, on a normal-sized body. They seem to be well disposed. There are both men and women in the group. Now the bill comes, and I put in an amount that seems fair to me in some currency unknown to me. Large grey notes on parchment paper.

I think it was before Toronto, why do I keep saying Seattle? I am standing in the usual dream set of a large dirty grey loft and a messenger in a slovenly dirty blue uniform with peaked blue cap has a message for me which is diverted by someone else claiming to be me and taking the message. Then another messenger arrives . . . old, with wrinkled yellow parchment skin like a mask showing under his cap, and this time the message is a visiting card with my name on it, all smudged and dirty . . . no dodging this one. *The Postman Always Rings Twice.* Yes, it was just before leaving for Toronto and not precisely an auspicious omen.

Then a dream, first night in Toronto at the Sutton Place Hotel in my luxurious suite. I am at a station and the train comes by and stops only a few seconds, no time to get on, and they are open at the sides like cattle cars. I finally board one and it stops at ARMY POST and everyone gets off. It's the end of the line. I find a macadam road leading down and ask someone if this road will take me to St. Louis. He says yes. How far? "About six miles." I figure I can make it in an hour, being all downhill. Some sections of the road are like a market, with vegetables and fruits and people milling around.

Several terrific attacks during the five days I passed in Toronto. Excruciating pain, radiating down the left arm and up to the jaw. Popping nitro pills like peanuts. It comes in waves and nails you down. No way to detach yourself since there is no place to detach yourself to. Bill Rich met me in K.C. and saw me through. Back through a hailstorm (tornado warning), Tuesday late afternoon. Hail like golf balls. The insurance companies had to pay out millions for dented cars and fractured roofs.

Saw Dr. Hiebert on Thursday after Toronto and straight to the hospital. Dye x-rays showed major artery ninety-eight percent blocked. Angioplasty Monday morning. Left St. Francis Hospital in Topeka on Tuesday afternoon.

A very close thing. Dr. Hiebert said he should not have allowed the Toronto trip. I had no idea just how serious the situation was. Another three or four days and . . . massive heart attack.

I think a lake in Nevada. I could see boats out a window. Last night a Visitor dream. Heard people talking in front room. Mort was there. Then I, Snubbie in hand, stepped out of bedroom and there were two men standing in the doorway to the front room. I went into the front room. Bedstead gone. A man in a red costume was lying on the floor and said something insulting. I said: "I could never shoot anyone without reason." There was a woman who was formed from white porcelain from the waist up. She is cavorting around. A man who announced himself without saying anything as a *Visitor* and leader of the group said: "You are causing trouble. You have too many irons in the fire." His face is grey and anonymous. His upper lip does not move when he talks but I can see grey teeth. Fletch, who is on my bed, says something enigmatic. There is a reference to Ted Morgan and a filter cigarette, half smoked in ashtray.

It often happens in a dream that two or more narrative lines are happening at the same time, but one intends to impose sequential structure so that one follows the other.

I am on a train. Allerton passes me going towards the back of the car in the other direction. He looks very young and handsome dressed in a light-brown suit. I call out: "Allerton!" but he doesn't hear me because of the train noise. So I get up and start after him. Into the next car, but I don't see him, and the car ends in a seat that runs all the way across. So I turn around and start back.

I am on a train going back to St. Louis. I have been drafted into the Army as a private and I am in uniform. I feel very disgruntled. How can they draft a man of seventy-two? The doctor has made a mistake. It is ridiculous. I have a feeling of having come full circle, back to this dreaded point. The train stops and I get out, walking under an arcade. I realize now that I don't have my passport with me.

I walk out of the station. There is a square in front of me and the mountains in the background. Looks like Colorado Springs. Just back from my search for Marker. There are long bunks along both sides of the car at the top. There are young boys in the bunks, all returning from school somewhere.

I walk into a large room like a gymnasium behind the train. The room is empty. I see some canes in one corner but when I go to look at them, they are gone. There is a closet or locker and a pair of high shoes.

Back on the train. There is a long ride and absolutely nothing to do. How can I endure the time? A feeling that there is nothing outside the train gives me a terrible sense of being enclosed in nothingness.

Back in the room, which opens into another room. "An overwhelming feeling of universal damage and loss." Just the shoes he used to wear. Dust and mold, and nothing outside the room.

I am groaning with grief and desolation.

"Oh my God. Nothing here. Nobody here. Just the empty shoes."

Whose empty shoes?

Well, let us contact the Muse. Come in, please . . .

Egypt. What am I doing here? It's terrible. I can't stand to be living in lodging houses with hostile innkeepers. They all hate me on sight, as do all dogs. I have to get out of this nightmare. But how? We will go upriver to Memphis to find the old Gods—terrible old frauds most of them, but some did have some items of value. Here is an amulet from Bast the Cat Goddess. There is also a male cat-God amulet. All dogs hate and fear it, for it brings the ancient hate into the open. What is a master of ten enraged cats?

He had achieved a modicum of serenity in Alexandria, but the dogs made his life a hell. Then he got two bodyguards with heavy clubs, but even this was not enough and they frequently had to use their short swords. Finally he captured a wild cat. He nurtured it and it became his cat. It rubbed itself against him and jumped into his lap.

Now it is time. He releases the cat and points to the dog. The cat streaks towards the target and leaps on the dog and tears its guts out.

The boys set up a guerrilla unit with the young Maize God. Traveling in time on the sacred books, they pick up allies: Tío Mate, an old assassin with eight deer on his gun, followed by El Mono, his adolescent Ka. Wild boys with eighteen-inch Bowie knives, head hunters and bandits, Castro and Chinese guerrillas, Black Panthers and hippies.

The priests have not been idle. They have opened negotiations with the United Fruit Company to arrange for a landing of Marines. They send in an agent to infiltrate the guerrillas.

The agent shows up at a guerrilla encampment:

"Shucks fellers, you got a *reefer?*"

"Who is this mother?"

A Black Panther with a submachine gun and a headhunter with a spear cover the stranger.

"You here to report to the head shrinker for a security check?"

The Security Department is divided down the middle into two sets. On one side is a brisk Scientology auditor with an E-Meter set up on a card table.

"Will you pick up the cans please. Thank you."

On the other side is a grass hut with shrunken heads on shelves. The headhunter takes up a stand facing the agent with his spear raised. Seated on a high chair is a Death Dwarf with larval flesh and skeleton face. He reaches forward and takes the agent's other hand with dry electric fingers.

"Do you know any CIA men personally?"

The agent looks wildly around at the shrunken heads of his predecessors.

"That reads . . . What do you consider that could mean?"

"The whole idea is repugnant to me. I'd as soon make a friend of a cobra."

"LIE. LIE. LIE," screams the Death Dwarf.

"Why, I've always been a Commie."

"That reads . . . What do you consider this could mean?"

"LIE. LIE. LIE."

"Do you have any unkind thoughts about M.O.B.? . . . That reads . . . What do you consider this could mean?"

"Why, all I ever wanted to do was mind my own business and smoke *reefers*."

"There's another read here."

"LIE. LIE. LIE."

"Are you connected to the CIA? Are you a CIA agent?"

"You got me wrong. I swear to you on my Scout's honor . . ."

"LIE. LIE. LIE."

"That ROCKSLAMS. What do you consider this could mean?"

The agent's head shrinks to the size of a fist and takes its place on the shelf.

With Alex Trocchi and Kafka. Kafka had cancer. We took a cab to the country club. Moroccan Ginger was the doorman and he said that Kafka could not come in. Inside, the members were eating at a cafeteria table. Walked around trying to find our way back out of the club. A sort of maze that ended up in a swimming pool and a Turkish bath. Finally found an exit and started down the road. Alex joined me with some firewood.

My analysis. Many years, a lot of money—one would be tempted to say complete waste of time and money, but no experience is ever lost on a writer. I would prefer not to discuss my horrible old condition at the beginning of a long period of analyses and psychotherapy, but on the other hand, I could get around, hold down jobs. Well, something happened and some little key was turned . . . perhaps so that I went on to do what I have done. Maybe no connection. It's like the one percent of penicillin in old Chinese prescriptions. They didn't know what the one percent was or more accurately *where*. And my gut feeling is that all there was in all this is a couch. This is the reason I am not buying a new couch, to save money. Anyhoo. There was a time . . . oh well . . . Dr. Federn, who killed himself. Nice old gentleman.

Did I seriously consider this any proof of telepathy?

I replied: "My dear shrink, I do not consider anything proof of anything, in any case, not involved in proving anything."

Like a young thief thinks he has a license to steal, a young writer thinks he has a license to write. You know what I mean right enough: riding along on it, it's coming faster than you can get it down and you know it's the real thing, you can't fake it, the writer has to have *been* there and make it back. Then it hits you, cold and heavy, like a cop's blackjack on a winter night: *Writer's Block*. Oh yes, he tried to warn me, the old hand, "You write too much, Bill. . . ." I wouldn't listen.

Then it slugs you in the guts. For a whole year I couldn't remember my dreams. Tried going without pot and everything. It was like some grey bureaucrat wiped away the dream before my eyes as I tried to grasp one detail that would bring the dream back, the outlines: dead. James complained I sat for hours in my chair at the end of the loft, doing absolutely nothing. Stagnating without tranquillity. The pages and pages with nothing in them: the writer has been nowhere and brought nothing back. The false starts, the brief enthusiasm. Books that died for the lack of any reason to stay alive after ten pages.

Then you get it back. It's there. You know. You can feel it, like the opening character . . . I was there on that mesa with Kim. Kim, my spacecraft for travels in the nineteenth century. I could see it from where I was, the arrowhead there in my hand. The dizzy awe, as if you could flash back through the millions or so years to the beginning, the caves, the hunger. Kim knew he had always been gay, making sex magic in front of the paintings to activate them, covered with animal skins he whines and growls and whimpers off, his sperm drips down the animals' flanks. Kim adored these animal impersonations. He was turning into the animals and found he had much more in common with the predators than the herbivores. You can see what a dog or cat is thinking, but the mind of a deer is a strange place, a strange green place. It's hard to get in there. The men swaying about with antlers on their heads are trying to get into it, mindless and beautiful.

Don't want to write this. Have said no honest autobiography has ever been attempted, much less written, and no one could bear to read it. At this point I guess the reader thinks I am about to confess some juicy sex practices. Hardly. Guess I was twenty-four, working in the shop at Cobble Stone Gardens, which I hate to remember, when this Jew woman sent me around to the servants' entrance and I drove away clashing the gears and saying: *"Hitler is perfectly right!"* So you want it honest? You vant? You vant? You vant?

One afternoon, Kammerer was there, and you could say about him, as Toots Shor said about Jimmy Walker at Walker's coffin: "Jimmy, when you walked in you brightened up the joint."

And I said: "Since I've had this job, my voice is changing."

And Dave says something about "the Catlins, you know them."

"I'm acquainted with the family," I said in my obsequious manner, and we had a laugh.

Stalling. Don't want to go on.

This context, one night in the house at Price Road. Went down to the icebox. (I was wretchedly unhappy. No sex. No work that meant anything—nothing.) Dad was there eating something. It's a suburban custom, raiding the icebox. "Hello, Bill." It was a little-boy voice pleading for love, and I looked at him with cold hate. I could see him wither under my eyes as I muttered, "Hello."

Looking back now, I feel an ache in the chest where the Ba lives. I reach out to him: *Dad! Dad! Dad!*

Too late. Over from Cobble Stone Gardens.

When Mother was in Chastains Nursing Home in St. Louis the last four years of her life, I never went to see her. Just sent mawkish cards from London on Mother's Day, and occasionally postcards from here and there. Remember years ago—fifty? don't remember—she once said to me: "Suppose I was very sick. Would you come to see me? Look after me? Care for me? I'm counting on that being true."

It wasn't. The telegram from Mort. I had gotten out of bed. For a moment I put it aside. "Mother dead." No feeling at all. Then it hit, like a kick in the stomach.

L. Ron Hubbard, the founder of Scientology, says that the secret of life has at last been discovered—by *him*. The secret of life is *to survive*. The rightest right a man could be would be to live infinitely long. And I venture to suggest that the wrongest wrong a man could be might well be the means whereby such relative immortality was obtained. To survive what, exactly? Enemy attack, what else?

We have now come full circle, from nineteenth-century crude literalism through behaviorism, the conditioned reflex, back to the magical universe, where nothing happens unless some force, being, or power wills it to happen. He was killed by a snake? Who murdered him? He dies of a fever? Who put the fever curse on him?

Many years ago my first contact with the Land of the Dead: It is in the backyard of 4664 Pershing Avenue. Darkness and patches of oil and smell of oil. In the house now, and I am bending over Mother from in front, eating her back, like a dinosaur. Now Mother comes screaming into the room: "I had a terrible dream that you were eating my back." I have a long neck that reaches up and over her head. My face in the dream is wooden with horror. It is like a segment of film underexposed. Not enough light. The light is running out. Dinosaurs rise from the tar pits on La Brea Avenue. Oil and coal gas.

Back through the sixties, slow letup in drug pressure . . . now back through the fifties . . . Anslinger in full swing. Morphine and Dilaudid scripts . . . Pantopon Rose . . . Old-time junkies at 103rd and Broadway . . . Back back clickety clack . . . Syrettes . . . World War II . . . The thirties . . . Heroin is $28 an ounce—back back . . . the Crash, the twenties . . . film stars on junk, Wally Read . . . Wilson Mizner . . . World War I . . . Keep the home fires burning though the hearts are yearning . . . back before the laws . . . another air . . . a different light . . . free lunch and beer at five cents a mug . . . back . . . no lines to the present . . . cut all lines . . . here come the lamplighters, ghostly private places . . . Westmoreland Place . . . Portland Place . . . empty houses, leaves blowing and drifting like shreds of time . . . radio silence on Portland Place . . . furtive seedy figures, rooming houses and chili parlors, hop joints, cathouses . . .

Afternoon Lake

July 27, 1991—after three weeks in the hospital in Topeka for triple bypass and fractured hip.

Flying over African set in a rickety old tin plane. I am in a windowless cubicle, jiggling about; if it turns upside down I will know this is It. But we land on the edge of a lake or inlet, in a basin. Standing there on the shore, I can see fish swimming in the clear, yellow water, twenty or thirty feet deep, and deeper towards the middle. Lily pads three feet across, yellow-grey in color, some dry on top—others soaked through, stems reaching down into the clear, still water. In the distance an inlet, in clear, golden afternoon light.

In that hospital there were interludes of blissful, painless tranquillity. (I start awake with a cry of fear.) Slipping, falling, deeper and deeper into easeful rest after the perilous journey, silent peace by the afternoon lake where the sun never sets and it is always late afternoon.

How did we get here, somewhere in Africa? In a rickety old tin plane. He was in a metal-lined cubicle, sheet iron, like the inside of an orgone accumulator. There were no windows but it was light. He could feel the vibrations and he knew the plane was in danger of a crash, but it lands and he gets out.

He is on the edge of a lake, sixty feet deep in the middle. About two hundred yards across. On the other side is a village. Black children trickling out along the shore of the lake, in little white suits and dresses. The water is a clear yellow, slanting steeply down to the center. There are large lily pads three feet across, and the stems reaching down to the bottom in a green-yellow haze where big, black fish swim around the stems. Fish range from one foot to three feet in length. The lake is in a basin. Away in the distance in a golden glow, I can see more water, a larger lake or river.

I am standing on the near side of the basin with the pilot, who wears shorts and knee-length socks. He says something about the white stones that litter the slope, none larger than a Ping-Pong ball. I cannot see over the edge.

Slowly a familiar odor fills my nostrils. Piss? *Piss!!! The lake is piss.* Years and years of strong yellow piss. And slowly the full desolate horror of that stagnant place hits him like a kick in the stomach.

"Fishing, anyone?" The scales are encrusted with crystals of yellow piss, the flesh yellow and oily with piss. Where is the plane? No plane here. He tries to reach the top of the basin. Keeps sliding back on white stones, smooth and slippery. Where is the pilot? No pilot here. The sun is not moving. Just a steady glow in the golden distance, on the great brown-yellow river of shit and piss.

The Duad! Out of the basin!? Beyond the basin? There is nothing beyond the basin!

A deep slough of clear, yellow urine, seepage of centuries from the Duad, there in the western distance, bathed in the golden glow of a sun that never sets.

Eternal vigilance and skill in the use of weapons that will never be needed here in this yellow stalemate where it is always late afternoon.

The city is vaguely reminiscent of New York, with the Land of the Dead superimposed. Dark, dirty streets littered with trash and garbage, but trash from what usage? And garbage from what foods and what containers? The smell of death and rot is here, from decay of unfamiliar offal. Many of the buildings appear deserted or semi-deserted. Many have stained marble facades and steps. The streets are narrow. A park in front of the traveler is a twisted tangle of roots and vines and misshapen trees.

I am leaving an old lover, who has taken a wife and has no further need of me. Looking at the tangled roots, the rotting fruit and phosphorescent excrement, I realize that I must face the nature of my own need.

Why do I need to be needed, and why can I not face and eliminate this abject need? For inexplicable and therefore inordinate need is always abject and unsightly. A man who suffers, however intensely, from frustrated sexual needs is always an object of contempt. He has only himself to blame. But it may be very difficult for him to face the parts of himself he can blame.

The pain of thinking about the lost lover and his new lover disporting themselves, with no thought of my pain and need, cuts like a salted wire whip.

Cabin on the Lake

Now I got no use for a big house, just two bedrooms, and one is my art studio . . . don't really want a guest room, 'cause I don't really want guests, they can sleep on the sofa . . . and I got me this cabin out on the lake. Got it cheap since I was able to put up cash, which the owners needed to put down on another house they is buying out in the country. Could easy sell it now, but what for? A few thousand profit? Nowadays what can you do with that kinda money?

My neighbor tells me right in front of my dock (I've got the *access,* and that is the thing matters here on the lake . . . a dock, see!), well, my neighbor tells me that right in front of my dock is the best catfish fishing in the lake, but I don't want to catch a catfish. They squawk when you pull them out of the water and snap at you like an animal, and I don't want to kill no animal. Besides which, they is a bitch to clean . . . have to skin them with a pair of pliers, and their guts is like animal guts. Course, I could turn the fish loose— unless he swallowed the hook, and then what I'd have to do is cut his head clean off with a machete and end his misery.

I could cope with a bass, or better, some bluegills—half pound, as tasty a fish as a man can eat—fresh from the lake, and I got me an aluminum flat-bottom boat, ten foot long, $270 . . . a real bargain. I likes to row out in the middle of the lake and just let the boat drift. I hear tell there's been flying saucers sighted out here on the lake, and I'm hoping maybe one will pick me up. These aliens the government is trying to hush up, they got no stomachs, nourish themselves from photosynthesis—so you can see why the scum on top of us want to hack that up. The whole fucking planet is built on eating, and if a surgical intervention could remove all stomachs, the whole shithouse would come crashing down and then we could look at Bush and that tight-assed bitch Thatcher and Mohamad Mahathir, that Malaysian bastard hangs people for smoking pot . . . would be flopping around like displaced catfish, only I wouldn't feel a thing for them, just stand there and watch them die. It would be my pleasure.

So I rows out and lets the boat drift, looking at the hill beyond the lake and just hoping for a flying saucer and humming to myself, "Swing low, sweet chariot, coming for to carry me home," and take out my stomach so I don't give a shit about no government. I can just set there from here on out . . . but nothing happens, leastwise nothing I can *feel* happening . . . but maybe it will happen when I go to sleep . . . but then I just wake up in my bed, to get up and feed my six cats. First thing would be to have their stomachs took out, so they would let up aggravating me.

Now lying comes as natural as breathing to a politician, and just as necessary for his survival. I reckon that's what happened with John F. Kennedy . . . he was on the edge of committing the criminal, unforgivable sin: he was about to tell the truth, and somebody called a special number in Washington.

Yeah, it sure would pleasure me to see the whole lot of them—Bennett, Bush, Thatcher, Mohamad Mahathir, Sad-Ass Hussein—flopping around out of their medium and gasping out their last lies.

One thing I hate more than other things is a liar. Maybe it's because I am not capable of lying. Even a simple everyday lie, like claiming I am sick to avoid a trip or an appointment, rings so hollow, even over the phone, that nobody will buy it.

It was a Thursday. For me, a portentous conjunction: I was born February 5, 1914, which was a Thursday. September 17 is also a special date for me. Arbitrary but significant, with potential for good or bad luck.

It was eight A.M. when I left my house in Lawrence, with Michael Emerton driving his BMW. The rain is coming down in sheets, and there is a yellow-grey haze across the sky. We pass the toll booth and the quarry lake, going 65 mph. Then the rain comes down so heavy and visibility is limited to the hood of the BMW and I *know* and start to say, "For Christ's sake, Michael, slow down and pull over," when the car hydroplanes and slams into the guard-rail and skids across the highway and into the ditch. *Stop!*

For a moment I can't move, and I mutter, "I need an ambulance," as if my need can conjure up such a contrivance. Then the door opens and a young man in a brown windbreaker says, "Can you walk?"

I find that I can indeed walk, with my cane and his supporting arm.

"Better move away," he says; "the car might catch fire." Another young man is helping Michael. They drive us ahead to the truckstop.

"You guys are lucky you're not dead."

Lawrence Journal-World, September 22, 1992; Classified Ads

Card of Thanks

To express our heartfelt thanks to the two young motorists who helped us out of a wrecked BMW 6 mi. E. of Lawrence on turnpike on Thurs., Sept. 17, 1992.

William Burroughs & Michael Emerton

Michael B. Emerton shot himself November 4, 1992.

An experience most deeply felt is the most difficult to convey in words. Remembering brings the emptiness, the acutely painful awareness of irreparable loss.

From my window, I can see the marble slab over Ruski's grave . . . Ruski, my first and always special cat, a Russian Blue from the woods of East Kansas. Every time I see the grave, I get that empty feeling where something was, and isn't anymore, and will never be again.

epilogue
by james grauerholz

After he revised the final edit of *My Education* in late 1994, William Burroughs never worked on a novel again. He turned instead to studio performances; in early 1995, he recorded an abridged version of *Naked Lunch* for an audiobook. His first cat, Ruski, died that spring, which hurt him deeply. In the fall, he flew to New York to see Paul Bowles, who had made a rare trip to the U.S. for arterial surgery on his legs. Burroughs made no secret of his expectation that this would be their last meeting. In early 1996, Burroughs recorded an audiobook of *Junky*. When Timothy Leary was dying of cancer that spring, he spoke often with Burroughs by telephone, and on the last phone call they talked openly of Leary's imminent death. The old junky priest was making his last rounds, taking confession and giving extreme unction.

By summer 1996, Burroughs' life had become a comfortably revolving schedule of dinners in his home with his close friends. The years had caught up with him, and he made allowance for the need to conserve his energy—despite the ever-growing demands of his celebrity. When the "Ports of Entry" museum exhibition, curated by Robert Sobieszek, was unveiled at the Los Angeles County Museum of Art that July, the retrospective show demonstrated a visual-arts continuity in Burroughs' life for the past three decades, beginning with his collage-scrapbooks and *The Third Mind*. Burroughs returned home from Los Angeles recharged with energy from these encomia. He received Allen Ginsberg in his home for a two-week stay, and they talked about the worsening condition of Herbert Huncke, who died in October.

Ginsberg returned to Kansas in November when the "Ports of Entry" show moved to the Spencer Art Museum at the University of Kansas. At the end of the month, KU's Lied Center for the Performance Arts hosted a "Nova Convention Revisited" performance night. The surviving veterans of the 1978 convention—Patti Smith (joined by Michael Stipe), John Giorno, Philip Glass, Ed Sanders, Debbie Harry and Chris Stein, Laurie Anderson—all performed in tribute to Burroughs' life accomplishment. Watching in state from his opera box, Burroughs was pleased and grateful for the recognition, and for the outpouring of love and appreciation from his adopted community of Lawrence.

In February 1997, Burroughs was eighty-three years old. He knew that his heart was going: it was his family heritage. Burroughs had already outlived his older brother by eleven years, and he now carried nitroglycerin tablets with him at all times. He was examined in March for a heart-valve problem, but the surgical options were of no further interest to him; he contemplated taking a dose of ketamine, for its promised preview of the near-death experience, but he concluded that the experiment might be fatal in itself. Burroughs had never approved of suicide, and especially not after experiencing the pain that Emerton's death caused to everyone who loved him. Burroughs had been relieved when Leary's announced plans for a public suicide, live on the Internet, came to nothing; he did not believe in any such display or intervention.

At the beginning of April, Allen Ginsberg, whose health had been failing for a few years, informed Burroughs by phone that his doctors had discovered inoperable liver cancer, and that he had only a few months to live—"but probably much less." How very much less became clear a few days later, when Ginsberg died, at home in New York, on April 5. Burroughs' reaction was philosophical, and more and more he spread a sense of calm and acceptance among his circle of friends. Ginsberg had told him: "I thought I would be terrified—but I am exhilarated!" Burroughs confessed that this had given him new courage in the face of death.

The spring and summer of 1997 were busy times, mostly with visitors. Burroughs continued writing every day in his private journals, by hand; his arthritis had made it impossible for him to use a typewriter. Even more friends than usual came through town, and some old comrades were welcomed back into the fold. Despite some people's fanciful beliefs, Burroughs was never isolated in Lawrence; during his sixteen years of residence there, he made dozens of trips and received at least a thousand visitors in his home. Because of his fame and a published address, in his latter years Burroughs heard from many long-forgotten friends, from all the times and places of his life. The grandniece of his first wife, Ilse Klapper, sent a photograph of Ilse, and the news that she had died peacefully in the 1980s; this information put Burroughs' mind to rest on a question that had long troubled him.

Not long after July 4, Burroughs found his favorite cat, fat old Fletch, dead in the yard by a little pond, apparently from heart failure. All that year, his cats were disappearing: Spooner, succumbing to feline leukemia; Senshu, swept away in a spring flood; Calico Jane, hit by a car. From his bedroom chair, where Burroughs read and wrote and took his afternoon cocktails, he could see all their graves around the pond. The death of Fletch was the worst, and Burroughs' heartache was tangible. In his journals, he wrote of his desire to be reunited with his familiars.

I spent all of the last day of July with Burroughs; the final round of visitors was gone, and although his energy had been subdued for weeks, he was very much our same old William. He had been target-shooting with friends that Tuesday, and due to his successful cataract surgery that spring, he was hitting the target better than ever. His arthritis troubled him, especially in his right hand, his writing hand; he was stooped from a lifetime of reading and writing; and he was easily winded. But he was not crippled, nor incontinent, nor senile. William said good night to me that Thursday night, with a hug, as always, and I left him there with three of our friends.

On the afternoon of Friday, August 1, when the painter George Condo called Burroughs to tell him that the paintings they'd made together would be shown in New York in December, Burroughs told him: "I am looking forward to some quiet time." At about four o'clock, he suffered a severe heart attack. In the diary he was writing, after an entry for August 1 about "no final answer," he wrote on the opposite page, in a struggling hand: "Love? What is it? The most natural painkiller what there is. LOVE."

Our close friend Tom Peschio happened by the house just at that moment, and called me, and summoned an ambulance. Burroughs was quickly aided by paramedics, sedated, and hospitalized at Lawrence Memorial. Our snake-expert friend Dean Ripa was in Lawrence, and he and Tom and I kept a vigil at William's bedside for twenty-four hours; William said nothing in all that time. He gave up breathing and died at 6:50 P.M. on August 2, 1997, very peacefully. We three were the only witnesses. I requested that his body lay untouched and undisturbed in the hospital for several hours, as the Buddhists recommend, and the hospital staff very kindly cooperated.

The news spread quickly around the world; Burroughs had come to seem literally immortal, and many people were shocked that he had actually died. The funeral in Lawrence was somber and brief; there were over two hundred mourners. According to Burroughs' express wishes, he was laid to rest in the Burroughs family plot at Bellefontaine Cemetery in St. Louis, alongside his grandfather, the inventor; his uncle Horace, the drug addict; his father, Mote; and his mother, Laura.

Born in middle America in 1914, William Burroughs lived eighty-three years— far longer than anyone might have expected, in view of the dangers he courted throughout his life. In many ways, he was supernaturally fortunate, for despite many years of drugs and alcohol, he retained his lucidity throughout his life. He came of age during the "Roaring Twenties," lived through World War II, actively participated in the cultural upheaval of the sixties, and witnessed the birth of the Space Age and the communications revolution of the late twentieth century. He lived in North and Central America, Africa, Europe, and England. He was a man for his times.

Burroughs was blessed with a strong constitution, but more than that, with the gift of prophecy—and he lived long enough to see many of his visions come true, and to know that his indelible point of view had put down deep roots in the cultural life of America and the Western world. His first book was published in 1953, when he was thirty-nine years old. Over the next forty-four years, he wrote some twenty novels, published hundreds of short pieces and essays, and left behind the materials for many posthumous works. A volume

of *Selected Letters* (1945–59), edited by Oliver Harris, was published by
Viking in 1993, and a second volume is projected to cover the period 1959–74.
A memoir begun by Burroughs, which he called *Evil River* (from the St. John
Perse line "My past was an evil river"), will be completed soon. And for the
last year of his life, Burroughs was writing daily in bound-book journals, con-
templating his own mortality; those texts will be published as *Last Words*.

Word Virus is the culmination of a lifetime of writing. When I began working with William Burroughs in 1974, he had already created an immortal body
of work. But the late 1960s and early 1970s in London were not a happy or
fruitful time for Burroughs personally, and his return to America, after twenty
years abroad, rejuvenated his career and gave him new energy. While *Naked
Lunch*, written in Tangier and Paris, is an untouchable achievement, many critics have opined that the "Red Night trilogy," which Burroughs wrote while
living in the United States in the late 1970s and the 1980s, is deserving of
consideration alongside his best work.

The idea of a "collected Burroughs" had been around for some time, but it
was not until the summer of 1997 that Ira Silverberg and I finally approached
the job of choosing a coherent selection from all of Burroughs' published work.
Providentially, we were able to show our work to William, in what turned out
to be the last week of his life; so we know that he saw and approved the texts
we have gathered here. With the exception of a six-page excerpt from the
beginning of the legendary, long-lost Burroughs-Kerouac manuscript, "And
the Hippos Were Boiled in Their Tanks," the *Word Virus* collection is made
up entirely of already-published work. The selections were chosen with an eye
to the author's first use, and later development, of certain characteristic themes
and images.

It is too early to write an authoritative assessment of the Burroughs cor-
pus, and in these introductory passages I have tried to confine myself to the
basic outline of his biography and some notes on the composition and bibliography of these pages. In my account of his life, I have relied heavily upon
the research done by Ted Morgan, Barry Miles, and Peter Swales, among others, and upon my innumerable conversations with William and my reading of
countless books and manuscripts. Inevitably, I will have erred in some places
in this text, and that I do regret; but I believe mine is the most accurate chronology yet published. My special thanks go to Ira Silverberg and Daniel Diaz,
for their patient encouragement and assistance during this difficult half year
of writing, which came so painfully soon for me after William's death. As always, I sincerely hope I have done him justice.

Not content to hew to an exhaused modernism, which seemed to require a
solitary, writerly "purity" in the lives of its practitioners, Burroughs collaborated widely, and branched out into several other mediums. His work stands
at the turning point between modernism and postmodernism, the movement
of which he is usually now considered a founding, if unwitting, member.
Working not only in writing per se, but also in art, performance, and multi-

media collaboration, he developed a recombinant art method. Even as postmodern criticism reassesses the presumed indivisibility of the author, Burroughs foresaw this evolution with his lifelong resort to multiple authorship. Indeed, much of his work is nonliterary, in media that are inherently collaborative, such as record albums and films, so his embrace of artistic partnerships is an essential element of his creation. Throughout a career that crossed so many boundaries—between art forms sometimes considered mutually exclusive, and between the thoughts and language of real people and the speech that is "acceptable" in polite society—Burroughs created an oeuvre that is by no means strictly literary. And yet, through it all, he considered himself, foremost, a *writer*—and it is in his writing that we will find the cornerstone of the edifice that is Burroughs' life's work, and the keys to every part of it.

Outcast from society, and moreover self-exiled, a perpetual student and seeker, William Seward Burroughs created himself. Homosexual, insecure, wounded by childhood mistreatment, haunted by an Ugly Spirit, he summoned every force whose name he knew to guide him on his path toward "the only goal worth striving for": immortality. And as his final writings show, on the long, hard journey to his own well-assured literary immortality, Burroughs finally glimpsed the meaning of human life: compassion for all life's endless suffering, and for its inexorable end.

selected bibliography
of current editions

WORKS BY WILLIAM S. BURROUGHS

The Adding Machine: Selected Essays. New York: Arcade, 1993.
Ah Pook Is Here and Other Texts. New York: Riverrun, 1982.
Blade Runner: A Movie. Berkeley: Blue Wind Press, 1979.
The Burroughs File. San Francisco: City Lights, 1984.
The Cat Inside. New York: Viking, 1992.
Cities of the Red Night. New York: Henry Holt and Company, 1995.
Exterminator! New York: Penguin, 1986.
Ghost of Chance. New York: High Risk Books, 1995.
Interzone. Ed. James Grauerholz. New York: Penguin, 1990.
Junky. New York: Penguin, 1985.
The Last Words of Dutch Schultz: A Fiction in the Form of a Film Script. New York:
    Arcade, 1993.
My Education: A Book of Dreams. New York: Penguin, 1996.
Naked Lunch. New York: Grove Press, 1992.
Nova Express. New York: Grove Press, 1992.
Painting and Guns. New York: Hanuman Books, 1992.
The Place of Dead Roads. New York: Henry Holt and Company, 1995.
Port of Saints. Berkeley: Blue Wind Press, 1980.
Queer. New York: Penguin, 1995.
The Soft Machine. New York: Grove Press, 1992.
The Ticket That Exploded. New York: Grove Press, 1992.
The Western Lands. New York: Penguin, 1989.
The Wild Boys: A Book of the Dead. New York: Grove Press, 1992.

CONVERSATIONS AND LETTERS

Bockris, Victor, with William Burroughs: *A Report from the Bunker.* New York:
    St. Martin's Press, 1996.
Burroughs, William S. *The Letters of William S. Burroughs.* Ed. Oliver Harris. New
    York: Penguin, 1994.

Burroughs, William S. *The Job: Interviews with William S. Burroughs.* Ed. Daniel Odier. New York: Penguin, 1989.

COLLABORATIVE AND ILLUSTRATED WORKS

Gale, Bob, and William S. Burroughs. *The Book of Breething.* Berkeley: Blue Wind Press, 1980.

Ginsberg, Allen, and William S. Burroughs. *The Yagé Letters.* San Francisco: City Lights Books, 1971.

Gysin, Brion, and William S. Burroughs. *The Third Mind.* New York: Viking, 1978.

Wilson, S. Clay, and William S. Burroughs. *Tornado Alley.* Cherry Valley, New York: Cherry Valley Editions, 1989.

BIOGRAPHIES AND CRITICISM

Lydenberg, Robin, and Jennie Skerl. *William S. Burroughs at the Front: Critical Reception 1959–1989.* Carbondale: Southern Illinois University Press, 1991.

Lydenberg, Robin. *Word Cultures: Radical Theory and Practice in William S. Burroughs' Fiction.* Chicago: University of Illinois Press, 1987.

Miles, Barry. *William Burroughs: El Hombre Invisible, a Portrait.* New York: Hyperion, 1993.

Morgan, Ted. *Literary Outlaw: The Life and Times of William S. Burroughs.* New York: Henry Holt and Company, 1988.

Murphy, Timothy S. *Wising Up the Marks: The Amodern William Burroughs.* Berkeley: University of California Press, 1997.

Skerl, Jennie. *William S. Burroughs.* Boston: Twayne Publishers, 1985.

Sobieszek, Robert A. Afterword by William S. Burroughs. Exh. cat. *Ports of Entry: William S. Burroughs and the Arts.* Los Angeles: Los Angeles County Museum of Art, 1996.

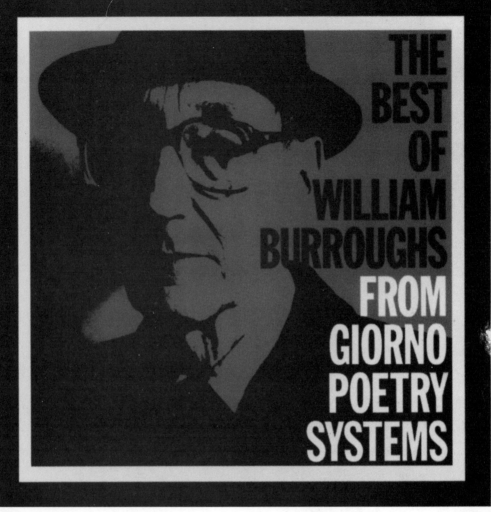

THE
BEST
OF
WILLIAM
BURROUGHS
FROM
GIORNO
POETRY
SYSTEMS

- The best spoken-word performances by William Burroughs
- Four CDs, each containing seventy-four minutes of amazing material
- Five extensively illustrated books with over seventy photographs and excerpts from Burroughs's works
- Includes rare recordings and archival photographs

THE BEST OF WILLIAM BURROUGHS is a four–CD box set bringing together material from Giorno Poetry Systems' vast archives and Burroughs's personal archives. It is the only complete collection of Burroughs's spoken-word performances, all packaged in a luxurious black-linen box complete with a sixty-four-page photographic retrospective on the achievements of this great author.

From Mouth Almighty/Mercury Records
Available at fine book and music retailers everywhere.
To order call 1-800-992-9673 or visit
www.mouthalmighty.com   www.polygram.us.com

mouth almighty
r e c o r d s

INDEPENDENT
LABEL SALES

Mercury
RECORDS

a PolyGram company